POLLUTION HAN

The 1999 edition of the *Pollution Handbook* h
Since the main text was completed there have been a number of leg
related, developments on which it might be helpful for readers to have information:

- **Integrated Pollution Prevention and Control** *(pages 19-21)*: The EU's 1996 Directive is to be implemented through the Pollution Prevention and Control Bill (PPC Bill), which was introduced into the House of Lords at the end of November. The legislation, which will repeal Part I of the Environmental Protection Act 1990, together with the detailed regulations, must be in place by 30 October 1999, the date by which new and substantially changed installations must meet the Directive's requirements. In England and Wales the regulatory role will be split between the Environment Agency and local authorities; all installations in Scotland covered by the Directive will be regulated by the Scottish Environment Protection Agency.

- **Integrated Pollution Control - authorisations** *(page 30)*: Processes regulated for IPC in England and Wales have had their authorisations varied to require them to submit annual reports on releases of 200 specified substances; the first report covering 1998 releases was due by 31 January 1999, with reports covering subsequent years also due on 31 January of the following year.

- **Integrated Pollution Control - charging** *(page 39)*: The Environment Agency is proposing to increase IPC charges for 1999/2000 by 15%. New charges will take effect from 1 April 1999, when the Agency will also begin charging monthly in arrears for routine monitoring.

- **EU - Air Quality Assessment and Management** *(pages 79-82)*: The European Commission is proposing a second "daughter directive" which would introduce a limit value of 5 $\mu g/m^3$ for benzene to be achieved by 2010 and 10 mg/m^3 for carbon monoxide to be achieved by 2005.

- **EU Controls on Substances that Deplete the Ozone Layer** *(pages 86-88)*: The European Commission has published a draft Regulation (COM(98) 398); this will replace the current 1994 Regulation and implement more stringent controls than those called for in the Montreal Protocol (see pages 71-73). The draft EU Regulation proposes:

  - 2% cap on consumption of HCFCs, with tighter controls on use and production and bigger cuts in consumption leading to phase-out in 2015;
  - to bring forward the 2001 phase-out date for methyl bromide;

- a ban on the sale and use of CFCs, halons, 1,1,1 trichloroethane, carbon tetrachloride and HBFCs.

- **National Air Quality Strategy** *(pages 97-98)*: In January 1999 the Government published its proposals for amending the National Air Quality Strategy; the main proposals (*with revisions in italics*) are as follows:

  - benzene: 5 ppb standard running annual mean *to be achieved by 31.12.03; indicative level of 1 ppb by 31.12.05;*
  - 1,3 butadiene: 1 ppb to be achieved *by 31.12.03*;
  - carbon monoxide: 10 ppm running annual mean to be achieved *by 31.12.03*;
  - Lead: 0.5 $\mu g/m^3$ annual mean to be achieved *by 31.12.04; 0.25* $\mu g/m^3$ *by 31.12.08;*
  - Nitrogen dioxide: *104.6 ppb (200* $\mu g/m^3$*) hourly mean to be achieved by 31.12.05, with maximum 18 exceedences; 21 ppb annual mean as objective for 31.12.05 (provisional)*;
  - Ozone: no change to 50 ppb running 8-hour mean as indicative level;
  - Fine particles (PM_{10}): no change to 50 $\mu g/m^3$ running 24-hour mean as 99th percentile indicative level; *annual limit of 31* $\mu g/m^3$ *and 24 hour limit of 50* $\mu g/m^3$ *(max 7-20 exceedences - to be decided) for 31.12.04;*
  - Sulphur dioxide: no change to 100 ppb 15 minute mean to be achieved by 31.12.05; *131 ppb 1 hour mean, not to be exceeded more than 24 times per year, and 46.8 ppb 24 hour mean, not to be exceeded more than 3 times per year, to be achieved by 31.12.04.*

- **Fuel Controls - N. Ireland** *(page 140)*: The Smoke Control Areas (Sale or Delivery of Unauthorised Fuel) Regulations (Northern Ireland) 1998 (SR 328) prohibit the sale or delivery of unauthorised fuels in smoke control areas; the Sulphur Content of Solid Fuel Regulations (Northern Ireland) 1998 (SR 329) ban the sale or delivery to households of solid fuels with a sulphur content exceeding 2%.

- **Agriculture Codes of Practice** *(pages 157-158)*: Revised Codes of Good Agricultural Practice covering: air, water and soil were published in 1998 and are available from MAFF.

- **Registration of Waste Carriers - N. Ireland** *(pages 305-307)*: Draft regulations, similar to the 1991 Regulations in force in the rest of the UK, have been issued for consultation; like the 1991 Regulations, the N. Ireland Regulations will also cover seizure of vehicles used for illegal dumping of waste.

- **Radioactive Substances Act - charging** *(page 335-336)*: The Environment Agency is proposing to increase the charges applicable to Band 1 and 2 premises (which are charged per inspector day) by 15% from 1 April 1999;

1999 POLLUTION HANDBOOK

Editor
Loveday Murley

NSCA POLLUTION HANDBOOK
National Society for Clean Air
and Environmental Protection

First published January 1985
Updated and reprinted
1986, 1987, 1988, 1989
Revised 1990, 1991, 1992, 1993, 1994, 1995, 1996, 1997,1998

Printed and published in Great Britain by
The National Society for Clean Air and Environmental Protection
136 North Street, Brighton BN1 1RG

ISBN 0 903474 42 5

charges for Band 3 and 4 premises are to rise by approximately 4%; in addition certain Band 4 premises are to be subject to an annual subsistence charge.

- **Drinking Water Directive** *(page 353-354)*: the new Drinking Water Directive was formally adopted by the EU Council of Ministers on 10 November 1998. The official text was published on 5 December in Official Journal L330, vol. 41.

- **Dumping Sludge at Sea** *(pages 394-395)*: In line with a commitment made at the 1990 North Sea Conference and included in the 1991 EU Directive on Urban Waste Water Treatment *(page 354-355)*, the UK ceased the dumping of sewage sludge at sea from 1 January 1999.

The *Pollution Handbook* is widely used by central and local government, industry, pollution control specialists, researchers and students. It aims, therefore, to provide an overview of pollution control legislation and related matters. Thus, it is not a detailed statement of the law and NSCA can accept no legal responsibility for any inaccuracies which may have arisen. Specialist professional advice should always be sought in dealing with specific problems or before taking legal action.

NSCA is always happy to receive comments and other suggestions to ensure that the *Pollution Handbook* meets the needs of all its users.

Loveday Murley
Editor
14 January 1999

CONTENTS

INTRODUCTION

CHAPTER 1: INTEGRATED POLLUTION CONTROL AND OTHER PRINCIPLES OF CONTROL

THE EUROPEAN UNION & WATER POLLUTION CONTROL

IMPLEMENTATION AND ENFORCEMENT AUTHORITIES

REGULATORY CONTROLS

MARINE POLLUTION

IPC

AND OTHER PRINCIPLES OF CONTROL

GENERAL PRINCIPLES

1.1 INTRODUCTION

The principles underlying the UK approach to pollution control evolved over many years, with the term "Best Practicable Means" (BPM) providing the fundamental basis for almost 150 years. More recently, "Best Practicable Environmental Option" and "Best Available Techniques Not Entailing Excessive Cost" have become major elements of industrial pollution control. There is now general acceptance that the polluter should pay – the "polluter pays principle" – and that environmental legislation should embody the concept of "sustainable development". All these principles – or control mechanisms – are applicable to the control of pollution across all environmental media – air, noise, waste and water pollution.

The first part of this chapter of the *Pollution Handbook* therefore explains some of the general principles of control which are applicable to all or some of the subsequent chapters and describes the main bodies concerned with the implementation and enforcement of UK pollution control legislation.

The second part of this chapter describes the legislative requirements of Integrated Pollution Control; finally this chapter covers those areas of UK pollution control, such as statutory nuisance and access to environmental information, which are of relevance in the control of air, noise, waste and water pollution.

1.2 EARLY CONTROLS

1.2.1 Alkali Acts & Best Practicable Means

Most of the UK's early pollution control measures were enacted as a result of the Industrial Revolution of the late 18th and 19th centuries, although both air and water pollution had been identified as problems many hundreds of years before (see chapters 2 and 5 respectively). The concept of "Best Practicable Means" (BPM) – which for many years was a fundamental principle of pollution control legislation – was often used to describe the whole approach of UK anti-pollution legislation towards industrial emissions, and indeed controlling other types of pollution, including noise. (See also chapter 2, 2.2.1 and chapter 3, 3.6.5)

The concept of BPM originated in a law applying in Leeds in 1842 under which a fine could be imposed on offenders who had not used the Best Practicable Means to prevent or abate smoke nuisance. In 1874 an amendment to the *Alkali Act 1863* required the use of BPM to prevent the discharge of all noxious or offensive gases arising from alkali works.

A schedule to the *Health and Safety (Emissions into the Atmosphere) Regulations 1983* (revoked in December 1996) listed all those processes ("works") which had to be registered with the pollution inspectorate; as an essential prior condition to registration, operators of scheduled works had to satisfy the inspectorate that the works were provided with the BPM for preventing the escape of noxious or offensive substances, and for rendering all such emissions harmless and inoffensive. BPM took into account the cost of pollution abatement and its effect on the viability of industry.

The essential elements of BPM so far as emissions to air were concerned could be defined as follows:

- no emission could be tolerated which constituted a recognised health hazard, either short or long term;
- emissions in terms of both concentration and mass, had to be reduced to the lowest practicable amount taking into account local conditions and circumstances, current state of knowledge on control technology and effects of substance emitted, financial considerations, and the means to be employed;
- having secured the minimum practicable emissions, the height of discharge should be arranged so that the residual emission was rendered harmless and inoffensive by dilution and dispersion.

The principle was extended to noise control. Under section 72 of the *Control of Pollution Act 1974*, it is a defence to prove that the BPM has been used to mitigate the effects of excessive noise from, for example, a factory. Section 80(7) of the *Environmental Protection Act* also allows a defence of BPM in respect of an action for nuisance from industrial, trade or business premises.

When working out the control details for any particular type of process, the pollution inspectorate would discuss ways of reducing emissions with representatives of the industry concerned, using their knowledge of control techniques and their own technical expertise. The conclusions were published in *Notes on Best Practicable Means*, which described treatment plant to be used and its maintenance, methods of operations and possibly a "presumptive limit" for emissions. Presumptive emission limits presumed that if an industry was discharging to the prescribed limit, then it would be meeting the BPM requirement. However, the intention was not that industry should pollute up to the limit, but rather that they should do whatever was practicable to reduce emissions below the limit.

BPM notes issued early in 1988 reflected for the first time European Community legislation on industrial emissions, in particular the 1984 framework Directive on air pollution from industrial plant

(84/360/EEC); BPM notes were not enshrined in legislation so the limits could be tightened by the inspectorate as required to keep up with advances in abatement technology, or in scientific understanding of the effects of pollutants.

1.2.2 Pollution Inspectorates

(a) England and Wales

Until 1 April 1987, the Alkali Inspectorate (renamed HM Industrial Air Pollution Inspectorate in 1983) was responsible for regulating processes scheduled under the *Alkali Acts*. From 1984-1987 the Inspectorate, together with the Factory Inspectorate, came under the Health and Safety Executive. Before that and from 1 April 1987 to 1 April 1996, the Inspectorate came under the direct control of the Department of the Environment (now Department of the Environment, Transport and the Regions).

On 1 April 1987 a unified HM Inspectorate of Pollution (HMIP) was established with the aim of providing a more integrated approach to pollution control; an important area of its work was to develop a method for determining the Best Practicable Environmental Option (BPEO) for dealing with industrial processes and the wastes which they produce. HMIP was a statutory body and brought together the inspectorates for air pollution, radiochemicals and hazardous waste; it was also responsible for the control of water pollution from particularly polluting processes. Thus HMIP was primarily responsible for enforcement of legislation under Part I of the *Environmental Protection Act 1990* and under the *Radioactive Substances Act 1993*. HMIP also had responsibilities under the *Alkali etc Works Regulation Act 1906, Control of Pollution Act 1974, Town and Country Planning (Assessment of Environmental Effects) Regulations 1988, Control of Industrial Air Pollution (Registration of Works) Regulations 1989* and *Air Quality Standards Regulations 1989*.

On 1 April 1996, HMIP's responsibilities were transferred to the Environment Agency (see 1.7.1 below).

(b) Scotland

Until 1 April 1996 HM Industrial Pollution Inspectorate (HMIPI) was responsible for enforcing legislation controlling emissions from industrial premises, for the *Radioactive Substances Act 1993* and for the implementation of IPC (together with the River Purification Authorities). The Inspectorate also provided scientific and technical advice on industrial pollution generally, radioactive waste management and environmental radioactivity. HMIPI contributed to the work of the Hazardous Waste Inspectorate (Scotland), which was responsible for the oversight of waste management in Scotland. Both HMIPI and the HWI worked within the Scottish Office.

On 1 April 1996 HMIPI's responsibilities were transferred to the Scottish Environment Protection Agency (see 1.7.2 below).

1.3 SUSTAINABLE DEVELOPMENT

The term "sustainable development" has now become the starting point – or key principle – in discussions on environmental policy and legislation. It was first introduced in the 1987 report of the World Commission on Environment and Development, *Our Common Future* (the Brundtland Report); this defined sustainable development as "meeting the needs of the current generation without compromising the ability of future generations to meet their own needs".

Many governments worldwide and the European Union have embodied the concept of sustainable development into policy making. In 1993 the European Commission published its *Fifth Action Programme on the Environment – Towards Sustainability*. This Programme runs from 1993-2000 and stresses the need for governments, industry and communities to become involved in and take responsibility for the protection of their environment. At their meeting in June 1997 EU Heads of State amended the Maastricht Treaty to strengthen the Union's commitment to the principles of sustainable development – see also Appendix 6.

In 1994 the UK Government published *Sustainable Development – the UK Strategy*. Here sustainable development is described as not implying "having less economic development" nor "that every aspect of the present environment should be preserved at all costs". Instead sustainable development requires that "decisions throughout society are taken with proper regard to their environmental impact". The Strategy document, which is to be regularly updated, reviews UK policies and sets out the agenda in all areas, including pollution control, for achieving a sustainable economy. This has been followed by *Indicators of Sustainable Development for the United Kingdom* (HMSO, 1996); this contains some 120 indicators, covering issues such as transport, the economy, air quality, climate change and energy, which can be used to monitor progress towards achieving the objectives set out in the UK Strategy.

Both the Environment Agency and SEPA are charged with contributing towards attaining the objectives of sustainable development in carrying out their functions; Ministerial Guidance addressed to the Environment Agency, published in November 1996, outlines how this should be done, with similar Guidance being addressed to SEPA; see also 1.7.1(a) below.

1.4 POLLUTER PAYS PRINCIPLE (PPP)

A key principle of the European Union's environment policy is that the cost of preventing pollution or of minimising environmental damage due to pollution should be borne by those responsible for the pollution. The principle originates from the proceedings of the UN Conference on the Human Environment, Stockholm 1972; in the European Community PPP was first mentioned in the First Action Programme on the Environment (1973-77) (see Appendix 6). As a signatory to the Treaty of Rome, the UK accepts the principle of PPP.

Amongst the elements of the principle as set out by the EU are:

- *payments* in the form of grants or subsidies from the public purse which may be made towards: investment in anti-pollution installations and equipment; the introduction of new processes; and the costs of operating and maintaining anti-pollution installations.
- *charges* which may be levied directly as taxes on the process which generates the pollution, or alternatively as the purchase price of a licence which entitles the holder to generate specific quantities of pollutants.

The cost recovery schemes implemented in the UK under which operators meet the costs of regulation for, for example, Integrated Pollution Control, air pollution control and waste management licensing are in line with the principle that the polluter should pay.

Environmental taxes, used by a number of EU Member States, are another means of charging for pollution control, or encouraging the use of less polluting alternatives; however, these must not be incompatible with the functioning of the Single European Market. Commission Communication COM(97) 9 outlines the circumstances in which such taxes may be used and those in which they are not permissible.

1.5 BEST PRACTICABLE ENVIRONMENTAL OPTION

The use of the "Best Practicable Environmental Option" (BPEO) as a means of controlling pollution was first proposed by the Royal Commission on Environmental Pollution in its fifth Report (1976), *Air Pollution Control: An Integrated Approach*. It suggested that a unified pollution inspectorate should be established whose aim would be "to achieve the best practicable environmental option taking account of the total pollution from a process and the technical possibilities for dealing with it". In its 12th Report (1988), *Best Practicable Environmental Option*, the RCEP described its concept of BPEO in more detail, including guidelines on its implementation. It defined the BPEO as

> "the outcome of a systematic and decision-making procedure which emphasises the protection and conservation of the environment

across land, air and water. The BPEO procedure establishes, for a given set of objectives, the option that provides the most benefit or least damage to the environment as a whole, at acceptable cost, in the long term as well as in the short term".

In applying for an IPC authorisation under Part I of the *Environmental Protection Act 1990*, process operators must demonstrate that their chosen abatement technique represents the BPEO; and in implementing Integrated Pollution Control the Environment Agency and Scottish Environment Protection Agency are required to set conditions which are commensurate with the BPEO. This specifies the pollution control technology which is the best practicable for the environment as a whole considering

- the total impact on water, land and air pathways together;
- the ability of the pathway to absorb the pollutant in the light of critical loads, where appropriate;
- the principles of sustainable development.

Technical Guidance Note E1 (Environmental), *Best Practicable Environmental Option Assessments for Integrated Pollution Control* (Stationery Office, 1997) describes a methodology for undertaking BPEO assessment for IPC in a consistent manner which is compatible with the requirements of the *Environmental Protection Act 1990*. Volume I provides guidance for assessing harm and comparing options for specific industrial processes to determine BATNEEC having regard to BPEO, as well as outlining the economic information required to gauge the practicality of process options. Volume II (which is still consultative) contains data that the Environment Agency has put together to support the methodology.

1.6 BEST AVAILABLE TECHNIQUES NOT ENTAILING EXCESSIVE COST (BATNEEC)

1.6.1 Euro-BATNEEC

Best Available Technology Not Entailing Excessive Cost (BATNEEC) was first used in the European Union (EU) Framework Directive on combatting air pollution from industrial plant (84/360/EEC). This requires that "all appropriate preventative measures against air pollution have been taken, including the application of best available technology, provided that the application of such measures does not entail excessive cost". "Technology" is interpreted as that which operating experience has adequately demonstrated to be the best technology commercially available as regards the minimisation of emissions to atmosphere; it should also be proven to be economically viable when applied to the industrial sector concerned.

The EU Directive on Integrated Pollution Prevention and Control (IPPC) (see 1.12 below), requires competent authorities to ensure that "installations are operated in such a way that all the appropriate preventive measures are taken against pollution, in particular through the application of best available techniques . . ." This is defined as

> "the most effective and advanced stage in the development of activities and their methods of operation which indicate the practical suitability of particular techniques for providing in principle the basis for emission limit values designed to prevent and, where that is not practicable, generally to reduce emissions and the impact on the environment as a whole.
>
> – "techniques" shall include both the technology used and the way in which the installation is designed, built, maintained, operated and decommissioned;
>
> – "available" techniques shall mean those developed on a scale which allows implementation in the relevant industrial sector, under economically and technically viable conditions, taking into consideration the costs and advantages, whether or not the techniques are used or produced inside the Member State in question, as long as they are reasonably accessible to the operator;
>
> – "best" shall mean most effective in achieving a high general level of protection of the environment as a whole."

1.6.2 UK-BATNEEC

The *Environmental Protection Act 1990* requires the use of Best Available Techniques Not Entailing Excessive Cost (BATNEEC) to minimise releases from all Part A processes (prescribed for Integrated Pollution Control) and Part B processes (prescribed for air pollution control) – see Appendix 1.1.

Integrated Pollution Control: A Practical Guide published by the Department of Environment and Welsh Office in 1993 and updated in 1996 defines BATNEEC as follows:

> **Best** means most effective in preventing, minimising or rendering harmless polluting releases. There may be more than one set of techniques that achieves comparable effectiveness – i.e. there may be more than one set of "best" techniques.
>
> **Available** should be taken to mean procurable by the operator of the process in question. It does not imply that the technique has to be in general use, but it does require general accessibility. It includes a technique which has been developed (or proven) at pilot scale

provided this allows its implementation in the relevant industrial context with the necessary business confidence. It does not imply that sources outside the UK are "unavailable". Nor does it imply a competitive supply market. If there is a monopoly supplier the technique counts as being available provided that the operator can procure it.

Techniques embrace both the plant in which the process is carried on and how the process is operated. It should be taken to mean the components of which it is made up and the manner in which they are connected together to make the whole. It also includes matters such as numbers and qualifications of staff, working methods, training and supervision and also the design, construction, lay-out and maintenance of buildings, and will affect the concept and design of the process.

Not Entailing Excessive Cost (NEEC) needs to be taken in two contexts, depending on whether it is applied to new processes or to existing processes.

So far as new processes are concerned, there will always be a presumption towards the use of BAT and BATNEEC, although the following principles should also be applied:

- the cost of the best available techniques must be weighed against the environmental damage from the process; the greater the environmental damage, the greater the costs of BAT that can be required before costs are considered excessive;
- the objective is to prevent damaging releases or to reduce such releases so far as this can be done without imposing excessive costs; if after applying BATNEEC serious harm would still result, the application can be refused; and
- as objective an approach as possible to the consideration of what is BATNEEC is required. The concern is with what costs in general are excessive; the lack of profitability of a particular business should not affect the determination.

With regard to existing processes, the main concern will be to establish timetables for upgrading to new plant standards, or as near as possible to such standards, or close down. Other factors to be taken into account for plant existing before July 1987 include:

- the plant's technical characteristics;
- its rate of utilisation and length of remaining life;
- the nature and volume of polluting emissions;
- the desirability of not entailing excessive cost for the plant

concerned, having regard to the economic situation of undertakings belonging to the category in question.

The BATNEEC for specific processes is described in the process guidance notes for both Part A and Part B processes (listed in Appendices 1.3 and 2.1).

IMPLEMENTATION AND ENFORCEMENT AUTHORITIES

The main bodies involved in implementation and enforcement of pollution control legislation are given below, together with an outline of their responsibilities. More specific detail is given in the individual chapters.

1.7 ENVIRONMENT AGENCIES

Proposals for establishing independent environment agencies in England and Wales and in Scotland were published for consultation in 1991 and confirmed in July 1992. Such Agencies would, it was suggested, be better able to develop a consistent and cohesive approach to environmental protection across all media as envisaged by the implementation of Integrated Pollution Control and taking account of the principles of sustainable development. The Agencies, which formally took over their pollution control and other functions on 1 April 1996, were established by the *Environment Act 1995*, Part I. The Act received Royal Assent on 19 July 1995. In exercising their powers, section 39 of the Act requires both Agencies to take into account the likely costs and benefits of exercising (or not exercising) a power.

The Government is currently reviewing (August 1998) whether the legislation under which the Environment Agency and SEPA operate act as a barrier to the Agencies being able to take an integrated approach towards the control of pollution; it is also considering whether rationalisation of the various regulatory regimes would enable them to provide a more efficient service to their customers. Issues to be considered include:

- harmonisation of procedures – e.g. for applications or variations of licences etc; enforcement action;
- rationalisation of charging schemes and public registers under different regimes;
- requirements for separate licences or authorisations for different activities at the same site;
- the need for separate regulatory regimes for radioactive and other major industrial processes.

Proposals for any amendments to the legislation resulting from the Government's review will be the subject of separate consultation in 1999.

1.7.1 England and Wales

The Environment Agency (in Welsh – Asiantaeth yr Amgylchedd) took over the responsibilities of HM Inspectorate of Pollution, the National Rivers Authority and the waste regulatory functions of local authorities on 1 April 1996. It is a non-departmental public body; members of the board are appointed by the Secretary of State for the Environment, Transport and the Regions, the Secretary of State for Wales and by the Minister of Agriculture, Fisheries and Food. The Agency's head office in Bristol is responsible for policies, standards, ensuring a consistent approach to environmental protection and overall financial control. There are eight regional offices arranged on the basis of water catchment areas for water management and political boundaries for pollution control and prevention and waste regulation; these latter have been drawn as close as possible to water catchment boundaries, using district rather than county boundaries where these provide a better match. In Wales, however, the boundary follows that of the Principality. The pollution control boundary is also the local "public face" of the Agency. Area offices within each region are largely responsible for the operational side of the Agency's work.

(a) Aims and Objectives (s.4)

The principal aim of the Agency in discharging its functions to protect and enhance the environment is to make a contribution towards "attaining the objective of achieving sustainable development" (s.4(1) of the Act); section 4(2) requires Ministers to give the Agency statutory guidance on its objectives (including guidance on its contribution to sustainable development) to which the Agency must have regard. This was formally issued in November 1996 and requires the Agency:

- to adopt, across all its functions, an integrated approach to environmental protection and enhancement which considers impacts of substances and activities on all environmental media and on natural resources;
- to work with all relevant sectors of society, including regulated organisations, to develop approaches which deliver environmental requirements and goals without imposing excessive costs (in relation to benefits gained) on regulated organisations or society as a whole;
- to adopt clear and effective procedures for serving its customers, including the development of single points of contact through which regulated organisations can deal with the Agency;
- to operate to high professional standards, based on sound science, information and analysis of the environment and processes which affect it;

- to organise its activities in ways which reflect good environmental and management practice and provide value for money for those who pay its charges and to taxpayers;
- to provide clear and readily available advice and information on its work;
- to develop a close and responsive relationship with the public, local authorities, representatives of local communities and regulated organisations.

In making a contribution towards the objective of attaining sustainable development the Agency should:

- take a holistic approach to the protection and enhancement of the environment;
- ensure that the longer term implications and effects of actions, particularly those which appear irreversible, or reversible at high cost over a long time, are fully taken into account;
- maintain biodiversity;
- protect the global atmosphere, having regard to UK commitments under the UN Convention on Climate Change and the Montreal Protocol;
- where possible, discharge its regulatory functions in partnership with business in ways which maximise the scope for cost-effective investment in improved technologies and techniques and encourage business to adopt high environmental objectives and standards;
- develop close and responsive relationships with all sectors of the community, maximising their contributions to the achievement of sustainable development;
- become a recognised centre of knowledge and expertise and provide readily accessible advice and information on its work and best environmental practice.

(b) Functions (ss.5-10)

In considering or formulating proposals relating to its functions (except pollution control – see next para) the Agency or Ministers should ensure that these will *further* the conservation and enhancement of natural beauty, flora and fauna etc (s.7(1)(a) of the Act).

In carrying out its pollution control responsibilities, the main objective is to prevent or minimise, remedy or mitigate the effects of pollution of the environment (s.5(1)); as well as ensuring it has sufficient information regarding the level, or potential level, of pollution of the environment, the Agency must also follow developments in technology and techniques for abating and preventing pollution or its effects. In formulating or considering proposals for pollution control the Agency or Ministers should have regard to the *desirability* of conserving and enhancing natural beauty, flora and fauna etc (s.7(1)(b)). Section 81 of the Act also requires the Environment Agency to have regard to the National Air Quality Strategy in discharging its pollution control functions.

With regard to water, the Agency also has a duty "to promote the conservation and enhancement of the natural beauty and amenity of inland and coastal waters ...; the conservation of flora and fauna ... dependent on an aquatic environment; and the use of such waters and land for recreational purposes."

(c) Pollution Control Responsibilities

- Authorisations, licences and consents for emissions, discharges and disposals to air, water and land; monitoring compliance and enforcement, including prosecutions under IPC and water legislation;
- Waste management licensing, including the registration of carriers; regulating the import and export of waste and control over the movement of waste, and the regulation of special waste; regulation of radioactive waste accumulation and disposal; assessing waste disposal needs and priorities; production of technical guidance on waste management;
- Regulation of contaminated land designated as "special sites"; report on the state of contaminated land and, as necessary, produce site-specific guidance to local authorities;
- Monitoring environmental conditions and publishing relevant statistics; research; advice to government in setting environmental quality and other standards and proposals for pollution prevention measures;
- Advice and guidance to industry and others on best environmental practice.

The Agency is also responsible for administering registration and exemption schemes for producer responsibility in accordance with regulations, and monitoring and enforcement of associated obligations (*Environment Act*, ss.93-95 – see chapter 4, 4.12).

(d) Consultation (ss.8 & 11-14)

Under section 8 of the Act, the Nature Conservancy Council for England, the Countryside Council for Wales or National Park (or Broads) Authority should notify the Environment Agency of any sites of special interest which might be affected by any of the Agency's activities or an authorisation. Where such notification has been received, the Agency must consult the relevant body before carrying out or authorising the activity. The Agency is also required to consult certain bodies before issuing an authorisation or discharge consent (this chapter 1.13.2(a) and chapter 5, 5.15.3(a), respectively).

The Agency is required to set up and consult Regional Environment Protection Advisory Committees (REPACs), Regional and Local Fisheries Advisory Committees and Regional Flood Defence Committees in England and Wales. Members of the REPAC will normally include a representative from the fisheries and flood defence committees, industry, local authorities, environmental organisations and persons with a particular interest in the air and land aspects of the Agency's work.

An Advisory Committee for Wales advises the Secretary of State on matters relating to the Agency's functions in Wales.

The Environment Agency and the local authority associations (now the Local Government Association) have signed a Memorandum of Understanding (1997) covering those aspects of environmental protection for which they both have some responsibility; these include: air quality; waste management and contaminated land; water resources and flood defence; planning; and information provision. Through the Memorandum, the parties are committed to

- making their workings as **transparent** as possible to each other;
- the free exchange of **information** for the discharge of their statutory responsibilities;
- the principle of **consultation**, both formal and informal, on any issue which affects the other;
- **cooperating** with each other at all levels for the well-being of the environment.

The Environment Agency has also signed (May 1998) a Memorandum of Understanding with the Association of Chief Police Officers; this aims to ensure effective cooperation during incidents in which the environment may be at risk of harm.

1.7.2 Scottish Environment Protection Agency

Plans for establishing a Scottish Environment Protection Agency (SEPA) were also issued for consultation in 1991.

As from 1 April 1996 SEPA took over the responsibilities of HM Industrial Pollution Inspectorate, the River Purification Authorities and the Hazardous Waste Inspectorate; SEPA also took over responsibility from local authorities for waste regulation and for the control of industrial air pollution under Part I of the EPA. For operational purposes, Scotland has been divided into three regions (West, East and North), each with a Regional Board to which SEPA may delegate certain functions subject to the approval of the Secretary of State. Regional boundaries have been based on river catchment areas and matched as far as possible with the boundaries of unitary authorities. SEPA's headquarters are in Stirling.

(a) Aims and Objectives

Under section 31 of the Act, the Secretary of State for Scotland will give SEPA Guidance, which it must have regard to, on the objectives to be pursued in carrying out its functions; this will include Guidance on SEPA's contribution to attaining the objective of sustainable development.

In considering or formulating proposals relating to its functions, SEPA and the Secretary of State have a duty to have regard to the desirability of conserving and enhancing the natural heritage of Scotland, and of protecting and enhancing buildings, sites and objects of interest (e.g. historic, architectural) and the effect which any proposals might have on the natural heritage etc (s.32).

In carrying out its pollution control responsibilities, the main objective is to prevent or minimise, remedy or mitigate the effects of pollution of the environment (s.33(1)); as well as ensuring it has sufficient information regarding the level, or potential level, of pollution of the environment, SEPA must also follow developments in technology and techniques for abating and preventing pollution or its effects. Section 81 of the Act also requires SEPA to have regard to the National Air Quality Strategy in discharging its pollution control functions.

With regard to water, SEPA also has a duty (s.34) to promote the cleanliness of rivers, inland, ground and tidal waters in Scotland and to promote the conservation and enhancement of the natural beauty and amenity of inland and coastal waters and the conservation of flora and fauna dependent on an aquatic environment.

Where land has been designated as a Natural Heritage Area or Scottish Natural Heritage considers an area of land to be of special interest, and which could be affected by an activity or authorisation of SEPA, it should notify SEPA of the fact. Where SEPA has received such notification, it must consult Scottish Natural Heritage prior to carrying out or authorising any activity on the land in question (s.35). SEPA and SNH have signed a formal Memorandum of Understanding which sets out arrangements for the coordination of their respective activities.

(b) Pollution Control Responsibilities

These are similar to those outlined for the Environment Agency, with the addition of the regulation of Part B processes for air pollution under Part I of the *Environmental Protection Act 1990*.

1.8 NORTHERN IRELAND

The Department of Environment (Northern Ireland) has overall responsibility for environmental protection and pollution control, conservation, and historic buildings and monuments. It aims "to protect and conserve the natural and built environment and to promote its appreciation for the benefit of present and future generations".

On 26 November 1997 *The Industrial Pollution Control (Northern Ireland) Order 1997* (SI 2777, NI 18) was made. It introduces a system of pollution control similar to the IPC and air pollution control regimes operating in the rest of the UK, although there are three tiers of control:

- "integrated central control": Part A processes with high pollution potential will be regulated for IPC by the Industrial Pollution and Radiochemical Inspectorate (IPRI) within the DOE(NI);
- "restricted central control": Part B processes with the potential to cause serious air pollution will be regulated for air pollution control, also by the IPRI;
- "local control": Part C processes with significant but less potential for air pollution will be regulated for air pollution control by district councils.

The Northern Ireland Order, and subsequent Regulations, are referred to as appropriate in the section on Integrated Pollution Control in this chapter (see 1.13), and in the section on local air pollution control in chapter 2 (see 2.12). The Regulations implementing the new legislation came into force on 2 March 1998; new processes were required to apply for an authorisation immediately; existing processes will transfer to the new regulatory règime by sector, with the final group required to apply for an authorisation by 31 December 2002.

1.9 LOCAL AUTHORITIES

Local authorities – usually environmental health departments or pollution control departments – have a wide range of responsibilities covering the whole spectrum of pollution control and environmental protection; these are detailed in the individual chapters of this book.

The local authority associations (now the Local Government Association) and the Environment Agency have signed a Memorandum of Understanding (1997) covering those areas of environmental protection for which they both have some responsibility – see 1.7.1(d) above.

The Public Health (Control of Diseases) Act 1984 gives Port Health Authorities similar responsibilities and powers to local authorities for legislation relating to public health and the control of pollution.

1.10 HEALTH AND SAFETY EXECUTIVE

The HSE, which is the executive arm of the Health and Safety Commission, is also involved with pollution legislation in that it enforces health and safety law for the majority of industrial premises for the protection of both the workforce and the general public. It operates mainly under the *Health and Safety at Work etc Act 1974* and regulations arising from the Act, e.g. the *Control of Substances Hazardous to Health Regulations 1994* (see chapter 2) and the *Noise at Work Regulations 1989* (see chapter 3). The HSE is also the licensing authority for nuclear installations (see chapter 4).

The HSE and the Environment Agency have signed a formal agreement which aims to minimise duplication in the regulation of industrial processes. HSE regulates industrial processes to protect workers and for safety issues.

1.11 BRITISH STANDARDS INSTITUTION

The BSI is an independent national organisation incorporated by Royal Charter. Through a Memorandum of Understanding with the Government, it is the national standards making body and produces all national standards. These include product and performance specifications, codes of practice, management systems, methods of testing, measurement, analysis and sampling, guides and glossaries. These standards are voluntary unless quoted in legislation, in which case they become mandatory. BSI also tests goods and services for industry and government.

The BSI has for some time participated in the work of the International Standards Organisation (ISO) and many ISO standards have been adopted as parallel British Standards. More recently there has been a shift in focus to European work, and the European Committee for Standardisation (CEN). Once a European Standard has been agreed, the BSI adopts it as a dual-numbered BS and withdraws any conflicting British Standards. Whilst it is not currently mandatory for UK bodies to use the European Standards, it is strongly advisable to do so as this provides a means of ensuring compliance with relevant European Directives.

See also, this chapter, 1.22, Environmental Management.

INTEGRATED POLLUTION CONTROL

1.12 INTEGRATED POLLUTION PREVENTION AND CONTROL

1.12.1 The EU Directive

On 24 September 1996, EU Environment Ministers formally adopted a Directive on Integrated Pollution Prevention and Control (96/61/EC). It came into force on 30 October 1996 and must be implemented by 30 October 1999 when it will apply to all new installations and those undergoing a substantial change. Existing installations (i.e. operating before 30 October 1996 or for which an authorisation existed or had been requested and the installation was brought into operation by 30 October 1997) must comply with the Directive by 30 October 2007. Existing installations wishing to carry out a substantial negative change (i.e. one with significant negative effects on human beings or the environment) between implementation of the Directive and 30 October 2007 must apply for a permit covering that part of the installation to be substantially changed.

The main purpose of the IPPC Directive is "to achieve integrated prevention and control of pollution" from listed activities. This will be done by preventing, or where that is not practicable, reducing emissions to the air, water and land by potentially polluting industrial and other installations "so as to achieve a high level of protection of the environment taken as a whole".

Annex I to the Directive lists the industrial activities to which the Directive applies; these are: energy industries; production and processing of metals; mineral industry; chemical industry; waste management; and other activities. This latter category includes pulp production, paper and board production, pretreatment or dyeing of fibres, tanning, slaughterhouses and disposal of animal carcases, various food processes and intensive poultry and pig rearing installations.

While IPPC and IPC are similar in a number of ways, a far greater number of installations are likely to fall within the scope of IPPC – about 4,600 in England and Wales: these include:

- installations currently regulated for IPC;
- installations currently regulated for air pollution control only under the *Environmental Protection Act 1990*;
- installations regulated for control of water pollution through discharge consents or trade effluent consents;
- waste sites currently regulated under the *Waste Management Licensing Regulations 1994*;
- pig and poultry units, some of which are subject to control under the *Control of Pollution (Silage, Slurry and Agricultural Fuel Oil) Regulations 1991*;
- food and drinks plants.

An application for a Permit will need to be made to the competent authority (i.e. enforcing authority); where there is more than one "competent authority" (e.g. Environment Agency and local authorities), steps must be taken to ensure an integrated approach to the procedure for granting a permit. Conditions attached to the Permit will relate to the operation of the plant, including emission limit values for certain substances and preparations listed in Annex III to the Directive based on best available techniques (BAT) (see 1.6.1 above); local environmental conditions, geographical location and other technical characteristics must be taken into account; other conditions should cover consumption of raw materials, energy efficiency, heat, noise, light and vibration, accident prevention, and waste management practices to avoid pollution following closure of the site. Permit conditions should ensure that there will be no breach of EU environmental quality standards or other EU legislation and ensure "a high level of protection for the environment taken as a whole". The permit must also contain monitoring requirements, specifying measurement methodology and frequency. Permits will be reviewed periodically and where necessary updated in line with BAT or to tighten permit conditions for various reasons. The Directive allows for Member States to use "general binding rules" as an alternative to individually tailored conditions. Public consultation requirements and access to permits and other data are similar to those under Part I of the *Environmental Protection Act 1990*.

Technical Guidance – or "Best Available Techniques Reference Documents" – are currently being drafted on behalf of the Commission and, once finalised, must be taken into account by competent authorities.

1.12.2 Implementation of the Directive

As mentioned above the Directive must be transposed by Member States into their national legislation by 30 October 1999. This is likely to be done through primary legislation which would also amend or replace some sections of Part I of the EPA to implement similar statutory regimes for IPPC and IPC/LAPC installations.

Among the issues being considered in implementing the Directive are the following:

- IPPC is wider than IPC, in that it seeks to regulate the entire environmental impact of an installation, not just polluting substances using the BPEO; IPPC includes issues such as site closure, energy efficiency, noise and vibration, accident prevention and environmental impact assessment, some of which are covered by other regulatory regimes; these need to be incorporated without introducing an unduly complex permit process;
- initially the Environment Agency should be the sole regulator for IPPC in England and Wales; existing LAPC processes would transfer to Agency control on being brought within IPPC or when a substantial change is made to the process; local authorities would be statutory consultees for those installations for which they have no direct regulatory responsibility. In Scotland, SEPA will be the sole regulator, with local authorities as statutory consultees;
- both the Environment Agency and SEPA would be required to justify any departures from LA recommendations on conditions relating to noise in IPPC permits;
- sectoral affordability as a criterion in BAT/BATNEEC decisions to be phased out gradually as sector-specific guidance with indicative standards to be expected from installations are produced which also take account of costs and benefits of different measures in different sectors; guidance would also include clear timetables for upgrading to meet standards. Operators would have to justify any departure from indicative standards and guidelines, and the regulator to explain acceptance of such arguments on the public register;
- the link between IPPC requirements for site restoration and the contaminated land provisions of the EPA, Part IIa will need clarifying;

A MAFF consultation document (also published in July 1997) looks at implementing the Directive in the pig and poultry sectors; it puts forward three possible approaches: site specific with individually tailored permit conditions; mainly general rules although individual installations could opt for site specific controls in agreement with the regulator; or general rules for certain emissions and site specific conditions for others.

1.13 ENVIRONMENTAL PROTECTION ACT, PART I

Proposals for an integrated approach to pollution control were first put forward by the Royal Commission on Environmental Pollution in their fifth report (*Air Pollution Control: An Integrated Approach*; 1976). The report drew attention to the cross-media movement of pollution, and the case was also made for a unified inspectorate "to ensure an integrated approach to difficult industrial problems at source, whether these affect air, water or land". Various consultation papers reviewing the control of air pollution and the establishment of HM Inspectorate of Pollution (HMIP) in England and Wales in April 1987 (see 1.2.1 above) culminated in the inclusion of Integrated Pollution Control (IPC) in the *Environmental Protection Act 1990*, Part I.

IPC covers all major solid, liquid and gaseous emissions to air, land and water from the most polluting and complex industrial processes – Part A processes. Thus, IPC recognises that reduction of a release to one environmental medium could well have implications for another. In cases of releases to more than one environmental medium from processes under central control, the enforcing authority is to set conditions to ensure that the Best Practicable Environmental Option (BPEO) – see 1.5 above – is secured to minimise pollution to the environment as a whole. Thus it should also be borne in mind that the objective is to set conditions which protect the environment – not workers: health and safety legislation is designed to protect workers.

From 1 April 1996 the Environment Agency in England and Wales and the Scottish Environment Protection Agency became the enforcing authorities for IPC.

Integrated Pollution Control (IPC) was progressively implemented from 1 April 1991 in England and Wales and from 1 April 1992 in Scotland with the various categories of processes required to apply for an authorisation within specified dates; the final tranche of processes had to apply for an authorisation before the end of January 1996. Prior to authorisation under the EPA, processes continued to be regulated under the *Alkali Act 1906* and regulations under it – this was finally repealed in England and Wales in December 1996.

Part I of the EPA also covers the control of air pollution from Part B processes by local authorities in England and Wales and by SEPA in Scotland – see chapter 2.

Northern Ireland

In Northern Ireland, processes with high pollution potential are to be regulated for integrated central control under the *Industrial Pollution Control (Northern Ireland) Order 1997*. These processes will be regulated by the Industrial Pollution and Radiochemical Inspectorate (IPRI), within the Department of the Environment (NI). The IPRI is also responsible for regulating processes with the potential to cause serious air pollution ("restricted central control") – see chapter 2.

Reference to the appropriate article of the Northern Ireland legislation is given throughout this section and is shown as follows: (NI: IPCO, Art.0).

1.13.1 Environmental Protection (Prescribed Processes and Substances) Regulations 1991 (SI 472) (as amended)

(Similar Regulations – The Industrial Pollution Control (Prescribed Processes and Substances) Regulations (Northern Ireland) 1998 (Statutory Rules of Northern Ireland no. 30) – have been made under Article 3 of the Industrial Pollution Control (NI) Order 1997; they came into force on 2 March 1998.)

These Regulations made under section 2 of the Act came into force in England and Wales on 1 April 1991 (Scotland – 1 April 1992). Schedule 1 of the 1991 Regulations (as amended) lists the processes prescribed for Integrated Pollution Control – Part A Processes – and those subject to control of air pollution only – Part B Processes – (Appendix 1.1).

The 1992 and 1993 amendment Regulations mainly relate to the definitions of prescribed processes in Schedule 1 attached to the 1991 Regulations – see Appendix 1.1. 1994 Amendment Regulations (SI 1271) are also mainly concerned with Schedule 1: some processes have been transferred from Part A to Part B or vice versa, some exempted from authorisation and some brought within the authorisation process for the first time. Although a consolidated version of the Regulations has been published, it should be noted that this is not a legal document; the original Regulations and subsequent amendments should be consulted where issues of legality, etc are concerned. 1995 Amendment Regulations (SI 3247, effective 8 January 1996) make further changes to the schedule of prescribed processes.

As at January 1996, about 2,000 processes were defined as Part A processes under current regulations.

As a general rule where a site in England and Wales contains both Part A and Part B processes, the Part B processes falling within the same section of the Schedule as the Part A processes will be scheduled for control by the Environment Agency (in Scotland both Part A and Part B processes are controlled by SEPA). Where operations at a site involve a number of processes falling within the same IPC section, a single authorisation will be issued if all the processes form an integral part of the end product or purpose of the operation. Processes falling within different sections of Schedule 1 will require separate authorisations (except for those in different sections of Chapter 4 – chemical industry, where only one authorisation will be required).

Schedules 4 and 6 of the 1991 Regulations list the substances to be controlled for air or land releases; Schedule 5 – releases to water – has been replaced by a new Schedule in the 1994 amendment Regulations (Appendix 1.2). The list for air applies to both IPC and air pollution control, and the lists for water and land releases to IPC. There is a requirement to use the Best Available Techniques Not Entailing Excessive Cost (BATNEEC – see 1.6 above) to minimise or prevent the release of all substances, whether prescribed or not, to the environment.

The timetable for bringing existing (i.e. in operation in the 12 months prior to April 1991 or 1992 in Scotland) Part A processes within IPC was also given in the 1991 Regulations. The final tranche of processes (Chapter 6 industries – see Appendix 1.1) were required to apply for authorisation between 1 November 1995 and 31 January 1996.

It is an offence to operate a process without an authorisation or in contravention of any conditions of the authorisation (EPA, ss.6(1) and 23; NI: IPCO, Art.6(1) and 23(1)(a)). Existing processes which have applied for an authorisation or are awaiting the outcome of an appeal may continue to operate.

Northern Ireland

Schedule 1 to the 1998 Regulations describes the prescribed processes to be regulated for Integrated Central Control (Part A processes); it also lists those for Restricted Central Control (Part B) and Local Control (Part C) – see chapter 2. While the processes prescribed for control are very similar to those in the rest of the United Kingdom, it is of course necessary to refer to the Schedule itself for details of classification.

As from 2 March 1998, all new processes had to apply for an authorisation from the relevant authority. Schedule 3 to the Regulations lists the dates within which existing processes must apply for an authorisation, with the first tranche required to apply before 31 December 1998. Others will be required to apply for authorisation as specified in Schedule 3, with the final tranche required to apply before 31 December 2002. Existing processes are defined as those operating in the 12 months before 2 March 1998; or the plant for which was in the course of construction, or for which contracts for construction had been exchanged in the 12 months to 2 March 1998; or are currently regulated under the *Alkali Act 1906*.

Schedules 4, 5 and 6 list the prescribed substances for release, respectively to air, water and land. These are identical to Schedules 4, 5 and 6 of the GB Regulations – see Appendix 1.2.

1.13.2 Environmental Protection (Applications, Appeals and Registers) Regulations 1991 (SI 507), as amended

(Similar Regulations – The Industrial Pollution Control (Applications, Appeals and Registers) Regulations (Northern Ireland) 1998 (SR NI 29) – have been made under The Industrial Pollution Control (Northern Ireland) Order 1997. They came into force on 2 March 1998.)

These Regulations came into force in England and Wales on 1 April 1991 (Scotland – 1 April 1992); they detail the procedure for applying for an authorisation and for a variation of the authorisation for both Part A and Part B processes as laid down by sections 6-15 of the EPA (as amended by the *Environment Act 1995*). The Regulations also cover the appeals procedure and the establishment of public registers of information. The 1996 Amendment Regulations (SI 667), which came into force on 1 April 1996, amend the 1991 Regulations with regard to advertising and consultation on applications and information to be placed on the public register. They also require companies applying for an authorisation for the first time and those seeking a variation to disclose the name of their parent company.

IPC adopts a preventative approach to pollution control. Before a prescribed process can be operated, prior authorisation must be obtained which will contain the specific conditions which must be met in operating the process.

As from 1 April 1991 in England and Wales (1 April 1992 in Scotland), all proposed new, and substantially changed existing, Part A processes required an IPC authorisation. (All large combustion plant, whether new or existing required an authorisation from 1 April 1991.) Authorisations for existing Part A plant were phased in over four years from 1 April 1992. Prior to authorisation existing plant could continue to operate under existing approvals, providing an application was made within the relevant period and pending a decision on that application. During that time they were not subject to IPC charges. The application procedure and charging structure are set out below.

It should be noted that the procedure for regulating processes for air pollution is much the same as that for Integrated Pollution Control (NI: Integrated Central Control) – see chapter 2.

Northern Ireland

The 1998 Regulations are similar to those applying in England, Scotland and Wales.

The Industrial Pollution Control (Authorisation of Processes) (Determination Periods) Order (Northern Ireland) 1998 (SR NI 30) varies the periods contained in the IPCO within which enforcing authorities should determine applications for authorisations. For existing Part A processes the period is extended from six to nine months. For new Part A processes the period is six months unless a longer period is agreed. Where a request is made for certain information on an application to be excluded from the public register for reasons of national security or commercial confidentiality, the period of determination does not begin until the request has been determined or withdrawn.

(a) Applications

(NI: IPCO, Art.6 & Sch. 1, Part I)

Applications for an IPC authorisation should be made on a form available from the enforcing authority. Prior to preparing an application – or at an early stage in its preparation – it is suggested that process operators should discuss it with the enforcing authority, thus ensuring that it will meet the requirements of the legislation.

In the case of planned new processes, operators are advised to make an application for an authorisation on the basis of design plans prior to construction of the plant. Where a novel or very complex process is under design, it is again suggested that the enforcing authority be involved at an early stage, and the use of a "staged" application procedure agreed – i.e. the application for an authorisation is submitted in stages as the plans for the process develop (*Integrated Pollution Control: A Practical Guide*, DOE/WO, 1996). The actual construction of the plant will be subject to separate approval under planning legislation – see 1.21.

In addition to general information about the plant (including the name and address of its parent company or ultimate holding company), and a description of the process, the application should have regard to the relevant IPR Process Guidance Note (England and Wales; see below and Appendix 1.3); it should also include:

- name and address of the local authority in which the process is to be carried on or, in the case of mobile plant, the local authority in which the applicant's principle place of business is located;

- a list of prescribed substances (and any other substances which might cause harm if released into any environmental medium) used in connection with or resulting from the process; the likely quantity and nature of releases from the process assuming the technology and controls have been fitted and are operational;
- description of the techniques to be used for preventing or minimising the release of prescribed substances and rendering harmless any substances which are released – i.e. the operator must show that the best available techniques not entailing excessive cost will be used (see 1.6 above);
- details of any proposed release of such a substance into any environmental medium and an assessment of the environmental consequences; where an IPC process releases substances to more than one environmental medium, an assessment must be undertaken to demonstrate that the application represents the Best Practicable Environmental Option (BPEO) (see 1.5 above); where the BPEO has not been selected, e.g. on cost grounds, this must be justified;
- proposals for monitoring the release of substances;
- in the case of existing plant, identification of areas requiring upgrading to comply with BATNEEC and new plant standards, together with provisional programme of improvements. (A detailed programme should be submitted within six months of receiving authorisation.)

The application plus eight copies must be sent to the enforcing authority; this will enable copies to be sent (within 14 days) to statutory consultees who will normally have 28 days (NI: 42 days) in which to comment; statutory consultees are

- the Health and Safety Executive
- Sewerage undertakers (sewerage authority in Scotland)
- Ministry of Agriculture, Fisheries and Foods, England, Secretary of State for Wales/Scotland (as appropriate)
- English Nature, Scottish Natural Heritage, Countryside Council for Wales (as appropriate)
- Harbour authority (if appropriate)
- the local authority in whose area the process (except mobile plant) will be carried on
- the local fisheries committee where the process may involve a discharge into territorial or coastal waters within its area.

In Northern Ireland, statutory consultees for Part A processes are:

- Department of Economic Development
- Department of Agriculture
- Department of the Environment, for processes which may involve a release into any underground strata or waterway, into a sewer, or of any substance into any environmental medium
- relevant district council
- relevant harbour authority for processes which may result in the release of any substance into the harbour.

Incomplete applications, those with insufficient information or accompanied by an incorrect fee will be returned to the applicant and it will be deemed as not having been submitted. In such instances it would be important for the applicant to resubmit the application as soon as possible so as not to risk prosecution for operating without an authorisation.

In submitting the application, the applicant may request that certain information should not be put in the register on the grounds of commercial confidentiality or national security (EPA, ss.21 & 22; NI: IPCO, Arts.21 & 22). Any request for exclusion should be accompanied by a full statement justifying the request. The enforcing authority has 14 days to consider the request. If it agrees, then the relevant information will be withheld (though it will be sent to the HSE); if the request is refused, the applicant has 21 days in which to appeal to the Secretary of State (see below); during this period the information in dispute will not be added to the register. Following determination or withdrawal of an appeal in respect of commercial confidentiality, a further seven days must elapse before the information is put in the register (*Env. Act 1995*, Sch. 22, para 58(2); IPCO, Art.22(5)). It should be noted that if the enforcing authority fails to respond to the request for information to be withheld within 14 days, then it automatically becomes commercially confidential (s.22(3) of the EPA; NI: IPCO, Art.22(3)).

Following acceptance of the application and resolution of any issues of commercial confidentiality, copies must be filed in the public register (see below), as the public also have a right to comment on the application – see also below (b) public consultation.

The Secretary of State (NI: DOE) may request the enforcing authority to forward a particular application, or class of applications, to him for determination (EPA, Sch. 1, para 3; NI: IPCO, Sch. 1, Part I, para 3). The enforcing authority should inform the applicant that this has been done; both parties have 21 days in which to request the Secretary of State to arrange either a local inquiry or a hearing in connection with the application.

Under the *Environmental Protection (Authorisation of Processes) (Determination of Periods) Order 1991* an application must be determined within four months from the day on which it is received or from when any issues of commercial confidentiality or national security are resolved (NI: 6 months – IPCO, Sch. 1, Part I, para 5); a longer determination period may, however, be agreed with applicants.

(b) Public Consultation

The public have a right to be consulted about applications for authorisations and proposals to vary an authorisation. Thus, the process operator must publish an advertisement in a local newspaper not less than 14 days but not more than 42 days following an application for authorisation or notification of, or application for, a variation. Applications for authorisations must also be advertised in the *London Gazette* (*Edinburgh Gazette* or *Belfast Gazette* – as appropriate). Applications or variations for mobile plant do not have to be advertised.

As well as brief details of the process, the advertisement should state where a copy of the application can be seen; it should also state that copies of any representations received will be put on the public register unless a request is made in writing that they should not. In such cases a statement will be put in the register saying that such a request has been made (without identifying the person making the request).

(c) Integrated Pollution Regulation Notes

• England & Wales

In addition to giving guidance on what constitutes the BATNEEC for each process, IPR Notes (see Appendix 1.2) include "achievable release levels (ARL)" for new plant using best available techniques. For existing plant a timetable for improvements towards meeting ARLs or for decommissioning the plant will normally form part of the authorisation. IPR Notes also include details of any environmental quality standards, European Union and international obligations etc which should be met (see chapter 2, 2.4); advice on techniques for pollution abatement and compliance monitoring is also given. Inspectors may take account of "site specific issues", such as the locality of the process with regard to emission effects.

IPR Notes are generally reviewed every four years.

A series of Technical Guidance Notes (see Appendix 1.4) provide guidance and background detail on a range of technical subjects and will be of interest to process operators, contractors used by the enforcing authorities and other regulatory bodies. Subjects dealt with by TG Notes include BPEO assessments, monitoring emissions of pollutants at source, solvent vapour emissions and pollutant abatement technology.

• Scotland

IPR Notes do not apply in Scotland; guidance on the implementation of IPC in Scotland issued by the Scottish Office (*A Practical Guide – Central Control*, 1992) notes that the IPR notes for England and Wales "represent an important source of information for the Scottish enforcing authorities and for applicants". It says that enforcing authorities will take note of their contents but may also prepare separate notes for Scotland. The Guide therefore suggests that applicants should discuss with the enforcing authorities the likely standards to be imposed and frame applications accordingly. General notes of guidance outlining information to be given on application forms are available from the Scottish Office.

(d) Authorisations

In granting an authorisation and setting conditions, the enforcing authority must have regard to any Directions from the Secretary of State implementing, for example, EU and other international obligations (EPA, s.7(b); NI: IPCO, Art.30), and to the National Air Quality Strategy (s.81 of the *Environment Act 1995* and see chapter 2, 2.9). Conditions may specify emission levels (including, where appropriate, for noise to prevent nuisance), the breaching of which constitutes an offence. Enforcing authorities are required to ensure that operators are using BATNEEC, that the conditions imposed will prevent or minimise release of the most polluting substances, and that any that are released are rendered harmless. There is also an implied condition (a residual duty) in all authorisations that operators will use BATNEEC to prevent or minimise pollution at all stages of plant design and operation. Conditions should not be attached regulating the final disposal of waste to land (EPA, s.28; NI: IPCO, Art.28); this activity will require a waste management licence under Part II of the EPA (NI: Part II of *Pollution Control and Local Government Order 1978* or *Waste & Contaminated Land Order 1997*, when implemented). However, authorisations under Part I of the EPA (NI: IPCO) for waste disposal and recycling processes should take account of the objectives of the waste framework Directive, including not causing nuisance through noise and odour (see also chapter 4, 4.6).

Authorisations should ensure compliance with any quality objectives or standards, emission limits and with national emission plans set by the Secretary of State for Environment, Transport and the Regions (e.g. for compliance with the EU Large Combustion Plant

Directive (EPA, s.3(5) – see chapter 2, 2.4.4); where the release of a substance is likely to affect more than one environmental medium, the authorisation must have regard to the BPEO.

If the enforcing authority is not convinced that an applicant will be able to carry on the process in compliance with the conditions to be imposed, it must refuse the application for an authorisation (EPA, s.6(4); NI: IPCO, Art.6(4)). An application for an authorisation should also be refused if the enforcing authority considers that a prescribed release might contribute or result in failure to achieve a statutory water quality objective (EPA, s.28(3)); *The Industrial Pollution Control Order 1997* extends this to cover pollution of any waters in Northern Ireland (Art.28(3)).

Authorisations may be transferred to another person who should notify the enforcing authority within 21 days (EPA, s.9; NI: IPCO, Art.9). However it is advisable to consult the enforcing authority prior to purchase of the plant to ensure that it has no objections to the transfer. A copy of the transfer notice will be put in the public register.

Generally, authorisations will be reviewed not less than every four years to take account of technological developments and to reflect new guidance notes.

(e) Variations

Conditions of an authorisation may be varied either at the request of the enforcing authority or of the operator.

Section 10 of the EPA (NI: IPCO, Art.10) empowers the enforcing authority to serve a variation notice in which it may vary conditions attached to an authorisation – for example, improved pollution control techniques and technology might make tighter emission limits feasible. The notice will specify the changes which the enforcing authority has decided should be made and the date(s) on which the variations are to take effect (unless the notice is withdrawn). Sch. 22, para 51(3) of the *Environment Act 1995* amends section 10 of the EPA to permit the enforcing authority to serve a notice varying a variation notice; this should specify the changes the enforcing authority wishes to make to the first variation notice and the date these are to take effect. The process operator must advise the enforcing authority of the way in which it is intended to meet the revised conditions. If the change is "substantial" (see below), then the normal application procedure for an authorisation will be followed and a fee become payable. There is a right of appeal (see (h) below) except if the variation notice implements a Direction from the Secretary of State.

Section 11 of the EPA and the *Environmental Protection (Applications, Appeals and Registers) Regulations 1991* (NI: IPCO, Art.11 and 1998 Regulations) apply where an operator wishes to make a change to the way in which the process is carried out and which could have implications for the authorisation. Such a request may be made when the process is already in use or at the design or construction stage. As a first step, the operator should send the enforcing authority written details of the changes being requested. If the enforcing authority considers that the changes require the conditions attached to the authorisation to be varied, then the operator must submit a formal application. An application to make a substantial change will then follow the procedure outlined above for applying for an authorisation; note: the application should include the name and address of the parent or ultimate holding company if this information is not already on the public register. There is a right of appeal if the enforcing authority refuses a section 11 variation (see below).

Statutory consultees (see (a) applications above) should be consulted concerning both proposed section 10 and section 11 variations and a copy of all representations received put in the public register, together with any received from the public – see above (b) public consultation.

Applications for variations (except those referred to the Secretary of State) must be determined within four months of receipt unless a different period is agreed. An application for a variation will be deemed to have failed if the enforcing authority fails to determine it within the agreed period and the applicant notifies the enforcing authority that he considers the failure to determine as refusal of the application (*Env. Act 1995*, Sch. 22, para 93(10)).

The *Environment Act 1995* (Sch. 22, para 93(5)) amends Schedule 1 of the EPA to permit the Secretary of State to call in applications for variations for determination. In doing so, he may either arrange for a local inquiry or give both the applicant and the enforcing authority the opportunity of a hearing.

Minor or "relevant" changes will be considered by the enforcing authority, without consulting statutory consultees, and any changes to conditions to be attached to the authorisation notified to the operator. "Relevant" changes relate to the way in which the process is carried on which may affect the substances released or affect the amount or characteristic of any substance released. "Substantial" changes are defined in the EPA (s.10(7); NI: IPCO, Art.10(8)) as those resulting in substantial changes "in the substances released from the process or in the amount or any other characteristic of any substance so released".

Copies of all variations and relating documentation must be put in the public register.

(f) Revocation of Authorisation

Following 28 days written notice, the enforcing authority may revoke an authorisation for failure to pay the annual subsistence charge, or if it has reason to believe that the process has not been carried on at all or carried on for 12 months; prior to the notice taking effect, the enforcing authority may either withdraw the notice or vary the date on which revocation is to take effect. (EPA, s.12; NI: IPCO, Art.12)

(g) Enforcement

If the enforcing authority believes conditions of an authorisation are being breached it can take any of the following actions under sections 13-14 of the EPA (NI: IPCO, Arts.13-14):

- serve an enforcement notice (s.13) reinforcing an existing condition or requiring the operator to remedy the cause of the breach of condition within a specified period; Sch. 22, para 53 of the *Environment Act 1995* amends the EPA to permit the enforcing authority by written notice to withdraw an enforcement notice.
- where it is felt that the continued operation of the process involves "an imminent risk of serious pollution of the environment", serve a prohibition notice requiring the operator to close down all or part of the process and take the necessary steps to stop the risk (s.14); written notice of the withdrawal of a prohibition notice will be given by the enforcing authority when it is satisfied that the necessary action to deal with the problems has been taken.

Where there is no immediate environmental risk, the enforcement officer will usually discuss the remedial action needed, and confirm it in writing. Prosecutions will normally only be undertaken for serious pollution incidents and contraventions of the law, including operating without an authorisation, failure to supply information or supplying false information, and obstructing an enforcement officer (Environment Agency draft Enforcement and Prosecution Policy, May 1998).

(h) Appeals

Section 15 of the EPA (NI: IPCO, Art.15) provides for a right of appeal against a decision of the enforcing authority to the Secretary of State (except when the decision implements a Direction from the Secretary of State – *Environment Act 1995*, Sch. 22, para 54(2)) in the following instances:

- refusal of authorisation or disagreement with conditions attached to the authorisation;
- terms of variation notice served by enforcing authority under section 10;
- refusal of request for variation of authorisation under section 11;
- revocation of authorisation;
- terms of enforcement or prohibition notice.

Section 22 (NI: IPCO, Art.22) provides a right of appeal with regard to decisions relating to whether information should be considered as commercially confidential and thus excluded from the public registers (see above – applications).

Where an appeal is lodged against a revocation notice or decision of the enforcing authority that information is not commercially confidential, implementation of the notice or decision is deferred pending determination or withdrawal of the appeal. All other notices take effect from the specified date and disputed conditions remain in place pending determination or withdrawal of the appeal. An appeal against conditions of an authorisation or refusal of an authorisation or variation must be made within six months, or in the case of enforcement, variation and prohibition notices, within two months. Where a revocation notice has been served, the appeal should be lodged before the date the notice takes effect. Appeals against a refusal to exclude information from the public register should be made within 21 days.

The Secretary of State may determine the appeal himself or appoint someone else for this purpose (*Env. Act 1995*, s.114 & Sch. 20). With effect from 1 September 1997 the Secretary of State delegated his powers for processes in England to the Planning Inspectorate. He has, however, reserved the right to recover appeals relating to the following for determination himself:

- processes or sites of major importance;
- those giving rise to significant public controversy or legal difficulties;
- those which can only be decided in conjunction with other cases over which inspectors have no jurisdiction;
- those which raise major or novel issues of industrial pollution control which could set a policy precedent;
- those which merit recovery because of the particular circumstances.

Appeals relating to issues of commercial confidentiality (s.22 of EPA) are also determined by the Secretary of State.

In Northern Ireland Article 15(3) and Schedule 2 of the *Industrial Pollution Control Order 1997* enables the DOE(NI) to refer appeals, or parts thereof, to the Planning Appeals Commission.

The Regulations (NI: 1998 Regulations) specify the information to be sent to the Secretary of State (England: Planning Inspectorate; NI: DOE) by the operator; this should include a notice of appeal, a statement setting out the reason for the appeal and a statement as to whether the appellant wishes the matter to be dealt with through written representations or by a hearing. A copy of these three documents should also be sent to the Agency/SEPA and the Secretary of State – or Planning Inspectorate – advised that this has been done. The Secretary of State (or Planning Inspectorate) should also be sent a copy of the application and of the authorisation (where this exists), together with any relevant correspondence and notices. Appeals may only be dealt with in writing if both parties agree; if either party request that the matter be dealt with by a hearing, then one will be arranged. A local inquiry may be held in connection with the appeal, either at the instigation of the Secretary of State's appointee or the Secretary of State may direct that a local inquiry be arranged (*Env. Act 1995*, Sch. 22, para 54).

Within 14 days of receiving notice of the appeal, the enforcing authority must send details of it to statutory consultees and others who submitted comments on the original application for the authorisation – they have 21 days in which to send any further comments to the Secretary of State (or Planning Inspectorate). These will then be copied to both the enforcing authority and the appellant and will also be put in the public register unless a written request is made that this should not happen. In such cases a statement will be added to the register saying that representations concerning the appeal have been received and are subject to a request to exclude from the register.

Where the matter is to be decided in writing, the enforcing authority must submit its comments to the Secretary of State (or his appointee) within 28 days of receipt of the appeal notice. The appellant will then have 17 days to comment on the statement. Both sides have 14 days from the date of receipt to comment on any other statements submitted in connection with the appeal.

Where a hearing is to be held, the Secretary of State (or Planning Inspectorate) will notify the appellant and the enforcing authority of the time, date and place – a minimum of 28 days notice will be given; details must be advertised in the local press and also sent to statutory consultees etc giving not less than 21 days notice. In the case of mobile plant, notice of the hearing must be given in the place in which the plant was operating when the enforcement/prohibition notice was served. Any further statements relating to the appeal should be submitted within six weeks of the appeal being lodged or not less than 21 days before the hearing (whichever is first). Most hearings will be held wholly or partly in public, unless matters of commercial confidentiality are involved (when the hearing will always be in private).

Following determination, copies of the decision and any report are sent to the appellant, the enforcing authority and statutory consultees; copies of the decision only are sent to others involved. In those cases where the Secretary of State has recovered an appeal, the Inspector will report to the Secretary of State who will then make a decision on the appeal. Documents relating to the determination of the appeal are put in the public register.

If an appeal is withdrawn, the enforcing authority should advise all those who were originally given notification of it.

(i) Public Registers

Sections 20-22 of the EPA (as amended by the *Env. Act 1995*, Sch. 22, paras 57-58) are concerned with the establishment of registers of IPC (and air pollution control – see chapter 2) information to be maintained by the enforcing authorities. Articles 20-22 of the *Industrial Pollution Control (Northern Ireland) Order 1997* contain similar provisions.

The 1996 Amendment of the *Applications, Appeals and Registers Regulations* (NI: IPCO, Art.20(1) and 1998 Regulations) list the documentation to be placed in the register:

- documentation relating to an application for an authorisation or for variation of the conditions of an authorisation; and subsequent information relating to the application for an authorisation requested by the enforcing authority;
- copy of advertisement relating to application for authorisation or variation or notification by enforcing authority to vary an authorisation; representations made as a result of the advertisement unless a request is made that they should not be put on the register; in such cases a statement to this effect should be put on the register without identifying the person making the request;
- authorisations and their conditions;
- written notice of transfer of authorisation to another person;
- revocation, variation, enforcement or prohibition notices issued by the enforcing authority; notification by the enforcing authority of withdrawal of enforcement or prohibition notice;
- documentation relating to an appeal, its determination and any accompanying reports;
- details of convictions relating to carrying on of a prescribed process with or without an authorisation;
- monitoring data collected by the enforcing authority or submitted

by an operator as a condition of the authorisation; where such information is omitted on grounds of commercial confidentiality, then the enforcing authority should put a statement on the register confirming or otherwise compliance with the relevant condition of the authorisation;

- information given to the enforcing authority on or after 1 April 1996 in compliance with a condition of an authorisation, variation, enforcement or prohibition notice;
- reports by the enforcing authority relating to the environmental consequences of a prescribed process in the locality of premises where the prescribed process is carried on under an authorisation;
- Directions from the Secretary of State.

Information affecting national security or which is accepted as being commercially confidential may be withheld and a note to this effect added to the register. The onus is on operators to prove that disclosure of specific information would be prejudicial to their commercial interests. Exclusion of data from the register on the grounds of commercial confidentially lasts for four years after which it will be added to the register unless a further four year exclusion is applied for and agreed.

Local authorities in England and Wales have copies of entries relating to IPC processes in their area in their registers, and also maintain registers for air pollution processes – Part B processes – under their control (see chapter 2). Registers held by district councils in Northern Ireland will also contain particulars of authorisations granted by the DOE's Chief Inspector (Industrial Pollution and Radiochemical Inspectorate).

Applications for an authorisation or variation which have been advertised in a paper should be put on the register within 14 days of receipt by the enforcing authority; notifications to vary an authorisation (which are also advertised) should also be put on the register within 14 days of notifying the operator. The Regulations do not specify the time within which other information should be placed in the register although guidance issued by the Department of Environment (now DETR) suggests that this should be done "as soon as possible". Information held on the registers may be inspected by the public free of charge and copies of entries obtained on "payment of a reasonable charge".

Information will be removed from the register in the following circumstances:

- withdrawal of application for authorisation prior to determination – all particulars to be removed not less than two months but within three months after the date of withdrawal;
- if a process ceases to be a prescribed process following amendment of the *Prescribed Processes and Substances Regulations* – all particulars to be removed not less than two months but within three months of the date on which the process ceases to be prescribed;
- monitoring information relating to a process – four years after entering in the register;
- information relating to a process which has been superseded – four years after the later information has been entered in the register.

1.13.3 Chemical Release Inventory

As a distinct, but related, part of the IPC register system, an annual Chemical Release Inventory covering England and Wales is prepared by the Environment Agency. This provides aggregated data on releases from industrial processes regulated for IPC (Part A processes) and will in due course cover those regulated under the *Radioactive Substances Act 1993*. The Inventory is prepared using data supplied by industrial processes on those releases for which limits have been set in their authorisations. The Inventory includes a commentary on the actual data in terms of emissions and their potential environmental effects, as well as brief information on figures extracted from the database in a geographical (i.e. by county) and industrial context.

The Inventory is in the form of an electronic database and staff will carry out a search on request.

1.13.4 Offences

It is an offence (EPA, s.23; NI: IPCO, Art.23) to operate a prescribed process without an authorisation or to contravene any conditions attached to an authorisation or other enforcement notice without reasonable excuse. Other offences include making a false or misleading statement and obstructing an inspector. Summary conviction carries a maximum fine of £20,000 and/or three months imprisonment, and conviction on indictment an unlimited fine and/or two years imprisonment.

1.14 ENVIRONMENT ACT 1995

1.14.1 Fees and Charges for IPC

Sections 41-43 of the Act, which came into force on 21 September 1995, enable the Environment Agency and SEPA to make schemes (to be approved by their respective Secretary of State) for the recovery of costs in respect of environmental licences. Such costs include:

- issuing authorisations;
- carrying out compliance monitoring and enforcing controls;
- sampling and analysis of releases;
- operation of the registers of information on IPC processes;
- administrative expenditure in support of the above functions.

Charges are levied according to the number of components a process contains. Levels of charges are reviewed each year. Where an authorisation is issued part way through the year, the charge will be calculated on a pro-rata basis. The financial year runs from 1 April - 31 March.

England and Wales

Fees for 1998/99 are set out in *The Environment Act (Environmental Licences) (Integrated Pollution Control) Charging Scheme 1998* which came into operation on 1 April 1998, and are as follows:

- **Application fee** (covering consideration of each IPC application): £4,420 per component, or £2,945 per component for processes holding a certificate of registration under s.9 of the *Alkali Act 1906*. (NB where the process is regulated for IPC only because of the amount of special waste arisings, it will be charged a flat rate fee of £4,420/£2,945, as appropriate.) Staged applications (see above 1.13.2a) – £1,058 per day.

- **Subsistence charge** (payable annually, covering the cost of inspection, monitoring and enforcement): £2,010 per component (or flat rate fee of £2,010 if IPC regulated because of special waste arisings). Processes involving a release to controlled waters are subject to an additional charge.

- **Substantial variation fee:** £1,480 normally applied to the number of components in the process as it would be following the proposed change. Variations necessitated by a non-substantial change to a process will not incur a charge, the costs being recouped through the annual subsistence charge.

The cost of any routine monitoring, e.g. to verify an operator's monitoring, is charged to the operator concerned. Ad hoc and reactive monitoring is covered by the subsistence charge.

If an operator withdraws an application within 56 calendar days of its receipt by the Environment Agency, then the fee will normally be refunded, though the Agency retains the right not to do so. Non-payment of statutory fees or charges may result in revocation of an operator's authorisation.

The Environment Agency is likely to propose some changes to the IPC charging structure, both to take account of the implementation of the IPPC Directive, as well as its work on a charging methodology for "Operator Performance and Risk Assessment". It has, however, already announced that from 1999/2000 it will be charging in arrears for independent monitoring work.

Scotland

A similar charging scheme applies in Scotland. The following fees were payable from 1 April 1998:

- **application fee**: £1,775;
- **subsistence fee**: £800;
- **variation fee**: £1,105.

Northern Ireland

A charging scheme in respect of applications for authorisations and variations and the level of subsistence charge will be made under Article 8 of the *Industrial Pollution Control (Northern Ireland) Order 1997*.

1.14.2 Powers of Entry

Sections 108-109 of the Act empower "a person who appears suitable to an enforcing authority to be authorised in writing ..." to enter premises where they have reason to believe a prescribed process is being or has been operated (with or without an authorisation) or where they believe there is a risk of serious pollution. Authorised persons may take photographs, samples etc of substances, and require access to relevant information and records. The authorised person may render harmless any substance or article from which it is considered there is imminent danger of serious harm; a written and signed report of what has been done and why should be given to a responsible person on the premises and a copy of the report served on the owner of the substance or article (if different).

Except in an emergency, a warrant should be obtained if entry has been or is likely to be refused and it is probable that force will be needed to gain entry.

Similar powers for inspectors in Northern Ireland are contained in Articles 17 and 18 of the *Industrial Pollution Control (Northern Ireland) Order 1997*.

NUISANCE

There are three types of nuisance: statutory nuisance where a particular nuisance has been made so by statute; and public and private nuisance which are within Common Law.

1.15 STATUTORY NUISANCE

Various Acts of Parliament have covered statutory nuisances; these included the *Public Health Act 1936* which was often used in respect of odour (see chapter 2, 2.33.1); the *Clean Air Act 1956* (now *Clean Air Act 1993*) in respect of smoke (see chapter 2, 2.13.2); the *Control of Pollution Act 1974* (noise nuisance – see chapter 3, 3.6); and in Scotland, until 1 April 1996, ss.16-26 of the *Public Health (Scotland) Act 1897*.

1.15.1 Environmental Protection Act, Part III

Part III of the *Environmental Protection Act 1990*, as amended by the *Noise and Statutory Nuisance Act 1993* (see chapter 3, 3.7) contains the main legislation on statutory nuisance and enables local authorities and individuals to take action to secure the abatement of a statutory nuisance. The *Noise Act 1996* enables action to be taken in respect of noise nuisance from dwellings between 11.00 pm and 7.00 am (see chapter 3, 3.8.1).

Part III of the EPA applied in England and Wales from 1 January 1991 and in Scotland from 1 April 1996 as a result of implementation of section 107 and Schedule 17 of the *Environment Act 1995*; these extend the relevant provisions of the EPA to Scotland.

Section 79 of the EPA, as amended, defines the following statutory nuisances:

a) any premises in such a state as to be prejudicial to health or a nuisance;

b) smoke emitted from premises so as to be prejudicial to health or a nuisance;

c) fumes or gases emitted from premises so as to be prejudicial to health or a nuisance (from private dwellings only);

d) any dust, steam, smell or other effluvia arising on industrial, trade or business premises and being prejudicial to health or a nuisance;

e) any accumulation or deposit which is prejudicial to health or a nuisance;

f) any animal kept in such a place or manner as to be prejudicial to health or a nuisance;

g) noise emitted from premises so as to be prejudicial to health or a nuisance;

ga) noise that is prejudicial to health or a nuisance and is emitted from or caused by a vehicle, machinery or equipment in a street or in Scotland, road;

h) any other matter declared by any enactment to be a statutory nuisance.

Action for nuisance defined in (b), (d) or (e) above may only be taken against a process registered for IPC or air pollution control (Part I of EPA) with the consent of the Secretary of State.

Action for smoke emissions can be taken under the *Clean Air Act 1993* (CAA) in certain instances and cannot therefore be dealt with as a statutory nuisance under the EPA. These instances are:

- smoke emitted from a chimney of a private dwelling in a smoke control area (s.20 of CAA);
- dark smoke from a chimney of a building or a chimney serving the furnace of a boiler or industrial plant attached to a building or installed on any land (s.1 of CAA);
- smoke from a railway locomotive steam engine (s.43 of CAA);
- dark smoke caused by industrial or trade burning (s.2 of CAA).

Also excluded from statutory nuisance action are dust, steam, smell etc (d above) from a railway locomotive steam engine and noise (g above) from aircraft other than model aircraft. Crown defence premises and those occupied by visiting forces are excluded from action under (b)-(g) above. Statutory nuisance legislation cannot be used to take action against land which is in a contaminated state (EPA, s.79(1A), *Env. Act 1995*, Sch. 22, para 89).

It should be noted that the EPA interprets “premises” as including “land”. Equipment (ga above) includes musical instruments. Guidance from the Department of the Environment, Transport and the Regions (Env. Circular 9/97, WO 42/97) suggests that loudspeaker tannoys, loudhailers, radios and “ghetto-blasters” should also be regarded as equipment.

There is a defence (ss.80(8) & 82(10) of the EPA) of Best Practicable Means in respect of nuisance from industrial, trade or business premises. This is interpreted as practicable given local conditions, technical knowledge and financial implications; means includes design, installation and maintenance of plant, buildings and structure and periods of operation.

Steam railway locomotives and recreational steam vessels are exempt from nuisance action in respect of steam and smoke; steam road vehicles (such as traction engines and steamrollers) used on a public highway are also exempt.

So far as action to deal with bonfire smoke is concerned, in certain instances it would be possible to use the *Highways (Amendment) Act 1986*: this makes it an offence to light a fire, permit or direct one to be lit, the smoke from which injures, interrupts or endangers anyone using a highway.

(a) Action by Local Authorities

Local authorities have a duty to inspect their areas from time to time to detect whether a nuisance exists or is likely to occur or recur (s.79(1) of EPA). (Port Health Authorities have the same powers to take action for nuisance, except for noise.) An authority must also take such steps as are reasonably practicable to investigate any complaint of statutory nuisance from a person living in its area. Section 81(2) enables a local authority to take action against a statutory nuisance outside its area if it appears to be affecting any part of its area.

Where the local authority is satisfied that a statutory nuisance exists, or is likely to occur or recur, it must serve an abatement notice on the person responsible for the nuisance or if that person cannot be found, on the owner or occupier of the premises (s.80(1)). If the nuisance is as a result of a structural problem, then the notice should be served on the owner of the premises. The *Noise and Statutory Nuisance Act 1993* amends the procedure for serving an abatement notice in respect of a nuisance from or caused by an unattended vehicle, machinery or equipment (VME) on the street to enable the notice to be affixed directly to it (see chapter 3, 3.7.1).

The notice should impose all or any of the following requirements (s.80(1)):

a) the abatement of the nuisance or prohibiting or restricting its occurrence or recurrence;

b) the carrying out of such works and other steps necessary to abate the nuisance.

The notice should specify the time or times within which the requirements of the notice must be complied with; it should also state that there is a right of appeal and that any appeal against a notice should be made within 21 days to the Magistrates' Court (Sheriff in Scotland) – see below.

Failure to comply with the terms of an abatement notice without reasonable excuse may result in prosecution in the Magistrates' Court (Sheriff in Scotland) (s.80(4)). Conviction may result in a maximum fine of £5,000, plus a daily fine of £500 for each day on which the offence continues after conviction. Where the conviction is for noise from industrial, trade or business premises, the maximum fine is £20,000.

If an abatement notice is not complied with, the local authority may take the necessary steps to abate the nuisance itself (s.81(3)). In the case of action to abate a noise nuisance (s.79(g) of the EPA), this can include seizure of the noise-making equipment – section 10(7) and Schedule 1 of the *Noise Act 1996* (this Act does not apply in Scotland); the procedure is set out in chapter 3, 3.8.2.

Any expenses reasonably incurred by a local authority in England and Wales in abating or preventing the recurrence of a statutory nuisance may be recovered by it from the person responsible for the nuisance (s.81(4)). The *Noise and Statutory Nuisance Act 1993* adds a new section 81A to the EPA enabling local authorities in England and Wales to charge interest from the date of serving the payment notice until full payment is received. If no payment has been received after 21 days, then the expenses plus accrued interest become a legal charge on the property. The charge on the property remains until the debt has been paid in full; if the property is sold, then the charge passes to the new owners. The person on whom the notice is served may appeal to the county court within 21 days of its service. New section 81B of the EPA enables local authorities in England and Wales to require the debt to be paid in instalments over a period of up to 30 years.

(b) Action by Individuals

Action to abate a statutory nuisance may also be taken by an individual through the Magistrates' Court (Sheriff in Scotland) (s.82 of EPA). The nuisance must exist or be likely to recur. Prior to taking action, the complainant must advise the alleged nuisance-maker that it is intended to take court action.

If proved, the court will serve an order which

a) requires abatement of the nuisance within a specified time, and the carrying out of any necessary works; and/or

b) prohibits a recurrence of the nuisance and requires the carrying out of any necessary works within a specified time to prevent a recurrence.

Again, failure to comply with an order without reasonable excuse is an offence and results in a fine, plus a daily fine for each day on which the offence continues after conviction.

1.15.2 The Statutory Nuisance (Appeals) Regulations 1995 (SI 2644)

An appeal against an abatement notice served under sections 80 and 80A of the *Environmental Protection Act 1990* (as amended by the *Noise and Statutory Nuisance Act 1993*) should be lodged with the Magistrates' Court within 21 days of service of the notice.

These Regulations, applicable in England and Wales, came into force on 8 November 1995, replacing 1990 Regulations; the 1995 Regulations are very similar to the 1990 Regulations, their main effect being to add further grounds for appeal against an abatement notice. The Regulations also outline the procedure to be followed when the appellant claims the notice should have been served on another person, and the action which the court may take to give effect to its decisions. Similar Regulations – the *Statutory Nuisance (Appeals) (Scotland) Regulations 1996* (SI 1076) – came into force on 2 May 1996 in Scotland.

Grounds for appeal include:

- unreasonable amount of time given for complying with a notice, or unreasonable requirements;
- an error or other irregularity in the notice;
- that it could or should have been served on someone else; in this instance the appellant should give a copy of the appeals notice to any other person referred to in it;
- in the case of a notice served on a trade or business premises that the best practicable means was used to prevent or counteract the effects of the nuisance. This can be used in defence of the following nuisances: premises in such a state as to be prejudicial to health etc; smoke emitted from a chimney; dust, steam, smell or other effluvia; the manner or place in which animals are being kept; noise; and noise from or caused by vehicles, machinery or equipment;

An appeal may also be lodged if it is felt that the requirements of an abatement notice in respect of noise from premises or VMEs are more onerous than the terms of a valid consent (e.g. for construction work or for the use of loudspeakers).

Where an appeal has been lodged, the notice will be suspended pending determination of the appeal if compliance would result in expenditure or the noise was caused due to carrying out a task imposed by law, except

- where there is a risk of injury to health;
- the cost of carrying out the work required by the notice is not considered disproportionate to the expected benefit;
- there is no point in suspending the notice because of its limited duration.

The Court also has powers to dismiss an appeal, or quash or vary the terms of an abatement notice.

1.16 PUBLIC NUISANCE

A public nuisance is both a tort (civil wrong) and a crime punishable by law, whereas private nuisance is a tort, a wrong for which there is remedy by compensation or damages. Where nuisance is alleged, the court will consider a variety of elements including the nature of the facts complained of, the location, and whether or not the complainant has lost the right to complain through acquiescence. The harm, inconvenience or discomfort suffered by the complainant must be material, and continuing or recurrent; the courts will also take into account the nature of the locality: what is acceptable in an area of substantial industrial activity may not be acceptable in the heart of a residential area; and indeed what is acceptable in a rural area may not be acceptable in an urban situation. Public nuisance takes into account primarily the number of persons affected. The nuisance should affect "all persons who come within the sphere of its operation".

In cases of public nuisance, criminal prosecution can be made by the Attorney General or other enforcing bodies including local authorities' environmental health departments; civil proceedings can be instituted by the Attorney General alone or at the request of a local authority or individual. Section 222 of the *Local Government Act 1972*, provides that a local authority "in the case of civil proceedings may institute them in their own name".

1.17 PRIVATE NUISANCE

Private nuisance actions are more common than public nuisance cases and rely on damage or unreasonable interference with an individual's right to use and enjoy their property. Action may be brought by the aggrieved person in the civil court (either the County or the High Court). Only the occupier of the land or person having a requisite interest is entitled to sue. This may include owner occupiers and tenants but not relatives or visitors even if living with the occupier.

In any proceedings, the person causing the nuisance will be responsible whether or not the nuisance arises from the property he/she occupies, provided that it affects the plaintiff's property. Ownership of land does not necessarily mean that the owner will be held responsible for the actions of others who may cause nuisance. However, the occupier of property may be liable for nuisance even if he/she did not cause it, if he/she allows it to continue during his/her occupation. Remedial action is principally an injunction (a court order restraining the convicted person from committing or continuing the act or omission complained about) and damages.

Eight important principles have been established in court in relation to private nuisance:

a) there must be material interference with property or personal comfort;

b) it is no defence for the defendant to show that all reasonable steps and care have been taken to prevent the nuisance;

c) the nuisance need not be injurious to health;

d) temporary or transient (noise) nuisance will not generally be accepted as a nuisance;

e) the courts do not seek to apply a fixed standard of comfort;

f) it is no defence to show that the plaintiff came to the nuisance;

g) the courts will not interfere with building operations conducted in a reasonable manner;

h) contrary to the general rule in the law of tort, malice may be a significant factor.

Generally speaking, nuisances caused by a person or organisation carrying out a duty imposed by statute are exempt from nuisance action.

ACCESS TO ENVIRONMENTAL INFORMATION

The establishment of Public Registers under, among others, the *Environmental Protection Act 1990*, has made a wide range of environmental information held by enforcement authorities publicly available. Information on the Registers includes applications for (and actual) authorisations and consents, enforcement notices, monitoring results. Only matters of genuine commercial confidentiality and national security may remain secret. Among the areas covered by Registers are Integrated Pollution Control, industrial air pollution control, waste management, water pollution and radioactive substances. In addition, the *Environment and Safety Information Act*

1988 provides for the maintenance of registers of notices relating to environmental and public safety matters issued under, for example, the *Health and Safety at Work Act 1974* and the *Food and Environment Protection Act 1985.*

1.18 EU DIRECTIVE ON PUBLIC ACCESS TO ENVIRONMENTAL INFORMATION

In 1990, the European Union adopted a Directive on Public Access to Environmental Information (90/313/EEC) which had to be implemented by 31 December 1992. Under the Directive members of the public are entitled to have access to all information about the environment held by government and public authorities in their own or another Member State (unless exempt on the grounds of commercial confidentiality or national security). The Directive defines this as information relating to the state of water, air, soil, fauna, flora, land and natural sites, as well as information relating to

- activities (including those which give rise to nuisances such as noise) or measures adversely affecting, or likely to affect these; and
- activities or measures designed to protect these, including administrative measures and environmental management programmes.

Information must be supplied within two months of a request; reasons for refusal must be given and there must be a right of appeal.

The Directive is now due for review, with any revisions also needing to take into account a UNECE Convention on Access to Environmental Information which has now been agreed – see next section.

1.19 UNECE CONVENTION ON ACCESS TO INFORMATION

This Convention, the full name of which is the Convention on Access to Information, Public Participation in Decision Making and Access to Justice in Environmental Matters, was adopted in June 1998 in Aarhus, Denmark; it covers information held by public authorities and will come into force after ratification by 16 countries. Its main requirements are:

- **access to information** – the definition of environmental matters is rather wider than that in either the EU Directive or the UK Regulations, and includes issues which may form part of the decision making process connected with the environmental issue, such as land use planning, health and safety and economic issues; information on biological diversity and genetically modified organisms are also covered by the Convention. Criteria for withholding information are very tightly defined; information should normally be released within one month of a request and there is a right of appeal in the event of refusal.

- **public participation** – the Convention lists projects where this would be obligatory; they include developments relating to waste management, energy and chemical industries and intensive farming.
- **access to justice** – the Convention aims to make it easier for people to take action through the courts or other public authorities if they feel that national environmental law is being contravened.

1.20 ENVIRONMENTAL INFORMATION REGULATIONS 1992 (SI 3240)

In the UK, the EU Directive has been implemented through the above Regulations made under the *European Communities Act 1972*. They came into force on 31 December 1992 and apply in England, Scotland and Wales with similar Regulations, which came into force in March 1993, applying in Northern Ireland. The Regulations place a duty on all those to whom they apply to make arrangements for dealing with requests for environmental information. The definition of environmental information is similar to that in the Directive; it includes all relevant information, as well as that collected before 31 December 1992 and information held in all forms – e.g. written, visual, aural, databases, computer records, registers and reports.

As of 31 December 1992, all information relating to the environment held by central and local government and other bodies with regulatory responsibilities for the environment became publicly accessible. This includes information held by bodies such as the Environment Agency and SEPA, Health and Safety Executive, English Nature, Countryside Council for Wales and Scottish Natural Heritage.

As well as exemptions for reasons of commercial confidentiality, international relations and public and national security, the Regulations exclude: internal communications and unfinished documents; judicial matters; personal data (unless the individual consents to disclosure); volunteered information; material relating to legal or other proceedings (including disciplinary proceedings and local or public inquiries); and material whose disclosure could itself lead to environmental damage.

The Regulations provide for the information to be made available in the most appropriate manner, e.g. registers and annual reports; all those to whom the Regulations apply must publish, from time to time, details of the main areas in which they hold unrestricted environmental information and a contact point for gaining access to it.

A request for information should be dealt with as soon as possible and within two months; reasons for refusal – such as the information is covered by one of the exemptions – must be given; other grounds for refusal include: that the request was too general or unreasonable; it is considered outside the scope of the Regulations; or the body does not have the requested information. There is no formal appeals system against refusal. Department of the Environment (now DETR) guidance suggests appealing to the head of the body concerned, to the local government ombudsman (in dealings with a local authority), to one's MP, or if all else fails, taking action in the courts. However, in response to a House of Lords Select Committee Report on Freedom of Access to Information on the Environment, consideration is to be given to establishing an independent appeals body.

As is the case with the Public Registers, inspection in person of publicly held information is free of charge. Where a request for information is met by providing copies of documents, a reasonable charge may be made to cover copying and associated staff costs.

It should also be noted that in those instances where other environmental legislation requires more or less information to be made publicly available than these Regulations, the legislation requiring greater public access takes precedence.

It is also possible to request access to environmental information under the 1994 Code of Practice on Access to Government Information. This is a non-statutory Code with different requirements and exemptions from the Regulations and can be used to try to gain access to information held by public bodies answerable to the Parliamentary Ombudsman. Where access to information is refused under the Code, the matter can be referred to the Parliamentary Ombudsman.

A White Paper on Freedom of Information published in December 1997 proposes extending the right to information on environmental matters to that held by courts and tribunals, local councils and some private industries and utilities; it also proposes reducing the number of exemptions where release can be refused and the appointment of an Information Commissioner with powers to order release of information.

PLANNING CONTROL AND ENVIRONMENTAL ASSESSMENT

1.21 GENERAL

Most new industrial developments – defined as "the carrying out of building, engineering, mining or other operations in, on, over or under land, or the making of any material change in the use of any building or other land" – require planning permission from the local planning authority. Applications for developments and projects with permitted development rights covered by the EU environmental assessment Directive (see 1.23.1a below) must be supported by an environmental statement, prepared on the basis of an environmental assessment. The public has a right to comment on planning applications which are advertised in the local press and copies placed on the planning register.

In considering the application, the planning authority will aim to ensure that there is no significant clash between domestic, commercial, industrial, agricultural or aesthetic interests and will approve or reject the application accordingly. While not primarily concerned with potentially polluting emissions, the planning authority will of course also take into account the overall effect of the proposed development on the neighbourhood.

When consent is given, it is usual to impose conditions relating to the construction and use of a new structure, or a changed use of an old one. Once a consent has been given for a particular use described under the Use Classes Order, that use cannot be changed from one class to another without obtaining a new permission from the planning authority.

If the application is refused, or granted subject to conditions which the applicant feels are unacceptable, there is a right of appeal to the Secretary of State. The appeal may be determined either by a written procedure, or by an inspector holding a public inquiry to determine the facts. The inspector will then report back with recommendations to the Minister who must make the final decision. With some particularly large or controversial projects, the Minister may call in the application for determination by holding a public inquiry.

Developers of new industrial sites on which it is proposed to operate a prescribed process (see Appendix 1.1) are also advised to liaise with the enforcing authority at an early stage in the project. This will ensure that new plant are developed to meet the legislative requirements of Integrated Pollution Control (see 1.13 above).

The main pieces of legislation in England and Wales covering planning are the *Town and Country Planning Act 1990* (and Regulations and Orders made under it) and the *Planning (Hazardous Substances) Act 1990* (and 1992 Regulations – see below). These Acts have both been amended by the *Planning and Compensation Act 1991*. In Scotland, the principal planning legislation is the *Town and Country Planning (Scotland) Act 1997*. In Northern Ireland, the relevant legislation is the *Planning (Northern Ireland) Order 1991* and the *Planning General Development Order (Northern Ireland) 1993* (as amended).

Planning Departments also need to have regard to the objectives of the National Air Quality Strategy when considering planning applications for new developments; if there is a likelihood that a new development could lead to an air quality standard being breached, then the application should be refused. LAQM.G4(97), *Air Quality and Land-Use Planning* (January 1998), provides guidance for local planning departments on this issue.

1.21.1 Planning Policy Guidance Notes

To assist planning authorities – and indeed applicants – there are a number of policy statements relating to planning and development issues. Planning Policy Guidance Notes (PPG) and Mineral Policy Guidance Notes are the main sources of information, providing advice on the points which should be taken into account when considering whether a particular type of development or activity would be appropriate for the locality. They are not statutory documents but nevertheless can play a very influential role in the operation of the planning system especially when considering draft development plans or in local planning appeals. PPG 1 (March 1992) covers general policy and principles and is currently under revision; other PPGs cover issues as diverse as noise, renewable energy and tourism and transport (see bibliography). They are published by the Department of the Environment, Transport and the Regions and the Welsh Office (often jointly) and by the Scottish Office. In Northern Ireland, planning policy guidance is contained in Planning Policy Statements (see bibliography).

PPG 23 on *Planning and Pollution Control* (1994) aims to inform planners on the various pollution controls with specific relevance to those industrial developments likely to pose a pollution risk. A main objective of this PPG is to provide guidance on avoiding duplication between planning and pollution controls. PPG 24 on Planning and Noise (1994) outlines how noise should be taken into account in the planning process (see chapter 3, 3.4.1).

1.22 PLANNING - HAZARDOUS SUBSTANCES

The Planning (Hazardous Substances) Act 1990 consolidates and amends certain provisions of the *Town and Country Planning Act 1971* and the *Housing and Planning Act 1986*. Under the Act, the presence of a hazardous substance on, over or under land above a specified quantity (the controlled quantity) will require a consent from the hazardous substances authority (HSA). The Act provides for local authorities to be appointed as the HSA; they will be required to take into account the current and contemplated use of the land, its surroundings etc in considering applications. The Act provides for public registers to be maintained containing full details of applications, consents, conditions etc.

The Act has now been implemented in England and Wales through the *Planning (Hazardous Substances) Regulations 1992* (SI 656), which came into effect on 1 June 1992. Similar Regulations – *the Town and Country Planning (Hazardous Substances) (Scotland) Regulations 1993* (SI 323) – came into effect in Scotland on 1 May 1993.

Storage of certain hazardous substances above the controlled quantity (both specified in the Regulations) requires a consent from the HSA; the procedure for obtaining a consent is set out in the Regulations. This is similar to the procedure for applying for an authorisation under Part I of the *Environmental Protection Act 1990* – i.e. a prescribed form must be used for the application which must be accompanied by the appropriate fee; the application must be publicised locally and statutory consultees asked for their views. In the case of refusal of an application, there is a right of appeal to the Secretary of State.

Applications, consents and their conditions, modifications, revocations etc will all be put on a public register.

The Regulations do not apply to controlled wastes or radioactive waste which are subject to control under the *Environmental Protection Act 1990* and *Radioactive Substances Act 1993*. Nor do they cover the storage of explosives where the licensing system is administered by the Health and Safety Executive. Contravention of the Regulations is subject to a maximum fine of £20,000 on summary conviction or an unlimited fine on conviction on indictment.

1.23 ENVIRONMENTAL ASSESSMENT

1.23.1 European and International Measures

(a) Assessment of Certain Public and Private Projects

European Union Directive 85/337/EEC on the assessment of the effects of certain public and private projects on the environment was implemented in England, Scotland and Wales through 1988 Regulations and in Northern Ireland in 1989; it requires an environmental impact statement to be prepared on all proposed developments which might have a significant effect on the environment. The statement should include a full description of the project; this might include measures to be taken to avoid, reduce or remedy any adverse effects of the development, and supporting data to enable full assessment by the public and various authorities. Annex I of the Directive lists types of projects for which EA is mandatory; a second list, Annex II, includes projects which "shall be made subject to an assessment where Member States consider their characteristics so require".

In March 1997 Environment Ministers formally adopted Directive 97/11/EC amending the 1985 Directive. This Directive, which must be implemented by 14 March 1999, gives more guidance as to the information to be provided by developers; it requires public consultation prior to authorisation of a project subject to environmental assessment (rather than before start of the work); the decision of the determining authority, together with reasons for it and measures required to offset any adverse impacts, must be made public.

Annex I now lists 20 types of project subject to mandatory EA (see box). Additional criteria for deciding whether or not an Annex II project should be subject to EA include: (a) is the project likely to have "significant" environmental effects (on the basis of preset thresholds); and (b) is it likely to have a "significant effect" on an area designated a special protection zone under other EU legislation. Annex II lists 50 types of project including: agriculture, extractive, energy, metal processing, glass making, chemical, food, textile, leather, wood, paper and rubber industries, tourism and leisure. It also includes the modification or expansion of authorised or completed Annex I or II projects "which could have a major or negative impact on the environment". Member States must put in place a formal mechanism for determining whether a particular Annex II project should be subject to EA – the outcome and the reasons for it must be made public.

Projects for which EA is Mandatory

(Annex I to Directive 97/11/EC)

- Power stations with a heat output of 300 MW or more, nuclear power stations and nuclear reactors (including decommissioning and dismantling);
- Crude oil refineries; facilities for gasification and liquefaction of coal or bituminous shale;
- Asbestos plants;
- Construction of motorways and express roads and widening of existing dual and single carriageways where new or widened section is more than 10 km in length;
- Long distance railway lines and airports with a planned runway length of 2100 metres or more;
- Inland waterways and inland waterway ports which allow the passage of vessels over 1,350 tonnes;
- Developments for the disposal of special waste, including incinerators, chemical waste treatment and landfill facilities, radioactive waste disposal sites and toxic waste facilities; non hazardous waste facilities with capacity of more than 100 tonnes per day;
- Projects for the reprocessing of irradiated nuclear fuels, for the production or enrichment of fuel, and the processing or storage of nuclear waste;
- Integrated chemical facilities (producing inorganic or organic chemical products, fertilisers, biocides, pharmaceuticals or explosives;
- Groundwater abstraction or artificial groundwater recharge with annual volume of at least 10 million cubic metres;
- Plant for the transfer of water between river basins;
- Waste water treatment plant with capacity exceeding 150,000 population equivalent;
- Extraction of oil (> 500 tonnes per day) and natural gas (> 500,000 m^3 per day);
- Gas, oil and chemical pipelines > 800 mm diameter and > 40 km in length;
- Dams storing in excess of 10 million cubic metres;
- Intensive pig and poultry rearing units;
- Industrial plant for production of pulp from timber or similar fibrous materials;
- Quarries and open cast mines > 25 hectares and peat extraction sites exceeding 150 hectares;
- Construction of overhead power lines with voltage of 220 kV or more and length > 15 km;
- oil, petrochemical or chemical products storage facilities with capacity of > 200,000 tonnes.

(b) Assessment of Certain Plans and Programmes on the Environment

Published in December 1996 this proposal for a Directive (COM(96) 511) would require an environmental assessment to be carried out, and an environmental statement prepared, before the adoption by public authorities of, or national legislation for, land-use development plans and programmes; in the UK this would include structure plans and unitary development plans and local plans; it would not apply to plans submitted to the Commission under the Structural Funds Regulation (EEC 2081/93) or to those plans which are not subject to formal adoption or legislation in the Member State concerned. The statement would need to include:

- environmental characteristics of any area which might be significantly affected;
- existing environmental problems;
- likely significant adverse environmental effects of implementing the plan or programme and measures to prevent, reduce or offset those effects;
- possible alternative ways of achieving the plan's objectives and why these are not considered appropriate.

The Directive includes requirements for consulting environmental authorities and other interested bodies, with the general public also being given an opportunity to comment. The Commission is hoping that the Directive can be adopted in time for implementation by Member States in 2000.

(c) UNECE Convention

A Convention on Environmental Impact Assessment in a Transboundary Context (Espoo Convention) came into force in 1998, 90 days after ratification by 16 countries. It applies solely to those projects with possible transboundary effects (e.g. off-shore oil production, new reservoirs or dams); it gives those likely to be affected by a project the right to be notified about the project, to participate in the EIA and then to be consulted about the transboundary impacts and measures to mitigate them.

The Convention was ratified by the European Community on 24 June 1997 and by the UK on 10 October 1997. The terms of the Convention have been taken account of in the amended EU Directive – see (a) above.

1.23.2 UK Regulations

The *Town and Country Planning (Assessment of Environmental Effects) Regulations 1988* (SI 1199), as amended, (and similar in Scotland – SI 1221 – and Northern Ireland) and other regulations specifying assessment of environmental effects for the various projects for which EA is required implement the 1985 Directive. 1994 amendment Regulations (SI 677) for England and Wales (and similar for Scotland) extend requirements for an EA to projects not listed in the Directive. These are privately financed toll roads for which EA will be mandatory; wind turbines, motorway and other service areas with restaurant facilities, and coastal protection works will require EA if their environmental effect is thought likely to be "significant" by the planning authority.

An environmental statement, together with the planning application should be submitted to the local planning authority, who should send a copy to the Department of the Environment, Transport and the Regions (or Welsh Office, Scottish Office Environment Department, as appropriate). The planning authority should also send copies to statutory consultees; these include English Nature, Countryside Council for Wales, Scottish Natural Heritage (as appropriate) and if relevant, the Environment Agency or SEPA.

Circulars issued by the Department of the Environment (15/88 and 7/94), the Welsh Office (23/88 and 20/94) and the Scottish Office (13/88) in 1988 detail the scope and content of environmental statements and consultation procedures. *Preparation of environmental statements for planning projects that require environmental assessment: a good practice guide* (DOE, 1995) provides advice on assessing environmental impacts and on presenting statements in a way which clearly separates facts, judgements and opinions.

The Government is currently consulting on its proposals for implementing the 1997 Directive's requirements for formal screening processes to be put in place for determining whether an Annex II project should be subject to environmental assessment (July and December 1997); among it proposals are the setting of statutory thresholds for most Annex II projects, below which an EA would not normally be required, subject to a power for the Secretary of State to determine that a particular project should be subject to EA; higher non-binding indicative thresholds where an EA may be required would be set for all Annex II projects. EA would also be required – as now – for projects within SSSIs or other sensitive locations, very large projects or those which could have an effect on the environment.

In accordance with the requirements of the 1985 Directive, but also in compliance with the 1997 Directive, the *Offshore Petroleum Production and Pipelines (Assessment of Environmental Effects) Regulations 1998* (SI 968) have now been made and came into force on 30 April 1998. These require mandatory assessment of certain projects relating to the extraction of oil and natural gas and gas, oil and chemical pipelines above the threshold (see box, p.55), as well as other projects below the threshold which are likely to have significant environmental effects. Guidance from the Department of Trade and Industry outlines those instances when environmental assessment is likely to be required.

It should be noted that the requirements for an EA (apart from the need for statutory consultation) also apply to major development projects promoted through the Parliamentary Private Bill system; proposals for new rail line developments, harbour projects are examples of projects for which approval is often sought in this way. Private Bills (which should not be confused with the Private Member's Bill procedure) can be a means of avoiding local planning procedures and public inquiries. In addition, the Secretary of State may, by regulations made under the *Planning and Compensation Act 1991*, require an EA to be carried out on other projects.

ENVIRONMENTAL MANAGEMENT AND AUDIT SYSTEMS

1.24 ENVIRONMENTAL MANAGEMENT

An essential part of a company's environmental policy is its environmental management system. This also forms part of the European Union's Eco-Management and Audit Regulation agreed at the end of 1992 which came into force in 1995 (see below).

The British Standards Institution (see above, 1.11) published in 1992 British Standard BS 7750, *Environmental Management System*; a revised version, compatible with the Eco-Management and Audit Regulation, was published in 1994 and in February 1996 the standard was formally recognised by the European Commission in accordance with Article 12 of the EU Regulation (Commission Decision 96/150/EC, Official Journal L34, 13.2.96). BS 7750 was withdrawn on 31 March 1997 following agreement on an International Standard on Environmental Management Systems (ISO 14001 – specification with guidance for use, and ISO 14000 – general guidelines on principles, systems and supporting techniques). This too has now been formally recognised by the Commission.

Companies wishing to be certified under ISO must ensure that

- they comply with environmental legislation and regulations;
- their products or services are produced, delivered and disposed of in an environmentally friendly manner – and thus any adverse effects on the environment are minimised;
- expenditure on environmental protection is timely and effective, and that planning for future investment and growth reflects market needs on the environment.

Participating bodies must prepare a written environmental management system which, it is suggested, should take into account the principles of sustainable development: it should include environmental policy, objectives and targets aimed at an on-going process of environmental improvement; evaluation procedures; staff training and awareness. Where the company has identified a "significant environmental effect" this should be entered on a register. All participating companies should carry out an environmental audit at least every three years or annually if there is "particular potential to cause environmental harm".

Certification for compliance with the Standard is voluntary; it is carried out by external assessors ("certifiers") who are formally accredited under a scheme run by the National Accreditation Council for Certification Bodies. NACCB is also responsible for accrediting verifiers for the environmental statements required under the Eco-Management and Audit Regulation (see below).

1.25 ENVIRONMENTAL AUDITING

The need for companies to be publicly seen to be acting in an environmentally responsible manner has resulted in a number carrying out environmental audits of their operations; some local authorities have also carried out audits of their operations.

The European Union has now approved a Council Regulation allowing Voluntary Participation by Companies in the Industry Sector in a Community Eco-Management and Audit Scheme. The Regulation (1836/93), which came into force in May 1995, aims to encourage industrial companies to continually evaluate and improve their environmental performance. The Commission is reviewing the Regulation with a view to making it more compatible with ISO 14001 and extending its coverage to non-industrial companies.

The Institute of Environmental Assessment is the UK Registration Authority; companies may choose whether or not to participate in the scheme and indeed whether to register all or only some of their sites. Those that are registered are required to carry out an assessment of operations at each site and the impact on the environment. This would form the basis of an environmental protection system (including an environmental policy, environmental management system and audit programme); this must be reviewed periodically to ensure the use of Best Available Technology. Issues to be covered include energy policy, waste and water management, product planning, safety, staff training and involvement in environmental issues, information to be made public and complaints handling; objectives and targets should be set and programmes for improvement drawn up. An environmental audit must be carried out not less than every three years by someone not directly involved in the activity with a report written (to be publicly available); in the intervening years an environmental statement should be published. Accredited verifiers will ensure compliance with all aspects of the Regulation and validate the environmental statement if satisfied with the way the company has complied with the Regulation. The verifier and the auditor should be independent of each other.

Companies satisfying the requirements of the Regulation and registering under the Scheme can use a "statement of participation". This cannot be used on actual products or packaging, or to advertise the product. The National Accreditation Council of Certification Bodies is responsible for accrediting verifiers for the environmental statements.

The Regulation provides for companies accredited under similar national schemes which have been recognised by the European Commission to receive accreditation under the Regulation; accreditation under a national scheme must have been granted by a recognised body.

1.26 ENVIRONMENTAL LIABILITY

In March 1993 the European Commission published for discussion a Green Paper (COM(93) 47) on Remedying Environmental Damage. The rationale for the document is the principle that the polluter should pay for any damage caused to the environment; the paper proposed strict (or no fault) liability where the polluter is known and the establishment of a compensation fund to cover damage where the polluter is not known or where damage is the result of pollution and cannot be attributed to a single party. A White Paper is being prepared outlining options for the way forward; these include: ratification of the Council of Europe Convention (see below); a Directive on environmental liability which would focus on site-clean up and ecological damage; or a Directive establishing a general environmental liability regime covering both personal injury and property and environmental damage.

The Council of Europe has already agreed (March 1993) a *Convention on Civil Liability for Damage Resulting from Activities Dangerous to the Environment* (the Lugano Convention). Although some countries have signed the Convention, it requires ratification by three before it comes into force. (In *Paying for our Past*, DOE, 1994, it was stated that there were no plans for the UK to sign the Convention.) The Convention applies to a wide range of industries, including research laboratories dealing with genetically modified organisms, who will be liable for any "intolerable" damage caused even though pollution legislation has been complied with. It provides for compensation to persons and property and for economic loss as a result of environmental damage; operators are required to have insurance cover and the Convention provides for environmental organisations to take legal action in pursuit of the Convention's requirements.

AIR

EARLY CONTROLS

2.1 INTRODUCTION

The development of air pollution control legislation in the UK has been a gradual process with most of it resulting from the Industrial Revolution of the late 18th and 19th centuries; air pollution was, however, first acknowledged to be a problem many hundreds of years earlier.

Coal was already used in England by the year 852 and a record of "Seacoales Lane" in London dates from 1228. The use of coal was prohibited in London in 1273 as being prejudicial to health; however the practice must have continued for early in the 14th century a Royal Proclamation prohibited the use of seacoal by artificers (craftsmen) in their furnaces. In 1648, Londoners petitioned Parliament to prohibit the importation of coal from Newcastle because of the injuries they experienced. After complaints of smoke from his neighbour, one baker was ordered to erect a chimney "so high as to convey the smoake clear of the topps of the houses".

In 1661 John Evelyn published his tract *Fumifugium or The Smoke of London Dissipated*. This suggested practical schemes to improve the air over London. These were ignored and it was not until 1819 that Parliament appointed a committee to enquire to what extent persons using steam engines and furnaces could erect them in a manner less prejudicial to the public health and comfort. However, nothing of significance emerged from the committee's deliberations.

2.2 ALKALI ACTS AND BEST PRACTICABLE MEANS

The Industrial Revolution, which was based on coal as the energy source, brought a worsening of urban squalor and appalling air pollution. Around 1860, discharges to the air from an early alkali works devastated the surrounding country, corroding material and tools and destroying vegetation and crops. Air pollution from the works could no longer be ignored. Following overwhelming public complaint and a Parliamentary Enquiry, the first *Alkali etc Works Act* was passed in 1863. This made no attempt to control smoke, but required that 95% of the offensive emissions should be arrested. The remainder, after adequate dilution, might be allowed to pass to atmosphere. This tolerance replaced the unworkable prohibition of all previous enactments and allowed a rapidly growing chemical industry the freedom to develop. The same Act set up a national inspectorate to enforce the legislation. The improvement in pollution levels was dramatic: acid emissions from alkali works were reduced from an annual rate of almost 14,000 tonnes to about 45 tonnes.

The second *Alkali Act* (1874) required, for the first time, the application of the Best Practicable Means (BPM) to prevent the escape of noxious or offensive gases. The Act was subsequently extended to all the major industries that pollute the air. The requirement applied whether the escapes arose indirectly from any part of the process or plant, or directly from the exit flues. The requirement also applied to "fugitive" or "uncontained" emissions; these could include gases or vapours leaking from process storage tanks, pumps, compressors, coking plant or streams of liquid effluent; they could also include dust from roadways, stockpiles or even materials carried out of works on the wheels of vehicles. The 1874 Act also introduced the first statutory emission limit – for hydrogen chloride (0.2 grains per cubic foot).

2.2.1 Scheduled Processes

A series of Acts then followed which were eventually consolidated by the *Alkali etc Works Regulation Act 1906*. This linked together a schedule of carefully defined and chosen processes – works – with an equally carefully chosen list of "noxious and offensive gases". The types of works scheduled were those thought most likely to cause pollution problems and included a substantial part of the chemical industry, petroleum refineries, petrochemicals, electricity generation, coal carbonisation, iron and steel works, non-ferrous metals, mineral processing works etc.

The *Public Health (Smoke Abatement) Act 1926* empowered ministers to make various additions to the list of scheduled works and noxious and offensive gases by an order laid before Parliament for approval and given legislative effect as a statutory instrument. As industrial technology advanced, seven such orders extended control over various processes between 1928 and 1963. These orders were consolidated in 1966 in the *Alkali etc Works Order*. In 1974 the *Health and Safety at Work etc Act* was passed. It was essentially an enabling measure and was intended to repeal the 1906 Act entirely, replacing it by regulations made under the 1974 Act, e.g. the *Health and Safety (Emissions into the Atmosphere) Regulations 1983*. The remaining sections of the 1906 Act were repealed in England and Wales on 16 December 1996 following completion of authorisation of all prescribed processes under Part I of the *Environmental Protection Act 1990* (see chapter 1, 1.13 and chapter 2, 2.11).

The legislation was administered in England and Wales by HM Inspectorate of Pollution (or its forerunners), with almost identical legislation in Scotland administered by HM Industrial Pollution Inspectorate. The control of scheduled processes by the Inspectorate had three distinct aspects:

Registration: Under the *Health and Safety (Emissions into the Atmosphere) Regulations* (SI 943, repealed December 1996) scheduled works had to be registered annually. As an essential prior condition to the first and all subsequent registrations, every scheduled works had to be provided, to the satisfaction of the chief inspector, with the Best Practicable Means for preventing the escape of any noxious or offensive substances, and for rendering all such emissions harmless and inoffensive. The *Control of Air Pollution (Registration of Works) Regulations 1989* (SI 318, repealed December 1996) specified the information that should be contained in applications to HM Inspectorate of Pollution for the registration of scheduled works under the *Alkali etc Works Regulation Act 1906* and the *Health and Safety at Work etc Act 1974* and in the register of works (which had to be made available for public inspection).

Inspection: Following registration, it was a requirement that the Best Practicable Means must always be in use, and that pollution control equipment must be maintained in good and efficient working order. Under the *Health and Safety at Work etc Act 1974*, inspectors were authorised to enter premises for examination or investigation without prior announcement. The emphasis was on prevention rather than cure.

If the inspector believed that provisions of the 1974 Act (or the *1906 Alkali Act*) were being contravened, an improvement notice could be issued specifying the problem, the period during which it should be put right and if appropriate, the remedial measures to be taken. Where toxic emissions were involved the process would generally be suspended or drastically curtailed. Inspectors could also issue a prohibition notice if there was believed to be a risk of personal injury.

Presumptive Limits: The remaining aspect of control was the setting, via the Notes on Best Practicable Means, of presumptive limits which specified the amount of pollutant per cubic metre of gas that could be emitted from the chimney stack. Although they were non-statutory limits, there was normally a presumption that if the limit was being met, then the legislation was being complied with in that the Best Practicable Means were being used. The fact that BPM Notes were non-statutory documents allowed the inspectorate to tighten emission limits in line with advances in abatement technology or scientific understanding of the effects of pollutants. For many processes there were, in addition, other limits based on subjective assessment, such as smoke emission or other visibility criteria. Most of the processes covered by the Act were prescribed for Integrated Pollution Control under Part I of the *Environmental Protection Act 1990* (see chapter 1, 1.13).

2.2.2 Smoke Control

While the *Public Health (Smoke Abatement) Act 1926* had enabled the Alkali Inspectorate to extend its influence to industrial smoke, there was no measure to control the far more widespread problem of smoke from domestic chimneys. Other legislation enabled smoke to be dealt with as a possible nuisance, but was largely ineffective because a nuisance had first to be proved in court. Thus the atmosphere of Britain's urban areas was still characterised by the pervading pall of smoke and sulphur fumes from countless stacks, chimneys and funnels. The lack of winter sunshine, the prevalence of pea-soup fogs, black buildings and even black snow, had become accepted as the price of progress and bronchitis, exacerbated by smoke and sulphur, was a common illness.

It was not until the infamous London smog of December 1952, which lasted for five days, that any real action was taken. The first casualties of the fog were prize cattle brought to London for the Smithfield Show – one died, 12 had to be slaughtered and some 160 required veterinary treatment. Even an opera performance at the Sadlers Wells Theatre had to be stopped after the first Act as the audience could not see the stage! More seriously, some 4,000 additional deaths were directly attributed to the episode.

The Government appointed a committee, under the chairmanship of Sir Hugh Beaver, to study the problem of air pollution. Its terms of reference were "to examine the nature, causes and effects of air pollution and the efficacy of present preventive measures; to consider what further measures are practicable; and to make recommendations". The committee issued two reports, the first in 1953 and the second in 1954; these recognised that the constituent parts of the problem were gaseous and particulate emissions, and recommended immediate legislation to reduce smoke, grit and dust.

The eventual result was the *Clean Air Act 1956* which was later amended and extended by the *Clean Air Act 1968*. These Acts (covering England, Scotland and Wales, with a similar 1964 Act for N. Ireland) constituted the operative legislation against pollution by smoke, grit and dust from domestic fires and other commercial and industrial processes not covered by the *Alkali Acts* and other subsequent pollution legislation. They regulated the combustion of solid, liquid and gaseous fuels and controlled the heights of new industrial chimneys that are not scheduled elsewhere. The legislation also prohibited the emission of "dark" smoke from any chimney, provided for Government funding for the conversion of domestic grates to smokeless operation, and regulated the fuels that could be burned on them.

The 1956 and 1968 Acts have now been consolidated and their provisions re-enacted in the *Clean Air Act 1993* which came into force on 27 August 1993. This applies in England, Scotland and Wales only. (s.30 – regulations about motor fuel – also applies in Northern Ireland: see 2.13.4 below.) In Northern Ireland, the 1964 Act has been replaced by the *Clean Air (Northern Ireland) Order 1981*.

INTERNATIONAL AND EUROPEAN INITIATIVES

2.3 INTERNATIONAL INITIATIVES

2.3.1 Environment and Development

Many pollution problems – depletion of the ozone layer, global warming, export of hazardous wastes and so on – are recognised as global problems requiring global solutions. Here the United Nations Organisation and its agencies, such as the United Nations Environment Programme (UNEP), have an important role in providing a forum for discussion and cooperation on global environmental problems. UNEP itself was founded in 1973 following the UN Conference on the Human Environment held in 1972 where the 113 participating countries expressed concern over the rapidly deteriorating environment.

A further conference – the United Nations Conference on Environment and Development (UNCED, or the Earth Summit) – was held in June 1992 in Brazil. This conference was a direct result of the UN Commission on Environment and Development whose report *Our Common Future* (often called the Brundtland Report, after its Chairman Gro Harlem Brundtland), was published in 1987. This identified the importance of "sustainable development" in eradicating poverty and halting further environmental degradation and moving to sustained economic growth.

The Earth Summit in Brazil was attended by world leaders, ministers, officials and representatives of environment non-governmental organisations from over 160 countries. The main aim of the Conference was to find ways to "halt and reverse the effects of environmental degradation" while increasing efforts "to promote sustainable and environmentally sound development in all countries". During the conference, world leaders endorsed the following:

- *Framework Convention on the Atmosphere (Climate Treaty):* Developed countries are required to take measures aimed at returning emissions of greenhouse gases (in particular carbon dioxide) to 1990 levels by 2000 and to provide assistance to developing countries. Other obligations include compiling inventories of emissions, producing and publishing national programmes of measures to limit emissions and to promote research and public education about climate change. The Convention came into force on 21 March 1994 following ratification by 50 countries; as at October 1996 the Convention had been ratified by 159 countries, including both the European Community and the UK.

In December 1997, in Kyoto, Japan, Parties to the Climate Treaty agreed to make legally binding cuts in emissions of six greenhouse gases – carbon dioxide, methane, nitrous oxide, hydrofluorocarbons, perfluorocarbons and sulphur hexafluoride. Between 2008-2012 developed countries will reduce their emissions by an average of 5.2% below 1990 levels (for the first three substances; any year between 1990-1995 for the last three). Different targets have been set for individual countries – e.g. EU 8%, Switzerland 8%, USA 7%, Japan 6%. The Protocol also permits emissions trading between countries as a means of meeting targets, although rules for doing this have still to be finalised. The Protocol will come into force 90 days after ratification by 55 countries which together account for 55% of the 1990 carbon dioxide emissions of developed countries. As at the end of April 1998, 34 countries had signed the Protocol.

(See also final para of this sub-section on UK commitments regarding the Climate Treaty and 2.4.2 for EU proposals with regard to the Protocol.)

- *Convention on the Conservation of Biological Diversity:* aims to protect and preserve endangered plants and species on land and in the oceans. This Convention came into force on 29 December 1993 following ratification by 30 countries; it became legally binding 90 days later. Countries will each draw up a list of "protected areas". Use of resources in protected areas – e.g. exploitation of plants for medicines – would need to be paid for with financial assistance additional to current levels of development assistance. It has been signed and ratified by the EC and the UK.

  The European Commission has published a Communication (COM(98) 42) to the Council of Ministers and European Parliament outlining a Community Biodiversity Strategy. This endorses the principles of the UN Convention and calls upon Member States to ensure they also act upon them.

- *Agenda 21* – a huge document setting out an "environmental work programme" into the 21st century. It aims to provide guidance for governments in establishing environmental policies that meet the needs of sustainable development; it covers all areas of pollution, energy policy, population and development issues.

In the UK, local authorities have been encouraged to adopt their own Agenda 21 – i.e. a strategy for sustainable development at local level – in consultation with business and community groups.

- *Sustainable Development Commission*, set up under the auspices of the UN, has as one of its main tasks to ensure progress on Agenda 21.
- *Statement of principles* for the sustainable management and conservation of forests aimed at preserving as much as possible of the world's forests.
- *Declaration of principles* for the pursuit of sustainable development as the prime means of alleviating Third World poverty and global environmental degradation.
- *Agreement on funding* with new environmental aid for developing countries.

In 1995 UK emissions of carbon dioxide totalled 148 m. tonnes, a reduction of 11 m. tonnes on 1990 levels. By 2000 it is expected that UK emissions of carbon dioxide will be between 4-8% lower than in 1990. The Government has pledged to reduce emissions of carbon dioxide by 20% of their 1990 level by 2010; this will be achieved through greater energy efficiency, renewable forms of power generation, and development of an integrated transport policy (Prime Minister's statement to House of Commons, June 1997).

The UK's national programme (*Climate Change – the UK Programme*, published January 1994) outlines a number of voluntary actions which various sectors (e.g. individuals, industry and commerce and the public sector) can take to reduce energy consumption and also government measures. Voluntary actions include encouraging energy conservation and efficiency; better use of transport and use of fuel efficient cars; central government can play its part by encouraging voluntary action, support for renewable energy, and regulatory and/or economic instruments where necessary. (See also below, 2.4.2 – carbon dioxide.) The UK's *Home Energy Conservation Act 1995* should also result in reduced carbon dioxide emissions; this Act requires local authorities to report to the Secretary of State on how "significant energy savings" – initially 30% – can be made from residential properties, including homes in multiple occupation, in their area.

2.3.2 Ozone Layer

Concern over depletion of the stratospheric ozone layer, particularly over Antarctica, was first raised in the 1970s. Increasingly scientific evidence pointed to the fact that the growing consumption of chlorine based chemicals – such as chlorofluorocarbons – may be largely to blame for the continuing damage to the ozone layer. It also became clear that action was needed on an international basis to protect the ozone layer from further damage to avert a more serious situation. More recently, preliminary results for research being carried out by the European Arctic Stratospheric Ozone Experiment reveal that ozone amounts in the Northern Hemisphere are also falling, thus confirming the need for urgent measures if further damage is to be halted.

The ozone layer which forms part of the earth's stratosphere, lies about 15-20 km above the earth's surface. Ozone molecules absorb some of the sun's ultraviolet radiation, thus acting as a protective filter. Research shows that increased ultraviolet light on earth as a result of ozone depletion can increase the risk of skin cancer and eye cataracts, depress the human immune system, and harm aquatic systems and crops.

A series of meetings held under the auspices of the UN Environment Programme culminated in Montreal in September 1987 with the signing of an Agreement on Substances that deplete the Ozone Layer – the Montreal Protocol. This has now been ratified by over 160 governments worldwide and committed industrialised nations to reduce consumption of CFCs by 50% by 1999 and to freeze production of halons in 1992. The Protocol is reviewed regularly (most recently in September 1997) and in the light of scientific evidence revised and strengthened. It currently provides for the following:

- **Chlorofluorocarbons:** based on 1986 consumption levels, 75% reduction by 1 January 1994; phase out by 1 January 1996. Less developed countries phase out by 2010.
- **Halons:** based on 1986 levels, phase out by 1 January 1994; less developed countries phase out by 2010.
- **Carbon Tetrachloride:** Based on 1989 levels, 85% reduction by 1 January 1994; phase out by 1 January 1996.
- **1,1,1-trichloroethane:** based on 1989 levels, 50% reduction by 1 January 1994; phase out by 1 January 1996.

In 1992 methyl bromide, hydrochlorofluorocarbons and hydrobromofluorocarbons were included in the Protocol, with further controls on the first two substances being agreed in 1995, and the timetable for methyl bromide being tightened further in 1997:

- **Methyl Bromide:** for developed countries, freeze on use at 1991 levels from 1 January 1995; 25% reduction by 1999, followed by 50% reduction by 2001, 70% by 2003 and phase out by 2005, subject to exemption for critical agricultural uses. Less developed countries are to reduce use by 20% by 2005 using a baseline of the average of 1995-98 consumption and phase out by 2015.

- **Hydrochlorofluorocarbons:** developed countries, freeze at 2.8% of CFC and HCFC consumption in 1989 from 1 January 1996 levels; 35% reduction by 2004; 65% by 2007; 90% by 2010; 99.5% by 2013; phase out by 2020, subject to limited exemptions for existing equipment. Less developed countries are to freeze their consumption of HCFCs in 2016 and phase them out entirely by 2040.
- **Hydrobromofluorocarbons:** phase out from 1 January 1996.

In ratifying the original Protocol, which came into force in August 1992, governments commit themselves to its requirements. The European Community implemented the revised Protocol through Regulation 3093/94/EC – see below 2.4.4.

In the case of the first four substances listed above, limited production for essential uses will be allowed after the phase out dates. An annual list of critical uses in developed countries is to be published by UNEP from 2004. Criteria to be taken into account in considering whether a use is essential include:

- the use must be necessary for the health and safety of society or critical for its functioning;
- no alternatives which are technically and economically feasible and which are acceptable on health and safety grounds;
- insufficient recycled material, both in terms of quantity and quality, available.

In 1997, Parties to the Protocol also agreed that with effect from 1 January 2000, imports and exports of new and recycled CFCs and halons, methyl bromide and HCFCs will require licensing. It is hoped this will curb the illegal trade in these substances.

The UK has been able to meet the requirements of the Protocols basically through the voluntary cooperation of industry and consumers in reducing their use of CFCs – see also 2.4.4.

2.3.3 Convention on Long-Range Transboundary Air Pollution

This Convention, which was adopted in Geneva in 1979, was drawn up under the auspices of the UN Economic Commission for Europe (which comprises all the countries of Europe and of North America); it came into force in 1983. The Convention was the result of concern – particularly from Norway and Sweden – that the long-range transport of certain pollutants (mainly sulphur dioxide and nitrogen oxides) was having an adverse effect on the environment of their countries. The Convention says that countries shall "endeavour to limit and, as far as possible, gradually reduce and prevent air pollution, including long range transboundary air pollution". This should be achieved through the "use of best available technology that is economically feasible".

The Convention also deals with the long-range transport of nitrogen and chlorine compounds, polycyclic aromatic hydrocarbons, heavy metals and particles of various sizes. Parties to the Convention are currently negotiating two new Protocols – see (d) and (e) below.

Critical Loads

There is a commitment that subsequent reductions in emissions of both sulphur dioxide and nitrogen oxides will be negotiated "taking into account the best available scientific and technical developments . . . and internationally accepted critical loads". The "critical loads" approach takes account of the level of pollutant that a receptor – e.g. ecosystem, human being, plant or material – can tolerate without suffering long term adverse effect according to current knowledge.

Critical loads maps covering the whole of Europe are being drawn up by the European Evaluation and Monitoring Programme (EMEP) under the LRTAP Convention. In the UK the Department of the Environment, Transport and the Regions (DETR) is preparing maps showing the levels of deposition at which soils in the UK are vulnerable to acidity. Other maps show actual estimates of deposition and where this is likely to exceed the critical load. Maps are also being drawn up for freshwaters.

In its revised *Air Quality Guidelines for Europe* (which were due to be published towards the end of 1997, the World Health Organisation has recommended the following critical levels and loads:

- *Sulphur dioxide*: critical level 10-30 $\mu g/m^3$ (annual) depending on type of vegetation; critical load 250-1500 eqS/ha/yr depending on the type of soil and ecosystem.
- *Nitrogen oxides*: critical level 30 $\mu g/m^3$ (annual); critical load 15-35 kgN/ha/yr depending on the type of soil and ecosystem.
- *Ozone*: critical level 0.5-10 ppm.h (5d-6m) depending on type of vegetation.

(a) Sulphur Protocol

The Helsinki Protocol adopted in 1985 came into force in 1987; it required signatories to reduce national sulphur emissions, or their transboundary fluxes by 30% on 1980 levels, by 1993. This Protocol was not ratified by either the UK or the European Community, although some individual Member States did do so. All signatories to the Protocol achieved reductions of more than 30%, as did a number of non-signatories including the UK with a reduction of 37% by the end of 1993 (45% by the end of 1994).

This Protocol has now been renegotiated using data based on critical loads assessments; countries are required to reduce, by the year 2000, their sulphur emissions to meet a UNECE-wide target of 60% of the gap between sulphur emissions and the critical load. Particularly sensitive areas of Scandinavia, Germany and The Netherlands where natural and unattributable emissions exceed the critical load have been excluded from the calculations.

Individual countries' target reductions are based on their contribution to acid deposition over the areas included in the calculations. To meet the 60% target, the UK has agreed to reduce its own sulphur dioxide emissions by 50% by 2000, 70% by 2005 and 80% by 2010 (on 1980 levels). (To meet the target by the year 2000 would have required the UK to reduce its emissions by 79%, a target to which the UK would not agree.)

The new Protocol was officially signed in Oslo in June 1994 and came into force on 5 August 1998; parties to the Protocol must submit their national strategies for meeting their targets to the UNECE monitoring committee within six months of ratification.

The UK ratified the Protocol on 17 December 1996, becoming the fifth country to do so; at the same time, the Government also published its national strategy for meeting the requirements of the Protocol: briefly, this suggests that current emissions reduction and control programmes will ensure the 2000 and 2005 targets are met, with advances in technology helping to meet the 2010 target. In 1995 UK emissions of sulphur dioxide were 52% lower than in 1980 (*Digest of Environmental Statistics*, No. 19, 1997).

In March 1997 The European Commission published a proposal for a decision to ratify the Protocol as part of its Strategy to combat Acidification (see 2.4.5a below).

(b) Nitrogen Oxides Protocol

The 1988 Sofia Protocol, which came into effect in 1991, freezes nitrogen oxides emissions, or their transboundary fluxes, by 1994 using a 1987 baseline. The UK ratified this Protocol in 1990 and the European Community in 1993. In 1994 UK NOx emissions were in fact 9% lower than in 1987, and in 1995 fell a further 5% (*Digest of Environmental Statistics*, No. 19, 1997).

A new multi-pollutants Protocol covering nitrogen oxides, VOCs and ammonia is currently being negotiated; critical loads will be used as a basis for setting national emissions ceilings to combat acidification, eutrophication and tropospheric ozone formation; it is hoped the new Protocol will be ready for signing during the first half of 1999.

(c) VOC Protocol

A further Protocol under the LRTAP Convention signed in Geneva in 1991 to control emissions of volatile organic compounds (VOCs) or their transboundary fluxes came into force on 29 September 1997, following ratification by 16 countries (the UK did so in June 1994).

VOCs are defined as "all organic compounds of anthropogenic nature, other than methane, that are capable of producing photochemical oxidants by reactions with nitrogen oxides in the presence of sunlight". VOCs are involved in the formation of ground level ozone and in depletion of the ozone layer. They also contribute to the greenhouse effect in that methane and photochemical oxidants produced from the use of VOCs are both greenhouse gases. Thus they have both local and regional/transboundary effects.

The new Protocol obliges most parties to secure a 30% overall reduction in their VOC emissions by 1999, using 1988 as a base (or another year between 1984 and 1990 to be specified when acceding to the Protocol). Other basic obligations include requirements,

two years after the Protocol enters into force

- to apply national or international emission standards to new sources of VOCs, taking account of guidance on control technologies given in the Protocol;
- to apply national or international measures to products that contain solvents and promote the use of products with low or nil content; and to foster public participation in VOC emission control.

no later than five years after entering into force

- to apply economically feasible best available technologies to existing stationary sources in those areas where ozone standards are exceeded or transboundary fluxes originate;
- to implement techniques to reduce VOC emissions from petrol distribution and motor vehicle refuellings and to reduce the volatility of petrol.

So far as these latter obligations are concerned, a European Union Directive controlling VOC emissions during petrol storage and distribution was adopted in late 1995 – see 2.20.8. A draft Directive (COM(96) 538) on reducing emissions of organic solvents from certain processes and industrial installations was published in December 1996, with Environment Ministers agreeing a Common Position in June 1998 – see below 2.4.5(c).

In November 1993, the UK Government published its strategy for meeting its commitments under the Protocol, which it is hoped will result in a 36% reduction in emissions of VOCs by 1999. The strategy includes: setting of emission limits in conditions attached to authorisations for both Part A and Part B processes regulated under the *Environmental Protection Act 1990*; implementation of EU measures to reduce evaporative emissions during petrol storage and distribution; information to the public on reducing usage – and thus emissions – of household products containing VOCs. By the end of 1995, the UK had achieved a 14% reduction in VOC emissions on 1988 levels (*Digest of Environmental Statistics*, No. 19, 1997).

(d) Heavy Metals

This Protocol was signed in June 1998 at Aarhus, Denmark, and will come into force 90 days after ratification by 16 countries. It requires emissions of cadmium, lead and mercury to be reduced to below their 1990 levels (or an agreed year between 1985 and 1995). It also aims to cut emissions from new and existing industrial sources and waste incinerators by laying down strict limit values based on the use of best available techniques.

(e) Persistent Organic Pollutants

This Protocol was also signed in June 1998 at Aarhus, Denmark, and will come into force 90 days after ratification by 16 countries. It aims to phase out production and use of a defined list of substances as well as imposing requirements to eliminate discharges, emissions and losses, and to ensure safe disposal methods. The list covers 16 substances in three categories:

- pesticides (including aldrin, dieldrin, endrin, chlordane, DDT, HCB and heptachlor);
- industrial chemicals (including PCBs);
- by-products and contaminants (including dioxins, furans and PAHs).

Annexes to the Protocol set emission limit values, as well as outline best available techniques for the various industrial sectors which emit substances covered by the Protocol.

(f) Evaluation and Monitoring Programme

A 1984 Protocol, which was ratified by the UK in 1985 and by the European Community in 1986, provides funding for the programme of monitoring and evaluation of the long-range transport of air pollution (EMEP). EMEP comprises some 100 monitoring stations in 25 countries which provide data on all Convention substances.

2.3.4 World Health Organisation

As mentioned below, the World Health Organisation's recommended air quality guidelines are being used as a basis for setting EU standards. They were also taken into account by the UK Expert Panel on Air Quality Standards when making recommendations for UK air quality standards (see this chapter, 2.10.2). Originally published in 1987 as *Air Quality Guidelines for Europe*, WHO's recommendations are not mandatory but are generally accepted as being levels not to be exceeded if healthy air quality is to be maintained. In 1993 WHO began reviewing the guidelines in the light of new scientific data and at a Consultation meeting in October 1996 revised guidelines (see box) were agreed; a fully revised version of *Air Quality Guidelines for Europe* was due to be published at the end of 1997.

WHO Air Quality Guidelines

(This table includes only those pollutants for which EU standards exist or are being proposed)

Substances	*Time-weighted average*	*Averaging time*
Classical air pollutants		
Nitrogen dioxide	200 $\mu g/m^3$	1 hour
	40 $\mu g/m^3$	annual
Ozone	120 $\mu g/m^3$	8 hour
Sulphur dioxide	500 $\mu g/m^3$	10 minutes
	125 $\mu g/m^3$	24 hour
	50 $\mu g/m^3$	annual
Carbon monoxide	100 mg/m^3	15 minutes
	60 mg/m^3	30 minutes
	30 mg/m^3	1 hour
	10 mg/m^3	8 hours
Particulate matter	exposure-effect information to be provided giving guidance on major health impacts for short and long term exposures at various levels	
Organic pollutants		
PAH (benzo-a-pyrene)	8.7×10^{-5} $(ng/m^3)^{-1}$	lifetime
Benzene	6×10^{-6} $(\mu g/m^3)^{-1}$	lifetime
Inorganic pollutants		
Lead	0.5 $\mu g/m^3$	annual
Arsenic	1.5×10^{-3} $(\mu g/m^3)^{-1}$	lifetime
Cadmium	5 ng/m^3	annual
Mercury	1.0 $\mu g/m^3$	annual

2.4 THE EUROPEAN UNION AND AIR POLLUTION CONTROL

The need to reduce emissions from all sources is a major thrust of the European Union's policy to improve air quality. More recently the global threats of climate change and depletion of the ozone layer have been an important factor in shaping EU policy. Details of EU measures to reduce traffic-related pollution are summarised later in this chapter at 2.20.

A summary of the institutions of the European Union, its legislative procedures and a list of the Directives on air pollution are given in Appendix 6 and 6.2, respectively.

2.4.1 Air Quality

(a) Assessment and Management

On 27 September 1996 a framework Directive on ambient air quality assessment and management (96/62/EC) was formally adopted; it came into force on 21 November 1996, and must be implemented by Member States by 21 May 1998. A main aim of the Directive is to protect human health and the environment by avoiding, reducing or preventing harmful concentrations of air pollutants; this will be achieved through

- the definition and fixing of objectives for air quality and setting of limit values and/or alert thresholds (and/or target values for ozone);
- assessing air quality in a uniform manner;
- making information available to the public;
- maintaining or improving ambient air quality.

The framework Directive requires the Commission to propose "Daughter" Directives setting air quality objectives, limit values, alert thresholds, guidance on monitoring, siting and measurement methods for individual pollutants as follows:

- Sulphur dioxide, nitrogen dioxide, fine particulate matter (PM_{10}), suspended particulate matter and lead by 31 December 1996; COM(97) 500 published October 1997, amended proposal COM(98) 386 – see (b) below.
- Ozone by 1 March 1998 in accordance with Article 8 of the 1992 ozone Directive; proposal expected end 1998.
- Benzene and carbon monoxide – proposal should have been brought forward no later than 31 December 1997; not expected before end of 1998.
- PAHs (benzo-a-pyrene as indicator), cadmium, arsenic, nickel compounds (classified as carcinogens) and mercury – as soon as possible but not later than 31 December 1999.

Pollutants to be considered at a further stage are dioxins, VOCs, methane, ammonia, nitric acid and PAHs (general). Proposals for other substances to be covered by daughter Directives will be considered on the basis of new scientific evidence on environmental or health effects.

Factors to be taken into account when setting limit values and alert thresholds include: degree of exposure of population (including sensitive groups); climatic conditions; sensitivity of flora and fauna and of historic heritage; economic and technical feasibility; and long-range transmission of pollutants. The World Health Organisation's guidelines (see above, 2.3.4) will also be used as a basis for setting air quality objectives.

Criteria for monitoring, modelling and estimation techniques will be fixed for individual pollutants. Monitoring will be mandatory in population centres of more than 250,000, in those areas where the level of the pollutant is above a certain proportion of its limit value, and in other areas where limit values are exceeded. Member States must designate the national, regional or local authorities to be responsible for implementation of the Directive and also accredit laboratories for quality assurance and assessment.

Member states must assess ambient air quality on the basis of the limit values and alert thresholds set, drawing up action plans indicating measures to be taken in the short term where there is a risk that these may be exceeded. Certain measures are required depending on measured air quality:

- in zones where levels exceed or are likely to exceed the limit value, plus the margin of tolerance (i.e. the percentage of the limit value by which the value may be exceeded) – plans and programmes to achieve the limit value within the specific time limit must be drawn up and implemented and the public given details of them;
- in zones where the levels are lower than the limit value – these levels should be maintained and the best ambient air quality compatible with sustainable development maintained;
- where the alert threshold is exceeded, steps must be taken to inform the public and a report sent to the Commission within three months of the episode, with details such as duration and levels of pollutants recorded.

(b) Air Quality Standards

The adoption in July 1980 of a Directive on health protection standards for levels of sulphur dioxide and suspended particulates in air resulted in an important change in UK policy. In effect, the Directive introduced into the UK the first air quality standards and was thus a break with the UK's tradition of setting non-statutory emission standards, via the pollution inspectorate. Similar Directives for nitrogen oxides and lead followed. The Directives fixed limit values (and non-mandatory guide values), all of which have now to be met.

Following adoption of the new Directive setting limit values for sulphur dioxide, oxides of nitrogen, particulate matter and lead (see below), various articles of these Directives will be repealed on 1 January 2000; the remainder (including those articles relating to limit values) will be repealed on 1 January 2005 (or 1 January 2010 in the case of the nitrogen dioxide Directive). The current standards are shown in the table below.

EU Air Quality Standards

Sulphur Dioxide and Suspended Particulates: EU Directive 80/779/EEC

	Reference period	*Limit values (to be met by 1.4.83)*
Sulphur dioxide	one year (median daily values)	120 μg/m³ if smoke less than 40 μg/m³ 80 μg/m³ if smoke more than 40 μg/m³
	winter (median of daily values)	180 μg/m³ if smoke less than 60 μg/m³ 130 μg/m³ if smoke more than 60 μg/m³
	year, peak (98 percentile of daily values)	350 μg/m³ if smoke less than 150 μg/m³ 250 μg/m³ if smoke more than 150 μg/m³
Smoke	one year (median of daily values)	80 μg/m³
	winter (median of daily values)	130 μg/m³
	year, peak (98 percentile of daily values)	250 μg/m³
		Guide values
Sulphur dioxide	24-hour mean	100-150 μg/m³
	one year mean	40-60 μg/m³

Nitrogen dioxide: EU Directive 85/203/EEC

Reference period	*Limit value (to be met by 1.7.87)*
one year (98 percentile of 1-hour mean)	200 μg/m³
	Guide values
1 year (50 percentile of 1-hour mean)	50 μg/m³
1 year (98 percentile of 1-hour mean)	135 μg/m³

Lead in the air: EU Directive 82/884/EEC

Limit value (to be met by 9.12.87): 2 μg/m³ annual mean

These standards have been implemented in the UK through *Air Quality Standards Regulations* – see this chapter, 2.8. The widespread introduction of smoke control areas (see 2.13.3 below) has played a major part in reducing levels of smoke.

Directive Relating to Limit Values for Sulphur Dioxide, Oxides of Nitrogen, Particulate Matter and Lead

The first proposal for a Daughter Directive (COM(97) 500) under the Air Quality Assessment and Management Directive (see above) was published in October 1997, and a Common Position (COM(98) 386) agreed in June 1998; it was hoped it would be formally adopted before the end of 1998 following a second reading in the European Parliament.

Forthcoming EU Air Quality Standards (COM(98) 386

Sulphur dioxide

- *Hourly limit value for the protection of human health:* 350 $\mu g/m^3$, not to be exceeded more than 24 times per calendar year (pcy) target date: 1.1.05.
- *Daily limit value for the protection of human health:* 125 $\mu g/m^3$, not to be exceeded more than 3 times pcy; target date: 1.1.05.
- *Alert threshold:* 500 $\mu g/m^3$ measured over 3 hours.
- *Annual limit value for the protection of ecosystems:* 20 $\mu g/m^3$; target date: 2 years after Directive enters into force.

Nitrogen dioxide

- *Hourly limit value for the protection of human health:* 200 $\mu g/m^3$, not to be exceeded more than 18 times pcy; target date: 1.1.10.
- *Annual limit value for the protection of human health:* 40 $\mu g/m^3$; target date: 1.1.10.
- *Alert threshold:* 400 $\mu g/m^3$ measured over 3 hours.
- *Annual limit value for the protection of vegetation:* 30 $\mu g/m^3$; target date: 2 years after Directive enters into force.

Particulate matter (PM_{10})

Stage 1:

- *Daily limit value for the protection of human health:* 50 $\mu g/m^3$, not to be exceeded more than 35 times pcy; target date: 1.1.05;
- *Annual limit value for the protection of human health:* 40 $\mu g/m^3$; target date: 1.1.05.

Stage 2:

- *Indicative daily limit value for the protection of human health:* 50 $\mu g/m^3$, not to be exceeded more than 7 times pcy; target date: 1.1.10.
- *Indicative annual limit value for the protection of human health:* 20 $\mu g/m^3$; target date: 1.1.10.

Lead

- *Annual limit value for the protection of human health:* 0.5 $\mu g/m^3$; target date: 1.1.05.

The Directive, which will come into force two years after its formal adoption, sets limit values for the above pollutants with the aim of avoiding, preventing or reducing their harmful effects on human health and on the environment as a whole. Where the limit value is likely to be exceeded on more than the permitted number of days per year then action programmes setting out plans to meet the limit value by the target date must be drawn up; where the limit value is exceeded, steps must be taken to ensure it is met by the target date; where air quality is below the limit value, it should not be allowed to deteriorate. When the alert threshold for sulphur dioxide or nitrogen dioxide is exceeded, specified information must be made available to the public. Information (updated hourly, or every three months for lead) on ambient concentrations of all the pollutants should be made available to the public, including exceedances of the public indicator threshold (i.e. the hourly or daily limit values below). The Directive recognises that some Member States may not be able to meet some of the limit values because of climatic or other special circumstances. The Commission is to review the Directive before 30 September 2003.

(c) Monitoring and Information - Ozone

In September 1992 a Directive on Air Pollution by Ozone (92/72/EEC) was adopted; it includes requirements for a monitoring network, exchange of information and for a warning system for when ozone concentrations exceed thresholds above which there is considered to be a health risk (see box). The values, which should not be exceeded, are based on WHO recommendations.

EU Ozone Thresholds

	$\mu g/m^3$	*or*	*as ppb*
Health protection			
8 hour mean	110		55
Vegetation protection			
1 hour mean	200		100
24 hour mean	65		32.5
Population information			
1 hour mean	180		90
Population warning			
1 hour mean	360		180

When the population thresholds are exceeded (see table) information must be available "on a sufficiently large scale as soon as possible to enable the population concerned to take all appropriate preventive protective action". Such information should include the area affected, forecast of length of episode and whether ozone levels are likely to increase further; information on what health precautions are advisable (e.g. the need to avoid strenuous exercise) should also be given.

This Directive has been implemented in the UK through the *Ozone Monitoring and Information Regulations 1994* – see this chapter, 2.9. In the UK ozone levels are monitored and information is made available to the public (see section 2.10.1).

(d) Exchange of Air Pollution Data

Decision 97/101/EC approved in January 1997 establishes a "reciprocal exchange of information and data from networks and individual stations measuring ambient air pollution within Member States". This supersedes an earlier 1982 Decision which aimed to achieve equality throughout the Community and harmonise measurements and, subsequently, techniques. The new scheme covers all the pollutants listed in the air quality assessment and management Directive (see above); Member States are required to submit to the Commission data collected and validated in accordance with the Decision; data for the year must be sent by October of the following year. The data will be stored by the European Environment Agency; a request for access to the data may be made to the EEA or to a Member State.

2.4.2 Carbon Dioxide

The members of the European Union have agreed that emissions of carbon dioxide (CO_2) – the major greenhouse gas, accounting for 66% of global greenhouse effect – should be stabilised at 1990 levels by 2000. This was in line with a commitment made at the 1992 Earth Summit and confirmed in the Framework Convention on the Climate – see above 2.3.1. In April 1998 the EU (together with individual Member States) signed a Protocol to the Convention (the Kyoto Protocol); this commits the members of the EU to reducing emissions of six greenhouse gases by 8% based on 1990 levels between 2008-2012. In June 1998 Member States agreed on how to apportion the 8% target cut and, as a result, the UK is to reduce its emissions by 12.5%.

The EU also has in place a number of other measures aimed at stabilising CO_2 emissions; these include:

- **reducing energy demand:** Directive to improve Energy Efficiency (93/76) implements the programme of Specific Actions for Vigorous Energy Efficiency (SAVE) and could reduce growth in CO_2 emissions by about 25%; the Directive requires, *inter alia*, regular inspections of cars and boilers; energy audits for business; thermal insulation of new buildings; certification of CO_2 emissions related to energy consumption in buildings. Decision 96/737, adopted in December 1996 outlines a multi-annual programme for the promotion of energy efficiency (SAVE II) from 1996-2000 It includes measures to improve energy efficiency and to encourage the exchange of experience and information at all levels.

- **carbon tax:** In 1992 the Commission proposed a Directive (COM(92) 226, amended by COM(95) 172) for a tax on carbon dioxide/energy; a principle objective of the Directive was to help meet the EU's commitments to returning CO_2 emissions to their 1990 levels by the year 2000. However Member States were unable to reach any consensus as to the form of any tax. As a result the Commission is now considering extending excise duty, which currently applies to mineral oils, to all energy sources, including biofuels (see also 2.20.10).
- **monitoring CO_2 emissions:** 93/389 is a Council Decision for a Monitoring Mechanism for Community CO_2 and other Greenhouse Gas Emissions to 2000; monitoring is seen as an integral part of the national programmes that EU Member States are preparing (see 2.3.1 above – *Framework Convention on the Atmosphere*); national programmes should include actions to increase energy conservation and efficiency, encourage a switch to low or no carbon fuels and implement Community legislation. Member States are required to report on and publicise their policies and actions to limit emissions of CO_2 and other greenhouse gases and to evaluate the impact of these measures. COM(98) 108, on which a Common Position was reached on 23 March 1998, is a proposal for a Council Decision to amend 93/389 and extend monitoring arrangements beyond 2000. This Decision also includes provisions for monitoring all manmade emissions of greenhouse gases not controlled by the Montreal Protocol; stabilisation of CO_2 emissions at 1990 levels by 2000; meeting EU commitments under the Kyoto Protocol and monitoring in this respect.
- **reducing CO_2 emissions from cars:** COM(95) 689 proposes voluntary agreements between the Commission and car manufacturers to reduce emissions from new cars by 25% by 2005; development of a framework of tax incentives; and labelling of fuel consumption – see 2.20.6.

2.4.3 Methane

Methane – CH_4 – is the second most important greenhouse gas (after carbon dioxide), accounting for 18% of the global greenhouse effect. In November 1996, the Commission published a Strategy Paper (COM(96) 557) for reducing methane emissions from the three sectors chiefly responsible for emissions: agriculture (45% of EU emissions), waste (32%) and energy (23%). It is hoped that the measures proposed for these sectors (see below) will lead to a reduction in methane emissions of 30% by 2005 and 41% by 2010.

- **Agriculture:** promotion of research and incentives to reduce emissions from, in particular, cattle and sheep; animal manure management, e.g. anaerobic digesters or covered lagoons.
- **Waste:** promotion of measures to encourage separate collection of organic wastes, composting and recycling; new anaerobic landfills to be equipped with methane recovery and use systems; wherever possible, existing landfills to be retrofitted with methane collection and use systems; otherwise encourage flaring.
- **Energy:** CH_4 reduction schemes promoting best available recovery techniques in coal mines. For natural gas, a minimum leakages standard and increased control frequency of pipelines.

In 1995 UK methane emissions fell slightly to 3.8 thousand tonnes, with landfill and cattle accounting for 46% and 21% respectively of the total (*Digest of Environmental Statistics*, No. 19, 1997).

2.4.4 Substances that Deplete the Ozone Layer

Over the past few years there have been a number of EU measures aimed at controlling the use of chlorofluorocarbons (CFCs) and other substances that deplete the ozone layer; in June 1988, the Council of Environment Ministers agreed on a Decision to ratify the Montreal Protocol of 11 September 1987 to the Vienna Convention for the protection of the ozone layer; this initiative had originated from the United Nations Environment Programme. The Protocol came into force on 1 January 1989 and aims to achieve a 50% reduction in CFC use by 1999; the Protocol was further strengthened at international meetings held in London in 1990 and Copenhagen in 1992; EU Regulations 594/91 and 3952/92 adopted in 1991 and 1992 respectively implemented the amendments and set a tighter timetable for phasing out the production and use of some of the various ozone depleting chemicals.

In December 1994, Environment Ministers formally adopted Regulation 3093/94/EC; this consolidates the 1991 and 1992 Regulations, which are now repealed as having been superseded; it also implements the revised Protocol (see 2.3.2) and extends controls on ozone depleting chemicals to cover hydrochlorofluorocarbons (HCFC), hydrobromofluorocarbons (HBFC) and methyl bromide. The current schedule leading to the phase-out of the main ozone depleting chemicals, together with the Commission's proposed amendments to the Regulation published in July 1998, is as follows:

- **Chlorofluorocarbons (11, 12, 113, 114, 115):** production banned from 1 January 1995. 1998 amendment proposes ban on their supply and use.

- **Other Fully Halogenated CFCs (13, 111, 112, 211, 212, 213, 214, 215, 216, 217):** as for other CFCs.
- **Halons:** production banned from 1 January 1994. 1998 amendment proposes ban on supply and use, except for fire retardants.
- **Carbon Tetrachloride:** production banned from 1 January 1995.
- **1,1,1-trichloroethane:** production banned from 1 January 1996.
- **Methyl Bromide:** using 1991 as a base level, freeze on production from 1 January 1995 and 25% reduction by 1 January 1998. 1998 amendment proposes production, supply and use phase-out by 1 January 2001, with an exemption for critical uses.
- **Hydrochlorofluorocarbons:** the limits refer to use and supply; from 1 January 1995 freeze at 2.6% (1998 amendment proposes 2%) of CFC and HCFC consumption in 1989. Using 1989 as a base level, 35% reduction from 1 January 2004, 60% reduction from 1 January 2007, 80% reduction by 2010; 90% reduction by 2013 and ban from 1 January 2015. In addition their use will be banned six months after implementation of the Regulation except as a solvent, refrigerant, for plastic foams, research and development and to protect human life. As from 1 January 1995 their use is banned except for a few specified uses such as in aerosols, cooling equipment, etc; 1998 amendment proposes extending ban to cover new refrigeration equipment from 1 January 2001, solvents and polyurethane foams from 1 January 2003; it is also proposed to freeze production of HCFCs at 1998 levels from 1 January 2000, reducing to 40% of that level in 2008, 25% in 2014, 15% in 2020, 5% in 2025, 1% in 2030 leading to a ban on production in 2040.
- **Hydrobromofluorocarbons:** production banned from 1 January 1996.

The limits apply both to the amounts of CFCs which can be produced within the European Union and to the amounts imported. Limited exceptions (to be updated annually) to the timetable will be allowed where substitutes have not been found for "essential uses", e.g. medical uses, in particular metered dose inhalers for asthma and other lung diseases – see also 2.3.2. "All practicable precautionary measures" have to be taken to ensure no leakages of ozone depleting substances from various commercial and industrial installations and manufacturing processes. Member States are required to make non-compliance with the Regulation an offence.

The draft amendment to the Regulation also proposes the introduction of an export licensing system, similar to that included in the Montreal Protocol, as a means of halting the illegal trade in CFCs etc.

The *Environmental Protection (Controls on Substances that Deplete the Ozone Layer) Regulations 1996* (SI 506) which came into force on 26 March 1996 implement the requirements of the EU Regulation; non-compliance with the Regulations is an offence and subject to a maximum fine of £5,000 on summary conviction or an unlimited fine on conviction on indictment.

Voluntary agreements between the UK Government and the aerosols, air conditioning & refrigeration, fire protection, and the foam industries ensure that where HFCs are used, any emissions to atmosphere will be minimised. The industries concerned have also agreed not to use HFCs where emissions are unavoidable if safe, practical and more environmentally acceptable alternatives exist.

2.4.5 Industrial Emissions

(a) Strategy to Combat Acidification

There has been considerable concern about the effects of acid deposition on parts of the EU for many years and various measures aimed at reducing discharges of pollutants thought to contribute to the problem have been put in place. These provide a framework for reduction of industrial air pollution and propose specific emission limits for pollutants such as sulphur dioxide, nitrogen oxides and suspended particulates. The EU's long-term objective, as stated in the Fifth Environmental Action Programme is that there should be no exceedance of critical loads for acidification anywhere in the EU. On the basis of measures in place prior to 1997, however, the Commission estimates that about nine million hectares of the Community will still exceed critical loads in 2010. In an effort to cut this deficit to 4.5 million hectares, the Commission published in March 1997 a Draft Communication on a Community Strategy to Combat Acidification (COM(97) 88); the main elements of Strategy are:

- A proposal for a Directive is to be drafted setting *national emission ceilings for critical atmospheric pollutants for each Member State* for sulphur dioxide, nitrogen oxides, ammonia and VOCs; limits to be consistent with the attainment of 50% gap closure target for acidification and the achievement of agreed air quality objectives for tropospheric ozone.

- Proposal for a Council Directive on the *sulphur content of certain liquid fuels*; COM(97) 88, amended by COM(98) 385; Common position agreed June 1998. This Directive maintains the limit for the sulphur content of gas oil at 0.2% by weight (as set in Directive 93/12 – see 2.20.7) as a minimum standard, reducing to 0.1% from 1 January 2008. The sulphur content of heavy fuel oils (used mainly in refineries, power stations and industry) will be limited to 1% by weight from 1 January 2003; the UK average is 2.3% (DETR, 1997). Operators of combustion plant burning heavy fuel oil with a sulphur content of more than 1% may continue to do so as long as total SO_2 emissions do not exceed 1700 mg/m^3. Member States which contribute very little (or nothing) to acidification have a derogation to use gas oils with a sulphur content of between 0.1-0.2%, and heavy fuel oils with a sulphur content up to 3% until 1 January 2013. Refineries may also continue to burn high sulphur fuels so long as total emissions do not exceed 1700 mg/m^3 (existing plant) or 1000 mg/m^3 (new plant).

- Ratification of *UNECE Sulphur Protocol*: COM(97) 88 also includes a draft proposal for a decision to ratify the Protocol was published by the Commission in March 1997 (see also 2.3.3a above).
- Revision of the 1988 *Large Combustion Plant Directive*: see (b) below.
- To negotiate for the inclusion of *"sulphur dioxide control areas"* in the current revision of the IMO's MARPOL Convention controlling maritime pollution (see also 5.20.2); in such areas ships would be required to use marine bunker fuel oil with a sulphur content not exceeding 1.5%.

(b) Large Combustion Plant

In 1988 agreement was reached on the Large Combustion Plant Directive (88/609/EEC) which commits Member States to specific reductions in emissions of sulphur dioxide and nitrogen oxides from large fossil fuel burning plant (50 MW or more) – mainly power stations. The UK is committed to reducing sulphur dioxide emissions from existing plant (i.e. licensed prior to 1 July 1987) in steps of 20, 40 and 60% of the 1980 baseline by 1993, 1998 and 2003 respectively. Reductions in nitrogen oxides emissions of 15% by 1993 and 30% by 1998 must also be achieved. Emission limits for sulphur dioxide and nitrogen oxides for new plant are included in an annex to the Directive.

The UK is on target to meet its commitments under the Large Combustion Plants Directive. By the end of 1995 UK sulphur dioxide emissions from LCP were 55% lower than in 1980 – i.e. 15% ahead of the 1998 target. Emissions of nitrogen oxides from LCP were 45% lower than 1980 – an improvement of 15% over the 1998 requirement (*Digest of Environmental Statistics*, No. 19, 1997). During the period 1980-93, total EU emissions of SO_2 and NO_X reduced by 52.5% and 45.8% respectively. See also 2.3.3a & b for the UK's commitments under the sulphur and nitrogen oxides protocols to the UNECE Convention on Long-Range Transboundary Air Pollution.

The 1988 Directive did not cover sulphur dioxide emissions from new solid fuel plant between 50-100 MW as agreement could not be reached on the limit to be applied to these plant. However in December 1994 an amendment Directive (94/66) covering such plant was adopted; this came into force on 24 June 1995 and sets an emission limit of 2000 mg/m^3 for such plant (i.e. those authorised to start after 1 July 1987). Proposals for a Directive covering emissions from small (up to 50 MW) combustion plant are under discussion.

In July 1998, the Commission published proposals for amending the 1988 Directive to take account of technical developments since the adoption of the 1988 Directive, and thus contribute to the goals of the acidification strategy in a cost effective manner and reduce health risks from LCP emissions; it proposes setting emission limit values for SO_2 and NO_X, based on best available techniques, from new large combustion plant (including gas turbines) coming into operation after 1 January 2000. For solid and liquid fuel plant with a capacity of less than 100 MW, an emission limit of 850 mg/m^3 SO_2 is proposed, and 200 mg/m^3 for those over 300 MW; emission limits for plant between 100 - 300 MW would be on a scale within the upper and lower limits. An emission limit of 400 mg/m^3 NO_X is proposed for solid fuel plant with a capacity of less than 100 MW and 300 mg/m^3 for plant between 100 -300 MW. Large combustion plant over 50 MW will be required to comply with the Integrated Pollution Prevention and Control Directive (see chapter 1, 1.12.1).

In the UK, a National Emissions Plan drawn up by the Secretary of State for the Environment under section 3 of the *Environmental Protection Act 1990* establishes emission limits and allocates quotas for the main sectors responsible for emissions – power stations and refineries, and for other industries. For power stations specific quotas/limits have been established for National Power, PowerGen, Scotland and N. Ireland. For refineries and other industry, quotas/limits are set for England/Wales and Scotland. The emission limits will be met by a variety of means including flue gas desulphurisation and the use of lower sulphur fuels. The *Large Combustion Plant (New Plant) Directions 1995* require conditions to be set in IPC authorisations ensuring compliance with the 1988 and 1994 Directives. In Scotland, the *Large Combustion Plant (Control of Emissions) (Scotland) Regulations 1991* (SI 562) implement the earlier Directive. In 1995 the National Emissions Plan was amended to make allowance for the transfer by National Power to Northern Ireland Electricity of some its surplus SO_2 and NO_X quota in 1995 and 1996. The Plan was further amended in December 1996 to ensure that future allocations of emissions quota for both SO_2 and NO_X are more closely in line with regulatory consents under IPC and thus based on BATNEEC.

In its Fifth Action Programme (see Appendix 6), the European Commission has set a target of reducing emissions of acidifying gases to ensure no exceedances of critical loads and levels. In addition to measures already in hand, the Commission proposes a Community-wide target of the stabilisation of nitrogen oxides at 1990 levels by 1994, and a 30% reduction by 2000; for sulphur dioxide a reduction of 35% by 2000 using 1985 as a base is proposed; other measures include the revision of municipal waste incineration standards; an inventory of ammonia emissions and standards for new farm buildings; and product standards for coal, fuel oils and residuals.

(c) Solvent Emissions

In December 1996, the European Commission published a proposal for a draft Directive on the limitation of emissions of volatile organic solvents in certain industrial activities. COM(96) 538, as amended by COM(98) 190, aims to reduce emissions of VOCs by two-thirds by 2007, based on 1990 levels, from various activities listed in an Annex to the Directive (see box). Environment Ministers adopted a Common Position on this proposal in June 1998 and it now returns to the European Parliament for a second reading .

Annex I to Draft Solvents Directive

adhesive coating; coating processes, coil coating; conversion of natural or synthetic rubber; dry cleaning; impregnation of wooden surfaces; manufacturing of coatings, varnishes, inks and adhesives; manufacturing of pharmaceutical products; printing; surface cleaning; vegetable oil extraction and fat and vegetable oil refining processes; vehicle refinishing; winding wire coating; wood and plastic lamination

Annex III specifies annual thresholds for solvent consumption for the activities and emission limits. The draft Directive gives Member States the option of meeting the overall reduction target through the establishment of a national plan for existing installations: this would enable Member States to set their own reduction targets for sectors taking into account national patterns of emissions, while still meeting the overall objectives of the Directive. New installations would be required to comply with emission limits for the sector concerned and to be registered with, or authorised by the appropriate authority upon implementation of the Directive (currently proposed as 31 December 1999); existing installations would have a further eight years to comply. Installations requiring a permit under the IPPC Directive would not also require authorisation under this Directive. Member States who already have measures reducing VOC emissions but which are incompatible with the Directive will have until 2010 to comply.

(d) Major Accident Hazards

Following a major explosion at a chemical factory in Seveso, Italy, in 1976, which resulted in health and other environmental problems in the area, the EU adopted a Directive on the Major Accident Hazards of Certain Industrial Activities (82/501/EEC). This Directive, commonly known as the Seveso Directive, was amended in 1987 and 1988; on 3 February 1999 it (and the subsequent amendments) were repealed, the date by which Member States had to have implemented its replacement – Council Directive 96/82/EC on the control of major accident hazards involving dangerous substances (Seveso 2), which was adopted on 9 December 1996. New Regulations – *the Control of Major Accident Hazards Regulations* – were due to come into force on 3 February 1999 (see this chapter 2.14.1).

The 1982 Directive aimed, through laying down requirements for notification of major hazard sites, hazard and risk assessments, safety reports and emergency planning, to prevent major accidents which may cause serious damage to the environment or human health. An amendment to the Directive (87/216/EEC) required owners of "top tier" sites – i.e. those storing above specified amounts of hazardous substances and those carrying out particularly toxic or hazardous activities – to provide information to the public on the nature of the hazard and on action to be taken in the event of an accident. The 1996 Directive aims to close some of the loopholes/shortcomings of the earlier Directives which were identified in the light of lessons learned from accidents since the 1982 Directive came into force; many of the accidents were felt to have been preventable given better management and operational procedures.

The 1996 Directive applies mainly to the chemical and petrochemical industries and to those which produce or use substances with flammable, toxic or explosive properties; warehouses and storage facilities for hazardous materials such as fuel oils and gases are included but nuclear and military installations are not. Land-use policies must take major hazard sites into account, and thus more attention must be given to the siting of potentially hazardous installations, ensuring that new installations are sited at an "appropriate distance" from residential or other areas used by the public.

The Directive defines "hazard" in terms of its potential to damage or harm human health and the environment (flora, fauna, water, soil etc); operators of those establishments where dangerous substances are present above a certain threshold (top tier sites) are required to identify possible hazards and to adopt appropriate management and staff training procedures and policies to prevent accidents or minimise harm caused by accidental releases. This information must be included in the detailed safety report required by the Directive to be submitted to the competent authority (in England, Scotland & Wales – the HSE, the Environment Agency or SEPA); this must also include "main possible major accident scenarios" and how they would be dealt with. The Directive also requires an on-site emergency plan to be prepared and sufficient information given to the competent authority to enable it to prepare an off-site emergency plan. The competent authority must identify those establishments where, because of their proximity or the combinations of substances, the occurrence of an accident becomes even more potentially dangerous.

Safety reports must be publicly available and inspected by the competent authority to ensure that they meet the Directive's requirements. The competent authority must reject the safety report if it is of the opinion that, on the basis of the report, the continued use (or the start up) of an installation would "involve an imminent risk of a major accident". The competent authority must carry out an inspection of the facility (using qualified and trained personnel) and prepare a report of any follow-up measures required, with a follow-up inspection taking place within three months.

2.4.6 Transport Policy

In 1992 the European Commission adopted a Green Paper on the *Impact of Transport on the Environment* (COM(92) 46 final). This outlines an EU strategy for "sustainable mobility" and highlights the expected growth in all forms of transport with a consequent rise in levels of pollution. Between 1990 and 2010, the Commission forecasts a growth in road/goods transport of 42%, in rail/goods transport of 33%, and in air/passenger transport of 74%. Private cars are predicted to increase 45% over the period 1987-2010 and vehicle kilometres 25% between 1990 and 2010.

The Green Paper while noting the EU's current and future legislative programmes on emission limits and standards, says that these will not be enough to contain likely environmental damage from increased transport. The Commission suggests the need for a more integrated approach to transport policy and policy in other areas on which transport has an impact, such as planning and economic policy.

Since 1970, the European Union has adopted a number of Directives aimed at reducing emissions of air pollutants from all classes of vehicle. These are summarised later in this chapter – see 2.20.

IMPLEMENTATION AND ENFORCEMENT AUTHORITIES

As was seen earlier in this chapter (section 2.2.1 and 2.2.2), HM Inspectorate of Pollution and its predecessors had most of the responsibility for controlling air pollution from a wide range of scheduled processes. The control of emissions from non-scheduled processes was the responsibility of local authorities, usually the environmental health department or its equivalent. *The Clean Air Acts* of 1956 and 1968 strengthened the powers of local authorities, previously contained in the *Public Health Act 1936*, to control such works, although it should be noted that the Acts covered only combustion processes and smoke, grit and dust emissions.

Implementation of Part I of the *Environmental Protection Act 1990* extended local authority powers to include the control of air pollution from a range of prescribed processes (see 2.11 below). Action to control smoke, dust, fumes and gases as a statutory nuisance can be taken under Part III of the EPA (see chapter 1, 1.15.1).

2.5 LOCAL AUTHORITIES

2.5.1 England and Wales

Local authorities became responsible for air pollution control under Part I of the *Environmental Protection Act 1990* (EPA) on 1 April 1991; processes prescribed for local authority control – Part B processes (see Appendix 1.1) – require an authorisation from their local authority.

In carrying out their functions under Part I of the EPA local authorities must have regard to the National Air Quality Strategy (new section (4)4A of EPA, *Environment Act 1995*, Sch. 22, para 46(5)) – see this chapter 2.7; they also have a duty to keep themselves up-to-date with regard to techniques and technologies for preventing and reducing releases to air from Part B processes (new section 4(9) of EPA, *Env. Act 1995*, Sch. 22, para 46(9)).

Local authorities are also responsible for

- air quality management and assessment (this chapter 2.7) under the *Environment Act 1995*;
- enforcing statutory nuisance legislation (see chapter 1, 1.15.1);
- enforcement of the *Clean Air Act 1993*, including the regulation of smoke, grit, dust and fumes from furnaces and for implementation and enforcement of smoke control (this chapter, 2.13);
- enforcing noise control legislation (see chapter 3)
- identification of and ensuring appropriate clean up of contaminated land following implementation of Part IIA of EPA (see chapter 4).

The *Public Health (Control of Diseases) Act 1984* gives Port Health Authorities similar responsibilities to local authorities in relation to those sections of the *Clean Air Act 1993* and the *Environmental Protection Act 1990* relating to the control of air pollution.

A Memorandum of Understanding between the Environment Agency and local authority associations agreed in February 1997 outlines working arrangements and communications on all the various areas in which both have responsibilities, including air quality management, waste management and contaminated land – see chapter 1, 1.7.1d.

2.5.2 Scotland

Scottish local authorities have similar responsibilities to authorities in England and Wales. However they are not responsible for local air pollution control (Part B processes) under Part I of the *Environmental Protection Act 1990*; since 1 April 1996 these have been regulated by the Scottish Environment Protection Agency (SEPA) (*Env. Act 1995*, section 21(1)(h)).

2.6 NORTHERN IRELAND

In Northern Ireland, the control of air pollution was the responsibility of the Department of the Environment and is currently regulated under the *Alkali Act 1906*. The *Industrial Pollution Control (Northern Ireland) Order 1997*, which received Royal Assent on 26 November 1997, establishes a system of air pollution control similar to that operating in the rest of the UK. There are, however, two tiers of air pollution control:

- processes with the potential to cause serious air pollution are to be regulated by the Industrial Pollution and Radiochemical Inspectorate (IPRI) within the DOE;
- processes with significant but less potential for air pollution are to be regulated by district councils.

New processes (i.e. those coming into operation on 2 March 1998 or after) were required to apply for an authorisation immediately; existing processes are being brought within the new controls between 1 October 1998 and 31 December 2002.

Local authorities (district councils) are responsible for the control of domestic emissions and for emissions from commercial and industrial premises not covered by the *Alkali Act 1906*, for statutory nuisance and noise legislation.

AIR QUALITY MANAGEMENT

A recent report from the Committee on the Medical Effects of Air Pollutants (*Quantification of the Effects of Air Pollution on Health*, The Stationery Office, 1998) suggests that short term air pollution may cause the premature death of between 12,000-24,000 vulnerable (i.e. the very old, very young or sick and those with respiratory diseases) people in Great Britain each year; the Committee also estimates that between 14,000 and 24,000 hospital admissions and readmissions may also be associated with short term air pollution each year. The effects of air pollution on health have, however, been recognised for more than three centuries – in 1648 Londoners petitioned Parliament to ban the importation of coal from Newcastle because of its injurious effects.

National and EU legislation (as well as international agreements) over the years has tended to focus on reducing pollution from a particular sector, e.g. from industry or from motor vehicles. Now, however, the emphasis is on maintaining or, where necessary, improving local air quality to protect public health: targets or limit values are set for individual pollutants and action plans drawn up for those areas where there is a risk that standards might be, or are being, exceeded – see above, 2.4.1a, the EU ambient air quality assessment and management Directive, and 2.7 below, the UK National Air Quality Strategy. The UNECE Convention on Long-Range Transboundary Air Pollution (see 2.3.3), whose signatories include most European countries, aims to reduce levels of certain pollutants to protect, and to prevent further damage to, sensitive ecosystems.

This section of the *Pollution Handbook* outlines the provisions of Part IV of the *Environment Act 1995*: the Secretary of State is required to draw up a National Air Quality Strategy; local authorities are required to review and assess local air quality against standards and objectives in the National Air Quality Strategy which have now been given statutory backing in Regulations. Brief details of the UK air quality monitoring networks and of the sources of research and advice on issues such as the health effects of pollutants on which Government policy is based are also given. Further sources of information on the effects of pollutants are listed in the bibliography at the back of this book.

As most people spend around 90% of their time indoors, the quality of indoor air is obviously also important. Indoor pollution can arise from a number of sources – heating, ventilation or cooking appliances, or from the structure or furnishings of the building. The presence of pollutants in the home environment is largely in the control of the householder and there are no regulations covering indoor air pollution; there are of course regulations and/or guidance relating to matters such as ventilation in homes (e.g. in areas where radon might be a problem) and the siting and servicing of appliances such as gas cookers and heaters. In the workplace, however, the *Control of Substances Hazardous to Health Regulations 1994* place strict controls on the use and storage of hazardous or toxic substances to ensure risks to health are prevented or minimised – see this chapter 2.14.3.

2.7 ENVIRONMENT ACT 1995, PART IV

National Air Quality Strategy (s.80)

This section of the Act was brought into force on 1 February 1996; it requires the Secretary of State to formulate a national air quality strategy in consultation with the Environment Agencies, representatives of local authorities and of industry and other relevant bodies or persons considered appropriate. Following a period of consultation in 1996, *The United Kingdom National Air Quality Strategy* was published in March 1997.

The Strategy outlines a national framework for reducing hazards to health from air pollution in the UK. It sets standards and objectives for the control and reduction of the eight main health-threatening pollutants; these have been set with regard to recommendations of the Government's Expert Panel on Air Quality Standards (see 2.10.2 below) or the WHO. The transport sector, local authorities and industry are identified as key contributors to meeting the Strategy's aims.

The objectives for each pollutant to be achieved by 2005 (apart from that for ozone) have been given statutory force in the *Air Quality Regulations 1997* (SI 3043); local authorities must take account of these objectives when reviewing local air quality and, where necessary, draw up an air quality management plan if standards are being breached or are at risk (see below). The Strategy recognises that ozone is not easily controlled by local measures and that strategies to reduce it will therefore need to be agreed at a European level.

As well as setting AQ standards and objectives, the Strategy includes:

- an assessment of current air quality, and describes the international and European framework within which the Strategy has been drawn up (see 2.3 and 2.4 above);
- what the Government is doing to achieve the Strategy's objectives;
- the contribution which other sectors – industry, transport, local government – can make towards achieving the objectives of the National Strategy.

National Air Quality Standards and Objectives

Pollutant	*Standard concentration*	*measured as*	*Objective to be achieved by 2005*
Benzene	5 ppb	running annual mean	5 ppb
1,3-Butadiene	1 ppb	running annual mean	1 ppb
Carbon monoxide	10 ppm	running 8-hour mean	10 ppm
Lead	0.5 $\mu g/m^3$	annual mean	0.5 $\mu g/m^3$
Nitrogen dioxide	150 ppb	1 hour mean	150 ppb, hourly mean*
	21 ppb	annual mean	21 ppb, annual mean*
Ozone	50 ppb	running 8-hour	50 ppb, measured as the
mean			97th percentile*
Fine particles (PM_{10})	50 $\mu g/m^3$	running 24-hour mean	50 $\mu g/m^3$ measured as the 99th percentile*
Sulphur dioxide	100 ppb	15 minute mean	100 ppb measured as the 99.9th percentile*

* provisional objectives – all to be reviewed in 1999; the percentiles mean: ozone target to be achieved on all but 10 days per year; particles target to be achieved on all but 4 days per year; Sulphur dioxide standard to be achieved on all but 35 periods of 15 minutes, assuming complete data capture in a year.

With regard to this latter point local authorities are advised (it is not a statutory requirement) to develop a local air quality strategy to ensure that air quality is integrated into planning and transport policy. This local strategy might cover: cooperation within and between local authorities; involving and informing business and the community; local statutory and voluntary measures.

The Environment Agency and SEPA are required to take account of the Strategy in carrying out their pollution control functions (s.81). Section 7(2) & (12) of the *Environmental Protection Act 1990*, as amended by the *Environment Act*, Sch. 22, para 49(2) place the same obligation on local authorities in England and Wales.

The Strategy is currently under review and proposals for its amendment were expected by the end of 1998; as well as looking at the feasibility of bringing forward the 2005 target dates, particular attention will be paid to those pollutants for which only provisional objectives have been set; it will also look at pollutants and their effects, policies for reducing them, the role of transport, industry and local authorities, and the costs of abatement etc.

Local Authority Functions and Duties (ss.82-84)

These sections of the Act, which place a duty on local authorities to review air quality in their area, were brought into force on 23 December 1997. The review should include the likely future air quality within the relevant period and an assessment of whether air quality standards and objectives are being achieved, or are likely to be achieved when measured against the national air quality strategy. It is hoped that local authorities will have completed their reviews and assessments within two years of this Part of the Act being brought into force (i.e by December 1999), with at least one further review and assessment being completed before 2005.

Any part of the authority's area in which standards or objectives are not being met, or are unlikely to be met over the relevant period (i.e. 2005) set out in the *Air Quality Regulations 1997*, should by Order be designated an "air quality management area". In such areas, the local authority must carry out a further assessment of the air quality in that area, identifying those standards and objectives which are not being met and the possible reasons. Within 12 months of designation, the local authority should draw up an action plan for each AQMA setting out the various measures, together with target dates, by which it aims to meet air quality standards. The plan may be revised as appropriate. AQM Orders may be varied by subsequent Order or revoked (where standards and objectives are being achieved or likely to be during the relevant period) only following a further air quality review.

In carrying out its functions in respect of an air quality review, assessment or preparing an action plan, the local authority must consult:

- the Secretary of State,
- the appropriate Environment Agency,
- in England and Wales, any highway authority affected by the review or plan,
- any local authority with whom it shares a border,
- in England, any relevant county council,
- appropriate National Parks authority,

and, as the local authority considers appropriate, any public authorities with functions within the area, representatives of business interests, or any other bodies or persons (Schedule 11 to the Act).

Schedule 11 also specifies that the local authority should ensure the public have free access to the following documents, with copies obtainable at a reasonable charge:

- results of air quality review
- results of any assessment made
- any Order designating an Air Quality Management Area
- any action plan
- any Directions from the Secretary of State
- in England, proposals and statements submitted by a county council under s.86 or any Secretary of State Direction.

The Secretary of State has published (January 1998) four guidance notes relating to local authorities' duties; these are attached to Environment Circular 15/97 (WO/63/97); the guidance notes, but not the Circular, also apply in Scotland:

- Framework for review and assessment of air quality (LAQM.G1(97));
- Developing local air quality action plans and strategies: principal considerations (LAQM.G2(97));
- Air quality and traffic management (LAQM.G3(97));
- Air quality and land-use planning (LAQM.G4(97)).

Four sets of technical guidance have also been published (the first three in May 1998 and the last in September 1998):

- Monitoring for air quality reviews and assessments (LAQM.TG1(98));
- Preparation and use of atmospheric emission inventories (LAQM.TG2(98));
- Selection and use of dispersion models (LAQM.TG3(98));
- Review and assessment: pollutant specific guidance (LAQM.TG4(98)).

Section 88(2) of the *Environment Act* requires local authorities to have regard to any guidance issued by the Secretary of State in carrying out their duties under this Part of the Act.

Reserve Powers of Secretary of State (E & W) and of SEPA (s.85)

This section of the Act (brought into force on 23 December 1997) provides powers for the Secretary of State/SEPA (acting with the approval of the Secretary of State) to carry out or to have carried out a review of air quality within the area of a local authority; to assess whether air quality objectives and standards are being met; to identify those parts of a local authority's area where it seems objectives and standards are not being met; and to make an assessment of the possible reasons why they are not being met either within the area of the LA or within a designated area.

If it appears to the Secretary of State/SEPA that a local authority is not meeting its obligations under ss.82-84, or that AQSs or objectives are unlikely to be achieved, the Secretary of State/SEPA may direct the local authority to:

- arrange for an air quality review to be carried out as specified by the Directions;
- arrange for a new air quality review to be carried out, covering such area as directed or in the way specified by the Directions;
- to revoke or modify an Order made under s.81 of the Act;
- to prepare or modify its action plan or to implement any measures in its action plan.

The Secretary of State/SEPA may also direct local authorities to take account of European or international commitments in their action plan.

County Council Functions (s.86)

This section of the Act came into force on 23 December 1997 and has been given effect through the *Air Quality Regulations 1997*; it applies in those districts in England covered by a district council which are also in an area comprising a county council.

The relevant county council may make recommendations to the district council with regard to the district council's duties under this part of the Act, which the district council must take into account.

Where the district council is preparing an action plan, the county council should submit its proposals, together with a statement outlining the timescale, for meeting air quality standards and objectives within the designated area. The *Air Quality Regulations 1997* require the county council to submit its proposals within nine months of first being consulted by the district council on its action plan.

If the Secretary of State is of the opinion that the council is not meeting its obligations under this section of the Act, he may through Directions require the county council to

- submit its proposals and statement of timescale for meeting AQSs and objectives;
- modify its proposals or statement in accordance with the Directions and to submit this to the district council;
- implement any measures in an action plan as required by the Direction.

Directions may also require county councils to take steps to implement international or European obligations with regard to air quality.

Schedule 11 to the Act requires county and district councils in England to provide each other with information "as is reasonably requested" in pursuit of their respective duties and functions.

Regulations (s.87)

This section of the Act (brought into force on 1 February 1996) provides for regulations covering all aspects of this Part of the Act, including air quality standards; objectives for restricting levels of particular substances in the air; prohibiting or restricting specified activities, vehicle or mobile equipment access in general or in certain circumstances; communicating AQ information to the public; regulations may also relate to air quality reviews, assessments, orders designating AQ management areas and action plans; vehicle emission spot checks; offences, penalties (including fixed penalty offences) and appeals.

(a) Air Quality Regulations 1997 (SI 3043)

These Regulations apply in England, Scotland and Wales and came into force on 23 December 1997. They incorporate the objectives contained in the National Air Quality Strategy, against which local authorities must review and assess air quality (see above, s.80 of the Act); they also specify the period within which county councils in England must submit proposals to district councils for inclusion in an air quality action plan (see above, s.86 of the Act).

(b) Road Traffic (Vehicle Emissions) (Fixed Penalty) Regulations 1997 (SI 3058)

These Regulations apply in England, Scotland and Wales and were brought into force on 26 December 1997, but for the first 12 months of their operation have applied only in the areas of seven local authorities (see 2.21.7).The application of these Regulations in the pilot authorities is to be reviewed, and if thought appropriate the Regulations will be amended to enable all local authorities to use them. The Regulations empower authorised officers to check that emissions from road vehicles comply with Construction and Use Regulations and to issue fixed penalty notices to drivers of vehicles failing the test; they also enable fixed penalty notices to be issued to drivers who leave their vehicle engine running unnecessarily – see also this chapter 2.21.7.

2.8 THE AIR QUALITY STANDARDS REGULATIONS 1989 (SI 317)

These Regulations (amended 1993), made under the *European Communities Act 1972*, came into effect on 31 March 1989 and apply to England, Scotland and Wales. *The Air Quality Standards Regulations (Northern Ireland) 1990* (amended 1994 and 1996) containing similar provisions came into operation on 31 May 1990. The Regulations implement EU Directives setting air quality limit values and guide values for sulphur dioxide and suspended particulates (80/779/EEC), a limit value for lead in air (82/884/EEC) and air quality standards for nitrogen dioxide (85/203/EEC); these were the first EU Directives to lay down mandatory air quality standards – the standards are detailed earlier in this chapter, 2.4.1b. These Directives are to be superseded by a "daughter" Directive under the Air Quality Assessment and Management Framework Directive – see this chapter 2.4.1a, and thus the Regulations will also need replacing to implement the new Directive.

The UK Regulations provided for specific areas to be temporarily exempted from complying with the air quality limits for suspended particulates and lead. With respect to the limit values for suspended particulates, a number of districts, mostly in the West Midlands, Yorkshire, North East England, and Glasgow in Scotland had until 1 April 1993 to comply, although programmes for meeting the Directive had to be drawn up in advance of this.

The Regulations require the Secretary of State to ensure that the amounts in the air of suspended particulates and sulphur dioxide (considered both separately and in association), lead, and nitrogen dioxide are measured and reduced below specified limit values. They do not apply to exposure to lead in the air as a result of a person's occupation, nor to nitrogen dioxide in the atmosphere at work or within buildings.

2.9 THE OZONE MONITORING AND INFORMATION REGULATIONS 1994 (SI 440)

These Regulations made under the *European Communities Act 1972* apply throughout the UK and came into force on 21 March 1994; they implement EU Directive 92/72 (see this chapter 2.4.1c).

The Regulations require the Secretary of State to either set up or designate monitoring stations for ozone – the Directive specifies the number and where they should be sited. Monitoring results must also be analysed and evaluated in accordance with the reference method (or method giving similar results) in the Directive.

When ozone levels exceed thresholds specified in the Directive, the public must be informed and health advice given.

2.10 AIR POLLUTION MEASUREMENT AND MONITORING

Measurements of air pollution have been made for many years in the UK, with monitoring (i.e. the systematic measurement of air pollution) begun in 1914 by the voluntary Committee for the Investigation of Atmospheric Pollution. This Committee included, among others, members from a few local authorities, the Coal Smoke Abatement Society (the forerunner of the National Society for Clean Air) and the Director of the Meteorological Office. Its work was put on an official footing in 1917, under the direction of the Met. Office with the aim of providing an adequate picture of smoke and sulphur dioxide, grit and dust in towns; this coordinating function was later passed to the Department of Scientific and Industrial Research, followed in turn by the Fuel Research Station, Warren Spring Laboratory and now the National Environmental Technology Centre (NETCEN) (part of AEA Technology – an agency of the DTI).

In 1961, the National Survey of Air Pollution was set up to monitor concentrations of both smoke and sulphur dioxide; measurements were made at about 1,200 urban and rural sites throughout the UK by local authorities and other bodies.

An annual National Atmospheric Emissions Inventory is prepared each year for the Department of the Environment, Transport and the Regions (DETR) by NETCEN. The Inventory covers black smoke, sulphur dioxide, nitrogen oxides, carbon monoxide, non-methane volatile organics, methane, carbon dioxide, lead, ammonia, metals and halogens; it provides estimates of pollution to atmosphere from all known sources and is used by government for policy formulation and for meeting European legislative requirements and international treaty obligations.

2.10.1 Monitoring Networks

In 1982, the National Survey was replaced by a more streamlined network – the UK Smoke and Sulphur Dioxide Monitoring Network. This Network comprises some 200 sites monitoring black smoke and sulphur dioxide; 156 are EU Directive sites monitoring in compliance with the Directive on air quality limit values and guide values for sulphur dioxide and suspended particulates (see 2.4.1b) and 151 comprise the Basic Urban Network (some sites are common to both networks). Like its predecessor, this Network is equipped and operated by local authorities, industries and other bodies; it is coordinated by

NETCEN who process and analyse the data on behalf of the DETR. Daily average concentrations of sulphur dioxide are measured using the acid titration method (BS 1747, Part 3) and smoke using the reflectance method (BS 1747, Part 11). Smoke and sulphur dioxide measurement data are available from the air quality archive website – http://www.aeat.co.uk/netcen/aqarchive/archome.html. The archive includes automatic and non-automatic monitoring data and the UK atmospheric emissions inventories, with some data going back to the 1960s.

Nitrogen dioxide is measured (using diffusion tubes) at approximately 1,200 urban background and roadside sites. In compliance with EU Directives, ground level concentrations of nitrogen dioxide and airborne lead are also monitored. Acid deposition and toxic organic micropollutants (dioxins, PCBs and PAHs) are also measured at a number of sites.

In January 1992 the Enhanced Urban Network (EUN) – now the Automatic Urban Network (AUN) – funded by the DETR, became operational, and a number of local authority sites were integrated into the Network. Sulphur dioxide, nitrogen oxides, carbon monoxide, ozone and particulate matter (PM_{10}) are monitored continuously using automatic instruments. The DETR also funds the Automatic Rural Network which monitors ozone by automatic UV absorption analysers. The main purpose of the sites is to provide up to date information on air quality which can be used to increase understanding of air quality problems, to assess personal exposure to air pollution and to assess the extent to which air quality standards and targets are met. As at 1 April 1998, there were 84 monitoring stations.

In April 1998, the Urban and Rural Networks were combined under the Central Management and Coordination Unit, with Stanger Science and Environment (environmental consultants) being contracted to carry out day to day management and control of the combined Networks – the UK Automatic Urban and Rural Air Quality Monitoring Networks (AURN); this includes specifying the monitoring equipment, site housings, data handling and maintenance requirements; NETCEN is responsible for quality assurance and quality control; sites are operated mainly by trained staff within local authorities. Data from the sites is coordinated by NETCEN on behalf of the DETR, with quality assurance and quality control carried out by the National Physical Laboratory. Air quality information is logged on a central computer system which gathers and analyses data from all the sites.

The Hydrocarbons Network which consists of 12 sites, is also funded by the DETR and monitors 25 VOCs, including benzene and 1,3 butadiene. The National Physical Laboratory is the Central

Management and Coordination Unit for this Network (as well as being responsible for quality assurance/quality control).

Measurement is carried out using the following methods:

- *Ozone*: UV absorption
- *Oxides of nitrogen*: Ozone chemiluminescence
- *Carbon monoxide*: IR absorption
- *Sulphur dioxide*: UV fluorescence
- PM_{10}: Tapered element oscillating microbalance
- *Hydrocarbons*: Gas chromatography.

In 1990, the DOE (now DETR) established an air quality information service to advise the public both on the quality of the air and on any precautions which should be taken during pollution episodes. In November 1997, a new system was launched, with air pollution bands reflecting effects on health (see next page). Data collected by the networks on ozone, sulphur dioxide, nitrogen dioxide, benzene and 1,3 butadiene is available via an air quality telephone line (freephone 0800 556677), on Ceefax (page 410-417) and Teletext (page 106); it is also sent to the media for inclusion in weather bulletins and is available on the Internet (http://www.environment.detr.gov.uk/airq/aqinfo.html). Data from automatic monitoring networks from 1972 onwards and from non-automatic networks (the National Air Quality Archive), as well as data from the National Atmospheric Emissions Inventory can also be accessed at this website.

2.10.2 Research and Advice

There are of course a wide range of independent and government sponsored bodies carrying out research in all areas relating to air pollution and air quality. Of particular interest to air quality are two groups set up under the auspices of the DOE (now DETR):

- *Quality of Urban Air Review Group* (QUARG): set up to review current knowledge of urban air quality and how it is assessed in the UK, especially in relation to public exposure and information to the public; QUARG makes recommendations to the Secretary of State for the Environment, Transport and the Regions as to any changes which need to be made to the monitoring networks, pollutants measured, advice to the public and identifies areas where more research is needed.

- *The Expert Panel on Air Quality Standards* consists largely of medical and air pollution experts. It was set up to recommend air quality standards for the UK; it has so far made seven recommendations:

Air Pollution Information "Bands"

Description "...air pollution"	low	Standard threshold moderate	Information threshold high	Alert threshold very high
Sulphur dioxide (ppb, 15 minute average)	Less than 100	100-199	200-399	400 or more
Ozone (ppb)	Less than 50 (8hr running av)	50-89 (hourly average)	90-179 (hourly average)	180 or more (hourly average)
Carbon monoxide (ppm, 8 hr running average)	Less than 10	10-14	15-19	20 or more
Nitrogen dioxide (ppb, hourly average)	Less than 150	150-299	300-399	400 or more
Fine Particles (μg/m³, 24 hr running average)	Less than 50	50-74	75-99	100 or more

Low: Effects unlikely to be noticed even by individuals who know they are sensitive to air pollutants;

Moderate: Mild effects, unlikely to require action, may be noticed amongst sensitive individuals;

High: Significant effects may be noticed by sensitive individuals and action to avoid or reduce these effects may be needed;

Very high: The effects on sensitive individuals described for "high" levels of pollution may worsen.

- *Benzene*: 5 ppb as a running annual average to be reduced to 1 ppb (1994);
- *Ozone*: 50 ppb as a running 8 hour average (1994);
- *1,3 butadiene*: 1 ppb measured as a running annual average (1994);
- *Carbon monoxide*: 10 ppm measured as a running 8-hour average (1994);
- *Sulphur dioxide*: 100 ppb measured over a 15 minute averaging period (1995);
- *Particles (PM_{10})*: 50 μg/m³ measured as a 24-hour running average (1995);
- *Nitrogen dioxide*: 150 ppb measured as an hourly average (1996);
- *Lead*: 0.25 μg/m³ measured as an annual average (1998).

These recommendations are reflected in the standards and objectives for air quality in the National Air Quality Strategy (see 2.7 above). A report on polyaromatic hydrocarbons was due in 1998.

The Department of Health's Committee on the Medical Effects of Air Pollutants (COMEAP) is an expert bodies set up in 1992 to advise the government on the effects of environmental factors on health. It has published a number of reports including *Asthma and Outdoor Air Pollution* and *Non-Biological Particles and Health* (both 1995), and *Quantification of the Effects of Air Pollution on Health in the United Kingdom* (1998); its views help to inform the work of EPAQS when recommending air quality standards. It also provides advice on the type of information which should be provided to the public during air pollution episodes.

2.10.3 Methods of Measuring

Although some measurement methods are relatively cheap and simple, others may involve the expenditure of thousands of pounds on equipment, the training of personnel to operate the instruments, and the careful analysis of results.

The choice of measurement method depends to a large extent on the finance and expertise available, but above all it has to be practical and relevant to the airborne contaminant under investigation. In each case the technique consists of two essential components: sample collection, and sample analysis.

There are two basic systems: the indirect, where sample collection and analysis are carried out separately and independently, and the direct, where two operations are combined simultaneously to give a direct reading. The direct method is most useful where immediate warnings are required of imminent danger and alarm circuits can be triggered, e.g. to protect workers or to check the compliance of emissions with legislation.

Environmental standards and legislative requirements will affect not only the method used, but also the duration of the monitoring. Essentially, effective monitoring requires both a sound knowledge of the instrumental and analytical methods employed and a full understanding of the behaviour of the pollutants in question, in terms of both the physical and chemical processes that they undergo in time and space in the ambient atmosphere.

A number of reference books on various methods of measuring air pollution are listed in the bibliography.

REGULATION OF INDUSTRIAL EMISSIONS

The *Environmental Protection Act 1990* gave local authorities powers to control air pollution from a range of prescribed (Part B) processes (see Appendix 1.1 and 2.11 below); in Scotland these powers were transferred to the Scottish Environment Protection Agency (SEPA) on 1 April 1996.

Much of the principal legislation for dealing with industrial smoke pollution is contained in the *Clean Air Act 1993* which came into force on 27 August 1993 and extends to England, Scotland and Wales only – 2.13 below. The provisions of this Act enabling local authorities to designate "Smoke Control Areas" also apply to residential areas; the content of motor fuel is regulated by Regulations made under section 30 of the Act (this section also applies to N. Ireland). The *Clean Air Act 1993* is a consolidating Act and replaces the *Clean Air Acts 1956 and 1968*, Part IV of the *Control of Pollution Act 1974, the Control of Smoke Pollution Act 1989*, as well as various sections of a number of other Acts. The *Clean Air (Northern Ireland) Order 1981* provides similar controls for Northern Ireland.

In general, legislation applying in England and Wales also covers Scotland, modified where necessary to take account of the Scottish administrative and judicial system. Thus, where appropriate, the name of the relevant Scottish legislation is given.

In Northern Ireland the *Industrial Pollution Control (Northern Ireland) Order 1997* establishes a system of industrial air pollution control similar to that applying in the rest of the UK – see 2.6 above. Industrial emissions are currently regulated under the *Alkali Act 1906* – this will be repealed in Northern Ireland following full implementation of the new legislation.

2.11 ENVIRONMENTAL PROTECTION ACT 1990, PART I

Under the *Environmental Protection Act*, which received Royal Assent on 1 November 1990, local authorities were given new powers to control air pollution from a range of industrial processes, including mobile plant (i.e. those designed to move or to be moved on roads or otherwise). Part I of the Act also introduced Integrated Pollution Control for more potentially polluting industrial processes – this is regulated by the Environment Agency and the Scottish Environment Protection Agency (see chapter 1, 1.13).

As from 1 April 1991 (1992 in Scotland), all new Part B processes and existing processes which were substantially modified after 1 April 1991/2, had to apply immediately for an authorisation from their local authority. Existing Part B processes were required to apply for an authorisation within specified dates between 1991 and 1993. As at early 1998, there were an estimated 13,000 authorised Part B processes in England and Wales.

In Scotland, the *Environment Act 1995* transferred responsibility for local air pollution control under Part I of the EPA to the Scottish Environment Protection Agency on 1 April 1996 (see chapter 1, 1.7.2).

Port Health Authorities in England and Wales have the same responsibilities and functions as local authorities for controlling local air pollution under Part I of the EPA.

The Department of Environment (now Department of the Environment, Transport and the Regions) has published five general guidance notes (see Appendix 2.1) which are intended to serve as a manual for local authorities on the operation of their air pollution control responsibilities. Issues covered include the procedure for applications for an authorisation, variations and appeals, as well as the establishment, content and access to the public registers. Revisions to general guidance notes are published in "upgrading guidance notes" – see Appendix 2.1.

The *Environment Act 1995*, Schedule 22, makes a number of amendments to the EPA and these are noted in the following text.

Northern Ireland

The *Industrial Pollution Control (Northern Ireland) Order 1997* establishes a system of air pollution control similar to that applying in the rest of the UK. There are however two levels of air pollution control: Part B processes – those with the potential to cause serious air pollution – are regulated by the Industrial Pollution and Radiochemical Inspectorate (IPRI) of the Department of the Environment (NI); Part C processes – those with significant but less potential for air pollution – are regulated by district councils. (A third category, Part A processes – those with high pollution potential – are regulated for Integrated Pollution Control also by the IPRI.)

Reference to the appropriate article of the Northern Ireland legislation is shown as follows: (NI: IPCO, Art.0).

2.11.1 Environmental Protection (Prescribed Processes and Substances) Regulations 1991 (SI 472) (as amended)

(Similar Regulations – The Industrial Pollution Control (Prescribed Processes and Substances) Regulations (Northern Ireland) 1998 (Statutory Rules of Northern Ireland no. 30) – have been made under Article 3 of the Industrial Pollution Control (NI) Order; they came into force on 2 March 1998.)

These Regulations made under section 2 of the Act came into force on 1 April 1991 in England and Wales and a year later in Scotland. Schedule 1 to the 1991 Regulations, as amended, lists Part A processes to be regulated for Integrated Pollution Control (see chapter 1, 1.13) and those to be regulated for the control of air pollution (Part B processes) (Appendix 1.1). Amendment Regulations (1992 – SI 614, 1993 – SI 1749 and SI 2405, 1994 – SI 1271 and 1995 – SI 3247) are mainly concerned with changing process descriptions or altering the categorisation of prescribed processes. 1996 Amendment Regulations (SI 2678) prescribe certain petrol storage and distribution processes for authorisation as Part B processes. (A consolidated version of the Regulations to 1994 was published in 1994, but it should be noted that this is not a legal document; thus, the original Regulations and subsequent amendment Regulations should always be consulted where matters of legality etc are concerned.)

In England and Wales, where both Part A and Part B processes within the same section of Schedule 1 are carried on at a site, the Environment Agency will normally be the regulatory body. Where a site has a number of processes in different sections of the Schedule, they will each require a separate authorisation.

Schedule 4 to the 1991 Regulations lists the substances to be controlled in relation to air pollution (see Appendix 1.2). There are separate lists for releases to land and water which apply to IPC. The Best Available Techniques Not Entailing Excessive Costs (BATNEEC – see chapter 1, 1.6.2) must be used to prevent or minimise the release of all substances – whether prescribed or not – to the environment to render them harmless.

The 1991 Regulations also detailed the dates within which existing processes had to apply for an authorisation; all existing (i.e. in operation prior to the 1991 or 1992 date from which they could apply for authorisation) have now been authorised. The subsequent amendment Regulations specify the dates by when existing processes coming under control as a result of the amendment Regulations had to apply for authorisation. Transitional arrangements permitted existing processes to continue operating prior to receiving (or being refused) an authorisation provided the application was made on time; in the event of a refusal existing processes can continue to operate pending the outcome of an appeal. Failure to apply for an authorisation renders the operator liable for prosecution under section 23(1)(a) of the EPA (NI: IPCO, Art.23(1)(a)).

It should be noted that certain processes, although included in the Regulations, are exempt; these include processes carried out at museums to demonstrate an historical activity; at an educational establishment or as part of a domestic activity in a private home.

Prescribed processes releasing substances in "trivial" amounts (except where the release results in an offensive smell outside the premises) are also exempt, as are engines for propelling most forms of transport (e.g. aircraft, road vehicles, ships etc).

Implementation of the 1996 EU Integrated Pollution Prevention and Control Directive will result in certain Part B processes requiring authorisation (or permitting) under IPPC – see chapter 1, 1.12.1.

Northern Ireland

Schedule 1 to the 1998 Regulations describes the prescribed processes to be regulated for Integrated Central Control (Part A) – see chapter 1; Restricted Central Control (Part B); and local control (Part C). While the processes prescribed for control are very similar to those in the rest of the United Kingdom, it is of course necessary to refer to the Schedule itself for details of classification.

As from 2 March 1998, all new processes had to apply for an authorisation from the relevant authority. Schedule 3 to the Regulations lists the dates within which existing processes must apply for an authorisation, with the first tranche required to apply before 31 December 1998. Others will be required to apply for authorisation as specified in Schedule 3, with the final tranche required to apply before 31 December 2002. Existing processes are defined as those operating in the 12 months before 2 March 1998, or the plant for which was in the course of construction or for which contracts for construction had been exchanged in the 12 months to 2 March 1998, or are currently regulated under the *Alkali Act 1906*.

Schedules 4, 5 and 6 list the prescribed substances for release, respectively, to air, water and land. These are identical to Schedules 4, 5 and 6 of the GB Regulations – see Appendix 1.2.

2.11.2 Environmental Protection (Applications, Appeals and Registers) Regulations 1991 (SI 507), as amended

(Similar Regulations – The Industrial Pollution Control (Applications, Appeals and Registers) Regulations (Northern Ireland) 1998 (SR NI 29) – have been made under The Industrial Pollution Control (NI) Order 1997. They came into force on 2 March 1998.)

These Regulations came into force in England and Wales on 1 April 1991 and a year later in Scotland; they detail the way in which applications for authorisations, variations and substantial changes are to be made for both Part A and Part B processes; they also set out the circumstances and procedures for appeals against decisions made by the enforcing authority and establish public registers of authorisations etc.

1996 Amendment Regulations (SI 667), which came into force on 1 April 1996, amend the 1991 Regulations with regard to advertising and consultation on applications, information to be placed on the public register and requirement to disclose name of parent or holding company on applications and variations.

With effect from 1 April 1996 responsibility for regulating Part B processes in Scotland transferred to the Scottish Environment Protection Agency (SEPA).

Northern Ireland

The 1998 Regulations are similar to those applying in England, Scotland and Wales.

The Industrial Pollution Control (Authorisation of Processes) (Determination Periods) Order (Northern Ireland) 1998 (SR NI 30) – varies the periods contained in the IPCO within which enforcing authorities should determine applications for authorisations:

- Existing Part A and Part B Processes: 9 months, instead of 6; where a request has been made for certain information to be considered as of importance to national security or as commercially confidential, the determination period begins when such matters have been resolved;
- Part C, new waste or recovered oil burners: 2 months, instead of 6.

Where a request is made for certain information on an application for authorisation to be excluded from the public register for national security or commercial confidentiality reasons, the 6 months (or longer as agreed) period of determination does not begin until the request has been determined or withdrawn.

(a) Applications

(NI: IPCO, Art.6 & Sch. 1, Part I)

All processes prescribed for local air pollution control (see Appendix 1.1) must apply for an authorisation from the local authority in which the process will be carried on (or in Scotland from SEPA); in the case of mobile plant in England and Wales (i.e. plant designed to move or to be moved by road or otherwise), this will be the local authority in which the applicant's principal place of business is situated.

For planned new processes, it is recommended that an application for an authorisation be made at the design stage (i.e. before construction); this will avoid the possibility of unnecessary expenditure due to the enforcing authority not approving, for example, the abatement technology. The actual construction of the site will be subject to separate approval under planning legislation (see chapter 1, 1.21).

In addition to general information about the plant, its location, name and address of operator and description of the process, the application should also identify the parent or ultimate holding company and its address. In making an application for authorisation the process operator should take account of the appropriate Process Guidance Note (see below and Appendix 2.1) and should include the following details:

- list of prescribed substances (and non-prescribed substances which might cause harm if released to the environment) to be used in connection with, or resulting from, the process; details of likely quantities and natures of releases should be given assuming the technology and controls have been fitted and are operational;
- description of techniques to be used for preventing or minimising the release of prescribed substances and rendering harmless any which are released;
- details of any proposed release and an assessment of the environmental consequences;
- proposals for monitoring, sampling and measurement of air emissions;
- for existing plant, outline programme for upgrading to meet new plant standards for BATNEEC.

An application for an authorisation for a waste oil burner with a net rated thermal input of less than 0.4 MW need only provide a list of specific information related to the appliance.

The application, relevant fee and copies (if requested) must be sent to the appropriate enforcing authority. If the application is considered to be incomplete – e.g. lacking in detail, sent without a fee or an incorrect fee – it will be returned to the applicant. Supplementary information in respect of applications for new or substantially changed processes should be requested in writing with a deadline by when the information should be submitted (EPA, Sch. 1, para 1(3)).

In submitting the application, the applicant may request that certain information should not be put in the register on the grounds of national security or commercial confidentiality (EPA, ss.21 & 22; NI: IPCO, Arts.21 & 22); the request for exclusion, which the enforcing authority has 14 days to consider, should be accompanied by a full statement justifying it. If it agrees, then the relevant information will be withheld; if the enforcing authority refuses the request, the applicant has 21 days in which to appeal to the Secretary of State (see below), during which time the information will not be added to the register. Following determination or withdrawal of the appeal, a further seven days must elapse before the information is added to the register (*Env. Act 1995*,

Sch. 22, para 58(2)). It should be noted that if the enforcing authority fails to respond within 14 days to the request for information to be withheld, then it automatically becomes commercially confidential (s.22(3) of the EPA and of the NI: IPCO). The period for determination of applications for which a request for commercial confidentiality has been made will begin from the date on which such matters have been resolved.

Following acceptance of the application and resolution of any issues of commercial confidentiality, the enforcing authority will file a copy of the application in the public register kept for the purpose (see below).

Copies of applications (except those for small waste oil burners will be sent to English Nature, Scottish Natural Heritage, and the Countryside Council for Wales (as appropriate) where an emission to air may affect a Site of Special Scientific Interest; these bodies – statutory consultees – will normally have 28 days in which to comment. Petroleum licensing authorities must be consulted over applications relating to petrol storage and distribution processes in their area (1996 Amendment to EP Prescribed Processes & Substances Regulations – SI 2678). Applications for mobile plant need only be sent to the consultees if the plant is likely to remain in the same place for at least six months and is within one kilometre of an SSSI; in such cases a copy of the application should be sent to the relevant branch/office which should be invited to comment in the usual way. The Health and Safety Executive should be advised that an application for an authorisation has been made (1996 Amendment Regulations).

In Northern Ireland, the Department of Economic Development is a statutory consultee for both Part B and Part C processes; the DOE(NI) should be consulted over applications relating to Part B and C processes where a release to air may affect an area of special scientific interest; the relevant district council is a statutory consultee in the case of a Part B process which may involve a release to air. Statutory consultees must be notified within 14 days of the application being received and have 42 days in which to comment.

The enforcing authority will normally have four months from the date of receipt to consider applications relating to new processes (14 days for new waste or recovered oil burners under 0.4 MW). Under the *Environmental Protection (Authorisation of Process) (Determination of Periods) (Amendment) Order 1994*, local authorities had nine months in which to decide applications for processes prescribed for their control as a result of the 1994 amendments to the *Prescribed Processes and Substances Regulations.*

The Secretary of State may request the enforcing authority to forward a particular application, or class of application, to him for determination. The enforcing authority should advise the applicant that this has been done; both parties have 21 days in which to request the Secretary of State to arrange either a hearing or a local inquiry in connection with the application (Schedule 1, para 3; NI: IPCO, Sch. 1, Part I, para 3).

(b) Public Consultation

The applicant must publish an advertisement in an appropriate local newspaper not less than 14 days and not more than 42 days after the application is made; this should include brief details of the application, where it can be seen in the public register and note that any comments made will be put on the public register unless a request is made for them to be excluded. A period of 28 days (NI: 42 days) will normally be allowed for receipt of any comments from the public. Applications relating to waste oil burners under 0.4 MW, petrol service stations and to mobile plant do not need to be advertised although a copy of the application will be placed in the public register.

(c) Process Guidance Notes

In addition to the General Guidance Notes covering various aspects of local authority air pollution control, Process Guidance Notes (PG Notes) cover each of the Part B process sectors – see Appendix 2.1. The PG Notes are issued by the Secretary of State under section 7 of the EPA and were drafted by the Department of Environment's (now Department of the Environment, Transport and the Regions) Local Authority Unit in consultation with relevant industry groups, local authorities and IPLA (the former HMIP/Local Authority Liaison Committee) to assist enforcing authorities in drawing up authorisations and setting appropriate conditions of operation.

Process Guidance Notes provide guidance on what constitutes BATNEEC for each category of process; they will usually include details of emission limits and controls, monitoring, sampling and measuring of emissions, materials handling and storage. They may also include general requirements for staff training, maintenance and response to abnormal emissions.

The Notes set the standards to be met by new plant and say that existing plant should be upgraded to new plant standards "whenever the opportunity arises", with the timetable for upgrading taking account of criteria laid down in the 1984 EU Directive on combatting air pollution from industrial plant. The PG Notes include an outside limit beyond which an upgrading programme may be extended "only in exceptional circumstances".

Process Guidance Notes are generally reviewed every four years with a view to updating to reflect advances in technology etc. General revisions and amendments are published in Additional Guidance Notes (AQ Notes) – see Appendix 2.2; these provide clarification on matters relating to PG Notes as well as general guidance on administrative procedures relating to the EPA.

In addition a number of technical guidance notes have been published by the Environment Agency (and earlier ones by HMIP). These provide background detail on a range of technical subjects – see Appendix 1.4. For instance, the TG note on *Guidelines on Discharge Stack Heights for Polluting Emissions* (published in 1993 by HMSO) covers a wide variety of pollutant discharges not dealt with by the *Memorandum on Chimney Heights*, which it complements; it is intended primarily as an aid for enforcing authorities (but is also of interest to industry) in setting conditions for authorisations.

(d) Authorisations

In considering whether to grant an authorisation, and the conditions which should be attached to it, the enforcing authority will take into account comments from statutory consultees and members of the public, as well as other relevant legislation, Directions from the Secretary of State, the National Air Quality Strategy and Process Guidance Notes, setting conditions as appropriate to ensure compliance with them. Where the Part B process consists of a waste disposal or recovery process, the enforcing authority should also ensure that the objectives of the Framework Directive on waste will be achieved – see chapter 4, 4.6.

In addition to factual details and a general description of the process, authorisations will include specific conditions for the operation of processes. Authorisations and their conditions should be written clearly and precisely to ensure their enforceability. Implicit in all authorisations is a duty (a residual duty) to use BATNEEC (see chapter 1, 1.6.2) to prevent or minimise the release to air of any prescribed substances and to ensure that any emissions are rendered harmless. If it is felt necessary, emission standards for specific pollutants can be included as well as conditions monitoring releases beyond the boundary of the plant. Reference to the need to adhere to other relevant legislation such as the *Clean Air Act 1993* and nuisance provisions of the EPA should also be noted on the authorisation; however conditions relating to aspects of pollution control other than air pollution should not be included; nor should conditions be included which are solely for the protection of health at work, or which relate to the final disposal of waste.

Authorisations for mobile plant will normally include a requirement for the operator to notify the enforcing authority in advance if it is proposed to relocate the plant, including details of the new location.

In general there is a requirement to review authorisations at least every four years, and immediately if complaints are felt to be the result of older standards in operation or if new information about the harmful effects of a pollutant becomes available. Copies of all authorisations will be placed in the public register (see below).

It is an offence (EPA, ss.6(1) & 23; NI: IPCO, Arts.6(1) & 23)) to operate a process without an authorisation or in contravention of any of its conditions, even if an appeal has been lodged against those conditions. If an authorisation has been refused and an appeal lodged, the process can continue to operate pending the outcome of the appeal. The enforcing authority must refuse to grant an authorisation if it is felt that the operator will be unable to meet the proposed conditions (EPA, s.6(4); NI: IPCO, Art.6(4)).

Operators of existing plant (i.e. those in operation prior to the date specified in the Regulations) are usually required to let the enforcing authority have a detailed upgrading plan within 6-12 months of receiving their authorisation. If this is not possible because, for example, further investigation of the technological options is needed, then the operator is allowed to submit a paper detailing expected progress leading up to a date for submitting the final upgrading plan. The enforcing authority would then issue a variation notice (see below) incorporating the programme into the authorisation.

Authorisations may be transferred to another person, who should notify the enforcing authority within 21 days of taking it over (EPA, s.9; NI: IPCO, Art.9). Details should be put in the public register.

(e) Inspections

Guidance (AQ 4/95) from the Department of Environment (now DETR) suggests that local enforcing authorities should aim to carry out a full inspection of authorised processes (except small waste oil burners) in their area approximately every six months; the main purpose is to check compliance with conditions of an authorisation, with compliance monitoring and in response to complaints; such visits may be unannounced.

Sites will also usually be visited in connection with applications for an authorisation, variation, etc.

(f) Variations

Sections 10 and 11 of the Act provide for authorisations to be varied by the enforcing authority or the process operator respectively.

Section 10 of the EPA (NI: IPCO, Art.10) requires the enforcing authority to vary an authorisation if it is of the opinion that conditions in the existing authorisation do not comply with BATNEEC or meet other objectives for minimising air pollution. In this instance, the enforcing authority will serve a variation notice specifying the changes it has decided should be made and the effective date. The *Environment Act 1995*, Sch. 22, para 51 amends the EPA to enable the enforcing authority to serve a variation notice varying a variation notice; this should specify the changes the enforcing authority wishes to make to the original variation notice and when these are to take effect. A variation notice will also require the operator to notify the enforcing authority how it proposes to meet the new requirements. If in the opinion of the enforcing authority this will result in a substantial change in the substances released from the process, or in the amounts released, then a procedure similar to applying for an authorisation (including disclosure of parent or holding company where this information is not already on the public register) is followed and a fee becomes payable (see below); varied variation notices do not however have to be sent to statutory consultees or advertised (*Env. Act 1995*, Sch. 22, para 93(4)). Where the action proposed to meet the variation notice is not considered substantial, the enforcing authority must decide whether it is acceptable; the enforcing authority has the option of issuing an amended variation notice proposing different action. Minor changes to an authorisation are likely to be decided by the enforcing authority alone and any alterations to the conditions attached to an authorisation advised to the operator.

There is a right of appeal except if the variation notice implements a Direction from the Secretary of State (see below).

Under section 11 of the EPA (NI: IPCO, Art.11), process operators must inform the enforcing authority if any substantial changes to the process are planned or if it is to be transferred to another person. While not a formal requirement, operators are advised to notify the enforcing authority if it is proposed to make a "relevant change" to the process – e.g. changing the way in which the process is operated – which might affect the amount and nature of emissions. Again, minor changes would be considered by the enforcing authority and a request for a more substantial change would follow the procedure outlined above for making an application. A process operator may appeal to the Secretary of State if a variation under section 11 of the EPA is refused.

Applications for variations (except those referred to the Secretary of State) must be determined within four months of receipt unless a different period is agreed. An application for a variation will be deemed to have failed if the enforcing authority fails to determine it within the agreed period and the applicant notifies the enforcing authority that he considers the failure to determine as refusal of the application (*Env. Act 1995*, Sch. 22, para 93(10)).

The *Environment Act 1995* (Sch. 22, para 93(5)) amends Schedule 1 of the EPA to permit the Secretary of State to call in applications for variations for determination. In doing so, he may either arrange for a local inquiry or give both the applicant and the enforcing authority the opportunity of a hearing.

Copies of variation notices and changes in conditions attached to an authorisation will be put in the public register.

(g) Revocation of Authorisation

Following 28 days written notice, the enforcing authority may revoke an authorisation in the following circumstances (EPA, s.12; NI: IPCO, Art.12):

- failure to pay the annual subsistence charge;
- it has reason to believe that the process has not been carried on, or not carried on for 12 months.

Prior to the notice taking effect, the enforcing authority may either withdraw the notice or vary the date on which revocation is to take effect.

(h) Enforcement

If the enforcing authority believes conditions of an authorisation are being breached it can take any of the following actions under sections 13-14 of the EPA (NI: IPCO, Arts.13-14):

- serve an enforcement notice (s.13) reinforcing an existing condition or requiring the operator to remedy the cause of the breach of condition within a specified period; Sch. 22, para 53 of the *Environment Act 1995* amends the EPA to permit the enforcing authority by written notice to withdraw an enforcement notice.

- where it is felt that the continued operation of the process involves "an imminent risk of serious pollution of the environment", serve a prohibition notice requiring the operator to close down all or part of the process and take the necessary steps to stop the risk (s.14); written notice of the withdrawal of a prohibition notice will be given by the enforcing authority when it is satisfied that the necessary action to deal with the problems has been taken.

(i) Appeals

The Secretary of State may determine appeals himself or appoint someone else for this purpose (*Env. Act 1995*, s.114 and Sch. 20). In Northern Ireland the DOE may refer an appeal to the Planning Appeals Commission for determination or for consideration prior to determination by the DOE (IPCO, Art.15(3) & Sch. 2). With effect from 1 September 1997, the Secretary of State delegated his powers on appeals for processes in England to the Planning Inspectorate. He has however, reserved the right to recover appeals relating to the following for determination himself:

- processes or sites of major importance;
- those giving rise to significant public controversy or legal difficulties;
- those which can only be decided in conjunction with other cases over which inspectors have no jurisdiction;
- those which raise major or novel issues of industrial pollution control which could set a policy precedent;
- those which merit recovery because of the particular circumstances.

Operators of Part B processes have a right of appeal under section 15 of the EPA (NI: IPCO, Arts.15 & 22) to the Secretary of State (or Planning Inspectorate in England; DOE in NI) against the decision of the enforcing authority, including refusal to authorise a process or imposition of a particular condition, the serving of variation, enforcement or prohibition notices, or revocation of an authorisation. There is also a right of appeal under section 22 of the EPA in relation to issues of commercial confidentiality – these appeals are determined by the Secretary of State. There is however no right of appeal where the notice implements a Direction from the Secretary of State (*Env. Act 1995*, Sch. 22, para 54(2)).

An appeal against refusal of an authorisation or a variation, or of conditions of an authorisation must be made within six months; for revocation notices, before the date on which the notice takes effect; for enforcement, prohibition or section 10 variation notices, within two months; appeals against a refusal to exclude information from the public register must be made within 21 days. Where an appeal has been lodged against a revocation notice or decision of the enforcing authority that information is not commercially confidential, implementation of the notice or decision is deferred pending determination of the appeal. All other notices or decisions take effect from the specified date; disputed conditions also remain in place pending the outcome of the appeal.

The Regulations specify the information to be sent to the Secretary of State (England: Planning Inspectorate) by the operator; this includes a notice of appeal; statement setting out the reason for the appeal; statement about whether the appellant wishes the matter to be decided by written representations or by a hearing; these three documents should be copied to the enforcing authority and the Secretary of State – or Planning Inspectorate – advised that this has been done. The Secretary of State (or Planning Inspectorate) should also be sent a copy of the application and of the authorisation (where this exists) and relevant correspondence and notices with the appeal documents.

Following notification that an appeal has been lodged, the enforcing authority must, within 14 days, notify the statutory consultees and others who commented on the original application for the authorisation and invite comments; the notice will also state that a copy of any representations made will be put on the public register unless a written request is made that this should not happen. Any representations must usually be submitted to the Secretary of State (or his appointee) within 21 days.

Both parties must agree to the matter being dealt with in writing but if either side requests a hearing, then this will be arranged. A local inquiry may also be held in connection with the appeal, either at the instigation of the Secretary of State's appointee, or the Secretary of State may direct that a local inquiry be arranged (*Env. Act 1995*, Sch. 22, para 54).

If the appeal is to be decided through written representations, the enforcing authority has 28 days (from receipt of the appeal) in which to submit any further statement; the appellant will then have 17 days on which to comment on this statement; both have 14 days on which to comment on any other representations submitted.

If a hearing is to be held, the Secretary of State (Planning Inspectorate in England) will notify the appellant and the enforcing authority of the date, time and place for the hearing (giving at least 28 days notice); not less than 21 days notice of it should be given in a local newspaper and the same notice given to statutory consultees, etc. In the case of mobile plant, notice of the appeal must appear in the place in which the plant was operating when the enforcement/prohibition notice was issued. Most hearings will be held wholly or partly in public, unless matters of commercial confidentiality are concerned (in which case the hearing will always be in private).

Following determination, copies of the decision and any report will be sent to the appellant, the enforcing authority and statutory consultees. In those cases where the Secretary of State has recovered an appeal, the Inspector will report to the Secretary of State who will then make a decision on the appeal. A copy of the decision only will be sent to others involved in the appeal. A copy of both the report and decision will be put on the public register.

(j) Public Registers

Sections 20-22 of the EPA (as amended by *Env. Act 1995*, Sch. 22, paras 57-58) are concerned with the establishment of registers of air pollution control (and IPC – see chapter 1) information to be maintained by the enforcing authorities. Articles 20-22 of the *Industrial Pollution Control (NI) Order* contain similar provisions.

The 1996 Amendment of the Applications, Appeals and Registers Regulations list the documentation to be placed in the register (NI: 1998 Regulations):

- documentation relating to an application for an authorisation or for variation of the conditions of an authorisation; and subsequent information relating to the application for an authorisation requested by the enforcing authority;
- copy of advertisement relating to application for authorisation or variation or notification by enforcing authority to vary an authorisation; representations made as a result of the advertisement unless a request made that they should not be put on the register in which case a statement to this effect should be put on the register without identifying the person making the request;
- authorisations and their conditions;
- written notice of transfer of authorisation to another person;
- revocation, variation, enforcement or prohibition notices issued by the enforcing authority; notification by the enforcing authority of withdrawal of enforcement or prohibition notice;
- documentation relating to an appeal, its determination and any accompanying reports;
- details of convictions relating to carrying on of a prescribed process with or without an authorisation;
- monitoring data collected by the enforcing authority or submitted by an operator as a condition of the authorisation; where such information is omitted on grounds of commercial confidentiality, then the enforcing authority should put a statement on the register confirming or otherwise compliance with the relevant condition of the authorisation;
- information given to the enforcing authority on or after 1 April 1996 in compliance with a condition of an authorisation, variation, enforcement or prohibition notice;
- reports by the enforcing authority relating to the environmental consequences of a prescribed process in the locality of premises where the prescribed process is carried on under an authorisation;
- Directions from the Secretary of State.

Information affecting national security or which is accepted as being commercially confidential may be withheld and a note to this effect added to the register. The onus is on the operator to prove that disclosure of specific information would be prejudicial to their commercial interests. Exclusion of data from the register on the grounds of commercial confidentially lasts for four years after which it will be added to the register unless a further four year exclusion is applied for and agreed.

Applications for an authorisation or variation which have been advertised in a paper should be put in the register within 14 days of receipt by the enforcing authority; notifications to vary an authorisation (which are also advertised) should also be put in the register within 14 days of notifying the operator. The Regulations do not specify the time within which other information should be placed in the register although guidance issued by the Department of Environment (now Department of the Environment, Transport and the Regions) suggests that this should be done "as soon as possible". Information held in the registers may be inspected by the public free of charge and copies of entries obtained on "payment of a reasonable charge".

Information will be removed from the register in the following circumstances:

- withdrawal of application for authorisation prior to determination – all particulars to be removed not less than two months but within three months after the date of withdrawal;
- if a process ceases to be a prescribed process following amendment of the *Prescribed Processes and Substances Regulations* – all particulars to be removed not less than two months but within three months of the date on which the process ceases to be prescribed;
- monitoring information relating to a process – four years after entering in the register;
- information relating to a process which has been superseded – four years after the later information has been entered in the register.

Local authority registers in England and Wales (but not Port Health Authorities) also have copies of entries relating to IPC processes in their area; they will also contain copies of authorisations covering Part A and Part B processes in a port health district in their area. In NI, registers of Part B processes are held by the DOE, with district councils having registers of Part C processes; district councils also hold details of Part A and Part B processes in their area. In Scotland, registers of processes regulated for air pollution are maintained by the Scottish Environment Protection Agency.

2.11.3 Offences

It is an offence (EPA, s.23; NI: IPCO, Art.23) to operate, without reasonable excuse, a prescribed process without an authorisation, in contravention of a condition attached to an authorisation, or other variation, enforcement or prohibition notice. Summary conviction may result in a fine of up to £20,000 and/or up to three months imprisonment (*Env. Act 1995*, Sch. 22, para 59(3)). Conviction on indictment may result in an unlimited fine and/or two years imprisonment.

2.11.4 Fees and Charges

(a) England and Wales

Section 8 of the *Environmental Protection Act 1990* enables the Secretary of State to set up a scheme enabling local enforcing authorities in England and Wales to recover costs related to carrying out their air pollution control responsibilities.

Operators of Part B processes are required to pay a fee when applying for an authorisation or to vary an existing authorisation. An annual subsistence charge (which may be paid in quarterly instalments) becomes payable each 1 April. In both cases a reduced charge will be made for small waste oil burners (less than 0.4 MW). The charge will cover compliance monitoring and enforcement costs, including sampling and analysis of emissions.

Fees and charges for air pollution control are set annually by the Secretary of State.

The Local Enforcing Authorities Air Pollution Fees and Charges Scheme (England and Wales) 1998 sets out the charges which applied from 1 April 1998:

Initial application for authorisation except	£1,065
- where process comprises one or more waste oil burning appliance under 0.4 MWth	£100
- where process relates to the unloading of petrol into storage tanks at a service station	£100
Substantial change except	£680
- where this results solely from implementing upgrading programme	£100
- where process comprises one or more waste oil burners under 0.4 MWth	£ 65
- where process relates to the unloading of petrol into storage tanks at a service station	£ 65

Annual subsistence charge	£660
except	
- where process comprises one or more waste oil burners under 0.4 MWth	£100
- where process relates to the unloading of petrol into storage tanks at a service station	£100
- odorising of natural gas	£240
- the charge is paid in quarterly instalments	£685

Initial application fees and annual subsistence charges for processes which comprise mobile crushing and/or screening plant are based on the number of authorisations held by the operator.

Non-payment of statutory fees or charges may result in revocation of an operator's authorisation.

(b) Scotland

Fees in Scotland are currently as follows:

- application fee	£1,175
except where previously regulated under IPC	£ 100
- subsistence charge	£ 800
- variation fee	£1,105

(c) Northern Ireland

A similar charging scheme will be made under Article 8 of the *Industrial Pollution Control (NI) Order 1997.*

2.12 ENVIRONMENT ACT 1995

Powers of Entry

The *Environment Act 1995*, sections 108-109, (effective 1 April 1996) empower "a person who appears suitable to an enforcing authority to be authorised in writing ..." to act under these sections of the Act. The Act also requires that, except in an emergency, a warrant should be obtained if entry has been or is likely to be refused and it is probable that force will be needed to gain entry.

Similar powers for inspectors in Northern Ireland are contained in Articles 17 and 18 of the *Industrial Pollution Control (NI) Order 1997.*

Authorised persons (warranted officers) are empowered to enter premises where they have reason to believe a prescribed process is being or has been operated (with or without an authorisation) or where they believe there is a risk of serious pollution. They may take photographs, samples etc of substances, and require access to relevant information and records. The authorised person may render harmless any substance or article from which it is considered there is imminent danger of serious harm; a written and signed report of what has been done and why should be given to a responsible person on the premises and a copy served on the owner of the substance or article (if different).

2.13 CLEAN AIR ACT 1993

This Act covers England, Scotland and Wales, with section 30 (regulations on motor fuel) applying also to Northern Ireland. It came into force in August 1993 and consolidates the 1956 and 1968 *Clean Air Acts* (which were repealed); it also incorporates clean air legislation contained in other Acts such as the *Control of Pollution Act 1974*, the *Control of Smoke Pollution Act 1989* (which is also repealed) and the EPA. Regulations made under the earlier Acts still apply.

Similar controls in Northern Ireland are provided in the *Clean Air (Northern Ireland) Order 1981*.

It should be noted that Parts I, II and III of the Act do not apply to processes prescribed for control under Part I of the *Environmental Protection Act 1990* from the date on which an authorisation has been granted, refused or refusal confirmed following an appeal (s.41).

Offences

Prosecutions for most offences under the *Clean Air Act 1993* are dealt with in the Magistrates' Court (Sheriff Court, Scotland); offences are subject to a fine on the standard scale as specified in the *Criminal Justice Act 1982/Criminal Procedure (Scotland) Act 1975*, both as amended; for offences under sections 10, 42 and 43, where conviction relates to an offence which is substantially a repetition or continuation of an offence for which the defendant has already been convicted, a cumulative fine of £50 per day may be substituted (s.50 of CAA).

2.13.1 Part I: Dark Smoke

Prohibition of Dark Smoke from Chimneys (s.1)

This section prohibits the emission of dark smoke from a chimney of any building; it also applies to chimneys not attached to a building serving furnaces of fixed boilers or industrial plant, and could include incinerators and crematoria. The Secretary of State may, by regulation, exempt prescribed lengths of emission from action under this section. Section 43 of the Act brings dark smoke emissions from railway engines within the scope of section 1.

There are four defences available in any proceedings for dark/black smoke emission. These are that the alleged emission was:

a) solely due to lighting a furnace from cold and all practicable steps had been taken to minimise emissions;

b) solely due to unavoidable mechanical failure of part of the plant, that this could not reasonably have been foreseen or if foreseen could not reasonably have been provided for and that the emission could not have been prevented after failure occurred;

c) solely due to unavoidable use of unsuitable fuel, suitable fuel not being available and the best available fuel being used; and all practical steps were taken to minimise the emission;

d) due to any combination of a, b and c.

It should be noted that these are not absolute defences and are available only if every practical effort is made to avoid and/or minimise emissions.

The Dark Smoke (Permitted Periods) Regulations 1958 (SI 498)

These Regulations were made under section 1(2) of the 1956 Act. Similar 1958 Regulations apply in Scotland and 1965 Regulations in Northern Ireland.

Specified permitted periods of emission are as follows:
a) Aggregate emissions of dark smoke

Number of furnaces served by the chimney	Permitted emission of dark smoke in any period of eight hours	
	If not soot blowing during period	If soot blowing during period
One	10 mins	14 mins
Two	18 mins	25 mins
Three	24 mins	34 mins
Four or more	29 mins	41 mins

Where a single boiler or unit of industrial plant is fired by more than one furnace discharging into the same chimney, those furnaces shall be deemed to be one furnace.
b) Continuous emission of dark smoke
The continuous emission of black smoke in excess of four minutes, caused otherwise than by soot blowing, is prohibited.
c) Aggregate emission of black smoke
No emission of black smoke exceeding two minutes aggregate in any period of thirty minutes is allowed. There are thus three standards of emission which are acceptable in relation to any one chimney.

(Soot blowing is a method of cleaning deposited carbon from the internal surfaces of large industrial boilers. It includes the use of a jet of steam onto heat exchange surfaces on a regular, usually daily basis.)

Prohibition of Dark Smoke from Industrial or Trade Premises (s.2)

Subject to certain exemptions, it is an offence to cause or permit the emission of dark smoke from industrial or trade premises (as distinct from chimneys). Unless the contrary is proved, an emission of dark smoke is deemed to have taken place if material is burned on those premises in circumstances where the burning would be likely to give rise to the emission of dark smoke. This can include night-time burning of cable and vehicles on open ground by removing the necessity for a local authority to prove by direct observation that dark smoke has been emitted.

"Industrial or trade premises" means premises normally used for industrial or trade purposes, or premises not normally so used, but which, at the time of the offence, were being used for industrial or trade burning, e.g. demolition sites. For the purposes of this section, land being used for commercial agriculture or horticulture constitutes trade premises (Code of Good Agricultural Practice for the Protection of Air, MAFF, 1992). Thus, for example, emitting dark smoke from the burning of tyres on a commercial farm would probably be an offence.

An offence under this section of the Act may result in a fine not exceeding £20,000 (*Environment Act 1995*, Sch. 22, para 195).

Clean Air (Emission of Dark Smoke) (Exemption) Regulations 1969 (SI 1263)

These Regulations (made under s.1(3) of the 1968 Act) apply to England and Wales. They exempt the emission of dark smoke caused by the burning of certain materials subject to specified conditions:

Exempted Matter	Conditions*
1. Timber and any other waste matter (other than natural or synthetic rubber or flock or feathers) which results from the demolition of a building or clearance of a site in connection with any building operation or work of engineering construction (within the meaning of section 176 of the Factories Act 1961).	A, B and C
2. Explosive (within the meaning of the Explosives Act 1975) which has become waste; and matter which has been contaminated by such explosive	A and C
3. Matter which is burnt in connection with: a) research into the cause or control of fire or b) training in fire fighting.	C
4. Tar, pitch, asphalt and other matter which is burnt in connection with the preparation and laying of any surface, or which is burnt off any surface in connection with re-surfacing, together with any fuel used for any such purpose.	C
5. Carcasses of animals or poultry which a) have died, or are reasonably believed to have died, because of disease; b) have been slaughtered because of disease; or c) have been required to be slaughtered pursuant to the Diseases of Animals Act 1950	A and C unless the burning is carried out by or on behalf of an inspector (within the meaning of section 84 of the Diseases of Animals Act 1950)
6. Containers which are contaminated by any pesticide or by any toxic substances used for veterinary or agricultural purposes; and in this paragraph "container" includes any sack, box or receptacle of any kind.	A, B and C

* Condition A	That there is no other reasonable safe and practicable method of disposing of the matter.
Condition B	That the burning is carried out in such a manner as to minimise the emission of dark smoke.
Condition C	That the burning is carried out under the direct and continuous supervision of the occupier of the premises concerned or a person authorised to act on his behalf.

The corresponding Regulations for Scotland are the *Clean Air (Emission of Dark Smoke) (Exemption) (Scotland) Regulations 1969.* In Northern Ireland, the *Clean Air (Emission of Dark Smoke) (Exemption) Regulations 1981 apply.*

Meaning of "Dark Smoke" (s.3)

Where legal standards of emission are prescribed for smoke, they refer to "dark" and "black" smoke.

Dark smoke is defined by reference to a shade on the British Standard Ringelmann Chart (see Appendix 2.3) and means smoke which if compared ... with the Ringelmann Chart would appear to be as dark as, or darker than shade 2 on the chart.

Black smoke (defined in the *Dark Smoke (Permitted Periods) Regulations 1958* and in the *Dark Smoke (Permitted Periods) (Vessels) Regulations 1958)* means smoke which, if compared ... with the Ringelmann Chart, would appear to be as dark as, or darker than shade 4 on the chart.

Although legislation defines dark and black smoke by reference to colour shades on the Ringelmann Chart, the use of the Chart is not compulsory. The 1993 Act says that "for the avoidance of doubt, it is hereby declared that ... the court may be satisfied that smoke is or is not dark smoke ... [even if] there has been no actual comparison of the smoke with a chart of the type mentioned".

For an illustration and description of how to use the Ringelmann chart see Appendix 2.3.

2.13.2 Part II: Smoke, Grit, Dust, and Fumes

Installation of Furnaces (s.4)

Before installing a furnace (except a domestic furnace) in a building or fixed boiler, the local authority must be informed; any such furnace must be capable of being operated continuously without emitting smoke when burning fuel of a type for which the furnace was designed.

There is no definition of "furnace", but a practical interpretation of this word whenever it appears in clean air legislation is usually taken as "any enclosed or partly enclosed space in which liquid, solid or gaseous matter is burned, or in which heat is produced". Domestic furnaces are defined as those with a maximum heating capacity of less than 16.12 kilowatts.

Limits on Rate of Emission of Grit and Dust (s.5)

The Secretary of State may by regulation prescribe limits on the rates of emission of grit and dust from the chimneys of all furnaces (except domestic furnaces); it is a defence to prove that the best practicable means were used to prevent any emission in excess of the permitted rates.

The Clean Air Act (Emission of Grit and Dust from Furnaces) Regulations 1971 (SI 162)

These Regulations (which do not cover N. Ireland) were made under section 2(1) of the 1968 Act and apply to:

a) boilers;

b) indirect heating appliances (being heating appliances in which the combustion gases are not in contact with the material being heated);

c) furnaces in which the combustion gases are in contact with the material being heated but that material does not in itself contribute to the grit and dust in the combustion gases.

The Regulations do not apply to incinerators burning refuse or waste matter (solid or liquid) whether or not the resulting heat is used for any purpose. (Incinerators are prescribed processes under the *Environmental Protection Act* – see earlier this chapter and chapter 1, 1.13.) Schedules 1 and 2 of the Regulations tabulate the quantities of grit and dust which may be emitted, and where the rating of the boiler or furnace is intermediate between the tabulated values, the minimum permitted emission is obtained by interpolation (see Appendix 2.4).

Arrestment Plant for Furnaces (ss.6-9)

Section 6 requires all furnaces (except domestic furnaces) to be equipped with grit and dust arrestment plant approved by the local authority and the arrestors to be properly maintained and used if used for the following purposes:

a) to burn pulverised fuel; or

b) to burn, at a rate of 45.4 kg or more an hour, any other solid matter; or

c) to burn, at a rate equivalent to 366.4 kilowatts or more, any liquid or gaseous matter.

The Secretary of State may by regulation prescribe limits on the rates of emission of grit and dust from the chimneys of furnaces, and prescribe different limits for different cases and according to different circumstances. Such regulations would not however apply to furnaces

Clean Air (Arrestment Plant) (Exemption) Regulations 1969 (SI 1262)

These Regulations were made under section 4(1) of the 1968 Act.

Class of Furnace

1. Mobile or transportable furnaces.

Purpose

a) providing a temporary source of heat or power during any building operation or work of engineering construction (within the meaning of section 176 of the *Factories Act 1961*);
b) providing a temporary source of heat or power for investigation or research;
c) providing heat or power for the purpose of agriculture (within the meaning of section 109(3) of the *Agriculture Act 1947*).

Class of Furnace

2. Furnaces other than furnaces designed to burn solid matter at a rate of 1.02 tonnes an hour or more, which fall within any of the following descriptions and in which the matter being heated does not contribute to the emission of grit and dust:

a) furnaces burning liquid matter, gas, or liquid matter and gas;
b) hand-fired sectional furnaces designed to burn solid matter at a rate of not more than 11.3 kg an hour for each square foot of grate surface;
c) magazine type gravity-fed furnaces designed to burn solid matter at a rate of not more than 11.3 kg an hour for each square foot of grate surface;
d) furnaces fitted with an underfeed stoker designed to burn solid matter at a rate of not more than 11.3 kg an hour for each square foot of the plan area of the combustion chamber;
e) furnaces fitted with a chain grate stoker designed to burn solid matter at a rate of not more than 11.3 kg an hour for each square foot of the grate surface;
f) furnaces fitted with a coking stoker designed to burn solid matter at a rate of not more than 11.3 kg an hour for each square foot of area covered by the fire bars excluding the solid coking plate.

Purpose

Any purpose except the incineration of refuse.

begun, or an agreement for the purchase or installation entered into, before the implementation of the regulations.

Section 7 of the 1993 Act specifies under what circumstances exemptions from section 6 will be permitted:

a) The Secretary of State has power to provide in Regulations that furnaces of any particular class, whilst used for a prescribed purpose, should be exempted. Here the *Clean Air (Arrestment Plant) (Exemption) Regulations 1969* are relevant (see below).

b) The local authority may, on application, exempt a specific furnace installation providing that it is satisfied that the emissions will not be prejudicial to health or a nuisance. The local authority must give a written decision within eight weeks, and an aggrieved applicant may appeal within a further 28 days, to the Secretary of State.

An offence occurs if a furnace is exempt and is then used for any purpose other than that prescribed in the exemption.

When considering an application for approval of a proposed arrestor plant (or an application for exemption from the need to install arrestor plant) the local authority will have regard to the probable grit and dust burden in the flue gases, and to the known efficiency of the proposed arrestor plant so that it can compare the probable emissions with any standard which might at the time be in force or which is under consideration. It should be noted that arrestor plant, unless very well maintained at all times, rarely operate at full design efficiency after a few years in use.

Measurement of Grit, Dust and Fumes (ss.10-11)

Grit is defined in the *Clean Air (Emission of Grit and Dust from Furnaces) Regulations 1971* as particles exceeding 76 µm in diameter; the *Clean Air Act 1993* (s.64) defines fumes as any airborne solid matter smaller than dust. British Standard BS 3405 defines dust as small solid particles between 1-75 µm in diameter.

Under section 10 if a furnace (or range of furnaces served by one chimney) is used to burn:

a) pulverised fuel,
b) any other solid matter at a rate of 45.4 kg, or more per hour, or
c) any liquid or gaseous matter, at a rate equivalent to 366.4 kilowatts or more,

the local authority may serve a notice on the owner of the plant or occupier of the building, requiring grit, dust and fume emissions to be measured from time to time, to adapt the chimney for that purpose, to provide and maintain the necessary measuring apparatus, and to inform the local authority of measuring results. The occupier of the building is under a duty to permit the local authority to be present during the measuring and recording of emissions. The local authority may revoke its notice at any time.

If the plant burns at a rate of:

a) less than 1.02 tonnes/hour of solid matter other than pulverised fuel, or
b) less than 8.21 Megawatts of liquid or gaseous matter,

the industrialist may serve a notice on the local authority requiring the authority from time to time to measure and record emissions at its own expense until such notice is withdrawn in writing.

The Clean Air (Measurement of Grit and Dust from Furnaces) Regulations 1971 (SI 161)

These Regulations were made under section 7(2) of the 1956 Act and prescribe the administrative process to invoke the above provisions (similar Regulations apply in Scotland):

a) A local authority must give at least six weeks' notice in writing to an industrialist requiring:

- adaptations to be made to the chimney or flues; and
- the provision of the necessary equipment, to enable measurements to be made in accordance with BS 3405 (Simplified) Method for Measurement of Particulate Emission Including Grit and Dust. The British Standard states the principles to adopt, sets out requirements to be met in designing apparatus and indicates basic sampling procedures.

b) When the sampling points have been installed and the equipment provided (or it is known that the firm are engaging a consultant who possesses the equipment), the local authority must give at least 28 days' notice in writing, requiring the tests to be carried out in accordance with the methods detailed in *Measurements of Solids in Flue Gases* (published by the Institute of Energy).

c) Before making the measurement the industrialist must give the local authority at least 48 hours' notice in writing of the date and time of the commencement of the tests.

d) The result of the test must be sent to the local authority within 14 days from the making of the measurements and the reports shall include:

- the date(s) of the test(s);
- the number of furnaces discharging into the chimney on that date;
- the results of the measurements expressed in lbs/hour of grit and dust emitted and, in the case of solid fuel fired plant, the percentage of grit in the solids.

A notice may require the making of measurements from time to time or at stated intervals, but not at intervals of less than three months unless, in the opinion of the local authority, the true level of emission cannot be determined without further measurement being made.

If an industrialist serves a "counter notice" on the local authority, he need only make adaptations to the chimney to enable the measurements to be made, including the provision of scaffolding where necessary, and the provision of facilities such as electrical connections to enable the measurements to be made. The local authority must provide the sampling equipment and conduct the test entirely at its own expense.

Information about Furnaces and Fuel Consumed (s.12)

Local authorities may serve a notice on the occupier requesting information about furnaces in a building and the fuel or waste being burned to be given to them within 14 days or longer.

Outdoor Furnaces (s.13)

This section notes that sections 5-12 apply to boilers or industrial plant furnaces attached to buildings or installed on land.

Height of Chimneys (ss.14-16)

At whatever height smoke and flue gases are discharged, gravity will eventually bring the larger particles of grit, dust and soot to the ground. Additionally, because of the natural turbulence of the atmosphere, a proportion of the gases and of the freely suspended fine particles will reach the ground although not affected by gravity. The higher the point of discharge and the greater the total heat content of the discharged gases, the more widespread and diluted will be the fine particles and gases by the time they reach ground level. The control of chimney heights enables local authorities to take into account a number of relevant factors in determining the height of a chimney. These include the need to avoid downdraught or downwash created by the chimney itself, or by buildings or topographical features; to avoid the ground level concentration of combustion products becoming prejudicial to health or a nuisance; in the case of smaller units to prevent the flue gases from entering nearby buildings in too high a concentration.

Under section 14 of the Act, unless the height of the chimney has been approved by the local authority and any conditions attached to approval adhered to, it is an offence to cause or knowingly permit a furnace to be used to

- burn pulverised fuel;
- burn at a rate of 45.4 kg or more an hour any other solid matter; or
- burn at a rate equivalent to 366.4 kilowatts or more any liquid or gaseous matter.

An application for chimney height approval must contain adequate information to enable the necessary calculations to be carried out. Additional information on the calculation of chimney heights is given in Appendix 2.5.

The local authority must consider an application for approval for a chimney height for a furnace and give a written decision within 28 days of its receipt, unless it is agreed in writing between the local authority and the applicant that a longer period may be allowed. Should the local authority fail to deal with the application within the agreed period, then approval without qualification will be deemed to have been given.

The local authority, however, must not approve the proposed chimney height unless it is satisfied that it will be sufficient to prevent, so far as is practicable, the smoke, grit, dust, gases or fumes emitted from the chimney from becoming prejudicial to health or a nuisance, having regard to:

a) the purpose of the chimney;
b) the position and descriptions of buildings near to it;
c) the levels of the neighbouring ground;
d) any other matters requiring consideration in the circumstances.

Any approval of the height of a chimney may be granted unconditionally or subject to conditions as to the rate and/or quality of emissions from the chimney. "Rate of emissions" is defined as the quantities of any specified substance which may be emitted in a period specified in the conditions attached to the approval, e.g. kg/hr of sulphur dioxide. Many other miscellaneous emissions may, of necessity, be considered for inclusion in conditions as to the rate of emission, but there will be cases where a limitation on "rate" alone will not sufficiently ensure against excessive pollution by materials other than normal combustion products; in those cases it might be appropriate to impose conditions as to the "quality" (i.e. concentration) of the emission. A limitation on the quality of emission would be appropriate if the products of combustion contain gases or acid mists resulting from abnormal reactions or breakdown of materials derived from chlorinated or sulphur-bearing compounds etc, or if products of combustion are mixed with waste gases from non-combustion processes.

There will also be occasions, particularly in relation to metallurgical processes, where the optical density of emissions may be regulated by reference to percentage obscuration or perhaps by reference to the Bacharach Scale (a scale of ten shades, from white to black, for the assessment of smoke in flues; a smoke stain is obtained by sampling flue gases through a filter paper in a prescribed manner, and graded according to the scale).

If the local authority decides not to approve the height of a chimney or to attach conditions to its approval, it must give the applicant a written notification of its decision, stating its reasons; it must additionally specify the lowest height, if any, which it is prepared to approve unconditionally and/or the lowest height it is prepared to approve with any specified conditions. The applicant may appeal against the decision to the Secretary of State within 28 days. The Secretary of State may confirm the local authority's decision, or may amend the height or conditions if this is thought to be appropriate. The

Secretary of State must also give a written notification of the decision stating the reasons and, where a chimney height is not approved, specifying what height, with and/or without conditions would be approved.

Section 16 applies where plans have been submitted in accordance with building regulations to the local authority to erect or extend a building outside Greater London or in an outer London borough, and the plans include a chimney outside the scope of section 15 above (i.e. one not serving a furnace). It does not cover residences, shops or offices. Again, the local authority must reject the plans if it is thought that the proposed height of chimney will not be sufficient, so far as practicable, to prevent emissions of smoke, grit, dust or gases from becoming prejudicial to health or a nuisance. The factors to be taken into account are the same as listed above. There is a right of appeal against the local authority's decision to the Secretary of State.

In Scotland such plans are submitted for approval with an application for a warrant under the *Building (Scotland) Act 1959*, and rejections are issued as a refusal of a warrant under the same Act.

The Secretary of State may by regulation exempt boiler or plant to be used for certain prescribed purposes from the above requirements so long as the chimney height has been approved for that purpose.

Clean Air (Heights of Chimneys) (Exemption) Regulations 1969 (SI 411)

These Regulations were made under section 6(1) of the 1968 Act. It is not necessary to apply for chimney height approval for any exempted boiler or plant specified in these Regulations. Such boiler or plant include those used:

a) as a temporary replacement for a boiler or plant which is under inspection or being maintained, repaired, rebuilt or replaced by another permanent boiler or plant;

b) as a temporary source of heat or power for building or engineering construction work;

c) as a temporary source of heat or power for investigation or research;

d) as an auxiliary plant used to bring other plant to an operating temperature;

e) as a mobile or transportable source of heat or power for agricultural operations.

Two other pieces of legislation are also of relevance where approval of chimney height is needed. These are

- **Building Act 1984:** Section 73 of this Act applies when a new building is erected which will over-reach the chimney of an adjoining building.

Providing that the chimney of the lower building is in the party wall between it and the taller building, or is six feet or less from the taller building, the local authority may by notice require the person who erects the taller building to raise the height of the chimneys of the adjoining building if it is reasonably practicable to do so, so that the chimneys are the same height as the taller building or its chimneys, whichever is the higher.

The notice will also require the owner or occupier of the adjoining building to allow the work to be done, but he may elect to do the work himself and charge the reasonable cost of so doing to the person on whom the notice was served. In the event of non-compliance with the notice, the local authority may do the work in default.

- **The Building Regulations 1991:** The *Clean Air Act 1993* controls chimney heights only if the fuel consumption exceeds 45.4 kg or 366.4 kilowatts or more per hour. *The Building Regulations 1991* (effective 1 June 1992) consolidate and replace the 1985 Regulations and subsequent revisions. They apply to all chimneys, irrespective of the capacity of the fireplace, furnace, or type of building. Part J of Schedule 1 of the Regulations applies to heat producing appliances, divided into two categories:

a) solid fuel and oil-burning appliances with a rated output up to 45 kW;
b) gas burning appliances with a rated input of up to 60 kW.

Approved Document J indicates that such an installation will meet the requirements of the Regulations if it is so installed that it:

a) receives sufficient air for the proper combustion of the fuel and operation of the flue;
b) is capable of normal operation without the products of combustion becoming a hazard to health;
c) is capable of normal operation without causing damage by heat or fire to the fabric of the building.

The relevant Regulations in Scotland are the *Building Standards (Scotland) Regulations 1990*. Part F deals with heat producing installations and storage of liquid and gaseous fuels.

Smoke Nuisances in Scotland (s.17)

This section was repealed on 1 April 1996 following implementation of section 107 and Schedule 17 of the *Environment Act 1995*. It enabled action to abate certain nuisances from smoke to be taken under the *Public Health (Scotland) Act 1897*.

2.13.3 Part III: Smoke Control

Creation of Smoke Control Areas (ss.18-19)

Section 18 allows a local authority to declare the whole or any part of its district a smoke control area by making a "Smoke Control Order". Before doing so it must publicise its intention, and the effect of the Order, in the *London Gazette* (or *Edinburgh Gazette*) and a local newspaper on two successive weeks. Unless postponed through resolution, the Order must come into effect not later than six months after it was made. The Order may specify to what area the Order applies, the types of buildings covered, and any exemptions (e.g. specified buildings or fireplaces).

Section 19 enables the Secretary of State (or in Scotland, the Scottish Environment Protection Agency, *Environment Act 1995*, Sch. 22, para 196) to direct a local authority to bring forward, within six months, proposals for making a Smoke Control Order for the purposes of abating smoke pollution in its area.

Local authorities may themselves subsequently revoke or vary Orders; Smoke Control Orders originally confirmed by the Secretary of State (Scotland, SEPA) can only be revoked or varied by a similarly confirmed Order.

Prohibition on Emission of Smoke in Smoke Control Area (ss.20-22)

When operative, it is an offence for an occupier of premises within a smoke control area to allow smoke emission from a chimney, unless the smoke is caused by the use of an "authorised fuel" (listed in Regulations – see Appendix 2.6a). It is recognised that there may be times when certain of these fuels may cause short periods of light smoke emission. Appliances which may be used in a smoke control area are defined in *Smoke Control (Exempted Fireplaces) Orders*. These conditionally exempt the emission of smoke from chimneys serving the various fireplaces (see Appendix 2.6b).

The implications of the law are that coal, oil and wood cannot be used as fuel in a smoke control area unless burnt on an exempted fireplace (unless they can be burnt without any emission of smoke). Refuse cannot be burnt in an incinerator in a smoke control area unless there is a specific exemption written into the Order, a general exemption for incinerators, or unless smokeless combustion can always be achieved. This prohibition would even apply to the simple incinerators which consist of a dustbin with a chimney.

The local authority may also include in the Smoke Control Order other exemptions, which it may feel are necessary, subject to reasonable conditions. One of these is to allow the lighting of domestic fires with sticks and paper if there is no gas in the dwelling.

Dealings with Unauthorised Fuel (s.23)

It is an offence to acquire for use or to sell by retail for delivery in a smoke control area any fuel other than an authorised fuel, unless in each case the premises or fireplace are exempt. It is a defence to prove that the sale for delivery of unauthorised fuel was carried out in the belief that either the building or the fireplace/boiler or plant was not covered by a Smoke Control Order.

It should be noted that this section does not ban the sale (e.g. from a shop) of unauthorised fuel in a smoke control area. Regulations were expected during 1997 banning the sale of unauthorised fuels in smoke control areas in Northern Ireland. This would help Northern Ireland to comply with EU air quality standards on smoke and sulphur dioxide (see 2.4.1 above). Similar legislation was planned for the rest of the UK but the need for it is being reconsidered.

Adaptation of Fireplaces (ss.24-29)

The local authority may serve a notice on the owner of a private dwelling in a smoke control area requiring work to be carried out to ensure compliance with a Smoke Control Order. So long as the work has been carried out to the local authority's satisfaction, it should repay seven-tenths of the reasonable cost of the adaptation, and it may repay all or any part of the remaining three-tenths. Grants are not available for "new dwellings" begun on or after 16 August 1964.

A local authority may designate as unsuitable any appliances for which suitable fuels are not fully available, and in those circumstances a grant is not available for installation of those appliances. The principles which local authorities must follow in assessing eligibility of works of adaptation for grant are contained in the Memorandum on Smoke Control Areas, as revised. The Department of Environment (now DETR) also set cost limits for local authority guidance in assessing "reasonable costs".

The Act enabled the Secretary of State to repay to the local authority a proportion of their expenditure in implementing a Smoke Control Order. Exchequer contributions for smoke control orders in England and Wales made after 31 March 1995 are not normally available. Claims for payments could be made up to 31 December 1996 for payment by 31 March 1997. In Scotland such grants were no longer available from 1 April 1993; applications for approval of schemes had to be submitted to the Scottish Office Environment Department by 31

March 1993 and contributions for all approved schemes claimed by 28 February 1995.

2.13.4 Part IV: Control of Certain Forms of Air Pollution

Regulations about Motor Fuel (s.30)

This section enables the Secretary of State to make regulations limiting the composition and content of motor fuel and preventing or restricting the production, treatment, distribution, import, sale or use of any fuel which fails to comply with the requirements and which is for use in the United Kingdom. (See also this chapter, 2.21.) Before making any regulations the Secretary of State must consult representatives of manufacturers, users of vehicles, producers and users of fuel for motor vehicles as well as air pollution experts.

The Motor Fuel (Composition and Content) Regulations 1994 (SI 2295)

These Regulations, which apply throughout the UK, came into effect on 1 October 1994. They revoke and replace the *Motor Fuel (Lead Content of Petrol) Regulations 1981* and the *Motor Fuel (Sulphur Content of Gas Oil) Regulations 1976* and their amending Regulations.

All leaded, unleaded and super (high octane) unleaded petrol and diesel fuels must meet certain requirements as to their composition and content specified in various British Standards (BS 4040:1988, BS EN 228:1993, BS 7800:1992 and BS EN 590:1993 respectively); these requirements vary according to the time of year; the distribution or sale of petrol not meeting the specifications is prohibited except if it is for tests or experiments, for use in an aircraft or for use in a vehicle solely used in competitions or trials.

The Regulations embrace the requirements of EU Directives on the lead content of petrol and sulphur content of gas oil (see this chapter, 2.20.8), previously contained in the revoked Regulations mentioned above. By early 1998, 75% of the petrol retail market was for unleaded petrol (DTI *Energy Statistics*, 1998).

Regulations about the Sulphur Content of Oil Fuel for Furnaces or Engines (s.31)

The Secretary of State is empowered to make regulations limiting the sulphur content of a wide range of fuel oils used in industry, commerce and in domestic boilers. The Secretary of State has a duty to consult similar to that outlined for section 30 above.

The Marketing of Gas Oil (Sulphur Content) Regulations 1994 (SI 2249)

These Regulations, which came into effect on 1 October 1994, apply throughout the UK and are enforced by local authorities. The Regulations implement EU Directive 93/12/EEC relating to the sulphur content of certain liquid fuels (see this chapter, 2.20.7). Under the Regulations it is an offence to market gas oil with a sulphur content in excess of 0.2% by weight. The Regulations do not apply to gas oil in the fuel tanks of vessels, aircraft or motor vehicles crossing a frontier between a third country and an EU Member State, or to gas oil for processing prior to final combustion; aviation kerosene is also outside the scope of the Regulations. To ensure compliance with the Regulations, local authorities are required to check the sulphur content of gas oils on the market in their area.

These Regulations replace the *Oil Fuel (Sulphur Content of Gas Oil) Regulations 1990* and similar 1991 Regulations in Northern Ireland.

Regulations limiting the sulphur content of domestic fuel are expected in Northern Ireland. The Regulations, which would be enforced by local authorities, would prevent wholesalers, distributors and retail outlets from supplying solid fuel with a sulphur content greater than 2% by weight (air dried basis) for use in domestic premises in Northern Ireland. Similar legislation was planned for the rest of the UK but the need for it is being reconsidered.

Supplementary Provisions (s.32)

This section notes that anyone contravening or failing to comply with the provisions of Regulations made under sections 30 and 31 shall be guilty of an offence and liable to a fine, subject to any exclusion for liability included in the Regulations. Regulations made under sections 30 and 31 apply to fuel used in the public service of the Crown.

Cable Burning (s.33)

Cable burning for the purposes of recovering the metal is illegal unless the burning is carried out as part of a process subject to authorisation under Part I of the *Environmental Protection Act 1990*.

2.13.5 Part V: Information about Air Pollution

Research and Publicity (s.34)

This enables local authorities to carry out or contribute towards the cost of, investigations and research relevant to air pollution. It can arrange lectures, addresses and discussions and publish information; organise exhibitions or other displays including films; prepare or contribute towards the cost of making a film or exhibition, etc. Care should be taken to ensure that any material published does not breach trade secrets, unless the written consent of the person providing the information has been obtained.

Obtaining Information (s.35)

In order to obtain information about emissions into the air – gaseous, liquid or solid or any combination (s.40) – the local authority may issue a notice under section 36 (see below); it can enter premises to measure and record emissions (either by agreement or using powers under section 56 of the Act which confers rights of entry and inspection); or it can agree with the occupiers of premises that they will measure and record emissions for the local authority. Private dwellings and caravans are excluded from this section.

The local authority may only use its powers of entry to measure and record emissions after serving and expiry of a 21 day notice on the occupier which

- specified the kind of emissions in question and how it was proposed to measure and record them;
- stated that it would monitor and record the emissions itself unless the occupier requested the local authority to serve a section 36 notice.

Investigation of emissions from processes subject to Part I of the *Environmental Protection Act 1990* may only be carried out following service of a section 36 notice or by contributing to the cost of such investigation, as provided for in section 34, without entering the premises.

In exercising its powers to obtain information, the local authority should set up a consultation committee of locally representative people with knowledge of air pollution problems or an interest in the local amenity; this should meet not less than twice a year to discuss the extent and way in which information collected should be made publicly available.

Notices Requiring Information about Air Pollution (s.36)

The local authority may by notice require an occupier of premises in its area to provide certain information about emissions of pollutants into the air at specified intervals. If the notice is served on a process for which authorisation under Part I of the EPA is required, only information certified by the appropriate enforcing inspector as being required under the EPA need be supplied. The person on whom a notice is served has six weeks within which to comply, or longer as agreed with the local authority.

Notices may require periodical renewal or single event emission data; but if periodical returns are requested, the interval between returns shall be not less than three months, and no one return is to cover a period of more than one year.

Section 36 applies to all premises, including Crown premises, unless specifically exempted by the Secretary of State. The *Control of Atmospheric Pollution (Exempted Premises) Regulations 1977* (SI 18) covering England and Wales list government research establishments to which this section does not apply.

Failure to comply with a notice, without reasonable excuse is an offence, as is the furnishing of false information.

Appeal against Notice (s.37)

A person on whom a section 36 notice is served may appeal to the Secretary of State on the grounds that

- disclosure would unreasonably prejudice some private interest, or be contrary to public interest, or
- the information is not readily available and cannot readily be collected without incurring undue expenditure.

Following consultation with representatives of local authorities, industry and air pollution experts, the Secretary of State may make regulations relating to the appeals process.

Regulations under the *Control of Pollution Act 1974* – the *Control of Atmospheric Pollution (Appeals) Regulations 1977* (SI 17) – set out the information to be submitted with the appeal, allow the Secretary of State to withhold certain, secret information from the local authority and indicate how the appeal should be determined. If an appeal is upheld, the Secretary of State may direct the local authority to withdraw or to modify the notice, or to take steps to ensure that the prejudicial information is not disclosed to the public. Similar Regulations (1982) apply in Scotland.

Regulations about Local Authority Functions under ss.34, 35 and 36 (s.38)

Following consultation with representatives of local authorities, industry and air pollution experts, the Secretary of State may make regulations prescribing emissions for which a section 36 notice may be issued, the information which such a notice may require and the way in which such notice is to be given. Regulations may also specify under what circumstances local authorities may arrange for the occupier of premises to measure and record emissions and the apparatus which local authorities may provide and use for measuring and recording emissions. Regulations would also provide for the setting up of a public register.

The Control of Atmospheric Pollution (Research and Publicity) Regulations 1977 (SI 19) limit the information to be required. Notices may only relate to sulphur dioxide or particulates from processes where stock does not contribute to the emission, or gas or particulates where stock does contribute to the emission, or gas or particulates from non-combustion processes. Also laid down is the information which can be required in respect of such emissions. The Regulations contain provisions relating to the service of notices and the maintenance of a register of information under these Regulations. Similar Regulations (1982) apply in Scotland.

Provision by Local Authorities of Information for Secretary of State (s.39)

This section enables the Secretary of State, after consultation with a local authority, to direct it to monitor air pollution and to send the information to the Secretary of State. Any capital expenditure incurred by the local authority in providing and installing apparatus to be able to comply with a direction may be reclaimed from the Secretary of State.

2.13.6 Part VI: Special Cases

Relation to Environmental Protection Act 1990 (s.41)

Parts I-III of the *Clean Air Act 1993* (dark smoke; smoke, grit, dust and fumes; smoke control areas) do not apply to a process prescribed for control under Part I of the EPA from the date of authorisation of the process, refusal of authorisation or confirmation of refusal following an appeal.

Colliery Spoilbanks (s.42)

The owner of a mine or quarry from which coal or shale is, has been, or will be obtained must use all practicable means to prevent combustion of refuse from the mine or quarry and to prevent or minimise emissions of smoke and fumes from the refuse.

The nuisance provisions of the *Environmental Protection Act 1990* and Parts I-III of the *Clean Air Act 1993* may not be applied to smoke, grit or dust arising from combustion of mine refuse.

This section of the Act does not apply to refuse from a mine or quarry deposited before 5 July 1956 if it was no longer in use and ownership had passed from the mine or quarry owner.

Railway Engines (s.43)

Emissions from railway engines are subject to the dark smoke provisions of section 1 of the 1993 Act and owners of railway engines are required to use any practicable means for minimising emissions of dark smoke. The remainder of Part I, together with Parts II and III of the 1993 Act do not apply to smoke, grit or dust from railway engines. However emissions could be the subject of a statutory nuisance action under section 79 of the EPA (see chapter 1, 1.15.1).

The Dark Smoke (Permitted Periods) Regulations 1958 made under section 19 of the 1956 Act are also applicable.

Vessels (s.44)

Vessels in water not navigable by sea-going ships and in waters within the seaward limits of the territorial waters (including docks, ports, harbours and rivers) of the UK, must comply with the dark smoke provisions of section 1 of the 1993 Act. This section does not apply to ships in HM Navy or "Government Shipping" (e.g. merchant shipping) being used by the Navy.

The Dark Smoke (Permitted Periods) (Vessels) Regulations 1958 made under section 1(2) of the 1956 Act specify the types of emissions which will be permissible and the length of time. There are similar Regulations for Scotland (1958) and for Northern Ireland (1965).

The Dark Smoke (Permitted Periods) (Vessels) Regulations 1958 (SI 878)

A vessel is not under way when it is at anchor or made fast to the shore or bottom. However a vessel which is aground is deemed to be under way. The Regulations include a proviso that continuous emissions of dark smoke caused otherwise than by the soot blowing of a water tube boiler shall not exceed (see box on next page):

a) in the case of classes 1 and 2: 4 minutes;
b) in the case of natural draught oil-fired boiler furnaces in class 4: 10 minutes; and
c) in no case shall black smoke be emitted for more than 3 minutes in the aggregate in any period of 30 minutes.

Exemption for Purposes of Investigations and Research (s.45)

The local authority may exempt a particular chimney, boiler or furnace etc or the acquisition or sale of a specified fuel from various provisions of the Act, for example to enable investigations or research relevant to air pollution to be carried out without making the applicant liable to proceedings. If the local authority refuses the exemption, the applicant

Class of Case	*Permitted Period for Emission of Dark Smoke*
1. Emissions from a forced draught oil-fired boiler furnace, or an oil engine.	10 minutes in the aggregate in any period of two hours.
2. Emissions from a natural draught oil-fired boiler furnace, (except in the case falling within class 4 below).	10 minutes in the aggregate in any period of one hour.
3. Emissions from a coal-fired boiler furnace:–	
a) when the vessel is not under way (except in the cases falling within class 4 below).	10 minutes in the aggregate in any period of one hour.
b) when the vessel is under way.	20 minutes in the aggregate in any period of one hour.
4. Emission from a natural draught oil-fired boiler furnace or a coal-fired boiler furnace in the following cases:– a) a vessel with funnels shortened for the purpose of navigating the Manchester Ship Canal; b) a tug not under way, but preparing to get under way or supplying power to other vessels or to shore installations; c) a vessel not under way but using main power for the purpose of dredging, lifting pumping or performing some other special operation for which the vessel is designed.	20 minutes in the aggregate in any period of one hour.
5. Emission from any other source.	5 minutes in the aggregate in any period of one hour.

has a right of appeal to the Secretary of State for the Environment, Transport and the Regions.

Crown Premises (s.46)

In the event of excessive emissions of smoke, grit and dust from Crown premises, the local authority should notify the Minister responsible for the premises who should take appropriate action to prevent or minimise the emission. This includes premises within a smoke control area and those being used by visiting forces (except for Parts IV and V); ships in the Navy or Government Ships (e.g. merchant shipping) being used by the Navy are also subject to the Act.

2.13.7 Part VII: Miscellaneous and General

Application of Certain Provisions to Fumes and Gases (s.47)

This enables the Secretary of State to make regulations extending the scope of sections 4, 5, 6, 7, 11, 42, 43, 44 and 46 (covering variously grit, smoke and dust) to fumes or prescribed gases.

Power to give effect to International Agreements (s.48)

The Secretary of State may make Regulations relating to any of the provisions of Parts IV, V and VII of the 1993 Act to enable compliance with international agreements.

Administration and Enforcement (ss.49-62)

These sections of the Act are mainly administrative, relating to such matters as improper disclosure of information by an officer (s.49), penalties for offences under the Act (s.50), county court powers to authorise works and order payments (s.54) and general provisions as to enforcement (s.55).

Duty to Notify Occupiers of Offences (s.51)

Where an offence has been or is being committed under sections 1, 2 or 20 (prohibition of certain smoke emissions), the local authority's authorised officer must notify the occupier of the premises, either verbally or in writing "as soon as may be". If notification is given verbally this should be confirmed in writing before the end of four days following that on which the officer became aware of the offence. In any subsequent proceedings it is a defence to prove that the notification procedure was not complied with.

Rights of Entry and Inspection (ss.56-57)

In order to carry out their duties under the Act, authorised officers of a local authority are allowed access to land (which includes premises) and vessels at any reasonable time; they may also carry out any necessary measurements and tests and remove samples for analysis. This section does not apply to private dwellings except in relation to work required to effect compliance with a smoke control order.

The local authority may apply to a Magistrate (Sheriff in Scotland) for a warrant to enter (if necessary by force) in the following circumstances:

- if refused entry despite seven days notice having been given;
- the land/vessel is unoccupied or the occupier absent;
- there is an emergency;
- to apply for admission would defeat the object of the exercise.

Power of Local Authority to Obtain Information (s.58)

The local authority may serve a notice specifying what information it requires and by when in relation to Parts IV and V of the Act (Control of Certain Forms of Air Pollution and Information about Air Pollution). Non-compliance with such a notice is an offence, as is furnishing false information.

Inquiries (s.59)

The Secretary of State may cause an inquiry to be held in connection with any part of the *Clean Air Act* or for preventing or dealing with air pollution.

SCHEDULES

The Act has the following Schedules appended to it:

- **Schedule 1:** Coming into Operation of Smoke Control Orders;
- **Schedule 2:** Smoke Control Orders: Expenditure on Old Private Dwellings;
- **Schedule 3:** Provisions having effect until repeal of *Alkali etc. Works Regulation Act 1906*;
- **Schedule 4:** Consequential Amendments;
- **Schedule 5:** General Transitional Provisions and Savings;
- **Schedule 6:** Repeals.

2.14 HEALTH AND SAFETY AT WORK ETC ACT 1974

The main purpose of this Act is to provide a comprehensive and integrated legal and administrative system for securing the health, safety and welfare of persons at work and for protecting other persons against risk to health or safety arising from the activities of persons at work. To this end all the various inspectorates and agencies involved in these matters were brought together in the Health and Safety Executive (established 1 January 1975) under the Health and Safety Commission which had been set up on 1 October 1974. The HSC is a public office responsible to the employment minister (Department for Education and Employment) for the working of the HSW Act and also for proposing new or revised legislation; the HSE is responsible for the day to day enforcement of health and safety legislation.

In Northern Ireland, the corresponding legislation is the *Health and Safety at Work (Northern Ireland) Order 1978.*

2.14.1 The Control of Major Accident Hazards Regulations (COMAH Regulations) *(draft published May 1998)*

These Regulations, which were due to come into force on 3 February 1999, implement the EU's 1996 Directive on the control of major accident hazards involving dangerous substances (Seveso II) – see this chapter, 2.4.5d. They apply in England, Scotland and Wales and replace 1984 Regulations (SI 1902) which implemented a 1982 Directive. The Regulations are enforced by the Environment Agency and the HSE in England and Wales and by the Scottish Environmental Protection Agency and the HSE in Scotland (the competent authorities).

The Regulations apply to establishments which keep (or transport) listed dangerous substances in quantities exceeding thresholds set in the Regulations; thus they apply mainly to the chemical and petrochemical industries and to those which produce or use substances with flammable, toxic or explosive properties, and those which are dangerous for the environment; explosives and chemicals on nuclear sites are included but hazards created by ionising radiation are not. They do not apply to military installations, certain activities of the extractive industries or to waste landfill sites.

Operators of companies covered by the Regulations are placed under a general duty to take all necessary measures to prevent major accidents and to limit their consequences to persons and the environment. They must prepare a "major accident prevention policy document" which should demonstrate that an adequate safety management system is in place. The enforcing authority should be sent details ("notification") of the name and address of the operator, the address of the site concerned and who is in charge, and details and amounts of dangerous substances held at the site; significant increases in the quantities held or in the nature or physical form of the substances held should be notified to the authority. Site operators holding larger amounts of hazardous substances (top tier sites) must provide the competent authority with a safety report for approval. This should demonstrate that the company's operational, and indeed emergency, procedures are of sufficiently high standard to prevent accidents and damage both inside and outside plants; the report should include major accident scenarios and safety management systems.

The Regulations also require the operator to prepare an "on-site emergency plan" (which should include details of site remediation and clean up following an accident); the local authority for the area in which the establishment is situated is required to prepare an "off-site emergency plan". Both plans must be reviewed and tested at intervals of not more than three years. The company must also notify all those living in the locality of the fact that there is a hazardous site in the area, and advise what action should be taken in the event of an accident; information and safety reports relating to the establishment must be made available to the public.

Separate Regulations – the *Planning (Hazardous Substances) Regulations 1992* – require the storage of certain hazardous substances above a "controlled quantity" to be covered by a consent from the Hazardous Substances Authority (usually the local authority) - see also chapter 1, 1.22.

2.14.2 The Control of Substances Hazardous to Health Regulations (COSHH Regulations) *(draft published May 1998)*

These Regulations, covering England, Scotland and Wales, were expected to come into force in January 1999; they replace and consolidate 1994 Regulations (SI 3246) which came into force in January 1995 and subsequent amendments. (The 1994 Regulations replaced the original 1988 regulations which came into force in October 1989). Similar Regulations (1990) apply in Northern Ireland.

An Approved Code of Practice (also updated at the same time as the Regulations) provides guidance on the application of the Regulations.

The Regulations apply to all "very toxic, toxic, harmful, corrosive or irritant" substances (defined in the *Chemicals (Hazard Information and Packaging for Supply) Regulations 1994* – SI 3247) and to all places of work; they provide a legal framework for controlling people's exposure to such substances. Hazardous substances may include gases, vapours, liquids, fumes, dusts and solids; they can be components of a mixture of materials including micro-organisms. COSHH also covers substances which have chronic or delayed effects such as those which are carcinogenic, mutagenic or teratogenic. The Regulations also apply to the use of pesticides, for which two codes of practice have been drawn up by the HSE (see chapter 5, pesticides), to the use of biological agents and to offshore oil and gas installations. Asbestos, lead, materials producing ionising radiations and inhalable dust below ground in coalmines are excluded as they are covered by separate legislation.

The Regulations require

- an assessment of the risk to health of employees arising from their work and what precautions are needed; this assessment must be regularly reviewed, particularly if it is suspected that the assessment is no longer valid or there has been a significant change in the work to which the assessment relates;
- the introduction of appropriate measures to prevent or control the risk;
- that control measures are used and equipment is properly maintained and procedures observed;
- monitoring the exposure of workers to hazardous substances; in general monitoring should be carried out every 12 months and more frequently for certain processes involving the use of local exhaust ventilation plant (see Schedule 4 to the Regulations); personal exposure monitoring records should be retained for 40 years and general monitoring records for at least 5;
- health surveillance of employees exposed, or likely to be exposed, to hazardous substances, with records being retained for at least 40 years;
- informing, instructing and training employees about the risks and the precautions to be taken, and providing them with results of monitoring and health surveillance;
- compliance with maximum exposure limits listed in HSE publication EH40, *Occupational Exposure Limits*.

Maximum Exposure Limits (MELs) are set for substances for which it is impossible to determine a "no adverse effect level" and must, therefore, not be exceeded. Occupational Exposure Standards (OESs) are set for those substances for which there is a clear "no adverse effect level", the standard representing a limit at which exposure may be harmful; exposure at a level below the standard is generally considered to be safe. HSE publication EH 40, *Occupational Exposure Limits*, which is published annually gives advice on short and long term exposure limits in the workplace, listing both control limits, recommended exposure limits and maximum exposure limits. The HSE uses these control limits in determining whether, in its opinion, the requirements of the relevant legislation are being observed. Failure to comply with control limits or, where practicable, to reduce exposure still further, may result in enforcement action. Recommended exposure limits are considered to represent good practice and realistic criteria. The Inspectorates use these as part of their criteria for assessing compliance with the HSW Act and other relevant statutory provisions.

The Regulations are enforced by HM Factory Inspectorate and any breaches prosecuted under the HSW Act.

The Health and Safety Commission has published (1995, revised 1997) three Approved Codes of Practice (in a single volume) relating to the 1994 Regulations, as amended; the first code is a general one which includes the full text of the Regulations; the other two codes cover the control of carcinogenic substances and control of biological agents.

2.14.3 The Control of Asbestos in the Air Regulations 1990 (SI 556)

These Regulations, effective 5 April 1990, apply to England, Scotland and Wales, and are made under the *Health and Safety at Work Act*. They implement the air pollution aspects of the EU Directive on the Prevention and Reduction of Environmental Pollution by Asbestos (87/217/EEC) which came into force on 31 December 1988. The Directive is being implemented in Northern Ireland through parallel legislation.

All scheduled asbestos works involving the "use of asbestos" are required to meet an emission limit of 0.1 mg m^{-3}. The "use of asbestos" is defined as the production of raw asbestos from ore, and the manufacturing and industrial finishing of a range of products using raw asbestos.

To comply with the Directive the Regulations impose the emission limit on amosite and crocidolite although the import, supply and use of these substances for use at work is banned in the UK by virtue of the *Asbestos (Prohibitions) Regulations 1992*. The Regulations require asbestos emissions to be monitored at intervals of not less than six months; operators are required to prevent significant environmental pollution from the working of products containing asbestos or from the demolition of buildings, structures and installations containing asbestos.

Occupational exposure to asbestos is regulated by the *Control of Asbestos at Work Regulations 1987* (SI 2115) (amended 1992) which came into force in March 1988 and implemented a 1983 Directive (83/477/EEC). They impose duties on employers, similar to those contained in the 1998 COSHH Regulations (see above), for the protection of employees who may be exposed to asbestos at work. 1992 amendment Regulations implementing EU Directives 91/382/EEC and 90/394/EEC (the Carcinogens Directive) came into force on 1 January 1993 and require employers to

- review assessments made under the Regulations at regular intervals;
- prepare a plan of work where the activity concerned entails the removal of asbestos from plant, buildings or other sources;
- put greater emphasis on preventing exposure to asbestos as a carcinogen by using alternative non- or less dangerous substances;
- ensure that only essential workers enter the affected area if there is an unforeseen escape or concentrations are likely to exceed limits.

The HSE is proposing (April 1998) to tighten these Regulations to ensure better protection for those employees likely to come into contact with asbestos in their normal work (e.g. plumbers and electricians); its proposals include improved training, maintenance and testing of respiratory equipment and more specific duties on employers to assess risk of exposure to asbestos; it also proposes reducing the action level at which employers must ensure extra safeguards to protect employees.

Guidance Note EH 10 from the Health and Safety Executive details exposure limits and the measurement of airborne dust concentrations.

2.14.4 The Control of Lead at Work Regulations 1998 (SI 543)

These Regulations replace 1980 Regulations and revoke various pieces of legislation dating back to 1907 which placed employment prohibitions on women and young people working with lead.

The Regulations require employers, who have the duty under the *Management of Health and Safety at Work Regulations 1992*, to assess risks from exposure to lead in the workplace and to take steps to prevent or adequately control such exposure. If the employer concludes from the assessment that the exposure of employees to lead is likely to be "significant", specific controls must be introduced; these include issuing protective clothing, monitoring of air and medical surveillance.

2.14.5 The Genetically Modified Organisms (Contained Use) Regulations 1992 (SI 3217)

These Regulations, made under the *Health and Safety at Work Act 1974*, came into force on 1 February 1993; The *Genetically Modified Organisms (Northern Ireland) Order 1991* amended by 1994 Regulations (SR 143) contain similar provisions. Further 1993 Regulations (SI 15; NI, 1994, SR 145) relate to environmental risk assessment for genetically modified plants and animals. The Deliberate Release of GMOs is covered by Regulations under the *Environmental Protection Act 1990* – see 2.15 below.

The Regulations implement EU Directive 90/219/EEC which requires the setting up of a notification, consent and emergency system to protect human health and the environment. "Contained Use" refers to any work with GMOs which takes place in conditions which are intended to prevent any escape of the organisms into the environment. COM(95) 640, on which a common position was reached in December 1996, is a proposal to amend the 1990 Directive to, where possible, streamline administrative arrangements, specify minimum containment and control measures for each risk class and to introduce the possibility of exemptions for safe GMOs. Following discussion in the European Parliament the Commission has published an amended proposal COM(97) 240 which includes some of the EP's amendments.

The *Contained Use Regulations* establish a consent procedure for work involving GMOs, as well as provisions for both the human health and environmental protection aspects of such activity. The main requirements on persons working with GMOs are to

- notify the HSE of an intention to carry out the work and, in certain cases, to await consent;
- classify operations and the organisms used according to a prescribed scheme;
- carry out a risk assessment;
- adopt controls, including suitable containment measures;
- draw up emergency plans and to notify the HSE of accidents involving GMOs.

Other provisions relate to the disclosure to the public of information given to HSE and the placing, subject to safeguards, of certain information relating to consents on a public register.

2.15 ENVIRONMENTAL PROTECTION ACT 1990, PART VI

Genetically Modified Organisms (ss.106-127)

This part of the EPA aims to prevent or minimise damage to the environment resulting from the escape or release (i.e. deliberate release) from human control of GMOs. (The contained use – i.e. any work in conditions intended to prevent any escape – is dealt with under Regulations made under the *Health and Safety at Work Act 1974* – see above). This part of the Act also applies to Northern Ireland.

The Act defines "organism" as any "acellular, unicellular or multicellular entity (in any form) other than humans or human embryos; and ... any article or substance consisting of or including biological matter". "Genetically modified" means "if any of the genes or other genetic material in the organism have been modified by means of an artificial technique ... or are inherited or otherwise derived, through any number of replications, from genes or other genetic material which were so modified".

The Act places certain duties on persons proposing to import, acquire, keep or release or market GMOs. These include the need to carry out a risk assessment of any potential damage to the environment as a result of the activity; notifying the Secretary of State of the intention to carry out the activity and in most instances applying for a consent; this may include conditions and other limits or restrictions on the activities permitted. Implicit in all consents is a requirement to use BATNEEC to control organisms and prevent damage to the environment; all reasonable steps should be taken to remain informed about any damage which the activity might have caused and to notify the Secretary of State if the risk appears more serious than was first apparent; if it appears that despite the use of BATNEEC for keeping the GMOs under control, damage might occur, then the activity should be ceased.

Other requirements of this part of the Act relate to enforcement and prohibition notices, offences and fees and charges, and are similar to those in Part I of the EPA.

The *Genetically Modified Organisms (Deliberate Release) Regulations 1992* (SI 3280), as amended by 1995 Regulations (SI 304) came into force on 1 February 1993 and implement EU Directive 90/220/EEC on the Release of Genetically Modified Organisms into the Environment. The Regulations also implement the requirements of the EPA relating to Secretary of State consents and a charging scheme, risk assessments and make certain information publicly available subject to various exclusions on the grounds of confidentiality. Similar provisions for Northern Ireland are contained in the *Genetically Modified Organisms (Northern Ireland) Order 1991*, amended by 1994 Regulations.

A proposal to amend Directive 90/220/EEC was published in February 1998. COM(98) 85 requires authorisations to be renewed every seven years and mandatory monitoring for environmental impact of products containing GMOs, with renewal of authorisation dependent on monitoring results. Other amendments relate to harmonisation of risk assessment and classification of risks, labelling and streamlining of administrative procedures, with a simplified authorisation procedure for certain categories of release (defined in an Annex to the Directive).

REGULATION OF AGRICULTURAL POLLUTION

2.16 GENERAL

A number of agricultural practices contribute to air pollution or cause a nuisance. Among the main problems are odour, smoke nuisance and water pollution. Controls on agricultural practices causing pollution are included explicitly, or by implication, in a number of statutes and codes of good practice. Most of these have been covered in other sections of the *Pollution Handbook*, and include the following:

- *Clean Air Act 1993, Part I*: section 2 prohibits the emission of dark smoke from industrial or trade premises; this includes land being used for commercial agriculture or horticulture (this chapter, 2.13.1).
- *Clean Air Act 1993, Part III*: farms falling within a smoke control area must comply with sections 18-29 of the Act which prohibit the emission of smoke from any building or chimney and require the use only of authorised fuels (this chapter, 2.13.3).
- *Clean Air (Emission of Dark Smoke) (Exemption) Regulations 1969*: these permit the burning, in certain circumstances, of various farm wastes; these include the burning of animal or poultry carcases and pesticide containers (this chapter, 2.13.3).
- *Environmental Protection Act 1990, Part I*: this requires the farming industry to obtain an authorisation from their local authority (Scotland – SEPA) for carrying on any of the following processes: waste oil burners; straw or poultry litter combustion processes between 0.4 and 3 MW net rated thermal input; animal carcase incineration under 1 tonne an hour (incinerators under 50 kg/hour do not require authorisation); treatment and processing of animal or vegetable matter including fur breeding, animal feed composting and composting, including production of compost for mushrooms (subject to extensive exceptions) (this chapter, 2.11.2).
- *Environmental Protection Act 1990, Part II*: the disposal of certain organic wastes to land requires a waste management licence from the waste regulation authority (Environment Agency or SEPA) – see chapter 4, 4.19.3.
- *Environmental Protection Act 1990, Part III*: this enables local authorities and individuals to take action against statutory nuisance;

statutory nuisances include smoke, odour, noise, accumulations or deposits and animals kept in such a way as to be prejudicial to health or a nuisance (see chapter 1, 1.15.1).

- *Highways (Amendment) Act 1986*: it is an offence to light a fire, permit or direct one to be lit, the smoke from which injures, interrupts or endangers anyone using a highway. This provision could also be used for bonfire smoke.
- *The Sludge (Use in Agriculture) Regulations 1989* (SI 1263) (as amended and Code of Practice dated 1989) control the spreading of sewage sludge on agricultural land, and restrict the planting, grazing and harvesting of some crops following application. The main aim of the controls is to prevent the accumulation of hazardous concentrations of heavy metals in soil and to prevent bacteriological contamination of crops; a Code of Practice specifies the way in which sludge is treated, utilisation practices on the farm and monitoring requirements for soils receiving sludge. Similar Regulations came into force in N. Ireland in July 1990.
- *Code of Practice for the Safe Use of Pesticides on Farms and Holdings 1990* (under review – 1995). This deals, among other things, with the disposal of waste pesticides and containers and aerial application of pesticides (see chapter 5).
- The control of water pollution from agricultural practices, in particular the use of nitrates and pesticides is covered in chapter 5.

It should be noted that implementation of the EU Framework Directive on Waste (chapter 4, 4.6) is likely to require further statutory controls on agricultural and farm wastes.

2.17 CODES OF PRACTICE

2.17.1 England and Wales

A *Code of Good Agricultural Practice for the Protection of Air* was published in 1992. It covers England and Wales and summarises the various pieces of legislation which farmers should be aware of; it gives practical guidance on reducing the problem of odours from housed livestock systems, slurry and manure storage, production of compost for mushrooms and land spreading of livestock wastes. There is also guidance on minimising the need to burn waste and other materials and alternative uses for straw. The Code describes ways of reducing emissions of ammonia and of the greenhouse gases. It does not cover noise nuisance (action for which can be taken under Part III of the *Environmental Protection Act 1990* (see chapter 1, 1.15.1; nor does it cover pesticide use for which there are separate codes of practice (see chapter 5).

The Code, which was prepared by the Ministry of Agriculture, Fisheries and Foods and the Welsh Office Agriculture Department, has no legal status; adherence to the Code is not a defence in a legal action.

A *Code of Good Agricultural Practice for the Protection of Soil* was published in December 1993. Like the Code covering the protection of the air. It summarises the legislative controls farmers should be aware of and suggests ways of preventing soil erosion and the loss of organic matter. The code gives a reminder that wastes and pesticides should not be applied in such quantities that they are likely to accumulate in the soil. It also provides advice on protecting soil from contamination and acidification.

Revisions of both these Codes were published for consultation in July 1997, together with a draft *Code of Good Agricultural Practice for the Protection of Water*; the revised codes were due for publication during 1998.

2.17.2 Scotland

In Scotland there is a single Code of Practice covering the prevention of air, soil and water pollution. *The Code of Good Practice on the Prevention of Environmental Pollution from Agricultural Activity* came into effect in 1992 (a revised version was due during 1997). Only those parts of the Code covering water pollution have been given statutory backing under the *Water (Prevention of Pollution) (Code of Practice) (Scotland) Order 1992* (see chapter 5).

The Code summarises all the various pieces of legislation in Scotland of relevance to the control of agricultural pollution. It provides advice and information on principles of land application and storage of livestock wastes, their management and disposal; silos and silage effluent; other organic wastes often disposed of to land; agricultural fuel oil and waste oil; waste treatment technology; sheep dip (use and disposal); pesticides; disposal of animal carcases; nitrates; straw and stubble burning and muirburn (a means of managing the vegetation of upland grazings); control of odours and ammonia emissions; disposal of waste products and litter; soil protection.

The various pollution problems caused by incorrect – or inadvisable – treatment and disposal practices are summarised, together with the advantages and disadvantages of various recommended good practices and action necessary to comply with legislation.

2.17.3 Northern Ireland

The 1994 codes for the protection of air, water and soil for Northern Ireland are similar to those for the rest of the UK.

2.18 STRAW AND STUBBLE BURNING

Section 152 of the *Environmental Protection Act 1990*, Part VIII enables Regulations to be made prohibiting or restricting the burning of crop residues on agricultural land and for exemptions relating to specified areas, specified crop residues, or in specified circumstances. The Regulations may impose requirements to be complied with before or after burning, and also make contravention of any Regulations an offence which on conviction is subject to a fine. Straw and stubble burning in England and Wales was previously controlled through local authority bye-laws; these were all repealed with effect from 2 April 1992.

2.18.1 The Crop Residues (Burning) Regulations 1993 (SI 1366)

These Regulations came into effect on 29 June 1993 and extend to England and Wales only and revoke earlier 1991 Regulations. The burning of cereal straw and stubble, and the residues of field beans and peas harvested dry and oilseed rape is banned. They may, however, be burnt in the following circumstances:

- for education and research purposes;
- in compliance with a notice served under the *Plant Health (Great Britain) Order 1993* (e.g. to eliminate pests);
- to dispose of broken bales and the remains of straw stacks.

The burning of linseed residues is currently exempted from the ban, but may subsequently be included in the light of the availability and practicability of alternative methods of disposal and the level of public complaint.

Any burning for education and research, in compliance with a plant health order or of linseed residues must be carried out in compliance with the conditions contained in Schedule 2 of the Regulations; these are:

a) No burning at weekends, bank holidays, or from one hour before sunset until the following sunrise.

b) No more than an area of ten hectares of straw and stubble and 20 hectares of other crop residues may be burnt in a single operation. Additional guidance from MAFF states that if sufficient fire-fighting equipment and manpower are available and fire-break requirements are observed, two or more burning operations may be undertaken simultaneously, so long as they are at least 150 metres apart.

c) No burning within certain distances of various "vulnerable" objects; these are:

- 15 metres for straw and stubble burn and 5 metres for other residues: tree trunks (including coppices or scrubland); fence belonging to another property; telegraph or telephone poles; electricity pole, pylon or substation.
- 50 metres for straw and stubble burn and 15 metres for other residues: residential buildings; thatched roofs; building, structure, fixed plant or machinery which could be set alight by heat from a fire; scheduled monument which could be set alight; hay or straw stack; accumulation of combustible material (other than crop residues) removed in making of fire-break; mature standing crop; woodland or land managed as a nature reserve; above ground gas or oil installation.
- 100 metres for burning of any residue: motorways, dual carriageways; A roads; and railway lines.

d) The area to be burnt must be completely surrounded by a fire-break. This must be 10 metres wide for cereal straw and stubble and 5 metres wide for other crop residues. Precautions should be taken to ensure that the fire will not cross the fire-break.

e) At least two adults who are familiar with the Regulations must be present during burning, one of whom must be in control of the operation and must be experienced in burning of crop residues.

f) At least one hour's notice (but not more than 24 hours' notice) must be given to the following: local environmental health department; occupiers of all premises adjacent to the area to be burned; air traffic control of any aerodrome within 800 metres.

g) At least 1000 litres of water must be available on the burning site, together with equipment to dispense the water in a spray or jet at a rate of 100 litres per minute; there must be five implements suitable for fire beating available and all vehicles used in connection with burning must be equipped with fire extinguishers.

h) Ash remaining from cereal straw and stubble burning should normally be incorporated into the soil within 24 hours of burning; if windy conditions mean that incorporating the ash might cause a nuisance, it should be incorporated as soon as conditions allow.

The maximum fine for each breach of the Regulations is currently £5,000.

The burning of broken bales and straw stack remains is still permitted, as is the burning of other crop residues not specifically mentioned, e.g. herbage seeds, reeds, lavender, hop bines and potato haulms. The local environmental health department must be notified of any permitted burning.

The Regulations do not ban burning when winds exceed certain speeds. However, guidance notes issued by MAFF suggest farmers should not burn when winds exceed, or are forecast to exceed, force 3 (8-12 mph). Farmers are also advised to pay attention to wind direction in order to minimise nuisance and hazard.

Action for burning on agricultural or horticultural land may also be taken under section 2 of the *Clean Air Act 1993* (see section 2.13.1 above), or under the nuisance provisions of the *Environmental Protection Act* (see chapter 1, 1.15.1 above).

In Scotland, there are no specific regulations covering straw and stubble burning as only a small percentage of stubble is burnt. A voluntary Code of Practice (*Straw and Stubble Burning and Muirburn Practice*) has however been agreed between the Scottish NFU and the Scottish Office Agriculture and Fisheries Department. Additional guidance is contained in the 1992 *Code of Good Practice on Prevention of Environmental Pollution from Agricultural Activity*. The advice given is similar to that contained in the Regulations for England and Wales.

Under the "set aside" arrangements, the burning of "set aside" is prohibited.

REGULATION OF POLLUTION FROM ROAD VEHICLES

2.19 INTRODUCTION

In 1996 there were over 26 million vehicles using nearly 470,000 km of road in Great Britain. This is forecast to rise by between 52-82% by 2025. Cars account for 82% of all road traffic, light vans for 9%, HGVs for 7% and buses and motorcycles for 1% each. (*Road Traffic Statistics Great Britain*, The Stationery Office, 1997). In its Green Paper on the Impact of Transport on the Environment (see also earlier this chapter 2.4.6) published in 1992, the European Commission predicted a probable growth in private cars in the European Union (EU) of 45% between 1987-2010 (i.e. from 115 million to a total of 167 million). Goods traffic is expected to increase by 42% between 1990-2010; total vehicle kilometres are predicted to grow 25% throughout the same period.

Road transport is an integral feature of modern life, moving people and goods for industry, commerce and pleasure; however, it is also a major source of a number of important air pollutants, including nitrogen oxides, hydrocarbons, carbon monoxide, particulate matter and carbon dioxide. The contribution from road traffic to total emissions of each of these pollutants in 1995 was as follows (1994 figures in brackets):

Hydrocarbons	30% (29%)
Nitrogen oxides	46% (49%)
Carbon monoxide	75% (88%)
Black smoke	50% (58%)
Particles (PM_{10})	26% (26%)
Carbon dioxide	20% (20%)

(*Source*: DETR Digest of Environmental Protection Statistics, No. 19, 1997 & No. 18, DOE, 1996)

As at the beginning of 1998, unleaded petrol accounted for 75% of the retail petrol market (DTI *Energy Statistics*, 1998). Levels of lead in the air resulting from petrol engined vehicles have halved since 1987 following the reduction in the permissible amount of lead in petrol from 0.40 g/l to 0.15 g/l; lead from this source is, however, still by far the most significant source of lead in the air, accounting for 73%, followed by lead/zinc/copper processes (9%) (EPAQS, 1998). In some areas noise from road transport is also a significant problem and there are various controls limiting noise emissions from vehicles (see chapter 3).

Early legislation in both the UK and EU limiting vehicle emissions was often based on model standards developed by the UN Economic Commission for Europe (which includes both EU and non-EU countries); the UNECE has no enforcement powers. A series of European Directives over the last 25 years has set progressively tighter emission standards for all road vehicles. However these gains have been more than offset by the rapid growth in the total volume of road traffic. Emissions from road transport therefore remain one of Europe's most pressing air pollution problems. Within the EU, this issue is being addressed through the Auto/Oil Programme (see below 2.20.1).

In the UK, attainment of the air quality objectives in the National Air Quality Strategy (this chapter, 2.7) will require a reduction in traffic related pollution. The emission of pollutants – including standards emanating from the EU – from road vehicles are governed by the *Road Vehicles (Construction and Use) Regulations* and the *Motor Vehicles (Type Approval) (Great Britain) Regulations* made under the *Road Traffic Act 1988*. Similar regulations made under the *Road Traffic (Northern Ireland) Order 1981* apply in Northern Ireland. The *Transport Act 1982* also specifies requirements for the manufacture of vehicles; Regulations made under the *Clean Air Act 1993* impose requirements as to the composition, content and marketing of fuel used in motor vehicles – see section 2.13.4.

In July 1998, the Government published a White Paper setting out its strategy for developing an integrated transport policy which aims to both improve public transport and cut road congestion and traffic generated pollution; *A New Deal for Transport* outlines the Government's policies for developing better and more integrated public transport systems, for more environmentally acceptable cars and car use, for more efficient and environmentally sustainable freight transport, and for the integration of transport and land-use planning policies. Similar documents for Scotland (*Travel Choices for Scotland*) and Wales (*Transporting Wales into the Future*) have also been published.

2.20 THE EUROPEAN UNION AND VEHICLE POLLUTION CONTROL

2.20.1 The Auto/Oil Programme

In 1992, the European Commission initiated a tripartite research programme with the European oil and motor industries. The aim of the programme was to identify technical measures to help achieve health-based air quality targets at least cost to society. The Auto/Oil programme was intended to consider not just motor and oil industry solutions but also the contributions of traffic management, public transport, new technologies and vehicle maintenance programmes.

Based on the results of the research, the Commission published proposals in June 1996 aimed at reducing emissions from road transport by up to 70% by the year 2010. Published as a Communication (COM(96) 248) "on a future strategy for the control of atmospheric emissions from road transport", the proposals take into account EU air quality targets, technological advances and improvements in fuel quality; the Communication also discusses the practicalities of measures such as fiscal incentives, traffic management and encouraging urban public transport as a means of reducing overall emissions. A number of Directives arising out of the Auto/Oil Programme were formally adopted in September 1998, with further draft Directives under discussion. These are summarised below at 2.20.2, 2.20.3 and 2.20.7.

2.20.2 Light Duty Vehicles

Light duty vehicles are cars and vans under 3.5 tonnes. As mentioned above a number of important EU Directives (see Appendix 6.2) and UNECE standards controlling vehicle emissions have been adopted: the first EU Directive (70/220/EEC) relating to measures to be taken against air pollution from positive ignition engines continues to be the basis for current Directives and proposals and has thus been amended and adapted a number of times; it applies to vehicles with no more than six seating positions and a maximum permissible mass of not more than 2500 kg. Directive 83/351/EEC enforces the latest UNECE regulations

(ECE R15-04). This series of Directives relating to the UNECE Regulations laid down increasingly tight emission standards for CO and HC, and later NOx. All new cars in the UK, including diesel cars, have met the 83/351/EEC standards since April 1991.

The 1988 Directive (88/76) known as the "Luxembourg Agreement", partially agreed in 1985, proposed limits for three classes of engine size: more than 2 litres, 1.4 to 2 litres, and less than 1.4 litres. New limits for CO, HC and NOx were proposed for new vehicles to be produced in the late 1980s/early 1990s. Agreement was reached immediately for the two larger classes; stricter limits for small (less than 1.4 litre) cars had to be agreed in two stages because of opposition from small car manufacturers. The stricter (2nd stage) limits were agreed in June 1989 (Directive 89/458/EEC) and were in line with US and Japanese standards. This Directive which applied to both petrol and diesel vehicles was largely superseded by the Consolidated Directive (91/441/EEC) – see below.

A 1988 Directive (88/436/EEC), on particulate emissions from diesel cars, agreed in December 1987, is also an amendment to the original 1970 Directive on vehicle emissions. It acknowledges health-related concerns and bases controls on the mass of soot emitted, rather than on some subjective judgement of smoke opacity, which is easier to measure and enforce. The standard is set by measuring the mass of emissions, rather than the opacity of smoke emitted. The standards, which applied from 1990, are 1.1g/test for new engine types and 1.4g/test for all new vehicles. However this does little more than enforce existing technology, and a second stage of stricter emission limits has been proposed. The introduction dates for indirect injection diesel cars under 2 litres was April 1991 and for direct injection diesel cars under 2 litres April 1997.

In June 1991 further, stricter, limits (see below) were agreed. This Directive (91/441/EEC - the Consolidated Directive) implemented new stricter limits for all passenger cars (except direct injection diesel vehicles) with no more than six seats, and under 2500 kg. It also contained an improved driving cycle with a high speed element as the basis for tests. Emission limits are expressed in grams per kilometre instead of grams per test (i.e. the amount of emissions allowable per km averaged over the whole test cycle). The new standards were mandatory and applied to all new cars from 31 December 1992, and to new models from 1 July 1992.

	Emission limit (g/km)		
	CO	*HC+NOx*	*Particulates*
Type approval	2.72	0.97	0.14
Conformity of production	3.16	1.13	0.18

From 1 July 1994 the above limits also applied to new model light duty direct injection diesel vehicles and to new models from 31 December 1994.

To meet the standards, new petrol driven cars registered after 1 January 1993 had to be fitted with three-way catalytic converters; these fit into the car exhaust and act by converting CO, HC and NOx into CO_2, water and nitrogen. Diesel engined vehicles will require "state of the art" technology. These requirements were implemented through an amendment to the *Type Approval Regulations* (see 2.21.3 below). Research by the former Warren Spring Laboratory (an agency of the Department of Trade and Industry) showed that a vehicle fitted with a catalytic converter which is in good condition will reduce emissions of carbon monoxide, hydrocarbons and nitrogen oxides by 90% each. However fuel consumption increases by between 3-9% and emissions of carbon dioxide by between 9-23%. It should be noted, however, that catalytic converters do not become effective until the car engine has warmed up.

The Directive also contains provisions for the introduction of tax incentives to promote the introduction of cleaner vehicles. Hydrocarbons – or volatile organic compounds (VOCs) – which evaporate from the fuel tank and fuel system are limited to less than 2g/test; this will require the fitting of "carbon canisters" (a fuel vapour collection system). Carbon monoxide emissions are limited to 3.5-4.5% by volume at idling.

In 1994 a further Directive (94/12/EC) amending the original 1970 Directive on vehicle emission limits was agreed. Different limits are set for petrol and diesel engined vehicles and for the first time no distinction is made between standards for type approval and conformity of production.

	Emission limit (g/km)		
	CO	*HC+NOx*	*Particulates*
Petrol engines	2.2	0.5	
Diesel engines			
- indirect injection	1.0	0.7	0.08
- direct injection	1.0	0.9	0.10
DI from 1.10.99	1.0	0.7	0.08

The new limits were mandatory from 1 January 1996 for new model vehicles and from 1 January 1997 for new registrations. The Directive has been implemented through a 1995 amendment (SI 2210) to the 1986 *Construction and Use Regulations*.

As with the 1991 Directive it was permissible to offer fiscal incentives to encourage manufacturers to meet the new standards before the deadline. Any such schemes had to be approved by the Commission prior to introduction and meet a number of criteria, including compatibility with the functioning of the internal market and be non-discriminatory.

The latest emission limits (see table below) for passenger vehicles (up to 2,500 kg) are contained in a Directive which originates out of the Auto/Oil Programme, and was formally adopted in September 1998. The 2000 and 2005 compliance dates are those for new model types, with compliance by new cars a year later in each case. Petrol-engined vehicles with electronically controlled catalytic converters will also be required to carry an onboard diagnostic system from 2000 and diesel engined vehicles from 2005. Tax incentives will be permissible for vehicles already meeting the 2005 standards from 2000.

Petrol fuelled vehicles to meet following limits (g/km) by

	2000	*2005*
CO	2.3	1.0
HC	0.20	0.10
NOx	0.15	0.08

Diesel fuelled vehicles to meet following limits (g/km) by

	2000	*2005*
CO	0.64	0.50
HC/NOx	0.56	0.30
NOx	0.50	0.25
Particles	0.05	0.025

The Commission is to publish further proposals by 31 December 1999 for implementation after 2005.

2.20.3 Light Commercial Vehicles

A further amendment to Directive 70/220/EEC (Directive 93/59) adopted by Environment Ministers in June 1993 sets emission limits for light commercial vehicles. Emission limits are as strict as those for private vehicles, with vehicles being categorised according to their reference mass, i.e. the mass of the unladen vehicle in running order, as follows:

- Category I: commercial vehicles with reference mass up to 1250 kg and vans/cars designed to carry up to nine people; limits for these vehicles are the same as those for light duty vehicles as set in the 1991 Consolidated Directive (see above);
- Category II: commercial vehicles with reference mass between 1250-1700 kg;

- Category III: commercial vehicles with reference mass between 1701-3500 kg.

The new emission controls for type approvals came into force on 1 October 1993 and applied to new vehicles from 1 October 1994. Petrol engined vehicles need three-way catalytic converters to meet the exhaust limits and carbon canisters to control evaporative hydrocarbon emissions; diesel engined vehicles need engine modifications or two-way catalysts.

In October 1996 the Council of Ministers formally adopted a Directive – 96/69/EC – tightening emission limits further to bring them into line with those of Directive 94/12/EC. For Category I the limits applied to new models from 1 January 1997 and to new vehicles from 1 October 1997; for Categories II and III the respective dates were 1 January 1998 and 1 October 1998. Member States may use tax incentives as a means of encouraging the introduction of vehicles meeting the new emission limits before the mandatory dates.

These Directives have been implemented by amendments to the Construction and Use and Type Approval Regulations (see below, 2.21.2 and 2.21.3).

	Emission limit (g/km)				
	CO		*HC+NOx*		*Particulates*
	*P**	*D**	*P*	*D***	*D***
Category I	2.2	1.0	0.5	0.9/0.7	0.10/0.08
Category II	4.0	1.25	0.6	1.3/1.0	0.14/0.12
Category III	5.0	1.5	0.7	1.6/1.2	0.20/0.17

* P = petrol; D = diesel
** the first limit value applies to direct injection vehicles until 30.9.99

In September 1998, a further Directive, also issued as part of the Auto/Oil Programme, was formally adopted. This will reduce emissions of NOx and of HC by 40% and of CO by 30% on the above standards for petrol engined vehicles; for gas powered vehicles the reductions are 20%, 65% and 30% respectively and 35% reduction in particulate matter. The new limits (see table) will apply to new type vehicles in category I from 1 January 2000 and a year later to new vehicles; new type vehicles in categories II and III will be required to meet the limits from 1 January 2001 and new vehicles a year later, with stricter limits applying to all categories from 2005 and 2006 respectively. Light commercial petrol engined vehicles will be required to carry onboard diagnostic systems, but these will be optional for diesel engined vehicles. Member States may use fiscal incentives to encourage early adoption of the tighter standards.

	Emission limit (g/km)						
	CO	*HC*	*HC+NOx*		*NOx*		*PM*
	P	*D*	*P*	*D*	*P*	*D*	*D*
Category I - 2000	2.3	0.64	0.20	0.56	0.15	0.50	0.05
2005	1.0	0.50	0.10	0.30	0.08	0.25	0.025
Category II - 2001	4.17	0.80	0.25	0.72	0.18	0.65	0.07
2006	1.81	0.63	0.13	0.39	0.10	0.33	0.04
Category III - 2001	5.22	0.95	0.29	0.86	0.21	0.78	0.10
2006	2.27	0.74	0.16	0.46	0.11	0.39	0.06

2.20.4 Heavy Duty Vehicles

This applies to lorries, buses etc over 3.5 tonnes. A 1972 Directive (72/306/EEC) set limits on smoke emissions from large diesels (excluding tractors and public works vehicles) using visibility criteria. Limits for diesel-engined tractors are covered by Directive 77/537/EEC. Limits for gaseous pollutants emitted from heavy duty vehicles were set in Directive 88/77, subsequently amended through the adoption in October 1991 of Directive 91/542/EEC, agreed in October 1991 which tightens standards in two steps. It also introduces a strict, mass-based, standard for particulate emissions. Dates for compliance with the first step ("EURO 1") reductions were 1 July 1992 (new models) and 1 October 1993 (all new vehicles). Dates for introduction of the second step ("EURO 2") have now been agreed by Environment Ministers (Directive 96/1/EC) – see below; these limits match the very stringent US 1994 diesel standards.

The agreed emission limits for heavy duty diesels, and dates for implementation, are as follows:

	Emission limit (g/kWh)			
	CO	*HC*	*NOx*	*Particulates*
Euro I type approval	4.5	1.1	8.0	0.36*
Euro I conformity of production	4.9	1.23	9.0	0.4*
Euro II, TA & COP	4.0	1.1	7.0	0.15**

* for engines of 85 kW or less, a coefficient of 1.7 is applied to the limit value for particulate emissions.

** until 30 September 1997 (new models) and from 1 October 1996 to 30 September 1998 for existing models the limit was 0.25g/kWh.

These limits will require an improvement in the quality of diesel fuel which emits sulphur as particulate sulphates. In 1993, a Directive was adopted reducing the sulphur content of diesel fuel to 0.2% by weight from 1 October 1994 and to 0.05% by weight from 1 October 1996. The Directive also required Member States to ensure that diesel fuels with the lower sulphur limit became available from 1 October 1994 to enable compliance with the tighter emission standards. In the UK the Directives are implemented through amendments to the *Type Approval Regulations* and *Construction and Use Regulations* (see 2.21.2 & 2.21.3 below).

In December 1997 the Commission published COM(97) 627, a proposal for a Directive to amend 88/77 again – this proposal also forms part of the Auto/Oil I programme. As well as heavy duty diesel vehicles, the proposal covers those fuelled by natural gas and liquefied petroleum gas (LPG). The new emission limits would apply to new vehicle and engine types from 1 October 2000 and a year later to new engines and vehicles. Further proposals for standards to be met by 1 October 2005 are expected to be made.

Two sets of limit values are proposed (see table below) – depending on the test cycle used: ESC and ELR test cycles for conventional diesel engines, including those fitted with electronic fuel injection equipment, exhaust gas recirculation and/or oxidation catalysts; ESC, ELR and ETC test cycles for diesel engines fitted with advance emission control systems, including de-NO_x catalysts and/or particulate traps, and also gas engines.

Limit values for engines tested on ESC and ELR test cycles (g/kWh, except smoke)

Mass of CO	2.1
Mass of HC	0.66
Mass of NOx	5.0
Mass of Particulates	0.10 (0.13 for engines with swept vol < 0.7dm^3 per cylinder and rated power > 3,000 min^{-1})
Smoke (m^{-1})	0.8

Limit values for engines tested on ESC, ELR & ETC test cycles (g/kWh)

Mass of CO	5.45
Mass of NMHC	0.78
Mass of methane	1.6 (for natural gas engines only)
Mass of NOx	5.0
Mass of Particulates	0.16 (0.21 for engines with swept volume < 0.7 dm^3 per cylinder and rated power of > 3,000 min^{-1}) (diesel engines only)

2.20.5 Non-Road Mobile Machinery

In December 1997 Environment Ministers adopted Directive 97/68 relating to emissions of gaseous and particulate pollutants from non-road mobile machinery. This Directive applies to agricultural and forestry equipment, snow ploughs, fork lift trucks, mobile cranes and construction equipment; agricultural and forestry tractors are to be covered by a separate Directive. Stage I limits (see below) are being phased in from 30 September 1998 to 31 March 1999 and Stage II limits between December 2000 and 31 December 2003.

		Emission limit (g/kWh)			
Net Power P (kW)	*Stage*	*CO*	*HC*	*NOx*	*Particulates*
130 ≤ P <560	I	5.0	1.3	9.2	0.54
	II	3.5	1.0	6.0	0.2
75 ≤ P <130	I	5.0	1.3	9.2	0.70
	II	5.0	1.0	6.0	0.3
37 ≤ P <75	I	6.5	1.3	9.2	0.85
	II	5.0	1.3	7.0	0.4
18 ≤ P <37	II	5.5	1.5	8.0	0.8

2.20.6 Reducing Carbon Dioxide Emissions from Cars

In June 1996 Environment Ministers agreed the Commission's proposal for *A Community strategy to reduce carbon dioxide emissions from passenger cars and improve fuel economy* – COM(95) 689. This forms part of the overall strategy to stabilise emissions of carbon dioxide at 1990 levels by the year 2000 – see this chapter 2.4.2. The main elements of the strategy are:

- agreement of auto industry to reach a specific CO_2 emission target for cars within an agreed timeframe – the Commission suggested a 33% reduction (186g/km to 120 g/km) in the average of CO_2 emissions of new cars sold in the EU by 2005 compared with 1990; the European Car Manufacturers Association (ACEA) has now agreed that average emissions should be reduced to 140 g/km by 2008 and to review in 2003 the possibility of meeting a target of 120 g/km by 2012;
- promotion of fuel efficient passenger cars and fuel economy labelling;

- research and development programmes to improve the performance of cars;
- promotion of alternative modes of transport.

2.20.7 Fuel Quality

Directive 85/210/EEC, set a maximum of 0.15 grammes per litre of lead in petrol, and limited benzene to 5% by volume; it also required that unleaded petrol was to be made available in Member States by 1989, new model cars designed to run on it from 1989, and all new cars to run on unleaded petrol from 1990. An amendment to this Directive (87/416/EEC) permitted Member States to ban the sale of regular grade leaded petrol with six months notice.

Directive (93/12/EEC) limits the sulphur content of all gas oils (except aviation kerosene) to 0.2% by weight as from 1 October 1994, with a further reduction in the sulphur content of diesel fuel to 0.05% by weight as from 1 October 1996. The Directive also required Member States to ensure that diesel fuel with a sulphur content of 0.05% or less became available from 1 October 1995, thus enabling compliance with EU Directive 91/542/EEC on emissions from heavy duty vehicles (see 2.20.4). (As part of its strategy to combat acidification (see 2.4.5a), a Common Position has been reached on amending Directive 93/12/EC to reduce the sulphur content of gas oil to 0.1% by weight from 1 January 2008.)

In September 1998, a Directive relating to the quality of petrol and diesel fuels and amending Directive 93/12/EEC, was formally adopted. This Directive arises out of the Auto/Oil Programme, and includes the following provisions:

- A ban on the marketing of leaded petrol from 1 January 2000; five year derogation for those Member States where this timetable may result in "severe socio-economic problems or would not lead to overall environmental or health benefits".
- Reducing the amount of benzene in petrol from 5% to 1% by volume by 2000; aromatics to be limited to 42% by volume and sulphur to 150 ppm (with a three year derogation for those Member States where this would cause "severe socio-economic problems"). For diesel, polyaromatics are to be limited to 11% by volume and sulphur to 350 ppm. Sulphur in petrol must be reduced to 50 ppm sulphur from 2005, to be phased in for diesel, and a limit of 35% aromatics.
- From 2000 Member States can give tax incentives for fuels already meeting the 2005 limits.

The Commission is to review these specifications and come forward with further proposals by 31 December 1999.

Fuel quality Directives are implemented in the UK through regulations made under the *Clean Air Act 1993*, Part IV – see this chapter, 2.13.4.

2.20.8 Petrol Storage and Distribution

In December 1994, Ministers formally adopted a Directive (94/63/EC) on controlling VOC emissions resulting from the storage of petrol and its distribution from terminals to service stations ("Stage I" controls). The Directive, which came into force on 31 December 1995, also covers the loading of petrol on to rail or new oil tanker lorries and inland waterways vessels. The Directive aims to reduce emissions from these sources by 90% over ten years through the use of technical measures such as vapour recovery, painting storage tanks with reflectance paint and bottom loading of tankers. Design and operating standards for installations and equipment have been set so as to reduce vapour losses to below a "target reference value" of annual throughput.

New storage installations, the loading and unloading of new road or rail tankers at new terminals or new petrol stations (i.e. not authorised or operated before 31 December 1995) had to comply with the new standards by 31 December 1995. Existing storage installations with an annual throughput of more than 50,000 tonnes, loading and unloading of rail tankers and barges at terminals with an annual throughput of more than 150,000 tonnes have a further three years to meet the Directive, as does the loading and unloading at petrol stations with an annual throughput of more than 1,000 m^3; where the annual throughput exceeds 25,000 tonnes at existing storage installations or terminals loading and unloading road and rail tankers and petrol stations with an annual throughput of more than 500 m^3, the compliance date is 31 December 2001; remaining installations, terminals and petrol stations have a further three years. Where vapour emissions at storage installations, terminals or petrol stations could cause adverse health or environmental effects, stricter requirements may be imposed.

Small service stations (below 1,000 m^3 annual throughput) have been given longer to meet the new standards; small rural service stations (100-500 m^3 annual throughput) have a limited derogation from controls where VOC emissions are likely to pose an insignificant threat to the environment; all service stations below 100 m^3 annual throughput have been given an absolute derogation.

Implementation of the Directive in the UK has been effected through an amendment to the *Environmental Protection (Prescribed Processes and Substances) Regulations 1991* – see below 2.21.4.

A further Directive ("Stage II") to reduce VOC emissions from vehicle refuellings at petrol stations is also to be prepared. All petrol stations with a throughput of more than 2500 m^3 a year, together with those in "sensitive" areas as evidenced by the 1992 ozone information Directive (see this chapter, 2.4.1c) would be required to fit vapour recovery equipment initially capable of recovering 70% of vapour. By 1 January 2006 compatibility of filling necks and petrol pump nozzles to ensure a hermetic seal would be mandatory, thus enabling 95% vapour recovery.

2.20.9 Roadworthiness Testing

The EU Roadworthiness Directive (77/143/EEC) applies to goods vehicles (including trailers and semi-trailers) over 3.5 tonnes gross vehicle weight, vehicles with more than eight passenger seats, taxis and ambulances. It was extended by Directive 88/449/EEC to apply to other goods vehicles with effect from 1 January 1993 in those Member States which already have testing schemes for such vehicles, and 1 January 1995 in other Member States. The Directive lays down the periodicity of testing and the items to be checked, including exhaust emissions. There is no need for an item to be checked if there is no in-use requirement in the Member State concerned. If, for example, a Member State does not require a vehicle to carry a fire extinguisher, the Directive does not force that item to be checked.

In addition, a Directive (91/328/EEC) agreed in June 1991 introduced common roadworthiness tests for private cars from 1998; it identifies the items to be checked and applies to all vehicles registered from 1994. The first test will be obligatory after four years and subsequently every two years.

Directive 92/55/EEC specifies the emission standards to be achieved by 1 January 1997. All vehicles fitted with a catalytic converter for which there is no manufacturer's standard must meet a carbon monoxide emission of 0.5% when the vehicle is running slowly and 0.3% when running at 2000 rpm. Where a manufacturer's standard is specified, this should not be exceeded when the car is running slowly and is again limited to 0.3% at 2000 rpm.

For cars without a catalytic converter for which no manufacturer's standard is given the limits to be met by 1 January 1994 were 4.5% for cars first used prior to 1986 and 3.5% for cars used after that date. A tolerance of + 0.5% will be allowed where a manufacturer's standard is specified. (See also vehicle testing, below.)

A visual inspection to ensure that the exhaust system is leak-free must also be carried out and applicable vehicles must be inspected to ensure the presence of an emission control system. The Directive also specifies emission standards for diesel engines, which will be measured according to opacity.

A further Directive – 93/116 – amends a 1980 Directive on fuel consumption; it sets out a new procedure for establishing carbon dioxide emissions, which are to be recorded in a document retained by the vehicle's owner.

In March 1998, the Commission published proposals for a draft Directive (COM(98) 117) on the roadside inspection of roadworthiness of commercial vehicles.

2.20.10 Biofuels

The European Commission has published an amended proposal for a Directive (COM(94) 147) on Excise Duties on Motor Fuels from Agricultural Sources. This would set excise duties for biofuels (i.e. fuels derived from agricultural products) at not more than 10% of that on unleaded fuel or diesel; excise duties on biofuels would be gradually cut to a maximum of 50% compared with fossil fuels. It is hoped this will encourage the further development of such fuels and thus reduce dependence on fossil fuels and so reduce air pollution. Biofuels already at an advanced stage of development include bioethanol (produced by fermentation of sugar or starch) and vegetable oils esterified with ethanol or methanol. The European Parliament want the scheme to be optional, a proposal to which the Commission is opposed. The European Parliament also suggest that tax relief be given only for biofuels produced on set-aside and in compliance with codes of practice under the Nitrates Directive (see chapter 5, 5.7.7) and that products produced by pyrolysis should be exempted from tax. The draft has yet to be formally approved by the Council of Ministers.

No agreement has yet been reached on this proposal and further progress is not expected in the near future.

2.21 UK REGULATIONS

2.21.1 Composition of Fuels

The composition of motor fuel is governed by the *Motor Fuel (Composition and Content) Regulations 1994*, and the *Marketing of Gas Oil (Sulphur Content) Regulations 1994*. The latter Regulations apply to gas oil used in diesel engined road vehicles (see section 2.13.4).

The lead content of petrol was reduced from 0.40 grammes per litre to 0.15 grammes as from 31 December 1985. In line with EU Directive 85/210/EEC – Directive on the approximation of the laws of the Member States on the lead content of petrol – unleaded petrol is now widely available throughout the UK. This Directive also specifies a benzene level of 5% volume maximum for all petrol marketed from 1 October 1989 (UK levels are between 3-4%).

2.21.2 Construction and Use

The main objectives of *Construction and Use Regulations* are to ensure vehicles are manufactured to high standards, to ensure such standards are maintained while vehicles are in-use; they also implement EU Directives on emission limits and roadworthiness testing.

(a) Use of Unleaded Petrol

The *Road Vehicles (Construction and Use) (Amendment No. 6) Regulations 1988, Motor Vehicles (Type Approval) (Great Britain) (Amendment) Regulations 1988* and *Motor Vehicles (Type Approval for Goods Vehicles) (Great Britain) (Amendment) Regulations 1988* which came into force on 1 October 1988 require that all new vehicles shall be capable of running on unleaded petrol in the 1990s. Implementation dates were 1 October 1989 for new type approvals and 1 October 1990 for existing model types. Special arrangements cover the small number of models that would need major engineering changes to comply.

(b) Compliance with Emission Standards

Under Regulation 61(5) of the *Road Vehicles (Construction and Use) Regulations 1986* it is an offence to use a vehicle if it is emitting "smoke, visible vapour, grit, sparks, ashes, cinders or oily substances" in such a way as is likely to cause "damage to any property or injury or danger to any person".

These Regulations have been amended a number of times. The *Road Vehicles (Construction and Use) (Amendment No. 2) Regulations 1990* which came into force in June 1990 give effect to the various EU Directives on gaseous and particulate emissions mentioned above. The Regulations also require vehicle users to keep engines in tune and any emission control equipment, such as catalysts, working efficiently. 1992 Amendment Regulations implement the emission limits contained in Directives 91/441/EEC and 91/542/EEC relating to cars and heavy duty vehicles, respectively. 1993 and 1997 amendment regulations implement 93/59/EC and 96/69/EC respectively on light commercial vehicles. 1995 amendments implement EU Directive 94/12/EC and introduce new in-service emissions requirements. A further 1997 amendment requires drivers to switch off their vehicle's engine when stationary to prevent exhaust emissions (as well as noise).

(c) Vehicle Testing

The Road Vehicles (Construction and Use) (Amendment) (No. 5) Regulations 1995 (SI 2210) tightened in-service emission requirements for cars and light goods vehicles with effect from 25 September 1995. Petrol engined vehicles first used before 1 August 1975 are tested visually and checks on vehicles first used after this date are by metered test; diesel engined vehicles first used before 1 August 1979 are tested visually and those first used after that date by metered smoke test. The standards which are enforced through Type Approval Regulations and checked at the annual MOT (roadworthiness check for HGVs) and at roadside checks are:

- for petrol engined vehicles first used on or after 1 August 1975 and before 1 August 1986, CO should not exceed 4.5% of the total exhaust emissions by volume and HC 0.12% vol;
- for petrol engined vehicles first used on or after 1 August 1986 and before 1 August 1992, CO should not exceed 3.5% of the total exhaust emissions by volume and HC 0.12% vol;
- diesel fuelled passenger cars and light commercial vehicles (< 3,500 kg) first used before 1 August 1979 – visual assessment;
- all other diesel fuelled vehicles – maximum smoke value (absorption coefficient measured under free acceleration) – 3.0 per metre (turbocharged engines); 2.5 per metre (naturally aspirated engines).

As from 22 April 1996, the latter standards also applied to London taxis; London taxis are tested annually at the Public Carriage Office and have to meet requirements which are equal to those of the MOT.

From 1 January 1996 the following standards (amended by 1996 Amendment Regulations) applied to certain other newer vehicles with advanced emissions control systems (e.g. catalytic converters):

- petrol-engined vehicles first used on or after 1 August 1992 and other vehicles first used on or after 1 August 1994 listed in Department of Transport (now DETR) publication *In-service Exhaust Emission Standards for Road Vehicles* (this is regularly updated) will be required to meet emission limits specified by the manufacturer of the particular model;
- petrol fuelled cars first used on or after 1 August 1992 and other petrol fuelled vehicles first used on or after 1 August 1994, for which no model specific information is given in the DETR publication, CO not to exceed 3.5% vol and HC 0.12% vol;
- petrol fuelled cars first used from 1 August 1995 (1998 amendment Regulations; was 1 August 1994) and other petrol fuelled vehicles first used from 1 August 1996, but for which no model specific

information is given in the DETR publication, CO not to exceed 0.5% vol under normal idling conditions and volume of CO and HC not to exceed 0.3% and 0.02% respectively with engine running between 2500-3000 rpm.

Since 1 August 1997, vehicles with more than five seats (plus the driver) or vans or other vehicles of 3.5 tonnes or less, first used from 1 August 1994 have also been required to meet the standards for vehicles with advanced emission control systems.

For all vehicles the Regulations require that "no excessive smoke" (dense blue or clearly visible black smoke) should be emitted from the exhaust after 5 seconds at idling.

Vehicle owners have 14 days in which to have the necessary repairs carried out and the vehicle rechecked, or face prosecution with a possible fine. Owners who have neglected to maintain their vehicles are prosecuted and face a fine as well as the cost of putting their vehicle right.

2.21.3 Type Approval

Before a new vehicle model is introduced on to the market it must be tested by the Type Approval Authority to ensure it complies with relevant EU Directives. All new vehicles produced must then meet Conformity of Production limits. These are set at 15-30% above type approval limits, depending on the pollutant.

Passenger cars, including three wheeled cars, first used on or after 1 August 1978 (and not manufactured before 1 October 1977) are subject to the *Motor Vehicles (Type Approval) (Great Britain) Regulations 1984* as amended. Goods vehicles are subject to the *Motor Vehicles (Type Approval for Goods Vehicles) (Great Britain) Regulations 1982*, as amended. The main effect of *Type Approval Regulations* is the enforcement of construction requirements and of construction requirements necessitated by EU and other legislation – e.g. to enable compliance with emission limits. Specimen vehicles are tested by the Department of the Environment, Transport and the Regions to ensure compliance with the international standards referred to in *Construction and Use Regulations*. No routine testing of new vehicles for this purpose is carried out under the Regulations.

2.21.4 Petrol Storage and Distribution

EU Directive 94/63/EC "on controlling VOC emissions resulting from the storage of petrol and its distribution from terminals to service stations" has been implemented through an amendment to the *Environmental Protection (Prescribed Processes and Substances) Regulations 1991*; under the 1996 Amendment Regulations (SI 2678), which came into effect on 1 December 1996, certain petrol stations are prescribed for air pollution control as Part B processes under the *Environmental Protection Act 1990*, as are those storage terminals not prescribed for IPC (see also this chapter, 2.12.2). Guidance from the DETR (AQ 6(97)) suggests that "petrol" includes all leaded, unleaded and lead replacement gasoline but excludes diesel motor fuel, kerosene and aviation fuels.

Existing installations (i.e. in operation or for which planning permission had been received before the end of 1995) require an authorisation, depending on annual throughput, by the end of 1998, 2001 or 2004. New service stations with an annual throughput of between 100-500 m^3 in rural areas of Northern Scotland (where vapour emissions are unlikely to have an adverse environmental or health effect) do not require an authorisation.

Proposals for reducing VOC emissions during vehicle refuellings at certain petrol stations (i.e. "Stage II" controls) are under consideration (DETR, March 1997).

2.21.5 Road Traffic Reduction Acts

The *Road Traffic Reduction Act 1997* puts local traffic authorities under a duty to prepare a report assessing local traffic levels and forecast growth; the report must specify targets for reducing local traffic levels or for reducing the rate of growth – these can be different for the different areas within an authority (e.g. specific to congested areas or rural areas). The report must also contain any other information or proposals relating to levels of local traffic or which the Secretary of State may specify in guidance. The Act enables the Secretary of State to issue guidance relating to preparation of the report and on those who should be consulted during its preparation. All reports on traffic levels should be sent to the Secretary of State and published.

The *Road Traffic Reduction (National Targets) Act 1998* requires the Secretary of State to prepare a national traffic plan to include targets for road traffic reduction in England, Scotland and Wales, aimed at reducing the adverse environmental, social and economic impacts of road traffic.

Neither of the above Acts extend to Northern Ireland.

2.21.6 The Road Traffic Regulation Act 1984

This Act enables a local authority to make a traffic regulation order for preserving or improving the amenities of an area through which a road runs. The *Environment Act 1995* amends the Act to ensure that such an order could be made for the purpose of meeting statutory requirements in respect of air quality – see this chapter 2.7.

2.21.7 Road Traffic (Vehicle Emissions) (Fixed Penalty) Regulations 1997 (SI 3058)

These Regulations apply in England, Scotland and Wales and were brought into force on 26 December 1997. For the first twelve months they have applied only in the areas of the following local authorities: Birmingham, Bristol, Canterbury, Glasgow and Westminster City Councils, Middlesbrough Borough Council and the City and County of Swansea. Their application in these authorities is now being reviewed, and if thought appropriate the Regulations will be amended to enable all local authorities to use them.

The Regulations enable authorised officers of a local authority (who have also received training in roadside emissions testing) to test that emissions from a road vehicle comply with regulation 61 of the *Road Vehicles (Construction and Use) Regulations 1986* (as amended), i.e. that they comply with MOT standards. Note, the help of a uniformed police officer will be needed as only they have the right to stop vehicles on the road. The Regulations apply to all vehicle classes, including heavy goods vehicles, public service vehicles, light goods vehicles, taxis and private vehicles. If the vehicle fails the emission test, the local authority officer may issue a fixed penalty notice for £60, increasing to £90 if not paid within 28 days. Drivers have a right to request a court hearing rather than pay the fixed penalty notice.

The Regulations also enable authorised officers of the local authority to issue a fixed penalty notice to drivers who leave their engines running unnecessarily, for example

- while waiting to pick up someone at a railway station;
- while waiting to pick up children from school;
- while waiting for a passenger to run an errand;
- on a coach to power the ventilation, heating or air conditioning system (except while actually picking up or dropping off passengers).

These would all be offences under section 98 of the *Construction and Use Regulations* which requires drivers to switch of their vehicle's engine when stationary to prevent noise emissions; a 1997 amendment to the Regulations extends section 98 to cover exhaust emissions. In this instance the fixed penalty is £20, rising to £40 if not paid within 28 days.

2.21.8 Measurement of Smoke Emissions from Diesel Engined Vehicles

The UK and EU standards for smoke emissions from diesel engined vehicles are based on visual observations of light obscuration. In 1963 the British Standards Institution used a panel of observers to grade vehicle emissions which were measured by smoke meter measurements of light obscuration. The purpose of the test was to define a British Standard which would deal with the problem of the visual appearance of the smoke emissions; the possible implications for health and the environment were not at that time taken into account. The standard established as BS AU 141 and amended to BS AU 141a was made legally binding in the UK *Construction and Use Regulations*. Subsequently an EU Directive, 72/306, based on regulations developed by the United Nations Economic Commission for Europe, was also adopted; the standard was however based on measurement of smoke made by a different smoke meter to that used in the UK. Agreement was reached that BS AU 141a was a satisfactory alternative to the standard of Directive 72/306. These standards apply to new vehicles as constructed. While subsequent performance on the road is subject to legal control governing smoke emission, roadside measurement checks used in other countries such as ECE regulation 24 have been considered unsatisfactory or impracticable for use in the UK.

Since 1 January 1993 (although suspended for technical reasons until 1 February 1994) smoke density from light-duty diesel engined vehicles has been tested by meter while the engine is run at its maximum governed speed.

2.21.9 Steam Road Vehicles

Steam road vehicles – such as traction engines and steamrollers – used on the public highway are not liable to statutory nuisance action under the *Environmental Protection Act 1990*. They are however, subject to the *Road Vehicles (Construction and Use) Regulations*.

2.22 PLANNING POLICY GUIDANCE

Planning Policy Guidance Notes are advice from the Secretary of State to local authorities and others on policies and the operation of the planning system. PPG 13, *Transport*, looks at the needs of all road users (including pedestrians and cyclists), and the way in which land use planning and transport planning can be integrated to make optimum use of the transport system thus reducing the need to use the car, and indeed the length of journeys.

Similar draft guidance for Scotland was published in June 1996 (*National Planning Policy Guidance: Transport and Planning*).

2.23 AIRCRAFT EMISSIONS

Relatively few complaints relating to air pollution at airports are recorded and research so far shows that compared with other domestic, transport and industrial sources, aircraft make a negligible overall contribution to air pollution. However, because pollutants are mainly emitted at high altitudes, where they take longer to disperse, their contribution to global problems (such as ozone depletion and the greenhouse effect) are more serious. This is an area which is now coming under increasing investigation; tighter emission controls in other areas and environmental pressures are likely to have an effect on air traffic movements in the future. In the UK studies are being carried out around various airports to establish levels of pollution.

Fuel combustion in aircraft engines is relatively efficient and jet exhausts are now virtually smoke free. Current jet engines do however produce significant quantities of nitrogen oxides which react with sunlight to form ozone, a greenhouse gas. Other emissions of note from aircraft include carbon monoxide, hydrocarbons, nitrogen dioxide, water, sulphur dioxide and carbon dioxide; according to a 1994 report from the World Wide Fund for Nature, global emissions of carbon dioxide from aircraft may well treble by 2040 on 1990 levels, with improvements in fuel efficiency being offset by increased air traffic. In Sweden, the Government has already decided to impose a tax on nitrogen oxide and hydrocarbon emissions from their domestic airlines. Regulations defining emission limits for smoke and exhaust gases from air traffic have been in force in Switzerland since 1985.

In December 1997, the European Commission published a proposal for a Directive on the limitation of oxides of nitrogen from civil subsonic aeroplanes – COM(97) 629. Although aircraft are thought to be responsible for only about 3% of manmade NOx, they are the only source in the upper troposphere and lower stratosphere and thus they have a disproportionate effect on ozone formation. Action to control emissions is also needed given the forecast increase in air transport movements of about 6% per annum to 2010.

The Directive would apply to aeroplanes fitted with engines of which the date of manufacture of the first production model is after 31 December 1999, or the individual engine manufactured after 31 December 2007. Member States would only be able to add to their Register aeroplanes fitted with engines complying with NOx emission levels meeting the ICAO's Committee on Aviation Environmental Protection's recommendation in December 1995. This, taken together with the ICAO's 1991 Agreement, would require individual aircraft to meet standards which reduced their NOx emissions by 33% compared to the 1986 ICAO Agreement. It is hoped that the draft will be adopted to enable its provisions to come into effect from 31 December 1999.

RADIATION

2.24 INTRODUCTION

Radiation of natural origin has always been present in our environment, and always will be. Natural radioactive materials are present in the earth, in the buildings we inhabit, in the food and water we consume, and in the air we breathe. Even our bodies contain natural radioactivity. Radiation of artificial origin has been used since the beginning of the century. There is no difference between the effects of radiation whether it is emitted from natural or from artificial radioactive materials. Natural radiation accounts for most of the public's exposure (about 86% of the total). Most of the exposure from artificial radiation is due to medical uses (about 14% of the total).

2.25 NATURAL SOURCES OF RADIATION

(a) Cosmic Rays

One part of natural radiation comes from the sun and outer space in the form of cosmic rays. The atmosphere acts as a partial shield against these rays, but those that reach the earth's surface easily penetrate buildings. About 10% of our exposure comes from this source.

(b) Radiation from the Ground and Building Materials

Another part of natural radiation comes from the earth. Soils and rocks contain radioactive materials such as uranium and potassium-40, a radioactive form of the element potassium. Most building materials are extracted from the earth, so these are also somewhat radioactive. About 13% of our exposure comes from this source, principally from building materials, but with a small contribution directly from the ground itself. The level of exposure therefore varies mainly according to the type of building materials used in the construction of houses. Exposures in granite buildings, for instance, are generally higher than those in brick buildings. The overall variation in exposure is as large as the average exposure to radiation of artificial origin.

(c) Internal Exposure

Potassium-40 and other natural radioactive materials (from the ground or produced by cosmic rays in the atmosphere) are present in our diet and thus cause some radiation exposure inside our bodies. About 12% of our exposure arises from these radioactive materials, there being some variation depending on the individual's build and bodily processes.

(d) Radon

Naturally-occurring uranium, present in certain rocks, such as granite, and building materials, produces a gas called radon; it is a colourless, odourless and almost chemically inert gas. A similar gas (thoron) is produced from naturally-occurring thorium, which is also present in rocks and building materials. Together radon and thoron contribute about 50% of total exposure. In the open air, radon is diluted to very low levels and poses no danger. However, it can also seep upwards and become trapped in houses where it can build up to dangerously high concentrations.

The level of exposure received mainly depends on the type of rock underneath homes and how well ventilated they are. When radon is breathed in, it is mainly people's lungs that are exposed to radiation; it is estimated that radon-induced lung cancer may be responsible for around 1,800 deaths in Britain annually – second only to the number of deaths from smoking induced lung cancer.

2.26 ARTIFICIAL SOURCES OF RADIATION

(a) Medical Procedures

Radiation is used in a wide range of diagnostic procedures, as in chest and dental x-rays. Radiation is also used for treatment purposes, for example, in killing off cancerous cells. Actual exposure in any year depends on how many examinations an individual is subjected to, and the type of examination, but an average figure would be 14%.

(b) Fallout

Most tests of nuclear weapons now take place underground. But in the 1950s and early 1960s many tests took place in the atmosphere. Fallout is the term used to describe the radioactive particles that are released and which eventually drop to earth from the atmosphere. This radioactivity can add to the radiation from the ground. It can also be breathed in, and eaten when taken up in food. In the UK, exposure due to fallout from weapons tests is now less than one-tenth of the highest level experienced, which occurred in the mid 1960s.

Some of the radioactivity released by the Chernobyl accident in 1986 was deposited on the UK, the deposition being heaviest in the areas where it was raining at the time that the radioactive cloud passed overhead. Some of this radioactivity was taken up in foodstuffs. In the first year after the Chernobyl accident the total exposure of a typical individual in the UK was increased by about one per cent. Some people might have received increases of up to 40%, depending upon where they lived and what they ate.

Fallout from weapons tests and Chernobyl now contributes about 0.2% of our exposure on average. There are some variations in this average due, for example, to differences in rainfall between areas.

(c) Discharges from the Nuclear Industry

These occur routinely from nuclear power stations and plant that manufacture or reprocess the fuel. On average less than 0.1% (one-thousandth) of total radiation exposure is due to such discharges. Some people will get higher exposures than this if they live near nuclear installations. In some cases, these higher exposures are due to the concentration of radioactivity in locally produced foodstuffs such as shellfish. In the mid-1980s the most exposed individuals were getting up to one-third of their total exposure from the nuclear industry, but by the late 1980s this had fallen to about one-tenth.

(d) Occupational Exposure

This covers workers who deal with radiation in the nuclear power industry, medicine, dentistry, research laboratories and general industry. There are also underground miners and aircrew who are exposed to increased levels of natural radiation. Miners in non-coal mines receive the highest average exposures of all workers. They typically get more than ten times the exposure of a worker in a nuclear power station. Overall, all these workers receive an average additional exposure amounting to nearly 50% of typical total exposure. Averaged out over the whole population, working with radiation contributes about 0.3% of the total population exposure.

(e) Miscellaneous Sources

This covers enhanced cosmic radiation exposure of aeroplane passengers, release of radioactive material through coal burning (mainly in power stations), and consumer products containing small amounts of radioactivity for various purposes (e.g. smoke alarms, and radioluminous watches and clocks). These combined sources are responsible for less than 0.1% of exposure.

2.27 EFFECTS OF RADIATION

If the exposure of the whole body to radiation is very high, death may occur within a matter of weeks. In this context "very high" means about 2000 times higher than a typical annual total exposure. Even if death does not occur, high exposures may soon lead to other effects such as reddening of the skin, cataracts and sterility. These same doses of radiation are given to individual organs in radiotherapy to kill cancer cells and prolong patients' lives.

If the radiation exposure is lower, or is received over a long period of time, immediate effects will not occur, but there may be risks that the exposure will lead to cancer later in life or to hereditary defects in future generations. A small increase in cancers has been observed in a number of population groups exposed to relatively high exposures. For instance, for the survivors of the Hiroshima and Nagasaki bombs, the cancer death rate is about 10% higher than that expected in a similar Japanese population.

For the purposes of controlling exposures it is assumed that the cancer risk increases in proportion to the exposure, even at very low levels of radiation. This is a cautious assumption, and deliberately so. It ignores the possibilities that very low levels of radiation may be incapable of causing damage or that the body may be able to repair any damage caused by low exposures. For the average person, radiation poses a very small risk and most of that risk is due to natural radiation.

2.28 RECOMMENDATIONS ON RADIATION EXPOSURE LIMITS

The basic assumptions about the risks from radiation exposure given in the previous section have led the International Commission on Radiological Protection (ICRP) to state three key recommendations for radiation protection. ICRP is the principle standard setting body for radiation protection and many countries throughout the world, including the UK, have adopted their recommendations. Their three key recommendations formulated in 1990 are:

a) *Justification:* no practice involving exposures to radiation should be adopted unless it produces sufficient benefit to the exposed individuals or to society to offset the radiation detriment it causes.

b) *Optimisation:* radiation doses and risks should be kept as low as reasonably achievable, economic and social factors being taken into account; constraints on risk or dose should be used to provide upper bounds to the optimisation process.

c) *Limits:* the exposure of individuals should be subject to dose or risk limits above which the radiation risk would be unacceptable.

All of these recommendations apply to all sources of radiation, except that exposure to normal levels of natural radiation and exposure due to medical practices are not subject to exposure limits, and thus only the first two recommendations should be applied. For example, public exposure due to both routine discharges of radioactivity to the environment and solid radioactive waste disposal is constrained by the application of all three principles. It should be noted that it is not sufficient merely to comply with the limits placed on exposure. The second principle ensures that efforts will be made to keep exposures well below these limits.

Nothing can sensibly be done about normal levels of exposure from natural radiation. But human activities can result in increased exposure to natural radiation. Examples of this include flying at high altitude resulting in elevated exposure to cosmic rays, and living in a house where there is a high concentration of radon. Where control of such exposures is feasible, it is given full consideration. This is the case with the relatively high levels of radon exposure which occur in some parts of the UK. Government-funded surveys are being carried out to identify buildings with high radon concentrations.

The National Radiological Protection Board has set an "action level" of 200 Bq m^{-3} average annual concentration above which it recommends measures to exclude radon from houses. Current estimates are that more than 1 in 100 homes in Cornwall, Devon, Somerset, Northamptonshire and Derbyshire are above this recommended action level – 80% of England's radon-affected homes are in these counties; the remaining 20% are in Avon, Cumbria, Dorset, Gloucestershire, Leicestershire, Lincolnshire, Northumberland, North Yorkshire, Nottinghamshire, Oxfordshire, Shropshire, Staffordshire and Wiltshire.

In new buildings seepage can be prevented by the use of suspended concrete floors. In existing buildings, such measures may involve improved underfloor ventilation by the installation of a fan and sealing of the floor to prevent the upward flow of radon gas. Home improvement grants are available towards the cost of carrying out remedial work, although these are strictly means-tested. With regard to new buildings in radon-affected areas, the Department of Environment (now Department of the Environment, Transport and the Regions) has produced a guidance document – *Building Regulations 1985 – Part C: Radon. Interim Guidance on Construction of New Dwellings* (1988). (The 1985 Regulations have now been consolidated and replaced by 1991 Regulations.)

The National Radiological Protection Board carries out scientific research on radiation hazards and advises the Government on whether or not recommendations made by bodies such as the ICRP should be applied in the UK. It provides information and advice about radiation protection to UK government departments and other interested parties.

2.29 REGULATORY CONTROLS

In the UK several government departments have responsibility for protecting the public from radiation exposure. No significant amount of radioactive waste can be discharged without a specific authorisation from the Environment Agency or the Scottish Environment Protection Agency (as appropriate). Discharges from major nuclear sites in England also require authorisation from the Minister of Agriculture, Fisheries and Food. The Secretaries of State for Scotland and Wales grant authorisations within their respective countries. The Department of the Environment is the regulatory body for Northern Ireland. Authorisations specify discharge limits, and inspectors check that the conditions of the authorisations are adhered to. Unless the level of discharge is extremely small, this includes a requirement to monitor the local environment (see chapter 4).

2.29.1 Ionising Radiations Regulations 1985 (SI 1333)

Responsibility for the control of radiation hazards at work falls on the Health and Safety Commission supported by the Health and Safety Executive which employs inspectors to enforce the *Ionising Radiations Regulations 1985* (made under the *Health and Safety at Work Act 1974*). These provide protection for the workforce from ionising radiations, including the handling and storage of radioactive waste; exposure to radiation must be kept as low as reasonably practicable, whether the source is artificial (e.g. nuclear reactor) or naturally occurring (e.g. radon). A schedule to the Regulations sets out the annual dose limits which should not be exceeded for both occupational exposure and exposure of the general public. The dose limits were prescribed in a 1980 Euratom Directive. The UK Regulations require continuous monitoring to be carried out and employers must make an assessment of the potential radiation hazard in the event of a possible accidental release or other accident.

As a result of recommendations from the ICRP, in May 1996 the European Union's Council of Ministers formally adopted Directive 96/29 "laying down the basic safety standards for the protection of the health of workers and the general public against dangers arising from ionising radiation"; the Directive must be formally implemented by 13 May 2000. The new limits are:

- nuclear and other industry employees: whole body – 50 mSv per year (but should not exceed 100 mSv over five years); hands, feet, etc – 500 mSv per year. These limits may be exceeded only in "exceptional circumstances";
- apprentices and students aged 16-18 working with dangerous materials: whole body – 6 mSv; hands, feet etc – 30% of adult limit;

- pregnant women: exposure to be as low as reasonably achievable and not to exceed 1 mSv over pregnancy;
- general public: whole body – 1 mSv a year; a higher limit may be authorised in a particular year so long as average exposure over 5 years does not exceed 1 mSv.

The 1985 Regulations are currently being amended to reflect the new limits; the Regulations will also require employers conducting certain types of work to obtain prior authorisation from the HSE, and to be able to justify new types of practice. The HSE is also preparing an Approved Code of Practice and Guidance to accompany the new Regulations.

2.29.2 Public Information for Radiation Emergencies Regulations 1992 (SI 2997)

These Regulations which came into force on 1 January 1993 implement Euratom Directive 89/68. Members of the public within an area from which it is reasonable to foresee the possibility of a radiation emergency should receive certain information, such as what to do in the event of an accident. The company carrying out the work is required to prepare this information and ensure its dissemination. In addition, county and regional councils must prepare and keep up to date arrangements which ensure that members of the public actually affected by a radiation emergency receive prompt and appropriate information. This information should cover facts of the emergency and advice on health protection measures.

CONTROL OF PROCESS ODOURS

2.30 INTRODUCTION

Complaints to local authorities about odour constitute a significant proportion of total complaints received. For the year 1996/97, the Chartered Institute of Environmental Health reports that there were 15,264 (1995/96: over 19,000) complaints of smell from industrial processes in England and Wales. A further 7,378 (1995/96: 9,005) complaints concerned agricultural practices, including slurry spreading and storage, and the keeping of livestock. Animal by-product plants are a serious source of odour pollution, particularly for people living near them. These plants process animal waste from abattoirs, other animal and meat processing and rendering plants etc, into products such as tallow, bonemeal and animal feedstuffs. The handling, storage and cooking of the raw waste material can give rise to particularly difficult odour control problems.

2.31 PROCESS ODOUR COMPOSITION

It is usual to describe the odour by the nature of the process causing it but process odours, especially where animal or vegetable matter is heated, are often complex mixtures in air of many substances present at very low concentrations. These substances may be individually malodorous and will occur with large numbers of other compounds including hydrocarbons which cause little or no odour response. Recent years have seen the development of techniques for the sampling and analysis of such mixtures containing perhaps only parts per million (ppm) or even parts per billion (ppb) quantities in air.

Analysis of the process odour is likely to involve pre-concentration on an adsorbent and then separation on a gas chromatographic column, followed by identification of the separated components. The most positive and comprehensive method of identification is a combined gas chromatograph-mass spectrometer linked to a computer-based data system. If part of the flow of separated components is delivered to an "odour port", then the odour, if any, of each component can be described.

2.32 ODOUR PROPERTIES AND EFFECTS

Most complaints about odour relate to annoyance about smells caused by emissions from a factory or farm reducing enjoyment of homes and gardens or making working conditions unpleasant. It is now appreciated that annoyance is the combined result of a number of odour properties.

Odour intensity is the strength of the perceived odour sensation and depends in a complex way on the concentration of the odorous substances present. It can be measured by comparison with reference samples but often an alternative measure of odour strength, the dilution to threshold value, is determined.

Odour character is the property that enables one to distinguish between different odours and it is said that an odour with a distinct recognisable character tends to be more annoying.

The acceptability – or "hedonic tone" – of an odour is an important factor in judging whether or not it is offensive or a nuisance. Not only the nature of the odour is taken into account (whether it is pleasant or unpleasant), but also its intensity, time and duration of release. It should also be borne in mind that a normally "pleasant" odour becomes less acceptable when exposed to it frequently; for example, a "pleasant" odour from a fragrance factory may be unacceptable if persistent in a residential area.

2.33 REGULATORY CONTROLS

2.33.1 Odour as a Statutory Nuisance

Prior to the *Environmental Protection Act 1990*, nuisance from odour was controlled through the nuisance provisions of the *Public Health Act 1936* (ss. 91-100). In order for an odour to constitute a statutory nuisance it had to be either prejudicial to health or a nuisance. The Act provided a defence of Best Practicable Means which allowed a defendant to prove that the accumulation or deposit was necessary for the effective carrying out of business, and that the BPM was used to prevent the odour being prejudicial to health or a nuisance to the neighbourhood.

Local authorities had a duty to carry out periodic inspections of their areas in order to detect any matters needing to be dealt with under the statutory nuisance and offensive trades provisions, and if satisfied that a statutory nuisance existed could serve a notice requiring steps to be taken to abate the nuisance. The notice could be enforced by order in a Magistrates' Court. If a nuisance had occurred on the premises in the past and was felt likely to recur, the local authority could serve a prohibition notice under section 1 of the *Public Health (Recurring Nuisances) Act 1969*.

Under the *Environmental Protection Act 1990* those sections of the *Public Health Act 1936* dealing with statutory nuisance were repealed, together with the whole of the *Public Health (Recurring Nuisances) Act 1969*. The "offensive trades" provisions of the PHA 1936 were repealed in 1995. Statutory nuisance legislation is now covered by Part III of the EPA (see chapter 1, 1.15.1).

2.33.2 Environmental Protection Act 1990

Many of the main sources of odour complaint – e.g. animal and plant treatment processes – will, however, be prescribed processes under Part I of the EPA; as such they must have an authorisation from their local authority (from 1.4.96, SEPA in Scotland – *Environment Act 1995*) who are responsible for air pollution control under the Act. Although prescribed processes which release a prescribed substance in "trivial" amounts do not need an authorisation, where this results in an offensive smell outside the premises, then an authorisation will be required (see chapter 2, 2.11.2).

2.34 SENSORY MEASUREMENTS (OLFACTOMETRY)

In recent years, increasing use has been made of odour strength measurements, determined as dilution to threshold values. Samples of the odorous air are diluted with odour-free air until the observers (panellists) cannot detect any odour. The dilution to threshold value might be taken as the dilution required to obtain a negative response from 50% of the panellists. Various forms of olfactometer have been developed for presenting a continuously diluted sample to the panellists ("dynamic dilution").

Odour strength measurements have a number of practical uses. Measurements in the ambient air can be used to locate odour sources and to study their distribution in the community. The different operations in a factory can be investigated to determine which contribute most to the total odour emission rate with a view to possible process changes. Where abatement equipment has been installed, measurements of odour strength on inlet and outlet samples show the efficiency of odour removal. A knowledge of the dilution to threshold value together with the volume flow rate can also be used to estimate the maximum distance over which the process emission is likely to cause complaints, and hence to indicate the removal efficiency required from abatement equipment.

2.35 GENERAL CONTROL METHODS

There are various ways in which the nuisance caused by process odours can be minimised or eliminated. Here we outline some of the principles involved in various odour abatement techniques; there is however a large amount of published information on process odour control and this section therefore provides an overview on the subject.

(a) Process and Plant Changes

This is taken to mean not only changes in operating parameters but also improved facilities and procedures for the storage and handling of raw materials, products and waste; better buildings may encourage good housekeeping and should confine the process air so that it does not escape to the surrounding community before any treatment required. Plant in the open may require special attention to eliminate potential leakage points by better maintenance or re-design. Where biodegradable material is being stored in the open in heaps or lagoons or spread on the land, the practices involved may need to be reviewed.

(b) Dilution by the Atmosphere

Dilution in air, so that the concentration of the malodorous compounds in the process emission are reduced below their detection thresholds is, in principle, another method of avoiding local complaints. This may be achieved by siting a new plant well away from housing etc but future housing developments may nullify the initial benefit of an isolated site. Alternatively, sufficient atmospheric dilution may sometimes be achieved by discharging the untreated process gases through a stack of suitable height. Of course, the variability of meteorological conditions is such that stack dispersion alone is not a totally dependable method for avoiding all complaints.

The first step is to calculate the required stack height in the absence of any abatement equipment; the calculation will be complicated by the presence of other buildings and local topography. In practice, this height could well prove excessive (either visually or in cost terms) and then the target efficiency for abatement equipment must be calculated so that discharge at an acceptable height is only required as the final stage of odour control.

(c) Odour Modification

This involves the addition of other chemicals which modify a person's response to the process odour because of changes in the perceived odour intensity (counteraction) or the perceived odour quality (masking). They are well known for indoor applications where they are dispersed as aerosol sprays, or evaporated from wick or gel-type dispensers. For process odour control, the odour modifier may be sprayed into stack emissions; if incorporated into the process, the modifier must be capable of withstanding the process conditions. The selection of odour modifiers and the dispensing rate would seem to be critical and the modifier should never prevent the perception of toxic or harmful substances.

2.36 ODOUR TREATMENT

It is often necessary to treat the process gases before discharge by one or more abatement techniques. Such techniques include thermal or catalytic incineration, absorption in chemical reagent solutions, adsorption on carbon and biological oxidation. All are considered to offer 90-99% efficiency although the use of recycling and clean technologies are likely to become increasingly important methods of solving odour problems. (*Odour Measurement and Control – an Update*, AEA Technology, NETCEN, 1994)

(a) Incineration

Effective odour control can usually be achieved by raising the process emission to a sufficiently high temperature for an appropriate length of time; this oxidises the malodorous compounds present to carbon dioxide and water, plus the small amounts of the oxides of sulphur and nitrogen which have little odour. The design of thermal afterburners has been the subject of extensive study and it is now better appreciated that odour destruction requires considerable temperatures, typically 650-

800 degrees Centigrade, good mixing (in, say, 0.3-0.5 s) to ensure that all the process gases reach the required temperature and then adequate time to allow completion of the oxidation reactions (say, 0.1-0.3 s). Specific temperatures and residence times have been designated by some statutory bodies, e.g. some US States require animal rendering emissions to be incinerated at 650 degrees Centigrade for at least 0.3 seconds.

A major disadvantage when treating large volumes (often containing little combustible material) can be the cost of fuel; three approaches have been adopted to lower operating costs: heat recovery, the use of an existing boiler (or kiln), or the incorporation of a catalyst. In practice, feeding the malodorous air stream to an existing boiler, even when the required temperature is apparently achieved, may be unsatisfactory because of poor mixing, insufficient residence time, corrosion etc.

Catalytic incineration may provide effective odour control at 350-400 degrees Centigrade, thereby saving perhaps 40-60% on fuel costs compared with thermal incineration but partly offset by higher capital and catalyst replacement costs. Catalytic incineration is unsuitable for process emissions containing catalyst poisons which cannot be economically removed or where the catalyst surface is liable to become blocked with particulates or polymeric material.

(b) Absorption in Reagent Solutions

Transfer of the malodorous compounds from the process air stream to the liquid phase is often the best method for treating large air flows using, for example, an absorption tower. Water is the usual liquid but commonly a chemical reagent is added to increase the transfer efficiency and the capacity of the liquid phase. The complexity of many process emissions such as those arising from the heat treatment of animal or vegetable matter, means that in practice a number of separate absorption stages with different reagents may be required. The specification of suitable chemical reagents for each particular application can be a problem.

(c) Adsorption on Activated Carbon

The principle involved is the removal of the malodorous compounds by adsorption on the carbon as the air being treated passes through the carbon bed. The use of activated carbon for solvent recovery is well known and is also the basis of many indoor systems, e.g. to treat domestic and restaurant odours. In treating process odours, activated carbon may be the primary abatement method, or placed after other abatement equipment to improve overall efficiency.

(d) Biological Treatment

Biological towers are similar in principle to packed absorbers except that odour removal is achieved by the use of micro-organisms grown on an inert packing rather than by chemical reagent solutions sprayed over the packing. The biological tower may be started up with a mixture of activated sewage sludge and nutrient solutions. An alternative form of biological treatment is where the odorous air is passed through a bed of soil, peat or compost. The mechanism of odour removal is believed to involve the dissolution of the odorants and oxygen in water followed by their reaction under the influence of enzymes, generated by, or forming part of, the micro-organisms.

NOISE

GENERAL NEIGHBOURHOOD NOISE

3.1 INTRODUCTION

In its widest sense, neighbourhood noise might be defined as any unwanted sound in the vicinity of the home or its locality. That definition might embrace industrial noise, noise from transport, as well as noise from domestic premises, which is the biggest source of noise nuisance and complaints. During 1996/97 there were 242,181 separate complaints about noise made to environmental health departments in England and Wales (1994/95: 217,179); this figure breaks down into 173,436 relating to noise from domestic premises; 50,636 from industrial and commercial premises; 3,407 complaints about noise in the street; 8,065 about construction noise; and 6,637 complaints about noise from vehicles, machinery and equipment in streets (Chartered Institute of Environmental Health, Environmental Health Report 1996/97). In Scotland, environmental health departments received nearly 8,000 complaints in 1996/97, with noise from industrial and commercial premises providing the biggest source of complaint, followed by domestic premises (DETR, *Digest of Environmental Statistics*, No. 20, published 1998).

The noise which affects people in the home varies according to the situation, and accepted habits and customs. Country dwellers expect to be far freer of industrial and traffic noise than city dwellers; they will accept some agricultural machinery noise although devices such as bird scarers (particularly when situated close to houses and left to operate throughout the night) can be obtrusive. However, country dwellers may also be affected by noisy, large-scale operations such as quarrying and open-cast mining. Usually, the noise implications of such developments are considered at the planning stage and conditions governing noise levels and methods of operation are attached to the planning consent.

In towns, traffic noise is usually inescapable, and to an extent it is tolerated as inevitable. Noise generated by long-established industrial or commercial operations will similarly be tolerated by long standing residents in the vicinity, although problems arise when houses or flats change hands: newcomers are usually more sensitive to the noise and more likely to find it stressful. On the other hand, newcomers can change the character of an area and the types and levels of noise in it: for example when there is an influx of students. Most people now have domestic appliances of one sort or another, sophisticated audio systems or do-it-yourself tools; all of these can cause a nuisance if used at unsocial hours or at high volume; problems may also arise or be exacerbated by inadequate sound insulation. In some instances action under statutory nuisance legislation may be necessary; in others changes in furnishings – e.g. wall to wall carpeting – can lessen the effect to some extent. Part E of Schedule 1 of the *Building Regulations 1991* specifies that floors and walls between new built houses and flats and buildings where there is a material change of use (e.g. flat conversions) should have reasonable resistance to airborne and impact sound. *Approved Document E – Resistance to the Passage of Sound* describes ways of meeting the requirements, with examples of widely used "satisfactory" constructions and test results. Similar Regulations, the *Building Standards (Scotland) Regulations 1990*, apply in Scotland; Part H to the Regulations deals with resistance to transmission of sound.

Legislative controls on noise pollution are of more recent origin than controls on other forms of pollution. Prior to the *Noise Abatement Act 1960* noise was largely dealt with locally as a nuisance and under local bye-laws. Under the 1960 Act, noise became a statutory nuisance for the purposes of the *Public Health Act 1936*, thus enabling local authorities to take action for noise nuisance, under a procedure not unlike current procedures for statutory nuisance.

The 1960 Act also introduced a complaints procedure whereby private individuals could take action: the Act required that three or more people, each of whom occupied land or premises affected by the noise nuisance, could complain direct to a magistrate. The "three neighbour rule" was to deter malicious and frivolous complaints. However this rule was not carried forward to either the *Control of Pollution Act 1974* or the *Environmental Protection Act 1990*; under both of these only one person need be affected for action to be initiated for statutory nuisance.

The 1960 Act was repealed by the *Control of Pollution Act 1974*, Part III. As well as dealing with statutory noise nuisance, it introduced provisions relating to noise from construction sites, street noise, the setting up of noise abatement zones and on drawing up codes of practice on specific noise problems (e.g. burglar alarms). The sections dealing with statutory noise nuisance have been repealed and re-enacted in the *Environmental Protection Act 1990*; in England and Wales this change took effect on 1 January 1991 and in Scotland on 1 April 1996 (see chapter 1, 1.15). The *Noise and Statutory Nuisance Act 1993* provides local authorities in England, Scotland and Wales with powers to control noise nuisance emitted from vehicles, machinery or equipment in the street – see below 3.7. The *Noise Act 1996* enables local authorities in England, Wales and Northern Ireland to make night-time noise nuisance a criminal offence and provides powers to confiscate noise-making equipment – see 3.8 below.

Later sections of this chapter cover the controls available to deal with noise from neighbours, entertainment noise, industrial and construction site noise, transport and occupational noise.

3.2 THE EUROPEAN UNION AND NOISE POLLUTION

3.2.1 Fifth Action Programme (1993-2000)

The Commission's Fifth Action Programme on the Environment, *Towards Sustainability* – (see also Appendix 6) proposes a number of measures aimed at reducing people's exposure to night-time noise. The Commission's targets are that

- exposure to more than 65 dB(A) should be phased out and at no time should 85 dB(A) be exceeded;
- those exposed to levels of between 65-55 dB(A), and those currently exposed to less than 55 dB(A), should not suffer any increase.

To achieve these levels the Commission proposes noise abatement programmes; standardisation of noise measurement and rating; Directives further reducing noise from transportation; measures related to infrastructure and planning (e.g. better zoning around airports, industrial areas, main roads and railways).

The World Health Organisation suggests that daytime noise levels of below 50 d(B)A L_{eq} cause little annoyance and it recommends a daytime level of 55 d(B)A L_{eq} for outside noise in residential areas; its recommendation for undisturbed sleep is 35 d(B)A L_{eq} (*Environmental Health Criteria 12, Noise*, WHO, 1980).

3.2.2 Green Paper on Noise Pollution

Published in November 1996, the Commission's Green Paper (COM(96) 540) recognises that current measures for reducing people's exposure to unacceptable levels of noise – particularly traffic noise – are not enough. Although recognising that noise is essentially a local issue, the Commission suggests that there are a number of areas where a Community-wide approach (such as harmonisation of measurement methods) is needed. The night-time noise level targets of the Fifth Action Programme are also reaffirmed.

To date, most action in this area has related to fixing maximum sound levels for road and air transport. As well as suggesting that noise from these sources (and from rail too) should be further reduced, the Green Paper proposes

- mapping to assess noise climate and noise exposure;
- common noise exposure index to be used throughout Europe (L_{Aeq}) to enable comparability of noise data;
- development of harmonised measurement methods for environmental noise sources;
- exchange of comparable information on noise exposure between Member States;

- a framework for the assessment of environmental noise;
- provision of information on noise exposure to the public;
- possible agreement on a limited number of minimum noise target values, with an obligation to take action to meet them.

3.2.3 Noise Control Directives

As in other areas of environmental policy, the European Union (EU) has adopted a number of Directives aimed at reducing noise in the environment, which the UK must implement. These include maximum permitted noise levels for motor vehicles (cars, trucks, buses, motorcycles and agricultural tractors) – see 3.14 below, and subsonic jet aircraft – see 3.16 below. A Directive relating to noise exposure at work was implemented in 1990 through Regulations under the *Health and Safety at Work Act 1974* (see 3.20.1 below).

A number of Directives establish maximum noise levels for different types of machinery and equipment, including construction machinery and lawn mowers. The aim is to reduce the noise level of individual machines and thus bring about an overall reduction in neighbourhood noise. In February 1998, the Commission published a proposal for a new Directive relating to the noise emission of equipment used outdoors – COM(98) 46. This Directive will eventually repeal all the existing Directives covering noise from outdoor equipment. As well as introducing consistent noise emission requirements, the Directive also aims to reduce overall noise exposure to and nuisance from outdoor equipment, thus protecting citizens' health and well-being. The Directive will require manufacturers to guarantee that the noise level of a product conforms to the specific level for that category of equipment, and for a label confirming this to be affixed to it. The Directive would enter into force 12 months after adoption, with implementation required a further 24 months later; noise limit values would then be reduced again after a further six years.

The Commission is also drafting a proposal for a Directive on Ambient Noise Exposure Assessment. The purpose of the Directive would be to establish a harmonised procedure for assessing ambient noise exposure (ANE), to ensure that information on ANE is available to the public, and to introduce measures to reduce ANE; the proposal is expected to relate to ANE in urbanised areas, areas along traffic (road, rail and aircraft) routes and around industrial installations.

A list of Directives and other EU measures relating to noise is at Appendix 6.3. Brief details of the institutions of the EU and of the legislative process are given in Appendix 6.

3.3 IMPLEMENTATION AND ENFORCEMENT AUTHORITIES

Much of the responsibility for practical action to prevent or abate noise rests with local authorities and in particular environmental health departments under the general direction of central government departments.

At central government level, responsibility for noise control is shared among a number of departments. The Department of the Environment, Transport and the Regions is responsible for the control of noise from fixed sources, the use of planning control to prevent noise problems, and general noise nuisance questions; it also deals with legislation and policy on road traffic noise and noise from civil aircraft. Occupational noise is the responsibility of the Health and Safety Commission and its operational arm, the Health and Safety Executive.

The police, while having no specific powers to deal with noise nuisance, provide some support to environmental health officers and other officials in carrying out their duties; they also have powers to noise-test road vehicles.

Guidance drawn up by the Chartered Institute of Environmental Health and the Association of Chief Police Officers – *Good practice guidance for police and local authority cooperation* – was published by the CIEH in February 1997. This provides guidance on what is considered as a minimum standard of cooperation between the police and LAs when dealing with noise complaints. It sets out the roles and responsibilities of each and gives examples of effective local liaison arrangements. It suggests that both local authorities and the police in each area should draw up an agreement covering liaison which includes:

- their respective responsibilities and powers relating to noise;
- their respective response criteria – LAs in dealing with out of hours complaints, and the police on dealing with complaints received in the control room;
- resources available – LAs in dealing with out of hours complaints and extra resources which could be made available; support which police can provide where risk of threat or assault;
- the circumstances in which the LA would require police assistance, with the police providing contact points for requesting assistance;
- the chain of command and level at which the police and the LA should make contact.

The CIEH has also published (1997) *Noise Management Guidance for Local Authorities*. As well as providing guidance on noise control policies, this guidance aims to encourage consistency in the way local authorities deliver noise control services, while still enabling them to respond to local circumstances and needs.

3.4 PLANNING CONTROLS

Effective use of planning controls and related guidance will go a long way towards preventing many noise-related nuisances arising in the first place. Before any development can take place, planning permission under the *Town and Country Planning Act 1990* (Scotland – 1972 Act) must be obtained. In some cases an environmental impact assessment may be required (see also chapter 1, 1.21-1.23). In either case noise will be one of the criteria to be considered.

The *Town and Country Planning General Development Order 1988* permits the use of a specific site for an activity (e.g. clay pigeon shooting, helicopter landing site) for up to 28 days a year without the need for planning permission. There is no limit as to the amount of shootings or number of take-offs and landings in any one day.

3.4.1 Planning Policy Guidance

Planning Policy Guidance: Planning and Noise (PPG 24, 1994) replaced the 1973 *Planning and Noise Circular* (10/73); it builds on the principles established in the earlier circular and suggests new mechanisms and guidelines for local authorities to adopt. General principles of how noise should be taken into account in the planning process are suggested, including the need for special attention to be given to proposed developments which could affect "quiet enjoyment" of areas of outstanding natural beauty, national parks etc. Examples of planning conditions are given and the various statutory and other noise controls listed. The PPG deals with noise from road traffic; aircraft; railways; industrial and commercial developments; construction and waste disposal sites; sporting, entertainment and recreational activities; and mixed noise sources. An Appendix to the PPG lists four categories of noise exposure for the assessment of new residential developments near a noise source. The categories are:

- A: noise need not be considered as a determining factor in granting planning permission, although the noise level at the high end of the category should not be regarded as a desirable level;
- B: noise should be taken into account when determining planning applications and, where appropriate, conditions imposed to ensure an adequate level of protection against noise;

- C: planning permission should not normally be granted. Where it is considered permission should be given, for example because there are no alternative quieter sites available, conditions should be imposed to ensure a commensurate level of protection against noise;
- D: planning permission should normally be refused.

For each of these categories the PPG recommends limits for both day (0700-2300) and night (2300-0700) time exposure for new dwellings which it is planned to develop near one of the following existing noise sources – road traffic, rail traffic, air traffic, or mixed source. Recommended exposure limits for category A are considerably lower than for category D.

3.4.2 British Standard 4142

BS 4142, which was last revised in 1995, describes a "Method for Rating Industrial Noise Affecting Mixed Residential and Industrial Areas" and is thus of particular use when considering planning applications. It can be used to determine the likelihood of a complaint from an industrial source under normal operating conditions using a mixture of calculations and measurements, including measurement of background noise levels. It can be used to assess noise levels from both existing and new or modified premises in the vicinity of existing housing. BS 4142 has no legal status as it has not been approved under section 71 of COPA.

REGULATORY CONTROLS ON NEIGHBOURHOOD NOISE NUISANCE

The principal legislative controls on excessive noise in and around the neighbourhood are:

- the *Environmental Protection Act 1990, Part III* which deals with noise as a statutory nuisance;
- the *Control of Pollution Act 1974, Part III* covers construction site noise and certain noise in the street;
- the *Noise and Statutory Nuisance Act 1993* which as well as amending the EPA and COPA also covers noise emitted from vehicles or equipment on the street, and burglar alarms.
- the *Noise Act 1996* makes certain night-time noise a criminal offence and provides powers to confiscate noise-making equipment.

3.5 GENERAL NOISE NUISANCE

Anyone living in the United Kingdom has a legal right to be protected against noise nuisance. Nuisance itself may be defined as "an unlawful interference with a person's use or enjoyment of land or of some right over, or in connection with it". Nuisance at law is a tort, i.e. a civil wrong, for which courts can provide a remedy, usually damages. In any action for noise nuisance the key factors are the need for an aggrieved person to establish that his occupation of land or property is affected by noise, and that each case will be considered on its merit.

General noise nuisance may be dealt with under sections 79-81 of the *Environmental Protection Act 1990* (as amended), which empowers local authorities to deal with noise from fixed premises: factories, shops, discos and dwellings. Individuals may take action under section 82 (see chapter 1, 1.15.1). Excessive noise from council dwellings can often be dealt with as a breach of tenancy agreement where this includes a clause restricting noise, and the tenants taken to court. The *Housing Act 1996* also enables both private and council landlords to evict tenants for anti-social behaviour – e.g. for causing a nuisance.

Minor noise nuisance is often restricted by local authority bye-laws, which the local authority enforces (although an individual may also prosecute). Bye-laws can be used to control such noise sources as: noisy conduct at night; noisy street trading; noisy animals; loud music; radios, television and other audio equipment; seaside pleasure boats; model aircraft; fireworks. Other regulations cover the use of loudspeakers and chimes.

It is also worth drawing attention to the use of independent mediation services as a means of solving neighbour noise disputes where a statutory noise nuisance has not been established. The Department of Environment (now DETR) has published an information paper (November 1994) on when mediation may be an option for dealing with noise and other disputes; in many cases mediation can be a quicker and more cost-effective way of tackling a range of neighbour nuisance disputes at an early stage and thus avoiding formal action. It should be reiterated that mediation is not a substitute for formal action where a statutory nuisance has been established: in such instances an abatement notice must be issued.

Scotland

In addition to the *Environmental Protection Act 1990*, action can also be taken under the *Civic Government (Scotland) Act 1982* which covers many aspects of minor (or neighbourhood noise).

Northern Ireland

The control of noise and noise nuisance is regulated under the *Pollution Control and Local Government (Northern Ireland) Order 1978* and the *Noise Act 1996.*

The 1978 Order enables a noise abatement notice to be served placing a prohibition or restriction on the noise and for an appeal to be lodged against such a notice within 21 days; for noise caused in the course of trade or business, it is a defence to prove that the best practicable means have been used to prevent the noise; the Order also covers construction site noise and the establishing of noise abatement zones and codes of practice.

3.5.1 Environmental Protection Act 1990, Part III

This part of the Act deals with statutory nuisance (including noise) in England, Wales and Scotland. Section 79 of the EPA places a duty on local authorities to require its area to be inspected from time to time to detect whether a statutory nuisance exists; this includes "noise emitted from premises so as to be prejudicial to health or a nuisance". Premises include land and vessels (except those powered by "steam reciprocating machinery") and noise includes vibration. Noise from aircraft other than from model aircraft is excluded. Similar powers to investigate noise in the street are provided through an amendment to section 79 of the EPA in the *Noise and Statutory Nuisance Act 1993* (see below, 3.7.1).

Local authorities must also take such steps as are reasonably practicable to investigate any complaints of statutory nuisance in their area. Where the local authority is satisfied that a statutory nuisance exists, or is likely to occur or recur, it must serve an abatement notice requiring

- the abatement of the nuisance or prohibiting or restricting its occurrence or recurrence; and/or
- the carrying out of such works or other action necessary to abate the nuisance.

Individuals may also take action against statutory nuisance. Information about this, together with details of local authority powers with regard to statutory nuisance are covered in chapter 1, 1.15.1.

3.6 CONTROL OF POLLUTION ACT 1974, PART III

This part of COPA is specifically concerned with the control of noise pollution. Sections 57-59, which covered local authorities' duty to inspect, noise abatement notices and individuals' rights to take action in respect of a noise nuisance were repealed on 1 April 1996. On that date the statutory nuisance provisions of the EPA were extended to Scotland through implementation of section 107 and Sch. 17 of the *Environment Act 1995*.

In Northern Ireland, the *Pollution Control and Local Government (Northern Ireland) Order 1978* covers the same areas as the remaining sections of Part III of COPA.

3.6.1 Construction Sites (ss.60-61)

Construction activities are inherently noisy and often take place in areas which are normally quiet. During 1996/97, environmental health officers in England and Wales received 8,065 complaints relating to construction noise (CIEH Environmental Health Report 1996/97). Section 60 gives local authorities the power to serve a notice imposing requirements as to the way in which construction works are to be carried out.

British Standard 5228, *Noise Control on Construction and Open Sites*, provides guidance to enable compliance with section 60 and is applicable throughout the UK. It is in five parts and includes 1996 codes of practice covering basic information and procedures for noise control, noise control applicable to surface coal extraction by opencast methods, and noise and vibration control applicable to piling operations. The earlier codes of practice which formed part of BS 5228 were approved under section 71 of COPA and approval is to be sought for the revised codes.

Neither COPA nor the related codes of practice set down specific limits for construction site noise, on the basis that the local authority knows its own locality best and would have a better idea of suitable noise limits. The person served with the notice may appeal within 21 days to the Magistrates' Court (Sheriff in Scotland; N. Ireland – Court of Summary Jurisdiction) and is guilty of an offence under the Act if, without reasonable excuse, any requirement of the notice is contravened.

Under section 61, the person intending to carry out works may apply in advance for a consent as to the methods by which the works are to be carried out.

If a local authority does not give consent to a building contractor/developer's own scheme of noise control, the contractor has a right of appeal to the court. Once a consent has been given, the contractor is effectively immune from action on noise grounds taken by the local authority so long as the terms of the consent are complied with.

The activities covered by these sections of the Act are:

a) the erection, construction, alteration, repair or maintenance of buildings, structures or roads;

b) breaking up, opening or boring under any road or adjacent land in connection with the construction, inspection, maintenance or removal of works;

c) demolition or dredging work; and

d) (whether or not also comprised in paras a, b, or c) any work of engineering construction.

Individual occupiers of premises (England, Scotland and Wales) may apply to a Magistrates' Court (Sheriff in Scotland) for an order under section 82 of the *Environmental Protection Act 1990*, on the grounds that the noise from the site nevertheless amounts to a statutory nuisance.

Construction work undertaken by statutory operators (i.e. on behalf of the government) is usually regarded as "emergency" and therefore exempt from COPA. However, in 1990 a local authority in London successfully used section 61, which resulted in homes with an exposure of 65-70 dB(A) being insulated against construction noise caused by work on the Docklands Light Railway.

3.6.2 Noise in Streets (s.62)

Sub-section 62(1) bans the use of a loudspeaker in a street (Scotland – road) between the hours of 9.00 pm and 8.00 am. A loudspeaker includes a megaphone or other amplifying instrument. Under the *Noise and Statutory Nuisance Act 1993* (NASNA), the Secretary of State may vary these times but not so as to permit the use of loudspeakers between these times; additionally, local authorities may adopt powers enabling them to grant a Consent for a loudspeaker to be used later than 9.00 pm but not for advertising or electioneering purposes (see below, 3.7.2).

Under COPA, it is an offence to use loudspeakers in the street at any hour for advertising any entertainment, trade or business. Sub-section 62(2) exempts the emergency services (fire, police, ambulance) as well as the water authorities and local authorities in certain circumstances. Also exempt are loudspeakers on ground being used by pleasure fairs and loudspeakers which form part of a public telephone system.

Vehicles which sell perishable foodstuffs (such as ice-cream) are exempted from this section, but may only use loudspeakers between noon and 7.00 pm; again, the loudspeaker must be operated in such a way as not to give reasonable cause for annoyance to persons in the vicinity. These times may be varied by local authority Consent under the *Noise and Statutory Nuisance Act 1993* – see below, 3.7.2.

This section of COPA has also been successfully used to prosecute motorists with in-car stereo systems played at excessively loud levels. However, at the National Society for Clean Air's Noise Update seminar in September 1998, a representative of DETR said that an amendment to reg. 97 of the *Road Vehicles (Construction and Use) Regulations 1986* was being prepared to make specific reference to noise from equipment such as car steroes and radios.

In 1996/97 local authorities in England and Wales received 3,407 complaints under this section of COPA (CIEH Environmental Health Report 1996/97).

3.6.3 Noise Abatement Zones (ss.63-67)

These sections of the Act are likely to need reviewing in the light of the requirement in the Integrated Pollution Prevention and Control Directive (see chapter 1, 1.12) that noise must be taken into account before granting an operating permit for an industrial installation.

A local authority may designate all or part of its area as a noise abatement zone (NAZ); the purpose of a NAZ is the long-term control of noise from fixed premises in order to prevent any further increases in existing levels of neighbourhood or community noise levels, and to achieve reduction of those levels wherever possible.

An order setting up a NAZ was subject to the confirmation of the Secretary of State, until that provision was repealed by the *Local Government Planning and Land Act 1980*. However, a local authority should still take account of any objections made about the establishment of a NAZ by people within the affected area.

Following the implementation of a noise abatement zone order, the local authority measures noise levels from those types of premises (specified in the order) within the zone (s.64). These are recorded in a register kept by the local authority for the purpose and open to public inspection. Details of methods of measurement and maintenance of the register are given in the *Control of Noise (Measurement and Registers) Regulations 1976.*

Once the noise level has been registered, it may not be exceeded except with the local authority's consent (s.65). Over a period of time, the local authority may seek to achieve a reduction in the initially registered levels of noise by serving a reduction notice under section 66 of the Act, but only if it is satisfied that a reduction is practicable at a reasonable cost and would afford a public benefit. Section 67 empowers the local authority to determine the acceptance level of noise for a proposed new building, which when constructed will be subject to a noise abatement order. Section 68 allows the Secretary of State to make regulations for the reduction of noise covered by plant or machinery, whether or not in a noise abatement zone and section 69 gives the local authority default powers in the case of failure to comply with a noise abatement or noise reduction notice. There is a right of appeal (s.70) to the Magistrates' Court for three months from the date on which a Noise Reduction Notice is served. It is a defence to prove that the best practicable means were used to prevent or counteract the effects of the noise.

While the main benefit of a noise abatement zone is in controlling community noise, and reducing it where possible, without having to prove that the noise amounts to nuisance, it nevertheless remains a little used method of control; this may be because the procedures required by the Regulations for setting up a NAZ are considered cumbersome in practice. In 1990 the Government's Noise Review Working Party (The Batho Report) recommended that the noise testing procedures be simplified to make it easier to set up a NAZ. A 1993 report from the Building Research Establishment confirmed this view but felt a more extensive appraisal was needed. To date there has been no further action.

3.6.4 Codes of Practice (s.71)

This section gives the Secretary of State powers to prepare and approve, and issue codes of practice for minimising noise, or to approve such codes issued by non-government bodies, such as the Code of Practice on the control of noise on construction and demolition sites. This Code (BS 5228) was prepared by the British Standards Institution and originally approved by the Secretary of State in 1975, but has since been revised – see 3.6.1 above.

The Department of Environment (now DETR) has itself issued three codes, all in 1982 (with similar codes in Northern Ireland issued under the 1978 Order):

- Noise from ice cream chimes, etc (limits the use of chimes to between 12 noon and 7.00 pm).
- Noise from burglar intruder alarms (see also below, 3.7.3).
- Noise from model aircraft.

Such codes, although having statutory recognition, do not have the force of regulations, and infringement does not constitute an offence. Non-compliance, however, will usually be taken into account in any proceedings for noise nuisance.

Other Codes

There are a number of other draft and finalised codes of practice which have been prepared by various interest groups which have not received approval under section 71, although some have been submitted for such approval. These codes can, however, be used as guidance in determining what constitutes good practice. Such codes include:

- *Noise from Organised Off-Road Motor Cycle Sport*: prepared by the Noise Council in association with various other bodies (1994);
- *Clay Target Shooting: Guidance on the Management and Control of Noise* (draft): CIEH, Clay Pigeon Shooting Association and the British Shooting Sports Council, 1997; this guidance is intended for use by both those organising shoots or involved in their management, as well as local authorities. It provides practical guidance on the ways in which noise from such shoots can be controlled to minimise or prevent intrusion. A recommended method for noise measurement and subsequent rating, produced by the Building Research Establishment, is also given. Following finalisation it is planned to seek Secretary of State approval of the Guidance as an Approved Code of Practice under COPA.
- *Bird Scarers* (National Farmers Union, 1992; 1997 – code being amended prior to submitting to DETR for approval under COPA): provides advice on siting and use of all types of bird scarers, including audible scarers.
- *Water Skiing and Noise* (British Water Ski Federation, 1996): provides guidance for clubs on avoiding significant impact from noise on surrounding community for both existing and new sites. Method for assessing noise from sites, advice on course layout, hours of operation, screening etc also provided.
- *Environmental Noise Control at Concerts* (Noise Council, 1994): it provides assistance for those planning concerts, for licensing authorities and for local authorities enforcing nuisance legislation. It includes music noise levels for both indoor and outdoor events and single as well as multiple events.
- *Guide to Health, Safety and Welfare at Pop Concerts and Similar Events* (HSE, Home Office, Scottish Office, 1993): this includes guidance on noise levels, covering the risks to health and safety (including noise) both to those at the concerts and to those living near the concert venue.
- *Short Oval Circuit Motor Racing* (NSCA's National Noise Committee, 1996): this covers stock car, hot rod, banger racing and similar events; it aims to help local authorities and organisers to

minimise the noise impact of such events on nearby premises; it also outlines legal controls. This code has been submitted to DETR for approval under section 71 of COPA.

- *Noise from Pubs and Clubs*: being drafted by Institute of Acoustics (1997).

3.6.5 Best Practicable Means (s.72)

The law recognises that there is a limit to what a person may reasonably be required to do or to spend to reduce noise, and also that there may be technical limits on what can be done. The intention is to ensure that, while a firm can be asked to take all reasonable action to control noise, it cannot be faced with disproportionately expensive requirements for remedial action.

It is, therefore, a defence in any summary proceedings relating to noise caused by a trade or business to prove that the Best Practicable Means (BPM) have been used to prevent or counteract the effect of noise. Part III of COPA defines BPM as "reasonably practicable, having regard among other things to local conditions and circumstances, to the current state of technical knowledge and to the financial implications". Means includes "the design, installation, maintenance and manner and periods of operation of plant and machinery, and the design, construction and maintenance of buildings and acoustic structures".

3.6.6 Other Sections

Section 73 deals with the interpretation of some of the terms used in Part III of COPA, and section 74 with penalties for offences under Part III.

3.7 NOISE AND STATUTORY NUISANCE ACT 1993

This Act which, apart from the burglar alarm provisions, came into force on 5 January 1994, covers England, Scotland and Wales. It amends sections 79-82 of the *Environmental Protection Act 1990* to make noise in a street (Scotland – road) a statutory nuisance. Section 62 of COPA dealing with the hours in which loudspeakers may be used is also amended and provision is made for regulating burglar alarms. The Act is enforced by local authorities; the procedure for taking statutory nuisance action and the appeals procedure are outlined in chapter 1, 1.15.1 and 1.15.2.

Department of the Environment, Transport and the Regions Circular (Environment Circular 9/97, WO Circular 42/97) provides guidance to local authorities on implementation of the Act and their duties; it also explains the operational role of the police.

3.7.1 Statutory Nuisance - Noise in Street (ss.2-5)

An additional subsection is added to section 79 of the *Environmental Protection Act 1990* so as to make noise emitted from or caused by a vehicle, machinery or equipment in a street (Scotland – road) a statutory nuisance. This could include, for example, noisy car repairs, car alarms, car radios and parked refrigerator vehicles – in 1996/97 there were 6,637 complaints to local authorities in England and Wales under these sections of the Act (CIEH Environmental Health Report, 1996 & 97). Traffic noise, noise by military forces or from political or other campaigning demonstrations (but not noise or disturbance as result of picketing) is excluded. Having satisfied itself that a statutory nuisance exists or is likely to occur or recur, the local authority must serve an abatement notice; the procedure for this is set out in chapter 1, 1.15.1.

The *Noise and Statutory Nuisance Act 1993* does, however, amend the EPA procedure for serving an abatement notice in respect of a nuisance from or caused by a vehicle, machinery or equipment (VME) on the street; if possible the notice should be served on the person responsible, but if the VME is unattended then the notice may be affixed directly to the VME. The enforcing officer should then spend one hour endeavouring to trace the person responsible for the VME to serve a copy of the notice on them; where the person is found additional time should be allowed before the notice takes effect to enable them to abate the nuisance; if the person cannot be found the enforcing officer may then take the necessary steps to abate the nuisance.

Authorised persons are empowered to gain entry to a vehicle in order to carry out the terms of an abatement notice (e.g. to turn off an alarm); before doing so the police should be notified; the vehicle should be left as secure as before entry or, if this is not possible, should be immobilised or removed to a secure place and the police notified of where it has been taken.

So far as excessively loud car stereos are concerned, an alternative to nuisance action could be use of section 97 of the *Road Vehicles (Construction and Use) Regulations 1986*; this says that "no motor vehicle shall be used on a road in such manner as to cause any excessive noise which could have been avoided" by the use of reasonable care.

3.7.2 Loudspeakers (ss.7-8)

Section 7 of the Act gives the Secretary of State powers to further restrict the hours in which loudspeakers may be used (8.00 am - 9.00 pm) in a street (Scotland – road) under section 62 of COPA (see above, 3.6.2).

Under section 8 local authorities may adopt powers enabling them to grant a Consent for a loudspeaker to be used outside the hours of 9.00 pm and 8.00 am (except for advertising or electioneering). Schedule 2 to the Act sets out the procedure for granting a Consent: anybody wanting to use a loudspeaker at a different time must apply for a Consent specifying the purpose, date, location and duration of use. The local authority must deal with the application within 21 days and may attach any conditions it feels appropriate to the Consent. A charge may be made and the local authority may require details of the Consent to be published in a local newspaper.

3.7.3 Audible Intruder Alarms (s.9)

This section and Schedule 3 of NASNA have not yet been brought into force. They enable a local authority, following consultation with its chief police officer, to resolve that section 9 and Schedule 3 of the Act should apply in its area. The local authority would then be able to impose certain obligations on owners of burglar alarms, including

- audible intruder alarms would need to comply with the requirements of *The Audible Intruder Alarms Regulations* (draft issued Autumn 1995). Audible intruder alarms must be fitted with a device which automatically stops the alarm 20 minutes after it first sounds;
- the local authority to be informed of its installation within 48 hours;
- the police to be notified of names, addresses and telephone numbers of keyholders and the local authority advised at which police station this information is held;
- if the alarm is still sounding after one hour and is "giving reasonable cause for annoyance", the local authority would be empowered to gain entry to the premises to turn off the alarm. If unable to gain entry with the help of a keyholder, the local authority may apply to a magistrate for a warrant to enter by force, having left a notice to this effect at the premises. A police officer should be present if the premises are to be entered by force. The premises should be left secure with a notice saying what has been done. The local authority may recover any reasonable expenses incurred in gaining entry to premises.

The 1982 Code of Practice on Noise from Audible Intruder Alarms (approved under s.71 of COPA) gives guidance on minimising nuisance from faulty alarms. It suggests that alarms should be fitted with a 20 minute cut-out device and that keyholders of properties with alarms should be notified to the police.

It should be noted that in London the *London Local Authorities Act 1991* empowers local authorities to prosecute owners or occupiers of buildings whose audible intruder alarms contravene specified requirements or cause annoyance to people in the vicinity. Burglar alarms must be fitted with a 20 minute cut-out device and owners/occupiers of buildings with intruder alarms must notify their local council that an alarm has been fitted and give the police names and addresses of keyholders. They must also notify the council at which police station this information is held. The Act empowers local authority officers, accompanied by a police officer, to enter a building to deactivate an alarm.

3.7.4 Recovery of Expenses (s.10)

This section of the Act applies in England and Wales only. Its effect is to add two additional sections (81A and 81B) to the *Environmental Protection Act 1990* enabling local authorities to recover expenses incurred in abating a nuisance by placing a charge on the property – see chapter 1, 1.15.1.

3.8 NOISE ACT 1996

This Act, covering England, Wales and Northern Ireland, was introduced into Parliament as a Private Members Bill in February 1996 and received the Royal Assent on 18 July 1996. It deals with noise nuisance – in particular night-time noise – from domestic premises. Sections 2-9 relating to the procedure for dealing with night-time noise nuisance are adoptive – i.e. the local authority must resolve to implement these sections for application in its area; alternatively, the Secretary of State may, by order, require a local authority to implement sections 2-9. Section 10 and the Schedule to the Act – confiscation of noise-making equipment – apply to all local authorities.

The Government has undertaken to review sections 2-9 (both their implementation in practice and the number of local authorities adopting them) within two years of these sections being brought into force (i.e. by 23 July 1999).

Department of the Environment, Transport and the Regions Circular (Environment Circular 8/97, WO Circular 41/97) published July 1997, provides guidance for local authorities on how they should carry out their duties under the Act.

The *Civic Government (Scotland) Act 1982* provides the police in Scotland with powers to abate noise nuisance from, among other things, musical instruments and sound-producing devices; see this chapter 3.10.7.

3.8.1 Night-time Noise Nuisance (ss.2-9)

These sections of the Act were brought into force on 23 July 1997, and could be used from 23 October 1997.

A local authority wishing to adopt these sections of the Act must pass a resolution stating from when the offence is to apply in its area – this should not be less than three months from the date of the resolution. It must publish a notice in a local newspaper on two consecutive weeks ending at least two months before the commencement date. The notice should state that a resolution has been passed, give the commencement date and summarise the effect of the resolution. An order from the Secretary of State requiring implementation of these sections must also allow three months from the date of the order before they are brought into force.

Section 2(6) defines night as 11.00 pm to 7.00 am the following morning. Local authorities have a duty to take reasonable steps to investigate a complaint from an individual about noise being emitted from another dwelling during night hours. Section 2(7) enables a local authority to investigate a complaint about night-time noise from a dwelling outside its area, whether or not these sections of the Act apply in that area. Section 11 defines dwelling as any building or part of a building used or intended to be used as a dwelling, or any garden, yard, outhouse or other appurtenance belonging to or enjoyed with the dwelling.

If it is thought that the noise exceeds, or might exceed, the permitted level as measured within the complainant's dwelling then a warning notice may be served on the person appearing to be responsible for the noise. (Note – it is not a requirement of the Act that the noise should be measured; for instance, there may be circumstances when it is obvious that the noise exceeds the permitted level.)

It should be noted that there may be circumstances that while the noise does not exceed the night-time permitted level, the investigating officer considers that it does constitute a statutory nuisance under section 80 of the *Environmental Protection Act 1990*; in such cases an abatement notice must be served – see chapter 1, 1.15.1a.

If a warning notice is to be served, it should state (s.3(1)) that

- in the opinion of the local authority officer, noise is being emitted during night hours and that the noise exceeds, or might exceed, the permitted level;
- any person responsible for the noise being emitted during the time specified in the notice (beginning 10 minutes after service of the notice until 7.00 am) may be guilty of an offence.

If it is not possible to identify the person responsible for the noise then the notice should be left at the offending dwelling. The notice should state the time at which it was served or left.

The "permitted level" of noise has been set by the Secretary of State in Directions made under section 5; this is 35 dB(A) where the background level does not exceed 25 dB(A) and 10 dB(A) above the background level where this exceeds 25 dB(A); the noise level should be measured over a period of not less than one minute and no more than five. Secretary of State Approval under section 6 of the Act for measuring devices and specifying the manner and purpose for which such devices are to be used came into force on 23 July 1997.

An offence is committed (s.4) if the noise, when measured from inside the complainant's dwelling, continues to exceed the permitted level during the time specified in the warning notice; if convicted the offender will become liable to a fine not exceeding level 3 on the standard scale (currently £1,000). However the local authority authorised officer may, if he thinks that an offence has or is being committed, issue a fixed penalty notice (s.8), set at £100; the offender has 14 days to pay the penalty and in which case will not be prosecuted further. If the noise continues after the fixed penalty notice has been issued, then the local authority officer can prosecute the offender.

3.8.2 Seizure of Noise-making Equipment (s.10)

This section and the schedule to the Act apply where a warning notice has been served and the noise continues to exceed the permitted level; it was brought into force on 23 July 1997. (Section 10(7) clarifies that the powers of a local authority to abate a noise nuisance under s.81(3) of the *Environmental Protection Act 1990* include being able to seize and remove the noise-making equipment; this was brought into force on 19 September 1996 – see chapter 1, 1.15.1a).

A local authority officer, or other authorised officer, may enter the offending dwelling and seize and remove – confiscate – any equipment which it is thought is or has been used to emit noise. If entry is refused, likely to be refused, or request for admission to the dwelling would defeat the object of the entry, the local authority authorised officer may obtain a warrant from a justice of the peace authorising entrance (s.10(4)). The authorised officer may take with him such other people or equipment as is necessary (s.10(5)). Prosecution for obstructing confiscation may result in a maximum fine of £1,000.

The seized equipment may be retained for 28 days or, if court proceedings are instigated, until the case has been dealt with or discontinued. If no court proceedings are begun, then the equipment should be returned to any person who appears to be the owner, or who makes a claim for the equipment within six months of the expiry of the 28 day period. The local authority should take reasonable steps to advise a potential claimant of their right to do so. If no claim is made within six months the local authority may dispose of the equipment.

Equipment seized at the time that a fixed penalty notice has been served under section 8 of the Act may not be retained if the fixed penalty is paid within the allowed period (14 days).

The court may make a forfeiture order if it convicts someone of a noise offence and is satisfied that the seized equipment was actually used for that offence; such an order can be made as the sole means of punishment for the offence. An offender loses all right to the equipment forfeited.

Where equipment has been forfeited, a claimant (other than the offender) may apply to the court within six months of the date of the forfeiture order, if the court is satisfied that

- the claimant had not given the offender permission to use the equipment; or
- did not know, or had no reason to suspect, that the equipment would be used in committing an offence.

If the court is satisfied that the claimant is the owner of the forfeited equipment it will make an order requiring the local authority to deliver the equipment to that person. Local authorities also have a duty to take reasonable steps to bring to the attention of any person entitled to claim the forfeited equipment their right to do so. If the equipment has not been claimed on the expiry of six months from the date of the forfeiture order, the local authority may dispose of it.

Regulations will provide for the retention and safekeeping of any equipment seized and the charges which the local authority may recover. The local authority will be able to keep any equipment until all charges have been paid; a person claiming seized or forfeited equipment will not be liable for charges if the local authority is satisfied that the person did not know and had no reason to suspect that their equipment was likely to be used to commit an offence.

ENTERTAINMENT NOISE

3.9 INTRODUCTION

All public places for music and dancing etc require a licence from the local authority under the *Local Government (Miscellaneous) Provisions Act 1982*. In addition, private events which provide music or dancing or other entertainment and are held for profit or gain require a licence under the *Private Places of Entertainment (Licensing) Act 1967*. In both instances, it is open to the local authority to impose noise limits as a condition of the licence. The nuisance provisions of the *Environmental Protection Act 1990* may also be used in respect of entertainment noise.

Responsibility for enforcement of licence conditions lies with local authorities; infringement, or absence, of a licence may result in a maximum fine of £20,000 and/or imprisonment under the *Entertainment (Increased Penalties) Act 1990* (this does not apply in N. Ireland). If convicted, the *Criminal Justices Act 1988 (Confiscation Orders) Order 1990* empowers Magistrates to confiscate proceeds of an event where these exceed £10,000.

It should, however, be noted that most of the undermentioned legislation can of course be applied to other types of entertainment such as concerts (both classical and contemporary music).

The *Criminal Justice and Public Order Act 1994* enables the police to confiscate sound equipment from illegal raves or gatherings where the music is "wholly or predominantly characterised by ... repetitive beats".

3.10 CONTROL OF NOISY PARTIES

Although complaints do arise from private parties, these can usually be dealt with under statutory nuisance legislation (see below and chapter 1, 1.15.1), the main problems arise from "pay parties". These are often large events with music and dancing, attracting anything between 100 and several thousand people and sometimes lasting several days. An entrance fee is normally charged, thus bringing them within the legislation mentioned above.

In its report to the Government in 1990 (The "Batho Report"), the Noise Review Working Party drew attention to the increasing number of noisy parties (particularly large-scale parties), and the difficulties facing local authorities in controlling them. In response to a recommendation from the Working Party, the Home Office and Department of Environment published in 1992 a *Joint Guidance Note on the Control of Noisy Parties*. This outlines the main powers available to local authorities in England and Wales for dealing with noisy parties and provides advice and guidance on how the legislation can be interpreted. The Guidance Note also outlines the role of the police and how they can help local authority officers in dealing with noisy parties.

3.10.1 Statutory Nuisance Legislation

Action for noise nuisance from both the smaller private parties and pay parties can be taken under Part III of the *Environmental Protection Act*

1990. Under section 80 of the EPA, an abatement notice can be served requiring abatement of the nuisance; the notice can be served on anyone involved with the organisation of the party, e.g. host, disc jockey, sound engineer; the notice can be addressed to the occupier of the premises or indeed simply affixed to the premises. An abatement notice can also be served in anticipation of a nuisance – in such cases the notice could prohibit the delivery of audio equipment to the party site or require its removal. Contravention of an abatement notice is an offence.

The EPA provides local authorities with powers under section 80(3) to take whatever action is necessary to abate a nuisance themselves. This might include confiscating the offending noise-making equipment, a power clarified under section 10(7) of the *Noise Act 1996* (see above, 3.8.2). Schedule 2 of the Act provides powers of entry to the premises, although where these are mainly or wholly used for residential purposes 24 hours' notice should be given or where entry is likely to be refused, a warrant obtained.

Section 43 of the *Powers of Criminal Courts Act 1973* also enables local authorities in England and Wales to seek a deprivation order from the court for the permanent confiscation of noise making equipment following a prosecution.

For further details regarding procedures under nuisance legislation, see chapter 1, 1.15.1.

3.10.2 Public Entertainment Licensing

Under the *Local Government (Miscellaneous Provisions) Act 1982* and the *London Government Act 1963*, local authorities have powers to license all places used for public music and dancing etc. The DOE/HO Guidance suggests that case law would indicate that the legislation would also apply to all parties where there is an admission charge and music and dancing. It should be noted that in London the legislation covers both indoor and outdoor events, but outside Greater London it applies to indoor events only.

Before applying the legislation to outdoor musical events held on private land, local authorities outside London must adopt the relevant provisions of the legislation. Outside London, local authorities, in granting a licence, may only attach conditions and other restrictions aimed at preventing unreasonable noise disturbance to people nearby, to ensure the safety of performers and those attending, to ensure access for emergency vehicles and to ensure adequate sanitation. Licences for events held indoors or outside in Greater London may include whatever conditions are considered reasonable in the circumstances.

Contravention of a licence, or absence of a licence, is an offence, the penalties for which are outlined above (3.9).

3.10.3 Private Parties for Gain

These include all "private" events for which an admission or other charge has been made and the event can be regarded as having been promoted for private gain. Such events are controlled by the *Private Places of Entertainment (Licensing) Act 1967* and contain similar powers for local authorities to those outlined in the section above. Before using these powers, it is necessary for local authorities to adopt the whole of the Act.

3.10.4 Private Parties Not for Gain

The main way of controlling these is through statutory nuisance legislation – Part III of the *Environmental Protection Act 1990* – see above and chapter 1, 1.15.1. The *Noise Act 1996* (England, Wales and Northern Ireland) sets a limit on the level of noise which can be made between 11.00 pm and 7.00 am from a dwelling; disobeying a warning notice is an offence – see above 3.8.1.

3.10.5 High Court Injunctions

Section 222 of the *Local Government Act 1972* empowers a local authority to seek a High Court injunction to prevent a party from taking place where it is felt that this is the only way of stopping a potential nuisance and thus promoting or protecting the interests of local inhabitants. In seeking an injunction, the Court will need to be convinced that action under other legislation (e.g. nuisance legislation) will be ineffective.

Section 81(5) of the EPA enables a local authority to seek an injunction for abating a nuisance in those instances where it is felt that taking action for contravention of an abatement notice would be ineffective.

Contravention of the terms of an injunction may lead to imprisonment or an unlimited fine.

3.10.6 Codes of Practice

A code of practice on *Environmental Noise Control at Concerts* (Noise Council, 1994) provides guidance for those planning concerts, for licensing authorities and for local authorities enforcing nuisance legislation. It includes music noise levels for both indoor and outdoor events and single as well as multiple events.

3.10.7 Scotland

Section 54 of the *Civic Government (Scotland) Act 1982* empowers uniformed police officers to request that noise from, for example, sound-producing devices be reduced if it is giving any other person "reasonable cause for annoyance". If the request is ignored then the police may confiscate the offending equipment as evidence for any prosecution. This section of the Act also covers annoyance caused by singing, playing musical instruments, televisions, radios etc. Loudspeakers used by the emergency services are exempt.

The Licensing (Scotland) Act 1976 enables the Licensing Board to include conditions limiting noise.

INDUSTRIAL AND CONSTRUCTION SITE NOISE

3.11 INTRODUCTION

Complaints about noise from industrial and commercial premises continue to rise in England and Wales with 49,543 complaints to local authorities in 1995/96 (1994/95: 49,248); however, complaints about noise from roadworks, demolition and construction works decreased – 7,716 complaints in 1995/96, compared with nearly 11,000 in 1994/95 (CIEH, Environmental Health Report 1995/96). In Scotland there were 3,634 complaints (1992/93: 2,515) about noise from industrial and commercial premises in 1996/97 and 885 complaints (1992/93: 401) about noise from roadworks etc (DETR *Digest of Environmental Statistics, No. 20*, 1998).

The use of the planning system in controlling noise has already been summarised – see this chapter 3.4.

3.12 REGULATORY CONTROLS

3.12.1 Control of Pollution Act 1974

Sections 60-61 cover noise from construction sites and enable local authorities to impose requirements, including noise limits on the way in which work is carried out – see 3.6.1 above.

Under sections 63-67 of COPA a local authority may by order designate all or part of its area a noise abatement zone; premises classified under the order – usually industrial premises – may not exceed their registered noise level (details of which are kept in a public register) – see 3.6.3 above. It is a defence to prove that the best practicable means have been used to counteract the effects of noise caused in the course of trade or business from premises in a NAZ.

3.12.2 Environmental Protection Act 1990

Statutory Nuisance

Action against noise (including vibration) from industrial or trade premises may be taken using Part III of the EPA. It is a defence to prove that the best practicable means were used to prevent or counteract the effects of the nuisance. See chapter 1, 1.15.1.

Waste Management Licensing

The EU's Waste Framework Directive (see chapter 4, 4.6) requires waste disposal processes to be regulated to ensure that they do not cause noise nuisance; relevant conditions are included in waste management licences. This, however, does not preclude action under statutory nuisance legislation.

3.12.3 EU Directive - Integrated Pollution Prevention and Control

This Directive was formally adopted on 24 September 1996 and must be incorporated into national legislation within three years. Noise and vibration are among the pollutants which operators of processes covered by the Directive will be required to control – see chapter 1, 1.12. The Directive defines pollution from noise and vibration as that "which may be harmful to human health or the quality of the environment, result in damage to material property or impair or interfere with amenities and other legitimate uses of the environment".

ROAD TRAFFIC NOISE

3.13 INTRODUCTION

A 1991 survey by the Building Research Establishment showed that while a higher percentage of those who heard it objected to noise from neighbours, road traffic noise was heard by considerably more people. (*Digest of Environmental Protection and Water Statistics, No. 16*, DOE, 1994)

Road traffic noise has two main components: the mechanical noise associated with the engine and transmission system of the vehicle, and the "rolling noise" of the vehicle – this latter is due to factors such as the frictional contact between the tyres and the road and the aerodynamic noise caused by the passage of the vehicle through the air. The noise levels caused by traffic on a road are dependent on the number of vehicles using the road, their speed and the proportion of heavy vehicles. Heavy vehicles are of course much noisier than cars and hence have a greater influence on overall traffic noise levels.

Other factors affecting traffic noise levels are road surface and the immediate topography of the street. Rough road surfaces cause more noise than smooth ones; asphalt surfaces, and in particular porous asphalt, tend to generate less noise than other conventional surfaces; nearby high walls or buildings also reflect noise causing an increase in the overall level. Noise from smoothly flowing traffic is less than noise from an interrupted flow because changes in engine speed and the use of low gears, necessary at traffic lights, junctions and hills, produce more noise than a steady cruising speed.

3.14 REGULATORY CONTROLS

3.14.1 Motor Vehicles

Maximum noise limits from the engines and exhausts of motor vehicles when new and in use are set out in regulations made under the *Road Traffic Act 1972; the Road Vehicles (Construction & Use) Regulations 1986* (and amendments), and the *Motor Vehicle (Type Approval) (Great Britain) Regulations. The Type Approval Regulations* set requirements to meet noise limits set in EU Directives. The latest Directive, 92/97/EEC, adopted in 1992 has reduced the limits set in a 1984 Directive (84/424/EEC) by between 2-5 dB(A) – see table below. The new limits applied to new model vehicles, cars, dual purpose vehicles and light goods vehicles with petrol engines from 1 October 1995 and to all new vehicles from 1 October 1996. Subject to the agreement of the European Commission, Member States were permitted to offer tax incentives until October 1996 for all vehicles meeting the new limits before the deadline. Directive 92/97/EEC has been implemented in the UK through amendments to the type approval and construction and use regulations which came into force on 1 October 1996 (see also chapter 2, 2.21.2). These regulations also implement Noise Directive 96/20/EC which makes certain changes to the method of noise level testing set out in the 1992 Directive.

The Commission is expected to make proposals for further reductions in noise emissions in the near future.

The Road Vehicles (Construction and Use) Regulations 1986 also make it an offence to use a motor vehicle in such a way as to cause excessive noise; the Regulations do not cover off-road uses, such as motorcycle scrambling. Maximum permitted levels for vehicles in use on the road are generally 3 dB(A) higher than the construction noise limits specified in Regulations, because of differences in measurement. Higher limits apply to older vehicles. Similar Regulations apply in Northern Ireland.

In addition the Regulations specify that motor horns may not be sounded in a restricted road between 11.30 pm and 7.00 am and not at

Maximum Noise Limits for Road Vehicles

Vehicle	*dB(A)*
Goods vehicles over 3.5 tonnes	
- over 150 kW engine power	80
- 75-150 kW engine power	78
- below 75 kW engine power	77
Goods vehicles below 3.5 tonnes	
- goods vehicles 2-3.5 tonnes	77
- goods vehicles below 2 tonnes	76
Buses	
- with over 9 seats, over 3.5 tonnes GVW and over 150 kW engine power	80
- with over 9 seats, over 3.5 tonnes GVW but below 150 kW engine power	78
Cars	74

all when a vehicle is stationary unless there is danger to another moving vehicle. Private vehicles must not be fitted with a gong, bell, siren or two-tone horn. For vehicles first used on or after 1 August 1973, no other multi-tone horns are permitted.

Car alarms are also covered by the Regulations; all car alarms fitted to vehicles must have a five minute cut-out device; if the alarm continues to sound then the police may prosecute the vehicle's owner.

3.14.2 Motorcycles

The first Directive to limit motorcycle noise was adopted in 1978 (78/1015/EEC) and set optional limits of between 86 dB(A) for motorcycles over 500 cc and 78 dB(A) for those less than 80 cc; these limits were reduced in two stages by Directive 87/56/EEC to 80 dB(A) for motorcycles over 175 cc, 77 dB(A) for those between 80-175 cc and 75 dB(A) for those under 80 cc. The 1978 Directive and its amendment have been repealed following implementation of Directive 97/24 which was adopted in mid-1997. This Directive, which also covers 2 and 3 wheel mopeds and tricycles, had to be complied with by 18 December 1998 and the limits observed by 17 June 1999 – see table.

A 1989 Directive (89/235 EEC) laid down standards for replacement exhausts and silencers and prohibited the marketing and use of those that did not meet the required standards from October 1990. Implementation was optional. The Commission is however expected to bring forward proposals for a Directive which would make implementation obligatory and require all replacement exhausts to meet EU standards.

Motorcycle Noise Limits

Vehicle	*dB(A)*
Motorcycles	
- < 80 cc	75
- 80 - 175 cc	77
- > 175 cc	80
Tricycles	80
Two Wheel Mopeds	
- up to 25 km/h	66
- > 25 km/h	71
Three Wheel Mopeds	76

In the UK, the construction and use requirements of the Directives are implemented through the *Road Vehicles (Construction and Use) Regulations 1986* and subsequent amendments (see also chapter 2, 2.21.2). So far as noise from motorcycles is concerned, the Regulations require silencers to be maintained in good and efficient working order; the silencer should not be altered so as to increase the noise made by the escape of exhaust gases. A silencer which forms part of the exhaust system of a motorcycle first used on or after 1 January 1985 shall be either the original one, or one that meets the relevant British Standard (and is so marked), or is of a make and type specified by the manufacturer. Older motorcycles (used after 1 April 1970) must be able to meet noise standards specified in the Regulations.

Regulations made under *the Motor Cycle Act 1987* (SI 2370), the *Motor Cycle Silencer Regulations 1995*, effective 1 August 1996, make it an offence to sell, supply, offer to supply, or have available for supply, exhaust systems and silencers that are not marked BS AU 193/T2, BS AU 193a: 1990/T2 or BS AU 193a: 1990/T3. The Regulations (which also apply to mopeds and scooters) do not apply to silencers and exhausts to be used by off-road motorcycles but must be clearly marked "Not for Road Use"; nor do they apply to motorcycles first used before 1 January 1985 and the silencer is marked "Pre 1985 MC only".

The Motorcycles (Sound Level Measurement Certificates) (Amendment) Regulations 1989 ensure that a certificate may only be issued when the relevant standards are met.

3.14.3 Other Controls

A number of other legislative measures are of importance for controlling and abating noise pollution from road traffic.

The Road Traffic Regulation Act 1984 gives local authorities powers to make a traffic regulation order for preserving or improving the amenities of an area through which a road runs.

Part I of the *Land Compensation Act 1973* provides for compensation in cases where property values can be shown to have fallen as a direct result of increased noise levels (and other specific factors). Part II, enables householders to claim a grant from their local authority to provide noise insulation if:

a) their property is within 300 metres of a new road or substantially improved roads and they experience increased noise levels as a result; and

b) the noise level reaches or exceeds 68 dB(A) $L_{10(18\text{ hour})}$ with at least 1 dB(A) resulting from the increase in traffic.

The Noise Insulation Regulations 1975 (and amendments – the latest dated 1988). These are made under Part II of the *Land Compensation Act 1973* and apply in England and Wales. They provide for grants to cover the costs of insulation. Grants are available for secondary glazing of eligible rooms of dwellings where it is estimated that maximum noise levels during the 15 years after the road opening will be at least 68 dB(A) $L_{10(18\text{ hour})}$, with a contribution of at least 1 dB(A) from traffic using the new road. However grants are not available to householders affected by increased traffic along existing roads resulting from re-routing or traffic management schemes, or from a general increase in traffic flow.

Similar legislation – the *Land Compensation (Scotland) Act 1973* and Regulations made under it, the *Noise Insulation (Scotland) Regulations 1985* – applies in Scotland.

AIRCRAFT NOISE

3.15 INTRODUCTION

In common with other forms of transport, air travel has an environmental impact, and with the growing awareness of and interest in environmental issues, increasing attention is being paid to the detrimental effects of heavy air traffic. In the UK we have two of the world's busiest international airports: in 1996 there were over 428,000 take-offs and landings at Heathrow and 212,000 at Gatwick; over 55 million people used Heathrow in 1996 and 24 million used Gatwick.

The most obvious environmental threat from aircraft is noise – ranging from the regular rumble of large jets to the buzz of microlights and other light aircraft. A 1991 survey by the Building Research Establishment found that the number of people reporting hearing aircraft noise was second only to those hearing noise from road traffic, with 76% of those hearing noise from aircraft being disturbed by the noise periodically (*Digest of Environmental Protection and Water*

Statistics, No. 16, DOE, 1994). In 1996/97, local authorities in England and Wales received 1,956 complaints about aircraft noise (CIEH Environmental Health Report, 1996/97). The impact of emissions to atmosphere from aircraft is briefly summarised in chapter 2, 2.23.

The noise generated by an aircraft is related to air velocity. Thus any fast moving components – propellers, compressor blades – as well as jet exhaust gases, will be efficient generators of noise.

Aircraft noise comprises a broadband background noise with the periodic components of rotating machinery noise superimposed on it. In newer aircraft with high by-pass ratio turbo-fan engines, these components operate at much lower speeds and are significantly quieter as a result.

Different aircraft produce different noise problems; for instance, jets produce more periodic component noise on landing than on take-off, when the broadband exhaust noise predominates; noise from the hull on landing tends to predominate in quiet-engined aircraft.

Jets currently in service are Chapter 2 and Chapter 3 aircraft – the term comes from the relevant annex of the Chicago Convention of 1944. Chapter 2 aircraft include the BAe 1-11, DC9 and Boeing 737-200. Chapter 3 aircraft include the Boeing 747, 757 and 767, DC10 and airbus. (Chapter 1 aircraft which are, on the whole, no longer in use include the DC8 and VC10.)

Noise standards are drawn up by the International Civil Aviation Organisation (ICAO) – a UN body – and by the European Civil Aviation Conference, whose members are drawn from throughout Europe, including the European Community. Their standards are then incorporated into European and national legislation. ICAO is also responsible for developing operating procedures, for example to minimise take-off and landing noise. It also carries out research and is currently looking at air quality around airports and emissions at high altitude.

3.16 THE EUROPEAN UNION AND AIRCRAFT NOISE

The European Union's first Directive on aeroplane noise (80/51/EEC) prevented the addition of any further non-noise certificated aeroplanes (i.e. Chapter 1 aircraft) to the civil registers of Member States, and required the removal of any such aeroplanes by 31 December 1986. A small number of exemptions enabled some of these aeroplanes to continue flying until 31 December 1988. An amendment to this Directive (83/206/EEC) prevented non-noise certificated aircraft registered outside the EU from landing within it from 1 January 1988 (with some exemptions until 31 December 1989). A 1989 amendment

Directive (89/629/EEC) limited noise from subsonic aircraft and permitted only Chapter 3 aircraft able to meet the tighter limits to be added to Registers.

A further Directive (92/14/EEC) limiting aircraft noise was agreed in March 1992, and an amendment (98/20/EC) adopted in March 1998. These ban all aircraft unable to meet Chapter 3 standards or Chapter 2 standards and are less than 25 years old, from operating into the EU after 1 April 1995; from 1 April 2002, all Chapter 2 aircraft will be banned. Various exemptions to the Directive cover such matters as extensions to an aircraft's life and aircraft from developing countries. This Directive is in line with a timetable agreed by the European Civil Aviation Conference in June 1991.

The Commission has now published a proposal for a Directive which would ban the addition to Member States' registers from 1 April 1999 of aircraft meeting the Chapter 3 standards through the use of "hushkits"; those fitted with hushkits and on registers prior to this date would be allowed to continue operating. The use of such aircraft in the EU is currently not widespread, and the Commission aims through this measure to prevent them from becoming so. The European Commission is also expected to publish proposals for a draft Directive reducing aircraft noise levels by 3 decibels; the reduction would apply to new aircraft applying for airworthiness certificates after a specified date.

3.17 REGULATORY CONTROLS

The Department of the Environment, Transport and the Regions (DETR) is responsible for policy on the control of aircraft noise. Section 78 of the *Civil Aviation Act 1982* gives the Secretary of State wide powers to enforce noise standards on aircraft, apply operational controls and restrictions and give directions to owners of designated airports in relation to operational requirements and noise insulation grant schemes. The policy is concerned with containing and effectively reducing aircraft noise by restrictions on aircraft movements, control of flight paths and use of certain operational procedures.

3.17.1 Civil Aviation Act 1982

While powers to control environmental noise are contained in Part III of the *Environmental Protection Act 1990*, section 79(6) specifically excludes noise from aircraft (other than model aircraft) from these controls which are designed to deal with noise from fixed rather than moving sources.

The principal legislation covering aircraft operations is the *Civil*

Aviation Act 1982. This contains three main powers aimed at aircraft noise control at particular airports. Section 76 does, however, exclude the properly controlled flight of aircraft from action in respect of trespass or nuisance provided that rules and regulations such as the *Rules of the Air* and *Air Traffic Control Regulations* have been observed.

Environmental Considerations (ss.5 & 6)

This requires the Civil Aviation Authority to take account of environmental aspects, such as noise and atmospheric pollution when exercising their licensing functions at aerodromes. When the CAA license or re-license an aerodrome, they are primarily concerned with whether it can operate safely; under section 5, the Secretary of State can also require them to take account of environmental matters.

Section 6 enables the Secretary of State to give directions to the CAA on a number of issues, including taking action to prevent or deal with noise, vibration, pollution or other disturbance attributable to aircraft used for civil aviation.

Requirement to provide Consultation Facilities (s.35)

Where the Secretary of State designates an airport under this power, the airport management is required to establish suitable consultation facilities with users, nearby local authorities, and local representative organisations. Forty-seven airports have been designated under section 35, covering all the national and regional airports and some of the general aviation airfields.

Direct Responsibility for Designated Airports (ss.78 & 79)

The Secretary of State is directly responsible for noise abatement measures for aircraft landing and taking off (including during the night) at airports designated for the purposes of section 78, and for noise insulation grant schemes for airports designated for the purposes of section 79. Heathrow, Gatwick and Stansted are designated for both sections.

• Daytime Noise Limits

Daytime noise limits were first introduced at Heathrow in 1959, at Gatwick in 1968 and at Stansted in 1993, and cover the period 0700-2300. The current limit is 97 dB(A). The airport companies are responsible for monitoring compliance with noise limits with breaches of the limit subject to financial penalty – currently £500 if the limit is exceeded by 3dB(A) or less, £1,000 if it is exceeded by more than 3dB(A).

The Government is now proposing (DETR, February 1998) to reduce the daytime noise limit to be complied with by all aircraft, except Concorde, to 94 dB(A). Aircraft exempted under the provisions of the EU Directive 92/14 until 31 March 2002 (e.g. on grounds of economic hardship or those registered in developing countries) will also be exempt from the new daytime limit.

- **Night-time Noise Limits and Flight Restrictions**

Night flights have been restricted at Heathrow since 1962, at Gatwick since 1988 and at Stansted since 1993, and cover the period 2300-0700. The current limit is 89 dB(A). In addition, the noisiest aircraft (i.e. those with a QC of 8 or 16 – see below) may not be scheduled to take-off or land during the night-time period. The airport companies are responsible for monitoring compliance, with the same financial penalties applying as for daytime exceedances of the limit. The Government is now proposing (DETR, February 1998) to reduce this limit to 87 dB(A) to be complied with by all aircraft.

Further restrictions, in the form of quotas covering the period 2330-0600 have also been in force since October 1993. Aircraft are categorised into three bands – NN/A, NN/B and NN/C – with NN/A representing the noisiest aircraft which are not normally allowed to operate between 2330 and 0600. Each airport is allocated a total number of flight movements covering the B and C bands which should not be exceeded. A night noise limit of 89 dB(A) applies and any exceedance results in a reduction in the airport's quota. If the quota is exceeded by more than 50, then the following season's quota is reduced.

In addition, all aircraft have been assigned a quota count (QC) of units for both take off and landing and each of the airports allocated an annual number of quota points for night (i.e. between 2330 and 0600) movements which should not be exceeded. Quota Counts range from 0.5 for aircraft with a certificated noise performance of less than 90 EPNdB (79 dB(A)) to QC 8 for those between 99-101 EPNdB (88 dB(A) or more) and QC 16 for those above 101.9 EPNdB. The noisier the aircraft, the more points are deducted from the airport's allocation. Certain jet aircraft and propeller aircraft with a certificated noise performance under 87 EPNdB are exempt from quota restrictions.

The quota are divided between summer and winter seasons, with airports allowed to carry forward up to 10% of the quota to the next season or to use 10% of the next season's quota to deal with any overrun. Any exceedance of the quota over 10% results in a loss of quota double the exceedance. Movement and noise quota have been set up to summer 1999.

The Government is currently reviewing (DETR, February 1998) the current regime for night restrictions, with detailed proposals to be put forward in the light of comments on the current regime.

3.17.2 Rules of the Air and Air Traffic Control Regulations

These cover general rules as to flight: usually, aircraft or helicopters may not fly over any congested area of a town or settlement below the height of 1,500 feet above the highest fixed object and within 2,000 feet of it, or at such height as would not permit the aircraft to glide clear of the area in the event of a failure of a power unit. Landing and take-off routes are prescribed by air traffic control procedures and these usually include a requirement as to the rate of height gain or loss and turning on track with the intention of minimising noise over built up areas. Aircraft are prohibited from flying within 500 feet of persons, vessels, vehicles or structures. The Regulations, which include Northern Ireland, are enforced by the Civil Aviation Authority.

International airports often have formal "minimum noise" routes, which are to be observed as far as possible.

3.17.3 Noise Certification

Relevant standards, drawn up by the International Civil Aviation Organisation, are enacted in the UK, and domestic regulations are tightened as the ICAO standards are revised. *Air Navigation (Noise Certification) Orders* prohibit non-certificated aircraft from taking off or landing in the UK and implement the latest international recommendations in respect of the control of aircraft noise at source.

Noise standards have also been introduced for light propeller driven aircraft, helicopters and microlights; in 1984 the British Microlight Association drew up a voluntary code of practice which gives advice on minimising the noise impact of microlights.

3.17.4 Helicopters

While the provisions of the *Civil Aviation Act 1982* apply to helicopters, their ability to land almost anywhere can be a particular source of noise nuisance in residential areas; currently very little can be done to alleviate the problem, except by use of planning controls (see below, 3.17.6).

3.17.5 Military Aircraft

In most cases legal liability in respect of nuisance by military aircraft is excluded by statute. Military airfields usually have their own schemes to limit disturbance, including sound insulation and compensation schemes.

3.17.6 Planning Controls

New airport developments are subject to planning permission under the *Town and Country Planning Act 1990*. However, airports which have established use operate without planning controls and increasing use does not require planning permission. Permanent helicopter landing sites require planning permission, although temporary use of land for up to 28 days per year is permitted under the *General Development Order 1988*. In this instance, there is no limit to the number of take-offs and landings in one day.

Private Aerodromes

Where private aerodromes are established by individuals and companies, normal planning procedures will apply except on those vested in or controlled by the British Airports Authority. Planning permission may include conditions to secure the abatement of noise and local authority bye-laws may also be used to restrict operations so as to limit or mitigate the effect of noise. The operating authority of the aerodrome may also make such bye-laws.

Compensation is payable in certain circumstances where there is a new runway or if there have been major changes to an existing runway/other features at the airport. Compensation will be paid where the value of an interest in land is depreciated by more than £50 as a result of noise and other physical factors. Compensation will only be payable where the authority responsible for the public works involved can claim statutory immunity from an action for nuisance in respect of the work.

3.17.7 Supersonic Aircraft

There are no noise regulations covering the operation of supersonic aircraft, such as Concorde, characterised by their sonic boom. Briefly, the sonic boom is a shock wave system produced by an aircraft flying at a speed faster than the local speed of sound. At a certain point the shock wave causes a sudden rise in atmospheric pressure followed by a gradual fall to below normal pressure before a sudden rise back to normal. The double sound of the sonic boom occurs when these pressure fluctuations occur at more than about 100 milliseconds apart. An aircraft in supersonic flight can trail a sonic boom audible over more than 50 km on either side of its ground track depending upon altitude and size of aircraft. Apart from Concorde, all supersonic aircraft in this country are military.

3.18 MONITORING AIRCRAFT NOISE

Since September 1990 the Department of Transport (now DETR) has used "equivalent continuous sound level" (L_{Aeq}) to measure the extent and intensity of noise disturbance around airports for the daytime period (0700-2300). This can be defined as the sound level of a steady sound having the same energy as a fluctuating sound over a specified measuring period (Batho Report, 1990).

RAIL NOISE

3.19 The introduction of high speed trains has created special noise patterns, especially when trains cross bridges or other structures which amplify the noise. Development of the high speed rail link from London to the Channel Tunnel is causing particular concern in South East England.

Under the *Noise Insulation (Railways and Other Guided Transport Systems) Regulations 1995* which came into force on 1 March 1996, an authority constructing a new railway (or other guided transport system) or additional track has a duty to provide insulation or a grant towards the cost of insulation for homes affected by the noise. Only residential buildings within 300 metres of the works for the new, altered or extended system are eligible for grant or insulation. The Regulations also include discretionary powers to provide grants for homes affected by altered lines or the noise of construction work. The level at which insulation should be provided or a grant paid towards its cost is 68 dB $L_{Aeq\ 18h}$ during the day (0600-midnight) and 63 dB $L_{Aeq\ 6h}$ at night (midnight-0600). Noise levels should be calculated using *Calculation of Railway Noise 1995* (HMSO), and based on expected normal traffic flows within a 15 year period; amendment Regulations will incorporate a supplement to the *Calculation of Railway Noise* into the Regulations.

OCCUPATIONAL NOISE

It is estimated that about one million people in the UK are working in conditions that may damage their hearing unless precautions are taken. People typically at risk are shipbuilders and steel workers using pneumatic hammers; workers engaged in rivetting or drop forging; workers in canning and bottling plants; and those who operate wood-working machinery.

3.20 HEALTH AND SAFETY AT WORK ETC ACT 1974

Occupational noise is controlled under statute by the *Health and Safety at Work Act 1974*. Part I provides a comprehensive and integrated system of law to deal with the health, safety and welfare of persons at work and the health and safety of the public as they may be affected by work activities, including protection from occupational noise exposure.

3.20.1 Noise at Work Regulations 1989 (SI 1790)

In 1986 the European Union adopted a Directive on the protection of workers from the risks related to exposure to noise at work (86/188/EEC) which had to be implemented in 1990. This has been done through the above Regulations which came into effect on 1 January 1990. The Regulations apply to all workers in Great Britain covered by the HSW Act, except the crews of sea-going ships and aircraft or hovercraft moving under their own power. Enforcement of the Regulations is mainly the responsibility of the Health and Safety Executive, and of local authorities. Similar 1990 Regulations apply in Northern Ireland; they are enforced by district councils, the Department for Economic Development and the Department of Agriculture for Northern Ireland.

The Regulations impose a duty on employers to assess and, where necessary, measure noise levels to identify workers to which its specific provisions apply. Three action levels are defined:

- *First Action Level* – a daily personal noise exposure (LEP,d) of 85 dB(A);
- *Second Action Level* – a daily personal noise exposure (LEP,d) of 90 dB(A);
- *Peak Action Level* – a peak sound pressure of 200 pascals (140 dB re 20 uPa).

LEP,d should be regarded as total exposure to noise throughout the day, taking account of the average noise level in the working area and the time spent in it, but not taking account of any reduction through the use of ear protectors. Peak pressure is the highest pressure reached by the sound wave.

Noise exposures are generally to be reduced to the lowest level reasonably practicable, taking account of technical progress and the availability of measures to control the noise, in particular at source.

Where average daily personal noise exposures reach or exceed 85 dB(A), personal ear protectors are to be made available to those employees who ask for them. At average daily personal noise exposures of 90 dB(A) and above, or where the peak sound pressure level exceeds 200 pascals, employers must ensure that personal ear protectors are used. At these levels the employee has a duty to use ear protectors; at all action levels the employee must use any other protective equipment supplied and report any defects to the employer. Areas where noise exposures exceed these levels must be marked with signs, and access to them restricted.

The Regulations require a noise assessment to be carried out where it is likely that employees will be exposed to noise at or above the First or Peak Action Level. The assessment must identify all employees likely to be exposed to the noise levels and provide sufficient information to enable appropriate action to be taken; employers must implement technical or organisational measures to reduce exposures as far as reasonably practicable. Assessments must be reviewed if significant changes are made to either the equipment or nature of the work. Records of assessments or noise measurements must be kept and employees given access to them.

The Regulations also place a duty on manufacturers, designers, importers and suppliers to supply adequate noise data with all new articles, such as tools and machinery, whenever their normal use at work is likely to result in daily noise exposures of 85 dB(A) or above.

The HSE has published detailed Guidance Notes for employers on implementation of the Regulations. The Guidance Notes also contain advice on the provision of information to employees covering health and safety, maintenance of ear protectors and provision of training and instruction programmes for employees in order to minimise the risk of damage to hearing.

People may qualify for industrial injuries benefit on the grounds of deafness, but since it is very difficult to decide whether deafness was incurred at work or elsewhere, the definition of what is accepted as occupational deafness is extremely restricted.

The 1986 Directive did not cover workers in either the air or maritime transport industries; in late 1992 the Commission published a draft Directive on Physical Agents at Work which, as well as extending protection to these sectors, introduces further requirements for monitoring workers' exposure to noise hazards; it requires information and training for workers, medical screening and measures to ensure that equipment and practices do not expose workers to excessive risks. Following adoption, this Directive will replace the 1986 Directive. (The Directive also covers protection from mechanical vibration, electromagnetic fields and optical radiation.)

3.21 REDUCING NOISE IN THE WORKPLACE

Prolonged exposure to high noise levels can lead to stress, fatigue or even deafness. While the best way of reducing the risk of hearing damage is obviously to reduce the noise, there are various steps which can be taken to mitigate the effects of excessive noise.

(a) Noise Reduction at Source

This is usually achieved by the use of absorptive treatments. Particular examples are:

- the lining with noise-absorptive material of cabinets, cladding and cover panels on all forms of machinery;
- the treatment of a wall panel and head lining within all forms of operator cab;
- the facing of panels on the noisy side of acoustic screen and on complete enclosure systems.

The materials most commonly used are mineral fibre, glass fibre, and open-cell polyurethane foams.

(b) Attenuation in Transmission

This is achieved by the insertion of a barrier or screen between the machine and areas to be protected. When a high degree of noise control is required, complete enclosure will be necessary; for limited control, integrally mounted covers for particularly noisy parts of the machine may suffice. Complete enclosures need to be lined with an absorptive material to reduce the reverberation. In the same way, covers may be lined with absorptive material and supported on anti-vibration mounts to improve performance.

(c) Silencers

In cases where noise is transmitted along ducting, (such as ventilator fan noise) a silencer in the ducting reduces noise received by attenuating the noise energy in transmission. There are several types of silencer for different applications, but most operate on the principle of sound absorption through the use of absorptive material.

(d) Vibration Isolation

This prevents the transmission of energy, through mechanical vibration, from the machine to the structure on which it is mounted. It can also prevent transmission of energy from one machine component to another. Vibration isolators vary according to the static deflection required; they may be simple composition pads, rubber unit mounts or steel springs.

(e) Personal Hearing Protection

The Noise at Work Regulations 1989 require personal hearing protection to be provided where noise levels reach 85 dB(A) or more. Personal hearing protectors must not only be maintained and used correctly but must also be worn for the entire period of exposure to the noise to be effective. Failure to wear the protection for only 15% of the exposure time renders it virtually useless: if a protector with an assumed protection of 20 dB(A) is removed for 30 minutes per day the actual reduction in dose received by the wearer will only be 12 dB(A).

There are various types of protectors available such as ear plugs which are inserted in the ear canal to block out unwanted noise; they usually provide adequate protection up to 105 dB(A); semi-insert protection (canal caps), usually of soft rubber, which are pressed into the openings of the ear canals by a resilient headband, are particularly suited for use in such industries as catering where the loss of an ear plug could prove dangerous. Again, they provide protection up to 105 dB(A).

For adequate protection from noise above 105 dB(A) ear muffs must be used. These are normally hard plastic cups which fit over the ears and are sealed to the head by cushion seals, with the inner surface being covered by sound absorbing material.

(f) Noise Cancellation Systems

In some professions ear protectors may not be practicable. For instance pilots need to be able to hear sounds around them, including instrument warning systems. Noise cancellation systems, which are currently being developed aim to reduce background sound levels, but allow users to otherwise hear normally. Special headphones with built in microphones and speakers pick up the sound, transmit it to a small electronic box, and analyse it for particular frequencies. An "anti-noise" signal is generated, which mixes with the original noise signal, and the two signals cancel each other out.

LOW FREQUENCY NOISE

3.22 A low frequency noise is very often characterised by a hum or rumble and may be confused with tinnitus. These sounds often have no obvious source though in some areas a number of people may complain about the same unidentified "noise". While many of these noises remain unidentified, sources of LFN can include ventilation and air conditioning systems in large buildings; domestic boilers; diesel powered transport, such as ships, locomotives and lorries; and even the vibration of high rise buildings in the wind. These can cause complaints for two reasons:

a) primary noise (low frequency or infrasonic) radiated from source and entering houses either through their structure or through open windows;

b) secondary noise, e.g. rattling windows and doors. This either causes disturbance in itself or wakes people up, whereupon they become conscious of the low frequency pulsation.

Although there is no convenient measurement unit to describe it, low frequency sound may be defined as having a frequency below 150

Hz. Low frequency sound has a long wavelength which radiates in a spherical manner, rather like the ripples caused by a stone being dropped into a pond. In this way it can cover a vast area.

It can be particularly difficult to track down the source of LFN and assess its magnitude – ordinary sound level meters may not be able to detect it on the decibel scale as its decibel level is often lower than background noise. Practical methods of control are technically difficult and often prohibitive in cost. Sound proofing in buildings is usually impracticable as the design – particularly of modern buildings – may enhance the effect. Enclosing the noise source is a better option and will provide a more comprehensive solution. This too is often difficult and expensive as it involves enclosing the source in a combination of massive structures to reduce sound transmission. LFN from machinery can sometimes be reduced by the use of vibration absorbing mountings.

In order to apply controls in a scientific manner, a standard measurement unit has to be established which describes the noise in a single number (such as is given by the A weighting curve when defining higher frequency noise.) The International Standards Organisation is studying a curve which approximates to the hearing threshold (the f weighting) and falls off by 12 dB per octave towards the low frequencies. However, as this curve tolerates very high sound pressures between 2 Hz and 4 Hz, it is also proposed to introduce another curve (N) which falls off at 6 dB per octave. Once these curves and their tolerances have been defined by the ISO each country will be free to prescribe its own limits for low frequency sound.

EFFECTS OF NOISE

3.23 Noise can cause annoyance, interfere with communication and sleep, cause fatigue, reduce efficiency and damage hearing. In 1980 the World Health Organisation recommended a level of less than 35 dB(A) L_{eq} "to preserve the restorative process of sleep". The WHO is expected to recommend a reduced guideline level of 30 dB(A) L_{eq} for undisturbed sleep, with a peak night- time maximum of 45 dB(A) L_{eq}.

Physiological effects of noise include constriction of blood vessels, tightening of muscles, increased heart rate and blood pressure and changes in stomach and abdomen movement. Exposure to constant or very loud noise can cause temporary or permanent damage to hearing. However, hearing sensitivity varies and the effects of exposure are therefore personal. Current legislation states that 90 decibels for eight hours a day will damage the hearing. It is not only unwanted sound that can be damaging. Entertainment noise can also cause problems: pop stars may suffer hearing loss due to prolonged exposure to loud music and recent research has raised concern at the detrimental effects that loud personal stereos can have on hearing.

So far as low frequency noise is concerned, it is not clear at what level it may be physically damaging; however, the unpleasant symptoms it can induce are sufficient to cause disruption and significant social and economic penalties to sufferers.

MEASUREMENT OF NOISE

3.24 The simple definition of noise as "sound which is undesired by the recipient" (Wilson Committee on the Problem of Noise, Cmnd 2056, 1963) requires the presence of three conditions – there must be a sound source, a transmission path, and a receiver who would have some adverse subjective reaction to the sound. It is this area of subjectivity which creates the major difficulty in the measurement and assessment of noise sources. There is no (nor is it likely there ever will be) equipment available which can measure "noise", but there are a wide range of instruments which measure sound levels and there are more sophisticated derivatives capable of carrying out statistical evaluations of total noise climates. Thus it is relatively easy, given suitable equipment, to measure sound but it is much more difficult to allow for the subjective reaction to noise, which varies widely within an exposed population.

3.24.1 The Decibel

The logarithmic scale on which sound levels are measured is called the decibel (dB). The fundamental unit is the Bel and this is the logarithm of the ratio of the intensity of the given sound and the reference level; 1 Bel equals 10 dB or a factor of 10 in intensity – a change of 10 dB roughly corresponds to a doubling or halving of the loudness of a sound, i.e. a sound of 80 dB sounds about twice as loud as one of 70 dB. 0 dB is the threshold of hearing and 140 dB the threshold of pain.

3.24.2 Effective Perceived Noise Level

EPNdB and PNdB are used to measure aircraft noise with 3 EPNdB representing a doubling of noise energy. The quietest aircraft currently generate less than 90 EPNdB (about 75 dB(A)). It includes corrections for the duration and tonal quality of aircraft noise which are dependent on the rotational frequency of propellers or fans. The measure is used internationally for noise certification of aircraft.

3.24.3 Frequency

Another physical parameter which it is often necessary to measure is the frequency of the sound. The ear has a nominal range of between 20 hertz (Hz) (formerly called cycles per second) and 20 kHz (20,000 Hz), although at very high levels sound outside this range may be sensed.

This sensitivity obtains only for the young, healthy, adult ear; as one gets older, the upper limit is reduced progressively perhaps to around 10 kHz. Because the ear does not respond equally to sound of different frequencies, being most sensitive around the 1,000 Hz region and least sensitive at very low frequencies, a measurement of sound without a frequency "weighting" would not indicate the likely response which the auditory mechanism might have to that sound.

In order that a sound level meter may approximate the response of the human ear, certain standardised filter networks are built into instruments and the most commonly utilised network is termed the "A" weighting. Measurements made when this circuit is switched on are referred to as dB(A) – decibels on the A weighted scale. Other weightings are occasionally used, of which the most important is the "D" network used for certain (approximate) aircraft noise measurements.

3.25 MEASUREMENT INDICES

Whilst the majority of measurements are made in terms of dB(A), most noise climates are dynamic – i.e. levels change frequently and simple "peak" noise measurement may not be enough. In addition the variable factors of on-time, duration and frequency components may make that noise more or less annoying. Accordingly, a composite noise rating known as the Corrected Noise Level (CNL) has been constructed whereby various correction factors can be applied to a measured level to allow for additional intrusiveness or greater annoyance potential.

British Standard 4142 (1967, subsequently amended with the latest revision published in 1995) describes a method for determining a noise level, together with procedures for assessing the extent to which an industrial noise is likely to affect people in its vicinity leading to complaints. This method of rating is only applicable to certain situations, and other noise rating indices have been formulated to allow different noise sources to be evaluated in a similar meaningful way. Thus for traffic noise, the L_{10} (18 hour) index has been devised. The L_{10} is the level just exceeded for 10 per cent of the time; the arithmetic average of the 18 individual hourly readings taken between 0600 and 2400 hours on a working day gives the L_{10} (18 hour), which index relates well to subjective response to this particular source.

When assessing occupational noise and risk of damage to the hearing mechanism, measurements are made in terms of "equivalent continuous sound level" (Leq). This is a notional level, in dB(A), that over a stated period of time contains the same amount of acoustic energy as the actual, fluctuating noise measured over that same period. The period is normally 8 to 12 hours. This "energy average" concept is finding favour in other measurement fields, including environmental noise assessment.

WASTE

WASTE - GENERAL

The need to protect the environment for current and future generations – i.e. to ensure that development is sustainable (see chapter 1, 1.3) – also impinges on the way in which waste is managed. A considerable amount of "waste" can in fact be recovered, re-used or recycled, thus reducing the amount of non-renewable resources needed for making the products – and their packaging – that have become an essential part of most people's lives. Poorly managed waste and waste disposal sites can adversely affect the environment by contaminating the air, soil or water; they can also pose a danger to human health.

Section 44A of the *Environmental Protection Act 1990* (s.92 of the *Environment Act 1995*) requires the Secretary of State to prepare a National Waste Strategy for England and Wales. *Less Waste, More Value*, published for consultation in June 1998, sets out some of the issues to be addressed by the Strategy. Waste minimisation is identified as a key element of sustainable production, but where waste is produced, it must be dealt with in a manner which causes minimum harm to the environment. Similar obligations to prepare a National Waste Strategy are placed on SEPA by section 44B of the EPA and on the Department of the Environment (NI) by Article 19 of the *Waste and Contaminated Land (Northern Ireland) Order 1997*; for more details, see later this chapter 4.19.4.

The term "waste" is used to cover anything from the contents of the household dustbin to high level radioactive waste and clinical and other hazardous waste from hospitals, factories and other industrial premises.

This chapter covers legislation relating to the disposal of controlled and special waste from industry, commerce and households, the disposal of radioactive waste, as well as legislation on contaminated land and litter.

In June 1997 the Department of the Environment (DOE) merged with the Department of Transport to become the Department of the Environment, Transport and the Regions (DETR); both names are used in this chapter, depending on whether the matter being referred to happened pre- or post-June 1997.

4.1 EARLY CONTROLS

Until 1972, when public concern about the dumping of toxic waste in the Midlands resulted in the *Deposit of Poisonous Wastes Act*, there had been no specific legislation in the UK dealing with the management of wastes on land, although local authorities had for many years had powers to control waste in the interests of public health. The *Deposit of Poisonous Wastes Act 1972* had made it an offence to deposit on land any poisonous, noxious or polluting waste in a manner likely to create an environmental hazard. The Act also required that the waste disposal authority or water authority be given prior notification of the composition, quantity and destination of the waste. The Act was repealed in 1981 and replaced by the *Control of Pollution (Special Waste) Regulations 1980* made under section 17 of the *Control of Pollution Act 1974*. These Regulations were themselves revoked in September 1996 following implementation of the *Special Waste Regulations 1996* on 1 September 1996 (see this chapter 4.19.6).

The *Public Health Act 1936* had given local authorities powers to remove house and trade refuse and to require removal of any accumulation of noxious matter. It also placed a duty on them to inspect their areas "for accumulation or deposit which is prejudicial to health or a nuisance", with powers to serve abatement notices and to prosecute offenders. The *Town and Country Planning Act 1947* included a requirement for waste disposal sites to have planning permission. Part I of the *Control of Pollution Act 1974*, which was the principal legislation governing the collection and disposal of waste, has now been replaced by Part II of the *Environmental Protection Act 1990*. The main objective of this part of COPA was to ensure that licensed activities did not cause pollution of water, danger to public health or detriment to local amenities.

4.2 DEFINITIONS OF WASTE

4.2.1 Controlled Waste Regulations 1992 (SI 588)

Section 75 of the *Environmental Protection Act 1990* (EPA) and the *Controlled Waste Regulations 1992* defined waste as including

a) any substance which constitutes a scrap material or an effluent or other unwanted surplus substance arising from the application of any process;
   and
b) any substance or article which requires to be disposed of as being broken, worn out, contaminated or otherwise spoiled.

However, following implementation of the 1991 European Union (EU) Framework Directive on waste (91/156/EEC), section 75 of the EPA has been amended by the *Environment Act 1995* (Sch. 22, para 88) to reflect the new definition:

> "Waste means any substance or object in the categories set out in Schedule 2B to this Act [i.e. EPA] which the holder discards or intends or is required to discard;..."

Schedule 2B to the EPA (*Env. Act 1995*, Sch. 22, para 95) reproduces Annex I to the 1991 Directive – see box. "Holder" is defined as the producer of the waste or the person who is in possession of it; and the "producer" is anyone whose activities produce waste or anyone who carries out pre-processing, mixing or other operations resulting in a change in the nature or composition of this waste.

EU Framework Directive on Waste: Substances or Objects which are Waste when Discarded etc.

Annex I to Directive 91/156; Schedule 2B to *Environmental Protection Act 1990*

1. Production or consumption residues not otherwise specified below.
2. Off-specification products.
3. Products whose date for appropriate use has expired.
4. Materials spilled, lost or having undergone other mishap, including any materials, equipment, etc, contaminated as a result of the mishap.
5. Materials contaminated or soiled as a result of planned actions (e.g. residues from cleaning operations, packing materials, containers, etc).
6. Unusable parts (e.g. reject batteries, exhausted catalysts, etc).
7. Substances which no longer perform satisfactorily (e.g. contaminated acids, contaminated solvents, exhausted tempering salts, etc).
8. Residues of industrial processes (e.g. slags, still bottoms, etc).
9. Residues from pollution abatement processes (e.g. scrubber sludges, baghouse dusts, spent filters, etc).
10. Machining or finishing residues (e.g. lathe turnings, mill scales, etc).
11. Residues from raw materials extraction and processing (e.g. mining residues, oil field slops, etc).
12. Adulterated materials (e.g. oils contaminated with PCBs etc).
13. Any materials, substances or products whose use has been banned by law.
14. Products for which the holder has no further use (e.g. agricultural, household, office, commercial and shop discards, etc).
15. Contaminated materials, substances or products resulting from remedial action with respect to land.
16. Any materials, substances or products which are not contained in the above categories.

DOE Guidance (Circular 11/94, SOED 10/94, WO 26/94) suggests the following be used as a starting point in deciding whether or not something is waste:

a) [has it been] discarded, disposed of or got rid of by the holder; or
b) [is it] intended to be discarded, disposed of or got rid of by the holder; or
c) [is it] required to be discarded, disposed of or got rid of by the holder.

A further consideration is whether "the substance or object [has] been discarded so that it is no longer part of the normal commercial cycle or chain of utility". Thus some items although eventually recycled will be treated as waste (discarded) because they need to be reprocessed before they can be brought back into re-use.

Waste subject to the provisions of COPA and the EPA is known as "controlled waste" and includes wastes arising from domestic, industrial and commercial premises, as well as "special waste" for which there are additional regulations (see this chapter 4.19.6). The types of waste to be treated under each of these classifications for the purposes of Part II of the EPA are defined in the *Controlled Waste Regulations 1992*, which took effect on 1 April 1992 and apply in England, Scotland and Wales:

- **Household waste** includes waste from: premises occupied by a charity; land belonging to domestic property, caravan or residential home, or a private garage for a car; private (domestic) premises; moored houseboat; camp sites; prisons and penal institutions; public meeting halls; royal palaces; litter collected under section 89 of the EPA. Local authorities may charge for the collection of certain types of household waste – see 4.19.5 below.

- **Industrial waste** includes waste from: commercial garages/maintenance premises (for vehicles, vessels, aircraft); laboratories and scientific research associations; workshops; dredging and tunnelling waste; clinical waste (other than from domestic property, residential home or houseboat); aircraft, vehicles, vessels not used for domestic purposes; leachate; poisonous or noxious waste from certain processes (e.g. dry cleaning, paint mixing/selling, pesticide sales); premises for breeding, boarding, stabling or exhibiting animals; waste oils, waste solvent, scrap metals (except from domestic premises); waste imports and waste from ships.

- **Commercial waste** includes waste from: offices; showrooms; hotels; private garages (more than 25 sq m); club/social premises; markets or fairs; courts, government departments, local and central government premises; corporate bodies; tents on land other than camp sites.

The *Waste Management Regulations 1994* (see below, 4.19.3) apply to disposal and recovery activities relating to "Directive Waste" – that is waste covered by the EU Framework Directive (91/156) (see below, 4.6).

It should be noted that waste from a mine or quarry and waste from premises used for agriculture are not "controlled waste" under the *Controlled Waste Regulations*, and thus do not require a waste management licence. However to comply with the Framework Directive it will be necessary to extend waste management controls to "non-natural" agricultural waste and non-mineral mining and quarry waste.

Clinical waste (healthcare waste or healthcare risk waste) – other than that from a private dwelling or residential home – is classified as industrial waste for legislative purposes. Handlers of clinical waste are also subject to the duty of care provisions of section 34 of the EPA: this places a duty on producers, handlers and disposers of waste to ensure it is disposed of safely and legally (see 4.19.2 below). Most clinical waste (except that from households) is also subject to the *Special Waste Regulations 1996* (see 4.19.6 below). The *Controlled Waste Regulations 1992* define clinical waste as

- any waste which consists wholly or partly of human or animal tissue, blood or other body fluids, excretions, drugs or other pharmaceutical products, swabs or dressings, or syringes, needles or other sharp instruments, being waste which unless rendered safe may prove hazardous to any person coming into contact with it; and
- any other waste arising from medical, nursing, dental, veterinary, pharmaceutical or similar practice, investigation, treatment, care, teaching or research, or the collection of blood for transfusion, being waste which may cause infection to any persons coming into contact with it.

A Department of Environment Circular, 14/92, (WO 30/92; SOED 24/92) defines in detail wastes to be treated as "controlled waste". Further guidance is contained in DOE Circular 11/94 (WO 26/94; SOED 10/94) on waste management licensing and the Framework Directive on waste. Guidance on the treatment and management of clinical waste is given in Waste Management Paper No. 25.

4.3 AMOUNTS OF WASTE GENERATED

Total waste arisings from all sources in the UK are currently estimated to be about 423 m. tonnes a year of which about 172 m. tonnes is controlled waste from municipal (28 m. tonnes), industrial (69 m. tonnes), construction and demolition (70 m. tonnes) and commercial (15 m. tonnes) sources. Other major sources of waste include agriculture (80 m. tonnes) and mining and quarrying (74 m. tonnes). Special waste arisings in the UK for 1993/4 are estimated at 2.07 m. tonnes (*Digest of Environmental Statistics*, No. 20, 1998). In England and Wales municipal waste arisings for 1996/97 totalled 28 m. tonnes, 90% of which was from household sources; 1.5 m. tonnes of household waste was collected separately for recycling or composting (Municipal Waste Management 1995/96, DETR, 1998).

About 86% of all controlled waste in the UK is landfilled, 4% incinerated with the remainder being dumped at sea or disposed of by other means. For special wastes the figures are 70% landfilled and 5% incinerated; 15% is physically or chemically treated and the rest disposed of at sea. Of controlled waste, approximately 26 m. tonnes a year (England & Wales) can be classified as municipal waste (see EU Directive definition, 4.2 and 4.6) – this is collected by waste collection authorities. Eighty-three per cent of municipal waste in England and Wales was disposed of to landfill, 12% had value recovered from it through recycling, composting or energy recovery, and the remaining 5% was incinerated without energy recovery (Municipal Waste Management 1995/96, DETR, 1998).

The increasing amount of waste being generated is resulting in more awareness, both at EU and UK level, of the need for policies aimed at waste minimisation – i.e. reduction or prevention of waste at source, thus eliminating the need to treat and dispose of it. In 1996 the European Commission updated its 1989 *Community Strategy for Waste Management* which outlines its policy on waste prevention and minimisation – see below). The National Waste Strategies for England and Wales, Scotland, and Northern Ireland (see below, 4.19.4) must also include proposals for encouraging the prevention or reduction of waste production.

Although about half of our domestic waste could be recycled or re-used, there are still only a few appropriate schemes in the UK although more are likely to be established: section 49 of the EPA, which was brought into force on 1 August 1991, requires waste collection authorities to investigate and draw up plans for recycling schemes (see 4.19.5 below). The 1990 White Paper (*This Common Inheritance*) set a national target of 50% recovery of the recyclable content of domestic refuse by the year 2000 (i.e. about 25% of all household waste).

Hospital clinical waste amounts to something between 200,000 and 400,000 tonnes a year, most of which is currently incinerated on site. Incinerators, depending on their size, are regulated for either integrated pollution control or air pollution control under Part I of the *Environmental Protection Act 1990* – see chapters 1 and 2 and Appendix 1.1.

4.4 WASTE DISPOSAL: SOME OPTIONS

4.4.1 Landfill

Approximately 84% of municipal waste in England and Wales is disposed of to landfill (*Digest of Environmental Statistics*, No. 20, 1998). If not properly managed landfill sites can give rise to a variety of pollution problems, including leachate (a liquid formed when waste is broken down by bacteria which can cause contamination of groundwater); rodent infestation, production of potentially explosive levels of methane gas (65%), dangerous levels of carbon dioxide (35%), plus trace concentrations of a range of organic gases and vapours, are other problems associated with landfill sites.

Growing concern over the hazards posed by landfill gas has led to a number of government initiatives specifically aimed at minimising the risks to people and property from explosions; in July 1989, the Department of the Environment and the Welsh Office issued a circular (17/89) on the use of planning powers to control hazards posed by landfill gas. This followed the inclusion in the *Town and Country Planning General Development Order 1988* of a requirement for planning authorities to consult waste disposal authorities about any proposed development within 250 metres of land which has been used for waste disposal within the past 30 years. The DOE circular also suggests that particular attention be paid to proposals for new developments within 250 metres of existing developments and draws attention to existing powers which can be used to mitigate the hazards of landfill gas. It is suggested that some attention also be given to the problem of existing developments on or near landfill sites.

It should, however, also be noted that landfill gas can be harnessed as a valuable source of renewable energy, resulting in significant energy savings; in 1994 approximately 587 kt of landfill methane was extracted and flared or used for energy recovery; methane capture and use is now practised at over 150 landfill sites and in 1996 generated 136 MW of electricity.

Advice on the control of landfill gas is given in Waste Management Paper No. 27 (HMSO, 1991): this provides information on the production of landfill gas, and a summary, including key points for licensing officers, of the technical aspects of landfill gas; there is a discussion of the main factors responsible for the formation of landfill gas, advice on monitoring, information on the options available for its management and guidance on development on or near landfill sites. The Paper also gives guidance to waste regulation authorities on the criteria to be met before accepting the surrender of a waste management licence for a closed landfill site (s.61 of the *Environmental Protection Act* – to be revoked by the *Environment Act*).

Landfill Tax

As from October 1996 all waste deposited in landfill sites has been subject to a tax. Landfill operators licensed under the EPA or the *Pollution Control and Local Government Order (Northern Ireland) 1978* (or *Waste Management and Contaminated Land (NI) Order 1997* once this is implemented) were required to register their liability for the tax by 31 August 1996. Landfill operators who also use their site for recycling, incineration or sorting waste may apply to have the relevant area designated a tax-free site.

The *Landfill Tax Regulations 1996* (SI 1527) cover registration procedures, credits, accounting and environmental trusts. The *Landfill Tax (Qualifying Material) Order 1996* (SI 1528) defines the categories of waste which are subject to the lower rate of tax. The *Landfill Tax (Contaminated Land) Order 1996* (SI 1529) sets out the provisions for exempting waste generated as a result of cleaning up historically contaminated land.

The tax is based on the weight of the waste to be deposited, thus applying the polluter pays principle; it also aims to promote a more sustainable approach to waste management by providing an incentive to dispose of less waste to landfill and to recover more value from waste, e.g. through recycling etc.

Active waste is taxed at £7 per tonne (£10 from 1 April 1999), except for the following lower risk wastes where the tax is £2 per tonne:

- Naturally occurring rocks and soils, including clay, sand, gravel, sandstone, limestone, clean building or demolition stone, topsoil, peat, silt and dredgings.
- Ceramic or cemented materials: glass, ceramics (including bricks, tiles, clay ware, pottery, china, bricks & mortar), concrete. Refractories (bricks lining certain types of furnace).
- Processed or prepared mineral materials which have not been used or contaminated: moulding sands and clays, clay absorbents, manmade mineral fibres, silica, mica and abrasives.
- Furnace slags.
- Certain ash: bottom ash and fly ash from wood or coal combustion, including incineration.
- Low activity inorganic compounds: titanium dioxide, calcium carbonate, magnesium carbonate, magnesium oxide, aluminium hydroxide, magnesium hydroxide, calcium hydroxide and salt (if disposed of in a brine cavity), iron oxide, ferric hydroxide, aluminium oxide, zirconium dioxide.
- Gypsum and calcium sulphate-based plaster, if disposed of in a separate containment cell on a mixed landfill site, and on inactive-only sites.

Certain wastes are exempt from the tax; these include: dredgings arising from the maintenance of inland waterways and ports; naturally occurring minerals arising from mining and quarrying; burial of domestic pets at pet cemeteries; and waste resulting from remediation of historically contaminated land. From October 1999 inert waste used in the restoration of sites is also to be exempt (Budget Statement, 17 March 1998).

Landfill site operators may contribute funds to approved environmental bodies for spending on relevant environmental projects; they may then reclaim 90% of their contributions up to a maximum of 20% of their annual landfill tax payment. To qualify as "approved", environmental bodies must be non-profit distributing and independent of any local authority or site operator interest and they will need to enroll with ENTRUST, the regulatory body set up to oversee distribution of funds. Examples of projects falling within the scheme include: the restoration of closed landfill sites (or of damage caused by such sites) where liability was unclear or the person responsible has insufficient funds for clean up; provision, maintenance or improvement of a public park or amenity near a landfill site; funds could also be made available for research into, and development of, more sustainable waste management practices.

HM Customs and Excise has produced a series of information notes (1996) covering all aspects of the landfill tax and the way in which it is to be applied. The series includes: registration, tax liability, calculating the weight of waste, record keeping, environmental bodies, reviews and appeals, contaminated land.

The *Waste Management (Miscellaneous Provisions) Regulations 1997* (SI 351, effective 14 March 1997) make conviction for evading payment of landfill tax a "relevant offence" in relation to the definition of a "fit and proper" person under section 74 of the *Environmental Protection Act 1990*. Thus an offender risks being deemed unfit to hold a waste management licence. See also 4.19.8.

4.4.2 Incineration

Incineration is the burning of waste at high temperatures. This reduces the weight of the waste by about two-thirds and its volume by 90%. Uncontrolled burning of waste can give off poisonous chemicals such as hydrochloric acid, dioxins and furans and heavy metals. Hydrochloric acid contributes locally to acid rain and is given off by the burning of plastics. If organic matter and plastics are burnt at low temperatures, dioxins and furans may also be emitted. These are poisonous substances and it is therefore essential that incinerators operate at high temperatures in order to reduce such emissions to a minimum. Grit, chars and dust must also be controlled by special equipment. Heavy metals – such as cadmium, lead, arsenic and chromium – which originate in the waste will be collected in the dust filter; mercury, also a heavy metal, may however escape as a vapour. This is best controlled by reducing the source of mercury in waste (mainly batteries).

In the UK, around 10% of all waste is incinerated, and currently less than 2% of toxic waste. A growing shortage of suitable landfill sites may well lead to more waste being incinerated.

Incineration can be a valuable source of energy; a number of European cities have successful Combined Heat and Power (CHP) schemes generating heat and electricity using incinerators.

4.4.3 Recycling

The 1995 White Paper, *Making Waste Work*, set a target of recovering value from 40% of municipal waste by 2005, and of recycling and composting 25% of household waste by 2000. These targets are being reviewed in the context of the Government's obligation to produce a National Waste Strategy (*Environmental Protection Act 1990*, s.44A), and on which a first consultation document was published in June 1998 – see 4.19.4). *The Environmental Protection Act 1990* (ss.49 & 52) requires waste collection authorities to draw up plans for recycling household and commercial waste and empowers waste disposal authorities to pay recycling credits as a result of waste collected for recycling by waste collection authorities (see this chapter 4.19.5).

The DETR has recently updated the 1991 Waste Management Paper No. 28 which provided guidance for local authorities on preparing a recycling plan and implementing a recycling strategy. *Waste Policy Guidance: Preparing and Revising Local Authority Recycling Strategies and Recycling Plans* (DETR, 1998) suggests ways in which local authorities can plan to achieve the target of recovering value from 40% of municipal waste by 2005. It also shows how waste disposal and collection authorities can together develop a coordinated approach to municipal waste management in their area, which integrates the various treatment and disposal options for municipal waste.

An EU Directive on packaging waste adopted in 1994 also has as a prime purpose the recycling of such waste; this has been implemented in the UK through the *Producer Responsibility Obligations (Packaging Waste) Regulations 1997* which place certain obligations on producers to recover and recycle packaging waste – see this chapter 4.12 and 4.20.2.

4.5 WASTE MANAGEMENT PAPERS

This series of papers, prepared by the Department of Environment (now Department of the Environment, Transport and the Regions), provide technical guidance on all aspects of waste management, including legislative requirements and advice on treatment and safe disposal of waste. The papers were first issued following enactment of the *Control of Pollution Act 1974*; they are now being updated to take account of the *Environmental Protection Act 1990* and other technical developments. There are currently over 30 papers in the series – see Appendix 4.1.

THE EUROPEAN UNION AND WASTE MANAGEMENT

According to a 1987 report from the European Parliament, the Member States of the European Union (EU) together produce approximately 2,200 million tonnes of waste annually. Of this, 66% of household waste is landfilled, 33% incinerated and 7% composted. Over 60% of industrial waste and 95% of agriculture waste is re-used.

The European Union has adopted a number of Directives aimed at harmonising waste disposal policies throughout the EU and preventing the development of measures that might distort competition. Since October 1993, however, proposals for waste legislation have been based on environmental protection (Article 130S) rather than harmonisation (Article 100A).

In December 1996, European Environment Ministers adopted by Resolution an updated version of the 1989 *Community Strategy for Waste Management* (COM(96) 399). The hierarchy of principles of the 1989 Strategy is reaffirmed: that is that the prevention of waste should be the first priority, followed by recovery and then the safe disposal of waste. Implementation of the hierarchy would depend on choosing the best environmental solution having regard to economic and social costs (see also box). The Strategy also highlights the important role of producers in preventing waste and discusses the use of economic instruments, regulation and voluntary agreements. The Strategy

European Union Principles of Waste Management

- **prevention:** the following measures should be developed: promotion of clean technologies and products; reduction of the hazardousness of wastes, establishment of technical standards, and possibly EC-wide rules to limit the presence of certain dangerous substances in products, the promotion of re-use and recycling schemes, the appropriate use of economic instruments, eco-balances, eco-audit schemes, life-cycle analysis and actions on consumer information and education as well as the development of the eco-label system.
- **recovery:** where environmentally sound, preference should in general be given to the recovery of material over energy recovery operations. This reflects the greater effect on the prevention of waste produced by material recovery rather than by energy recovery.
- **final disposal:** particular care should be taken to avoid as much as possible incineration operations without energy recovery. Uncontrolled landfilling and contaminated land are two problems requiring special and strong actions at different levels.

Source: Executive Summary, Community Strategy for Waste Management, COM(96) 399, 30 July 1996.

reaffirms that controls on waste shipments need to be properly enforced and that waste generated within the EU should be disposed of within it and in the nearest appropriate facility (the self-sufficiency and proximity principles).

A list of EU measures relating to waste is at Appendix 6.4. Brief details of the institutions of the European Union, and of the legislative process are given in Appendix 6.

4.6 FRAMEWORK DIRECTIVE ON WASTE

Among the most important of the Directives adopted on waste was the 1975 "Framework" Directive which established general rules for waste management. This has been amended by a Directive adopted in 1991 (91/156/EEC) and should have been implemented by Member States by 1 April 1993. The Directive identifies 16 specific categories of waste, which is defined as "any substance or object ... which the holder discards or intends or is required to discard" (see 4.2.1 above). The Commission has drawn up a list of materials to be treated as waste: the *European Waste Catalogue* (Council Decision, 94/3/EC, January 1994) categorises waste by industry sector or process. Further work on the list is likely to classify materials as hazardous, non hazardous or potentially hazardous according to their physical, chemical and biological properties.

An important objective of the Directive is to ensure "that waste is recovered or disposed of without endangering human health and without using processes or methods which could harm the environment and in particular without

- risk to water, air, soil, plants or animals;
- causing nuisance through noise or odours; or
- adversely affecting the countryside or places of special interest".

Greater emphasis is placed on the prevention, reduction, re-use and recycling of waste, and on the use of waste as a source of energy. With the ultimate aim of the EU becoming self-sufficient in waste disposal, the Directive calls on Member States to establish a network of disposal facilities.

Member States are required to establish competent authorities who must draw up waste disposal plans in collaboration with other Member States and the Commission; the designated competent authorities are also to be responsible for issuing authorisations and waste management licences. Specified waste recovery operations and businesses which dispose of their waste on site do not require an authorisation but must be registered with the relevant authority; before permitting exemption from authorisation, Member States must have appropriate Regulations specifying the types of activity exempted, quantities of waste, disposal and recovery methods permitted and other conditions.

The Directive has been largely implemented through Part II of the *Environmental Protection Act 1990* and the *Waste Management Licensing Regulations 1994* – see later this chapter, 4.19.3. Department of Environment Circular 11/94 (WO 26/94; SOED 10/94) provides a detailed interpretation of the Directive's requirements and how these have been incorporated into national legislation.

4.7 INCINERATION

4.7.1 Municipal Waste Incinerators

Two Directives adopted in June 1989 require both new and existing municipal waste incinerators to meet much tighter emission standards. Municipal waste is defined as "domestic refuse as well as commercial or trade refuse and other waste which, because of its nature or its composition, is similar to domestic refuse". A municipal waste incinerator is defined as "any technical equipment used for the treatment of municipal waste by incineration, with or without recovery of the combustion heat generated but excluding plants used specifically for the incineration of sewage sludge, chemical, toxic and dangerous waste, medical waste from hospitals or other types of special waste, on land or at sea, even if these plants may burn municipal waste as well". This definition covers the whole site.

The Directive covering new plant (89/369/EEC) applies to all new municipal waste incinerators for which authorisation was granted after 30 November 1990. An objective of the Directive is to harmonise controls across the EU by setting standards which can be achieved with proven abatement technology and at a reasonable cost – i.e. Best Available Technique Not Entailing Excessive Cost (BATNEEC) (see chapter 1, 1.6). It sets emission limits which vary with the size of the plant, as well as operating and monitoring requirements. Requirements for meeting emission limits (see below) are included in authorisations under Part I of the *Environmental Protection Act 1990* (see chapters 1 and 2).

The Directive specifies measuring and monitoring requirements for the various categories of incinerator: for incinerators with a capacity of one tonne per hour or more, there must be continuous measurement of dust, carbon monoxide, oxygen and hydrogen chloride. For these incinerators too, periodic monitoring for heavy metals, hydrofluoric acid and sulphur dioxide will be required. There is also a general duty on Member States to specify maximum permissible periods during which emission limits may be breached due to "technically unavoidable stoppages", and to publish the results of emissions measurements.

Emission Limits for New Municipal Waste Incinerators: Directive 89/369 EEC

Pollutant	*Less than 1 tonne/h*	*1 tonne/h or more but less than 3 tonnes/h*	*3 tonnes/h or more*
Total dust	20	100	30
Heavy metals			
- Pb + Cr + Cu + Mn	-	5	5
- Ni + As	-	1	1
- Cd and Hg	-	0.2	0.2
Hydrochloric acid (HCl)	250	100	50
Hydrofluoric acid (HF)	-	4	2
Sulphur dioxide (SO_2)	-	300	300
Carbon monoxide (CO)	100	100	100
Organics (as total carbon)	20	20	20

Emission limits are in mg/Nm^3 as a function of the nominal capacity of the incineration plant. Combustion gases in combustion chambers must be kept after the last injection of combustion air at least 850 degrees C for two seconds in the presence of at least 6% oxygen. All measurements to be based on a standard gas condition of 101.3 kPa, 273 K (0 degrees C) 11% oxygen, or 9% carbon dioxide, dry gas.

The Directive covering existing plant (89/429/EEC) required standards to be progressively improved to meet those set for new plant. Existing incinerators – i.e. those for which authorisation was granted before 30 November 1990 – with a capacity of six tonnes/hour or more had to meet the standards applicable for new plant by 1 December 1996, or close down.

A two-stage improvement programme has been set for incinerators with a capacity of less than six tonnes/hour. Interim emission limits and operating standards had to be met by 1 December 1995, with full compliance with the standards set for new plant by 1 December 2000.

Other provisions of the Directive relate to emission limits in the case of technical stoppages, monitoring, and public access to information.

Both Directives are implemented in the UK through the *Municipal Waste Incineration Directions Order 1991* made under the *Environmental Protection Act*: those with a capacity of 1 tonne an hour or more are subject to Integrated Pollution Control (see chapter 1, 1.13); those less than 1 tonne an hour are subject to Local Air Pollution Control (see chapter 2, 2.11) – see also 4.23 below.

In October 1998, the Commission adopted a proposal for a Directive on waste incineration (COM(98) 281). This will replace the Directives on both new and existing municipal waste incinerators and cover the incineration of all wastes not covered by the 1994 Directive on hazardous waste incineration (including used oils, solvents and hospital wastes), municipal waste and other non-hazardous wastes. Strict emission limits, based on best available techniques, similar to those for hazardous waste incinerators are to be required, as well as compliance with the IPPC Directive. Limit values, are to be set for hydrogen chloride, hydrogen fluoride, heavy metals, sulphur oxides, nitrogen oxides, dioxins and furans, as well as discharges into water and leachate from residues. The Directive will also introduce strict requirements for the co-incineration of waste (i.e. the incineration of waste as an additional fuel in plants for energy generation) to ensure that operational standards are as high as for other plant; the incineration of biomass (wood and wood residues) is excluded from the Directive.

4.7.2 Hazardous Waste Incineration

This Directive (94/67/EC) was formally adopted in December 1994; it came into force on 31 December 1994 and should have been transposed into national legislation by 31 December 1996. Decision 97/283/EC specifies a harmonised measurement method to determine the mass concentration of dioxins and furans in atmospheric emissions in accordance with Article 7(2) of the Directive. This Directive has been implemented through the *Environmental Protection (Prescribed Processes and Substances) Amendment (Hazardous Waste Incineration) Regulations 1998* and through a statutory Direction to the Environment Agency and SEPA requiring them to include the Directive's obligations in conditions of authorisations – see 4.23 below.

The Directive specifies stricter standards for all incinerators of hazardous waste, including plant which burn such waste as a fuel in the industrial process. In aiming to minimise risks to human health and the environment, the Directive also has as an objective the adoption of an integrated approach to controlling emissions from incinerators to air, land and water.

A further aim is to raise the standards of hazardous waste management by introducing tighter standards, thus preventing the disposal of hazardous waste in older or less efficient incinerators. Specific standards are laid down for operating conditions and emissions (which are to be reviewed before the end of 2000) – see box below; there is a general requirement to use the best available technology. New plant had to meet operating standards from 1 January 1997 and existing plant must meet the standards by 30 June 2000. Operators of existing incinerators who notified the Environment Agency (or SEPA) by 30

June 1997 of their intention to operate for no more than 20,000 hours over the next five years and then close do not have to upgrade. Other Articles of the Directive – such as licensing and public access to information – are compatible with the UK's Integrated Pollution Control requirements. An environmental impact assessment must be carried out before a licence can be granted.

EU Standards for Hazardous Waste Incineration

Daily average value (100% compliance), mg/m³

Total dust	10
Total organic carbon	10
Hydrogen chloride	10
Hydrogen fluoride	1
Sulphur dioxide	50

Half-hourly average value, mg/m³, 100% and 97% compliance

Total dust	30	10
Total organic carbon	20	10
Hydrogen chloride	60	10
Hydrogen fluoride	4	2
Sulphur dioxide	200	50

Averages over sample period, minimum 30 mins, maximum 8 hours

Hg	0.05 mg/m³ (total)
Cd + Tl	0.05 mg/m³ (total)
Sb+As+Pb+Cr+Co+Cu+Mn+Ni+V+Sn	0.5 mg/m³ (total)

(new incinerators only; limits double for existing incinerators which must meet new standards within 42 months of Directive taking effect)

Dioxins and furans to be "reduced by the most progressive techniques"; from 1 January 1997 must not exceed 0.1 ng/m³ over min. 6 hrs, max. 8 hours sampling period.

Combustion gases in combustion chamber must be kept after the last injection of combustion air at least at 850 degrees C (or 1,100 degrees C for waste containing at least 1% halogenated organic substances) for 2 seconds in the presence of at least 6% oxygen or 3% when fed with liquid wastes.

Municipal waste incinerators are excluded from the Directive as they are already covered by two 1989 Directives (see above); also excluded are combustible liquid waste burning plant; sewage sludge and small clinical waste incinerators (so long as their contents do not make the incinerator hazardous in terms of the Directive); crematoria; and incinerators for animal carcasses.

The Commission is now proposing (COM(97) 604) to amend the Hazardous Waste Incineration Directive to extend controls on emissions of heavy metals and dioxins to the aquatic environment.

Specific emission limits – see below – are to be set for pollutants in the waste water generated by exhaust gas cleaning systems. All waste waters discharged from an incineration plant will require authorisation with strict conditions based on BAT, and operational controls parameters must be set for pH, temperature, flow and turbidity. The Directive requires instantaneous daily measurement for total suspended solids at the point of discharge, daily and monthly measurement of mercury, cadmium and thallium and daily measurements of the other heavy metals. For the first two months of operation of the incinerator, dioxins and furans must be measured every two months, and thereafter at least two measurements must be taken annually.

Proposed Limit Values for Discharges to Water from HW Incinerators

	Daily	*Monthly*
	average value (mg/l)	
Total suspended solids	20	
Mercury & its compounds	0.02	0.01
Cadmium & its compounds	0.05	0.02
Thallium & its compounds	0.05	0.02
Antimony, arsenic, lead, chromium, cobalt, copper, manganese, nickel, vanadium, tin	5	
Dioxins and furans	Annual measurements not to exceed 0.5 ng/l	

4.8 HAZARDOUS WASTE

In 1975 and 1978, Directives were adopted on the disposal of waste oils (75/439/EEC), and on toxic and dangerous waste (78/319/EEC) respectively. The latter established a list of 27 substances which in certain circumstances might cause waste to be toxic and dangerous. This Directive, which was repealed upon implementation of the 1991 Directive, also prohibited uncontrolled dumping and tipping and made provision for the labelling of packages containing waste; the licensing of storage, treatment and/or disposal establishments; control of the transport of wastes; and the planning by competent authorities within the Member States of a programme of disposals.

The current Hazardous Waste Directive (91/689/EEC) was adopted in December 1991 but implementation was deferred until 27 June 1995 owing to difficulties in drawing up a definitive list of hazardous wastes. This was finally adopted in December 1994 (Council Decision 94/904/EC) and includes 200 types of waste split into 20 categories; inclusion of a waste on the list assumes that it is dangerous unless a

Member State can prove otherwise. The European Commission is currently considering additions to the types of waste on the list.

The Directive redefines "hazardous waste" and aims to achieve greater harmonisation in the management of hazardous waste. All wastes with characteristics which render them hazardous, e.g. corrosive, infectious or ecotoxic substances, would be covered. Annexes to the Directive list the categories of waste to be covered, the various components which would make it hazardous; a third annex lists 15 characteristics of which one or more must be present for the waste to be hazardous. Domestic waste from domestic premises is exempt from this Directive. A common list of wastes relating to both this and the Framework Directive (see 4.6 above) has been prepared by the Commission.

The Directive prohibits the mixing of hazardous waste with other waste except where it is a necessary part of the disposal operation and places stricter controls on carriers of hazardous waste. Hazardous waste producers will be subject to periodic inspection and they and waste carriers must keep records of waste transactions for one and three years respectively; waste transfers must comply with the EU's 1993 Transfrontier Shipment of Waste Regulation which came into force in May 1994 – see below.

Compliance with the Directive in the UK is effected through the *Special Waste Regulations 1996* (see this chapter, 4.19.6) with similar 1998 Regulations in N. Ireland. Other requirements of the Directive, such as licensing and duty of care are already included in Part II of the *Environmental Protection Act 1990* covering England, Scotland and Wales and in N. Ireland by Part II of the *Waste and Contaminated Land (Northern Ireland) Order 1997,* once implemented.

The Commission is currently formulating a proposal for an amendment to the Hazardous Waste Directive which would require the separate collection of hazardous municipal wastes, including that from households. Manufacturers would be required to mark products which can become hazardous when disposed of with an identifying logo to enable their separate collection.

4.9 TRANSFRONTIER SHIPMENT OF WASTE

4.9.1 EU Regulation 259/93

A 1984 Directive on the Transfrontier Shipment of Hazardous Wastes (84/631/EEC), amended in 1986 (86/279/EEC), required pre-notification of transfrontier shipments of hazardous waste; they had to be sent only to facilities that could dispose of them without danger to human life or the environment, their passage documented, and exports of hazardous waste outside the European Union prohibited unless the receiving country had given its prior consent. The 1984 Directive has been replaced by Regulation 259/93 on the Supervision and Control of Shipments of Waste within, into and out of the EU which came into force in May 1994. The earlier Directives were implemented in the UK by Regulations (1988) of the same name; these have now been repealed and replaced by 1994 Regulations. As EU Regulations are directly applicable by all Member States they do not need transposing into national legislation; thus the 1994 UK Regulations cover such matters as designation and powers of competent authority, offences and penalties etc – see 4.25 below.

The EU's 1993 Regulation while building on the terms of the 1984 Directive tightens up the procedure for transfrontier shipments of waste; unlike the 1984 Regulation it covers all waste (as defined by the Framework Directive) and thus enabled the Community to ratify the 1989 Basel Convention on the Control of Transboundary Movements of Hazardous Wastes and their Disposal – see below.

The Regulation covers the movement of all wastes (i.e. not just hazardous waste) although there are various exemptions such as civil aviation waste, radioactive waste and waste covered by other EU legislation; different requirements apply depending on whether the shipment is between, into or outside (including transit through) Member States. There is a general requirement on Member States to ensure appropriate arrangements for dealing with movements of waste within Member States. The import of waste into, and export of waste out of, the EU for disposal except to EFTA countries which are a party to the Basel Convention is banned. Shipments to African, Caribbean and Pacific countries covered by the Lomé Convention are also banned. Waste exported by an ACP country for reprocessing can be returned to that country following reprocessing.

In line with the EU's aim that States should become self-sufficient in waste disposal, all waste should be treated or disposed of in an appropriate facility nearest to where it was produced. An exception to this is where it would not be economically feasible to set up a facility for a particular type of waste because of the small amounts involved.

The Regulation includes detailed procedures for pre-notification, authorisation and documentation describing the waste and prior consent for transfrontier shipments. The person sending the waste (the notifier) is obliged to take it back if the person to whom it was sent (the consignee) is unable to deal with it appropriately; within 180 days of receiving the waste the consignee must send the notifier a certificate confirming that the waste has been dealt with in an environmentally sound manner. Multiple shipments of a similar nature may be covered by a single consignment document though the regulatory authority may require each shipment to be accompanied by specimen documentation. All shipments must be covered by financial guarantee in case the shipment has to be returned to the originator or sent elsewhere – this guarantee must be agreed with the waste regulation authority who will issue a certificate to this effect. This financial guarantee is in addition to any other insurance or financial guarantee covering the shipment and its disposal or recovery.

Waste for recovery or recycling is divided into three categories – red, amber and green – according to how hazardous it is; red wastes include PCBs, dioxins and asbestos; amber wastes include waste oils and petrol sludges, and green wastes include paper, glass, wood waste, waste from mining operations, textiles and rubber. For red and amber wastes intended for recovery or recycling the controls are the same as for shipments of waste for disposal with the added requirement that wastes on the red list must have the written consent of the authorities in the receiving country prior to shipment; amber wastes may be shipped within 30 days of the authorities in the receiving country acknowledging notification and no objections having been raised. Green wastes for recovery or recycling should be accompanied by basic information about the shipment, including a description and the quantities involved.

In January 1997 EU Environment Ministers adopted an Amendment to the 1993 Regulation (120/97/EC). This implements an amendment to the Basel Convention (see below): exports to non-OECD countries of hazardous waste for disposal have been banned with immediate effect; exports for recovery are banned from 1 January 1998. A further amendment to the Regulation (COM(97) 685, published January 1998), which extends the control procedures for red and amber wastes to certain exports of green wastes, was formally adopted in June 1998. The amendment covers exports of green wastes to non-OECD countries who have indicated that they do not wish to receive some or all types of green wastes for recovery and also non-OECD countries who have not responded to Commission communications regarding acceptance of green wastes for recovery.

A Department of Environment Circular 13/94 (revised by DOE letter 26.1.95; WO 44/94; SOED 21/94; NI WM 1/94) explains in detail the requirements of both the EU and UK Regulations (see 4.25 below).

The transfrontier shipment of radioactive waste is regulated by a European Atomic Energy Union Directive 92/3/Euratom, adopted in February 1992 – see this chapter 4.31.6. The shipment of radioactive wastes within the EU is regulated by Euratom Regulation 1493/93 of June 1993.

4.9.2 Basel Convention

The *Convention on the Control of Transboundary Movements of Hazardous Wastes and their Disposal*, prepared under the auspices of the UN Environment Programme, came into force on 5 May 1992. There are currently 120 parties to the Convention, including the European Community and the UK, who both ratified it in February 1994.

The Convention takes as a basic principle the need to reduce both the generation of hazardous wastes and their transboundary movement to a minimum. It says that all states have the right to ban the import of hazardous waste and there are extensive pre-notification requirements for all transfrontier movements of household and industrial wastes. The exporting state has a duty to ensure that all wastes, whether for recovery or disposal, can be dealt with in an environmentally sound manner; it also has a duty to arrange for the return of any wastes failing to go to an appropriate treatment or disposal plant. The Convention permits parties to it to agree bi-lateral arrangements for trade in hazardous waste and prohibits such arrangements with others. Hazardous wastes which are to be exported must be packaged, labelled and transported in accordance with recognised international standards.

In September 1995, parties to the Convention agreed an amendment to the Convention which will come into force 90 days after ratification by 65 Parties to the Convention. As at 20 October 1998, there had been 20 ratifications (including the European Community and the UK). The amendment provides for an immediate ban on exports of hazardous waste for disposal from OECD to non-OECD countries and a similar ban on exports for recovery or recycling from 1 January 1998, although such exports may be continued by agreement between an OECD and non-OECD country. Non-OECD countries which wish to continue importing hazardous waste for recycling or recovery must notify the Convention Secretariat of the types and quantities of waste it will accept, processes to be used and method of final disposal of the residues. Lists of hazardous and non-hazardous wastes covered by the ban to be annexed to the Convention were agreed by Parties to the Convention in February 1998. List A includes over 50 categories of waste defined as hazardous; List B covers those waste categories which the Basel Convention does not define as hazardous but which nevertheless may contain hazardous characteristics and thus be covered by the ban. A further list – List C – covers wastes "awaiting classification". This latter amendment to the Convention was implemented in the UK in November 1998 (Command Paper 4061).

4.10 DANGEROUS SUBSTANCES

Directives have been adopted on polychlorinated biphenyls (PCBs) and polychlorinated terphenyls (PCTs) – 96/59/EC which repeals a 1976 Directive (76/403/EEC); on wastes from the titanium dioxide industry (1978 and 1982); and on the use of sewage sludge in agriculture (1986). This latter was implemented in the UK in September 1989 through the *Sludge (Use in Agriculture) Regulations* (amended 1990) – see chapter 2, 2.16.

The 1996 Directive on PCBs and PCTs, adopted in September 1996, aims to reduce risks to human health and the environment through stricter controls on their disposal; it includes requirements for inventories, labelling and treatment of all significant PCB holdings and tighter regulation of all treatment facilities. See also chapter 5, 5.21 regarding avoiding marine pollution in the disposal of PCBs.

A number of Directives dealing with the discharge of hazardous substances to water have been adopted and information about these is contained in chapter 5 on water pollution.

4.10.1 Batteries

A Directive (91/157/EEC) adopted in March 1991 aims to reduce the level of heavy metals in batteries and to ensure separate collection of both single use and rechargeable cells for recovery or disposal. In 1993 Member States had to begin drawing up an identification scheme for batteries and accumulators for separate collection, recycling and heavy metal content. The UK has implemented part of the Directive through Regulations made under the *European Communities Act 1972* – see this chapter, 4.24.

The Commission is expected to bring forward proposals for a further Directive which would set new collection and recycling targets for all types of batteries; it would also impose marketing restrictions on batteries containing more than the background level of mercury, phase-out batteries containing cadmium by 2008, and oblige Member States to set up schemes for collecting waste batteries separately from other household waste.

4.11 LANDFILL

In June 1994 Environment Ministers agreed by qualified majority a draft Directive (COM(93) 275) on the landfill of waste. However in May 1996 the European Parliament rejected the draft Directive on the grounds that exemptions and waivers agreed by Ministers could result in existing legislation in some countries being seriously weakened. In May 1997, the Commission published a revised proposal for a draft

Directive, COM(97) 105 (as amended by COM(98) 189) which aims to reduce the amount of waste landfilled and to promote recycling and recovery. EU Ministers formally adopted a common position on the draft Directive in June 1998.

The new Directive will require Member States to implement strategies to reduce the amount of biodegradable waste sent to landfill to 75% of its 1995 total by 2006, 50% by 2009 and 35% by 2016. The final target will be reviewed in 2014. Member States (including the UK) who currently landfill a majority of waste would have an extra four years to meet each target.

Three types of landfill site are defined – for hazardous waste, non-hazardous waste and inert waste, with the Directive also covering underground and mine storage. All waste would need to be pretreated prior to landfilling unless this would have no environmental benefit or is not feasible (e.g. for inert wastes); co-disposal of hazardous and domestic waste is also banned. The disposal of the following wastes to landfill would be banned: liquid waste; explosive, corrosive or inflammable waste; infectious hospital waste; used whole and shredded tyres (two years and five years respectively after the Directive takes effect); and other waste not meeting certain criteria set out in an Annex to the Directive. Monitoring schemes to establish the amounts of waste being sent to landfill, and its biodegradable content, would need to be set up within two years of the Directive entering its force. Charges for landfilling would have to reflect the full costs of management of the site, as well as closure and aftercare for up to 50 years. A system of operating permits is proposed, many of the features of which are similar to the UK's current waste management licensing procedures. All sites will require licensing; existing sites not conforming to the Directive will need to do so within eight years of its incorporation into national law, or stop operating.

Member States would be able to exempt from the Directive landfills with a total capacity of less than 10,000 tonnes serving islands; also exempt are landfills serving isolated settlements – i.e. those with fewer than 500 inhabitants per municipality, and no more than 5 per sq. km, and more than 50 km from the nearest urban area with more than 250 inhabitants per sq. km.

4.12 PACKAGING WASTE

The Directive on Packaging and Packaging Waste (94/62/EC) was adopted in December 1994 and came into force on 31 December 1994. It applies to all waste packaging – household, commercial and industrial – and had to be implemented by 30 June 1996, when Directive 83/339/EEC (containers of liquids for human consumption) was repealed. Decision 97/129/EC established an identification system for packaging materials as required by the Directive; Decision 97/138/EC relates to the formats of databases on packaging and packing waste established under the Directive with the aim of making these compatible throughout the EU.

The EU produces about 50 m. tonnes of packaging waste annually, of which only about 18% is recycled. The Directive therefore places a strong emphasis on the prevention of packaging waste and on reducing the amount of packaging used (while safeguarding consumer safety and product quality); in promoting the use of recyclable and reusable materials and the use of packaging likely to have the least impact on the environment, an annex to the Directive lays down standards for manufacture, composition, etc to be complied with by the end of 1997. The composition by weight of lead, cadmium, hexavalent chromium and mercury in packaging and packaging waste must be reduced over five years.

A principle aim of the Directive is to harmonise the recovery and recycling targets to be achieved by Member States to ensure no barriers to trade and at the same time to achieve a high level of environmental protection. Within five years of coming into force a target of 50-65% recovery of packaging materials in waste should be met and a target of 25-45% recycled with a minimum of 15% of each material. The Council of Ministers will be looking for substantial increases in these percentages within ten years.

Also within five years of entering into force, the Directive requires all packaging to be labelled with its recyclable or recoverable content; Directives outlining marking and identification systems are currently being prepared. Member States must set up suitable systems for the collection of packaging and packaging waste and its recycling or reuse and should ensure that consumers have adequate information regarding the marking of packaging, the benefits of reusable packaging and about return systems.

Member States may use economic instruments as a means of achieving the Directive's objectives but only "in accordance with the principles governing Community policy on the environment, such as the polluter pays principle, and with full respect for obligations stemming from the Treaty".

The Directive has been implemented in England, Scotland and Wales through the *Producer Responsibility Obligations (Packaging Waste) Regulations 1997* (SI 648) which came into force on 6 March 1997, with a draft of similar Regulations for Northern Ireland published in 1998; and the *Packaging (Essential Requirements) Regulations 1998* (SI 1165) which apply throughout the UK – see this chapter 4.20.2.

In 1996, the Commission issued a proposal for a draft Directive on marking of packaging and on the establishment of a conformity assessment procedure for packaging (COM(96) 191); only packaging meeting the 1994 Directive would be able to use the approved symbols – one for reusable packaging and one for recyclable packaging – with all other symbols being prohibited; manufacturers would be required to prepare a statement of compliance with the 1994 Directive to be available for inspection by national authorities.

4.13 CIVIL LIABILITY ON WASTE

The text of a Draft Directive on civil liability for damage caused by waste was published in 1989 (and an amended version – COM (91)219 – in 1991), but there has been no progress for some time. The draft proposes making the waste producer strictly liable for any damage (to people or property) and "impairment of the environment" – i.e. lasting harm to the environment – until the waste has been transferred to a licensed waste disposal facility; in certain instances the waste carrier or waste holder would also be liable, e.g. if the waste producer could not be found. Waste producers would also remain liable for any damage to the environment if the waste disposal facility can prove that it was given incorrect or false information about the waste. Nuclear waste, waste covered by international conventions on oil pollution damage and domestic waste would be excluded. The draft also proposes investigating the feasibility of establishing a European fund for compensation to cover those cases where the liable person either cannot be found or is unable to bear the full costs of compensation.

The draft Directive would enable environmental, nature protection and common interest groups or associations to take legal action to ensure any environmental harm is remedied; it will be left to Member States to introduce legislation implementing this right.

IMPLEMENTATION AND ENFORCEMENT AUTHORITIES

4.14 ENVIRONMENT AGENCY

As from 1 April 1996 the Environment Agency took over responsibility for waste regulation from the local authority waste regulation authorities. As well as ensuring high standards of waste management and implementing the forthcoming National Waste Strategy, the Environment Agency's responsibilities include

- issuing waste management licences and enforcement of licences and any conditions attached to them; surrender of licences (4.19.3 below);
- compliance with the 1991 duty of care regulations (4.19.2 below);

- registration of waste carriers and brokers (4.22.1 & 2 below).

The Agency is also responsible for those areas of contaminated land designated as "special sites" because of the nature of contamination – see below 4.28.3.

Details of the Environment Agency's objectives and other responsibilities are given in chapter 1, 1.7.1.

4.15 SCOTTISH ENVIRONMENT PROTECTION AGENCY

As from 1 April 1996, SEPA also took over responsibility for the regulation of waste, including those areas of contaminated land designated as "special sites".

Details of SEPA's objectives and other responsibilities are given in chapter 1, 1.7.2.

4.16 LOCAL AUTHORITIES

The *Environment Act 1995*, section 57, adds a new Part IIA to the *Environmental Protection Act 1990* on contaminated land. Local authorities have a duty to inspect their land from time to time to identify whether any of it is contaminated and to ensure its suitable remediation – see later this chapter, 4.28.3.

Local authorities – acting as principal litter authorities – have a statutory duty to keep road, land, open highways etc free of litter and refuse; see later this chapter, 4.29.

4.16.1 Waste Disposal Authorities

Waste disposal authorities – county or district councils or unitary authorities as appropriate – are responsible for arranging for the disposal of all controlled waste in their area collected by the waste collection authority.

Under the *Environmental Protection Act*, local authorities in England and Wales had either to privatise their disposal operations, set up a joint operation with the private sector or set up local authority waste disposal companies (LAWDCs) as "arms length companies" to be run as commercial undertakings; waste disposal operations are subject to competitive tendering.

4.16.2 Waste Collection Authorities

Waste collection is the responsibility of district, metropolitan or city councils, or of the appropriate unitary authority. Waste collection authorities have a duty to arrange for the collection of household and, if requested, commercial waste. WCAs are also responsible for drawing up and implementing recycling plans. Many local authorities have privatised their collection facilities.

4.17 NORTHERN IRELAND

Under the *Pollution Control and Local Government (NI) Order 1978* district councils in Northern Ireland currently have a duty to arrange for the collection and disposal of controlled waste; they are also responsible for licensing private waste disposal facilities, for monitoring special waste and transfrontier shipment of waste movements, and for drawing up ten year waste disposal plans for their area.

New legislation – the *Waste and Contaminated Land (Northern Ireland) Order 1997* – received Royal Assent on 26 November 1997; when implemented it will introduce controls on waste management and contaminated land similar to those operating in the rest of the United Kingdom. The legislation will be enforced by the Northern Ireland Department of the Environment (Waste and Contaminated Land Inspectorate which is part of the Environment and Heritage Service).

WASTE ON LAND: REGULATORY CONTROLS

4.18 PLANNING CONTROLS AND ENVIRONMENTAL ASSESSMENT

As is the case with any use of land (apart from agricultural or defence activities) planning permission under the *Town and Country Planning Act 1990 (Town and Country Planning (Scotland) Act 1972)*, or exemption from its requirements, must be obtained. Application for planning permission, together with a copy of the environmental assessment where necessary (see chapter 1, 1.21 and 1.23) is made to the district council and this must be advertised locally. A public inquiry may be held if sufficient objections are received, if the developer appeals against a refusal or if the Secretary of State "calls in" the application. Where the local authority is the developer it must pass a resolution in council to give itself planning permission whereupon the normal requirements to advertise and receive objections still apply and the Secretary of State may still call in the application for a public inquiry if so minded.

Where a site was in use for waste disposal in July 1948, planning permission need not be sought as it is deemed to have an established use for that purpose. However if the nature of the operations on the site changes – e.g. if an incinerator is to be built where only landfill operations have been carried out – new planning permission must be obtained.

Planning permission, if and when granted, will usually contain conditions on the use of the site such as the limits of the area involved in the operations and, where relevant, the provisions to be made for the restoration of the land after operations have ceased. For land which may already be contaminated, the planning permission may be granted subject to conditions relating to the remedial action required. Specific details as to how a site should be operated will be included in the conditions attached to a waste management licence issued under the *Waste Management Licensing Regulations 1994* – see below 4.19.3.

Planning Policy Guidance Note on *Planning and Pollution Control* (PPG 23) outlines the responsibilities of planners and their relationship with statutory pollution control bodies and advises on avoiding duplication between planning and pollution control authorities. In particular it provides guidance on those industrial developments posing a risk of pollution, waste treatment and disposal sites, and the redevelopment of contaminated land; there is also guidance on development proposals near such sites. A new PPG on planning and waste disposal and management (PPG 10) is currently being finalised; it outlines the implications of landfill for long term land use planning and summarises the responsibilities of local authorities as land use planning authorities and the Environment Agency as the waste management licensing authority; wherever possible it is suggested that the two authorities should deal with applications simultaneously to avoid duplication.

In Scotland, *National Planning Policy Guidance 10, Planning and Waste Management* (March 1996) reminds planning authorities of the need to take account of the Framework Directive on Waste (see above, 4.6) – i.e. that waste should be recovered, or disposed of in the nearest suitable facility, without risk to the environment or human health. Planners are urged to safeguard groundwater when developing plans for all new waste facilities and to consult SEPA at appropriate stages. Guidance is also given on which decisions belong to planning and which to pollution control.

4.19 ENVIRONMENTAL PROTECTION ACT 1990, PART II

With the implementation of the *Waste Management Licensing Regulations 1994* in May 1994 Part I of the *Control of Pollution Act 1974* was finally replaced by Part II of the *Environmental Protection Act 1990* (EPA).

As noted above (4.17), the *Waste and Contaminated Land (Northern Ireland) Order* 1997 will introduce similar controls to those applying in the rest of the UK. Reference to the appropriate article of the Northern Ireland legislation is given throughout this chapter and is shown as follows: (NI: WCLO, Art.0).

The EPA builds on the system put in place by COPA with stricter licensing controls and other provisions aimed at ensuring waste handling, disposal and recovery operations do not harm the environment. Responsibility for waste rests on the person who produces it and everyone who handles it, right through to final disposal or reclamation. Only "fit and proper" persons may run waste sites and responsibility for a closed landfill site will continue until all risks of pollution or harm to human health and safety are past.

As well as reorganising local authority responsibilities for waste management, the EPA increased the former HM Inspectorate of Pollution's role in this area by giving it responsibility to oversee the activities of local waste regulation authorities. As from 1 April 1996, however, waste regulation became the responsibility of the Environment Agency in England and Wales and of the Scottish Environment Protection Agency (*Env. Act 1995*, ss.5(5) & 21(1)); thus, all references to a waste regulation authority in the EPA as amended are references to the Environment Agency or SEPA, as appropriate. In Northern Ireland, the *Waste and Contaminated Land (Northern Ireland) Order 1997* will be enforced by the Department of the Environment (Waste and Contaminated Land Inspectorate of the Environment and Heritage Service).

Part II of the EPA, as amended by the *Environment Act 1995*, Sch. 22, paras 62-88, applies to the disposal of all "controlled waste"; this includes household, industrial and commercial waste as defined by the *Controlled Waste Regulations 1992* and the 1991 EU Framework Directive (see 4.6 above); it also covers "special waste" – i.e. waste that is difficult or dangerous to dispose of – for which special provisions are made.

This part of the EPA (NI, WCLO, Part II) also introduces a duty of care for producers and handlers of waste; the separation of local authority regulatory and disposal functions; and amends waste disposal planning requirements and licensing controls.

It should be noted that incinerators with a capacity of 1 tonne/hour or less are regulated by local authorities under Part I of the EPA 1990 (in Scotland by SEPA) – see chapter 2, 2.11. Larger incinerators – with a capacity of more than 1 tonne an hour, chemical recovery, and waste derived fuel manufacturing processes – are prescribed for Integrated Pollution Control under Part I of the EPA and thus the responsibility of the Environment Agency or SEPA (see chapter 1, 1.13). Other legislation of relevance to incinerators is given later in this chapter, see 4.23. In Northern Ireland, incinerators are regulated by the DOE(NI).

In this chapter of the *Pollution Handbook*, unless otherwise stated, the term "regulatory authority", means the Environment Agency, SEPA, or the DOE(NI), as appropriate.

4.19.1 Prohibition on Unauthorised or Harmful Depositing, Treatment or Disposal of Waste (s.33) *(NI: WCLO, Art.4)*

Under this section

- it is an offence to deposit, knowingly cause or permit the disposal of controlled waste on land without a waste management licence;
- any waste to be deposited must be treated, kept or disposed of in accordance with the terms of the waste management licence, and
- waste must be dealt with in such a way that it is unlikely to cause pollution or harm to human health.

This sub-section – 33(1) – of the Act does not apply to household waste which is treated, kept or disposed of within an area attached to a domestic property (and with the permission of the occupier). Under the *Controlled Waste Regulations 1992*, this exclusion does not extend to clinical waste, asbestos, or any mineral or synthetic oil or grease.

The latter sub-section was brought into force on 1 April 1992, and the first two on 1 April 1993 (E, W & S).

It is however, a defence to prove that an act (e.g. unauthorised deposit, treatment or disposal etc) in relation to the waste was done in an emergency and appropriate steps taken to minimise environmental pollution and harm to human health, and that full details of the act were given to the waste regulation authority as soon as practicable (*Env. Act 1995*, Sch. 22, para 64). It is also a defence for an employee to show that waste was deposited illegally under instructions or that there was no reason to believe anything was wrong.

Dumping of any waste (including special waste) or treating it without a licence may result in a maximum fine of £20,000 and/or six months in prison on summary conviction or an unlimited fine and/or two years in prison (five years if special waste is involved) on conviction on indictment.

4.19.2 Duty of Care etc as Respects Waste (s.34) *(NI: WCLO, Art.5)*

This section, aimed at curbing the illegal disposal of controlled waste, has been implemented through Regulations which came into force on 1 April 1992 (E, S & W). A legal duty of care is imposed on anyone – from producers, to carriers and disposers of waste – to ensure that

- waste is not illegally disposed of or dealt with without a licence or in breach of a licence or in a way that causes pollution or harm;
- waste does not escape from a person's control;

- waste is transferred only to an "authorised person", such as a local authority, a registered carrier or a licensed disposer;
- when the waste is transferred, it is accompanied by a full written description so that each person who has it knows enough to deal with it properly and thus avoids committing an offence under section 33 of the Act.

The duty does not apply to domestic householders in respect of their own domestic waste; nor does it apply to animal waste collected and transported under the *Animal By-Products Order 1992*. The duty does however apply to a householder who disposes of household waste from a neighbour's property and to builders disposing of rubble etc from a house in which they are working. The duty of care also applies to the Crown – i.e. government departments etc – and since 1 October 1995 has applied to scrap metal yards. Special waste is covered by the duty of care; such waste must of course also comply with the requirements of the *Special Waste Regulations 1996* – see 4.19.6 below.

Environmental Protection (Duty of Care) Regulations 1991 (SI 2839)

These Regulations cover England, Scotland and Wales and came into force in April 1992. They provide for a mandatory system of signed transfer notes and require all those subject to the duty of care to keep records of waste received and transferred. Information to be recorded on the transfer note must include a full description of the waste – its special features, hazardous substances, source, how it was produced etc. Other details to be recorded include quantity of waste (by weight if possible), whether/how containerised, names and addresses of those involved in the transfer, and place and date of transfer. In summary, sufficient information should be given to ensure that anybody coming into contact with it has enough detail to deal with it properly and in compliance with the duty of care.

A transfer note, together with the full description of the waste must accompany each consignment of waste. Regular or multiple transfers of waste between the same people need not be individually documented provided that the details on the transfer note remain unchanged (amendment to EPA by s.33 of *Deregulation and Contracting Out Act 1994*); in the case of regular transfers, the transfer note should be renewed at least once a year. Records of all waste must be kept for at least two years.

Before transferring waste to a waste carrier it is important to check that a valid registration certificate is held; waste holders should assure themselves that their waste falls within the scope of the licence or exemption at the site to be used.

Where a waste regulation authority (i.e. Environment Agency or SEPA) wishes to assure itself that the duty of care is being complied with, or to follow up a suspected unlicensed dumping of waste, it may serve notice on a waste holder requesting copies of relevant documents within seven days.

A statutory code of practice (1991, updated 1996) giving practical guidance on how to discharge the duty of care has been drawn up by the Department of Environment (now DETR) and the Welsh Office, and a similar code for Scotland by the Scottish Development Department. (A code is also to be drawn up for Northern Ireland.) This gives step by step advice on following the duty of care and what to do if it is suspected that the waste does not correspond to its description or is being handled incorrectly. The code also outlines the law with regard to the duty of care and the regulations on keeping records.

Breach of the code is not an offence (although breach of the duty of care is). It is however admissible in court as evidence in deciding if a breach of the duty has occurred. An offence under this section of the Act may result in a £5,000 fine on summary conviction, or an unlimited fine on conviction on indictment.

A joint circular from the Department of Environment (19/91), Welsh Office (63/91) and Scottish Office (25/91), gives advice on the operation of the duty of care. It complements the advice for producers and holders of waste given in the code of practice.

4.19.3 Waste Management Licences (ss.35-44) *(NI: WCLO, Arts.6-18)*

These sections of the EPA have been implemented through the *Waste Management Licensing Regulations 1994* which came into force on 1 May 1994. They replace and repeal sections 3-11 of the *Control of Pollution Act 1974* which covered site licensing, and under which almost anybody could get a site licence provided planning permission had been obtained for use of the land. Changes to procedures and the regulation of waste management licensing as a result of amendments to the EPA in Schedule 22 to the *Environment Act 1995* are reflected in the text below.

1995 Amendment Regulations (SI 288) extend the licensing regulations to the scrap metal industry; 1996 Amendment Regulations (SI 634) and similar in Scotland (S.100) and 1997 Amendment Regulations (SI 2203) are largely concerned with amending the provisions relating to qualifications for fit and proper persons (see below, 4.19.8). 1997 Regulations – *the Waste Management (Miscellaneous Provisions) Regulations 1997* (SI 351) – make evasion of landfill tax a "relevant offence" for the purposes of whether someone is "fit and proper" to hold a waste management licence (EPA, s.74; see

4.19.8 below). 1998 Amendment Regulations (SI 606) relate to registration of waste brokers and charging schemes for registration of scrap metal recovery and vehicle dismantling sites (see 4.22.2 below).

In Northern Ireland, Articles 6-18 of the *Waste and Contaminated Land (Northern Ireland) Order 1997* will have the same effect as sections 35-44 of the EPA as amended by the *Environment Act 1995*.

Fees and charges in relation to waste management licences are fixed in accordance with sections 41-43 of the *Environment Act 1995* (NI: WCLO, Art.15) – see 4.20.1 below.

The Waste Management Licensing Regulations 1994 (SI 1056)

The *Waste Management Licensing Regulations 1994* (WML Regulations) apply in England, Scotland and Wales. They came into force on 1 May 1994 and ensure the UK's compliance with the EU's Framework Directive on Waste 75/442, as amended by 91/156 (see 4.6 above). The Regulations set out the procedure for obtaining a licence and also deal with revocations and suspensions of licences, appeals, public registers (EPA: ss.64-66; NI: WCLO, Art.34-36) and the definition of fit and proper persons (EPA: s.74; NI: WCLO, Art.3). The Regulations list the offences under which if a person has been convicted they would not be considered a fit and proper person to be a licence holder. They also introduce a system for the registration of waste brokers – see below 4.22.2.

Much of the detailed procedure on compliance with the Regulations is contained in the EPA itself and in schedules attached to the Regulations, as amended by the *Environment Act 1995*.

A Department of the Environment Circular 11/94 (SOED 10/94; WO 26/94) gives guidance on the EU Framework Directive on Waste and its incorporation into UK legislation and also on implementation of the UK Regulations. Waste Management Paper No. 4, *The Licensing of Waste Facilities* (published 1994), provides guidance for the regulatory authorities on how they should carry out their licensing functions; under section 35(8) of the EPA, the regulatory authorities are under a duty to have regard to this guidance (or any other issued by the Secretary of State).

It should be noted that waste from a mine or quarry and waste from premises used for agriculture are not "controlled waste" under the *Controlled Waste Regulations*, and thus do not require a waste management licence. However to ensure compliance with the Framework Directive it will be necessary to extend waste management controls to "non-natural" agricultural waste and non-mineral mining and quarry waste.

(a) Requirement for a Licence

Under the EPA, the deposit, keeping, treatment or disposal of controlled waste (i.e. Directive Waste – see above, 4.2 and 4.6 – in or on land (including treatment or disposal in mobile plant) requires a waste management licence. There are various exemptions (see below). It should be noted that certain waste installations will fall within the scope of the IPPC Directive and will thus require a permit in accordance with that Directive; the IPPC Directive has to be implemented by 30 October 1999 – see chapter 1, 1.12.

The licence is issued by the waste regulation authority within which the waste disposal facility is situated (i.e. the appropriate office of the Environment Agency or SEPA). In the case of mobile plant, this will be the office in which the operator's principal place of business is located. The WML Regulations define mobile plant as incinerators which are exempt under Part I of the EPA (Section 5.1 of Schedule 1 of *Prescribed Processes & Substances Regulations 1991* – see Appendix 1.1) and "which are designed to be moved on roads or other land". The definition does not include any other kind of mobile plant.

Disposal licences granted under COPA have been converted into waste management licences under section 77 of the EPA and as such become subject to the EPA. Operators of such sites were automatically deemed "fit and proper" for the purpose of holding a licence under the Regulations – see also 4.19.8 below.

(b) Exclusions from Licensing

Certain activities do not require a waste management licence where these are part of a process registered or authorised under other legislation. These are:

- recovery or disposal of waste from a process authorised for Integrated Pollution Control under Part I of the EPA;
- disposal of waste from incinerator authorised for control of air pollution under Part I of the EPA (see Appendix 1.1, section 5.1, Incineration);
- disposal of liquid waste under a consent for discharge to water (but not to a sewer) granted under Part III of the *Water Resources Act 1991*;
- recovery or disposal of waste where activity forms part of operation requiring licence under Part II of the *Food and Environment Protection Act 1985* (dumping at sea).

In July 1996 the Government announced that the following activities would also not require a waste management licence:

- operators of waste effluent treatment plant where disposal is subject to a discharge consent under Part III of the *Water Resources Act 1991* (Part II of COPA in Scotland), or a discharge consent under Part IV of the *Water Industry Act 1991*;
- discharges of effluent covered by the *Urban Waste Water Treatment (England & Wales) Regulations 1994* (1995 Regulations in Scotland and Northern Ireland) – see chapter 5, 5.18.

These exclusions, which do not have to be registered (see next section) also apply where the activity involves special waste; however a waste management licence will be required if the activity involves the final disposal of waste in or on land.

(c) Exemptions from licensing

Schedule 3 to the WML Regulations lists the activities for which a waste management licence will not normally be required – see box.

Recovery or reuse of waste: glass manufacture and production; scrap metal furnaces; scrap metal and waste motor vehicle dismantling; burning as fuel; packaging or containers; burning waste as fuel in a small appliance; burning waste oil as fuel in an engine; waste for the benefit of land; sludge and septic tank sludge on land; sewage and water treatment works; preparatory treatment of certain wastes; composting waste; construction and soil materials; manufacture of finished goods; use of waste; Diseases of Animals (Waste Food) Order 1973; storage of waste in a secure place; waste in secure containers; waste for construction; recovery of textiles; preparatory treatments of waste plant matter; recovery of silver; animal by-products.

Operations leading to recovery/reuse or disposal: crushing, grinding or size reduction of bricks, tiles or concrete; waterway dredging; recovery or disposal as part of the production process; baling, compacting or pulverising; storing returned goods.

Disposal of own waste at the place of production: disposal by incineration at the place of production; burning waste in the open; waste from railway sanitary conveniences or sinks; peatworking; railway ballasts; waste from prospecting.

Other deposits of waste: temporary storage of ships' garbage or tank washings; pet burial, storage of medicines, and medical, nursing or veterinary waste; storage of waste not at the place of production; storage of waste at the place of production.

It should be noted that an activity falling into one of the exempted categories will not necessarily be exempt and thus the Schedule to the Regulations (or in the case of scrap metal, the 1995 Amendment Regulations, SI 288) should be consulted for details of any limitations or other requirements affecting the exemption. In most cases the exemptions do not apply to special waste and the person carrying on the exempt activity must have the permission of the occupier of the land or be entitled to use the land for the activity. Amendments to the Schedule are being considered in connection with the recovery/recycling of wastes which are now special wastes under the *Special Waste Regulations 1996*.

All establishments or undertakings (i.e. not private individuals) carrying on an exempted activity had to register with the appropriate registration authority (Environment Agency or SEPA) by 31 December 1994 (for smaller scrapyards the deadline was 1.10.95); non-registration is an offence. Registered sites are usually inspected by the Agency/SEPA once a year; exempted activities forming part of a process authorised by a local authority (England and Wales only) under Part I of the EPA will be registered with the local authority; exempted activities relating to other licensed operations should be registered with the appropriate licensing authority.

The register, which is open to the public, will contain details of the establishment or undertaking, the exempt activity and where it takes place. Registration is valid indefinitely.

(d) Licence Applications

An application for a licence (EPA, s.36) may only be made if planning permission has been granted, or the land in question has an "established use" certificate (see 4.18 above). Applications must be made on a form provided by the appropriate Agency (*Env. Act 1995*, Sch. 22, para 68(2), brought into effect 1 April 1998); as well as general details of the site and of the operator, the application should include:

- details of the nature and quantities of wastes to be dealt with;
- details relating to the operation and management of the site;
- any other information required by the regulatory authority.

The licence application should demonstrate that the applicant is a "fit and proper" person (EPA, s.74 – 4.19.8 below), and should be accompanied by the appropriate fee (*Env. Act 1995*, s.41 – see 4.20.1 below).

(e) Consideration of Applications

The regulatory authority may refuse to deal with an application if the information which it requires to accompany the application has not been provided, or until the information is provided (s.36(1A), see *Env. Act 1995*, Sch. 22, para 68(2)). The regulatory authority has four months (or longer if mutually agreed) in which to consider the application – the four months beginning once all the information has been received (ss.36(9) & 36(9A) – *Env. Act*, Sch. 22, para 68(5)). If at the end of that time the regulatory authority has neither advised the applicant of acceptance of the application, nor that it intends to reject it, then the application is deemed to have been refused.

The regulatory authority may only reject a licence in order to prevent pollution of the environment, harm to human health or serious detriment to local amenities. A licence application may also be rejected if the regulatory authority is of the opinion that the applicant is not a fit and proper person or has insufficient financial resources to comply fully with licence conditions. The applicant has a right of appeal (s.43 – see (j) below, & *Env. Act 1995*, s.114) to the Secretary of State with regard to any refusal of licence.

If the regulatory authority plans to grant a licence it must first consult both the appropriate planning authority and the Health and Safety Executive. If any of the land falls within a Site of Special Scientific Interest, English Nature, Scottish Natural Heritage or the Countryside Council for Wales (as appropriate) should be consulted. All consultees have 28 days from the day on which the regulatory authority received the application in which to submit any comments (*Env. Act 1995*, Sch. 22, para 68(6)).

If granted, the licence will include conditions relating to types and quantities of waste covered by the licence, treatment methods, operation and management, hours of operation, record keeping and security provisions. The conditions will also cover standards to be achieved and measures to ensure site activities cause no pollution or other harm to the environment or human health. Licences must also ensure compliance with the 1991 Framework Directive on Waste, with the 1980 Groundwater Directive and with any Directions from the Secretary of State including waste management papers.

Licence conditions will remain in force even after closure of the site and until a certificate of completion has been issued (see below – s.61 to be revoked by *Env. Act 1995*). In addition site operators will also be required to provide financial guarantees covering care of the site following its closure and until surrender of the licence is accepted.

It is an offence to breach any of the conditions of a waste management licence. Summary conviction may result in a fine of £20,000 and/or six months in prison, or an unlimited fine and/or two years in prison on conviction on indictment.

Details of licence applications, and of any comments on the application, as well as full details (subject to certain exemptions) of all licences, conditions, etc must be kept by the regulatory authority on a register open to public inspection (see below, 4.19.7).

Licence conditions will normally be reviewed annually to ensure they remain appropriate to the activities carried out at the site. Unless otherwise revoked or surrendered, the waste management licence and any accompanying conditions apply to closed disposal sites, with operators retaining a duty of care for them.

The *Environment Act 1995*, Sch. 22, para 69 (brought into force on 1 April 1998), adds new section 36A to the EPA: if the regulatory authority plans to issue a licence which includes a condition requiring work which the applicant may not be entitled to do, it should notify all those with an interest in the land (e.g. the owner, lessee or occupier); the notice should set out the condition, the work required in connection with it, by when it has to be done and the date by which any representations must be received (the length of time allowed for such representations to be set in Regulations); the regulatory authority must take any such representations into account. A similar requirement is imposed by Article 9 of the *Waste and Contaminated Land (Northern Ireland) Order 1997.*

(f) Variation of Licence

Section 37 of the EPA (NI: WCLO, Art.10) places a duty on the regulatory authority to take the necessary steps to ensure that licence conditions are being met and that licensed activities are not causing any pollution or harm to human health; if necessary the regulatory authority may by notice modify the licence conditions, stating when the modification is to be effected. Licence holders may also apply (with the appropriate fee) for licence conditions to be varied. However, if after two months (or longer as mutually agreed), the regulatory authority has neither approved nor rejected the application for modification, it must be assumed that it has been rejected. In all instances there is a right of appeal to the Secretary of State.

New section 37A (*Env. Act 1995*, Sch. 22, para 71, brought into force on 1 April 1998) (NI: WCLO, Art.11) requires the regulatory authority to consult anyone with an interest in the land where it proposes to vary a licence by adding a new condition requiring certain works which the site operator may not be entitled to do. In such instances the regulatory authority should serve a notice on the interested persons setting out the new condition and the work which might be required to meet it. The notice should specify the date by which any representations should be received (the period allowed for such representations to be set in Regulations); any representations received must be taken into account before finally issuing the licence variation.

(g) Revocation and Suspension of Licence

Under the Environment Agency's 1996 code of practice an enforcement officer should give 10 working days notice of intention to take formal enforcement action unless there is an immediate environmental risk. This is to enable the waste operator to make representations to the enforcement officer's manager if it is thought that the proposed enforcement action should be changed or is inappropriate.

Where the regulatory authority has reason to believe that the licence holder has ceased to be a fit and proper person, that licence conditions are being breached or that the activities covered by the licence are, or are likely to, cause serious harm to human health or the environment, it may serve notice that it intends to suspend or partially revoke the licence (EPA: s.38; NI: WCLO, Art.12). In suspending, or partially suspending a licence, the regulatory authority may require the licence holder to take the necessary steps to deal with or avert the pollution; section 36A of the EPA (see above) – consulting those with an interest in the land – applies in this instance, though such consultation or notification may be postponed in an emergency (EPA s.38(9A-C), *Env. Act 1995*, Sch. 22, para 71(1)). If emergency remedial action is required, the regulatory authority may carry out the necessary work and recover the expenditure from the licence holder, or in the case of a surrendered licence from the former licence holder.

Notices suspending, or partially or totally revoking a licence, or modifying its conditions to prevent pollution or harm take immediate effect, whether or not an appeal has been lodged (see below). Failure to pay fees or charges also results in immediate revocation.

Where a licence has been suspended or revoked, and action required by the regulatory authority for remedying a situation has not been carried out, it may prosecute the licence holder, who on summary conviction may be liable to a maximum fine of £20,000 (and/or six months' imprisonment if special waste involved); on conviction on indictment, the offender becomes liable to imprisonment for up to two years (five years in relation to special waste) and/or an unlimited fine.

Copies of all enforcement notices and convictions will be put on the public register.

(h) Surrender of Site Licence

Section 39 of the EPA, as amended by the *Environment Act 1995* (Sch. 22, para 73), (NI: WCLO, Art.13), applies to all sites for which a waste management licence is required. An application to surrender a licence must be made on a form provided by the regulatory authority, together with any information and evidence required by them, and the appropriate fee.

Prior to making such an application, however, and despite the fact that the site is no longer in use, the site operator will need to maintain any pollution control systems and continue regular monitoring until the site has stabilised – this may take 30 years or more. Once this state has been reached, and in agreement with the regulatory authority, it is considered that the site no longer requires a pollution control system, a period of completion monitoring may be commenced to confirm the site's stability and safety. The period of completion monitoring will be decided by the regulatory authority – probably two years if regular monitoring data exists or five years in other instances.

Schedule 1 to the *Waste Management Licensing Regulations* specifies the information to be given on the application: this includes full details of the site location, licence number, activities carried out on the site and when and estimated quantities of each type of waste dealt with; details should also be given on landfill gas and leachate production and quality of surface water and groundwater; in the case of special wastes, plans should be included showing where the waste was deposited and information about possible contamination.

In considering whether to accept the surrender of a licence, the regulatory authority has a duty to inspect the site to determine whether the condition of the land is likely to cause pollution or harm to human health. If the regulatory authority plans to accept an application for surrender, it must refer the proposal to the appropriate planning authority which has 28 days from the day on which the regulatory authority receives the application (*Env. Act 1995*, Sch. 22, para 73(3)) to make any comments, or longer if mutually agreed. Where the regulatory authority has neither accepted nor rejected an application for surrender within three months of its receipt (or longer if mutually agreed), then it is deemed to have been rejected. If the appropriate planning authority wishes the application to be rejected because it is of the opinion that there is a risk of pollution, then either it or the regulatory authority may refer the matter to the Secretary of State for determination.

Surrender of a licence for a closed site will only be accepted after the site has been certified safe and a "certificate of completion" issued. Section 61 (to be revoked by the *Env. Act 1995*) of the EPA imposed various duties on the Agency/SEPA to monitor and secure the safety of closed landfill sites.

The requirements for surrendering waste management licences apply to all sites; Waste Management Paper 26A (1994) provides detailed guidance on the completion of waste management licences for landfill sites in view of their potential to cause more serious pollution. It outlines the requirements for monitoring completed landfill sites up to and including applying to surrender the licence. Under section 35(8) of the EPA, the Agency/SEPA has a duty to take account of guidance, such as WMPs, issued by the Secretary of State.

Full details of applications to surrender a licence etc must be put on the public register kept by the regulatory authorities.

(i) Transfer of Licences

Where it is proposed to transfer a licence (EPA, s.40; NI: WCLO, Art.14), the current and proposed licence holders must make a joint application to the regulatory authority (on the form provided), together with the relevant fee (*Env. Act 1995*, Sch. 22, para 74). Schedule 2 to the WML Regulations specifies the information to be given on the application: this should include full details of the licence and information to demonstrate that the proposed licence holder is a fit and proper person (EPA, s.74, 4.19.8 below). If within two months (or longer as mutually agreed) from the date of receiving the transfer application, the regulatory authority has neither agreed to nor rejected the transfer, then it is deemed to have been refused. Again, full details will be put on the public register.

(j) Appeals

There is a right of appeal (EPA: s.43; NI: WCLO, Art.17) to the Secretary of State (NI: Planning Appeals Commission) against a decision of the regulatory authority in the following instances:

- an application for a licence or modification of licence conditions is rejected;
- disagreement about licence conditions;
- disagreement over modification of licence conditions;
- a licence is suspended;
- a licence is revoked because it is thought the licence holder is no longer a fit and proper person or the licensed activities may cause environmental pollution or harm to human health and subsequent requirements to remedy the situation have not been carried out;
- rejection of an application for surrender of a licence;
- rejection of an application to transfer a licence.

There is also a right of appeal under section 66 of the EPA (NI: WCLO, Art.36(5)) where the regulatory authority rejects a request for information to be kept off the public register on the grounds of commercial confidentiality.

The WML Regulations prescribe that appeals should be made in writing to the Secretary of State; section 114 (& Sch. 20) of the *Environment Act 1995* enables the Secretary of State to appoint someone else to handle the appeal on his behalf. As from 1 April 1996, the Secretary of State transferred his powers to take decisions on waste management licensing appeals to the Planning Inspectorate which is based in Bristol. The Secretary of State will determine only those appeals of "major importance" or where difficulties arise.

The written statement should include the reasons for the appeal, copies of relevant documents and a statement as to whether the appellant wishes the appeal to be determined by means of a hearing or by correspondence. Appeals relating to licences should be made within six months of the action precipitating the appeal; those relating to information for the public register should be made within 21 days of the regulatory authority's initial decision.

Details of the appeal etc should be copied to the regulatory authority who will put a copy on the public register. Copies of all appeal decisions will also be put on the public register.

NB. The *Waste Management Licensing Regulations 1994* also deal with the following:

- Registration of waste brokers and dealers (see 4.22.2).
- Public registers (ss.64-66 of the Act): see below, 4.19.7).
- Fit and Proper Person (s.74 of the Act: see below, 4.19.8).
- Implementation of certain parts of the EU Directive on protection of groundwater against pollution by certain dangerous substances – see chapter 5.

(k) Supervision of Licensed Activities

Section 42 of the EPA (as amended by the *Env. Act 1995*, Sch. 22, para 76) (NI: WCLO, Art.16) places a duty on regulatory authorities to ensure that licences and their conditions are being complied with and that authorised activities are not causing pollution, harm to human health or having a detrimental effect on local amenities.

If the regulatory authority is of the opinion that emergency work is needed to prevent pollution etc, it may carry out the work itself, recovering any expenditure from the licence holder or as the case may be the former holder of the licence.

Where the regulatory authority is of the opinion that a licence condition is not being complied with, or is likely not to be complied with, it should serve a notice on the licence holder stating this; the notice will detail the activities constituting the non-compliance or likely non-compliance, the remedial steps to be taken and the time within which those steps must be taken. Non-compliance with the notice may result in partial or total revocation of the licence or in its suspension; if it is felt that this would be an ineffectual remedy, the regulatory authority may take action in the High Court to secure compliance (EPA, s.42(6A), see *Env. Act 1995*, Sch. 22, para 76(7)).

See also above, Revocation and Suspension of Licences and Appeals.

4.19.4 National Waste Strategy (ss.44A-B)

These sections of the EPA, together with Schedule 2A, are added by the *Environment Act 1995*, section 92 and Schedule 12. (It should be noted that the requirement for waste regulation authorities to prepare waste disposal plans under s.50 of the EPA was revoked by the *Env. Act*, Sch. 22, para 78 with effect from 1 April 1996.)

Section 44A requires the Secretary of State for the Environment, Transport and the Regions to prepare a National Waste Strategy for England and Wales; section 44B places a similar obligation on the Scottish Environment Protection Agency as regards Scotland; in Northern Ireland, the Strategy will be prepared by the Department of the Environment (NI) under Article 19 and Schedule 3 of the *Waste and Contaminated Land (Northern Ireland) Order 1997*. Preparation of the Strategies will implement Article 7 of the 1991 Framework Directive on Waste. The Strategies should include policies for meeting the following objectives:

- ensuring that waste is recovered or disposed of without endangering human health or using processes or methods which could harm the environment (including causing noise or odour nuisance).
- establishing an integrated and adequate network of waste disposal installations taking account of BATNEEC; the network should also aim to help the EU meet its objective of becoming self-sufficient in waste disposal, and that waste is disposed of in the nearest appropriate installation.
- encouraging the prevention or reduction of waste through the development of clean technologies, the technical development and marketing of products with the least impact on the waste stream, and the development of techniques for the final disposal of dangerous substances in waste for recovery.
- encouraging recovery, reuse, reclamation, recycling etc and the use of waste as a source of energy.

The Strategy should also include details of the amounts of waste to be recovered or disposed of, general technical requirements and requirements for specific types of waste.

The Environment Agency must be consulted in the preparation or modification of the Strategy, together with representatives of local government and industry; others may be consulted as considered appropriate. SEPA and the DOE(NI) should consult similar bodies.

The Secretary of State may require the Environment Agency to advise on the policies to be included in the Strategy and to carry out an investigation and report on the amount and types of likely waste arisings, the facilities which are or may be needed to deal with them. Before carrying out its investigation, the Agency should consult representatives of local planning authorities and of industry, and should report its findings to them. *Waste Management Planning – Principles and Practice*, (DOE, 1995), sets out good practice for the conduct and design of surveys to obtain key information on waste arisings and waste management facilities; the guidance suggests that surveys should be carried out every three years.

In Scotland, the Secretary of State may direct SEPA as to the policies to be included in the Strategy as well as requiring it to carry out an investigation with similar objectives to those for England and Wales.

In June 1998, the Government published a first consultation paper on its proposals for a National Waste Strategy for England and Wales. *Less Waste, More Value* highlights the need to develop sustainable waste management practices based on reducing the amount of waste produced and encouraging more recycling and recovery of waste; waste which cannot be recycled or recovered must be disposed of in such a way that it causes minimum harm to the environment. Thus the Strategy will be developed on the following principles:

- substantial increases in recycling and energy recovery;
- increased public involvement in re-use and recycling of household waste;
- the need for challenging but realistic targets;
- strong emphasis on waste minimisation;
- the use of the waste hierarchy (reduce – recycle – dispose) as a guide, not a prescriptive set of rules;
- use of economic incentives (such as the landfill tax);
- increased public involvement in decision-making.

The Strategy will need to consider the Best Practicable Environmental Option (BPEO) for disposing of waste, taking account of issues such as environmental and economic costs and benefits for different disposal options; whether the waste can be reduced or re-used; and whether any value can be derived from the waste. It is also likely to include a number of key targets for waste management and reduction; the following included in the 1995 White Paper *Making*

Waste Work: A Strategy for Sustainable Waste Management in England and Wales, are being reviewed:

- to reduce the amount of controlled waste going to landfill to 60% by 2005;
- to recover 40% of municipal waste by 2005;
- 25% of household waste to be recycled by 2000;
- 40% of domestic properties with a garden to carry out home composting by 2000;
- easily accessible recycling facilities for 80% of households by 2000.

A draft Strategy is expected to be published for consultation early in 1999, with the final version issued before the end of 1999.

Scotland's Strategy, *A Blueprint for Progress 1997-2001* was published for consultation in 1997 and was expected to be finalised during 1998. Northern Ireland's draft Strategy was published for consultation in July 1998.

4.19.5 Collection, Disposal or Treatment of Controlled Waste

Collection of Controlled Waste (ss.45-48)

Most of these sections came into effect on 1 April 1992 (E, S & W). They detail the duties of waste collection authorities for collecting controlled waste, and the provision of bins for both household and commercial or industrial waste. Similar provisions for Northern Ireland are contained in Article 20 of the *Waste and Contaminated Land (Northern Ireland) Order 1997*; the waste collection authority is the district council.

The WCA may charge for the collection of commercial and industrial waste, and under the *Controlled Waste Regulations 1992* (E, S & W), may charge for the collection of certain types of household waste or from those premises whose waste is classified as household waste (see 4.2.1 above). Examples of when a charge may be made include: garden waste; clinical waste from a domestic property; waste from camp sites or self-catering accommodation; waste from residential hostels, homes, educational establishments or premises forming part of a hospital or nursing home; asbestos; dead domestic pets; waste from halls used for public meetings; and waste from royal palaces.

Waste Management Plans (NI: WCLO, Art.23)

Each district council in Northern Ireland will be required to carry out an investigation with a view to deciding what arrangements are needed for the purpose of treating, recovering or disposing of controlled waste within its area; the need to prevent or minimise environmental pollution and harm to health is a prime objective. In drawing up an appropriate plan the council will need to take account of the Waste Strategy (Art.19).

The plan should include information on types and quantities of waste to be disposed of; methods of disposal and treatment with costs and savings attributable to each method; quantities of waste which the district council expects to be disposed of or treated in its area, including waste to be brought into its area or taken out of it. Wherever possible priority should be given to recovering waste. In preparing the plan, the district council should consult the DOE(NI), any other district council which might be affected by its plans as well as others (e.g. local business or industry) who might have an interest in it. Before finalising the plan, the district council must publicise it locally to give the public an opportunity to comment on it. The draft must be sent to the DOE(NI), as must a copy of the final version, which should also be publicised locally. The district council should keep a copy of the plan, to which members of the public should have free access; a charge may be made for copies of the plan.

Section 50 of the EPA, which was repealed by the *Environment Act 1995* on 1 April 1996, contained similar provisions for England, Scotland and Wales. Locally based waste disposal plans have been replaced by a Waste Strategy for England and Wales and similar for Scotland – see sections 44A and 44B of the EPA, above.

Waste Recycling (s.49, s.52 and ss.55-56)

Under section 49 which was brought into force on 1 August 1991, waste collection authorities are required to draw up plans for recycling household and commercial waste.

The plan should include details of the amounts and types of controlled waste it is expected to recycle, arrangements for dealing with it and costs. Following its finalisation, the waste collection authority must ensure that copies of the plan are available for public inspection and must also send a copy to the local waste disposal authority and to the regulatory authority.

Scottish councils are to be required to produce recycling plans as necessary, following the publication of guidance and of the Scottish Waste Strategy (This Common Inheritance: UK Annual Report, 1997).

Section 52 of the Act (which mainly applies in England only), introduces a system of "recycling credits"; where the WDA avoids disposal costs due to recycling initiatives by the WCA, it must pay the WCA a sum equivalent to that saved. Similarly, if the WDA retains waste for recycling, thus saving the WCA collection costs, the WCA must pay the WDA an equivalent sum. Both the WCA and WDA may pay a third party to recycle waste on their behalf (this latter point applies in Scotland and Wales also).

Article 24 of the *Waste and Contaminated Land (Northern Ireland) Order 1997* makes provision for the district council to pay another person in respect of waste collected by them for recycling; the payment should represent the council's net saving in not collecting and disposing of the waste itself.

Waste collection and disposal authorities may buy and sell waste for the purpose of recycling and make arrangements for the production of heat and electricity from waste (EPA: s.55; NI: WCLO, Art.26).

The Environmental Protection (Waste Recycling Payments) Regulations 1992 (SI 462)

These Regulations which cover Great Britain came into force on 1 April 1992. They specify how waste recycling credits are to be valued. However, they implement only that part of section 52 requiring the WDA to pay recycling credits to WCAs for savings as a result of waste recycled. WDAs are also encouraged to pay similar credits to other organisations for recycling but such payments are not mandatory. A Schedule to the Regulations provides figures (updated annually) for determining the net saving of expenditure in those areas where sufficient information is not available or could only be determined at disproportionate cost – for 1998/99 figures see the *Environmental Protection (Waste Recycling Payments) (Amendment) Regulations 1998* (SI 607).

Land Occupied by Disposal Authorities (Scotland) (s.54)

This section of the Act is revoked by the *Environment Act 1995*. Scottish district and island councils were responsible for both waste regulation and waste disposal though the functions had to be separated internally. This section of the Act detailed the additional provisions applying in Scotland with regard to the deposit of waste on land occupied by WDAs.

Acceptance of Waste (s.57-58) (NI: WCLO, Art.27)

These sections empower the Secretary of State (NI: DOE) to require holders of waste management licences (and in Scotland a WDA) to accept and keep/treat or dispose of controlled waste as directed by the Secretary of State.

Removal of Unlawfully Deposited Waste (s.59) (NI: WCLO, Art.28)

Waste regulation authorities and waste collection authorities may by notice require the removal or treatment within 21 days of waste deposited unlawfully on any land in their area. Failure to comply with the notice without adequate excuse is an offence. Where there is a danger of pollution or harm to health, the regulatory authority or WCA may arrange for removal of the waste and recover the costs from the occupier of the land.

The occupier of the land may appeal against the notice to the appropriate Magistrates' Court (Sheriff Court in Scotland; Court of Summary Jurisdiction in NI). The court may quash the notice if the occupier proves that the waste was not deposited by them or that it was deposited without their permission. In this instance, or where the occupier of the land is unknown, or to prevent pollution or harm to health, the regulatory authority or WCA may arrange for removal of the waste.

Interference with Waste and Waste Sites (s.60) (NI: WCLO, Art.29)

It is an offence for an unauthorised person to interfere with waste put out for collection or at a disposal site, unless consent has been obtained from the WCA, WDA or waste disposal company.

Closed Landfill Sites (s.61)

This section of the Act, which was never brought into force, is to be revoked by the *Environment Act 1995*. It would have applied to those sites for which the licence was surrendered prior to the *Waste Management Licensing Regulations* coming into force and to those sites for which surrender of the licence was accepted under the Regulations. It would have imposed certain duties on WRAs.

4.19.6 Special Waste and Non-Controlled Waste

Special Waste (s.62) (NI: WCLO, Art.30)

This section of the EPA (which came into force on 11 August 1995), as amended by the *Environment Act 1995* (Sch. 22, para 80) empowers the Secretary of State to make regulations for the treatment, keeping or disposal of particularly dangerous or difficult wastes. The regulations may impose, among other things, requirements on consignors and consignees relating to their handling of the waste, as well as provisions relating to record keeping and public registers and the penalty for contravening the regulations. Provision may also be made relating to the supervision by regulatory authorities of the activities authorised by the regulations or of the persons carrying out the activity, for the recovery of costs incurred by the regulatory authorities in carrying out their regulatory functions and for appeals in respect of their decisions.

It should be noted that all producers, handlers and disposers of special waste are subject to the duty of care provisions (EPA: s.34; NI: WCLO, Art.5).

Special Waste Regulations 1996 (SI 972)

These Regulations, which came into effect on 1 September 1996 (together with amending regulations – SI 2019 – which came into effect on 31 August 1996) apply in England, Scotland and Wales; further amendment Regulations (SI 251), and in Scotland (SI 257) came into force on 28 February 1997. The Regulations replace the *Control of Pollution (Special Waste) Regulations 1980* (SI 1709). The 1996 Regulations implement the 1991 EU Hazardous Waste Directive (91/689/EEC) and the EU List of Hazardous Waste (4.8 above). Similar Regulations, *The Special Waste Regulations (Northern Ireland) 1998* (SR 289), made under Article 30 of the WCLO, came into force on 18 September 1998, replacing the 1981 Northern Ireland Regulations; they are enforced by the DOE(NI) – Environment and Heritage Service (EHS).

The Regulations apply to all movements of controlled waste (as defined by s.75 of EPA; Art.2 of WCLO) which is also special waste, including movements of waste to and from storage, treatment and recycling facilities and movements of waste to final disposal sites. The Regulations also apply to imports and exports of special waste between Great Britain and Northern Ireland or Gibraltar and special waste landed by ship. Household waste (including clinical waste and waste oil, but not asbestos, generated by households) is exempted but most non-domestic hospital and laboratory waste is not. Unless authorised by a waste management licence (or exempted from licensing) or an authorisation under Part I of the EPA, the mixing of different categories of special waste is prohibited as is the mixing of special and other waste.

Controlled waste is defined as special if it is on the EU's Hazardous Waste List and has one or more of the following hazardous characteristics:

> explosive; oxidising; highly flammable and flammable; irritant; harmful; toxic; carcinogenic; corrosive; infectious; teratogenic; mutagenic; substances and preparations which release toxic or very toxic gases; substances and preparations which after disposal can produce a hazardous characteristic; and ecotoxic.

In addition the Regulations define controlled waste which has any of the following characteristics above a certain threshold as special: highly flammable, irritant, harmful, toxic, corrosive and carcinogenic; medicinal products (as defined by the *Medicines Act 1968*, s.130) are also included in the definition of special waste; it should also be noted that some wastes not on the EU's list may be classified as special, particularly if they contain one or more hazardous characteristic. Examples of special wastes are: waste oils, photographic chemicals, acids, alkaline solutions, industrial solvents, fly ash, pesticides, batteries, prescription-only medicines, pharmaceutical compounds and wood preservatives.

The Regulations require the Environment Agency or SEPA ("the Agency"; in NI, the Environment & Heritage Service) to assign to each consignment or carrier's round of special waste a unique code which must be used on all documentation. (A carrier's round is defined as a journey made by a carrier during which more than one consignment of special waste is collected for transportation to the same consignee; each type of waste must be listed on a schedule to the consignment note; the round must be completed within 24 hours, though a 1998 consultation document proposes extending this to 72 hours.) The Agency need not issue a code until the relevant fee has been paid and, in any event, fees must be paid within two months of requesting a code.

All movements of special waste (unless exempt, see next paragraph) must be prenotified through completion of the relevant part of the standard consignment note to the office of the Agency in the area to which the special waste is being sent; this should be done at least three working days, but not more than one month in advance of any movement of the waste. Repeat consignments of the same waste to the same destination can be notified at the time of the first consignment with no further notification being required for 12 months; waste carriers collecting similar consignments of special waste from various premises need only complete one prenotification which again will last for 12 months.

Certain types of special waste movements are exempt from prenotification; these include:

- special waste movements (except by waste management businesses) within a company where the waste is to be stored prior to recovery or disposal;
- special waste products or materials being returned to their originator because they do not meet the required specifications;
- lead acid vehicle batteries.

Each consignment of special waste should be recorded on the consignment note which has five sections (Parts A to E) for completion at various stages in the procedure and of which there are five copies. Following completion of Parts A and B, the consignor should send one copy to the office of the Agency in whose area the waste is to be sent.

The carrier should complete Part C of the remaining four copies, and the consignor Part D; the consignor should keep one copy, with the carrier having the remaining three copies. These three copies should accompany the waste during transportation and should be given to the consignee on delivery of the waste; he should complete the remainder of the consignment note (Part E), retain one copy, give one to the carrier and send the fifth copy to the local office of the Agency. A similar procedure is followed for the second and subsequent removals of repeat consignments or carrier's rounds (for which a schedule in quadruplet must also be prepared) of special waste, and for removals of ships' waste to reception facilities.

The consignor should normally send the (prenotification) copy of the consignment note to the relevant office of the Agency not more than one month, but not less than 72 hours, before removal of the consignment; the consignee should send a copy of the consignment note (or an explanation as to why the delivery has been refused – see also next para) to the relevant office of the Agency within one day of receipt of the special waste.

If for any reason the consignee does not accept the consignment, he should give his reasons on Part E of the consignment note and retain one copy; one copy should be sent to the local office of the Agency/EHS (within one day of receipt of the waste) and one copy given back to the carrier. If there is no consignment note, the consignee should send the Agency a written explanation of his reasons for refusing the waste. The receiving Agency should, within two weeks, send a copy of the consignment note (or explanation of refusal of consignment) to the office of the Agency from which the waste was transported.

Where a delivery has been refused, the carrier should also inform both the consignor and the Environment Agency (or SEPA/EHS) of the fact and get instructions from the consignor as to where the waste should be taken; the consignor should also inform the Agency of the action to be taken.

A fee of £15 (NI: £24), (or £10 for automotive lead-acid batteries), will apply to most consignments and carrier's rounds of special waste, to be paid when the Agency assigns a code to the consignment. No fee is payable for:

- second or subsequent carrier's rounds if the carrier is also the consignee for all rounds, only one consignment is collected from any consignor during the succession, the total weight collected in each round does not exceed 400 kg, or there is less than one week between collection of the first consignment and delivery of the last consignment in a round;

- the removal of a single consignment of special waste if it does not meet the specifications of the person to whom it was supplied;
- the removal of special waste from a ship in a harbour area to a conveyance for transportation outside the area, to reception facilities within the harbour area, or by pipeline to reception facilities outside the harbour area.

Registers containing a copy of all consignment notes and where relevant a copy of the carrier's schedule must be kept by consignors, carriers and consignees. Data must be retained on the registers of consignors and carriers for three years. Consignees must retain all data on their registers until their waste management licence is revoked or surrendered; they should then send their register to the Agency (NI: local district council) for the site which should keep it for not less than three years. In addition details of all consignments of special waste are to be entered on a national database enabling both the Environment Agency and SEPA/EHS to have access to up-to-date information on all special waste movements.

Regulation 16 requires that full site records be kept of all deposits of special waste; this should include a site plan marked with a grid, or with overlays on which deposits are shown. Descriptions of deposits should accord with those on the register of consignment notes; where the waste is disposed of by pipeline or at the place of production, a full record of the quantity, composition and date of disposal should be kept. A written statement of quantity, composition and date of disposal should be prepared of any liquid waste discharged without containers into underground strata or disused workings. All site records must be kept until a waste management licence is surrendered or revoked, when they should be sent to the Environment Agency (or SEPA, or in NI the local district council).

It is an offence not to comply with the regulations; it is a defence to prove that non-compliance was due to an emergency or grave danger and that all steps were taken to minimise any threat to the public or the environment and that subsequent compliance took place as soon as reasonably practicable. Summary conviction renders the offender liable to a fine not exceeding level 5 on the standard scale; conviction on indictment may result in a fine and/or imprisonment for up to two years.

DOE Circulars 6/96 and 14/96 (SO 13/96 & 26/96; WO 21/96 & 39/96) provide guidance on the Regulations, on the criteria to be used in deciding whether waste is special or not and on administrative procedures. The Environment Agency, SEPA and DOE (NI), Environment and Heritage Service have produced a draft Technical Guidance Note on special wastes (May 1998); it provides guidance on the definition and classification of special wastes to establish whether or not they fall under the Regulations; it updates and expands Waste Management Paper 23 on special waste and will also replace the 1996 Circulars.

A number of amendments to the 1996 Regulations have been proposed (DETR, April 1998), including:

- movement of a consignment of special waste between islands, or between islands and the mainland will be defined as a single journey, although two or more carriers are usually involved, and thus attract only one fee; the consignment note will need to carry details of all carriers;
- in those cases where a consignment of waste has been refused and it is then to be taken to a place other than the original collection or delivery address specified on the consignment note, a new consignment note and fee will be required;
- the £10 fee which currently only applies to automotive lead-acid batteries will be extended to all lead-acid batteries.

The Transfrontier Shipment of Waste Regulations 1994 (see 4.25) are also of relevance to the control of special waste.

Non-Controlled Waste (s.63) (NI: WCLO, Art.31)

It is an offence to deposit or knowingly cause or permit the deposit of non-controlled waste which, if it were controlled, would be special waste. Such a deposit done in accordance with a condition of a waste management licence or other consent is not an offence. The penalty for an illegal deposit is the same as that for an illegal deposit of special waste – see above section 33 of EPA.

4.19.7 Public Registers (ss.64-66) (NI: WCLO, Arts.34-36)

These sections (as amended by the *Env. Act 1995*, Schedule 22, paras 82-83) have been implemented through the *Waste Management Licensing Regulations 1994*. Similar provision for public registers in Northern Ireland is made in Articles 34-36 of the *Waste and Contaminated Land (Northern Ireland) Order 1997.*

Waste regulation authorities must maintain public registers containing copies of applications for waste management licences and supporting documentation, as well as copies of the actual licences. In Northern Ireland the register will be maintained by the DOE(NI), with district councils having registers relating to the keeping, treatment and disposal of waste in their areas. The registers must also include details of variations of licence conditions and notices relating to breaches of licence conditions; revocations, suspensions and convictions; monitoring data and inspectors' site reports; appeals and other written representations etc; applications for surrender of a licence and completion certificates (issued once a closed landfill site has been declared safe). Information relating to the *Special Waste Regulations 1996* will also be put on the register. Registers should also show when a person authorised under section 108 of the *Environment Act 1995* (powers of entry) has exercised his powers, for what purpose, the information obtained and action taken. Written reports relating to articles or substances seized and rendered harmless (s.109(2)) should also be put on the register.

Exemption may be sought for exclusion of information from the register on the grounds of commercial confidentiality or national security (EPA, ss.65 & 66). In the latter case the Secretary of State may give directions as to the types of information to be excluded or types of information which he will determine whether or not should be excluded. A person may give notice to the Secretary of State that they wish certain information excluded on the grounds of national security; such information will then remain off the register until the Secretary of State has made his decision. The Agency should be advised that a request is being made to the Secretary of State for the exclusion of certain information on grounds of national security.

Where a request is made for information to be excluded on the grounds of commercial confidentiality, the Agency should consider the request within 14 days; if it does not the information automatically receives that classification. If the Agency does not agree that information is commercially confidential, the information should not be placed on the Register for 21 days, thus allowing time for an appeal to the Secretary of State; section 114 of the *Environment Act 1995* enables the Secretary of State to appoint someone to deal with the appeal on his behalf. The appeal statement should be in writing and should include copies of the material in dispute (see above – Appeals under *Waste Management Licensing Regulations 1994*). A further seven days should elapse following determination or withdrawal of the appeal before information is placed on the Register (*Env. Act 1995*, Sch. 22, para 83(1)).

Information excluded on the grounds of commercial confidentiality loses this classification after four years unless an application is made for classification to continue. Where information has been excluded, a statement to this effect will be included on the register; if the exclusion relates to the terms and conditions of the licence, a statement confirming, or otherwise, compliance with licence conditions will be included.

Waste collection authorities in England and Wales are also required to maintain public registers relating to the treatment, keeping or disposal of controlled waste in their area. The WRA has a duty to supply waste collection authorities with the relevant information to enable them to maintain their registers.

The registers are open to the public free of charge and copies of information available for a "reasonable charge". The Secretary of State may prescribe where such Registers are to be available (*Env. Act 1995*, Sch.22, para 82(5)).

Information relating to licences will be retained on the register for the duration of the licence plus twelve months. Rejected applications will be retained on the register for twelve months from the date of rejection. Monitoring data is retained for four years and for four years if superseded by new data.

Annual Reports (NI: WCLO, Art.37)

The DOE(NI) must prepare an annual report covering its regulatory responsibilities for waste management, including income and expenditure; reports should also include information relating to implementation of waste disposal and recycling plans and prosecutions. The report should be published not later than six months after the end of the year to which it relates.

Section 67 of the EPA, which placed a similar duty on waste regulation authorities, was revoked on 1 April 1996 following implementation of the *Environment Act 1995*.

4.19.8 Fit and Proper Person (s.74) (NI: WCLO, Art.3)

Section 36 of the EPA (NI: WCLO, Art.8(4)) states that (subject to compliance with certain other conditions), a WRA cannot reject an application for a waste management licence if it is satisfied that the applicant is a fit and proper person. A person should not be treated as fit and proper (EPA, s.74, NI: WCLO, Art.3(3)) if they are not technically competent to manage the site concerned, do not have adequate financial resources (to manage the site in compliance with licence conditions) or have been convicted of a relevant offence (see reg.3 of WML Regulations); this includes an offence under various sections of the EPA, COPA and the *Transfrontier Shipment of Hazardous Waste Regulations 1994*; evasion of landfill tax is also a relevant offence (see this chapter 4.4.1).

A person will be considered as technically competent if they hold a certificate of competence at the appropriate level from the Waste Management Industry Training Board (WAMITAB); for instance, an applicant for a licence for a landfill site which receives biodegradable or special waste which requires substantial engineering works would need to have a certificate of technical competence in managing landfill sites at level four. Similar appropriate qualifications from another industry board may also be acceptable. For some smaller landfill sites and waste treatment operations, formal qualifications will not be a necessity; instead the regulatory authority will need to be satisfied that the site management has appropriate knowledge and understanding of the operations. Persons considered technically competent to handle waste which has subsequently become special as a result of the *Special Waste Regulations 1996* do not have to apply for a new certificate of competence (*Special Waste (Amendment) Regulations 1997*, SI 251).

The *Waste Management Licensing Regulations 1994* (as amended in 1996 – SI 634 England & Wales; SI 100 in Scotland) prescribe that an existing manager (i.e. someone who has been manager of a relevant facility in the twelve months prior to 1 October 1996 and is registered with WAMITAB) will be exempt from the requirements and permitted to manage the same type of facility until 1 October 2001. People 55 and over on 1 October 1996 with at least five years relevant experience at a particular type of facility over the last ten years will be treated as technically competent until 1 October 2006. The management at sites where COPA licences have been converted into EPA licences will be deemed technically competent for that site only. 1997 Amendment Regulations (SI 2203) specify the type of certificate required to be considered technically competent for different types of treatment plant.

Section 74 of the EPA requires the management of the licensed activity to "be in the hands of a technically competent person". DOE (now DETR) guidance interprets this as being in the hands of one or more individuals who together make up the technical competence required for the site or sites and are in a position to ensure proper management of the site on a day to day basis.

To be considered a fit and proper person, the licence applicant must also demonstrate to the regulatory authority that adequate financial provision has been made to ensure that licence conditions, including post-closure monitoring and pollution control obligations, can be met. DOE guidance suggests that the regulatory authority should let the applicant have a draft copy of the licence to enable a suitable financial plan to be submitted.

The Waste Management Licensing Regulations (see above) list the various Acts under which, if an offence was committed, it would be considered relevant to the holding of a licence; these include legislation relating to waste disposal and transportation, *Public Health Acts*, certain sections of the EPA and of the *Water Resources Act 1991*.

Further guidance on what constitutes a fit and proper person is given in Waste Management Paper No. 4, *Licensing of Waste Facilities* (published 1994).

4.20 ENVIRONMENT ACT 1995

4.20.1 Fees and Charges for Licences

Section 41 of the EPA was repealed on 1 April 1996 following implementation of sections 41-43 of the *Environment Act 1995* which contain powers for the Environment Agency and SEPA to make charging schemes for environmental licences; such schemes have to be approved by the Secretary of State. In Northern Ireland, a charging scheme will be made under Article 15 of the *Waste and Contaminated Land (Northern Ireland) Order 1997.*

In common with other charging schemes for pollution control, the aim is to enable the Agencies to recover their costs for both assessing applications for licences (or alterations to them) and to fulfill their duty (EPA, s.42) to supervise licensed activities (e.g. inspections and monitoring). Charges are not intended to cover duties such as maintenance of public registers and enforcement activities. The level of charges and fees is reviewed annually.

The Waste Management Licensing (Fees and Charges) Scheme (originally made under the EPA) was first introduced on 1 May 1994 and covers:

a) application fee for waste management licence;

b) application fee for varying or modifying licence (where the request comes from the licence holder);

c) application fee to surrender a licence;

d) annual subsistence charge (for landfill sites this will be based on whether the site is active, or closed but no certificate of completion issued);

e) application fee to transfer a licence.

In those instances where the Agency (or SEPA) has a duty to consult the appropriate planning authority, the fee payable will include an amount to cover their costs. The subsistence charge will also include an amount to cover the costs of the planning authority if it is consulted because of concern that a licensed activity may, or is causing pollution.

The fee payable is based on the quantity and type of waste to be dealt with and on the activity to be carried out – i.e.

- treatment of controlled waste in or on land;
- keeping of controlled waste in or on land;

- disposal of controlled waste in or on land;
- disposal of controlled waste in or on land where disposal operations have ceased;
- treatment or disposal of controlled waste by mobile plant.
- sites authorised to take waste newly defined as "special" under the *Special Waste Regulations 1996.*

Where the application (or subsequent licence) is for the keeping and treatment of waste, only one charge will be payable and that will be the higher of the two. However, where the activity relates to either the keeping and disposal of waste or the treatment and disposal of waste, separate fees will be payable. An operator requiring both a site licence and a mobile plant licence will also have to pay two fees. However in certain circumstances where more than one site licence is held by the same person only one standard component is payable. Detailed schedules of the amounts which apply in each instance are appended to the Scheme document.

With regard to the annual subsistence charge, the Agency (or SEPA) should serve a notice on the licence holder detailing the charge and when it becomes due. If after a minimum of 31 days no payment is received, the Agency (or SEPA) may suspend or revoke the licence.

4.20.2 Producer Responsibility Obligations (Packaging Waste) Regulations 1997 (SI 648)

A 1994 European Union Directive on packaging waste aims to increase the use of reusable and recyclable packaging and sets targets to this end; the UK is required to recover a minimum 50% by weight of packaging material and to recycle a minimum of 25% by weight of the total waste flow by 2001 – see earlier this chapter 4.12.

The *Environment Act 1995*, sections 93-95 (which came into force on 21 September 1995) relate to producer responsibility for packaging and packaging waste. The Secretary of State may, after consultation with bodies likely to be affected, make Regulations imposing an obligation on producers to increase the reuse, recycling or recovery of products and materials (at a time when it becomes, or has become, waste). Regulations should only be introduced if they will result in significant economic and environmental benefit, when weighed against the cost of imposing producer responsibility; the Regulations should impose the minimum burden necessary on business to achieve the desired result. The Regulations may specify:

- the classes or descriptions of persons to whom the producer responsibility applies and of products or materials covered;

- targets to be met by weight, volume or other method;
- registration of persons subject to producer responsibility and of exemption schemes and associated requirements; the registers would be the responsibility of the Environment Agency and SEPA, and in Northern Ireland, the Environment and Heritage Service;
- fees, application for registration and appeals procedure, etc.

The *Producer Responsibility Obligations (Packaging Waste) Regulations 1997* (SI 648) came into force on 6 March 1997 and apply in England, Wales and Scotland, with similar draft Regulations for Northern Ireland published in June 1998 (see below). The Regulations (including the draft NI Regulations) are currently under review to ensure that the UK will be able to meet the recovery and recycling targets set in the 1994 EU Directive. Issues under review include the apportionment of percentage targets to be met by each of the activities in the packaging chain; and the possibility of separation of targets for recycling of household and commercial/industrial packaging waste.

The Regulations apply to all businesses involved in the packaging chain (see box) and which handle more than 50 tonnes of packaging material and/or packaging in a year, and with an annual turnover of £5 million or more; from 1 January 2000, businesses with an annual turnover of £1 million or more will also have to comply with the Regulations; wholesalers are exempted from the Regulations until 1 January 2000.

Businesses covered by the Regulations had to join a registered compliance scheme or register as an individual business with the Environment Agency or the Scottish Environment Protection Agency by 31 August 1997. From 1998 registration must be renewed each year

Producer Obligations

Recovery and Recycling Targets:

1998, 1999:	38% recovery and 7% recycling by material
2000:	43% recovery and 11% recycling by material
2001 onwards:	52% recovery (of which at least half must be recovered through recycling) and 16% recycling by material

(the targets for recovery of UK packaging waste for the above years are 32%, 40% and 50%, respectively)

Packaging Chain: % of recovery and recycling target to be met by each:

- raw materials manufacturers	6%
- converters	11%
- packers/fillers	36%
- seller/wholesalers	47%
- secondary provider	83%

by 1 April. Compliance schemes had themselves to register with the Environment Agency or SEPA by 31 August 1997 (and to provide aggregated data for 1996); registration must be renewed each year by 1 April. Both individual businesses and compliance schemes must pay the Agency a fee and re-register annually. Both the Environment Agency and SEPA will keep publicly available registers with names and addresses of individual businesses and compliance schemes and details of their recovery and recycling obligations.

The Environment Agency and SEPA are required to monitor compliance with the Regulations and to maintain a public register containing details of individual businesses and schemes registered under the Regulations; from 1999 the register should also contain a statement confirming that evidence of compliance has been received.

Guidance on compliance with the Regulations is to be issued by the Environment Agency and SEPA.

Northern Ireland

Draft *Producer Responsibility (Packaging Waste) (Northern Ireland) Regulations* were issued for consultation in June 1998 and were expected to come into force before the end of 1998. These Regulations mirror those in force in the rest of the UK. Producers must either join an approved compliance scheme or register as an individual. In either case, those covered by the Regulations must register with the Environment and Heritage Service before 30 June 1999 (and in subsequent years, for renewals or new registrations by 1 April). Data on the previous year's recovery and recycling of packaging waste must be sent to the EHS by 31 January.

Compliance Schemes

A business may choose to become a member of a compliance scheme; such schemes will be responsible for meeting the aggregated targets of its members and will be required to provide data demonstrating compliance to the relevant Agency – the first date for compliance with targets is 31 December 1998. Scheme members are charged a joining fee and required to provide the scheme with packaging data. Registered compliance schemes are required to let the appropriate Agency have aggregated packaging data and a certificate of compliance with the Regulations by 31 January of the following year to which the data applies. Records and returns to the Agencies must be kept for at least four years.

A scheme which commits an offence under the Regulations, e.g. by knowingly submitting false data, will be de-registered by the appropriate Agency; individual members of the scheme then become liable for meeting their own recycling and recovery obligations.

Individual Business

Alternatively, a business may choose to take on the obligation of meeting the recovery and recycling targets on its own. As mentioned above registration with either the Environment Agency or SEPA, together with payment of a fee (1997: £750), was required by 31 August 1997, with data on 1996 packaging handled provided by the same date. From 1998 the date for payment of the annual fee and data provision is 1 April. Also from 1998, the business must calculate its recovery and recycling obligation for meeting by 31 December. Evidence of compliance must be submitted to the relevant Agency by 31 January of the following year.

An individual business who commits an offence under the Regulations, such as knowingly supplying false data to the appropriate Agency, is liable for prosecution; a fine not exceeding the statutory maximum (currently £5,000) may be levied on summary conviction or an unlimited fine on indictment.

The *Packaging (Essential Requirements) Regulations 1998* (SI 1165), which came into force throughout the UK on 31 May 1998, apply to all packaging manufactured after 31 December 1994. They specify the "essential requirements" to which all packaging must comply, including that

- it is the minimum necessary to meet safety and hygiene criteria for the product concerned;
- it can be re-used, recycled or recovered and will have minimal environmental impact if disposed of;
- it has been made with the minimum use of substances which become noxious or hazardous when incinerated or landfilled.
- limits for concentrations of lead, mercury, cadmium and hexavalent chromium of packaging or its components do not exceed 600 ppm after 30 June 1998, 250 ppm after 30 June 1999 and 100 ppm after 30 June 2001.

Technical documentation showing compliance with the Regulations must be kept for four years following the placing of the packaging on the market.

4.20.3 Powers of Entry

Sections 108-109 of the *Environment Act 1995* empower "a person who appears suitable to an enforcing authority" to be authorised in writing to enter premises etc where they have reason to believe that an activity for which a licence is required is being, or has been, operated without a licence or where they believe there is a risk of serious pollution. Except in an emergency, a warrant should be obtained if entry has been or is likely to be refused and it is probable that force will be needed to gain entry. See also chapter 1, 1.14.2.

In Northern Ireland, Article 72 and Schedule 4 of the *Waste and Contaminated Land (Northern Ireland) Order 1997* provide similar powers for authorised persons.

4.21 THE COLLECTION AND DISPOSAL OF WASTE REGULATIONS 1988 (SI 819)

These Regulations came into force in October 1988 and replaced the *Control of Pollution (Licensing of Waste Disposal) Regulations 1976* and 1977 Amendment Regulations which were revoked. The 1988 Regulations, which apply in England and Wales only, prescribe wastes to be treated (or not to be treated) as household, industrial and commercial waste; the *Waste Management Licensing Regulations 1994* amend these Regulations to refer to "Directive Waste" (see above, 4.2, definitions of waste). The Regulations gave effect to certain provisions of the EU Directive on the disposal of waste oils.

4.22 CONTROL OF POLLUTION (AMENDMENT) ACT 1989

This Act deals with the registration of waste carriers and provides new powers to control fly-tipping (illegal dumping of waste). The Act empowers the Secretary of State to make Regulations dealing with applications for registration, renewal, maintenance of registers and access to them, and appeal procedures etc.

The Act and Regulations under it are the responsibility of the Environment Agency in England and Wales and the Scottish Environment Protection Agency in Scotland.

In Northern Ireland, Articles 38-43 of the *Waste and Contaminated Land (Northern Ireland) Order 1997* cover the registration etc of waste carriers. The legislation will be enforced by the DOE(NI).

4.22.1 The Controlled Waste (Registration of Carriers and Seizure of Vehicles) Regulations 1991 (SI 1624), amended 1998 (SI 605)

These Regulations which implement the above Act apply in England, Scotland and Wales and came into force on 14 October 1991. Articles 40-43 of the *Waste and Contaminated Land (Northern Ireland) Order 1997* provide for similar regulations to be made for Northern Ireland.

From April 1992, it became an offence to transport controlled waste in the course of business or for profit unless registered with the regulation authority. Waste carriers – including producers of building and demolition waste (which includes waste arising from improvements, repairs or alterations) – are subject to section 33 (prohibition on unlicensed deposits of waste etc) and section 34 (duty of care) of the EPA (NI: WCLO, Arts.4 & 5).

Waste carriers, including those operating in Great Britain who do not have, or are not proposing to have, a place of business in Great Britain, must apply for registration from the office of the regulatory authority (i.e. Environment Agency or SEPA) appropriate to the location of their principal place of business; waste carriers should also register with it. Schedule 22, para 37(2), of the *Environment Act 1995* (brought into force on 1 April 1998) adds section 2(3A) to the *Control of Pollution (Amendment) Act 1989*; this empowers the regulatory authority to prescribe the application form and the information to be included (1998 amendment Regulations). An application to register should be made by all (including prospective) partners in the business. Persons wishing to register, or renew registration, as a carrier and as a broker (see below) can make a single application covering both.

There are a number of exemptions to registration; these include:

- charities and other voluntary organisations;
- waste regulation, disposal and collection authorities;
- ferry operators in respect of waste on a vehicle being carried on the ferry;
- ship operators carrying waste for disposal at sea under licence;
- persons authorised under the *Animal By-Products Order 1992* to hold or deal with animal waste; (carriers whose sole business is carrying animal waste are not exempt).

The regulatory authority has two months (or longer, as agreed mutually) in which to consider the application. Registrations may only be refused if:

- the application procedure has not been complied with;
- the applicant or another relevant person has been convicted of a "prescribed offence" (e.g. contravening environmental pollution control legislation) and is, therefore, in the opinion of the waste regulation authority not suitable for registration as a waste carrier.

Registrations are valid for three years and apply throughout Great Britain. Transporting waste without a valid registration makes the offender liable to a maximum fine of £5,000.

The charging scheme for registration is made under section 41 of the *Environment Act 1995* (1998 amendment Regulations). The current charge for registration as either a carrier or broker is £114 and £78 for renewal; there is an additional charge of £25 if registering as a carrier and broker (see below).

The Code of Practice on the Duty of Care suggests that every vehicle used by a waste carrier should carry a numbered copy of the registration certificate (obtainable from the regulatory authority – photocopies are not valid). This will facilitate checking of registration details by, for example, the police or a waste producer.

The Regulations provide for appeal to the Secretary of State when an application for registration or renewal is refused, or registration revoked; in the latter two cases registrations remain valid until the appeal is determined. (In Northern Ireland appeals will be made to the Planning Appeals Commission, WCLO, Art.41). Any appeal must be made within 28 days (NI: 2 months). Section 114 of the *Environment Act 1995* enables the Secretary of State to appoint someone to handle the appeal on his behalf. On 1 April 1996 the Secretary of State transferred determination of registration appeals to the Planning Inspectorate (based in Bristol).

The Regulations – and a Circular published jointly by the Department of Environment (11/91), Welsh Office (34/91) and Scottish Office (18/91) – detail the action a regulatory authority can take if it has reasonable grounds to believe that controlled waste is being carried by an unregistered carrier or that a vehicle has been used for the illegal disposal of waste (fly-tipping). In the former instance, authorised officers of the regulatory authority and police constables have powers to stop vehicles and to request production of the registration certificate. They can also take samples of the waste for analysis (NI: WCLO, Art.42).

Where the regulatory authority believes a vehicle has been used for fly-tipping, it must first try to obtain the name and address (through the DVLA) of any person who would be able to provide information as to who was using the vehicle at the time the offence was committed – for instance the vehicle might have been hired out to a third party. If this proves unsuccessful, or the regulatory authority has reasonable grounds for believing a particular vehicle has been used for an illegal deposit – and thus committed an offence under section 33 of the EPA – it can apply to a Justice of the Peace (E & W) or Sheriff (Scotland) (*Control of Pollution (Amendment) Act 1989*, s.6) for a warrant to seize the vehicle. In Northern Ireland, a warrant would be obtained from a Justice of the Peace under Art.43 of the WCLO. Note: any seizure of vehicle on a road should only be carried out by a uniformed police officer as only the police have powers to stop vehicles on public roads.

The Regulations provide for the return of vehicles and their contents subject to certain conditions, e.g. establishment of ownership and carrying out of such other requirements as may be ordered. The regulatory authority may sell or otherwise dispose of or destroy the vehicle and/or its contents only after efforts have been made to inform the owners and following a notice in a newspaper and after a prescribed period (*Env. Act 1995*, Sch. 22, para 37(4)); however the regulatory authority may arrange immediate disposal where the condition of the vehicle's contents so require.

Details of registrations, amendments, renewals, offences etc, will be filed on a register to be maintained by the regulatory authority; the registers will be open to public inspection free of charge.

4.22.2 Registration of Waste Brokers and Dealers

The European Union Framework Directive on Waste (91/156/EEC – see above 4.6) requires that, in addition to waste carriers, waste brokers and dealers – i.e. those who recover or dispose of waste on behalf of somebody else – should be registered; brokers may also apply to be carriers. This requirement has been implemented in Great Britain through the *Waste Management Licensing Regulations 1994* (Reg.18 & Sch.5), as amended by the *Waste Management Licensing (Amendment) Regulations 1998* (SI 606) which came into force on 1 April 1998. Brokers of controlled waste must use a form prescribed by the Environment Agency (or SEPA) in applying for registration or for registering exempt activities. The 1998 Regulations also amend the 1994 Regulations to require charges to be paid in accordance with a scheme made under section 41 of the *Environment Act 1995*. Charitable and voluntary organisations, and waste regulation, collection and disposal authorities are exempt from registering.

Waste brokers and dealers include:

- companies which buy and sell scrap metal and other recoverables either operating from a yard, or as middleman finding both buyer and seller and making all the necessary arrangements for the transaction;
- companies which arrange for the disposal of waste to an appropriate facility on behalf of either another company or waste producer;
- waste disposal operators, carriers etc who arrange for the disposal of waste not covered by their own operating licence.

4.23 INCINERATION: REGULATORY CONTROLS

4.23.1 Environmental Protection Act 1990, Part I

Prior to implementation of the *Environmental Protection Act 1990*, many of the provisions of Part I of the *Control of Pollution Act 1974* – e.g. site licensing and preparation of waste disposal plans etc – applied to disposal of waste by incineration. Now all incinerators with an aggregate works capacity of one tonne per hour or more are regulated by the Environment Agency or Scottish Environment Protection Agency for Integrated Pollution Control under Part I of the EPA. Incinerators with a capacity of less than one tonne per hour, but designed to burn at a rate of more than 50 kg/hour, are controlled for air pollution under Part I of the EPA by local authorities in England and Wales and by SEPA in Scotland; this includes most clinical waste incinerators and crematoria. Details of the regulatory controls are contained in chapters 1 and 2 respectively.

The Municipal Waste Incineration Directions 1991 made under section 7(2) of the EPA require the enforcing authorities to include in authorisations conditions complying with standards and emission limits in the two 1989 EU Directives on new and existing municipal waste incinerators (see 4.7.1). A copy of the 1991 Directions is appended to the air pollution control Process Guidance Note for general waste incineration processes (PG5/4(95)).

The EU's 1994 Hazardous Waste Incineration Directive has been implemented through the *Environmental Protection (Prescribed Processes and Substances) (Amendment) (Hazardous Waste Incineration) Regulations 1998* (SI 767); these apply in England, Scotland and Wales and came into force on 13 April 1998. All hazardous waste incineration processes (including those currently prescribed for air pollution control only) are prescribed for IPC. Authorisations for incineration processes granted before 31 December 1996 must be varied (or in the case of a Part B process, a new authorisation in place) by 30 June 2000, to ensure compliance with the Directive; authorisations granted after 31 December 1996 had to be varied as soon as possible or, in the case of a Part B process, a new authorisation applied for before 13 July 1998. *The Hazardous Waste Incineration Direction 1998*, dated 29 January 1998, requires the Agency to include conditions in compliance with the Directive in authorisations, or to issue variations as appropriate.

4.23.2 Environmental Protection Act 1990, Part III

This part of the Act (Statutory Nuisances and Clean Air) can be used to control certain aspects of incineration not covered by the provisions of other Acts – for instance action in respect of recurring odorous and gaseous emissions which may be prejudicial to health or a nuisance (see chapter 1, 1.15.1).

4.23.3 Clean Air Act 1993

(a) Chimney Height

Local authorities must take grit, dust, and gas emissions into account when accepting plans for new chimneys serving furnaces of 100 lb/hr or more. Chimney height is broadly calculated in relation to the probable future sulphur content of the refuse and the hourly burning rate. Reference to the *Memorandum on Chimney Heights* provides a general guide, and particular attention should be given to the interrelationship of chimney heights, gas plume height, wind velocity and direction, the nature of the terrain and other industry in the area. (See also Appendix 2.5)

(b) Solids Emissions

Smoke emissions from incinerators must be no darker than Shade 2 on the Ringelmann Chart. In smoke control areas, unless special exemption has been made, it is an offence to emit smoke.

Section 5(5) of the *Clean Air Act 1993* makes it an offence not to use the Best Practicable Means for minimising the emission of grit and dust from a chimney. There are no specific limits on grit and dust emissions from incinerators – the *Grit and Dust Regulations 1971* do not apply. However, the DOE issued draft regulations in May 1977 which may be used as a Best Practicable Means guideline for local authorities. A table sets out prescribed maximum rates of emission in kilograms per hour related to the melting rate of the furnace in metric tons per hour. Gas conditions are standardised at 10% carbon dioxide, NTP, dry. The heat release figures are arrived at using, for convenience, a calorific value of 5,000 Btu/lb, but it should be borne in mind that raw refuse, even in a given location, often changes substantially in composition and moisture content.

(c) Sulphur Content of Fuel Oil

Section 31 of the *Clean Air Act 1993* empowers the Secretary of State for the Environment, Transport and the Regions to impose regulations limiting the sulphur content of fuel oil used in furnaces and engines. *The Marketing of Gas Oil (Sulphur Content) Regulations 1994* came into effect on 1 October 1994, replacing the *Oil Fuel (Sulphur Content of Gas Oil) Regulations 1990*. Among other things, these Regulations make it an offence to market gas oil with a sulphur content in excess of 0.2% by weight (see chapter 2, 2.13.4). Section 36 of the Act also empowers local authorities to require the owner of plant to provide information on emissions to atmosphere, subject to certain restrictions.

4.24 THE BATTERIES AND ACCUMULATORS CONTAINING DANGEROUS SUBSTANCES REGULATIONS 1994 (SI 232)

European Union Directive 91/157/EEC requires Member States to set up schemes for the separate collection of spent batteries and accumulators containing specified amounts of lead, mercury or cadmium with a view to recycling or controlled disposal. A further Directive (93/72) deals with the marking system to be adhered to.

The above Regulations apply in England, Scotland and Wales and were made under the *European Communities Act 1972*. They

- prohibit the sale of alkaline manganese batteries with more than 0.025% mercury by weight; button cells and batteries composed of button cells and alkaline manganese batteries containing 0.05% mercury by weight and intended for prolonged use under extreme conditions are exempted;
- require that appliances using batteries covered by the Directive must be designed to ensure that the batteries can be easily removed;
- introduce a marking system for batteries covered by the Directive to indicate separate collection and heavy metal content; this will not apply to those manufactured or imported into the EU before 1 August 1994; nor will it apply to those marketed in Great Britain on or before 31 December 1995.

The first two provisions came into force on 1 March 1994 and the third on 1 August 1994.

The Government has yet to announce how it is to implement the remainder of the Directive – i.e. to set up a scheme for collection of spent batteries for recycling or controlled disposal.

4.25 TRANSFRONTIER SHIPMENT OF WASTE REGULATIONS 1994 (SI 1137)

In 1996 the UK imported almost 76,136 tonnes of hazardous waste for treatment and disposal and exported 12,072 tonnes (originating in E & W & N1). Approximately 61% was imported for recovery and the remainder for final disposal at specialist facilities. (*Digest of Environmental Statistics*, No. 20, 1998).

The above Regulations which came into effect in May 1994 were made under the *European Communities Act 1972* and replace the *Transfrontier Shipment of Hazardous Waste Regulations 1988* (N. Ireland 1989). They apply throughout the United Kingdom and amplify various parts of the EU Waste Shipments Regulation (259/93) to ensure its full implementation in the UK. (NB EU Regulations are binding in their entirety on Member States and thus do not require transposing into national legislation.) The main requirements of the EU Regulation, which covers the supervision and control of waste shipments between Member States and into and out of the European Union, are detailed earlier in this chapter – see 4.9 above. The Environment Agency, SEPA and local authorities in Northern Ireland are the competent authorities for imports and exports of waste, and the Environment Agency for transit shipments.

All shipments of waste will normally be covered by a contract between the notifier (person "who proposes to ship waste or have the waste shipped") and the consignee (person who is going to finally dispose or effect recovery of the waste). Under the UK Regulations, waste regulation authorities are designated as the competent authorities of dispatch and destination. They are thus responsible for ensuring documentation procedures (consignment notes and movement/tracking forms) are complied with and that the waste is handled in accordance with the documentation and with the EU Regulation. In addition the Regulations require enforcement authorities to raise objections to any shipments which do not conform to the *UK Management Plan for Exports and Imports of Waste* (see below). The UK Regulations provide for the enforcing authority to issue a certificate confirming that the shipment is or will be covered by a financial guarantee or insurance.

To comply with the EU Regulation, the enforcing authority may serve a notice

- on the notifier requiring the return of a waste shipment to the UK,
- on the consignee to dispose of, or recover the waste, in an environmentally sound manner.

Copies of all consignment notes must be sent to the Secretary of State, with a statement saying whether the shipment received authorisation or not. A Department of Environment Circular 13/94, revised by letter dated 26.1.95 (WO 44/94; SOED 21/94; NI WM 1/94) advises that information given on consignment notes is environmental information for the purposes of the *Environmental Information Regulations 1992*; it will thus normally be accessible to the public, subject to various exemptions in those Regulations such as commercial confidentiality.

It is an offence to contravene either the EU or UK Regulations; summary conviction may lead to a maximum fine of £5,000 (£2,000 in N. Ireland); conviction on indictment may result in an unlimited fine and/or imprisonment for up to two years.

The Department of Environment Circular mentioned above provides detailed guidance on both the EU and UK Regulations, including full advice on the documentation procedures and other requirements.

4.26 UK MANAGEMENT PLAN FOR EXPORTS AND IMPORTS OF WASTE

This document, prepared in accordance with the Waste Framework Directive and the above UK Regulations, sets out Government policy with regard to imports and exports of waste. It is a statutory document and has been legally binding since 1 June 1996. The Plan also provides technical guidance and assessment criteria to enable decisions to be taken on proposed shipments. It does not apply to radioactive waste.

Under the Plan all exports of waste for final disposal are banned; exports of waste for recovery are permitted only to OECD countries but exports of hazardous waste for recovery to non-OECD countries are permitted only in very limited circumstances.

In line with the principle that all countries should aim for self-sufficiency in waste disposal, the UK has adopted a general policy of importing waste only for "genuine recovery operations" including energy recovery. Imports for disposal to landfill will only be permitted if it is considered that the exporting country does not have the necessary technical capacity and facilities to dispose of the waste in an environmentally sound way; imports for incineration from all countries will only be accepted in an emergency. Hazardous waste imports for incineration from Portugal and Eire are to be allowed indefinitely (because of the small amounts involved) and from other EU countries for three years in diminishing amounts. Imports of clinical waste from Eire were also permitted until the end of 1997.

CONTAMINATED LAND

4.27 INTRODUCTION

Land may become contaminated as a result of a variety of human activities, and the polluted soil present problems for centuries. The metal extraction industries are well known for causing soil contamination and mineral processing also frequently leads to contamination. Indeed, the toxic effects of spoil from Roman lead and silver mines are still visible in parts of North Wales while the more recent extraction of zinc in the Shipham area of Somerset resulted in high levels of cadmium in soil – and hence in home grown vegetables – in the area.

The depositing of wastes, both industrial and domestic, into landfill sites can in some instances result in contamination of ground or surface waters unless properly contained: as different materials decompose, they react together and form leachate, a noxious liquid. A more serious problem with landfill sites can be the build up of methane gas to potentially explosive levels, posing a danger to nearby housing.

The contamination of soil with toxic chemicals may have direct effects on human health if houses and gardens are built on the land in question. Particles of soil handled or ingested by adults or children may carry irritant or poisonous chemicals while the inhalation of such particles, or vapours from the pollutants, provide another absorption route. Vegetable gardens sited on polluted land may produce crops contaminated by the direct uptake of toxins or the deposition of contaminated particles on the growing plants.

Once a pollutant reaches the soil a number of things may happen to it. It may break down or be neutralised; it may be washed out by rain or, if volatile, evaporate; or it may remain in the soil, building up to high concentrations with successive additions. The fate of a pollutant and its concentration are determined by the balance between the rate of input and the rate of removal. Removal mechanisms are, in turn, determined by the chemical, physical and biological properties of the contaminant and of the soil medium, together with the presence and activity of soil organisms, the amount of rainfall and its composition, and the nature of any other materials subsequently deposited.

Pollutant breakdown, by various chemical and microbiological processes, can be an important removal mechanism. Phenols, for instance, can be destroyed by micro-organisms providing that they are not present at concentrations sufficient to inhibit or kill the organisms concerned. Certain herbicides are also decomposed microbiologically and their frequent use leads to the establishment of populations of soil flora particularly adept at breaking them down.

Materials not broken down by micro-organisms – and the breakdown products of those that are – may be leached out if they are soluble in water at the prevailing pH. The type of soil and its permeability affect the rate of leaching with higher rates observed in sandy soils with a low organic content. Leaching through clay soils, and those with large amounts of humus, is much slower as contaminants tend to be more tightly bound to soil particles. Leaching can be prevented by properly lining landfill sites and covering them to prevent rainwater penetration.

Where breakdown and/or leaching do not occur to any great extent, the accumulation of contaminants in the upper layers of the soil occurs and high levels may be reached if repeated or continuous additions of materials are made. This build-up may not be permanent, as subsequent changes in conditions may cause the remobilisation of some materials bound to soil particles under the original circumstances, but in most instances soil contaminated with persistent materials remains damaged indefinitely.

With regard to contamination from landfill sites, the buried biodegradable matter decomposes anaerobically, producing large quantities of carbon dioxide and methane. Depending on the geology of the area, these gases can seep underground or rise to the surface. Methane, as mentioned earlier, is potentially explosive and can cause fires; methane from landfill sites can either be vented to the atmosphere, collected and used as a fuel supply, or simply burned off.

The total restoration of contaminated land to an "unpolluted" state is rarely achievable and, in many cases, unnecessary. Instead, a remedial approach tailored to the intensity and extent of the contamination found and the intended end-use of the site is adopted. In some cases it may be necessary to zone the land for specified non-residential purposes, endorsing the title deeds to that effect. The use of lightly contaminated land for amenity purposes may be possible if the materials present are largely inorganic and a sealing sward of tolerant grasses can be planted to prevent both human contact with the soil and the windborne transport of polluted dust.

More heavily contaminated sites may only be usable for purposes such as car parks, warehouses and other industrial developments where a layer of tarmac or concrete would be laid on the surface, thereby sealing off the pollution. In certain instances, such as the occurrence of highly contaminated pockets in otherwise fairly clean sites, or small sites badly contaminated throughout, the polluted soil may be removed in its entirety to a licensed waste disposal site and replaced with cleaner material.

Guidance based on the "suitable for use" principle on the redevelopment and after-use of contaminated land is provided by the Department of the Environment, Transport and the Regions' Interdepartmental Committee on the Redevelopment of Contaminated Land (ICRCL). It publishes information on problems relating to the redevelopment of landfill sites, gasworks and scrap yard sites, sewage works, farms, and on fire hazards. It has also published guidance on the hazards posed by the presence of specific substances on land, including asbestos, mercury, lead, sulphur, PAHs and arsenic. ICRCL also provides advice on the concentrations at which specific contaminants would make a site unsuitable (without remedial action) for particular purposes.

Chapter 8 of the Royal Commission on Environmental Pollution's 19th report, *Sustainable Use of Soil* (HMSO, 1996), looks at the industrial contamination of soil and also outlines a number of remediation processes, including:

- **solidification**, where a binder (e.g. cement) is used to enclose the contaminated soil in a solid form, reducing its solubility, mobility and toxicity; this method is suitable for dealing with heavy metals but not mercury or organic compounds.
- **physical**, where contaminants are isolated or concentrated, but not destroyed, e.g. by vapour extraction or soil washing.
- **chemical**, where reactants are used to destroy, immobilise, extract or neutralise contaminants.
- **thermal treatment** at 800-2,500 degrees C to destroy contaminants.
- **biological methods** to produce degradation of organic contaminants; to transform to less harmful or mobile forms; or convert to more mobile form to allow separation.

4.28 REGULATORY CONTROLS

4.28.1 Planning Controls

The main means of ensuring contaminated land is not used for any unsuitable purposes has been through the planning system; thus controls or conditions could be put on the use of land for a particular purpose or remedial work specified as part of the development permission. The fact that no – or only very patchy – records exist of former uses of land means that this system of control is not very satisfactory, particularly with the increasing pressures for release of land for development purposes.

PPG 23, *Planning Policy Guidance: Planning and Pollution Control* (June 1994) highlights the need to be aware of the previous use of land in considering development plans. Where contamination is suspected, developers should investigate the land to determine what remedial measures are necessary to ensure its safety and suitability for the purpose proposed.

4.28.2 Environmental Protection Act 1990, Part II

Section 34 (effective 1 April 1992) places a duty of care on all those involved in dealing with waste from its generation to its disposal (see this chapter, 4.19.2). The duty of care extends to closed landfill sites where the site operator remains responsible for the site until it has been declared safe and a "certificate of completion" issued.

Section 61 of the Act, which was never implemented and is to be repealed by the *Environment Act 1995*, placed a duty on waste regulation authorities to identify and inspect closed landfill sites to ensure their condition was not likely to cause pollution of the environment or harm to human health.

Section 143 of the EPA, which came into effect in England and Wales on 14 February 1992 and is also to be repealed by the *Environment Act 1995*, provided for the establishment by local authorities of public registers of land in their area which has been, or is being, put to contaminative use.

4.28.3 Environmental Protection Act 1990, Part IIA

A consultation document, *Paying for our Past* (DOE, 1994), reviewing arrangements for dealing with contaminated land proposed a "suitable for use" approach – i.e. it should be "treated to deal with unacceptable actual or perceived threats to health, safety or the environment, taking account of the actual or intended use of the site"; and that where practical such land should be brought back into beneficial use. This would not preclude a developer or owner from carrying out more extensive remedial work, nor a regulatory body from requiring it.

These proposals have been given effect through section 57 of the *Environment Act 1995*, which has yet to be brought into force; this adds Part IIA (ss.78A-78YC) to the EPA and contains the legislative framework for identifying and dealing with contaminated land.These sections of the Act are expected to be brought into force in July 1999.

Five sets of draft Regulations were published in November 1996 covering special sites, form and content of remediation notices, appeals, compensation, and remediation registers; it was suggested that all or some of the Regulations might be consolidated. Draft statutory guidance (for England and Wales and also for Scotland) on how various sections of the Act were to be implemented was issued for consultation in September 1996. The draft Guidance covered:

- Determination of contaminated land and definition of "significant harm" (s.78A(2) and (5));
- Inspection and identification of contaminated land (s.78B (1) and (2));
- Determination of who should be responsible for remediation; apportionment of costs (s.78F, K);
- Considerations which might lead to liability being mitigated in certain circumstances.

The Act requires the Secretary of State to issue a draft of the Guidance for prior consultation with the appropriate Agency and others considered appropriate. A draft must then be laid before both Houses of Parliament with 40 days being allowed for either House to resolve that the Guidance should not be issued (s.78YA). The enforcing authorities are required to act in accordance with the Guidance.

The Agencies may issue Guidance to a local authority in respect of its functions in relation to a specific piece of contaminated land (EPA: s.78V; NI: WCLO, Art.67).

This Part of the Act does not apply (unless Regulations state otherwise) to harm, or pollution of controlled waters as a result of the radioactive properties of any substance (EPA: s.78YC; NI: WCLO, Art.71).

Local authorities (district councils and unitary authorities) are the enforcing authority for contaminated land and the Environment Agency or Scottish Environment Protection Agency for any land designated a special site due to the nature of its contamination.

Northern Ireland

Part III of the *Waste and Contaminated Land (Northern Ireland) Order 1997*, Articles 49-71, makes similar provision for dealing with contaminated land; district councils are the main enforcing authority, except for land designated as a "special site", which is the responsibility of the DOE(NI). The DOE(NI) is also responsible for preparing Guidance on relevant Articles of the Order in accordance with Article 69. Reference is made throughout the text to the relevant Articles of the Northern Ireland legislation, which has also yet to be implemented.

Identification of Contaminated land and Designation of Special Sites (ss.78A-78D) (NI: WCLO, Arts.50-52)

Local authorities have a duty to inspect their land to identify whether any is contaminated and whether any such land should be designated as a "special site" (to be defined in Regulations) because of the nature of the contamination. In identifying contaminated land, local authorities will be required to act in accordance with Guidance from the Secretary of State. Section 78A(2) defines contaminated land as

> "land which appears . . . to be in such a condition, by reason of substances in, on or under the land, that –
>
> (a) significant harm is being caused or there is a significant possibility of such harm being caused; or
>
> (b) pollution of controlled waters is being, or is likely to be, caused."

Draft Statutory Guidance defines what "harm" is to be regarded as "significant" to:

- **human beings**: death serious injury, cancer or other disease, genetic mutation, birth defects, or the impairment of reproductive functions. Disease is to be taken to mean an unhealthy condition of the body or some part thereof;
- **living organisms or ecological systems**: an irreversible or other substantial adverse change in the functioning of the habitat or site;
- **property (livestock, other owned animals, wild animals which are the subject of shooting or fishing rights, crops)**: death, disease or other physical change such that there is a substantial loss (10%) in their value;
- **property (buildings)**: structural failure or substantial damage making them unfit for their intended purpose.

The Department of the Environment (now Department of the Environment, Transport and the Regions) has produced a number of industry profiles detailing the likely types of contamination to be found, and the materials and processes which would have been used by the industry sector concerned.

It should be noted that while two or more sites if considered individually would not be considered to be contaminated, but if considered together would, then each site should be treated as being contaminated (s.78X(1)). Also if land adjoining or adjacent to the area of a local authority appears contaminated, it may act as though the land were within its boundary (s.78X(2)). (NI: WCLO, Arts.68(1) and 68(2) respectively.)

Following identification, the local authority should then by notice inform the Environment Agency/SEPA or DOE(NI) as appropriate, the owner of the land, the occupiers of any part of the land and any other appropriate person.

If the local authority considers that any of the land which it has identified as being contaminated warrants being designated a special site, it should seek the appropriate Agency's advice in making its decision. Regulations will describe the types of land which should be designated as special sites. The local authority should also notify the relevant persons that it considers a site should be designated a special site. The Agency may also advise the local authority that it considers certain land should be designated as a special site.

Following a decision to designate land as a special site, the local authority should notify the appropriate Agency/DOE(NI) and other relevant persons (as above). The decision then takes effect on the day after the expiration of 21 days of the notification, or the day after notification is received from the appropriate Agency/DOE(NI) that it agrees with the designation (whichever is the soonest). All the relevant persons should then be notified that the decision has taken effect.

However, if the Agency/DOE(NI) disagrees with the local authority over whether land should be designated a special site, it has 21 days from the date of notification of the decision to notify the local authority that it disagrees and to give a statement of its reasons for doing so. The matter is then referred by the local authority to the Secretary of State (NI: Planning Appeals Commission) for decision. The Agency/DOE(NI) should send the local authority a copy of its notification and statement. The local authority should also notify all relevant persons that a decision has been referred to the Secretary of State (or Plannning Appeals Commission in NI); decisions to designate special sites do not take effect until the referral is determined and then take effect (as confirmed, revised, etc) the day after notice of determination has been sent to the relevant persons and to the local authority.

Remediation Notices (ss.78E, F, G, H(1)-(4)) (NI: WCLO, Arts.53 & 70)

Following designation of land as being contaminated land or a special site, the enforcing authority should serve a Remediation Notice on the appropriate person(s) specifying what needs to be done and the period within which the various pieces of work should be done. Regulations will prescribe the form and content of the notices.

The appropriate person so far as responsibility for remediation is concerned will normally be the person(s) who knowingly caused or permitted the presence of a substance in, on or under the land, thereby causing it to become contaminated. However if after inquiry the person who knowingly caused or permitted the contamination cannot be found, then the appropriate person is the person(s) who currently occupy or own the land. Where more than one person is required to carry out remediation work because of the presence of different substances, a Notice should be served on each person specifying what each needs to do. Where more than one person is to be responsible for cleaning up the same contamination, the Notice should specify the proportion of works and costs to be borne by each in accordance with Guidance from the Secretary of State (or DOE(NI)).

Before serving the remediation notice, however, the enforcing authority should endeavour to consult the appropriate persons about the remediation to be done and, where necessary to consult any other person who might be required to give consent or grant rights (e.g. of access) for certain work to be done. Such rights or consent should be granted to the person on whom the remediation notice is served (s.78G); the person granting consent or rights may be entitled to compensation from the person on whom the remediation notice has been served. Regulations are to be made outlining the procedure and way in which compensation is to be determined.

In specifying what it is reasonable to do by way of remediation, the enforcing authority must take into account the likely costs of the work and the seriousness of the harm, or pollution of controlled waters; the enforcing authorities should have regard to any Guidance from the Secretary of State (or DOE(NI)) as to what should be considered as "reasonable", the remediation to be done in any particular case and the standard to which land or waters should be remediated.

It should be noted that a Remediation Notice may not be served before the expiry of three months except when the enforcing authority considers that the condition of the land warrants it, there is imminent danger of serious harm, or of serious pollution to controlled waters.

It is an offence (EPA: s.78M; NI: WCLO, Art.59) not to comply with the terms of a Remediation Notice without reasonable excuse; on summary conviction this may result in a fine not exceeding level 5 on the standard scale, plus an amount equal to one-tenth of level 5 for each day the offence continues following conviction. Where the offence relates to industrial, trade or business premises, a fine not exceeding £20,000 may be imposed, plus a further fine of one-tenth of £20,000 for each day the offence continues following conviction.

A remediation notice should not be served if contamination has arisen as a result of non-compliance with an IPC authorisation, or enforcement or prohibition notice served under Part I of the EPA (NI: *Industrial Pollution Control Order 1997*). In such circumstances, the appropriate Agency (as IPC enforcing authorities) may with the written permission of the Secretary of State and of any other person whose land is affected, take remedial action and recover costs from the offender. Similarly where land becomes contaminated as a result of a breach of a waste management licence issued under Part II of the EPA NI: Part II of WCLO), the offence should be dealt with under that Part of the Act (EPA: s.78YB (1)-(3); NI: WCLO, Art.70). Contamination due to unlawful waste deposits (e.g. fly-tipping) will normally be dealt with under section 59 of the EPA (see 4.19.5 above).

A remediation notice should not require any action which could impede or prevent a discharge permitted under a consent granted under Part III of the *Water Resources Act 1991* or Part II of the *Control of Pollution Act 1974* in Scotland (EPA: s.78YB (4)). In Northern Ireland Art.70(4) of the WCLO contains the same provisions in relation to the

Water Act (Northern Ireland) 1972 and the *Water and Sewerage Services (Northern Ireland) Order 1973.*

Remediation Declarations and Statements (s.78H(5)-(9)) (NI: WCLO, Art.56(5)-(9))

A remediation notice will not be served in the following circumstances (see also above):

(a) where it appears to the enforcing authority that there is nothing by way of remediation that could be specified in the notice taking into account such matters as cost, seriousness of harm or pollution, standard of remediation, what it is reasonable to do, etc;

in this instance the enforcing authority must publish a Remediation Declaration saying what it would have specified in a Remediation Notice if it could have, and its reasons for not doing so.

(b) if the appropriate person is already carrying out the necessary remediation work or it has been done or is planned;

(c) if it appears that the appropriate person on whom to serve the remediation notice is the enforcing authority itself;

(d) if the enforcing authority is to carry out the remediation work itself for various reasons – see below;

in the case of (b) above the person(s) carrying out the remediation should publish a Remediation Statement or in the case of (c) and (d) the enforcing authority. The Statement should say what is, has or is likely to be done and the timescale, and the names and addresses of all those involved in the remediation work.

If, however, the appropriate person in (b) above does not publish a Remediation Statement within a reasonable time after the date on which a Remediation Notice could have been served, then the enforcing authority may publish the Statement, recovering its costs from the appropriate person. The enforcing authority may also then serve a Remediation Notice.

Appeals (s.78L) (NI: WCLO, Art.58)

A person on whom a Remediation Notice has been served may appeal within 21 days to the Magistrates Court/Sheriff (NI Court of Summary Jurisdiction) in the case of a notice served by a local authority; appeals against notices (relating to special sites) served by the Environment Agency/SEPA should be sent to the Secretary of State. (Section 114 of the *Environment Act 1995* enables the Secretary of State to appoint someone to handle the appeal on his behalf. In Northern Ireland appeals in relation to special sites will be dealt with by the Planning Appeals

Commission (Art.58). On appeal, the Remediation Notice may be quashed if it has a material defect, confirmed or modified. Regulations will outline the appeals procedure, cases when the Remediation Notice may be suspended pending determination of the appeal etc.

Powers of Enforcing Authority to carry out Remediation (s.78N & P) (NI: WCLO, Arts.60 & 61)

The enforcing authority may carry out the remediation work itself in the following circumstances:

- to prevent occurrence of serious harm, or serious pollution of controlled waters, of which there is imminent danger;
- where the appropriate person has given written agreement that the enforcing authority should carry out the remediation work (at his/her expense);
- failure to comply with remediation notice;
- contamination has resulted from water from an abandoned mine or where the owner or occupier of land has not caused or knowingly permitted the presence of contaminating substances in on or under land which have subsequently contaminated other land;
- where the enforcing authority decides to carry out certain work itself but does not intend to recover all or part of the cost of remediation work;
- where, after reasonable inquiry, the appropriate person cannot be found to do the particular work.

Where the enforcing authority has carried out the remediation work itself, it may recover all or part of its costs, bearing in mind the degree of hardship this may cause to the person concerned and with regard to any Guidance from the Secretary of State. The enforcing authority should serve a Charging Notice on the person concerned detailing the amount of the charge and any interest payable. The charging notice should also be copied to anyone who might have an interest in the premises affected by the charge. The charge becomes a charge on the premises 21 days after the service of the notice or, if there is an appeal, following its determination. (Any appeal should be made within 21 days of its service.) Where the charge is a charge on the premises, the enforcing authority may by order recover the costs over a period of up to 30 years.

Special Sites (s.78Q) (NI: WCLO, Art.62)

If contaminated land is designated a special site after a remediation notice has been served, the appropriate Agency may adopt the

Remediation Notice, notifying the local authority and any appropriate person of its decision to do so. If the local authority has already begun doing some remediation work, it may continue to do so and the appropriate Agency (NI: DOE) may inspect the land from time to time to review its condition.

Where the Agency considers that contaminated land no longer requires to be designated as a special site, it should notify both the Secretary of State and the local authority. In Northern Ireland, the DOE will notify the district council. The land may subsequently be redesignated as a special site if its condition requires.

Public Registers (s.78R-T) (NI: WCLO, Arts.63-65 & Sch.2)

Each enforcing authority will maintain a public register containing particulars relating to contaminated land and special sites for which it is the enforcing authority; local authority registers will also contain details relating to special sites in its area. The registers which may be in any form should be available for inspection by the public, with copies of documents available at a reasonable charge. Regulations will specify the content, location of and other procedural and administrative matters relating to the keeping of the registers.

Information on the registers will include:

- remediation notices and appeals against such notices;
- remediation statements and declarations; any other notifications given to the enforcing authority relating to work which has been done, or is claimed to have been done, as a result of a remediation notice;
- notices relating to the designation of land as a special site, or withdrawal of that designation;
- convictions for offences under this part of the Act;
- in England, Wales & NI, appeals against charging notices.

Information may be excluded from the registers on the grounds of national security or commercial confidentiality. In the former case, the enforcing authority should notify the Secretary of State of any information excluded on these grounds; or the person concerned may notify the Secretary of State direct of the information to be excluded on these grounds and notify the enforcing authority accordingly.

Where a person requests that information be treated as commercially confidential but the enforcing authority disagrees, 21 days should elapse before putting the information on the register. An appeal against the enforcing authority's decision may be made to the Secretary of State (NI Planning Appeals Commission) in which case the information in question will not be put on the register until seven days following determination or withdrawal of the appeal. Where either party requests a hearing, or the Secretary of State (NI Planning Appeals Commission) decides on a hearing, this must be held in private. Information remains commercially confidential for four years, but the person concerned may apply to the enforcing authority for this classification to be extended.

Reports on the State of Contaminated Land (s.78U) (NI: WCLO, Art.66)

The Environment Agency, SEPA and the DOE(NI) are required to prepare and publish from time to time reports on the state of contaminated land in their respective countries. They may request local authorities to provide information to enable them to prepare their reports.

4.28.4 Water Resources Act 1991

Anti-Pollution Works (s.161)

The Environment Agency is empowered to take remedial action to deal with any pollution affecting controlled waters, including from contaminated land and to recover the costs from the person responsible for the pollution. The *Control of Pollution Act 1974*, sections 46A-C, give the same powers to SEPA in Scotland. See chapter 5.

LITTER

4.29 ENVIRONMENTAL PROTECTION ACT 1990, PART IV

This introduces strict controls in England, Scotland and Wales to deal with the problem of litter. Prior to the Act, this was mainly regulated under the *Control of Pollution Act 1974* and in England and Wales under the *Litter Act 1983* and in Scotland under provisions contained in the *Local Government and Planning (Scotland) Act 1982*; all remain of relevance though certain sections are repealed as a result of the new legislation. In Northern Ireland the comparable legislation is the *Litter (Northern Ireland) Order 1994* which came into effect on 1 October 1994.

Responsibility for enforcement of the legislation lies with local authorities – principal litter authorities; they have a statutory duty (s.89) to keep open land and roads and highways under their control free of litter and refuse, and to ensure roads and highways are kept clean in accordance with the *Code of Practice on Litter and Refuse* (see below). The duty to keep land free of litter, which also applies to statutory undertakers, designated educational establishments and national parks to which the public have access, became effective on 1 April 1991. This duty was extended to statutory transport undertakers from 1 May 1991. (Note: the duty applied to British Rail but was not carried through when BR was privatised. Thus neither Railtrack nor the train operators have a duty to keep rail tracks free of litter. Legislation is to be brought forward to deal with this, and it will also make water companies responsible for rubbish etc on river banks.)

Section 90 of the Act, brought into force on 1 July 1991 through the *Litter Control Areas Order 1991* (N. Ireland: The *Litter Control Areas Order (Northern Ireland) 1995*, effective 5 July 1995), enables local authorities to designate as Litter Control Areas the main categories of land to which the public is entitled or permitted to have access. These include

- land or buildings used as car parks;
- shopping centres of 100,000 sq. ft or more of retail space. This is primarily intended to cover "out-of-town" retail parks and not high street shopping centres;
- business parks, industrial estates etc with a floor space of 100,000 sq. ft or more;
- cinemas, theatres, bingo halls, etc, skating rinks, amusement arcades, indoor and outdoor sports centres;
- inland beaches and seashores;
- aerodromes;
- marinas or similar boating facilities;
- land on which markets are held (other than on a highway or public road);
- camping and caravan sites;
- picnic areas on trunk roads;
- land to which the public has access and which is under the control of e.g. parish councils, NHS, police, national parks authorities, waste disposal authorities.

Land in such areas must be kept free of litter and refuse to the standards required by the designated zone into which the land falls (see below). Where standards are not met, members of the public may apply to the Magistrates' Court (Sheriff Court in Scotland) for a litter abatement order (s.91), having first given the offender five days notice of intention to do so. Failure to comply with a litter abatement order without adequate excuse may lead to further prosecution and a maximum fine of £1,000, plus a maximum daily fine of £50 for each day the offence continues after conviction.

Principal Litter Authorities may serve a litter abatement notice (s.92) specifying a timescale within which the litter or refuse must be cleared up, or prohibiting the land in question from becoming defaced by litter or refuse. Offenders may appeal against the terms of the notice within 21 days to the Magistrates'/Sheriff Court. Again failure to comply with the notice without adequate excuse may result in prosecution and a fine.

In addition, sections 93 and 94 of the Act, also brought into force on 1 July 1991 through the *Street Litter Control Notices Order 1991*, empower local authorities to issue Street Litter Control Notices to various premises with a street frontage which may cause a litter problem. These include take-away food premises, service stations, cinemas, theatres and other recreational premises; banks and building societies with cash machines on an outside wall are also covered. Local authorities must give 21 days' notice of their intention to serve a Notice and must take into account any representations made. The Notice can specify the length of street covered, as well as cleansing practices such as the number of litter bins, frequency of emptying and street washing. Any appeal against the terms of a Notice must be made to the Magistrates'/Sheriff Court. Once again, failure to comply with the terms of a Notice may result in prosecution and a fine.

A further deterrent to dropping litter is provided by the *Litter (Fixed Penalty) Order 1996* (SI 3055); this replaces a 1991 Order and came into effect on 1 January 1997. This enables enforcement officers to issue a fixed penalty notice of £25 to anyone who drops litter. If it is not paid within 14 days, the offender is liable to prosecution, for which the maximum fine on conviction is £2,500.

Code of Practice on Litter and Refuse

The legislation is backed up by a statutory code of practice, which is currently being reviewed. It applies in England, Wales and Scotland and came into force on 1 April 1991. It describes the extent of the duty placed on local authorities and others covered by the Act to keep their land clear of litter and refuse. Advice is given on standards of cleanliness to be achieved for particular zones, and the timescale within which a Grade A standard (see below) should be achieved for each zone (see below). For instance for Zone 1 areas, Grade A should be achieved immediately after cleaning and within six hours of falling to Grade B, within three hours of falling to Grade C and within one hour of falling to Grade D; Zone 5 (beaches) should be predominantly free of litter from May - September.

The standards of cleanliness (or for the last two grades, dirtiness) are:

- *Grade A:* No litter or refuse;
- *Grade B:* Predominantly free of litter, apart from small items such as cigarette ends;

- *Grade C:* Widespread distribution of small items and larger items (such as beverage containers etc) and animal faeces;
- *Grade D:* Heavily littered.

Zones have been classified as follows:

1) Town centres, shopping areas, railway and bus stations, public car parks and other open public spaces;
2) High density residential areas, recreational areas, suburban car parks, railway and bus stations;
3) Low density residential areas, public parks and industrial estates;
4) All other areas;
5) Local authority beaches;
6) Motorways and other main routes;
7) Other roads;
8) Educational establishments;
9) Railway embankments (within 100 m of platform ends);
10) Railway embankments within urban areas (other than above);
11) Canal towpaths (paved) in urban areas.

RADIOACTIVE WASTE

4.30 INTRODUCTION

Radioactive materials are used in the generation of electricity, in industry – including the food processing industry – in medicine, research and defence. Their use results in gaseous, liquid and solid wastes which can be divided into three categories:

- *high level (or heat generating) waste (HLW)*: this results from reprocessing of spent nuclear fuels; about 97% is recycled into new fuel;
- *intermediate level waste (ILW)*: this includes scrap metal, sludge and residues from fuel storage ponds, plutonium contaminated materials and fuel cladding;
- *low level waste (LLW)*: this includes paper towels, protective clothing, laboratory equipment and soils.

Strict safety standards have been set by the Government with which any disposal scheme for radioactive waste must comply. The National Radiological Protection Board advises the Government on radiological protection criteria to be applied to the disposal of all types of solid radioactive waste and in 1992, it published new objectives for its land-based disposal. This includes the following recommendations:

a) future generations should not be subjected to risks which would be considered unacceptable today, i.e. people alive at any time in the future should be given a level of protection at least equivalent to that accorded to members of the public alive now;

b) the radiological risk from one disposal facility to the most exposed group of people should not exceed a risk of serious health effects in the individuals or their descendants of 1 in 100,000 per year;

c) the radiological risks to members of the public should be as low as reasonably achievable (ALARA), economic and social factors being taken into account.

All high-level wastes must be stored for at least 50 years to allow them to cool. They are currently kept in liquid form in double-walled cooled stainless steel tanks enclosed in thick concrete walls at Sellafield in Cumbria and Dounreay in Scotland. In 1990 British Nuclear Fuels brought into operation a vitrification plant at Sellafield; HLW will be converted into glass blocks and sealed in stainless steel containers and stored for at least 90 years before eventual disposal. Current research worldwide is looking at emplacement in deep geologic formations on land or beneath the seabed which must remain impermeable for tens of thousands of years.

In June 1998, the Government announced that Dounreay is to be closed on scientific and economic grounds, and also because of safety concerns. Reprocessing of waste currently stored at the plant is expected to be completed by 2006; decommissioning and clean-up of the plant will then take at least another 50 years, with monitoring of parts of the site needed for at least 100 years.

The volume of ILW produced annually is currently about 5,000 cubic metres and of LLW, 40,000 cubic metres. Very low level solid waste can be collected and deposited at local authority landfill sites, provided its activity is below authorised limits. Other low level waste of a higher activity may be buried in a "near surface facility", such as that owned by British Nuclear Fuels at Drigg; this comprises concrete lined trenches which will be capped and earthed over when full. BNFL estimate that Drigg should be able to accommodate all the UK's LLW until around 2050. Conditions attached to such authorisations limit the intensity of radiation detectable at the surface of the site to specified limits. There are other conditions, one of which specifies the minimum depth at which the waste must be buried.

In 1982, the Government set up UK NIREX Ltd – the Nuclear Industry Radioactive Waste Executive – to implement Government strategy for disposal of LLW and ILW produced by the UK nuclear industry, and by users of radioactive materials in hospitals, industry, research and defence. In 1985, it was reconstituted as a company, UK Nirex Ltd, with the same remit. Following a period of public consultation and initial investigations of sites at Dounreay and Sellafield, Nirex chose the latter as its preferred site for the underground storage of ILW. However, in 1997, following a public inquiry, the Environment Secretary refused planning permission, mainly on scientific grounds, but also because he considered the proposal unacceptable for the Lake District National Park. Nirex will now need to consider alternative sites.

An independent committee – the Radioactive Waste Management Advisory Committee (RWMAC) – advises "the Secretaries of State for the Environment, Scotland and Wales on the technical and environmental implications of major issues concerning the development and implementation of an overall policy for all aspects of the management of civil radioactive waste, including research and development; and on any such matters referred to it by the Secretaries of State".

Sources and effects of both natural and artificial radiation are summarised in chapter 2, sections 2.25 and 2.26.

4.31 REGULATORY CONTROLS

Under the *Radioactive Substances Act 1993*, anybody wishing to keep or use radioactive materials requires to be registered by the Environment Agency in England and Wales, the Scottish Environment Protection Agency in Scotland and the Department of the Environment in Northern Ireland; the accumulation or disposal of radioactive waste also requires an authorisation from the same bodies.

4.31.1 Nuclear Installations

The Nuclear Installations Act 1965 requires that before a site can be used for a commercial nuclear installation, it must obtain a nuclear site licence. The *Nuclear Installations Regulations 1971* (SI 381) prescribe the types of installations and activities covered by the Act. HM Nuclear Installations Inspectorate (which is part of the Health and Safety Executive) is responsible for licensing and may attach specific conditions to licences to ensure appropriate standards are maintained. The NII continuously monitors sites for which it is responsible to ensure compliance with conditions and also ensures that emergency procedures are up to date and staff familiar with them. In setting conditions both the appropriate Agency and the Ministry of Agriculture, Fisheries and Food will be consulted. This Act does not cover radioactive waste or discharges from nuclear sites, which are licensed separately under the *Radioactive Substances Act 1993*.

4.31.2 Ionising Radiation

The Ionising Radiations Regulations 1985 (SI 1333) (made under the *Health and Safety at Work Act 1974*) provide protection for the workforce from ionising radiations, including the handling and storage of radioactive waste. These Regulations are currently being amended (see also chapter 2, 2.29.1).

4.31.3 Radioactive Substances Act 1993

The Radioactive Substances Act 1993 (RSA) which consolidates and replaces the 1960 Act came into force on 27 August 1993 and applies to the whole of the UK. It brings together under a single Act the provisions of the 1960 RSA (which is repealed), together with all the various amendments to it made under other Acts. Consolidating Acts, such as this, do not amend legislation but may make minor changes for the purposes of clarification or consistency of approach.

The Act controls the keeping and use of radioactive materials and the accumulation and disposal of radioactive wastes through authorisation and registration systems; it also provides for public access to information held by the enforcing authorities.

This Act applies to Crown premises, except those occupied for navy, army or air force purposes, visiting forces or the Secretary of State for Defence.

The Act is enforced, on behalf of the Secretary of State by the Environment Agency in England and Wales, the Scottish Environment Protection Agency in Scotland, and by the Department of the Environment in Northern Ireland. Sites in England which are also registered under the *Nuclear Installations Act* will be jointly controlled with the Minister of Agriculture, Fisheries and Food, and those in Northern Ireland with the Department of Agriculture for N. Ireland.

A number of amendments were made to the RSA by the *Environment Act 1995*, Schedule 22, paras 200-230; these are noted in the following text and most came into effect on 1 April 1996.

Registration for Users of Radioactive Materials (ss.6-12 & 19-20)

Anybody who keeps or uses radioactive materials, including mobile radioactive apparatus, must apply for registration under the RSA. The application must include details of the premises (or mobile apparatus), what they are used for, the materials being kept or used and likely quantities, and how the materials are to be used. The application must be accompanied by the appropriate fee (see below). A copy of the application, and the subsequent registration certificate, should be sent to all those local authorities in whose area the premises fall except where the Secretary of State has decided that national security could be compromised (s.25).

In granting a certificate of registration, the appropriate Agency may impose such conditions as it thinks fit; these may include alterations to the premises, requirements as to apparatus or equipment used or to be used, restrictions on selling or supplying radioactive materials from the premises. Sections 23-24 enable the Secretary of State (in the case of nuclear sites, with the Minister of Agriculture, Fisheries and Food) to direct the appropriate Agency as to how an application for registration is to be determined – see below. Copies of the certificate of registration should be prominently displayed so that all those with duties on the premises will see it (s.19).

Applications not dealt with within the prescribed determination period (or other period as agreed) should be deemed to have been refused. Section 12 of the Act enables the appropriate Agency to cancel or vary registrations and to notify the operator; the appropriate local authorities should also be advised that such action has been taken.

The appropriate Agency may, by notice, require an operator to retain records of operations for a specified period after ceasing those activities to which registration relates; where registration has been cancelled, authorisation revoked or activities ceased, the operator may by notice be required to give the appropriate Agency copies of relevant records (s.20).

Holders of licences under the *Nuclear Installations Act* do not require registration under section 7 although the appropriate Agency may direct that conditions in accordance with section 7 should be imposed on the licensee; premises which keep or use watches and clocks which are radioactive material do not require registration although their repair or manufacture using luminous materials does (s.8(4) & (5)).

It should be noted that any radioactive materials kept or used on premises for more than three months will be considered to be accumulated for subsequent disposal and thus require authorisation under section 14(4).

Authorisation of Disposal and Accumulation of Radioactive Waste (ss.13-18 & 19-20)

The disposal of any radioactive waste (including disposal from mobile radioactive apparatus) and accumulation of radioactive waste for subsequent disposal requires a certificate of authorisation.

Exceptions to the above are the accumulation and disposal of radioactive waste from clocks and watches, although its accumulation and disposal from premises using luminous materials to repair clocks and watches does (s.15). The disposal of radioactive waste from educational establishments and from hospitals is also exempt from authorisation – conditions and restrictions relating to disposal from such premises are set out, respectively, in the *Radioactive Substances (Schools etc) Exemption Order 1963* (SI 1832) and in the *Radioactive Substances (Hospitals) Exemption Order 1990* (SI 2512, amended 1995, SI 2395).

Applications for authorisations for the accumulation and disposal of radioactive waste will be determined by the appropriate Agency. Applications should be accompanied by the prescribed charge (see 4.31.4a below) – this will be refunded in full should the application be withdrawn within eight weeks of the regulator receiving it.

Section 16(3) – determination by the appropriate Minister of authorisations for disposal of radioactive waste from a nuclear site in England, Wales and N. Ireland – has been revoked by the *Environment Act 1995*, Sch. 22, para 205(3); in its place, section 16(4A) (Sch. 22, para 205(5)) requires the appropriate Agency to consult both the relevant Minister and the Health and Safety Executive prior to making a decision on whether to grant an authorisation and if minded to grant an authorisation on what terms and conditions etc; before granting an authorisation the appropriate Agency should forward a copy to the relevant Minister. Sections 23 and 24 of the Act enable the Secretary of State (and Minister of Agriculture, Fisheries and Food if a nuclear site – *Env. Act 1995*, Sch. 22, para 211(2) and 212(2)) to give directions to the appropriate Agency as to how a registration or authorisation is to be determined, or conditions to be imposed or to call in an application for his determination.

All applications (and subsequent authorisations), subject to the usual considerations of national security (s.25), should be copied to those local authorities within whose areas it is intended to accumulate or dispose of radioactive waste. In addition, before granting a disposal authorisation in respect of a nuclear site other local authorities public bodies and water bodies as is thought appropriate should be consulted.

Authorisations will set conditions for the operation of such plant, including discharge limits for radioactive waste and the manner in which it is to be disposed. The authorisation may permit the radioactive waste to be removed from the premises for disposal in a local authority disposal site; in such instances the local authority has a duty to accept the waste and to deal with it as specified in the authorisation. Authorisations will normally take effect not less than 28 days after a copy of it would have been received by the relevant local authorities.

A copy of the certificate of authorisation must be prominently displayed where all those with duties on the premises will see it (s.19). Failure to do so renders the offender liable to prosecution and a fine (s.33).

Applications (other than those relating to disposal of radioactive waste from a nuclear site – *Env. Act 1995*, Sch. 22, para 205(7)) not dealt with within the prescribed period (or such other period as has been agreed) are deemed to have been refused. Following notice, an authorisation may be varied or revoked and the relevant local authorities advised. However, before varying an authorisation relating to disposal of radioactive waste from a nuclear site, the appropriate Agency must follow the same consultation procedure as for an authorisation – see above: *Env. Act 1995*, Sch. 22, para 206(1). Authorisations and their conditions will normally be reviewed every four years in case updating is needed in the light of new knowledge, experience or technology.

Enforcement and Prohibition Notices (ss.21-22)

The Environment Agency and SEPA may issue enforcement, prohibition and revocation notices where conditions of a registration or authorisation are being contravened, or where there is a risk of environmental harm. The notice will state the problem and action to be taken to remedy the situation and the timescale within which this should be done. If there is considered to be an imminent risk of pollution or harm to human health, the authorisation or registration may be withdrawn in whole or in part. A copy of any notice will be sent to the relevant local authority. Once the appropriate Agency is satisfied that any risk has been dealt with, it can withdraw the notice; the local authority should be advised that this has been done. A similar procedure applies to registrations issued by MAFF.

Secretary of State Powers (ss.23-25)

These sections have been dealt with above. They deal with the Secretary of State's powers to give the Agency and SEPA directions as to how various matters relating to registrations and authorisations are to be determined. Section 25 enables the Secretary of State to declare data confidential on grounds of national security.

Appeals (ss.26-27)

An operator may appeal to the Secretary of State (MAFF for nuclear sites) if an application for authorisation or registration has been refused, conditions are considered unreasonable or in respect of the terms of an enforcement, prohibition, variation or revocation notice. It should be noted that the terms of all notices issued take immediate effect, except for those relating to revocation of authorisation or registration which are dependent on the outcome of any appeal. There is no appeals procedure in respect of

- decisions imposed by direction of the Secretary of State (s.23);
- applications etc determined by the Secretary of State (s.24);
- in N. Ireland, prohibition or other enforcement notices issued under sections 21-22.

The Radioactive Substances (Appeals) Regulations 1990 require that any appeal be made to the Secretary of State within two months of the appropriate Agency's decision (28 days in the case of revocation); the appellant may specify a preference for the appeal to be decided by written representations or by a hearing. Section 27 enables the Secretary of State to refer an appeal (except where it relates to a decision or notice served by SEPA – *Env. Act 1995*, Sch. 22, para 215) to another person appointed by himself). In Scotland, where an appeal has been made in respect of a decision or notice of SEPA, the Secretary of State may appoint someone to handle the appeal on his behalf under section 114 of the *Environment Act 1995*.

Where the matter is to be decided through written representations, the appropriate Agency has 28 days to comment on the appellant's statement, and the appellant a further 17 days to respond to those comments. All public authorities who commented on the original application for a registration or authorisation may also comment on the appeal; both the appropriate Agency) and the appellant have 14 days in which to comment on any such statements received.

Where the matter is to be dealt with in a hearing, the Secretary of State must give 28 days' notice of its date, time and place and must also publish details in a local newspaper. Public authorities who commented on the original application must be given 21 days' notice. The person conducting the hearing may decide if it should be held wholly or partly in public depending on whether matters of national security or commercial confidentiality are involved.

Powers of Secretary of State to deal with Accumulation and Disposal of Radioactive Waste (ss.29-30)

Section 29 empowers the Secretary of State to arrange for adequate facilities to be provided (by the state or another person) for the safe accumulation or disposal of radioactive waste, to consult with relevant local authorities and to charge for the site's use.

Under section 30 the appropriate Agency (*Env. Act 1995*, Sch. 22, para 217) may dispose of radioactive waste in certain circumstances;

these include where premises are empty, the owner is insolvent or there is a risk that the waste may be disposed of unlawfully. Costs may be recovered from the owner or occupier of the premises.

Offences (ss.32-38)

It is an offence not to comply with the conditions of registration or authorisation, or with the terms of an enforcement or prohibition notice; summary conviction may result in a maximum fine of £20,000 or maximum six months imprisonment or both for each offence or an unlimited fine or maximum five years imprisonment or both on conviction on indictment.

Failure to display a copy of registration or authorisation is also an offence, punishable by fine; failure to retain or produce records as specified by the appropriate Agency is also punishable by fine and/or imprisonment.

It is also an offence to disclose information relating to a process unless the person giving it has agreed, disclosure is in accordance with a direction from the Secretary of State, or is in connection with legal proceedings. Summary conviction is subject to a fine not exceeding the statutory maximum and/or up to three months in prison; conviction on indictment is subject to an unlimited fine and/or a maximum two year prison sentence.

Public Access to Documents and Records (s.39)

The Environment Agency and SEPA are required to keep, and to make publicly available, copies of all applications, authorisations and registrations under the RSA, and other relevant documentation, including details of enforcement or prohibition notices, and records of any convictions. Information may be withheld on the grounds of commercial confidentiality or national security and a note to this effect put on the file. Local authorities who have been sent copies of registrations and authorisations etc are also required to make these publicly available.

The public should be allowed access to documents at all reasonable times and may be charged for copies of any documents.

4.31.4 Environment Act 1995

(a) Fees and Charging (ss.41-42)

Prior to implementation of these sections of the *Environment Act 1995*, charging schemes for premises regulated by the *Radioactive Substances Act 1993* and the *Nuclear Installations Act 1965* were made under section 43 of the RSA. This has been replaced by sections 41-42 of the *Environment Act* which contain powers for the Environment Agency and SEPA to make charging schemes for environmental licences and for their approval by the Secretary of State.

The *Charging Scheme for Radioactive Substances Act Regulation 1998-99* enables the enforcing agencies and MAFF to recover their costs in respect of the following (Scotland and N. Ireland have similar schemes):

- considering applications, issuing authorisations or registration certificates, including related inspection visits;
- ongoing costs related to authorisations and registrations, e.g. inspection, assessment, reviews, monitoring related to discharges (but not general environmental monitoring), enforcement controls and various administrative costs.

Operators are categorised into four bands for charging purposes:

- *Band 1:* British Nuclear Fuels Ltd Sellafield plant;
- *Band 2:* All nuclear sites licensed under the *Nuclear Installations Act 1965* (except Sellafield), together with UK Atomic Energy Authority premises.
- *Band 3:* All other premises authorised under sections 13 or 14 of the RSA to dispose of or accumulate radioactive waste, e.g. hospital or university laboratories).
- *Band 4:* factories and other holders of minor radioactive sources, e.g. small hospitals, registered under section 7 of the RSA or section 10 in respect of mobile equipment.

Premises in Bands 1 and 2 are charged individually by MAFF and the enforcing agency on the basis of the actual regulatory time and costs incurred (estimated at £1,058 per day).

Premises in Bands 3 and 4 (all regulated by the appropriate Agency) pay an initial application fee and then an annual subsistence charge. For 1998/99 the application fee for Band 3 premises is £1,540; for a major variation to an authorisation, the fee is £1,540, for an intermediate variation £765; no charge is made for minor variations.The annual subsistence charge is £1,205; a lower subsistence charge of £95 per registration applies where the registered holding does not exceed 20 MBq or is solely for the use of Technetium 99M and the registered holding does not exceed 10 GBq.

For Band 4 premises, the fee for an application for registration or for a major variation is £555 with no charge being made for a minor variation. The annual subsistence charge in Band 4 (£95 per registration) will only apply to those operators holding larger closed sources, any one of which exceeds 4 TBq, or measuring, testing and investigative mobile equipment; the majority in Band 4, with smaller closed sources, will not pay an annual charge since these sources do not require routine inspection.

Fees and charges are usually revised annually with new rates applying on 1 April each year.

Failure to pay fees and charges will constitute a breach of authorisation or registration and may result in revocation or other enforcement action. A full refund will often be made if an application is withdrawn within eight weeks of receipt.

(b) Powers of Entry (ss.108-110)

Provisions relating to right of entry to premises regulated under the *Radioactive Substances Act 1993* were formerly set out in section 31 of the RSA. This section of the Act was repealed by the *Environment Act 1995* on 1 April 1996.

The Environment Agency or SEPA or other authorised person must be given access to premises to which a registration or authorisation relates in order to carry out their duties under the Act and in emergency (or possible emergency) situations. Photographs and samples may be taken; the occupiers can be required to leave certain parts of the premises undisturbed and to give the Agency (or SEPA or other authorised person) such assistance as is needed. An offence under this section is subject to a fine. See also chapter 1, 1.13.4.

4.31.5 Remediation of Radioactively Contaminated Land

A DETR consultation document published in February 1998 proposes a similar regulatory regime to that to be introduced for non-radioactively contaminated land, with regulations to be made under section 78YC of the *Environmental Protection Act 1990* (see 4.28.3 above).

The regulations would apply only to sites which are radioactively contaminated through an industrial process (i.e. not by, for example, naturally occurring radon). The Environment Agencies would be the lead enforcement agency. Where a site is contaminated by both radioactive and non-radioactive pollutants, the choice of enforcement authority would depend on which contamination posed the more serious risk. Guidance on risk assessment and when a site can be considered suitable for use will be prepared. The regulations would not apply to contaminated sites licensed under the *Nuclear Installations Act 1965*, as these remain licensed until all risk of radioactivity has gone.

4.31.6 Transfrontier Shipment of Radioactive Waste

The Transfrontier Shipment of Radioactive Waste Directive (92/3/Euratom) lays down standards for authorisation, information exchange and monitoring such transfers both between Member States and into and out of the European Union. A principle aim of the Directive is to protect the health of both citizens and workers from any dangers from ionising radiation.

The Directive has been implemented in the UK through the *Transfrontier Shipment of Radioactive Waste Regulations 1993* (SI 3031), which came into effect on 1 January 1994. The Regulations are enforced by the Environment Agency (and its counterparts in Scotland and Northern Ireland). All shipments require prior authorisation and notification of arrival at destination using EU standardised consignment documentation. The Regulations provide for prohibition of any shipments into the UK unless the holder (i.e. originator) guarantees to take back the waste if the shipment cannot be completed or if the authorisation is not complied with. There is a similar requirement on UK holders wishing to export waste. Shipments to African, Caribbean or Pacific states party to the Lomé Convention may not be authorised; shipments are also banned to third countries which it is considered are unable to deal with radioactive waste safely. Other provisions of the Regulations deal with appeals, offences and other procedural matters.

The shipment of radioactive *substances* within the EU is regulated by Euratom Regulation 1493/93 of June 1993; this deals with such things as documentation, information exchange etc.

The European Atomic Energy Community was founded in 1957 by the six founder members of the then European Economic Community – see Appendix 6.

WATER

INTRODUCTION TO CONTROLS ON WATER POLLUTION

5.1 LEGISLATIVE CONTROLS - 1388-1973

Legislation to control water pollution has been developed over a number of centuries. The earliest recorded legislation prohibiting the pollution of water dates from 1388 with an Act forbidding the dumping of animal remains, dung and garbage into rivers, ditches and streams because of the "great annoyance damage and peril of the inhabitants" – the penalty for non-compliance being death. *The Bill of Sewers* in 1531 laid a duty on persons responsible for sewers "to cleanse, and purge the trenches, sewers and ditches, in all places necessary" with a view to protecting public health.

However, it was not until the 19th century when the effects of increasing industrialisation and, as a consequence, the increasing concentration of the population in towns and cities and industrial areas, that more attention was paid to the problems of industrial pollution of water and the need to protect public health through the provision of proper sanitation. A series of Acts in 1847, known as the "Clauses Acts" variously provided a framework for legislative control of both industrial and domestic water pollution. The first *Public Health Act* in 1848 also aimed to improve sanitation by providing for a system of local management of water supply, sewerage etc which would be subject to overall national control; subsequent legislation between 1858 and 1875 amended and extended the provisions of the 1848 Act with the *Public Health Act 1875* remaining the primary piece of legislation in respect of sanitation facilities until the *Public Health Act 1936*.

The first statute specifically aimed at controlling water pollution was the *Salmon Fisheries Act 1861* which made it an offence to discharge sewage into salmon fishing waters; its main objective was however the protection of salmon and fishing interests, rather than protection of public health. This was followed by the *Rivers Pollution Prevention Act 1876* under which it became a criminal offence to pollute water. Part I of the Act dealt with pollution by solid matter, Part II with sewage pollution and Part III with pollution from manufacturing and mining. The Act provided for local authorities to take legal proceedings against offenders after having obtained permission from central government. The court could require the offender to abstain from committing the offence or order him to treat the discharge in a specific manner in future. The Act also included a defence of "best practicable and available means". Thus, if it could be shown that the best practicable and reasonably available means had been used to render harmless sewage or other polluting matter before discharging to water, no offence was committed.

In the years following the 1876 Act as the population became more urbanised, the use of waterborne sanitation became increasingly common. Simultaneously there was a corresponding rise in the demand for water for abstraction purposes both for domestic and industrial use. Consequently it became necessary to create local bodies responsible for the management of the rivers which served the various towns and districts. Initially these authoritative bodies were created piecemeal, starting with the rivers serving the major urban and industrial areas, but by the 1930s they existed for most of the more important rivers. The *River Boards Act 1948* established river boards for the whole of England except the Thames and London area. They acquired functions relating to land drainage, fisheries and river pollution within defined catchment areas. The boards were superseded by 27 river authorities as a result of the *Water Resources Act 1963*.

Other Acts, such as the *Salmon and Freshwater Fisheries Act 1923*, the *Water Act 1945* and the *River Boards Act 1948* laid down various powers to prevent pollution of water but in the main the procedure outlined in the 1876 Act remained in use until 1951 when the *Rivers (Prevention of Pollution) Act* was passed. This repealed virtually the whole of the 1876 Act and established a procedure whereby anyone wishing to make a new discharge of sewage or trade effluent to a stream was required to seek the consent of the river board (subsequently the regional water authority).

The Public Health Acts of 1936 and 1961 and the *Public Health (Drainage of Trade Premises) Act 1937* made it an offence to discharge into public sewers any matter which by its nature or its temperature was likely to damage the sewer or the treatment process; in order to safeguard the condition of the water to which the treated mixed effluents would ultimately discharge, authorities were empowered to impose conditions on discharges of trade effluent. *The Clean Rivers (Estuaries and Tidal Waters) Act 1960* extended the control system to all discharges commenced or altered after that date to most major estuaries.

The Rivers (Prevention of Pollution) Act 1961 strengthened the control system by bringing within it the pre-1951 discharges for which specific consent had not been required by the earlier Act. *The Water Resources Act 1963* extended the control system to cover discharges to underground strata via wells, pipes or boreholes, and gave river authorities specific powers to take emergency measures in the event of pollution of the water.

The river authorities in England and Wales remained in existence until 1973 when the *Water Act* of that year replaced them with ten regional water authorities. Each Authority was made responsible for one or more of the major river systems (e.g. Thames, Severn Trent), including the management of the entire hydrological cycle within its area and the adjacent coastal waters. The responsibility included water conservation and supply, pollution control, sewerage, sewage treatment the development and control of aquifers, land drainage, flood prevention, freshwater and sea fisheries, and the use of the water for amenity and recreation. As a result of privatisation, ownership of the water authorities was transferred to the private sector and a new regulatory framework instituted in 1989 (see 5.15 below).

5.2 CONTROL OF POLLUTION ACT 1974, PART II

Until the enactment of the *Water Act 1989* (see below), Part II of COPA contained much of the legislation covering water pollution control in England and Wales. It re-enacted and extended earlier controls in the *Rivers (Prevention of Pollution) Acts 1951* and 1961 and sections 72 and 76 of the *Water Resources Act 1963*.

This part of COPA is still the main legislation (although substantially added to and amended since 1974) controlling water pollution in Scotland (see 5.10 below and references to COPA throughout 5.15 below). Its main objectives are

a) to extend the control system to all inland waters, estuaries, tidal rivers, the sea within a three-mile limit (and in certain cases beyond) and specified underground waters;

b) to ensure that, subject to a few exceptions, the entry of poisonous, noxious or other polluting matter through casual or spontaneous acts, (e.g. dumping waste in a river) is totally prohibited;

c) to permit discharges of trade or sewage effluent providing that consent is obtained and that any conditions attached to that consent observed;

d) to enable water authorities to carry out operations to prevent the pollution of water or, where pollution has already occurred, to remedy its effects and to recover the costs of so doing from those responsible;

e) to expand and open procedures for the control of effluent discharges to public involvement, including provision for public advertisement, third party representations and, exceptionally, call-in by the Secretary of State and public enquiry.

5.3 WATER ACT 1989

This Act, which applied to England and Wales, paved the way for the sale of the utility functions of the existing water authorities to the private sector. The Act established the National Rivers Authority (NRA) – a statutory body – to take over the responsibilities of water authorities in England and Wales in relation to water pollution, water resource management, flood defence, fisheries, and in some areas navigation; the Act removed the regulatory functions of water authorities, and provided for terms of appointment and financial arrangements for new limited companies to provide water and sewerage services; provision was made for the division of the property, rights and liabilities of the water authorities between the successor water and sewerage companies and the NRA, and for the sale of the new companies; the Act also provided for the appointment of a Director General of Water Services responsible for the provision of water and sewerage services.

The Act also established a new statutory framework for the control of drinking water quality, river quality and other standards, and required the NRA to take specific steps, such as controlling polluting discharges in order to attain objectives set by the Secretary of State for maintaining and improving river quality.

Most of the *Water Act* has now been repealed by, and re-enacted in, the *Water Industry Act 1991* and the *Water Resources Act 1991*. These Acts took effect on 1 December 1991 and apply in England and Wales only. The former Act deals with the functions of the water and sewerage undertakers, the Director General of Water Services and local authority responsibilities for water supplies. The latter Act covered the duties of the National Rivers Authority, which from 1 April 1996 became the responsibility of the Environment Agency – see 5.9 below. The main purpose of these two Acts, together with three others enacted at the same time, is to consolidate all the legislation covering water, which was previously spread over some 20 statutes.

5.4 RIVER QUALITY SURVEYS

Since 1958 surveys have been periodically carried out to establish the overall state of rivers, estuaries and canals in England and Wales. More recently, these surveys were carried out every five years (1980, 1985 and 1990), with similar surveys being carried out in Scotland.

Under a National Water Council scheme rivers and canals were classified as good (1A and 1B), fair (2), poor (3) and bad (4). Waters classified as good were suitable for potable supply abstractions, game and high class fisheries and had high amenity value; waters classified as fair were suitable for the same purposes although their quality was not so high. Poor quality waters were probably unable to support fish life and waters of bad quality were "grossly polluted and likely to cause a nuisance".

River and canal water quality is now surveyed every five years using the General Quality Assessments Scheme; this is not a statutory scheme. In England and Wales the Environment Agency is responsible for the scheme and in Scotland, SEPA. Chemical quality is assessed on the basis of dissolved oxygen, biochemical oxygen demand (BOD) and ammoniacal nitrogen. Biological quality is assessed on the basis of the number and diversity of tiny animals (macro-invertebrates) which live in or on the beds of rivers.

The *Digest of Environmental Statistics* (No. 19, 1997) reports that in 1995 91% of freshwater rivers and canals in England and Wales were of good or fair chemical quality, 8% poor and 1% bad. Ninety-three per cent of rivers and canals were of good or fair biological quality and 7% poor or bad. In Northern Ireland 88% of freshwater rivers were of good or fair chemical quality and 12% of poor quality; all (100%) were assessed as being of good or fair biological quality.

Using a different chemical grading scheme, 99% of freshwater rivers and canals in Scotland were graded as being unpolluted or of fairly good quality in 1995. The biological quality of 98% was of good or moderate quality and 2% poor or bad.

Surface waters in England and Wales are surveyed and classified according to the *Surface Waters (River Ecosystem) (Classification) Regulations 1994* – see below 5.15.2a.

THE EUROPEAN UNION AND WATER POLLUTION CONTROL

The reduction and control of water pollution and contamination has always been an important priority in the European Union's (EU) environmental programme. As with other areas of EU pollution control legislation, Directives emanating from the EU are having a growing influence on UK legislation. European Union controls on water pollution can be classified in three categories: discharge of dangerous substances (including wastes); quality objectives; and by sector or industry (to date only one industry – the titanium dioxide industry – has been covered). In March 1997 the Commission published a proposal for a Framework Directive on Water (see below 5.5); some of the earlier Directives will be repealed ten years after its formal adoption.

The European Commission's Fifth Action Programme, *Towards Sustainability*, (see also Appendix 6) builds on current EU policies aimed at securing sufficient water supplies and maintaining and improving quality. In particular, policies to 2000 will be aimed at:

- prevention of pollution of fresh and marine surface waters and groundwater;

- restoration of natural ground and surface waters to an ecologically sound condition;
- ensuring that water demand and water supply are brought into equilibrium on the basis of more rational use and management of water resources.

Also, in line with the basic principles of the Fifth Action Programme, the Commission will aim to integrate water policy into other areas of Community policy.

Brief details of EU institutions and legislative processes are given in Appendix 6. Water-related Directives are listed in Appendix 6.5.

5.5 FRAMEWORK DIRECTIVE ON WATER POLICY

In March 1997 the Commission published a proposal for a Directive establishing a Framework for Community Action in the field of Water Policy (COM(97) 49, as amended by COM(97) 614 and COM (98) 76). The Commission were originally aiming for the Directive to be formally adopted by 31 December 1997 for implementation by Member States by 31 December 1999. The overall purpose of the draft Directive is to establish a framework for the protection of surface fresh water, estuaries, coastal waters and groundwater in the Community; the objective is to prevent further deterioration and protect and enhance the status of aquatic ecosystems; to promote sustainable water consumption; and to contribute to the provision of a supply of water in the qualities and quantities needed for sustainable use of resources. The Directive defines guiding principles for the qualitative and quantitative protection of groundwater, adopting a more integrated approach to water policy and applying both the precautionary and polluter pays principles. Environmental quality objectives using Best Available Techniques (BAT) would be set so as to ensure consistency with emission limits required by other legislation, e.g. the IPPC Directive and that on pollution caused by dangerous substances to water (76/464/EEC) – see 5.6 below.

Member States will be required to designate river basin management areas and to set up arrangements for cooperation where use of water within a river basin has transboundary effects. Member States would then need to establish a river basin management plan within 10 years of the Directive coming into force which meets the objectives of the Directive and achieves good ground and surface water status six years later; for groundwater this would be on the basis of chemical and quantitative status and for surface water on the basis of ecological and chemical status – these are defined in an annex to the Directive together with monitoring and other requirements. Member

States unable to meet the deadline would be able to apply for a derogation. Other requirements to be carried out for each river basin district by 31 December 2001 (and reviewed and updated every six years) include

- an analysis of the characteristics of each river basin;
- a review of the impact of human activity on the status of surface and groundwater for each river basin district; this should include estimates of point source pollution, diffuse source pollution, and of water abstractions, and an analysis of other anthropogenic influences on the status of water;
- an economic analysis of water use.

The Directive includes requirements for a register of those areas within each river basin district requiring special protection and monitoring programmes for such areas, as well as the establishment of monitoring of surface and ground water status. By 2010, Member States must ensure full cost recovery for all services provided for water use. Exemptions would be allowed to ensure the basic level of water use for households remained affordable, for climatic or geographical reasons or for certain infrastructure projects.

Among the Directives (or drafts) to be repealed ten years after adoption of the framework Directive are:

- 75/440/EEC – surface water
- 78/659/EEC – freshwater fish
- 79/923/EEC – shellfish waters
- 80/68/EEC – protection of groundwater from dangerous substances
- COM(93) 680 – draft on ecological quality

5.6 DANGEROUS SUBSTANCES

Discharges to surface and other waters are covered by the Framework Directive on pollution caused by certain dangerous substances discharged into the aquatic environment (76/464/EEC), and subsequent "daughter" Directives. Discharges to groundwater are dealt with by Directive 80/68/EEC. There are also various Directives (76/769/EEC and amendments) which relate to the marketing and use of certain dangerous substances with the primary objective of reducing risks to human health as well as protecting the aquatic environment; these are implemented through Regulations under the *Environmental Protection Act 1990* – the *Environmental Protection (Control of Injurious Substances) Regulations*. See also chapter 4, 4.10, Directive on the disposal of polychlorinated biphenyls and polychlorinated terphenyls.

5.6.1 Black List Substances

The Framework Directive (76/464/EEC) listed 129 substances considered to be so toxic, persistent or bio-accumulative in the environment that priority should be given to eliminating pollution by them. Included are substances such as organohalogens, organophosphorus, cadmium and mercury and their compounds. Control of these substances is to be achieved largely through the setting of limit values or environmental quality standards in subsequent "Daughter" Directives, thus formally giving the substance List I – or Black List – categorisation. From the original list of 129 substances, Daughter Directives have now been adopted for discharges of mercury, cadmium, hexachlorocyclohexane (HCH) (which includes lindane), DDT, pentachlorophenol (PCP), carbon tetrachloride, the 'drins' group of pesticides (aldrin, endrin, dieldrin and isodrin), hexachlorobenzene (HCB), hexachlorobutadiene and chloroform. In 1990, a further Daughter Directive covering 1,2-dichloroethane, trichloroethylene, perchloroethylene and trichlorobenzene was adopted.

In all cases, the Directives provide for emission limits and quality objectives, and they encourage the use of best available technology in new plant.

The remaining substances from the priority list which have not yet been given formal List I status in a Daughter Directive are in the meantime treated as List II substances for regulatory purposes.

In the UK, the *Environmental Protection (Prescribed Processes and Substances) Regulations 1991* (as amended) list a number of Black List substances whose releases to water are prescribed for Integrated Pollution Control (see chapter 1 and Appendix 1.2). The same substances, together with carbon tetrachloride, are also prescribed substances under the *Trade Effluents (Prescribed Processes and Substances) Regulations 1989* (as amended; see later this chapter, 5.17.3). All processes producing these substances, sometimes referred to as Red List substances in the UK, must use BATNEEC (Best Available Techniques Not Entailing Excessive Costs) to control polluting releases – see chapter 1, 1.6. Discharge consents will also have to ensure that strict environmental quality standards are met. *The Surface Waters (Dangerous Substances) (Classification) Regulations 1989*, as amended, and similar in Scotland (see this chapter, 5.15.2a) implement the environmental quality standards laid down in the 1990 Directive.

A Department of Environment Circular (DOE 7/89) gives guidance on the implementation of the various Directives setting specific environmental quality standards and discharge limits. The Circular emphasises that the aim should be "minimisation of inputs of the most dangerous substances to the aquatic environment".

5.6.2 Grey List Substances

List II substances – the "Grey List" – on the 1976 Framework Directive covers those substances considered less harmful when discharged to water. Included here are metals, such as zinc, nickel, chromium, lead, arsenic and copper; various biocides and substances such as cyanide and ammonia. It also covers those substances awaiting formal List I categorisation. The EU Directive requires Member States to establish pollution reduction programmes and to provide environmental quality objectives and standards for List II substances. Department of Environment Circular 7/89 also includes environmental quality standards for all Grey List substances. Concentrations of Grey List substances in freshwater should not be at such a level that freshwater fish cannot be supported.

The *Surface Waters (Dangerous Substances) (Classification) Regulations 1997* (SI 2560) and 1998 (SI 389) set statutory quality objectives for a total of 21 List II substances (see 5.15.2a below).

5.6.3 Groundwater

In 1979, a Directive (80/68/EEC) on the protection of groundwater against pollution caused by dangerous substances was adopted, for compliance in December 1981. This Directive will be repealed ten years after adoption of the Framework Directive on water (see 5.5 above).

The Directive requires the prevention of the discharge of List I substances to groundwater, and investigation of List II substances prior to direct or indirect discharge. (The Lists I and II referred to in this Directive are not identical to those contained in the dangerous substances Directive; also, unlike the dangerous substances Directive, List I status is definitive and does not need confirmation in a Daughter Directive.)

The Commission has also published (July 1996) a proposal for an "action programme for integrated groundwater protection and management" (COM(96) 315); this emphasises the need for

- licensing systems and other instruments providing an appropriate system of national management of groundwater;
- measures to provide for preventive, comprehensive groundwater protection;
- general provisions for the safety of installations handling substances harmful to water;
- general provisions to promote agricultural practices consistent with groundwater protection.

Member States would be expected to draw up national programmes meeting the above objectives in the light of national, regional and local conditions and needs. Some elements of the Groundwater Action Plan have also been included in the Framework Directive – see above, 5.5.

In a consultation paper published in October 1990, the Government outlined its proposals for a national classification scheme for dangerous substances in groundwater. It suggests using numerical threshold values to assess whether substances are List I or List II. Substances which are carcinogenic, mutagenic and teratogenic (unless the risk is solely from inhalation) would automatically remain on List I. Toxicity, persistence and bioaccumulation will also be used as criteria for assessing whether a substance should be on List I or List II.

Brief details of the National Rivers Authority *Policy and Practice for the Protection of Groundwater* (published 1992) are given below at 5.15.2b (*Water Resources Act 1991*, protection of groundwater).

The Waste Management Licensing Regulations 1994 (see chapter 4, 4.19.3) require waste regulation authorities to review all landfill licences, and to vary or revoke conditions as appropriate to prevent pollution of groundwater by List I and List II substances. 1998 Groundwater Regulations require disposal or tipping of controlled substances to be authorised and enable the Environment Agencies to issue notices prohibiting activities to prevent the entry of List I substances to groundwater or its pollution by List II substances – see 5.15.2b. In Northern Ireland, the Directive is implemented in part by the *Pollution of Groundwater by Dangerous Substances Regulations (Northern Ireland) 1994*.

5.7 QUALITY OBJECTIVES FOR WATER USED FOR PARTICULAR PURPOSES

A number of Directives define the acceptable quality of water for particular purposes and make provision for both achieving and monitoring the quality of the water. Directives have been adopted concerning the quality of surface water intended for the abstraction of drinking water, for bathing water, freshwater fish, shellfish and for water intended for human consumption.

The European Commission has now published a proposal for a Framework Directive (see above, 5.5) which would cover both the integrated management of surface and groundwater supplies, as well as water quality; it will eventually replace both the surface and groundwater Directives as well as the proposed Directive on Ecological Quality (and thus the Freshwater Fish and Shellfish Waters Directives).

5.7.1 Ecological Quality

The European Commission has issued a proposal for a Directive on the Ecological Quality of Surface Waters (COM(93) 680); it is intended that it should complement other water Directives including the urban waste water Directive and that on nitrate pollution (see below) as well as the Directive on Integrated Pollution Prevention and Control (see chapter 1, 1.12.1); the Directive aims to ensure a harmonised approach to controlling pollution of surface waters and thus achieve high ecological quality. Ecological quality is defined as "the structure and function of the biological community, geographical and climatic factors, physical and chemical parameters and impacts resulting from human activity". Ecological quality would be achieved through the setting of targets and through surveillance and monitoring of inland and territorial surface waters. When adopted this Directive will replace those on freshwater fish and shellfish. This Directive will itself be repealed ten years after adoption of the Framework Directive on Water (see above 5.5).

5.7.2 Surface Water

A Directive (75/440/EEC) adopted in 1975 classified the quality of surface waters intended for the abstraction of drinking water, and specified the treatment and timetable necessary to bring such waters up to drinking water quality. A1 waters required simple filtration and disinfection; A2 required normal physical and chemical treatment, and disinfection; and A3 waters intensive physical and chemical treatment and disinfection. This Directive will be repealed ten years after adoption of the Framework Directive on water (see above 5.5).

This Directive was initially partly implemented in England and Wales through the *Surface Waters (Classification) Regulations 1989* (and similar 1990 Regulations in Scotland and Northern Ireland). The 1989 Regulations have been revoked and the Directive implemented through new Regulations, *The Surface Water (Abstraction for Drinking Water) (Classification) Regulations 1996* (see below, 5.15.2a).

5.7.3 Bathing Water

This Directive (76/160/EEC) was adopted in December 1975, with Member States being given until December 1985 to bring designated bathing waters up to the required quality. Bathing waters are defined as fresh or sea water (other than swimming pools) where bathing is "traditionally practised by a large number of bathers". An annex to the Directive sets out sampling frequencies, guideline and mandatory values, as well as analysis and inspection methods for a number of microbiological and physio-chemical parameters (see Appendix 5.1a).

Proposals for a new Directive (COM(94) 36), to replace the 1976 Directive, were published by the Commission in 1994, and a revised proposal (COM(97) 585 in November which takes account of some of the amendments adopted by the European Parliament. In aiming to clarify the present Directive, which has been amended a number of times, the new Directive is also particularly concerned with ensuring protection of bathers' health.

The draft Directive requires monitoring and measurement for contamination and pollution as indicated by 12 instead of the current 19) parameters; these are: escherichia coli, faecal streptococci, enteroviruses, bacteriophages, pH, colour, mineral oils, surface active substances reacting with methylene blue, phenols, transparency, dissolved oxygen and tarry residues and floating materials. All except enteroviruses would have to be sampled at a minimum frequency of every fortnight during the bathing season, with sampling for enteroviruses carried out monthly.

In England and Wales, the *Bathing Waters (Classification) Regulations 1991* (and comparable Regulations in Scotland) implement the current Directive – see this chapter, 5.15.2a. In Northern Ireland the Directive is implemented through the *Quality of Bathing Waters Regulations (Northern Ireland) 1993.* In 1998, 89% of UK bathing waters met EU mandatory coliform bacteria standards.

5.7.4 Freshwater Fish and Shellfish Waters

Directives adopted in 1978 and 1979 lay down quality requirements for freshwater fish (78/659/EEC) and shellfish waters (79/923/EEC), respectively. These Directives are to be replaced by the Framework Directive on Water – see above 5.5.

The freshwater fish Directive requires Member States to designate fresh waters needing protection or improvement in order to support fish; an annex to the Directive lists a number of physical and chemical parameters – some mandatory and some guidelines. Implementation of the Directive in England, Scotland and Wales has been through the *Control of Pollution Act 1974* and in Northern Ireland by 1993 Statutory Order. New regulations are likely to be made under the *Water Resources Act 1991* following the finalisation of statutory water quality objectives under section 82-83 of that Act. In 1995, about 97% of the total length of designated rivers in the UK complied with standards in the freshwater fish Directive.

The shellfish waters Directive also requires Member States to designate shellfish waters and lays down water quality objectives aimed at ensuring that such waters "contribute to the high quality of shellfish products directly edible by man". The UK has so far designated 29 shellfish waters, but in July 1998 the DETR issued proposals for designating a further 60 waters in England and Wales. The *Surface Waters (Shellfish) (Classification) Regulations 1997* prescribe a system for classifying the quality of controlled waters in order to support shellfish – see 5.15.2a below.

5.7.5 Water Intended for Human Consumption

The 1980 Directive (80/778) relates to the quality of water intended for human consumption – the drinking water Directive. Quality standards have been set for some 60 substances (including some pesticides), as well as requirements for sampling frequency, measuring methods etc. Three types of standard – Guide Levels (GL); Maximum Admissible Concentrations (MAC); and Minimum Required Concentrations (MRC) – are laid down in respect of certain "parameters", which include:

- organoleptic parameters, e.g. colour, taste;
- physico-chemical parameters, e.g. conductivity, chlorides;
- substances undesirable in excessive amounts, e.g. nitrates, phenols;
- toxic substances, e.g. arsenic, mercury, lead;
- microbiological parameters, e.g. coliforms, streptococci;
- minimum required concentration (MRC) for softened water, e.g. hydrogen ion concentration, alkalinity.

The actual values set in the Directive for the substances within each parameter are listed in Appendix 5.2a.

In early 1995, the Commission published its proposals for a new Directive concerning the quality of water intended for human consumption (COM(94) 612), with an amended proposal being published in June 1997 (COM(97) 228). Environment Ministers reached a common position on this proposal in October 1997, and it was approved by the European Parliament in May 1998. National legislation implementing the new Directive would have to be in place within two years of the Directive entering into force; the current Directive would be repealed five years after the new Directive enters into force. The new proposal covers all water for domestic use (whether from tap, bottle or container) and water used by the food industry where this affects the final product and, thus consumers' health; it does not apply to water for agricultural purposes, natural mineral water or medicinal waters. An important objective of the Directive is to contribute towards achieving sustainable development by ensuring a sufficient supply of water of adequate quality, with Member States having a duty to ensure that drinking water is wholesome and clean.

The draft Directive reduces the number of parameters from 67 to 48 (including 13 new parameters), retaining only those essential for the protection of water quality and health; these are divided into three groups: microbiological, chemical and indicator parameters and would be reviewed at least every five years. Parametric values have been based largely on WHO guidelines adopted in 1992. The maximum permitted concentration of lead is to be reduced from 50 μg/l to 25 μg/l over five years and to 10 μg/l within 15 years; the lengthy period for compliance takes account of the costs involved in replacing lead pipes and fittings. (Plans for replacing lead pipes in homes must, however, be submitted to the Commission within five years.) Most other parameters would have to be complied with within five years of the Directive entering into force. Other limit values include 0.5 μg/l for nitrate concentrations and a maximum concentration of 0.5 μg/l of total pesticides and 0.1 μg/l for individual pesticides; a limit of 0.1 μg/l is set for PAHs (0.01 μg/l for benzo(a)pyrene). Member States would be free to set additional parameters in the light of local environmental conditions; enforcement authorities would be obliged to inform consumers when water quality fell below standard, of any danger to health, and advice on what to do; consumers would also have to be advised when action had been taken and water quality restored. As now, monitoring would be required to check on water quality and assess that measures taken to ensure quality are operating correctly; monitoring would also be required to verify the efficiency of disinfection treatment of water intended for human consumption and to ensure no contamination from disinfection by-products.

In England and Wales the current Directive is implemented through the *Water Supply (Water Quality) Regulations 1989* (Scotland, 1990), as amended and the *Private Water Supplies Regulations 1991* (Scotland, 1992), and in Northern Ireland by 1994 Regulations – see 5.17.1c below.

5.7.6 Urban Waste Water Treatment

A Directive (91/271/EEC) adopted in 1991 lays down minimum requirements for the treatment of municipal waste water and for the disposal of sludge. The Directive also aims to control the discharge of industrial waste waters which are of a similar nature to municipal waste water but which do not enter municipal waste water treatment plants before discharge. The release of treated or untreated sludge from treatment plants in fresh or seawater will be banned from 31 December 1998.

Receiving waters are classified according to "sensitivity". In most cases secondary biological treatment prior to discharge will be required as a minimum, with tertiary treatment for waters which are, or are likely to become, eutrophic. Primary treatment – such as the settlement of suspended solids – may be considered sufficient for discharges from treatment processes serving less than 150,000 inhabitants into coastal waters less sensitive to pollution. Limit values for various industrial sector discharges to rivers, estuaries and coastal waters should be set in regulations.

Member States should have drawn up plans for implementation of the Directive by the end of 1993 with the aim of achieving the various deadlines for treatment standards. However, in England, Scotland and Wales designation of "sensitive" and "less sensitive" areas was not completed until 1994.

This Directive has been implemented in England and Wales through *The Urban Waste Water Treatment (England and Wales) Regulations 1994* and by similar Regulations in Scotland and Northern Ireland – see below 5.18. Discharges to controlled waters are regulated under IPC (chapter 1, 1.13) and consents issued under regulations made under the *Water Resources Act 1991* (see this chapter 5.15.3a).

5.7.7 Nitrate Pollution

Directive 91/676/EEC places restrictions on the use of natural and chemical fertilisers to reduce the risk of nitrate pollution of river, coastal and sea waters and ensure a level of no more than 50 mg/l of nitrates in fresh water sources used for abstraction purposes. Catchment areas in which nitrate levels exceed the requirements of the Directive at any time in the year will be designated vulnerable zones. In such areas, an annual limit of 210 kg/ha of organic manure will be mandatory, reducing to 170 kg/ha four years later. Designation of such zones should have been completed by the end of 1993; action programmes to control nitrate leaching should have been in place by December 1995 to begin no later than December 1998 to ensure annual limits on nitrogen fertilisers are complied with by the implementation date of December 1999; programmes must be reviewed every four years.

The Directive also requires the drawing up of codes of good agricultural practice which must, as a minimum, include

- details of periods when use of fertilisers would be inappropriate;
- guidelines on use of fertilisers on sloping, flooded, frozen or snow covered ground;
- guidelines on use of fertilisers near water courses;
- measures to prevent run-off and seepage into rivers of manure-containing liquids and other effluents;
- conditions for general use of fertilisers.

Finally the Directive requires monitoring programmes to be established and reports on implementation progress to be sent to the Commission every four years.

The Protection of Water Against Agricultural Nitrate Pollution (England and Wales) Regulations 1996 (SI 888), which came into force on 17 April 1996, designate 68 nitrate vulnerable zones (NVZs). There is also one NVZ in Scotland. A review of these zones had to be carried out before 19 December 1997, with further reviews every four years to revise or add to the list as necessary.

The Environment Agency is required to monitor the concentrations of nitrates in freshwaters at designated sampling stations and to review the eutrophic state of fresh surface waters, estuarial and coastal waters before 19 December 1997 and thereafter on a monthly basis over a period of a year every four years. Where previous monitoring has shown nitrate concentrations to be consistently below 25 mg/l, the dates for monitoring by the Environment Agency are 19 December 2001 and thereafter every eight years. The Regulations designate relevant sections of the 1991 *Code of Good Agricultural Practice for the Protection of Water* (see below 5.15.5d) as the code of good practice required by the Directive.

The Regulations also require the establishment of action programmes to control nitrate leaching; these must be in place by 19 December 1998 to ensure limits are met by 19 December 1999; a draft for consultation was published for England and Wales at the end of 1997, with similar expected for Scotland. Action programmes are likely to include measures such as

- no inorganic fertilisers to be applied between 1 September and 1 February;
- no more than 250 kg per hectare of manure to be applied to grass; for other fields no more than 210 kg per hectare, reducing to 170 kg four years later;
- sufficient storage capacity for when manure and slurry spreading is restricted;
- records to be kept of fertiliser and manure use.

These measures, to be enforced by the Environment Agency, are mandatory unlike participation in the scheme establishing nitrate sensitive areas (NSAs) – see below 5.15.5c, *Water Resources Act 1991*, nitrate sensitive areas.

In Scotland the *Code of Good Practice on the Prevention of Environmental Pollution from Agricultural Activity*, implemented in 1992, also meets the requirements of the Directive. Those parts of the Code which relate to water pollution have statutory backing (see below 5.15.5d).

5.8 MARINE ENVIRONMENT

The European Union participates in various international Conventions relating to the protection of the marine environment and the prevention of oil spills; another part of its work is the harmonisation of national programmes regarding the elimination of pollution. With the enlargement of the EU, bringing in countries bordering the Mediterranean, efforts are also being directed towards the protection of that region, where the environment is sensitive and already severely overloaded locally (see also this chapter, 5.20).

IMPLEMENTATION AND ENFORCEMENT AUTHORITIES

Overall responsibility for the maintenance and management of water resources in England and Wales rests with the Secretary of State for the Environment, Transport and the Regions: this includes responsibility for national policy on all matters of conservation and supply, sewerage and sewage disposal; the control of pollution in both inland and coastal waters; the use of inland waters for recreation and navigation; the control of marine pollution by oil. The Minister of Agriculture, Fisheries and Food is responsible for land drainage, the protection of freshwater and marine fisheries, the dumping of waste at sea, and the safe use of agricultural pesticides.

The effects of individual acts of pollution are usually most noticeable within the locality where they take place and it was considered that they could best be controlled by authorities with a detailed knowledge of the area; thus the first statute to control water pollution – *the Rivers Pollution Prevention Act 1876* – laid down the statutory framework for controlling water pollution but gave the responsibility for enforcement to local government bodies, such as town and district councils.

The River Boards Act 1948 had established river boards for the whole of England (except the Thames and London area); these were superseded by river authorities following the *Water Resources Act 1963*, which were in turn replaced by ten regional water authorities (nine in England and one in Wales) by the *Water Act 1973*.

Following privatisation of the water industry, the ten water authorities were transferred to the private sector (water undertakers), together with their responsibilities for water supply and sewerage, and sewage disposal. Responsibility for pollution control of rivers and watercourses passed to the National Rivers Authority following its establishment on 1 September 1989. In Scotland the River Purification Authorities were given similar responsibilities.

On 1 April 1996 the responsibilities and functions of the NRA and RPAs were transferred to the Environment Agency and the Scottish Environment Protection Agency, respectively.

5.9 ENGLAND AND WALES

5.9.1 Environment Agency

The Environment Agency for England and Wales was established by the *Environment Act 1995* which received the Royal Assent on 19 July 1995. On 1 April 1996 the Agency assumed all the responsibilities and functions of the National Rivers Authority which was abolished. The Agency also has responsibility for Integrated Pollution Control and waste regulation (see chapters 1 and 4 respectively).

The Environment Agency is charged with preventing deterioration of water quality and seeking its improvement; it has a duty to promote, as it considers desirable, the conservation and enhancement of the water environment (inland and coastal waters). As well as pollution control, the Agency's responsibilities include water resource management, planning and conservation, flood defence, forecasting and warning, abstraction licences, fisheries and in some areas navigation. It also has certain duties in relation to promoting conservation; amenity and recreational facilities. The Agency and SEPA should consult and collaborate on matters of common interest.

5.9.2 Drinking Water Inspectorate

This Inspectorate was established within the Department of Environment (now Department of the Environment, Transport and the Regions – DETR) in January 1990; its principal task is to ensure that water undertakers in England and Wales are fulfilling their statutory requirements for the supply of wholesome drinking water.

The Inspectorate carries out annual technical audits of each water company; this includes an assessment (based on information supplied by the company) of the quality of water in each supply zone, arrangements for sampling and analysis, and progress made on achieving compliance with UK and EU requirements.

The Inspectorate monitors compliance with the standards set in the *Water Supply (Water Quality) Regulations 1989* (amended 1991) – see 5.17.1c below. The Inspectorate investigates incidents affecting water quality and water companies are required to notify the Inspectorate of any significant pollution incidents.

The DWI's annual report (*Drinking Water, 1997*) shows that 99.75% (1996: 99.70%) of the three million drinking water tests carried out in 1997 met national and EU standards.

5.10 SCOTLAND

5.10.1 Scottish Environment Protection Agency

SEPA was also established by the *Environment Act 1995* and assumed the responsibilities and functions of the river purification authorities on 1 April 1996. Its functions mirror those of the Environment Agency – see 5.9.1 above. SEPA also has responsibility for Integrated Pollution Control, Local Air Pollution Control (Part I, EPA 1990) and waste regulation (see chapters 1, 2 and 4 respectively).

The Water Act 1989 introduced new provisions into the *Water (Scotland) Act 1980* so as to make provision in Scotland in relation to the quality of water broadly equivalent to the quality of water provisions for England and Wales. The control of water pollution in Scotland is regulated by Part II of the *Control of Pollution Act 1974*, as amended.

Regulations implementing various EU Directives on water quality, and similar to those for England and Wales, have been made in Scotland and are referred to throughout this chapter.

5.10.2 Drinking Water

Monitoring and policy on drinking water in Scotland is the responsibility of the Scottish Office. Unitary authorities are responsible for the supply of "wholesome" water for domestic and other purposes (*Water (Scotland) Act 1980*).

In 1996, 98.6% (1994: 98.7%) drinking water tests in Scotland met the required standards (*Drinking Water Quality in Scotland 1996*, The Stationery Office).

5.11 NORTHERN IRELAND

The control of water pollution and water quality, together with drinking water are the responsibility of the Department of the Environment (NI); water supply and sewerage services are managed by the DOE's Water Service.

The main legislation for controlling water pollution is the *Water Act (Northern Ireland) 1972*. A consent must be obtained from DOE (NI) for a discharge of any trade or sewage effluent or any other poisonous or noxious matter. This can include conditions to ensure that the receiving waterway can sustain the discharge and that the quality of the aquatic environment will not be damaged or EU standards breached. The maximum fine on conviction in the Magistrates' Court for pollution of water is £20,000.

Proposals published by the DOE in 1994 would amend the *Water Act (Northern Ireland) 1972*, to provide for more effective controls safeguarding water quality and supply. The draft *Water (Northern Ireland) Order 1998* has now been published for consultation and provides for:

- the existence of a potentially hazardous development (as distinct from discharge) (e.g. marine fish cages which could harm fauna) to be taken into account in considering an application for a discharge consent;
- powers for the Environment Service to request the Water Appeals Commission to hold a public inquiry where objections to a proposed discharge have been received;
- an application for a discharge consent to be legal only if it had been publicly advertised; details of public inquiries and appeals would also have to be advertised;
- the determination period for an application for a consent to be extended to four months, with a right of appeal in default of a decision;
- public registers to be extended to include applications, sampling and analysis data, as well as consents and their conditions;
- length of consents to be increased from three to four years;
- the UK Government to prohibit by notice an existing discharge in order to ensure compliance with EU or other international obligations;
- prosecution for non-compliance with a notice served to prevent pollution, even if no pollution has occurred;
- cost recovery charging to be introduced.

5.12 LOCAL AUTHORITIES

Under sections 77 and 78 of the *Water Industry Act 1991*, local authorities have a statutory duty to take all such steps as they consider appropriate for keeping themselves informed about the wholesomeness and sufficiency of both public and private supplies of water in their area.

If the public supply is likely to become unwholesome or insufficient, the local authority must advise the water undertaker who must take appropriate remedial action (s.79). In the case of private supplies, the *Water Industry Act* gives local authorities the power to serve notice requiring improvements (s.80). *The Private Water Supplies*

Regulations 1991 set out local authorities' duties with regard to safeguarding water quality (see 5.17.1c below).

Local authorities are also responsible for the quality of bottled mineral waters for drinking. Sources have to be approved and standards as set out in the *Natural Mineral Waters Regulations 1985* complied with.

As from April 1992, local authorities also took over responsibility from MAFF for enforcing certain provisions of the *Control of Pesticides Regulations 1986*, as amended (see 5.28.2 below).

In Scotland water supplies, sewage disposal and sewerage are the responsibility of regional/unitary authorities, operating under the *Sewerage (Scotland) Act 1968*.

REGULATORY CONTROLS

Privatisation of the water industry in England and Wales in 1989 resulted in major changes to the legislation dealing with the control of water pollution. *The Water Act 1989*, which received the Royal Assent on 6 July 1989, largely replaced the water section (Part II) of the *Control of Pollution Act 1974* in England and Wales. On 30 November 1991 the *Water Act 1989*, together with a number of other statutes controlling water pollution in England and Wales, was repealed and their provisions consolidated in the following:

* *Water Resources Act 1991*
* *Water Industry Act 1991*
* *Land Drainage Act 1991*
* *Statutory Water Companies Act 1991*

A fifth Act – *the Water Consolidation (Consequential Provisions) Act 1991* – provides for consequential amendments and repeals and other transitional matters. These Acts took effect on 1 December 1991.

In Scotland, legislation dealing with water is contained in the *Water (Scotland) Act 1980* and Part II of the *Control of Pollution Act 1974*; both have been amended by sections 168 and 169 of the *Water Act 1989* to make provision, respectively, for water quality and the control of water pollution in Scotland similar to those in England and Wales. COPA has also been amended by the *Environment Act 1995* (Sch. 16 & Sch. 22, para 29). Reference is made to the appropriate provisions of COPA etc in the text below covering the *Water Resources Act 1991* and the *Water Industry Act 1991*.

In Northern Ireland the relevant legislation is the *Water Act (Northern Ireland) 1972* (currently under review). This is administered by the DOE (NI).

5.13 PUBLIC HEALTH ACT 1936

Section 259 makes the following matters statutory nuisances in England and Wales for the purposes of water pollution:

a) any pond, pool ditch, gutter or watercourse which is so foul or in such a state as to be prejudicial to health or a nuisance;

b) any part of a watercourse, not being a part ordinarily navigated by vessels employed in the carriage of goods by water, which is so choked or silted up as to obstruct or impede the proper flow of water and thereby to cause a nuisance, or give rise to conditions prejudicial to health.

Complaints about statutory nuisances are dealt with by local authorities who may take action through the Magistrates' Court for abatement of a nuisance (see also chapter 1, 1.15.1).

Section 260 enables parish and community councils to take action to deal with filthy or stagnant water which may be prejudicial to health.

5.14 ENVIRONMENTAL PROTECTION ACT 1990

Certain processes discharging to water are subject to Integrated Pollution Control as a result of their potential to pollute the air and/or land. For details of the processes and substances concerned and of the regulatory procedure, see chapter 1 and Appendix 1.1 and 1.2.

5.15 WATER RESOURCES ACT 1991

This Act which applies in England and Wales came into effect on 1 December 1991 and replaced corresponding sections of the *Water Act 1989*. It has subsequently been amended by the *Environment Act 1995*. The WRA deals with some of the responsibilities of the Environment Agency. (Sections 1-14 covering the functions of the NRA were repealed on 1 April 1996 following the abolition of the NRA and the establishment of the Environment Agency; its functions are set out in the *Environment Act 1995* – see chapter 1, 1.7.1.)

In Scotland water pollution is controlled under Part II of the *Control of Pollution Act 1974*, as amended by the *Environment Act 1995*, and is the responsibility of the Scottish Environment Protection Agency (SEPA) – see also chapter 1, 1.7.2.

5.15.1 Control of Pollution of Water Resources (Part III)

This part of the WRA is concerned with maintaining and enhancing the quality of "controlled waters" (i.e. relevant territorial, coastal, inland freshwaters (including lakes and ponds) and groundwaters.

The Controlled Waters (Lakes and Ponds) Order 1989 (SI 1149) which came into force on 1 September 1989 brings within the definition of "controlled waters" reservoirs not discharging into a watercourse, other than those containing water which has been treated prior to entering the supply.

5.15.2 Quality Objectives (ss.82-84)

(a) Statutory Water Quality Objectives (ss.82-83)

Section 82 of the *Water Resources Act* provides for the establishment, via regulations, of systems of classifying water quality according to various criteria; section 83 provides for the setting of statutory water quality objectives (SWQOs) for individual stretches of water, on the basis of one or more of the classifications, together with a date by which the classification should be achieved. SWQOs will eventually be set for some 40,000 km of rivers and canals, as well as estuaries, coastal waters, lakes and groundwaters.

For Scotland, similar powers are contained in section 30B, C, D and E of COPA (see Sch. 23, para 4 of *Water Act 1989* as amended by the *Environment Act 1995*, Sch. 22, para 29(1)-(5)).

The Surface Waters (Dangerous Substances) (Classification) Regulations 1989 (SI 2286), amended 1992

These Regulations, applicable in England and Wales, came into effect on 1 January 1990. They implement various EU Daughter Directives relating to inputs to inland and coastal and territorial waters of specific Black List (List I) substances listed in Directive 76/464 (see 5.6 above). The substances concerned and the standards set are at Appendix 5.3. These Regulations have been amended by 1992 Regulations made under section 83 of the *Water Resources Act 1991*. These implement statutory environmental quality standards for four substances covered by the 1990 EU Daughter Directive – ethylene dichloride, trichloroethylene, perchloroethylene and trichlorobenzene (see this chapter, 5.6.1). Similar 1990 Regulations (SI 126) apply in Scotland.

The Surface Waters (Dangerous Substances) (Classification) Regulations 1997 (SI 2560) and 1998 (SI 389)

These Regulations for England and Wales set water quality objectives for a total of 20 List II substances in EU Directive 76/464/EEC (see 5.6 above). Schedules to the Regulations specify the limits of dangerous substances which must not be exceeded to meet criteria for classification as inland freshwaters and for coastal waters and relevant territorial waters – see Appendix 5.3; the aim is to reduce pollution by the dangerous substances listed in the Schedules. The 1997 Regulations came into force on 26 November 1997 and the 1998 Regulations on 25 March 1998.

The Environment Agency is responsible for ensuring compliance with the Regulations, including sampling and analysis and monitoring the effect on waters of discharges containing the dangerous substances and of determining whether the requirements of each classification are being met.

In Scotland, the *Surface Waters (Dangerous Substances) (Classification) (Scotland) Regulations 1998* (SI 250), which came into force on 1 April 1998 and further 1998 regulations (SI 1344), which came into force on 1 July 1998, mirror the 1997 and 1998 E&W Regulations. Similar Regulations are to be made for Northern Ireland.

The Bathing Waters (Classification) Regulations 1991 (SI 1597)

These Regulations implementing EU Directive 76/160/EEC came into force in August 1991 in England and Wales (see above, 5.7.3). There are similar 1991 Regulations in Scotland (SI 1609) and 1993 Regulations in Northern Ireland (SR 205). They set out a system for classifying the quality of UK territorial, coastal and inland waters which are designated bathing waters (currently 505 in the UK) – classified as BW1 waters – in compliance with the Directive. Schedule 1 to the Regulations specifies criteria for BW1 classifications and Schedule 2 sampling requirements. Schedule 3 (see Appendix 5.1b) sets out quality and additional sampling requirements.

The criteria for BW1 classification include:

a) at least 95% of samples taken and tested in accordance with sampling requirements must conform to the parametric values in Schedule 3;

b) no sample which fails when tested for compliance with the phenols parameter by the absorption method or with the transparency parameter should have a value which deviates by more than 50% from that in Schedule 3;

c) consecutive samples taken at suitable intervals should not deviate from the parametric values specified in Schedule 3.

Sampling should be carried out at the same place and as specified in Schedule 3 from 1 May - 30 September with a minimum of 20 samples taken at each site; additional samples should be taken if it is suspected that the water quality is deteriorating. Sampling results can be disregarded if they do not meet the requirements due to abnormal weather conditions.

Water companies are also required to comply with the Environment Agency's *Policy for Consents for Sewage Effluent Discharges Affecting Bathing Waters* (1997); under this policy treatment plants must use high standards of conventional treatment and discharge from an outfall well away from bathing waters; if an outfall near a bathing water is used, then very high standards of treatment followed by ultraviolet light disinfection is required. The Agency also requires water companies to meet the requirements of the EU's urban waste water Directive (and of the UK regulations) to ensure identified bathing waters meet the standards set in the bathing water Directive – see 5.7.3, 5.7.6 and 5.18.

The Surface Waters (River Ecosystem) (Classification) Regulations 1994 (SI 1057)

These Regulations, covering England and Wales, came into force on 10 May 1994. They prescribe a system for classifying inland rivers and watercourses, replacing a previous classification devised by the National Water Council (see this chapter, 5.4). The classifications are:

RE1 Water of very good quality suitable for all fish species
RE2 Water of good quality suitable for all fish species
RE3 Water of fair quality suitable for high class coarse fish populations
RE4 Water of fair quality suitable for coarse fish populations
RE5 Water of poor quality which is likely to limit coarse fish populations.

Eight parameters are used for assessing quality: dissolved oxygen; BOD; total ammonia; un-ionised ammonia; pH; hardness; dissolved copper; and total zinc – see Appendix 5.4. Frequency, location, methods of sampling and other procedures for compliance were set out in the NRA's *Water Quality Objectives: Procedures used by the National Rivers Authority for the purpose of the Surface Waters (River Ecosystem) (Classification) Regulations 1994* (30 March 1994).

The Environment Agency is responsible for proposing water quality objectives for specific stretches of water to the Department of the Environment, Transport and the Regions (DETR). Following a minimum public consultation period of three months, the Secretary of State will by notice confirm the SWQOs and target dates for achievement. SWQOs remain binding for five years unless the Agency requests a review. SWQOs will also be taken into account by the Agency in taking decisions on discharge consents.

Eight river catchments in England and Wales are to take part in a pilot scheme; this will commence following agreement on the SWQOs to be achieved. Following consultation in 1996 in the eight pilot areas, the Environment Agency recommended to the Secretary of State SWQOs to be met by a target date of 2006.

In addition river and canal quality is surveyed every five years using the "General Quality Assessments Scheme" – see 5.4 above.

The Surface Waters (Abstraction for Drinking Water) (Classification) Regulations 1996 (SI 3001)

These Regulations, made under sections 82 and 102 of the WRA, came into force on 6 January 1997. They implement EU Directive 75/440/EEC on the quality of surface water intended for the abstraction of drinking water, which set mandatory and guideline quality requirements (see above, 5.7.2). Earlier 1989 Regulations (SI 1148), which dealt with the mandatory requirements of the Directive have been revoked. Similar legislation is being drafted for Scotland and Northern Ireland. The earlier Regulations (and the Northern Ireland Order) will then be repealed.

The Regulations prescribe the system of classifying the quality of inland freshwaters according to their suitability for abstraction by water undertakers for supply (after treatment) as drinking water (see Appendix 5.5). Sampling must be carried out at points chosen by the Environment Agency with the frequency for each parameter set in Schedule 3 to the Regulations; Schedule 2 details the measurement method to be used for each parameter. Analysis of the samples must be carried out to ascertain compliance with the parameters in Schedule 1 (see Appendix 5.5) – i.e. 95% of the samples should comply with the limit, none exceed it by more than 50%, and where any of the samples exceed the limit, there should be no danger to public health. The Environment Agency can decide to reduce sampling frequency where there is no pollution of waters, no risk of deterioration in quality or it is of a better quality than the parameter required for waters classified as DW1 (see Appendix 5.5).

The Surface Waters (Fishlife) (Classification) Regulations 1997 (SI 1331)

These Regulations for England and Wales came into force in June 1997, with similar Regulations (SI 2471) for Scotland coming into force on 18 November 1997, and for Northern Ireland (SR 448). They implement the EU freshwater fish Directive (see above 5.7.4), prescribing a system for classifying the quality of inland waters which need protection or improvement to support fishlife. A Schedule to the Regulations lists 13 parameters and the requirements to be satisfied for salmonid and for cyprinid waters, as well as methods of analysis or inspection and minimum sampling and measurement frequency.

The Surface Waters (Shellfish) (Classification) Regulations 1997 (SI 1332)

These Regulations came into force on 12 June 1997 and apply in England and Wales. Similar Regulations (SI 2470) for Scotland came into force on 18 November 1997, and for Northern Ireland (SR 449). They implement the 1979 Shellfish Waters Directive (see above 5.7.4) by prescribing a system for classifying the quality of controlled waters which are coastal or brackish waters and which need protection or improvement in order to support shellfish life and growth. A Schedule to the Regulations lists 11 parameters and the mandatory values assigned to them in the Directive; it lists reference methods of measurement, and the minimum frequency required for sampling and analysis, also laid down in the Directive.

In July 1998, the DETR issued proposals for the designation of an additional 60 waters in England and Wales in accordance with the 1979 Directive.

(b) Protection of Groundwater (s.84)

Section 84 of the *Water Resources Act* gives the Agency a duty to protect the quality of groundwater and conserve its use for water resources.

The NRA's *Policy and Practice for the Protection of Groundwater* (published in 1992) outlined policy for protecting groundwater supplies from various sources of pollution and defines source protection zones as zone I (inner source protection); zone II (outer source protection) and zone III (source catchment). Also detailed are those activities which it is considered would pose a threat to groundwater within each source protection zone and should therefore be stopped or restricted. Maps are being compiled showing groundwater areas and their vulnerability to pollution.

The NRA's policy paper is not a statutory document and thus its status is to provide advice for industry, developers, planners and regulatory authorities on the effect of a particular activity on a groundwater source. While the Environment Agency has no direct control over how an area is used, it can try to influence, for example planning decisions, through its position as a statutory consultee, or for conditions to protect groundwater quality to be included in an authorisation.

Scotland's strategy for protection of groundwater was published in 1995 and uses the same approach as the NRA in identifying protection zones.

The *Groundwater Regulations 1998*, cover England, Scotland and Wales; they are designed to protect groundwater from pollution from the industrial and farming sectors, thus implementing in full the 1980 groundwater Directive (see above 5.6.3). Direct discharges of List I substances are prohibited and indirect discharges (from tipping or disposal) only authorised with appropriate conditions to prevent discharges into groundwater and if results of prior investigation show this to be feasible. List II discharges will only be authorised, with conditions, if prior investigation shows that groundwater pollution can be prevented. The Regulations are enforced by the Environment Agency/SEPA, and include requirements for compliance monitoring, powers to serve variation and enforcement notices and revocation notices. There is a right of appeal if the Agency refuses an authorisation and against enforcement notices. Activities controlled under the provisions of the *Waste Management Licensing Regulations* (see 4.19.3) are excluded from these Regulations.

5.15.3 Pollution Offences (ss.85-91)

Under section 85 of the WRA (Scotland – s.30F of COPA: see *Env. Act 1995*, Sch. 16, para 1), it is an offence to cause or knowingly permit

a) any poisonous, noxious or polluting matter or any solid waste matter to enter any controlled waters;

b) any matter, other than trade effluent or sewage effluent, to enter controlled waters by being discharged from a drain or sewer in contravention of a relevant prohibition;

c) any trade effluent or sewage effluent to be discharged –

   into any controlled waters; or

   from land in England and Wales (or Scotland), through a pipe, into the sea outside the seaward limits of controlled waters;

d) any trade effluent or sewage effluent to be discharged, in contravention of any relevant prohibition, from a building or from any fixed plant on to or into any land or into any waters of a lake or pond which are not inland waters;

e) any matter whatever to enter any inland waters so as to tend (either directly or in combination with other matter which he or another person causes or permits to enter those waters) to impede the proper flow of the waters in a manner leading or likely to lead to a substantial aggravation of pollution due to other causes, or of the consequences of such pollution.

Contravention of this section of the Act or of conditions attached to a consent to discharge given under the Act may result in a fine not exceeding £20,000 and/or three months' imprisonment on summary conviction or an unlimited fine and/or two years' imprisonment on conviction on indictment.

Defences include:

- that the discharge or entry of matter into water was caused or permitted in an emergency to safeguard life or health;
- that all such steps as were reasonably practicable were taken to minimise the extent and effect of the discharge or entry;
- that the Environment Agency were given details of the entry or discharge as soon as reasonably practicable.

Under section 88 of the Act (Scotland, s.30I of COPA, see *Env. Act 1995*, Sch. 16), it is a defence to prove that a discharge to controlled waters did not contravene conditions imposed in accordance with other legislation under which the process is regulated – e.g. IPC authorisations under Part I of the *Environmental Protection Act 1990*. Section 89 of the WRA (as amended by s.60 of the *Env. Act 1995*, effective 1 July 1998), (Scotland, s.30J of COPA – *Env. Act*, Sch. 16), excludes from section 85 (s.30F COPA, *Env. Act*, Sch. 16) any person who allows water from a mine or part of a mine abandoned before 31 December 1999 to enter controlled waters; thus, mines abandoned after this date will be subject to control through discharge consents etc.

(a) The Control of Pollution (Applications, Appeals and Registers) Regulations 1996 (SI 2971)

Discharges of trade or sewage effluent and other matter to water are regulated through a system of consents. (See also 5.17.3 below relating to trade effluents.)

The above Regulations came into force on 31 December 1996 and apply in England and Wales; they were made under sections 90A, 91, 190, 191 and Schedule 10 of the WRA, as amended by the *Environment Act 1995*, Sch. 22, paras 142-144 and 183 (which replaces the original Schedule 10 to the WRA). The Regulations revoke the *Control of Pollution (Consents for Discharges) Regulations 1989, the Control of Pollution (Consents for Discharges by the National Rivers Authority) Regulations 1989* and the *Control of Pollution (Registers) Regulations 1989.*

- **Application for a Consent to Discharge**

An application for a consent to discharge has to be made on a form provided by the Agency, and submitted to it with any other information required together with the appropriate fee (see below). The Agency may refuse to process the application if all the information requested has not been provided (WRA, s.90A, see *Env. Act.* Sch.22, para 142).

A notice that an application for, or variation of, a discharge consent has been made must be advertised in one or more local newspapers and in the *London Gazette*; this should normally be done within 42 days, but not before 14 days after its receipt by the Agency. Exceptions to this are:

- where the Agency notifies the applicant that it refuses to proceed with the application or variation until further information is received, the period for advertising begins 14 days after receipt by the Agency of the additional information;
- where it is agreed that the application has implications for national security or is commercially confidential, the period for advertising begins 14 days later; where the applicant requests exclusion from the public register of those parts of the application considered to be commercially confidential, the date for advertising will begin when the Agency has notified the applicant of its decision, the date on which the period allowed for appeal expires, is determined or withdrawn.

The Agency may decide that the application may not be advertised if it is to be excluded from the public register on grounds of national security or that the activities to which the application relate "are unlikely to have an appreciable effect on controlled waters in the locality...".

Where it appears to the Agency that a discharge has been caused in contravention of section 85 or 86 of the WRA and is likely to happen again, it can issue a discharge consent (together with conditions) without having first received an application. Schedule 1 to the Regulations sets out the procedure (advertising, consultation, etc) which is similar to that for normal applications to discharge.

Where the Agency itself wishes to apply for a discharge consent, this should be done in writing to the Secretary of State; Schedule 2 to the Regulations sets out the procedure to be followed; this is similar to that for applicants to the Agency.

- **Consultation and Determination**

A copy of the application should be sent to all affected local authorities and water undertakers in whose area it is proposed to discharge; to relevant ministers if it is proposed to discharge to coastal waters or relevant territorial waters; to any harbour authority or local fisheries committees whose waters might be affected by the discharge. Unless otherwise specified, a period of six weeks will normally be allowed for representations.

Copies of all applications will be put on the public register kept by the Agency. However, an applicant may apply to the Secretary of State for data to be withheld on the grounds of commercial confidentiality or that publishing such data would not be in the public interest.

An application for a consent must be considered within four months of receipt; if it is not and a longer period has not been agreed with the applicant, it is deemed to have been refused. In considering whether to grant a consent, the Agency will take into account whether statutory water quality objectives will be met; it will also need to be assured that the discharge will not result in deterioration of water quality or adversely affect uses of the water downstream.

The Secretary of State may call in the application for determination as a result of objections or representations made; a local inquiry or hearing will then be arranged as a means of enabling a decision to be made on the application.

If consent is granted, conditions will be included to ensure compliance with statutory water quality objectives (including EU legislation), absolute limits set for discharges and other conditions such as

a) the place to which the consent to discharge relates;

b) the nature, origin, composition, temperature, volume and rate of discharge, and the periods during which the discharge may be made;

c) steps to be taken to minimise the polluting effects of the discharge;

d) provision of facilities for sampling and monitoring;

e) provision, maintenance and testing of meters for measuring or recording discharges,

f) keeping of detailed records relating to the discharge and conditions attaching to the consent;

g) provision of information to the enforcing authority in respect of the discharge.

Consents and their conditions are reviewed from "time to time" and, following review, the Agency may serve a notice revoking or modifying a consent, modifying its conditions or adding some conditions to it; however, apart from a notice revoking a consent, such a notice will not normally be served within four years of the consent being issued without the agreement of the discharger; exceptions to this are to ensure compliance with EU legislation, other international obligations, or health or environmental protection reasons.

The holder of a consent may apply (on a form provided by the Agency) for it to be varied; the consent may also be transferred to another person with the person transferring it advising the Agency within 21 days. A person taking responsibility for a consent following the death or bankruptcy of the holder should advise the Agency of the fact within 15 months. (Holders of consents transferred prior to 1 April 1996 had until 1 October 1996 to register their ownership with the Environment Agency; failure to register renders the current holder liable to prosecution as the discharge is deemed to be illegal as the consent to discharge is in the name of another person.)

In Scotland, consents to discharge are issued by SEPA under Regulations made under Part II of the *Control of Pollution Act*, section 34 – the *Control of Pollution (Consents for Discharges) (Secretary of State Functions) Regulations 1984* (SI 865) and the *Control of Pollution (Discharges by Islands Councils) (Scotland) Regulations 1993*. The procedure is similar to that outlined above.

- **Appeals**

Where an application for consent to discharge has been refused, revoked or otherwise varied, a variation has been refused, or an enforcement notice served, the applicant has a right of appeal to the Secretary of State. Any appeal should be submitted in writing (together with supporting documentation) to the Secretary of State within three months of the decision which is being appealed against, with copies also being sent to the Agency at the same time. Appeals in respect of a revocation notice should be submitted before the revocation takes effect; in respect of an enforcement notice or refusal for information to be excluded from the public register, within 21 days.

The Secretary of State may then require the appellant to submit further documentation supporting the appeal within 28 days and will also advise the Agency that an appeal has been lodged. The Agency has 21 days in which to submit its own representations in respect of the appeal.

The Agency should notify all those who made representations concerning the application for discharge consent or variation and statutory consultees within 14 days of receiving notice of the appeal; it must also inform the Secretary of State within a further 14 days to whom it has sent notification of an appeal. Any representations (which will be copied to the Agency, the appellant and put on the register) should be sent to the Secretary of State within 21 days.

The appellant may choose to have the appeal dealt with by written representation or a hearing. In the case of written representation, information supporting an appeal should be submitted within 28 days (or 14 days in respect of an enforcement notice). If there is to be a hearing, the Secretary of State should give both the appellant and the

Agency 28 days' notice of its date, time and place and at least 21 days before should publish a notice in a local newspaper and send notice of it to all who have submitted representations. Section 114 and Schedule 20 of the *Environment Act 1995* enable the Secretary of State to appoint someone to carry out all or some aspect of the appeal on his behalf, including arranging a hearing or local inquiry. With effect from 1 January 1997, appeals relating to discharge consents, works and enforcement notices were transferred to the Planning Inspectorate. The Secretary of State will notify the appellant in writing of his decision concerning the appeal, as well as notify the Agency and others who made representations.

It should be noted that the terms of an enforcement notice, must be complied with pending determination of the appeal. Revocations, variations or the addition of conditions to consents will not take effect until determination or withdrawal of the appeal unless the Agency is of the opinion that to delay might result in the entry of any polluting, poisonous or noxious matter into controlled water or harm to human health.

In Scotland the relevant sections of COPA are s.39 and s.49B (*Env. Act*, Sch. 22, para 29(26)). The appeals procedure is set out in the *Control of Pollution (Consents for Discharges) (Secretary of State Functions) Regulations 1984* (SI 865).

- **Consents for Discharges by the Agency**

Applications etc by the Agency itself to discharge into controlled waters are made in writing to the Secretary of State. Schedule 2 of the Regulations outlines the requirements and procedures, which are similar to those for applicants to the Agency.

- **Pollution Control Registers**

The Agency is required to maintain registers, open to public inspection, with details of

a) notices of water quality objectives and other Secretary of State notices and directions;

b) applications for discharge consents or for their variation and supporting data;

c) consents for discharges and any conditions, and information obtained or given in pursuance of conditions, and any variations thereof;

d) data relating to samples of water or effluent, including results of analysis, and steps taken by the Agency or another person as a consequence.

e) prohibition and enforcement notices, revocations, appeals and details of relevant convictions;

e) results of analysis of samples of effluent and of samples of water taken by the enforcing authority in carrying out their pollution control functions;

f) information acquired by the enforcing authority with respect to samples taken by other persons.

Information should normally be placed on the register within 28 days, or seven days in the case of enforcement notices. Information relating to a withdrawn application for a consent or variation should be removed from the Register not less than two months and not more than three months after its withdrawal.

The Agency should inform the Secretary of State of any information excluded on the grounds of national security; or a person wishing to have information excluded on these grounds may notify the Secretary of State direct and pending his decision, the information concerned should not be put on the register (*Env. Act 1995*, Sch. 22, para 170, adds s.191A to the WRA).

Where a person requests that certain information given in connection with an application for a discharge consent be excluded for commercially confidential reasons, the Agency must determine the request within 14 days; if it does not the information automatically becomes commercially confidential. Where the Agency has obtained information in pursuit of its duties which it considers could be commercially confidential, it should notify the appropriate person "giving him reasonable opportunity" to object to its inclusion. If the Agency considers information not to be commercially confidential, it should notify the relevant person, allowing 21 days before putting the information on the register, during which time an appeal may be made to the Secretary of State. Following determination or withdrawal of the appeal, seven days should elapse before the information is placed on the register (*Env. Act 1995*, Sch. 22, para 170 adds new s.191B to the WRA).

Where information is excluded from the Register, for instance on the grounds of commercial confidentiality, a notice should appear on the register to that effect.

The Agency is required to keep information on the Register for up to four years after it has been superseded; it is also required to keep monitoring information for up to four years.

The corresponding regulations in Scotland are the *Control of Pollution (Registers) (Scotland) Regulations 1993* (SI 1155) and sections 41 and 42A-B of COPA (*Env. Act 1995*, Sch. 22, para 29(17)-(20)).

(b) Enforcement Notices (s.90B)

This section of the WRA is added by the *Environment Act 1995*, Sch. 22, para 142. It was brought into force by Commencement Order (No. 8, SI 2909) on 1 January 1997. For Scotland the relevant section of COPA is s.49A (*Env. Act*, Sch. 22, para 29(26)).

The Agency may serve an enforcement notice if it is of the opinion that the conditions of a consent are being, or may be contravened; the notice will specify the nature of the contravention or why it is considered that a contravention is likely, the steps to be taken to remedy the matter and the period within which this must be done. The Agency will normally give ten days' notice of its intention to serve an enforcement notice. New Regulations (see 5.14.6(d) below) will require enforcement notices to be placed on the public register within seven days of service.

Failure to comply with a notice is an offence subject to a fine not exceeding £20,000 and/or up to three months' imprisonment on summary conviction or up to two years' imprisonment and/or a fine on conviction on indictment.

5.15.4 Abandoned Mines

Sections 91A and 91B were added to the WRA by section 58 of the *Environment Act 1995* which was brought into force on 1 July 1998. They cover mines (including tourist mines and those for commercial mineral extraction) in England and Wales abandoned on or after 1 January 1999. For Scotland, section 59 of the Act adds ss.30Y-Z to the *Control of Pollution Act 1974* and has the same effect for abandoned mines in Scotland. Similar legislation for Northern Ireland is to be made.

"Abandoned" includes stopping all or some of the mining or related activities at a mine, or stopping or substantially changing operations for the removal of water from a mine.

The Mines (Notice of Abandonment) Regulations 1998 (SI 892)

These Regulations apply in England and Wales and came into force on 1 July 1998, with similar Regulations (SI 1572) taking effect in Scotland on 31 July.

A mine operator is required to give at least six months' notice of intention to abandon a mine to the appropriate Agency. The Notice should include the following details:

- name and address of the mine operator, and of the owner if this is different;

- location and description of the mine, pumping rates, etc;
- consequences of abandonment;
- proposals for monitoring groundwater quality and water quality in the mine;
- proposals for treating, lessening or preventing discharges from the mine.

Details of the proposed closure should also be published in at least one local newspaper.

Failure to give the required notice is an offence except if the mine is abandoned in an emergency to safeguard life or health or in some cases of insolvency. Notice of abandonment should be sent to the appropriate Agency as soon as practicable.

If the appropriate Agency considers that the proposed or actual abandonment is likely to result in surrounding land becoming contaminated as defined by Part IIA of the EPA 1990 (see chapter 4, 4.28.3), the relevant local authority should be advised.

It should be noted that sections 161A-C (Scotland – COPA, ss.46A-C) enable the Agencies to serve a works notice requiring certain anti-pollution works to be carried out to prevent or deal with polluting matter entering controlled waters from, *inter alia*, abandoned mines; it will however only apply to mines abandoned after 31 December 1999 – see below 5.15.6b.

5.15.5 Powers to Prevent and Control Pollution (ss.92-97)

(a) The Control of Pollution (Silage, Slurry and Agricultural Fuel Oil) Regulations 1991 (SI 324)

These Regulations to prevent water pollution from farms, were made under section 110 of the *Water Act*. This has been replaced by section 92 of the WRA. The Regulations came into effect on 1 September 1991 and apply to England and Wales, with equivalent Regulations applying in Scotland (SI 346).

New silage, slurry and agricultural fuel oil storage facilities have to be designed and built to minimum standards to prevent the pollution of controlled waters. Existing installations – i.e. those in use or constructed before 1 March 1991, or a contract for construction, or actual construction begun, before 1 March 1991 and completed before 1 September 1991 – are largely exempt from the Regulations except where the Agency considers that there is a serious risk of pollution. In such instances the Agency may require (subject to a right of appeal) that all or some of the standards for new installations are met. Substantially extended or reconstructed facilities must meet the new standards.

Silage can only be made in a silo with an impermeable base surrounded by a system to collect any effluent and take it to a storage tank. Silage can also be made in bales in a tower silo or an existing installation. Any other methods of silage making (e.g. field silage making) had to be registered with the Agency under transitional arrangements and could continue until 31 August 1996 unless considered to be a serious pollution risk.

Farms producing slurry must have a minimum four months storage capacity unless the Agency is satisfied that less does not represent a serious pollution risk. There are also minimum standards for loading and height limits for slurry lagoons.

Tanks for storing more than 1500 litres of fuel oil on a farm must be surrounded by an impervious wall called a bund to prevent leaks reaching watercourses.

The penalty for contravening the Regulations is a fine of up to £20,000 and/or three months in prison on summary conviction or an unlimited fine and/or two years in prison on conviction on indictment.

A DOE consultation document published in June 1996 proposed amending the Regulations to permit field silage making – production and storage would be prohibited within a 50 metre radius of a groundwater source and, as currently, within 10 metres of watercourses. Farmers would be required to give the Agency 14 days notice of their intention to use a new site for field silage to enable the Agency to advise on pollution prevention measures. A further amendment to the Regulations will enable the Agency to serve a notice (instead of immediate prosecution) on a farmer requiring measures to be taken to prevent pollution of water from all slurry, silage and agricultural fuel oil stores.

(b) Water Protection Zones (s.93)

This section provides powers for areas to be designated water protection zones, which would enable the Agency to have control over the application of pesticides and other potential pollutants in surrounding areas. (See also above, 5.15.2b)

(c) Nitrate Sensitive Areas (ss.94-95)

These sections provide powers for the establishment of nitrate sensitive areas (NSAs) in England and Wales in which controls can be introduced over agricultural activity in order to reduce the amount of nitrate leaching from agricultural land into water sources.

The Nitrate Sensitive Areas (Designation) Order 1990 (revoked with effect from 1 June 1996 by 1995 Regulations – see below) established a pilot scheme of ten NSAs in North East and Central England under which farmers were eligible for payments if they adopted measures to reduce nitrate leaching. Under the basic option they could continue their usual cropping systems but were restricted as to the amounts of fertiliser and manure they could apply; under the premium option, farmers were compensated for converting arable production to grassland and could also claim towards the cost of storage and transportation of manure from pig and poultry units. The scheme was due to end in 1995 but was extended for a further five years.

The Nitrate Sensitive Areas Regulations 1994 (SI 1729)

These Regulations (as amended in 1995 SI 2095, 1996 SI 3105 and 1998 SI 79) establish 32 NSAs (including the 10 in the pilot scheme) around water supply boreholes mainly in the East Midlands, North Yorkshire, Lincolnshire and Staffordshire. Annual payments are made to farmers on the basis of their agreement to one of the following options:

- **arable conversion** – similar to the premium option outlined above; or
- **low nitrogen grassland** – change from intensive to extensive grassland management; or
- **low nitrogen arable** – arable crops to be restricted to 150 kg/ha per year of inorganic fertiliser; potato and vegetable brassicas prohibited; organic manure prohibited; cover crops to be grown when needed to prevent bare land in autumn and winter.
- **set-aside** – no nitrogen fertilisers to be applied to grassland or land planted with grass seed; no grass cutting between 1 April and 15 July and restrictions on grass cutting; no grazing; no use of land for non-agricultural purpose for money or otherwise.

Farmers participating in the scheme are expected to observe other environmental requirements, such as retention of hedges, trees, woodlands, etc. Farmers in the pilot scheme were able to transfer to the new scheme.

Participation in this scheme is voluntary and additional to the mandatory measures being introduced in compliance with the nitrates Directive to protect nitrate vulnerable zones – see above 5.7.7.

In Scotland, section 31(b) of COPA includes powers to designate nitrate sensitive areas.

(d) Codes of Practice (s.97)

This section of the Act enables the Secretary of State to approve codes of practice which give practical guidance to those engaged in agricultural activities that may affect controlled waters, and to promote desirable practices to control pollution. Breach of a code would not be an offence, but may be taken into account by the Agency in determining whether to serve a notice to prohibit pollution by discharges to water, or to require that precautions are taken against potential pollution.

The Water (Prevention of Pollution) (Code of Practice) Order 1991 is a statutory code of practice covering England and Wales; it was drawn up by MAFF and the Welsh Office and took effect in October 1991; it is currently being revised to reflect legislative changes, etc, with publication due in 1998. The code provides guidance on avoiding water pollution from various farming practices, such as pesticide and fertiliser use, silage, sheep dip and disposal of animal carcases. Breach of the code is not an offence although it can be used as evidence in any prosecution for polluting water. A code covering air pollution from agricultural sources was published in 1992 (see chapter 2, 2.17) and a code on soil pollution in 1993 – revised versions of both were due in 1998.

In Scotland the *Code of Practice on the Prevention of Environmental Pollution from Agricultural Activity* covers air, soil and water pollution. It came into effect in March 1992 and a revised version is being prepared. Only those sections covering water pollution have been given statutory backing under the *Water (Prevention of Pollution) (Code of Practice) (Scotland) Order 1992*. Compliance with the Code is not a defence in any action for water pollution. The water sections of the Code cover similar issues to that for England and Wales, and also recommend good practices to prevent water pollution from nitrates. This is in line with EU Directive 91/676/EEC which places restrictions on the use of certain fertilisers (see this chapter, 5.7.7).

5.15.6 Miscellaneous Provisions Relating to Water Pollution

(a) Radioactive Substances (s.98)

The Control of Pollution (Radioactive Waste) Regulations 1989 (SI 1158) were brought into force on 1 September 1989. They apply in England and Wales and brought radioactive waste within the scope of the following sections of the *Water Act* (now *Water Resources Act)*:

- classification of quality of waters (s.82);
- general duties to achieve and maintain objectives etc (s.84);
- offences of polluting controlled waters etc (ss.85-87);

- requirements to take precautions against pollution (s.92);
- consents and applications to the Agency (s.99);
- anti-pollution works and operations (s.161);
- registers (s.190);
- information and assistance (s.202);
- exchange of information with respect to pollution incidents etc (s.203);
- local inquiries (s.213).

The radioactive properties of such waste remain subject to control under the *Radioactive Substances Act 1993*.

The corresponding Regulations in Scotland are the *Control of Pollution (Radioactive Waste) (Scotland) Regulations 1991*.

(b) Anti-Pollution Works (s.161)

Under this section of the *Water Resources Act*, the Agency is empowered to take remedial action to deal with actual or potential pollution affecting controlled waters. It could be used to deal with pollution from sources such as contamination from landfill sites, old mine workings, chemical discharges etc. (Scotland, COPA, s.46)

Section 60(3) of the *Environment Act 1995* (effective 1 July 1997, Commencement Order No. 9) amends this section of the Act to enable the Agency to carry out an investigation to establish the source of the polluting matter and the person responsible. Costs and expenses in respect of the investigation and in dealing with the pollution may be recovered from the person who caused or knowingly permitted the pollution. (It should be noted that the recovery of costs in respect of investigating or dealing with pollution from legally abandoned mines is specifically excluded from the Act s.161(4) & *Env. Act 1995*, s.60(5)).

Sections 161A-D (*Env. Act 1995*, Sch. 22, para 162) – Scotland, COPA 46A-D (*Env. Act*, Sch. 22, para 29(22)) – enable the Agencies to serve a "works notice" on the person responsible for causing or knowingly permitting poisonous, polluting or noxious matter to enter controlled waters or to be likely to enter controlled waters.

The works notice should specify the action to be taken to remedy the situation and the period within which each action specified in the notice must be carried out. Before serving the notice the Agency should make reasonable efforts to consult the responsible person on the works to be undertaken. There is a right of appeal to the Secretary of State within 21 days of the service of the works notice.

If the person responsible for the actual or potential pollution cannot be found, or if the Agency considers the situation should be dealt with "forthwith", it may carry out the works itself and recover the costs and expenses incurred.

A works notice may not be served on an operator in respect of water from mines or part of a mine abandoned before 31 December 1999.

The Anti-Pollution Works Regulations *(draft August 1997)*

As well as the name and address of the person on whom the notice is being served, and identifying the controlled waters to which the notice applies, the notice should specify

- that in the opinion of the Agency, poisonous, noxious or polluting matter or solid waste matter has entered, or is likely to enter, the identified waters;
- the works or operations to be carried out;
- that the person on whom the notice is served has a right of appeal within 21 days from the date the notice is received to the Secretary of State;
- the Agency's entitlement to recover costs in carrying out its investigations;
- consequences of non-compliance with a works' notice; i.e. that is an offence which on summary conviction may result in a fine not exceeding £20,000 and/or three months imprisonment; conviction on indictment may result in up to two years imprisonment and/or a fine. Where a notice has not been complied with the Agency may carry out the work and recover the costs and expenses incurred.

Works Notices are not suspended during determination of an appeal; in sending written notice of appeal to the Secretary of State, the appellant should send relevant documents and should state whether the appeal is to be determined by written representations or a hearing; in the former case the Agency has 14 days to respond to any enquiries from the Secretary of State regarding the matter.

Where a person is required to grant rights of entry to a person on whom a works notice has been served in order that that person can comply with the notice, compensation is payable; the Regulations deal with the way in which compensation payments are to be calculated. Disputes over compensation payments are determined by the Lands Tribunal.

Copies of works notices, appeals and relevant documentation and appeal decisions, as well as convictions under the Regulations are held on the pollution control register maintained by the Environment Agency.

(c) Powers of Entry and Collecting Evidence

Sections 169 and 170 of the WRA empower an authorised person to enter any premises to determine whether any provisions of the *Water Resources Act* have been or are being contravened. Where entry is required for enforcement purposes, no advance notice need be given though, except in emergencies, entry should be sought at a "reasonable time"; in all other cases seven days' notice should be given (Schedule 20 to the WRA). The inspector may carry out tests, install monitoring equipment or take away samples for further analysis.

Under s.111 of the *Environment Act 1995* any apparatus used for recording or registering information shall be deemed to be accurate unless the contrary is proved. Where an authorised person has been unable to gain entry to monitor observance with a condition, this will be taken as evidence that the condition is not being complied with.

There is no longer a requirement for samples to be divided into three – one each for the discharger, the regulator and one for future comparison – as was the case under s.209 of the WRA, repealed by the *Env. Act*. In practice the Agency does still follow this procedure where "reasonably practicable" for samples to be used in court evidence.

Where entry is required in relation to the Agency's pollution control functions (including s.161-161D) of the WRA, the powers of entry provisions of the *Environment Act 1995* (ss.108-109) apply (*Env. Act*, Sch. 22, para 165); these provisions are set out in chapter 1, 1.14.2.

SCHEDULES

The *Water Resources Act 1991* has 26 Schedules appended to it, of which the following are of particular relevance to pollution control:

- **Schedule 10:** Discharge Consents (Schedule in WRA superseded by new Schedule 10 in *Environment Act 1995*, see Sch. 22, para 183);
- **Schedule 11:** Water Protection Zone Orders;
- **Schedule 12:** Nitrate Sensitive Area Orders –
  Part I, Applications by the Authority for Designation Orders and Part II, Orders Containing Mandatory Provisions;
- **Schedule 13:** Transitional Water Pollution Provisions;
- **Schedule 20:** Supplementary Provisions with Respect to Powers of Entry.

5.16 ENVIRONMENT ACT 1995

Charging Scheme

Section 41 of the *Environment Act* empowers the Agencies to make charging schemes in respect of environmental licences (including consents to discharge), variations of such licences etc; such schemes are approved by the Secretary of State under section 42 of the Act.

The Scheme for England and Wales described below (made under ss.131 & 132 of the *Water Resources Act 1991*, repealed by the *Env. Act)* is currently under review with consideration being given to the use of economic instruments to improve water quality, including

- charges being related to pollution;
- dischargers to be able to buy and sell the right to discharge to achieve environmental targets;
- charges to control the use of pesticides and fertilisers.

The purpose of charging for applications and consents for discharges of sewage and trade effluent to controlled waters is to enable the Environment Agency to recover its costs in respect of monitoring, sampling, analysing and other regulatory functions related to discharge consents. The current scheme came into effect on 1 July 1991 and was reviewed in March 1994. Charges are reviewed annually.

Applications for a new or revised discharge consent are subject to a standard charge per effluent (1998/9 £589 or £84 for smaller discharges, both plus VAT). In addition an annual fee, also per effluent, is payable; when treatment or monitoring is carried out together the annual fee will be calculated on the basis of the highest content and aggregated volume of the discharge. The annual fee is based on the volume and content of the discharges as specified in the consent, and on the nature of the receiving waters with the amount payable depending on the complexity of the discharge and the sensitivity of the receiving waters: each of the three categories of the annual charge has been banded into factors reflecting complexity and sensitivity or in the latter case, type of receiving water; the annual charge payable is the number of factors multiplied, multiplied again by the financial factor (1998/9 £455).

In Scotland charges are based on the volume and content of the discharge and the nature of the receiving water, multiplied by a financial factor: 1998/9 - £220, 1999/00 - £275, 2000/1 - £345.

5.17 WATER INDUSTRY ACT 1991

This Act came into force on 1 December 1991 and applies in England and Wales only. It consolidates various enactments relating to the appointment of water and sewerage undertakers, conditions of appointment, supply of water and the provision of sewerage services. It also sets out the functions of the Director General of Water Services, and the duties of local authorities with regard to the supply of wholesome and sufficient water.

In Scotland, the *Water (Scotland) Act 1980* as amended by the *Water Act 1989* covers similar areas. Sewerage and drainage services are covered by the *Sewerage (Scotland) Act 1958*. This legislation is the responsibility of the North, East, and West of Scotland Water Authorities.

5.17.1 Quality and Sufficiency of Supplies (ss.67-86)

(a) General Obligations of Undertakers (ss.68-70)

Section 68 places a duty on water undertakers to supply only water which is "wholesome at the time of supply" to any premises for domestic purposes. Section 69 empowers the Secretary of State through Regulations to specify minimum requirements for the monitoring and recording of water quality, to forbid or regulate the use of substances, processes and products which might affect the quality of water supplied, and to require provision of certain information to the public about its quality.

Section 70 makes it an offence to supply water which is unfit for human consumption unless it can be shown that there were no reasonable grounds for suspecting that the water would be used for human consumption, or took all reasonable steps to ensure it was fit, or was not used for human consumption.

(b) Waste, Contamination, Misuse of Water (ss.71-75)

Under these sections, it is an offence for an owner or occupier of premises either through negligence or intentionally to allow water fittings to remain in disrepair so as to cause the contamination, wasting or misuse of water. The Secretary of State is empowered to make Regulations with regard to water fittings, and representatives of water undertakers or local authorities will be able to enter any premises to ensure compliance with those regulations and to check the installation of any water fittings. To prevent damage to persons or property, or contamination or waste of water, water authorities will be entitled either to cut off a supply of water, or to serve a notice on a consumer requiring action to remedy the problem.

(c) Local Authority Functions (ss.77-85)

Where existing supplies of water are insufficient or unwholesome, and piped water supplies would not be practicable at reasonable cost, section 79 entitles local authorities to require water undertakers to supply water for domestic purposes other than through pipes. Sections 78-82 place a general duty on local authorities to monitor the quality and sufficiency of water supplies in their area and where this is found to be below standard, empowers them to serve a notice on the water undertaker specifying what steps they consider necessary to effect improvements. There is a right of appeal to the Secretary of State against any action by a local authority in relation to private supplies.

Under section 86 the Secretary of State may appoint technical assessors to carry out investigations of drinking water quality matters and advise whether any duty imposed on a water undertaker in relation to such matters has been or might be contravened.

The Water Supply (Water Quality) Regulations 1989 (SI 1147) (amended 1991)

These Regulations were made under sections 52, 53, 56 and 65 of the *Water Act 1989* (WIA: ss.67-69, 77-78) and apply to England and Wales. Most of the provisions of the Regulations came into effect on 1 September 1989, and the remainder on 1 January 1990. Similar Regulations (1990 – SI 119, amended 1991 – SI 1333) apply in Scotland, and in Northern Ireland (1994).

The Regulations are primarily concerned with the quality of public supplies of water for drinking, washing and cooking and with arrangements for the publication of information about water quality. They also give effect to EU Directive 80/778/EEC which relates to the quality of water intended for human consumption, and in part, to EU Directive 75/440/EEC (quality required of surface water intended for the abstraction of drinking water).

Part II of the Regulations prescribes standards of wholesomeness in respect of water supplied by the water companies for drinking, washing or cooking. In particular, it provides that water is to be regarded as wholesome if it contains concentrations or values in respect of various properties, elements, organisms and substances (including pesticides and related products) which do not contravene prescribed maximum and, in some cases, minimum concentrations or values, as specified in Directive 80/778/EEC – see Appendix 5.2b.

Part III enables the Secretary of State or the appropriate local authority, to relax the requirements of Part II in certain circumstances; these are

- in an emergency to maintain supplies for human consumption;
- in exceptional meteorological conditions;
- because of the nature or structure of the ground from which the supply emanates;
- where the supply is used solely for the purpose of food production.

Part IV provides for the monitoring of water supplies by reference to analysis of samples taken from consumers' taps, with Part V providing additional provisions with regard to sampling. Part VI deals with the treatment of water and regulates the substances, processes and products that may be used by water undertakers in connection with the supply of water.

Part VII of the Regulations relates to the provision of information by water companies and Part VIII imposes requirements on local authorities in the performance of their duties in relation to the quality of water supplied by water companies.

The 1991 Amendment Regulations, separate versions of which apply in England/Wales and in Scotland, extend the scope of the 1989 Regulations to include the quality of water used for food production. There are also more stringent requirements relating to the sampling of water to establish its wholesomeness for drinking water. Local authorities are also empowered to comment on any application by a water undertaker for relaxation of obligations under the Regulations.

In England and Wales only, the Amendment Regulations require water undertakers to give customers information regarding the public register of authorisations, discharge consents etc and how it can be consulted. This must be done at least once a year and, it is suggested should be sent out with customers' bills.

The Private Water Supplies Regulations 1991 (SI 2790)

These Regulations (made under ss.67 & 77 of the *Water Industry Act 1991*) relate to the quality of water from private supplies for drinking, washing, cooking or for food production. They apply in England and Wales only and came into force on 1 January 1992. They contain similar requirements to those of Parts II and III of the *Water Supply (Water Quality) Regulations 1991*. Similar (1992, SI 575) Regulations apply in Scotland, and 1994 Regulations in Northern Ireland.

Local authorities are required to monitor the quality of private water supplies by reference to two categories: water supplied for domestic purposes; and water supplied for food production, to staff canteens, hospitals, hostels, boarding schools etc and camp sites. The Regulations specify factors to be taken into account in monitoring programmes – sampling frequency, point of sampling, analysis, and charging for sampling and analysis. Where quality is found to be below standard, local authorities must ensure that the necessary remedial action is taken. They are also required to keep a register of all private water supplies in their area.

Private supplies are those not provided by a water undertaker (company) – i.e. not connected to a mains pipe (for example, borehole into an underground aquifer, a surface reservoir).

Sampling of Water

British Standard 6068, section 6.5, 1991, gives guidance on sampling drinking water and water used for food and beverage processing. It includes guidance on the design of sampling programmes and techniques, handling and preservation of samples, water processing treatment plant (including the analysis of raw water), supervision of the treatment plant and the distribution system, and the identification of defects in the system.

5.17.2 Sewerage Services (ss.94-117)

Provision of Sewerage Services (ss.94-101)

Every sewerage undertaker has a general duty to provide and maintain a system of public sewers and sewage disposal, and to have regard to its existing and likely obligations to allow for the discharge of trade effluent into its public sewers, and the disposal of such trade effluent. The Secretary of State may make Regulations detailing the extent to which breaches of specific sewerage service obligations are to amount to breaches of the general duty. Regulations may also prescribe individual standards of performance in relation to the sewerage service. If these standards are not met, payments are to be made by the undertaker to the persons affected. Sewerage undertakers must comply within six months with any request to provide a public sewer to be used for drainage of premises for domestic purposes, provided that certain financial conditions are met.

5.17.3 Trade Effluent (ss.118-134)

Occupiers of trade premises may not discharge any trade effluents into a public sewer unless authorised by the sewerage undertaker. An application to discharge should include details of the effluent, quantity to be discharged in any one day, and the highest rate at which it is proposed to discharge. (The sewerage undertaker must refer all applications covering special category effluent – see below – to the Environment Agency who will decide if the discharge should be prohibited or permitted subject to conditions.)

In granting an application, the sewerage undertaker may impose conditions covering the rate, quantity and composition of effluent and the sewer into which it may be discharged, and the time or times of day. Conditions may also relate to provision and maintenance of inspection chambers and meters and of other apparatus for testing the effluent, record keeping and payments to the sewerage undertaker.

There is a right of appeal to the Director of Water Services where an application is refused, has not been considered within two months, or conditions are considered unreasonable. In the case of special category effluent, appeals should be directed to the Secretary of State. A sewerage undertaker may vary conditions attached to a consent; again there is a right of appeal to the Director General of Water Services.

Where a process regulated under Part I of the *Environmental Protection Act 1990* proposes to discharge trade effluent into a sewer, it also requires a consent from the sewerage undertaker.

Trade Effluents (Prescribed Processes and Substances) Regulations 1989 (SI 1156) (amended 1990, 1992)

These Regulations came into force on 1 September 1989 and were made under sections 74 and 185 of the *Water Act*; they apply to England and Wales only and enable compliance with EU Directives on pollution caused by discharges to the aquatic environment (76/464/EEC) and the prevention and reduction of environmental pollution by asbestos (87/217/EEC).

The Regulations specify two categories of trade effluent which are subject to control over their discharge into public sewers and for which an authorisation to discharge is required from the Environment Agency.

The first category for which authorisation to discharge is required is effluent which contains concentrations of "red list" substances (see Appendix 1.2 – substances controlled for release to water under IPC) exceeding those that would be present regardless of the activities within the premises from which the effluent is discharged. The second "special" category consists of effluent from the following prescribed processes:

- any process for the production of chlorinated organic chemicals;
- any process for the manufacture of paper pulp;
- any industrial process in which cooling waters or effluents are chlorinated;
- any process for the manufacture of asbestos cement;
- any process for the manufacture of asbestos paper or board.

The 1992 Regulations added effluent containing more than 30 kg/year of trichloroethylene or perchloroethylene to "special category" effluent.

The Regulations also require sewerage undertakers to notify the Environment Agency if they propose to vary existing trade effluent discharge consents so as to permit the discharge of effluent containing "red list" substances at levels in excess of background concentrations. This will enable the Agency to exercise stricter controls over discharges to watercourses via the sewage system, thus enabling the UK to meet its commitment (agreed at the North Sea Conference – see 5.21 below) to reduce such discharges by 50% between 1985 and 1995.

The 1990 amending Regulations tightened up the notification procedure further to require agreements by which sewerage undertakers can accept trade effluents under the *Public Health (Drainage and Trade Premises) Act 1937*, also to be notified to the Agency. Under the Regulations, the Agency must also be notified where it is proposed to vary a consent for a trade effluent discharge containing asbestos or chloroform from any of the processes mentioned above at a level in excess of background concentrations.

In addition, a Department of Environment Circular (7/89) contains advice on implementation of the EU Directive on environmental pollution by asbestos. Water authorities were required to satisfy themselves that producers of asbestos cement, and of paper and board products, had appropriate effluent treatment or recycling technology in operation by mid-1991, or had phased out the use of raw asbestos by then.

In Scotland the 1987 EU Directive on the prevention and reduction of environmental pollution by asbestos has been implemented through the *Trade Effluents (Asbestos) (Scotland) Regulations 1993* (SI 1446). Asbestos discharges should be "reduced at source and prevented ... using BATNEEC, including where appropriate recycling or treatment". Specified limits on asbestos discharges can be included in discharge authorisations, with specific conditions to be included where the discharge relates to "special category" activities (see above).

5.18 URBAN WASTE WATER TREATMENT (ENGLAND & WALES) REGULATIONS 1994 (SI 2841)

These Regulations, made under the *European Communities Act 1972*, came into force on 30 November 1994, with similar (1994, SI 2842) Regulations applying in Scotland and in Northern Ireland (1995, SR 12). They implement the 1991 EU municipal waste water Directive (91/271/EEC) – see above 5.7.6.

Regulation 3 required the Secretary of State to review the identification of "sensitive areas" and "high natural dispersion areas" before 31 December 1997 and then at intervals of no more than four years. Schedule 1 to the Regulations lists criteria for identification: sensitive areas include natural freshwater lakes, estuaries and coastal waters and surface freshwaters intended for the abstraction of drinking waters. A high natural dispersion area is a marine body or area where the discharge of waste water will not adversely affect the environment as a result of morphology, hydrology or specific hydraulic conditions in the area; in identifying a high natural dispersion area account should be taken of the discharge being transferred to an area where it could have an adverse effect.

Unless it would have no environmental benefit or would involve excessive cost, collecting systems satisfying Schedule 2 to the Regulations must be in place (Regulation 4) –

- by 31 December 1998 where the discharge is into receiving waters in a sensitive area for agglomeration with a population equivalent (pe) of more than 10,000;
- by 31 December 2000 for agglomeration with pe of more than 15,000;
- by 31 December 2005 for agglomeration with pe of 2,000-15,000.

Regulation 5 specifies the dates by which suitable treatment plant must be provided, with Schedule 3 detailing the requirements for discharges from treatment plants.

The Regulations also impose requirements relating to discharges of industrial waste water with sewerage undertakers being empowered to modify trade effluent consents and agreements to ensure compliance. The dumping of sewage sludge at sea has to be phased out by 31 December 1998 and its toxic, persistent and bioaccumulable properties progressively reduced before then.

The appropriate Agency must ensure that monitoring and other studies of discharges is carried out and certain documents made available for public inspection.

MARINE POLLUTION

5.19 INTRODUCTION

The importance of protecting the marine environment is now recognised as a priority by many governments. Inadequate sewage disposal, the build-up of chlorinated hydrocarbons from pesticides, the dumping of polychlorinated biphenyls (PCBs) and other chemicals, as well as the incineration of hazardous waste at sea all pose a threat to human health and to marine life.

The 1982 UN Convention on the Law of the Sea defines pollution of the marine environment as

> ". . . the introduction by man, directly or indirectly, of substances or energy into the marine environment, including estuaries, which results or is likely to result in such deleterious effects as harm to living resources and marine life, hazards to human health, hindrance to marine activities, including fishing and other legitimate uses of the sea, impairment of quality for use of sea water and reduction of amenities."

The Convention covers all aspects of the preservation and protection of the marine environment and sets out the duties of states in this respect. Some of its articles – or aims – are similar to those in other conventions (see below) or have already been incorporated into national legislation.

This Convention came into effect in 1994 following ratification by the required number (60) of countries. On 23 March 1998 the Council of Ministers adopted a decision which approves the Convention and Agreement of 28 July 1994 on implementation of Part XI of it.

5.20 INTERNATIONAL CONVENTIONS

The concern over increasing levels of pollution led to a number of international conventions, the latest of which was signed in 1992.

5.20.1 The London Convention on the Prevention of Marine Pollution by Dumping of Wastes and other Matter

This Convention, signed in London in 1972, applies worldwide. It aims to ban or restrict the dumping (i.e. deliberate disposal) of various polluting substances according to their potential to harm either human or marine life or otherwise impair the marine environment. This includes the disposal of ships, aircraft and manmade structures and the residues of incineration at sea.

The London Convention also imposed an immediate ban on the dumping of high level radioactive waste at sea and in 1983 agreed a 10 year voluntary moratorium on the dumping of low and intermediate level radioactive waste. In February 1994 it was agreed that this too should be banned and the ban* reviewed on scientific grounds in 25 years (i.e. 2019). The dumping of industrial waste was banned from 31 December 1995; the 1991 ban on the incineration of industrial waste at sea has now been made permanent.

A Protocol to the Convention, which has yet to be ratified, aims to "secure enhanced measures to protect the marine environment"; only those wastes listed in the Protocol may be dumped at sea and signatories may not export waste for dumping at sea to non-signatories.

*The UK which had secured an opt-out to the ban, announced in September 1997 that it would give up its opt-out and no longer permit the dumping of low and intermediate level radioactive waste at sea; the dumping of harmful chemicals would be stopped by 2020 and that "there would be a presumption against" the disposal of redundant gas and oil installations at sea (House of Commons written answer). Enforcement of these decisions is the responsibility of the Department of Trade and Industry.

5.20.2 International Convention for the Prevention of Pollution from Ships 1973

This Convention – the MARPOL Convention – was adopted following the 1973 international conference on marine pollution held under the auspices of the International Maritime Organisation. Included were articles dealing with oil, chemical, sewage and other pollution from ships. However, it was not ratified because many governments felt it would be too difficult to implement. A further conference in 1978 agreed a protocol to the Convention which included a number of amendments and improved the annex relating to oil pollution. The Convention and its protocol (MARPOL 73/78) have now been ratified by a number of governments. In the UK it has been implemented through the 1996 *Merchant Shipping (Prevention of Oil Pollution) Regulations* – see below, 5.22.1.

Further measures aimed at reducing pollution from ships have now been agreed by the IMO and were incorporated in MARPOL for implementation from January 1992. These measures include reducing pollutants in ships' exhaust gases, banning the use of CFCs in refrigeration units and of halons in new fire extinguishers.

A new annex VI to the MARPOL Convention was signed in London in September 1997; this aims to control emissions of air pollutants from shipping. The sulphur content of bunker oil is limited to 4.5%, with a lower limit of 1.5% to apply in the Baltic Sea; limits on emissions of nitrogen oxides from diesel engines are set and the incineration at sea of contaminated packaging materials and PCBs is banned. Voluntary emissions of ozone depleting gases are also banned as are new installations with ozone depleting substances on board ships although those containing hydrochlorofluorocarbons are permitted until 1 January 2020. Before it can come into force, the annex requires ratification by 15 (out of a possible 100) member states who together account for 50% of the world's merchant tonnage.

The MARPOL Convention, in allowing certain oil discharges from ships, also allows for special areas to be declared in which stricter rules for discharges apply. The IMO has agreed that the seas around the UK and north west European coastline should have special area status; thus from 1 August 1999 almost all oil pollution from ships in this area will be banned.

A further treaty put forward by the IMO was agreed in London at the end of 1990. *The International Convention on Oil Pollution Preparedness Response and Cooperation 1990* lays down the principles of prompt and effective action in the event of an oil spill. Ships, off-shore installations, ports and other facilities which handle oil should establish emergency plans and all pollution incidents should be reported. This Convention came into force on 13 May 1995, 12 months after ratification by the required 15 states; as at 13 May 1995, 21 member states had ratified the Convention. In the UK this Convention has been partly implemented through the *Merchant Shipping (Oil Pollution Preparedness, Response and Cooperation Convention) Regulations 1998* (SI 1056); these came into force on 15 May 1998 – see 5.23.3 below.

5.20.3 Convention on the Protection of the North Sea and North East Atlantic 1992 (the OSPAR Convention)

This Convention, which was signed in Paris in September 1992, replaces the 1972 Oslo *Convention for the Prevention of Marine Pollution by Dumping from Ships and Aircraft* and the 1974 Paris *Convention for the Prevention of Marine Pollution from Land-Based Sources*. Both Conventions covered the North Sea and North East Atlantic and were monitored by London based Commissions which also took a leading role in ensuring follow-up of actions agreed at the North Sea Conferences (see below). A Commission – the OSPAR Commission (i.e. drawn from the Oslo and Paris Commissions) – has been set up to implement and monitor the 1992 Convention; the members of OSPAR are Belgium, Denmark, Finland, France, Germany, Iceland, Ireland, Luxembourg, The Netherlands, Norway, Portugal, Spain, Sweden, Switzerland and the UK. It was expected that the Convention would be brought into force in July 1998 following ratification.

The main objective of the 1992 Convention is the protection of the marine environment so as to safeguard human health through the elimination or prevention of pollution. Conservation and repair of the marine ecosystem are equally important objectives and a strategy to combat eutrophication is to be drawn up. Potentially polluting activities covered by the Convention are listed as are the substances for which control programmes must be implemented with a view to reducing marine concentrations by 2020; these include pesticides, heavy metals, oil and hydrocarbons, organohalogen compounds and various chemicals. A list of priority substances for control to which the 2020 target will apply has been agreed. Both dumping and incineration at sea are to be banned, as are radioactive discharges thus giving extra weight to the agreements reached at the North Sea Conferences (see below).

At the 1998 meeting of the Commission, Ministers agreed a total ban on sea dumping of large steel installations (gas and oil rigs); levels of radioactive discharges to sea from Sellafield are to be reduced to near zero by 2000 taking account of technical feasibility; the UK and France also withdrew their opt-out from a ban on dumping nuclear waste at sea, which is to be phased out by 2020.

In drawing up action programmes to deal with polluting discharges, signatories must also have regard to both BAT (Best Available Technique) and BEP (Best Environmental Practice); this latter includes information to the public, product labelling and collection and disposal systems. One of the tasks of the Commission implementing and monitoring the Convention will be to draw up documents specifying BAT for disposal, reduction and elimination of a range of substances from various industrial sectors.

5.21 NORTH SEA CONFERENCES

In Europe, apart from the Directives which apply throughout the EU (see 5.6 & 5.7 above and Appendix 6.5), further initiatives have been taken by the countries bordering the North Sea which is the receiving water for a number of effluent-laden rivers which flow into it; these rivers include the Rhine, Elbe, Humber, Forth, Tyne, Tees and the Thames.

This growing concern resulted, in 1984, in the Government of the former West Germany convening a conference of countries bordering the North Sea (Belgium, Britain, Denmark, France, The Netherlands, Norway, Sweden and Germany) to draw up measures aimed at reducing pollution of the North Sea. This was followed by a second conference in 1987 in London; among other measures, agreement was reached on ending the dumping of harmful wastes by the end of 1989 and ending incineration by 1994.

The Third North Sea Conference was held in The Hague in 1990, and was attended by all the North Sea States plus Switzerland, whose industries along the Rhine contribute significantly to pollution levels. For the first time, the cuts agreed at the meeting are to be legally binding. Among the measures agreed were:

- by 1995, to make cuts of 50% or more (on 1985 levels) in inputs via rivers and estuaries of 39 hazardous substances;
- by 1995, a 50% cut (on 1985 levels) of inputs of dangerous substances from the air;
- by 1995, a 70% cut (on 1985 levels) of substances deemed to pose a major threat, and including dioxins, mercury, cadmium and lead;
- to aim for a substantial reduction in the quantities of pesticides reaching the North Sea;
- to phase out and to destroy in an environmentally safe manner all identifiable PCBs as soon as possible with the aim of complete destruction by 1995; and by 1999 at the latest, to ensure that the

time between taking out of service and destruction is as short as practicable. It was also agreed that each country should provide its own destruction facilities;

- municipal sewage discharges, as well as effluent discharges from industry, should receive secondary treatment before discharge.

The European Commission's Fifth Action Programme on the Environment, *Towards Sustainability* (see also Appendix 6) includes as an objective to reduce emissions of cadmium, lead and mercury in line with the North Sea Agreement.

In the UK, the reductions will largely be achieved through controls on discharges under Integrated Pollution Control (see chapter 1) and by controls on discharges under the *Water Resources Act 1991* (see 5.15 above). The *Urban Waste Water Treatment (England and Wales) Regulations 1994* (and similar in Scotland) require the phasing out of the disposal of sewage sludge to sea by 31 December 1998 (5.18 above).

Commitments relating to the phasing out and destruction of PCBs and PCTs are to be met by voluntary action on the part of industry and other users. The UK action plan, which also takes into account the requirements of the EU Directive (96/59/EC) on the disposal of PCBs and PCTs, circulated by the DOE (now DETR) in March 1997 proposes

- progressive withdrawal of existing exemptions from the ban on the sale and use of PCBs;
- requirement to register PCBs with a competent authority by 16 March 1996 and to agree a date for their destruction;
- a complete ban on supply, use and storage of PCBs from 31 December 1999;
- the compilation of an inventory of equipment containing PCBs of more than 5 dm^3.

Regulations giving statutory force to the action plan, and covering registration and labelling requirements, in compliance with the EU Directive are to being made.

At the Fourth North Sea Conference in June 1995, there was a further commitment to achieve the reduction targets agreed at the Third Conference with a number of measures agreed for reducing discharges of priority substances (cadmium, mercury etc); there was also a call for on-going reductions in discharges and emissions of hazardous substances leading to their cessation within 25 years.

5.22 FOOD AND ENVIRONMENT PROTECTION ACT 1985, PART II

This part of the Act repealed the *Dumping at Sea Act 1974* which was the first UK legislation to impose statutory controls on the dumping of waste at sea; it gave effect to various international conventions (Oslo and London, 1972 – 5.20.1 and 5.20.3 above) imposing obligations relating to the disposal of waste, the dumping of hazardous pollutants and incineration at sea. The Act applies to the whole of the United Kingdom. (The UK ended incineration at sea in 1990 and the dumping of industrial waste in 1992.)

Part II of the *Food and Environment Protection Act* (FEPA) which covers dumping and incineration at sea and/or under the seabed within UK waters, and also the scuttling of vessels, was amended by section 146 of the *Environmental Protection Act 1990.* (The amendment mainly relates to the inclusion of UK controlled waters as well as UK waters.) FEPA applies to dumping etc whether by a UK or foreign ship, aircraft, hovercraft, marine structure or floating container.

5.22.1 Licensing Requirements for Dumping at Sea

Under the Act, the prescribed activities require prior approval by licence from the Ministry of Agriculture, Fisheries and Food. In most instances, the requirement for a licence includes activities prior to the dumping or incineration, such as the loading of ships and aircraft etc within the UK, UK waters or UK controlled waters. Exempted activities are listed in the *Deposits in the Sea (Exemptions) Order 1985* (SI 1699), and include activities such as returning to the water matter taken out during fishing and dredging or deposited for coastal protection or harbour works, and the disposal of "victual or domestic waste" from ships and hovercraft etc. As from 31 December 1994 exempted activities had to be registered with MAFF (amendment to Exemptions Order by *Waste Management Regulations 1994*).

In considering whether to issue a licence, MAFF will take into account the need to protect the marine environment, the living resources which it supports, and human health. The licence may include conditions to meet these requirements, and the Act provides for fees to be charged in respect of administrative expenses, monitoring and sampling. Where a licence has been breached, MAFF may revoke it and criminal proceedings may be instituted. Summary conviction carries a fine not exceeding £50,000; conviction on indictment carries a fine and/or imprisonment not exceeding two years.

5.22.2 Public Registers

Part II of FEPA requires each licensing authority to maintain a public register containing details of licences issued relating to deposits and incineration at sea. This provision has been amended by section 147 of the *Environmental Protection Act 1990* which specifies that the register must contain applications for licences, those issued, variations and revocations as well as details of convictions for breaches of licence conditions. Information may be excluded from the register on grounds of commercial confidentiality or national security. These requirements have been given effect through *The Deposits in the Sea (Public Registers of Information) Regulations 1996* (SI 1427) which came into force on 1 July 1996. The Regulations apply in England and Wales only. The register is to be held by MAFF in London with access available at reasonable times. A charge may be levied for copies of entries on the register.

5.23 OIL POLLUTION

5.23.1 Prevention of Oil Pollution Act 1971

This Act makes it an offence (subject to various defences) to discharge oil or any substance containing oil into UK territorial waters, either from a place on land or from sea-based explorations or into harbour waters; discharges under and escapes authorised by Part I of the *Environmental Protection Act 1990* are not subject to this part of the Act (*Env. Act 1995*, Sch. 22, para 15, England, Scotland and Wales only). The Act introduced requirements for record keeping covering transfers of oil and placed restrictions on when such transfers can take place; it also covers liability for soil pollution and requires compulsory insurance against liability. A 1986 Act extended the 1971 Act to cover discharges from vessels.

Section 148 of the *Environmental Protection Act 1990* amended the 1971 Act to enable action to be taken against foreign owned ships for illegally discharging oil into UK territorial waters or ports and harbours.

Merchant Shipping (Prevention of Oil Pollution) Regulations

These Regulations implement the MARPOL Convention (see above); they apply to UK ships worldwide and to others while in UK waters.

The *Merchant Shipping (Prevention of Oil Pollution) (Limits) Regulations 1996* (SI 2128), which came into force on 5 September 1996, establish a UK "pollution zone"; this extends beyond the 12 nautical mile territorial limit to up to 200 nautical miles from the coastline. Any foreign ship suspected of committing a pollution offence within the pollution zone which calls at a port in the UK will then be liable to prosecution by the UK courts.

The *Merchant Shipping (Prevention of Oil Pollution) Regulations 1996* (SI 2154) came into force on 17 September; they provide for the enforcement of oil pollution offences committed within the pollution zone and consolidate earlier 1983 and 1993 Regulations. These introduced record keeping requirements as well as survey and certification for oil tankers and other UK ships above a certain size. There is a duty to maintain ships and their equipment in compliance with the Regulations; other provisions relate to powers of inspection and penalties. New oil tankers must be fitted with double hulls and existing ones must be fitted with additional protection against grounding or collision once they are 25 years old. Oil pollution emergency plans must be carried and stricter rules regarding discharges of oil complied with. The 1996 Regulations also include measures aimed at improving the provision and use of port waste reception facilities, tighten the regulations on legal discharges from ships, improve the enforcement of the Regulations and increase the maximum fines for illegal discharges.

5.23.2 Merchant Shipping (Salvage and Pollution) Act 1994

This Act received the Royal Assent in July 1994; from 1 October 1994 the owners of all vessels (except laden oil tankers) became liable for any oil pollution and resultant pollution prevention measures. It also implemented, with effect from 1 January 1995, a number of international marine conventions and declarations, including:

- the 1990 Convention on Oil Pollution Preparedness, Response and Cooperation (see 5.20.2 above);
- a 1992 Declaration from the North Sea Conference calling for implementation of various provisions of the 1982 UN Convention on the Law of the Sea (see above 5.21).

5.23.3 Merchant Shipping (Oil Pollution Preparedness, Response and Cooperation Convention) Regulations 1998 (SI 1056)

These Regulations, which apply throughout the UK, came into force on 15 May 1998; they implement in part the 1990 IMO Convention of the same name (see above 5.20.2). They apply to harbours and oil handling facilities with an annual turnover of more than £1 million, and to those which are able to handle tankers above a certain threshold or are designated by the Secretary of State; they also apply to off-shore installations in UK waters.

The Regulations require harbour authorities and operators of oil handling facilities to prepare and submit an oil spill contingency plan to the Government's Marine Pollution Control Unit by 15 August 1999; off-shore installations have until the same date to submit a similar plan to the Department of Trade and Industry's Oil and Gas Office in Aberdeen; local people and organisations, local authorities and environmental organisations must be consulted during the plan's preparation. Plans must be reviewed every five years.

Ships' masters and those in charge of harbours, oil handling facilities and off-shore installations must report any oil spills to their nearest Coastguard station.

5.24 MERCHANT SHIPPING AND MARITIME SECURITY ACT 1997

This Act, which received the Royal Assent in late March 1997, aims to tighten UK controls on shipping which poses a pollution risk, e.g. because of an accident, collision or other internal or external damage. It includes provisions to:

- require the Secretary of State to draw up and implement a national marine pollution contingency plan;
- establish temporary exclusion zones at sea to allow safety zones to be placed around ships or structures on grounds of safety and/or pollution;
- widen the Coastguard's intervention powers to cover any risk of significant pollution;
- permit charging for maritime functions such as emergency pollution response and standard setting activity in line with the polluter pays and user pays principles;
- enable regulations to be made requiring port and harbour authorities to prepare waste management plans and to charge ships for the use of waste reception facilities;
- enable regulations to be made requiring local authorities to draw up contingency plans to deal with oil spills;
- give powers to move ships on if they pose a threat to safety or the environment;
- increase the maximum penalty for marine pollution offences from £50,000 to £250,000.

Regulations which came into force on 27 January 1998 – *The Merchant Shipping (Port Waste Reception Facilities) Regulations 1997* (SI 3018) – require port and harbour authorities to prepare waste management plans which have to be approved by the Secretary of State. The Regulations also require the authorities to ensure they have adequate facilities (having regard to their waste management plan and to Guidance from the Secretary of State) for receiving prescribed wastes from ships.

The *Merchant Shipping (Prevention of Pollution by Garbage) Regulations 1998* (SI 1377) require all ships above 400 gross tonnage and those certified to carry more than 15 people to have a garbage management plan, and to keep disposal records. Illegal disposal carries a maximum fine of £25,000.

PESTICIDES

5.25 INTRODUCTION

Pesticides are toxic chemicals intended to control insect, rodent and other pest infestations. Their main use is for agricultural purposes where benefits can be said to include less disease and increased yields. However, their overuse and misuse in some instances has resulted in various pests becoming resistant to certain pesticides; the widespread use of pesticides can also mean that some crops may receive multiple applications; and while workers may risk occupational exposure, the general public may be exposed to spraydrift from aerial applications of pesticides. Pesticide use can also result in environmental damage to rivers, wildlife and vegetation.

The term "pesticides" commonly includes insecticides, rodenticides, fungicides, herbicides etc as well as substances used as growth regulators, fumigants, insect repellants or attractors and defoliants and desiccants. In addition the European Commission uses the term "biocides" to cover a range of non-agricultural pesticides such as disinfectants, textile and consumer product preservatives and air conditioning biocides; it proposes regulating these in much the same way as the more traditional pesticides.

5.26 EUROPEAN UNION AND INTERNATIONAL MEASURES

At EU level, there are a number of Directives relating to the discharge of dangerous substances, including pesticides to water (see 5.6 above and Appendix 6.6). In addition there are various Directives covering pesticide residues in products of plant origin (e.g. fruit and vegetables) and in animal feeds and products. A 1979 Directive (79/117/EEC) which has subsequently been amended a number of times prohibits the placing on the market and use of plant protection products (i.e. pesticides etc) containing certain active substances; among the substances so far covered are the "drins" group of pesticides, DDT, chlordane, hexachlorocyclohexane, heptachlor, hexachlorobenzene and various mercury compounds. The marketing and use of various dangerous substances, including pentachlorophenol (PCP), is also controlled under Directive 76/769/EEC; in the UK the marketing and use of PCP and its supply for domestic use (which is banned) is regulated under the *Environmental Protection (Control of Injurious Substances) Regulations 1993*.

In 1991, a Directive (91/414/EEC) concerning the placing of plant protection products on the market was adopted; its main purpose is to regulate agricultural pesticides through the establishment of an EU-wide list of approved active ingredients, harmonise approval procedures and to allow for mutual recognition of individual Member States' authorisation procedures. The list of active ingredients will be drawn up progressively as pesticides currently on sale within the EU are examined on human and environmental health and safety grounds. The Directive has been amended a number of times with Directive 94/43 outlining uniform principles for evaluating and authorising pesticides to ensure uniformity throughout the Community. Following a complaint from the European Parliament, the European Court of Justice annulled Directive 94/43 on the basis that it did not adequately protect groundwater, a requirement of the 1991 Directive. The 1994 Directive has now been replaced by Directive 97/57/EC which was adopted in mid-1997. These Directives have been implemented by the *Plant Protection Products Regulations 1995* (SI 887) and subsequent amendments.

A Directive on the placing of biocidal products on the market – 98/8/EC – was adopted in March 1998 and must be implemented by Member States within 24 months. This Directive uses a similar approach to the plant products Directive in aiming to standardise the way in which biocides are registered throughout the EU, protecting human health and the environment; the Directive covers chemicals, including disinfectants, "avicides", "piscicides" and dirt inhibitors (but not biocides for agricultural use) not covered by existing legislation. An annex to the Directive sets out the common principles, including risk assessment criteria, to be applied when authorising biocidal products to enable mutual recognition of authorisations throughout Member States. Member States may however apply stricter standards to protect human health or the environment. Only biocidal products containing an active substance approved under the Directive (on the basis of how safe it is for human health and the environment) may be authorised for use. However products already on the market remain authorised for use until the active substance they contain has been reviewed; the Directive allows Member States ten years to review existing active substances. The Health and Safety Executive will be drawing up Regulations to implement the Directive.

In addition, the European Commission's Fifth Action Programme, *Towards Sustainability*, includes as an objective the "significant reduction of pesticide use . . . and conversion of farmers to methods of integrated pest control".

In the UK, the pesticide related Directives have been implemented mainly through Part III of the *Food and Environment Protection Act 1985* and the *Control of Pesticide Regulations 1986* and 1997 Amendment Regulations made under the Act, and the *Plant Protection Product Regulations 1995* (SI 887). The pesticide residues Directives are implemented through the *Pesticides (Maximum Residue Levels in Food) Regulations 1988* in England, Scotland and Wales, with similar Regulations applying in Northern Ireland.

In 1990 the Third North Sea Conference (see 5.21 above) also agreed measures to reduce discharges of certain pesticides into the North Sea. In 1985 the United Nations Food and Agriculture Organisation adopted a *Code of Practice on the International Distribution and Use of Pesticides*. This is mainly concerned with ensuring that pesticides restricted or banned in the country of origin are not freely available or dumped on other countries.

In September 1998, the International Convention on Trade in Hazardous Chemicals and Pesticides was approved with 95 signatories, including the EU. Amongst other things, the Convention bans the export of any chemical or pesticide which has itself been banned or severely restricted in at least two other countries, unless the importing country gives its specific (prior) consent; the Convention will initially apply to a list of 22 pesticides and five industrial chemicals. The Convention will need ratification by 50 states before it can come into force, but is likely to be implemented on a voluntary basis until it formally comes into force.

5.27 REGULATORY CONTROLS

The main legislation controlling the use of pesticides is Part III of the *Food and Environment Protection Act 1985* (FEPA), and Regulations made under it. Also of relevance are the *Control of Substances Hazardous to Health Regulations 1994* which are intended to safeguard employees' health (see this chapter, below, and chapter 2, 2.14.2). The disposal of pesticides and pesticides containers is covered by Part II of the *Environmental Protection Act 1990* and by the *Water Resources Act 1991* (Scotland – COPA) (see this chapter and chapter 4). The *Water Supply (Water Quality) Regulations 1989* include maximum admissible concentrations for pesticides and related products – see this chapter 5.17.1c and Appendix 5.3b.

Additional controls on the use of pesticides in designated Environmentally Sensitive Areas are contained in the *Agriculture Act 1986*.

5.27.1 Food and Environment Protection Act 1985, Part III

This Part of the Act aims to protect the health of human beings, creatures and plants, to safeguard the environment and to secure safe, efficient and humane methods of controlling pests. Pesticides are defined as any substance, preparation or organism prepared or used for destroying any pest. The definition therefore includes herbicides, fungicides, insecticides, wood preservatives etc.

The Act provides Ministers with power, by regulation or order, to control the import, sale, supply, storage, use and advertisement of pesticides; to set maximum pesticide residue levels in food, crops and feeding stuffs; to make information supplied in connection with the control of pesticides available to the public. Under the Act an Advisory Committee on Pesticides was established and Codes of Practice published.

The Advisory Committee on Pesticides (ACP) consists of government appointed experts. The ACP considers manufacturers' applications for approval of pesticides and makes recommendations to government; it also reviews existing approvals, reviews safety and can make recommendations regarding revocation or amendments to approvals. A number of expert advisory panels advise the ACP on various issues relating to pesticide approvals.

There is limited public access to information on pesticides data: since 1986 evaluation data on newly approved or reviewed pesticides has been published, with manufacturers' supporting data available on request. In 1992, public access was extended to cover pesticides approved before 1986; fact sheets on older pesticides are also to be published. It should be noted that access to manufacturers' data is limited: information is not available on active ingredients and formulation specification and composition; production methods; names and addresses of laboratories, sites, personnel and individual medical records. People requesting access have to sign an undertaking that they will make no commercial use of the information; access is by "reading room facility" and while notetaking is allowed, photocopying is not.

The monthly Pesticides Register gives information on regulatory and other policy issues and the ACP publishes reports on items discussed at its meetings.

5.27.2 Control of Pesticides Regulations 1986 (SI 1510), as amended

These Regulations, define the types of pesticides subject to control; they apply in England, Scotland and Wales and came into force in October 1986, with similar legislation (1987) applying in Northern Ireland. The Regulations implement those sections of FEPA relating to the approval, advertisement, sale, supply, storage and use (including aerial spraying) of pesticides – all these activities are prohibited unless products have been formally approved for use, conditions of approval observed and additional conditions set out in "Consents" are met. Two statutory codes of practice – see below – were issued by MAFF in 1990 giving guidance on implementation of the Regulations.

The Control of Pesticides (Amendment) Regulations 1997 (SI 188), which came into force on 31 January 1997, amend the 1986 Regulations to:

- clarify that they apply to: any pesticide, or substance, preparation or organism prepared or used as plant or wood protection product; plant growth regulator; to give protection from harmful creatures or to make them harmless; to control organisms with harmful or unwanted effects on water systems or buildings, other structures or manufactured products; to protect animals against ectoparasites;
- require Consents for the advertisement of pesticides, the sale, supply, storage of pesticides, and for their use (including aerial use – see also 5.28.4b below) to include the conditions which are set out in Schedules 1 - 4 of the Regulations;
- clarify that in the event of breach of an approval or of a Consent, Ministers may require persons to recover pesticides from the market; empower Ministers to seize and dispose of a pesticide or require the holder of an approval or other person to dispose of it; where a pesticide has been imported into Great Britain or Northern Ireland in contravention of the Regulations (1987 Regulations in NI), to require, in writing, that it is exported again within a specified period;
- amend the rules covering access to information: Ministers may make evaluation documents available to the public and may charge a fee for supplying a copy; a person who has either inspected or paid or received a copy of an evaluation document may then make a request to the Minister to inspect the relevant study report; access to studies commissioned by government (including those produced to meet data requirements set in the course of a reviews or approvals are included; the use for commercial purposes or publication of any data is prohibited unless approval in writing has been received from the Minister.

"Consents" are prepared by the Pesticides Safety Division of the Ministry of Agriculture, Fisheries and Food and updated from time to time. They are regularly updated and published in the Pesticides Register and the annual MAFF/HSE reference book on Pesticides – this latter also lists the pesticides approved under the Regulations. MAFF also publishes The COPR Handbook – a Guide to the Policies, Procedures and Data Requirements relating to their Control under the *Control of Pesticides Regulations 1986*. This also provides detailed information on pesticide legislation and guidance on registration under the Regulations.

Since April 1992 local authorities have been responsible for enforcing those sections of the Regulations which relate to the advertisement, sale, supply, storage and use of pesticides from a variety of commercial premises (e.g. shops, garden centres, sports grounds, hotels) and also domestic premises. Those parts of the Regulations relating to health and safety (e.g. storage and use) are dealt with by environmental health departments; the advertising, sale and supply of pesticides are the responsibility of trading standards departments.

The actual enforcement powers are contained in section 19 of FEPA. Authorised officers of the local authorities have powers of entry and inspection where they suspect infringement of the Regulations. While they may take photocopies of documents and records and photographs, they do not have powers to seize and destroy pesticides – only Ministers have this power. Where the local authority enforcement officer is of the opinion that an offence has been committed in respect of Regulation 4, e.g. breach of consent, it can serve a notice detailing infringements, and time within which remedial action should be taken.

5.27.3 Control of Substances Hazardous to Health Regulations 1994 (SI 3246)

These Regulations came into force on 16 January 1995, replacing the original 1988 Regulations which came into force on 1 October 1989. They apply in England, Scotland and Wales and cover a wide range of substances, including agricultural and non-agricultural pesticides; their purpose is to prevent exposure to all toxic or hazardous substances used in the work place which can harm health. New Regulations replacing and consolidating the 1994 Regulations and subsequent amendments were due to come into force in January 1999. A summary of requirements under COSHH is given in chapter 2, 2.14.2. The Regulations are enforced by the Health and Safety Executive.

Suspected cases of poisoning or death from exposure to pesticides in the course of work should be reported to the HSE and to the Pesticides Incidents Appraisal Panel (PIAP). Incidents within the home or outside should be reported to the local environmental health department and to the PIAP.

5.27.4 Codes of Practice

(a) Code of Practice for Suppliers of Pesticides to Agriculture, Horticulture and Forestry 1990

The Code covers construction of storage facilities, transportation of pesticides and disposal; a revised version was expected during summer 1997. Anyone involved in supplying or selling pesticides, or who stores more than 200 kg or litres of pesticides must hold a certificate of competence from the British Agrochemical Standards Inspection Scheme. Before storing pesticides, the relevant water authority, water undertakers, environmental health departments and emergency services must be consulted over safety and pollution control requirements.

While failure to observe both this Code and the one following is not in itself an offence, breach of them may be taken as evidence in any proceedings for breach of the Regulations.

(b) Code of Practice for the Safe Use of Pesticides on Farms and Holdings 1990

This Code deals with responsibilities under both the *Control of Pesticide Regulations 1986* and the *Control of Substances Hazardous to Health Regulations 1994* (see chapter 2). The main areas of the Code of relevance to pollution control are the prevention of spraydrift and the disposal of waste pesticides and containers. Other areas covered by the Code include user training and certification, application methods, protection of wildlife and protection of local residents and walkers, and record keeping. A similar Code (1992) applies in Northern Ireland.

A revised Code which is likely to include methods of integrated pest management and good plant protection practice is being finalised.

Prevention of Spraydrift

Aerial application of pesticides requires an Aerial Application Certificate under the *Air Navigation Order 1985* and approval of the pesticide specifically for aerial application under the *Control of Pesticides Regulations* (see above, 5.28.2). Additional conditions to be complied with are set out in Schedule 4 to the 1997 COP Amendment Regulations and will be reiterated in the Code of Practice.

Among the organisations and individuals to be notified in writing in advance if spraying is to take place within a specified distance or adjacent to their land or buildings are:

- local, marine or national nature reserves and Sites of Special Scientific Interest (not less than 72 hours' notice);
- if spraying is adjacent to or within 250 metres of water, the

appropriate area office of the Environment Agency or SEPA (not less than 72 hours' notice); specific consent must be obtained if it is intended to spray aquatic weeds or weeds on the banks of watercourses or lakes;

- local chief environmental health officer, farmers, growers, landowners, residents, hospitals and schools (24 - 48 hours' notice); local beekeepers spray warning scheme (not less than 48 hours' notice).

Details to be included on the notification include name, address and telephone number of person carrying out spraying; pesticide to be used; time and date of spraying; confirmation that similar information has been sent to the chief environmental health officer. Records of aerial spraying (including details of the pesticide used, aircraft, name and address of pilot, flight times, unusual occurrences which affected the application) must be retained for not less than three years. The conditions of the Consent also specify that aircraft be at least 200 feet above and 60 metres horizontally (30 metres with written consent of the occupier) from any occupied building and its curtilage, children's playgrounds, sportsgrounds and buildings with livestock; the aircraft should also be no less than 250 feet from ground level when over a motorway, or no less than 100 feet from other public highways. Other requirements relate to wind velocity, ground markers and warning signs for pedestrians and motorists.

Disposal of Waste Pesticides and Containers

In this respect, both the *Water Resources Act 1991* and Part I of the *Control of Pollution Act 1974* (re-enacted in Part II of the *Environmental Protection Act 1990*) are also applicable.

Under section 85 of the *Water Resources Act*, it is an offence to abandon or dispose of poisonous, noxious or polluting waste on any land (including agriculture premises) where it is likely to pose an environmental hazard; it is also an offence to cause or knowingly permit any poisonous, noxious or polluting matter to enter controlled waters, and in any case this requires a Consent to Discharge from the Environment Agency (see 5.15.3a above). Discharge of pesticide waste to sewers requires a trade effluent consent.

The Code of Practice says that on the whole, empty containers should not be re-used, but should be thoroughly cleaned, and then punctured or crushed; such containers can then usually be disposed of at licensed disposal sites.

In certain cases, pesticide containers may be buried on site with special attention being paid to ensuring no risk of pollution to surface or groundwater; the burial site should also be clearly marked for future identification.

Where it is proposed to burn pesticide containers, care must be taken to adhere to relevant clean air legislation and the Code gives guidance on minimising smoke and nuisance from any burning.

(c) Code on the Safe Use of Pesticides for Non-Agricultural Purposes

This Code drawn up by the Health and Safety Executive was published in 1991 and provides advice on compliance with the COSHH Regulations (see chapter 2, 2.14.2). It is aimed at all those involved in the use of non-agricultural pesticides, including those engaged in amenity horticulture, wood preservation, the application of anti-fouling paints, public hygiene pest control and commercial forestry. Topics covered include undertaking a COSHH assessment, prevention or control of exposure, use of control measures, health surveillance and information, and instruction and training for operators.

APPENDICES

APPENDIX 1.1

ENVIRONMENTAL PROTECTION (PRESCRIBED PROCESSES AND SUBSTANCES) REGULATIONS 1991 (AS AMENDED)

Schedule 1 to the 1991 Regulations (as amended, 1992, 1993, 1994 and 1995) details the processes subject to integrated pollution control (Part A processes), and those subject to air pollution control (Part B processes).

Process Guidance Notes for Part A and Part B processes are listed in Appendices 1.3 and 2.1, respectively.

PRESCRIBED PROCESSES

CHAPTER 1: FUEL PRODUCTION PROCESSES, COMBUSTION PROCESSES (INCLUDING POWER GENERATION)

1.1 Gasification and Associated Processes

PART A

(a) Reforming natural gas.
(aa) Refining natural gas if that process is related to another Part A process or is likely to involve the use in any 12 month period of 1000 tonnes or more of natural gas.
(b) Odorising natural gas or liquified petroleum gas if that process is related to another Part A process.
(c) Producing gas from coal, lignite, oil or other carbonaceous material or from mixtures thereof other than from sewage or the biological degradation of waste, unless carried on as part of a process which is a combustion process (whether or not that process falls within section 1.3 of this schedule).
(d) Purifying or refining any product of any of the processes described in paragraphs (a), (b) or (c) or converting it into a different product.

In this section "carbonaceous material" includes such materials as charcoal, coke, peat and rubber.

PART B

(a) Odorising natural gas or liquified petroleum gas, except where that process is related to a Part A process.
(b) Blending odorant for use with natural gas or liquified petroleum gas.
(c) Any process for refining natural gas not falling within paragraph (aa) of Part A of this Section.

In paragraph (c) of Part B of this section "refining natural gas" does not include refining mains gas.

1.2 Carbonisation and Associated Processes

PART A

(a) The pyrolysis, carbonisation, distillation, liquefaction, partial oxidation or other heat treatment of coal (other than the drying of coal), lignite, oil, other carbonaceous material (as defined in section 1.1) or mixtures thereof otherwise than with a view to gasification or making of charcoal.
(b) The purification or refining of any of the products of a process mentioned in paragraph (a) or its conversion into a different product.

Nothing in paragraph (a) or (b) refers to the use of any substance as a fuel or its incineration as a waste or to any process for the treatment of sewage.

In paragraph (a), the heat treatment of oil does not include heat treatment of waste oil or waste emulsions containing oil in order to recover oil.

PART B

No Processes.

1.3 Combustion Processes

PART A

(a) Burning any fuel in a combustion appliance with a net rated thermal input of 50 megawatts or more;
(b) [omitted - 1995 amendment Regulations]
(c) Burning any of the following in an appliance with a net rated thermal input of 3 megawatts or more otherwise than as a process which is related to a Part B process -
  (i) waste oil;
  (ii) recovered oil;
  (iii) any fuel manufactured from, or comprising, any other waste.

For the purposes of paragraph (a) above, where

(i) two or more boilers or furnaces with an aggregate net rated thermal input of 50 megawatts or more (disregarding any boiler or furnace with a net rated thermal input of less than 3 megawatts); or
(ii) two or more gas turbines or compression ignition engines with an aggregate net rated thermal input of 50 megawatts or more (disregarding any such turbine or engine with a net rated thermal input of less than 3 megawatts),

are operated by the same person at the same location those boilers or furnaces or, as the case may be, those turbines or engines, shall be treated as a single combustion appliance with a net rated thermal input of 50 megawatts or more.

Nothing in this part of this section applies to the burning of any fuel in a boiler, furnace or other appliance with a net rated thermal input of less than 3 megawatts.

PART B

The following processes unless carried on in relation to and as part of any Part A process -

(a) Burning any fuel in a boiler or furnace with a net rated thermal input of not less than 20 megawatts (but less than 50 megawatts);
(b) Burning any fuel in a gas turbine or compression ignition engine with a net rated thermal input of not less than 20 megawatts (but less than 50 megawatts);
(c) Burning as fuel in an appliance with a net rated thermal input of less than 3 megawatts waste oil or recovered oil;
(d) Burning, in an appliance with a net rated thermal input of less than 3 megawatts solid fuel which has been manufactured from waste by a process involving the application of heat;
(e) Burning, in any appliance, fuel manufactured from, or including, waste (other than waste oil or recovered oil or such fuel as is mentioned in paragraph (d)) if the appliance has a net rated thermal input of less than 3 megawatts but at least 0.4 megawatts or is used together with (whether or not it is operated simultaneously with) other appliances which each have a net rated thermal input of less than 3 megawatts and the aggregate net rated thermal input of all the appliances is at least 0.4 megawatts.

In paragraph (c) of Part A and paragraph (e) of Part B, "fuel" does not include gas produced by biological degradation of waste; for the purpose of this section -

"net rated thermal input" is the rate at which fuel can be burned at the maximum continuous rating of the appliance multiplied by the net calorific value of the fuel and expressed as megawatts thermal; and

"waste oil" means any mineral based lubricating or industrial oil which has become unfit for the use for which it was intended and, in particular, used combustion engine oil, gearbox oil, mineral lubricating oil, oil for turbines and hydraulic oil; and

"recovered oil" means waste oil which has been processed before being used.

1.4 Petroleum Processes

PART A

(a) The loading, unloading or other handling of, the storage of or the physical, chemical or thermal treatment of -

(i) crude oil;
(ii) stabilised crude petroleum;
(iii) crude shale oil;
(iv) if related to another process described in this paragraph, any associated gas or condensate.

(b) [omitted - 1994 amendment Regulations.]

(c) Any process not falling within any other description in this Schedule by which the product of any process described in paragraph (a) above is subject to further refining or conversion or is used (otherwise than as a fuel or solvent) in the manufacture of a chemical.

PART B

The following processes unless falling within a description in Part A of this Section -

(a) the storage of petrol in stationary storage tanks at a terminal, or the loading or unloading of petrol into or from road tankers, rail tankers or inland waterway vessels at a terminal;

(b) the unloading of petrol into stationary storage tanks at a service station, other than an exempt service station, if the total quantity of petrol unloaded into such tanks at the service station in any 12 month period is likely to be equal to or greater than 100 m^3.

Paragraph 2(1) of Schedule 2 shall not apply to a process described in paragraph (b) of this Section.

In this part of this section:

"inland waterway vessel" means a vessel, other than a sea-going vessel, having a total dead weight of 15 tonnes or more;

"petrol" means any petroleum derivative, with or without additives, having a reid vapour pressure of 27.6 kilopascals or more which is intended for use as a fuel for motor vehicles, other than liquefied petroleum gas;

"service station" means any premises where petrol is dispensed to motor vehicle fuel tanks from stationary storage tanks;

"exempt service station" means a service station:

(a) which was not in operation, and for the construction of which planning permission was not granted, before 31 December 1995;

(b) at which the total quantity of petrol unloaded into stationary storage tanks does not exceed 500 m^3 in any twelve month period; and

(c) which

i is situated in one of the following local government areas established by section 1 of the Local Government etc (Scotland) Act 1994:
- Argyll and Bute;
- Moray;
- Orkney Islands;
- Shetland Islands;
- Western Isles; or

ii is situated in the local government area of Aberdeenshire established by that section and outside the Aberdeen area the boundary of which is shown as "the derogated boundary: Aberdeen area" on the maps contained in the volume of maps entitled "Volume of maps indicating the extent of derogated areas for new small petrol stations under the Environmental

Protection (Prescribed Processes and Substances Etc) (Amendment) (Petrol Vapour Recovery) Regulations 1996" ("the maps"); or

iii is situated in the local government area of Highland established by that section and outside the Inverness area the boundary of which is shown on the maps as "the derogated boundary: Inverness area"; or

iv is situated in the local government area of Angus, Perth and Kinross or Stirling established by that section and to the north of the line shown on the maps as "the derogated boundary: Central Scotland";

"terminal" means any premises which are used for the storage and loading of petrol into road tankers, rail tankers or inland waterway vessels;

and other expressions which are also used in European Parliament and Council Directive 94/63/EC on the control of VOC emissions resulting from the storage of petrol and its distribution from terminals to service stations have the same meaning as in that Directive.

CHAPTER 2: METAL PRODUCTION AND PROCESSING

2.1 Iron and Steel

PART A

(a) Loading, unloading or otherwise handling or storing iron ore except in the course of mining operations;
(b) Loading, unloading or otherwise handling or storing burnt pyrites;
(c) Crushing, grading, grinding, screening, washing or drying iron ore or any mixture of iron ore and other materials;
(d) Blending or mechanically mixing grades of iron ore or iron ore with other materials;
(e) Pelletising, calcining, roasting or sintering iron ore or any mixture of iron ore and other materials;
(f) Making, melting or refining iron, steel or any ferrous-alloy in any furnace other than a furnace described in Part B of this Section;
(g) Any process for the refining or making of iron, steel or any ferrous-alloy in which air or oxygen or both are used unless related to a process described in Part B of this Section;
(h) The desulphurisation of iron, steel or any ferrous-alloy made by a process described in this Part of this Section;
(i) Heating iron, steel or any ferrous-alloy (whether in a furnace or other appliance) to remove grease, oil or any other non-metallic contaminant (including such operations as the removal by heat of plastic or rubber covering from scrap cable), if related to another process described in this Part of this Section;
(j) Any foundry process (including ancillary foundry operations such as the manufacture and recovery of moulds, the reclamation of sand, fettling, grinding and shot-blasting) if related to another process described in this Part of this Section;
(k) [omitted - 1994 amendment Regulations.]
(l) Handling slag in conjunction with a process described in paragraph (f) or (g).
(m) Any process for rolling iron, steel or any ferrous alloy carried on in relation to any process described in paragraph (f) or (g), and any process carried on in conjunction with such rolling involving the scarfing or cutting with oxygen of iron, steel or any ferrous alloy.

Nothing in paragraph (a) or (b) of this Part of this Section applies to the handling or storing of other minerals in association with the handling or storing of iron ore or burnt pyrites.

A process does not fall within paragraph (a), (b), (c) or (d) of this Part of this Section unless -

(i) it is carried on as part of or is related to a process falling within a paragraph of this Part of this Section other than paragraph (a), (b), (c) or (d); or

(ii) it consists of, forms part of or is related to a process which is likely to involve the unloading in any 12 month period of more than 500,000 tonnes of iron ore or burnt pyrites or, in aggregate, both.

PART B

(a) Making or refining iron, steel or any ferrous-alloy in -
  (i) an electric arc furnace with a designed holding capacity of less than 7 tonnes; or
  (ii) a cupola, crucible furnace, reverberatory furnace, rotary furnace, induction furnace or resistance furnace;
(b) Any process for the refining or making of iron, steel or any ferrous alloy in which air or oxygen or both are used, if related to a process described in this Part of this Section;
(c) The desulphurisation of iron, steel or any ferrous-alloy, if the process does not fall within paragraph (h) of Part A of this Section;
(d) Any such process as is described in paragraph (i) of Part A above, if not falling within that paragraph but a process does not fall within this paragraph if -
  (i) it is a process for heating iron, steel or any ferrous-alloy in one or more furnaces or other appliances the primary combustion chambers of which have in aggregate a net rated thermal input of less than 0.2 megawatts;
  (ii) it does not involve the removal by heat of plastic or rubber covering from scrap cable or of any asbestos contaminant; and
  (iii) it is not related to any other process described in this Part of this Section.
(e) Any foundry process (including ancillary foundry operations such as the manufacture and recovery of moulds, the reclamation of sand, fettling, grinding and shot-blasting) if related to another process described in this Part of this Section;
(f) Any other process involving the casting of iron, steel or any ferrous alloy from deliveries of 50 tonnes or more at one time of molten metal.

Any description of a process in this Section includes, where the process produces slag, the crushing, screening or grading or other treatment of the slag if that process is related to the process in question.

In this Section "net rated thermal input" has the same meaning as in Section 1.3.

In this Section and Section 2.2; "ferrous alloy" means an alloy of which iron is the largest constituent, or equal to the largest constituent, by weight, whether or not that alloy also has a non-ferrous metal content greater than any percentage specified in Section 2.2 below, and "non-ferrous metal alloy" shall be construed accordingly.

2.2 Non-ferrous Metals

PART A

(a) The extraction or recovery from any material -
  (i) by chemical means or the use of heat of any non-ferrous metal or alloy of non-ferrous metal or any compound of a non-ferrous metal: and
  (ii) by electrolytic means, of aluminium,

if the process may result in the release into the air of particulate matter or any metal, metalloid or any metal or metalloid compound or in the release into water of a substance described in Schedule 5 [see Appendix 1.2] and does not fall within a description set out within paragraph (b) of Part B of this Section.

In this paragraph "material" includes ores, scrap and other waste.

(b) The mining of zinc or tin where the process may result in the release into water of cadmium or any compound of cadmium.
(c) The refining of any non-ferrous metal (other than the electrolytic refining of copper) or

non-ferrous metal alloy except where the process is related to a process falling within a description in paragraphs (a), (c) or (d) of Part B of this Section.

(d) Any process other than a process described in paragraphs (b), (c) or (d) of Part B of this Section for making or melting any non-ferrous metal or non-ferrous metal alloy in a furnace, bath or other holding vessel if the furnace, bath or vessel employed has a designed holding capacity of 5 tonnes or more.

(e) Any process for producing, melting or recovering by chemical means or by the use of heat lead or any lead alloy, if -

 (i) the process may result in the release into the air of particulate matter or smoke which contains lead; and

 (ii) in the case of lead alloy, the percentage by weight of lead in the alloy in molten form exceeds 23% if the alloy contains copper and 2% in other cases.

(ee) Any process for recovering any of the elements listed below if the process may result in the release into the air of particulate matter or smoke which contains any of those elements -
gallium
indium
palladium
tellurium
thallium.

(f) Any process for producing, melting or recovering (whether by chemical means or by electrolysis or by the use of heat), cadmium or mercury or any alloy containing more than 0.05% by weight of either of those metals or of both of those metals in aggregate.

(g) Any manufacturing or repairing process involving the manufacture or use of beryllium or selenium or any alloy of one or both of those metals if the process may occasion the release into the air of any substance described in Schedule 4 [see Appendix 1.2]; but a process does not fall within this paragraph by reason solely of its involving the melting of any alloy or beryllium if that alloy contains less than 0.1% by weight of beryllium in molten form and the process falls within a description in paragraph (a) or (d) of Part B of this Section.

(h) The heating in a furnace or other appliance of any non-ferrous metal or non-ferrous metal alloy for the purpose of removing grease, oil or any other non-metallic contaminant (including such operations as the removal by heat of plastic or rubber covering from scrap cable) if related to another process described in this Part of this Section.

 (i) Any foundry process (including ancillary foundry operations such as the manufacture and recovery of moulds, the reclamation of sand, fettling, grinding and shot-blasting) if related to another process described in this Part of this Section.

(j) [omitted - 1994 amendment Regulations.]

(k) Pelletising, calcining, roasting or sintering any non-ferrous metal ore or any mixture of such ore and other materials.

PART B

(a) The making or melting of any non-ferrous metal or non-ferrous metal alloy (other than tin or any alloy which, in molten form, contains 50% or more by weight of tin in any furnace, bath or other holding vessel with a designed holding capacity of less than 5 tonnes (together with any incidental refining).

(b) The separation of copper, aluminium, magnesium or zinc from mixed scrap by differential melting.

(bb) The fusion of calcined bauxite for the production of artificial corundum.

(c) Melting zinc or a zinc alloy in conjunction with a galvanising process.

(d) Melting zinc, aluminium or magnesium or an alloy of one or more of these metals in conjunction with a die-casting process.

(e) Any such process as is described in paragraph (h) of Part A above, if not related to another process described in that Part; but a process does not fall within this paragraph if -

(i) it involves the use of one or more furnaces or other appliances the primary combustion chambers of which have in aggregate a net rated thermal input of less than 0.2 megawatts; and
(ii) it does not involve the removal by heat of plastic or rubber covering from scrap cable or of any asbestos contaminant.

(f) Any foundry process (including ancillary foundry operations such as the manufacture and recovery of moulds, the reclamation of sand, fettling, grinding and shot-blasting) if related to another process described in this Part of this Section.
(g) [omitted - 1995 amendment Regulations]

The processes described in paragraph (a), (c) and (d) above include any related process for the refining of any non-ferrous metal or non-ferrous metal alloy.

Nothing in this section shall be taken to prescribe the processes of hand soldering or flow soldering.

In this section "net rated thermal input" has the same meaning as in Section 1.3.

2.3 Smelting Processes

[omitted - 1994 amendment Regulations.]

CHAPTER 3: MINERAL INDUSTRIES

3.1 Cement & Lime Manufacture and Associated Processes

PART A

(a) Making cement clinker.
(b) Grinding cement clinker.
(c) Any of the following processes, where the process is related to a process described in paragraph (a) or (b), namely blending cement; putting cement into silos for bulk storage; removing cement from silos in which it has been stored in bulk; and any process involving the use of cement in bulk, including the bagging of cement and cement mixtures, the batching of ready-mixed concrete and the manufacture of concrete blocks and other cement products.
(d) The heating of calcium carbonate or calcium magnesium carbonate for the purpose of making lime where the process is likely to involve the heating in any 12 month period of 5,000 tonnes or more of either substance or, in aggregate, of both.
(e) The slaking of lime for the purpose of making calcium hydroxide or calcium magnesium hydroxide where the process is related to a process described in paragraph (d) above.

PART B

(a) Any of the following processes, if not related to a process falling within a description in Part A of this Section -
(i) storing, loading or unloading cement or cement clinker in bulk prior to further transportation in bulk;
(ii) blending cement in bulk or using cement in bulk other than at a construction site, including the bagging of cement and cement mixtures, the batching of ready-mixed concrete and the manufacture of concrete blocks and other cement products.
(b) The slaking of lime for the purpose of making calcium hydroxide or calcium magnesium hydroxide unless related to and carried on as part of a process falling within another description in this Schedule.
(c) The heating of calcium carbonate or calcium magnesium carbonate for the purpose of making lime where the process is not likely to involve the heating in any 12 month period of 5,000 tonnes or more of either substance or, in aggregate, of both.

3.2 Processes involving Asbestos

PART A

(a) Producing raw asbestos by extraction from the ore except where the process is directly associated with the mining of the ore.

(b) The manufacture and, where related to the manufacture, the industrial finishing of the following products where raw asbestos is involved -
asbestos cement
asbestos cement products
asbestos fillers
asbestos filters
asbestos floor coverings
asbestos friction products
asbestos insulating board
asbestos jointing, packaging and reinforcement material
asbestos packing
asbestos paper or card
asbestos textiles.

(c) The stripping of asbestos from railway vehicles except -
(i) in the course of the repair or maintenance of the vehicle;
(ii) in the course of recovery operations following an accident; or
(iii) where the asbestos is permanently bonded in cement or in any other material (including plastic, rubber or a resin).

(d) The destruction by burning of a railway vehicle if asbestos has been incorporated in, or sprayed on to, its structure.

PART B

The industrial finishing of any product mentioned in paragraph (b) of Part A of this Section if the process does not fall within that paragraph.

In this section, "asbestos" means any of the following fibrous silicates -

actinolite, amosite, anthophyllite, chrysotile, crocidolite and tremolite

3.3 Other Mineral Fibres

PART A

Manufacturing

(i) glass fibre;
(ii) any fibre from any mineral other than asbestos.

PART B

No Processes.

3.4 Other Mineral Processes

PART A

No Processes.

PART B

(a) The crushing, grinding or other size reduction (other than the cutting of stone) or the grading, screening or heating of any designated mineral or mineral product except where -

(i) the process falls within a description in another Section of this Schedule;
(ii) the process is related to and carried on as part of another process falling within such a description; or
(iii) the operation of the process is unlikely to result in the release into the air of particulate matter.

(b) Any of the following processes unless carried on at an exempt location or as part of a process falling within another description in this Schedule -
(i) crushing, grinding or otherwise breaking up coal or coke or any other coal product;
(ii) screening, grading or mixing coal, or coke or any other coal product;
(iii) loading or unloading petroleum coke, coal, coke or any other coal product except unloading on retail sale.

(c) The crushing, grinding or other size reduction with machinery designed for that purpose of bricks, tiles or concrete.

(d) Screening the product of any such process as is described in paragraph (c).

(e) Coating roadstone with tar or bitumen.

(f) Loading, unloading, or storing pulverised fuel ash in bulk prior to further transportation in bulk, unless carried on as part of or in relation to a process falling within another description in this Schedule.

In this section -

"coal" includes lignite;

"designated mineral or mineral product" means -

(i) clay, sand and any other naturally occurring mineral other than coal or lignite;
(ii) metallurgical slag;
(iii) boiler or furnace ash produced from the burning of coal, lignite, coke or any other coal product;
(iv) gypsum which is a by-product of any process; and

"exempt location" means -

(i) any premises used for the sale of petroleum coke, coal, coke or any coal product where the throughput of such substances at those premises in any 12 month period is in aggregate likely to be less than 10,000 tonnes; or
(ii) any premises to which petroleum coke, coal, coke or any coal product is supplied only for use there.

"retail sale" means sale to the final consumer.

Nothing in this section applies to any process carried on underground.

3.5 Glass Manufacture and Production

PART A

The manufacture of glass frit or enamel frit and its use in any process where that process is related to its manufacture and the aggregate quantity of such substances manufactured in any 12 month period is likely to be 100 tonnes or more.

PART B

(a) The manufacture of glass at any location where the person concerned has the capacity to make 5,000 tonnes or more of glass in any 12 month period, and any process involving the use of glass which is carried on at any such location in conjunction with its manufacture.

(b) The manufacture of glass where the use of lead or any lead compound is involved.

(c) The making of any glass product where lead or any lead compound has been used in the manufacture of the glass except -
(i) the making of products from lead glass blanks;

(ii) the melting, or mixing with another substance, of glass manufactured elsewhere to produce articles such as ornaments or road paint;

(d) Polishing or etching glass or glass products in the course of the manufacturing process if -
(i) hydrofluoric acid is used;
(ii) hydrogen fluoride may be released into the air.

(e) The manufacture of glass frit or enamel frit and its use in any process where that process is related to its manufacture if not falling within Part A of this Section.

3.6 Ceramic Production

PART A

Firing heavy clay goods or refractory material in a kiln where a reducing atmosphere is used for a purpose other than coloration.

PART B

(a) Firing heavy clay goods or refractory material (other than heavy clay goods) in a kiln where the process does not fall within a description in Part A of this Section.

(b) Vapour glazing earthenware or clay with salts.

"clay" includes a blend of clay with ash, sand or other materials;

"refractory material" means material (such as fireclay, silica, magnesite, chrome-magnesite, sillimanite, sintered alumina, beryllia and boron nitride) which is able to withstand high temperatures and to function as a furnace lining or in other similar high temperature applications.

CHAPTER 4: THE CHEMICAL INDUSTRY

Except where paragraph 2 or 8 of Schedule 2 applies, nothing in this chapter of this Schedule applies to the operation of waste treatment plant.

4.1 Petrochemical Processes

Where a process in this chapter falls within descriptions in different sections, it should be taken to fall within the description in whichever relevant section is first mentioned in the sequence 4.5; 4.2; 4.1; 4.4; 4.3; 4.6; 4.7; 4.8; 4.9.

PART A

(a) Any process for the manufacture of unsaturated hydrocarbons.

(b) Any process for the manufacture of any chemical which involves the use of a product of a process described in sub-paragraph (a).

(c) Any process for the manufacture of any chemical which involves the use of a product of a process described in paragraph (b) otherwise than as a fuel or solvent.

(d) Any process for the polymerisation or co-polymerisation of any unsaturated hydrocarbons (other than the polymerisation or co-polymerisation of a pre-formulated resin or pre-formulated gel coat which contains any unsaturated hydrocarbons, or which contains any product of a process mentioned in paragraph (b) or (c) of Part A of this section) which is likely to involve, in any 12 month period, the polymerisation or co-polymerisation of 50 tonnes or more of unsaturated hydrocarbons or of any such products or, in aggregate, of any combination of those materials or, in aggregate, of any combination of those materials and products.

(e) Any process, if related to and carried on as part of a process falling within another paragraph of this Part of this Section, for the polymerisation or co-polymerisation of any pre-formulated resin or pre-formulated gel coat which contains any unsaturated hydrocarbons, or which contains any product of a process mentioned in paragraph (b) or (c) of Part A of this section, which is likely to involve, in any 12 month period, the polymerisation or co-polymerisation of 100 tonnes or more of unsaturated hydrocarbons or of any such products or, in aggregate, of any combination of those materials and products.

PART B

Any process, unless related to and carried on as part of a process falling within Part A of this section, for the polymerisation or co-polymerisation of any pre-formulated resin or pre-formulated gel coat which contains any unsaturated hydrocarbons, or which contains any product of a process mentioned in paragraph (b) or (c) of Part A of this section, which is likely to involve, in any 12 month period, the polymerisation or co-polymerisation of 100 tonnes or more of unsaturated hydrocarbons or of any such products or, in aggregate, of any combination of those materials and products.

In this section and in section 4.2 "pre-formulated resin or pre-formulated gel coat" means any resin or gel coat which has been formulated before being introduced into the polymerisation or co-polymerisation process (whether or not the resin or gel coat contains a colour pigment, activator or catalyst).

4.2. The Manufacture and Use of Organic Chemicals

PART A

Any of the following processes unless falling within a description set out in Section 6.8 -

(a) The manufacture of styrene or vinyl chloride.

(aa) The polymerisation or co-polymerisation of styrene or vinyl chloride (other than the polymerisation or co-polymerisation of a pre-formulated resin or pre-formulated gel coat which contains any styrene) where the process is likely to involve, in any 12 month period, the polymerisation or co-polymerisation of 50 tonnes or more of either of those materials or, in aggregate, of both.

(ab) Any process, if related to and carried on as part of a process falling within another paragraph of this section, for the polymerisation or co-polymerisation of any pre-formulated resin or pre-formulated gel coat which contains any styrene, which is likely to involve, in any 12 month period, the polymerisation or co-polymerisation of 100 tonnes or more of styrene;

(b) Any process of manufacture involving the use of vinyl chloride.

(c) The manufacture of acetylene, any aldehyde, amine, isocyanate, nitrile, any carboxylic acid or any anhydride or carboxylic acid, any organic sulphur compound or any phenol if the process may result in the release of any of these substances into the air.

(d) Any process for the manufacture of a chemical involving the use of any substance mentioned in paragraph (c) if the process may result in the release of any such substance into the air.

(e) The manufacture or recovery of carbon disulphide.

(f) Any manufacturing process which may result in the release of carbon disulphide into the air.

(g) The manufacture or recovery of pyridine, or of any substituted pyridines.

(h) The manufacture of any organo-metallic compound.

(i) The manufacture, purification or recovery of any designated acrylate.

(j) Any process for the manufacture of a chemical which is likely to involve the use in any 12 month period of 1 tonne or more of any designated acrylate or, in aggregate, of more than one such designated acrylate.

In this part of this Section, "designated acrylate" means any of the following, namely, acrylic acid, substituted acrylic acids, the esters of acrylic acid and the esters of substituted acrylic acids.

PART B

Any process, unless related to and carried on as part of a process falling within Part A of this section, for the polymerisation or co-polymerisation of any pre-formulated resin or pre-formulated gel coat which contains any styrene, which is likely to involve, in any 12 month period, the polymerisation or co-polymerisation of 100 tonnes or more of styrene.

4.3 Acid Processes

PART A

(a) Any process for the manufacture, recovery, concentration or distillation of sulphuric acid or oleum.

(b) Any process for the manufacture of any oxide of sulphur but excluding any combustion or incineration process other than the burning of sulphur.

(c) Any process for the manufacture of a chemical which uses, or may result in the release into the air of, any oxide of sulphur but excluding any combustion or incineration process other than the burning of sulphur and excluding also any process where such a release could only occur as a result of the storage and use of SO_2 in cylinders.

(d) Any process for the manufacture or recovery of nitric acid.

(e) Any process for the manufacture of any acid-forming oxide of nitrogen.

(f) Any other process (except the combustion or incineration of carbonaceous material as defined in section 1.1 of this Schedule) which is not described in Part B of this Section, does not fall within a description in Section 2.1 or 2.2 of this Schedule and is not treated as so falling by virtue of the rules in Schedule 2, and which is likely to result in the release to air of any acid forming oxide of nitrogen.

(g) Any process for the manufacture or purification of phosphoric acid.

PART B

Any process for the surface treatment of metal which is likely to result in the release into the air of any acid-forming oxide of nitrogen and which does not fall within a description in Section 2.1 or 2.2. of this Schedule and is not treated as so falling by virtue of the rules in Schedule 2.

4.4 Processes Involving Halogens

PART A

The following processes if not falling within a description in any other Section of this Schedule -

(a) Any process for the manufacture of fluorine, chlorine, bromine or iodine or of any compound comprising only -
   (i) two or more of these halogens; or
   (ii) any one or more of those halogens and oxygen.

(b) Any process of manufacture which involves the use of, or which is likely to result in the release into the air or water of, any of the four halogens or any of the compounds mentioned in paragraph (a) other than the use of any of them as a pesticide (as defined in Schedule 6 [see Appendix 1.2]).

(c) Any process for the manufacture of hydrogen fluoride, hydrogen chloride, hydrogen bromide or hydrogen iodide or any of their acids.

(d) Any process for the manufacture of chemicals which may result in the release into the air of any of the four compounds mentioned in paragraph (c);

(e) Any process of manufacture (other than the manufacture of chemicals) involving the use of any of the four compounds mentioned in paragraph (c) or any of their acids, which may result in the release of any of those compounds into the air other than the coating, plating or surface treatment of metal.

PART B

No Processes.

4.5 Inorganic Chemical Processes

PART A

(a) The manufacture of hydrogen cyanide or hydrogen sulphide other than in the course of fumigation.

(b) Any manufacturing process involving the use of hydrogen cyanide or hydrogen sulphide.

(c) Any process for the manufacture of a chemical which may result in the release into the air of hydrogen cyanide or hydrogen sulphide.

(d) The production of any compound containing any of the following -
Antimony
Arsenic
Beryllium
Gallium
Indium
Lead
Palladium
Platinum
Selenium
Tellurium
Thallium,
where the process may result in the release into the air of any of those elements or compounds or the release into water of any substance described in Schedule 5 [see Appendix 1.2] in a quantity which, in any 12 month period, exceeds the background quantity by more than the amount specified in relation to the description of substance in column 2 of that Schedule.

(e) The recovery of any compound referred to in paragraph (d) where the process may result in any such release as is mentioned in that paragraph.

(f) The use in any process of manufacture other than the application of a glaze or vitreous enamel, of any element or compound referred to in paragraph (d) where the process may result in such a release as is mentioned in that paragraph.

(g) The production or recovery of any compound of cadmium or mercury.

(h) Any process of manufacture which involves the use of cadmium or mercury or of any compound of either of those elements or which may result in the release into the air of either of those elements or any of their compounds.

(i) The production of any compound of -
Chromium
Manganese
Nickel
Zinc.

(j) The manufacture of any metal carbonyl.

(k) Any process for the manufacture of a chemical involving the use of a metal carbonyl.

(l) The manufacture or recovery of ammonia.

(m) Any process for the manufacture of a chemical which involves the use of ammonia or may result in the release of ammonia into the air other than a process in which ammonia is used only as a refrigerant.

(n) The production of phosphorus or of any oxide, hydride or halide of phosphorus.

(o) Any process for the manufacture of a chemical which involves the use of phosphorus or any oxide, hydride or halide of phosphorus or which may result in the release into the air of phosphorus or of any such oxide, hydride or halide.

(p) The extraction of any magnesium compound from sea water.

PART B

No Processes.

4.6 Chemical Fertiliser Production

PART A

(a) The manufacture of chemical fertilisers.

(b) The conversion of chemical fertilisers into granules.

In this section "chemical fertilisers" means any inorganic chemical to be applied to the soil to promote plant growth; and "inorganic chemical" includes urea; and "manufacture of chemical fertilisers" shall be taken to include any process for blending chemical fertilisers which is related to a process for their manufacture.

PART B

No Processes.

4.7 Pesticide Production

PART A

The manufacture or the formulation of chemical pesticides if the process may result in the release into water of any substance described in Schedule 5 [see Appendix 1.2] in a quantity which, in any 12 month period, exceeds the background quantity by more than the amount specified in relation to the description of substance in column 2 of that Schedule.

PART B

No Processes.

In this section "pesticide" has the same meaning as in Schedule 6 [see Appendix 1.2].

4.8 Pharmaceutical Production

PART A

The manufacture or the formulation of a medicinal product if the process may result in the release into water of any substance described in Schedule 5 [see Appendix 1.2] in a quantity which, in any 12 month period, exceeds the background quantity by more than the amount specified in relation to the description of substance in column 2 of that Schedule.

PART B

No Processes.

In this section, "medicinal product" means any substance or article (not being an instrument, apparatus or appliance) manufactured for use in one of the ways specified in section 130(1) of the Medicines Act 1968.

4.9 The Storage of Chemicals in Bulk

PART A

No Processes - reclassified as Part B - 1994 Amendment Regulations.

PART B

The storage in a tank or tanks, other than as part of a Part A process, and other than in a tank for the time being forming part of a powered vehicle, of any of the substances listed below except where the total capacity of the tanks installed at the location in question in which the relevant substance may be stored is less than the figure specified below in relation to that substance:

any one or more designated acrylates	20 tonnes
acrylonitrile	20 tonnes
anhydrous ammonia	100 tonnes
anhydrous hydrogen fluoride	1 tonne
toluene di-isocyanate	20 tonnes
vinyl chloride monomer	20 tonnes
ethylene	8,000 tonnes

In this Section, "designated acrylate" has the same meaning as in Part A of Section 4.2.

CHAPTER 5: WASTE DISPOSAL AND RECYCLING

5.1 Incineration

PART A

(a) The destruction by burning in an incinerator of any waste chemicals or waste plastic arising from the manufacture of a chemical or the manufacture of a plastic.

(b) The destruction by burning in an incinerator, other than incidentally in the course of burning other waste, of any waste chemicals being, or comprising in elemental or compound form any of the following -
bromine
cadmium
chlorine
fluorine
iodine
lead
mercury
nitrogen
phosphorus
sulphur
zinc.

(bb) The incineration of hazardous waste in an incineration plant, other than in an exempt hazardous incineration plant.

(c) The destruction by burning of any other waste, including animal remains, otherwise than by a process related to and carried on as part of a Part B process, on premises where there is plant designed to incinerate such waste at a rate of 1 tonne or more per hour.

(d) The cleaning for reuse of metal containers used for the transport or storage of a chemical by burning out their residual content.

PART B

(a) The destruction by burning in an incinerator other than an exempt incinerator of any waste, including animal remains, except where related to a Part A process.

(b) The cremation of human remains.

In this section -

"exempt hazardous waste incineration plant" means:

(i) an incineration plant for animal carcases or remains;

(ii) an incineration plant for infectious clinical waste, provided that such waste is not rendered hazardous as a result of the presence of constituents listed in Annex II to Directive 91/689/EEC on hazardous waste other than constituents C35 in that list (infectious substances); or

(iii) a municipal waste incineration plant also burning infectious clinical waste which is not mixed with other wastes which are rendered hazardous as a result of one of the properties listed in Annex III to Directive 91/689/EEC other than property H9 in that list (infectious);

"exempt incinerator" means any incinerator on premises where there is plant designed to incinerate waste, including animal remains, at a rate of not more than 50 kgs per hour, not being an incinerator employed to incinerate clinical waste, sewage sludge, sewage screenings or municipal waste (as defined in Article 1 of EC Directive 89/369/EEC); and for the purposes of this section, the weight of waste shall be determined by reference to its weight as fed into the incinerator;

"hazardous waste" means any solid or liquid waste as defined in Article 1(4) of Directive 91/689/EEC but shall not include the following waste:

(i) combustible liquid wastes, including waste oils as defined in Article 1 of Directive 75/439/EEC on the disposal of waste oils, provided that they meet the following three criteria:

(a) the mass content of polychlorinated aromatic hydrocarbons, e.g. polychlorinated biphenyls or pentachlorinated phenol, amounts to concentrations not higher than those set out in the relevant Community legislation;
(b) these wastes are not rendered hazardous by virtue of containing other constituents listed in Annex II to Directive 91/689/EEC in quantities or concentrations which are inconsistent with the achievement of the objectives set out in Article 4 of Directive 75/442/EEC on waste; and
(c) the net calorific value amounts to at least 30 MJ per kilogramme;

(ii) any combustible liquid wastes which cannot cause, in the flue gas directly resulting from their combustion, emissions other than those from gas oil, as defined in Article 1(1) of Directive 75/716/EEC relating to the sulphur content of liquid fuels or a higher concentration of emissions than those resulting from the combustion of gas oil as so defined;
(iii) hazardous waste resulting from the exploration for and the exploitation of oil and gas resources from off-shore installations and incinerated on board;
(iv) municipal waste covered by Directives 89/369/EEC and 89/429/EEC relating to air pollution from, respectively, new and existing municipal waste incinceration plants;
(v) sewage sludges from the treatment of municipal waste waters which are not rendered hazardous by virtue of containing constituents listed in Annex II to Directive 91/689/EEC in quantities or in concentrations which are inconsistent with the achievement of the objectives set out in Article 4 of Directive 75/442/EEc on waste;

"incineration of hazardous waste in an incineration plant" means the incineration by oxidation of hazardous wastes, with or without recovery of the combustion heat generated, including pretreatment as well as pyrolysis or other thermal treatment processes, for example, plasma process, insofar as their products are subsequently incinerated, and includes the incineration of such wastes as a regular or additional fuel for any industrial process;

"waste" means solid, liquid wastes or gaseous wastes (other than gas produced by biological degradation of waste); and

"clinical waste" in the definition of exempt incinerator means waste (other than waste consisting wholly of animal remains) which falls within sub-paragraph (a) or (b) of the definition of such waste in paragraph (2) of regulation 1 of the Controlled Waste Regulations 1992 (or would fall within one of those sub-paragraphs but for paragraph (4) of the regulation).

5.2 Recovery Processes

PART A

(a) The recovery by distillation of any oil or organic solvent.
(b) The cleaning or regeneration of carbon, charcoal or ion exchange resins by removing matter which is, or includes, any substance described in Schedule 4, 5 or 6.

Nothing in this part of this Section applies to -

(i) The distillation of oil for the productionn or cleaning of vaccum pump oil; or
(ii) A process which is ancillary and related to another process which involves the production or use of the substance which is recovered, cleaned or regenerated.

PART B

No Processes.

5.3 The Production of Fuel from Waste

PART A

Making fuel from waste by any process involving the use of heat other than making charcoal.PART B

No Processes.

CHAPTER 6: OTHER INDUSTRIES

6.1 Paper and Pulp Manufacturing Processes

PART A

(a) The making of paper pulp by a chemical method if the person concerned has the capacity at the location in question to produce more than 25,000 tonnes of paper pulp in any 12 month period.

(b) Any process associated with making paper pulp or paper (including processes connected with the recycling of paper such as de-inking) if the process may result in the release into water of any substance described in Schedule 5 [see Appendix 1.2] in a quantity which, in any 12 month period, exceeds the background quantity by more than the amount specified in relation to the description of substance in column 2 of that Schedule.

In this paragraph "paper pulp" includes pulp made from wood, grass, straw and similar materials and references to the making of paper are to the making of any product using paper pulp.

PART B

No Processes.

6.2 Di-Isocyanate Processes

PART A

(a) Any process for the manufacture of any di-isocyanate or a partly polymerised di-isocyanate.

(b) Any manufacturing process involving the use of toluene di-isocyanate or partly polymerised toluene di-isocyanate if -
  (i) 1 tonne or more of toluene di-isocyanate monomer is likely to be used in any 12 month period; and
  (ii) The process may result in a release into the air which contains toluene di-isocyanate.

(c) [omitted - 1994 amendment Regulations]

(d) The flame bonding of polyurethane foams or polyurethane elastomers, and the hot wire cutting of such substances where such cutting is related to any other Part A process.

PART B

(a) Any process not falling within any other description in this Schedule where the carrying on of the process by the person concerned at the location in question is likely to involve the use in any 12 month period of 5 tonnes or more of any di-isocyanate or of any partly polymerised di-isocyanate or, in aggregate, of both.

(b) Any process not falling within any other description in this Schedule involving the use of toluene di-isocyanate or partly polymerised toluene di-isocyanate if -
  (i) less than 1 tonne of toluene di-isocyanate monomer is likely to be used in any 12 month period; and
  (ii) The process may result in a release into the air which contains toluene di-isocyanate.

(c) The hot wire cutting of polyurethane foams or polyurethane elastomers, except where this process is related to any other Part A process.

6.3 Tar and Bitumen Processes

PART A

Any process not falling within any other description in this Schedule involving -

(a) The distillation of tar or bitumen in connection with any process of manufacture; or
(b) The heating of tar or bitumen for the manufacture of electrodes or carbon-based refractory materials,

where the carrying on of the process by the person concerned at the location in question is likely to involve the use in any 12 month period of 5 tonnes or more of bitumen or, in aggregate, of both.

PART B

Any process not falling within Part A of this Section or within any other description in this Schedule involving -

(a) The heating, but not the distillation, of tar or bitumen in connection with any process of manufacture; or
(b) (unless the process is related to and carried on as part of a process falling within Part A of Section 1.4 of this Schedule) the oxidation of bitumen by blowing air through it,

where the carrying on of the process by the person concerned at the location in question is likely to involve the use in any 12 month period of 5 tonnes or more of tar or of bitumen or, in aggregate, of both.

In this Section the expressions "tar" and "bitumen" include pitch.

6.4 Processes Involving Uranium

[omitted - 1994 amendment Regulations.]

6.5 Coating Processes and Printing

PART A

(a) The application or removal of a coating material containing one or more tributyltin compounds or triphenyltin compounds, if carried out at a shipyard or boatyard at which vessels of a length of 25 metres or more can be built, or maintained or repaired.
(b) The treatment of textiles if the process may result in the release into water of any substance described in Schedule 5 [see Appendix 1.2] in a quantity which, in any 12 month period, exceeds the background quantity by more than the amount specified in relation to the description of substance in column 2 of that Schedule.
(c) [omitted - 1994 amendment Regulations.]

PART B

(a) Any process (other than for the repainting or respraying of or of parts of aircraft or road or railway vehicles) for the application to a substrate of, or the drying or curing after such application of, printing ink or paint or any other coating material as, or in the course of, a manufacturing process where -
    (i) the process may result in the release into the air of particulate matter or of any volatile organic compound; and
    (ii) the carrying on of the process by the person concerned at the location in question is likely to involve the use in any 12 month period of -
        (aa) 20 tonnes or more applied in solid form of any printing ink, paint or other coating material; or
        (bb) 20 tonnes or more of any metal coatings which are sprayed on in molten form; or,

cc) 25 tonnes or more of organic solvents in respect of any cold set web offset printing process or any sheet fed litho printing process or, in respect of any other process, 5 tonnes or more of organic solvents.

(b) Any process for the repainting or respraying of or of parts of road vehicles if the process may result in the release into the air of particulate matter or of any volatile organic compound and the carrying on of the process by the person concerned at the location in question is likely to involve the use of 1 tonne or more of organic solvents in any 12 month period.

(c) Any process for the repainting or respraying of or of parts of aircraft or railway vehicles if the process may result in the release into the air of particulate matter or of any volatile organic compound and the carrying on of the process by the person concerned at the location in question is likely to involve the use in any 12 month period of -

(i) 20 tonnes or more applied in solid form of any paint or other coating material; or

(ii) 20 tonnes or more of any metal coatings which are sprayed on in molten form; or

(iii) 5 tonnes or more of organic solvents.

In this section -

"aircraft" includes gliders and missiles;

"coating material" means paint, printing ink, varnish, laquer, dye, any metal oxide coating, any adhesive coating, any elastomer coating and any metal or plastic coating and any other coating material; and the amount or organic solvents used in a process shall be calculated as -

(a) The total input of organic solvents into the process, including both solvents contained in coating materials and solvents used for cleaning or other purposes; less

(b) Any organic solvents that are removed from the process for re-use or for recovery for re-use.

6.6 The Manufacture of Dyestuffs, Printing Ink & Coating Materials

PART A

Any process for the manufacture of dyestuffs if the process involves the use of hexachlorobenzene.

PART B

Any process

(a) For the manufacture or formulation of a printing ink or any other coating material containing, or involving the use of, an organic solvent, where the carrying on of the process by the person concerned at the location in question is likely to involve the use of 100 tonnes or more of organic solvents in any 12 month period;

(b) For the manufacture of any powder for use as a coating material where there is the capacity to produce 200 tonnes or more of such powder in any 12 month period.

In this section "coating material" has the same meaning as in section 6.5, and the amount of organic solvents used in a process shall be calculated as -

(a) The total input of organic solvents into the process, including both solvents contained in coating materials and solvents used for cleaning or other purposes; less

(b) Any organic solvents (not contained in coating materials) that are removed from the process for re-use or for recovery for re-use.

6.7 Timber Processes

PART A

(a) The curing or chemical treatment as part of a manufacturing process of timber or of products wholly or mainly made of wood if any substance described in Schedule 5 [see Appendix 1.2] is used.
(b) [omitted - 1994 amendment Regulations.]

PART B

The manufacture of products wholly or mainly of wood at any works if the process involves the sawing, drilling, sanding, shaping, turning, planing, curing or chemical treatment of wood relevant processes and the throughput of the works in any 12 month period is likely to exceed -

(i) 10,000 cubic metres, in the case of works at which wood is sawed but is not subjected to any other relevant processes or is subjected only to relevant processes which are exempt processes; or
(ii) 1,000 cubic metres in any other case.

For the purposes of this paragraph relevant processes other than sawing are "exempt processes" where, if no sawing were carried out at the works, the activities carried on there would be treated as not falling within this Part of this Section by virtue of Regulation 4(2). "Throughput" shall be calculated by reference to the amount of wood which is subjected to any of the relevant processes: but where, at the same works, wood is subject to two or more of the relevant processes, no account shall be taken of the second or any subsequent processes; "wood" includes any product consisting wholly or mainly of wood; and "works" includes a sawmill or any other premises on which relevant processes are carried out on wood.

6.8 Processes Involving Rubber

PART A

No Processes.

PART B

(a) The mixing, milling or blending of: -
  (i) natural rubber; or
  (ii) synthetic organic elastomers, if carbon black is used.
(b) Any process which converts the product of a process falling within paragraph (a) into a finished product if related to a process falling within that paragraph.

6.9 The Treatment & Processing of Animal or Vegetable Matter

PART A

Any of the following processes, unless falling within a description in another Section of the Schedule or an exempt process, namely the processing in any way whatsoever, storing or drying by the application of heat of any dead animal (or part thereof) or any vegetable matter if the process may result in the release into water of any substance described in Schedule 5 [see Appendix 1.2] in a quantity which, in any 12 month period, exceeds the background quantity by more than the amount specified in relation to the description of substance in column 2 of that Schedule; but excluding any process for the treatment of effluent so as to permit its discharge into controlled waters or into a sewer unless the treatment process involves the drying of any material with a view to its use as an animal feed stuff.

PART B

(a) Any process mentioned in Part A, of this Section unless an exempt process - but
- (i) where the process has the characteristics described in regulation 4(1)(ii); but
- (ii) may release into the air a substance described in Schedule 4 [see Appendix 1.2] or any offensive smell noticeable outside the premises on which the process is carried on.

(b) Breeding maggots in any case where 5 kg or more of animal or of vegetable matter or, in aggregate, of both are introduced into the process in any week.

In this section -

"animal" includes a bird or a fish; and

"exempt process" means -

(i) any process carried on on a farm or agricultural holding other than the manufacture of goods for sale;

(ii) the manufacture or preparation of food or drink for human consumption but excluding -
- (a) the extraction, distillation or purification of animal or vegetable oil or fat otherwise than as a process incidental to the cooking of food for human consumption;
- (b) any process involving the use of green offal or the boiling of blood except the cooking of food (other than tripe) for human consumption;
- (c) the cooking of tripe for human consumption elsewhere than on premises on which it is to be consumed;

(iii) the fleshing, cleaning and drying of pelts of fur-bearing animals;

(iv) any process carried on in connection with the operation of a knacker's yard, as defined in article 3(1) of the Animal By-Products Order 1992;

(v) any process for the manufacture of soap not falling within a description in Part A of Section 4.2 of this Schedule;

(vi) the storage of vegetable matter otherwise than as part of any prescribed process;

(vii) the cleaning of shellfish shells;

(viii) the manufacture of starch;

(ix) the processing of animal or vegetable matter at premises for feeding a recognised pack of hounds registered under article 10 of the Animal By-Products Order 1992;

(x) the salting of hides or skins, unless related to any other prescribed process;

(xi) any process for composting animal or vegetable matter or a combination of both, except where that process is carried on for the purposes of cultivating mushrooms;

(xii) any process for cleaning, and any related process for drying or dressing, seeds, bulbs, corms or tubers;

(xiii) the drying of grain or pulses;

(xiv) any process for the production of cotton yarn from raw cotton or for the conversion of cotton yarn into cloth;

"food" includes drink, articles and substances of no nutritional value which are used for human consumption, and articles and substances used as ingredients in the preparation of food. and "green offal" means the stomach and intestines of any animal, other than poultry or fish, and their contents.

APPENDIX 1.2

ENVIRONMENTAL PROTECTION (PRESCRIBED PROCESSES AND SUBSTANCES) REGULATIONS 1991 (AS AMENDED)

Schedules 4, 5 and 6 of the Regulations list the prescribed substances for releases to, respectively, air, water and land. Schedule 4 applies to those processes which are regulated for air pollution only (Part B processes); all three schedules apply to processes regulated for Integrated Pollution Control.

These substances are also prescribed for control under the *Industrial Pollution Control (Prescribed Processes and Substances) Regulations (Northern Ireland) 1998.*

Schedule 4: Releases into the Air

Oxides of sulphur & other sulphur compounds
Oxides of nitrogen & other nitrogen compounds
Oxides of carbon
Organic compounds & partial oxidation products
Metals, metalloids & their compounds
Asbestos (suspended particulate matter & fibres), glass fibres & mineral fibres
Halogens & their compounds
Phosphorus & its compounds
Particulate matter

Schedule 5: Releases into Water

Substance	*Amount in excess of background quantity released in any 12 month period (Grammes)*
Mercury & its compounds	200 (expressed as metal)
Cadmium & its compounds	1000 (expressed as metal)
All isomers of hexachlorocyclohexane	20
All isomers of DDT	5
Pentachlorophenol & its compounds	350 (expressed as PCP)
Hexachlorobenzene	5
Hexachlorobutadiene	20
Aldrin	2
Dieldrin	2
Endrin	1
Polychlorinated biphenyls	1
Dichlorvos	0.2
1,2-Dichloroethane	2000
All isomers of trichlorobenzene	75
Atrazine	350*
Simazine	350*
Tributyltin compounds	4 (expressed as TBT)
Triphenyltin compounds	4 (expressed as TPT)
Trifluralin	20
Fenitrothion	2

Azinphos-methyl	2
Malathion	2
Endosulfan	0.5

*Where both Atrazine and Simazine are released, the figure in aggregate is 350 grammes.

Schedule 6: Releases to Land

Organic solvents
Azides
Halogens & their covalent compounds
Metal carbonyls
Organo-metallic compounds
Oxidising agents
Polychlorinated dibenzofuran & any cogener thereof
Polychlorinated dibenzo-p-dioxin & any cogener thereof
Polyhalogenated biphenyls, terphenyls & naphthalenes
Phosphorus

Pesticides, that is to say, any chemical substance or preparation prepared or used for destroying any pest, including those used for protecting plants or wood or other plant products from harmful organisms; regulating the growth of plants; giving protection against harmful creatures; rendering such creatures harmless; controlling organisms with harmful or unwanted effects on water systems, buildings or other structures, or on manufactured products; or protecting animals against ectoparasites.

Alkali metals and their oxides and alkaline earth metals and their oxides.

APPENDIX 1.3
CHIEF INSPECTOR'S GUIDANCE TO INSPECTORS
INDUSTRY SECTOR GUIDANCE NOTES

These notes are intended to give general guidance to the Environment Agency in England and Wales on specific industry sectors to enable them to deal with applications for authorisations for new processes and for substantial changes to existing processes. More detailed guidance is given in the process guidance notes.

IPR 1	Fuel and Power Industry
IPR 2	Metal Industry
IPR 3	Mineral Industry
IPR 4	Chemical Industry
IPR 5	Waste Disposal Industry

PROCESS GUIDANCE NOTES

IPR Process Guidance Notes are available from The Stationery Office. IPR Notes are normally reviewed every four years to take account of new technology etc - revised notes have been given a prefix S2 (Series 2). The notes listed here only apply to processes in England and Wales; there are no comparable notes for processes in Scotland.

Combustion Processes (1.3)

S2 1.01	Large boilers & furnaces 50 MW(th) & over (1995) [supersedes IPR 1/1]
IPR 1/2	Gas turbines (revised September 1994)
S2 1.03	Compression ignition engines 50 MW(th) & over (1995) [supersedes IPR 1/3]
S2 1.04	Waste and recovered oil burners 3 MW(th) & over (1995) [supersedes IPR 1/4]
S2 1.05	Combustion of fuel manufactured from or comprised of solid waste in appliances 3 MW(th) and over (1995) [supersedes IPR 1/5, 1/6, 1/7 and 1/8]
S2 1.12	Reheat and heat treatment furnaces 50 MW(th) and over (1995) [supersedes IPR 1/17]

Carbonisation & Associated Processes (1.2)

S2 1.06	Coke manufacture (1995) [supersedes IPR 1/09]
S2 1.07	Smokeless fuel, activated carbon and carbon black manufacture (1995) [supersedes IPR 1/10]

Gasification Processes (1.1)

S2 1.08	Gasification of solid & liquid feedstocks including gasification combined cycle (1995) [previously IPR 1/11]
S2 1.09	Refining of natural gas (1995) [previously IPR 1/12]
IPR 1/13	The refining of natural gas at liquified natural gas sites

Petroleum Processes (1.4)

S2 1.10	Oil refining and associated processes (1995) [incorporates IPR 1/14 on the odorising of natural gas or liquified petroleum gas and IPR 1/15 crude oil refineries]
S2 1.11	On-shore oil production (1995) [supersedes IPR 1/16]

Iron and Steel (2.1)

IPR 2/1	Integrated iron and steel works
IPR 2/2	Ferrous foundry processes
IPR 2/3	Processes for electric arc steelmaking, secondary steelmaking and special alloy production

Non-Ferrous Metals (2.2); Smelting Processes (2.3)

IPR 2/4	Processes for the production of zinc and zinc alloys
IPR 2/5	Processes for the production of lead and lead alloys
IPR 2/6	Processes for the production of refractory metals
IPR 2/7	Processes for the production, melting, recovery of cadmium, mercury and their alloys
IPR 2/8	Processes for the production of aluminium
IPR 2/9	Processes for the production of copper and copper alloys
IPR 2/10	Processes for the production of precious metals and platinum group metals
IPR 2/11	The extraction of nickel by the carbonyl process and the production of cobalt and nickel alloys
IPR 2/12	Tin and bismuth processes

Cement & Lime Manufacture & Associated Processes (3.1)

S2 3.01	Cement manufacture, lime manufacture & associated processes (1996)

Processes Involving Asbestos (3.2)

S2 3.02	Asbestos processes (1996) [supersedes IPR 3/2]

Other Mineral Fibres (3.3) and Glass Manufacture & Production (3.5)

S2 3.03	Manufacture of glass fibres, other non-asbestos mineral fibrés, glass frit, enamel frit and associated processes (1996) [incorporates former IPR 3/4 and 3/5]

Ceramic Production (3.6)

S2 3.04	Ceramic processes (1996) [formerly 3/6]

Petrochemical Processes (4.1)

IPR 4/1*	Petrochemical processes

Manufacture and Use of Organic Chemicals (4.2)

IPR 4/2*	Processes for the production and use of amines, nitriles, isocyanates and pyridines
IPR 4/3*	Processes for the production or use of acetylene, aldehydes, etc
IPR 4/4*	Processes for the production or use of organic sulphur compounds, and production, use or recovery of carbon disulphide
IPR 4/5*	Batch manufacture of organic chemicals in multipurpose plant
IPR 4/6*	Production and polymerisation of organic monomers
IPR 4/7*	Processes for the manufacture of organo-metallic compounds

Acid Processes (4.3)

IPR 4/10*	Processes for the manufacture, use or release of oxides of sulphur and the manufacture, recovery, condensation or distillation of sulphuric acid or oleum
IPR 4/11*	Processes for the manufacture or recovery of nitric acid and processes involving the manufacture of or release of acid-forming oxides of nitrogen
IPR 4/12*	Processes for the sulphonation or nitration of organic chemicals

Processes involving Halogens (4.4)

IPR 4/13*	Processes for the manufacture of, or which use or release halogens, mixed halogen compounds or oxohalocompounds
IPR 4/14*	Processes for the manufacture of, or which use or release hydrogen halides or any of their acids
IPR 4/15*	Processes for the halogenation of organic chemicals

Inorganic Chemical Processes (4.5)

IPR 4/18*	Processes for the manufacture of ammonia
IPR 4/19*	Processes involving the use, release or recovery of ammonia
IPR 4/20*	The production of and use of, in any process for the manufacture of a chemical, phosphorus and any oxide, hydride, or halide of phosphorus

IPR 4/21* Processes involving the manufacture or use of, or which may release, hydrogen cyanide or hydrogen sulphide

IPR 4/22* Processes for the manufacture and use of antimony, arsenic, beryllium, gallium, indium, lead, palladium, platinum, selenium, tellurium, thallium and their compounds

IPR 4/23* Processes involving the manufacture, recovery, use or release of cadmium or any compounds of cadmium

IPR 4/24* Processes involving the use or release of mercury or any compounds of mercury

IPR 4/25* Processes for the production of compounds of chromium, magnesium, manganese, nickel and zinc

Chemical Fertiliser Production (4.6)

IPR 4/16* Processes for the manufacture of chemical fertilisers or their conversion into granules

Pesticide Production (4.7)

IPR 4/8* Pesticide processes

Pharmaceutical Production (4.8)

IPR 4/9* Pharmaceutical processes

The Storage of Chemicals in Bulk (4.9)

IPR 4/17* Bulk storage installations

* The Guidance Notes on chemical processes are being revised and consolidated into four IPC Guidance Notes, which were due for publication in December 1998:

S2 4.01 Large volume organic chemical processes

S2 4.02 Speciality organic chemical processes

S2 4.03 Inorganic Acid and Halogen Processes

S2 4.04 Inorganic Chemical Processes

Incineration (5.1)

S2 5.01 Waste to energy plants and incineration plant for the following wastes: chemical and hazardous; clinical; municipal; animal carcasses; sewage sludge; and drum residues (1996) [replaces 5/1, 5/2, 5/3, 5/4, 5/5 and 5/11]

Recovery Processes (5.2)

S2 5.03 Cleaning and regeneration of carbon (1996) [replaces IPR 5/7]

S2 5.04 Recovery of organic solvents and oil by distillation (1996) [replaces IPR 5/8 & 5/10]

IPR 5/9 Regeneration of ion exchange resins [not being revised; only one IPC authorisation. HMIP research report DOE/HMIP/RR/95/028 *Technical & Economic Study of Recovery Processes* contains up to date information on their environmental performance]

Production of Fuel from Waste (5.3)

S2 5.02 Making solid fuel from waste (1996) [replaces IPR 5/6]

Other Industries (chapter 6)

IPR 6/1 Application or removal of tributyltin, or triphenyltin coatings at shipyards or boatyards

IPR 6/2 Tar and bitumen processes

IPR 6/3 Timber preservation processes

IPR 6/4 Di-isocynate manufacture

IPR 6/5 Toluene di-isocyanate use and flame bonding of polyurethanes

IPR 6/6 Textile treatment processes

IPR 6/7 Processing of animal hides and skins

IPR 6/8 The making of paper pulp by chemical methods

IPR 6/9 Papermaking and related processes, including mechanical pulping, recycled fibres and de-inking

APPENDIX 1.4

TECHNICAL GUIDANCE NOTES

These notes provide further guidance to those involved in implementing Part I of the *Environmental Protection Act*; they will however also be of interest to process operators and others with an interest in the operation of the EPA. Further TG notes are planned. They are available from The Stationery Office.

Dispersion

D1 Guidelines on discharge stack heights for polluting emissions (1993)

Monitoring

M1 Sampling facility requirements for the monitoring of particulates in gaseous releases to atmosphere (1993)
M2 Monitoring emissions of pollutants at source (1994)
M3 Standards for IPC monitoring: Part 1 - standards organisations and the measurement infrastructure (1995)
M4 Standards for IPC monitoring: Part 2 - standards in support of IPC monitoring (1995)
M5 Routine measurement of gamma ray air kerma rate in the environment (1995)
M The Measurement of Di-Isocyanates in Stack Emissions (draft, 1998)
M The Monitoring of Tar Fume (draft, 1998)

Abatement

A1 Guidance on effective flaring in the gas, petroleum, petrochemical and associated industries (1993)
A2 Pollution abatement technology for the reduction of solvent vapour emissions (1994)
A3 Pollution abatement technology for particulate and trace gas removal (1994)
A4 Effluent treatment techniques (1997)

Environmental

E1 Best Practicable Environmental Option Assessments for Integrated Pollution Control; Vol. I: Principles and Methodology; Vol. II: Technical Data (for consultation) (1997)

APPENDIX 2.1

AIR POLLUTION CONTROL: SECRETARY OF STATE'S GUIDANCE NOTES

GENERAL GUIDANCE NOTES

These notes (GG Notes) give guidance to local authorities and port health authorities in England and Wales and to the Scottish Environment Protection Agency in Scotland) on their responsibilities under Part I of the *Environmental Protection Act 1990.*

GG1(91)	Introduction to Part I of the Act
GG2(91)	Authorisations
GG3(91)	Applications and Registers
GG4(91)	Interpretation of terms used in process guidance notes
GG5(91)	Appeals

PROCESS GUIDANCE NOTES

Process Guidance (PG) Notes are issued by the Secretary of State under section 7 of the *Environmental Protection Act 1990*; they provide guidance on BATNEEC for each category of process, and will usually include emission limits, monitoring and sampling requirements etc. PG Notes were originally produced in 1991 and 1992 in advance of processes applying for authorisation from their local authority and most have now been revised. The revised notes supersede any earlier versions. PG notes are reviewed approximatly every four years. PG Notes are published by The Stationery Office for the DETR, Welsh Office and Scottish Office.

PG 1/1(95)	Waste oil burners, less than 0.4 MW net rated thermal input
PG 1/2(95)	Waste oil or recovered oil burners, 0 .4-3 MW net rated thermal input
PG 1/3(95)	Boilers and furnaces, 20-50 MW net rated thermal input
PG 1/4(95)	Gas turbines, 20-50 MW net rated thermal input; see also AQ 1(97)
PG 1/5(95)	Compression ignition engines, 20-50 MW net rated thermal input
PG 1/10(92)	Waste derived fuel burning processes less than 3 MW net rated thermal input
PG 1/11(96)	Reheat and heat treatment furnaces, 20-50 MW net rated thermal input
PG 1/12(95)	Combustion of fuel manufactured from or comprised of solid waste in appliances between 0.4 and 0.3 MW net rated thermal input [replaces 1991 PG 1/6, 1/7, 1/8 and 1/9]
PG 1/13(96)	Processes for the storage, loading and unloading of petrol at terminals; see also AQ 6(97)
PG 1/14(96)	Unloading of petrol into storage at service stations; see also AQ 6(97)
PG 1/15(97)	Odorising natural gas and liquefied petroleum gas
PG 2/1(96)	Furnaces for the extraction of non-ferrous metal from scrap
PG 2/2(96)	Hot dip galvanising processes
PG 2/3(96)	Electrical, rotary, crucible and reverberatory furncaces
PG 2/4(96)	Iron, steel and non-ferrous metal foundry processes
PG 2/5(96)	Hot and cold blast cupolas
PG 2/6(96)	Processes for melting and producing aluminium, magnesium and their alloys
PG 2/7(96)	Zinc and zinc alloy processes
PG 2/8(96)	Copper and copper alloy processes
PG 2/9(96)	Metal decontamination processes

PG 3/1(95)	Blending, packing, loading and use of bulk cement
PG 3/2(95)	Manufacture of heavy clay goods and refractory goods
PG 3/3(95)	Glass (excluding lead glass) manufacturing processes
PG 3/4(95)	Lead glass, glass frit and enamel frit manufacturing processes
PG 3/5(95)	Coal, coke, coal product and petroleum coke processes
PG 3/6(95)	Processes for the polishing or etching of glass or glass products using hydrofluoric acid
PG 3/7(95)	Exfoliation of vermiculite and expansion of perlite
PG 3/8(96)	Quarry processes
PG 3/12(95)	Plaster processes
PG 3/13(95)	Asbestos processes; see also AQ 3(96)
PG 3/14(95)	Lime processes
PG 3/15(96)	Mineral drying and roadstone coating processes [amends and replaces 3/15(96)]
PG 3/16(96)	Mobile crushing and screening processes
PG 3/17(95)	China and ball clay processes including the spray drying of ceramics [amends and replaces 3/10(91) and 3/11(91)]
PG 4/1(94)	Processes for the surface treatment of metals
PG 4/2(96)	Processes for the manufacture of fibre reinforced plastics; see also AQ 1(97)
PG 5/1(95)	Clinical waste incineration processes under 1 tonne an hour
PG 5/2(95)	Crematoria
PG 5/3(95)	Animal remains incineration processes under 1 tonne an hour
PG 5/4(95)	General waste incineration processes under 1 tonne an hour
PG 5/5(91)	Sewage sludge incineration processes under 1 tonne an hour [not being updated: no relevant incinerators; if any enquiries or applications, DETR suggest also refer to IPR 5/11]
PG 6/1(91)	Animal by-product rendering; (see also AQ 3(94)
PG 6/2(95)	Manufacture of timber and wood based products
PG 6/3(97)	Chemical treatment of timber and wood based products
PG 6/4(95)	Processes for the manufacture of particleboard and fibreboard
PG 6/5(95)	Maggot breeding processes; see also AQ 1(97)
PG 6/6(91)	Withdrawn (fur breeding processes)
PG 6/7(97)	Printing and coating of metal packaging
PG 6/8(97)	Textile and fabric coating and finishing processes
PG 6/9(96)	Manufacture of coating powder
PG 6/10(97)	Coating manufacturing processes
PG 6/11(97)	Manufacture of printing ink
PG 6/12(91)	Production of natural sausage casings, tripe, chitterlings and other boiled green offal products
PG 6/13(97)	Coil coating processes
PG 6/14(97)	Film coating processes
PG 6/15(97)	Coating in drum manufacturing and reconditioning processes
PG 6/16(97)	Printworks
PG 6/17(97)	Printing of flexible packaging
PG 6/18(97)	Paper coating processes; see also AQ 4(98)
PG 6/19(97)	Fish meal and fish oil processes
PG 6/20(97)	Paint application in vehicle manufacturing; see also AQ 4(98)
PG 6/21(96)	Hide and skin processes
PG 6/22(97)	Leather finishing processes
PG 6/23(97)	Coating of metal and plastic
PG 6/24(96)	Pet food manufacturing processes
PG 6/25(97)	Vegetable oil extraction and fat and oil refining processes
PG 6/26(96)	Animal feed compounding processes; see also AQ 1(97)

PG 6/27(96)	Vegetable matter drying processes
PG 6/28(97)	Rubber processes
PG 6/29(97)	Di-isocyanate processes ; see also AQ 3(97)
PG 6/30(97)	Production of mushroom substrate
PG 6/31(96)	Powder coating processes, including sheradising
PG 6/32(97)	Adhesive coating processes
PG 6/33(97)	Wood coating processes
PG 6/34(97)	Respraying of road vehicles; see also AQ 4(98)
PG 6/35(96)	Metal and other thermal spraying processes
PG 6/36(97)	Tobacco processing
PG 6/37(92)	Withdrawn (knackers yards)
PG 6/38(92)	Blood processing
PG 6/39(92)	Animal by-product dealers
PG 6/40(94)	Coating and recoating of aircraft and aircraft components
PG 6/41(94)	Coating and recoating of rail vehicles
PG 6/42(94)	Bitumen and tar processes, as amended by "green note" dated November 1996
UG-1 (92)	Revisions/additions to existing process and general guidance notes: no. 1. However, this is now relevant only inrelation to PG 1/10 - all other references in UG-1 having been included in PG Note revisions.

APPENDIX 2.2

LOCAL AIR POLLUTION CONTROL: ADDITIONAL GUIDANCE NOTES

These notes are prepared by the Air and Environment Quality Division at the Department of the Environment, Transport and the Regions (until mid-1997, the Department of the Environment); they supplement and clarify information contained in Process Guidance Notes and provide additional guidance on the way in which Part I of the *Environmental Protection Act 1990* and its Regulations should be interpreted. Only those notes which remain valid as at July 1998 are listed here.

AQ 5(91)	Registers - Rehabilitation of Offenders Act
AQ 7(91)	Meaning of "existing process"
AQ 8(91)	Obtaining further information: specimen notice
AQ 9(91)	VAT on charges
AQ 3(92)	Radioactive substances
AQ 5(92)	Foundries - triviality
AQ 7(92)	Amendments to applications
AQ 8(92)	Rubber processes - meaning of "if carbon black is used"
AQ 9(92)	Mobile plant
AQ 1(93)	EPA Part I - advising operators on their rights of appeal. See also AQ 7(94) and 8(96)
AQ 3(93)	Triviality and zinc diecasters
AQ 4(93)	Transfer of authorisations under s.9 of EPA
AQ 7(93)	Small coal mines - triviality
AQ 8(93)	Mobile plant - necessity for consultation with English Nature and Countryside Council for Wales
AQ 9(93)	Variation notices - consolidation of authorisations
AQ 10(93)	Notification of publication of TG note *Guidelines on Discharge Stack Heights for Polluting Emissions* (see also AQ 18(93))
AQ 12(93)	Obtaining additional information
AQ 14(93)	Service of notices etc - advice on
AQ 15(93)	Appeals: costs; commercial confidentiality
AQ 16(93)	Submission of draft authorisations to operators
AQ 18(93)	Errors in Technical Guidance D1 (see also AQ 10(93))
AQ 1(94)	Notification (to operators) of triviality exemption, together with specimen
AQ 2(94)	Solvent substitution [of 1,1,1 trichloroethane or methyl chloroform to another solvent] in vapour degreasing equipment
AQ 3(94)	Animal by-product rendering (PG 6/1(91)) - amendment of para 2 of clause 33 relating to self-closing doors
AQ 4(94)	Availability of HMIP Technical Guidance Note M2 of monitoring of pollutants at source
AQ 5(94)	Content of public registers (should only include information specified in Reg. 15 of Applications, Appeals & Registers Regs 1991; working files not to be used as public registers)
AQ 6(94)	Notification of availability of HMIP TG Note A2 *Pollution Abatement Technology for the Reduction of Solvent Vapour Emissions*
AQ 7(94)	Appeals arrangements: initial stages of appeals in England under Part I of EPA to be handled by Planning Inspectorate

AQ 9(94)	Availability of HMIP TG Note A3 *Pollution Abatement Technology for Particulate and Trace Gas Removal*
AQ 11(94)	Additional guidance on *Waste Management Licensing Regulations 1994* and their implications for LAAPC
AQ 12(94)	Establishment of Environmental Technology Best Practice Programme
AQ 15(94)	Explicitly informing operators of their right to appeal against EPA Part I decisions of the LA and suggested form of wording
AQ 17(94)	Recirculation of workroom air and triviality - exemption from LAPC authorisations (so long as satisfy COSHH requirements)
AQ 18(94)	Triviality
AQ 2(95)	Delays in deciding applications and considering upgrading submissions (should aim to deal with within 4 months of receipt of all relevant information)
AQ 3(95)	Refractory materials: further guidance on defining; see also section 3.6 of Schedule 1 to 1994 Prescribed Processes & Substances Regulations
AQ 4(95)	Inspection frequency - basic principles: to check compliance with conditions usually every 6 months, announced or unannounced; in connection with applications etc, prearranged visit
AQ 5(95)	Four-yearly review of authorisations under s. 6(6) of EPA: aspects to be considered
AQ 7(95)	Placing of commercially confidential information on public register on expiry of 4 year limit; see also AQ 1(93), 15(93) & 15(94). Removal of details of convictions from public register in accordance with *Rehabilitation of Offenders Act 1994*
AQ 10(95)	PG 5/5(91) not being updated as no sewage sludge incinerators under 1 tonne/hr in operation
AQ 11(95)	Amendments to LAAPC as a result of *Environment Act 1995* and note re air quality provisions of the Act
AQ 14(95)	Publication of HMIP Technical Guidance Notes M3 and M4 on standards for IPC Monitoring
AQ 16(95)	Authorisation conditions relating to odour
AQ 17(95)	Summary of recent LAPC appeals decisions (see also 10(96) & 7(98))
AQ 18(95)	Amended EPA sections 10 and 13 relating to variation and enforcement notices effective 12.10.95 - see *Environment Act 1995*, Sch. 22, paras 51 and 53
AQ 20(95)	Monitoring of processes and emissions by local authorities
AQ 1(96)	The determination of chimney heights for process heaters
AQ 2(96)	Amendments to LAPC coming into force on 1 April as result of *Environment Act 1995*
AQ 3(96)	Asbestos processes (PG 3/13(95)) - clause 14, second sentence should read "A fibre is defined as any object of length greater than 5 μm, breadth less than 3 μm ..."
AQ 8(96)	Amendment to specimen notes on appeal (dated November 1992) and AQ 1(93); appeals should be received by the Secretary of State within the appropriate time limit (not sent within the limit)
AQ 10(96)	Summary of recent LAPC appeal decisions (see also 17(95) & 7(98))
AQ 1(97)	Corrections to PG 1/4(95), 4/2(96), 6/5(95) and 6/26(96)
AQ 3(97)	Corrections to PG 6/29(97)
AQ 4(97)	Categories of process operated by different local authorities
AQ 5(97)	Appeals (Secretary of State powers delegated to Planning Inspectorate wef 1 September 1997); guidance on appeals procedure
AQ 6(97)	Petroleum processes (PG 1/13(96) & PG 1/14(96)): definition of petrol and advice on when modifying of existing process should trigger "new process" requirements
AQ 7(97)	Categories of process operated by different local authorities (additions to AQ 4(97)
AQ 1(98)	Information about LAPC on Internet at

	http://www.aeat.co.uk/netcen/airqual/info/labrief.html
AQ 2(98)	New address for AEQ Division
AQ 3(98)	List of current and outdated AQ notes as at July 1998
AQ 4(98)	Corrections to PG 6/18(97), PG 6/20(97) and PG 6/34(97)
AQ 5(98)	Advice on the calculation of chimney heights available from Stanger Science and Environment in assocation with University of Greenwich; tel: 0181 256 4972; Email: modelhelp@stanger.co.uk
AQ 6(98)	Temporary advice service (5/10-13/11/98) on PG 6/23
AQ 7(98)	Summary of recent appeal decisions (see also 17(95) & 10(96))
AQ 8(98)	Proposed changes to 1998/9 LAPC statistical returns
AQ 9(98)	BATNEEC for unloading petrol at stations with older types of tank gauging (modification of advice given in PG 1/14(96)
AQ 10(98)	Procedures for tank connections at petrol stations (confirmed as stated in PG 1/14(96)
AQ 11(98)	Guidance in response to LAPC action plan
AQ 12(98)	Application of the emission limit value for amines in PG 2/4

APPENDIX 2.3

THE RINGELMANN CHART

The method of visual assessment of smoke emission by comparison of the darkness of the smoke with the standard shades of grey on a chart placed in a suitable position was devised by Professor Ringelmann of Paris towards the end of the 19th century. Professor Ringelmann obtained the shades of grey by cross-hatching in black on a white background so that a known percentage of the white was obscured.

The British Standard Ringelmann Chart (BS 2742C) is printed for the BSI so that the shades obtained in use are both consistent and near the average of those to which users were accustomed when using the previously available commercially-printed Ringelmann Charts, including those issued by the US Bureau of Mines.

The Chart consists of a cardboard sheet 581 mm x 127 mm on which are printed five 101 mm squares, four of which are cross-hatched by 20 horizontal and 20 vertical lines so that in use the cross-hatched black lines merge into the white background and produce for each shade, apparently, a uniform grey.

The number of shades - the Ringelmann numbers - range from 0 to 4, each shade increasing by comparison with the previous number by 20% obscuration so that

Ringelmann 1 = 20% obscuration
Ringelmann 2 = 40% obscuration
Ringelmann 3 = 60% obscuration
Ringelmann 4 = 80% obscuration

"Dark smoke" is smoke which is as dark or darker than shade 2 on the Chart; "black smoke" is smoke which is as dark or darker than shade 4 on the Chart.

The Use of the Ringelmann Chart

The use of the Ringelmann Chart is described in BS 2742:1969.

The Ringelmann Chart should be firmly mounted onto a backing holder - aluminium is suitable - similar to that described in BS 2742. Protective coverings must not be applied to the Chart in use and nothing should impair the luminance of its working surface.

It should be used under daylight conditions and held in a vertical plane in line between the observer and the chimney top, at a distance of more than 15 metres to ensure that cross-hatched lines merge into shades of grey.

Where possible the general illumination of the sky should be uniform, but if the sun is shining or the sky bright on one side, the British Standard recommends that the bright source of illumination should be approximately at right angles to the line of vision and not in front of or behind the observer. Under hazy conditions observations should not be taken at extreme distance as there will be a tendency for the readings to be low. The angle of view of the Chart and smoke should be as low as possible; observations at a steep angle should be avoided.

The darkness of the smoke at the chimney terminal should be compared with the Chart; the Ringelmann number which most closely matches the darkness of the smoke, and the time and duration of the emission, should be noted. In favourable conditions it is possible to estimate smoke darkness to the nearest quarter Ringelmann.

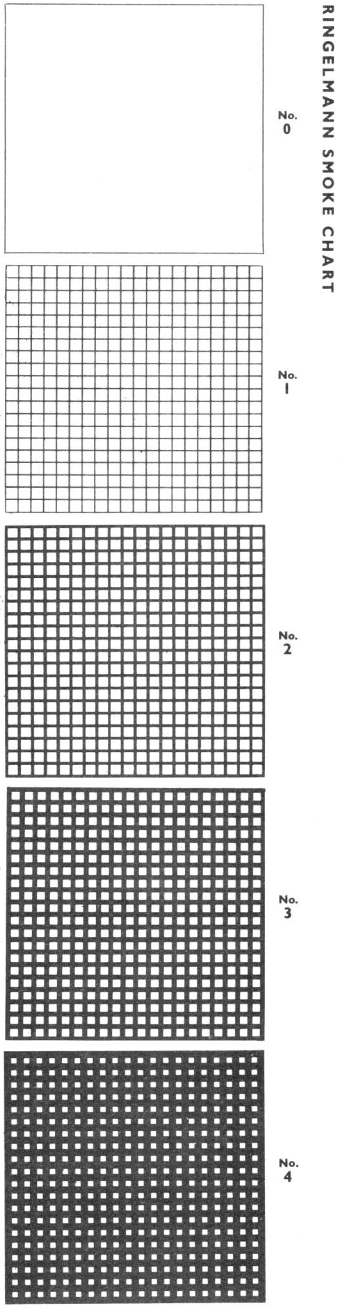

APPENDIX 2.4

THE CLEAN AIR ACT (EMISSION OF GRIT AND DUST FROM FURNACES) REGULATIONS 1971

Schedule 1 - Furnaces Rated by Heat Output

This Schedule applies to boilers and also indirect heating appliances in which the material being heated is a gas or a liquid (e.g. an air heater); where an indirect heating appliance falls also within the provisions of Schedule 2, it should be treated as a Schedule 1 furnace.

Max. continuous rating in lbs of steam/hr (from & at 100°C (212%F) in thousands BTU/hr)*		Max. permitted quantities of grit and dust per hour Furnaces burning			
		solid matter		liquid matter	
000 Btu/hr	MW	lbs	kg	lbs	kg
825	0.24	1.10	0.55	0.25	0.11
1,000	0.29	1.33	0.60	0.28	0.12
2,000	0.58	2.67	1.21	0.56	0.25
3,000	0.87	4.00	1.81	0.84	0.38
4,000	1.17	5.33	2.41	1.12	0.50
5,000	1.46	6.67	3.02	1.4	0.63
7,000	2.19	8.50	3.85	2.1	0.95
10,000	2.93	10.00	4.53	2.8	1.27
15,000	4.39	13.33	6.04	4.2	1.90
20,000	5.86	16.67	7.56	5.6	2.54
25,000	7.32	20.0	9.07	7.0	3.17
30,000	8.79	23.4	10.61	8.4	3.81
40,000	11.72	30	13.60	11.2	5.08
50,000	14.65	37	16.78	12.5	5.66
100,000	29.30	66	29.93	18	8.16
150,000	43.96	94	40.97	24	10.88
200,000	58.61	122	55.37	29	13.15
250,000	73.42	149	67.58	36	16.32
300,000	87.92	172	78.01	41	18.59
350,000	102.57	195	88.45	45	20.41
400,000	117.22	217	98.42	50	22.67
450,000	131.88	239	108.40	54.5	24.72
475,000	139.20	250	113.39	57	25.85
1 Watt = 3.41214 Btu/hr					

Schedule 2 - Furnaces Rated by Heat Input

This schedule applies to indirect heating appliances and to furnaces in which combustion gases are in contact with the material being heated, but that material does not in itself contribute to the grit and dust in the combustion gases.

		Max. permitted quantities of grit and dust emissions per hour Furnaces burning			
		solid matter		liquid matter	
in millions ofBtu/hr	MW	lbs	kg	lbs	kg
1.25	0.36	1.1	0.49	0.28	0.12
2.5	0.73	2.1	0.95	0.55	0.24
5.0	1.46	4.3	1.95	1.1	0.49
7.5	2.19	6.8	3.08	1.7	0.77
10	2.93	7.6	3.44	2.2	0.99
15	4.39	9.7	4.39	3.3	1.49
20	5.86	11.9	5.39	4.4	1.99
25	7.32	14.1	6.40	5.5	2.49
30	8.79	16.3	7.39	6.6	2.99
35	10.25	18.4	8.34	7.7	3.49
40	11.72	20.6	9.34	8.8	3.99
45	13.18	22.8	10.34	9.8	4.44
50	14.65	25	11.33	10.9	4.94
100	29.30	45	20.51	16	7.25
200	58.61	90	40.82	26	11.79
300	87.92	132	59.87	35	15.87
400	117.22	175	79.37	44	19.95
500	146.53	218	98.88	54	24.49
575	168.51	250	113.39	57	25.85

Note: typically, a large power station is 2000-4000 MW.

The Regulations limit the grit in the sample of grit and dust to the following proportions:

- **Schedule 1 furnaces:**

Grit not to exceed 33% where maximum continuous rating does not exceed 16,800 lbs/hr of steam or 16,800,000 Btu/hr (4.92 MW);

Grit not to exceed 20% in any other case.

- **Schedule 2 furnaces:**

Grit not to exceed 33% where designed heat input of the furnace does not exceed 25,000,000 Btu/hr (7.32 MW);

Grit not to exceed 20% in any other case.

Notes:

1. Multiflue chimneys are defined and for the purpose of the Regulations each flue is to be taken as a separate chimney for the purpose of calculating acceptable emissions.
2. Where a chimney serves a furnace to which the Regulations apply and also a furnace to which the Regulations do not apply, the emissions from the latter shall be disregarded.
3. The prescribed limits apply to any period of standard operation of the furnace, including periods during which it is at or close to the loading to which it is subject for the greater part of its working time, or at any higher loading to which it is regularly subject for a limited time (whether or not this exceeds the furnace maximum combustion rating or designed heat input).

APPENDIX 2.5
CALCULATION OF CHIMNEY HEIGHT

This appendix supplements the details given in chapter 2, 2.13.2 relating to chimney height, sections 14-16 of the *Clean Air Act 1993*, and also has relevance to the requirements for BATNEEC in section 7(2) of the *Environmental Protection Act 1990.*

Chimney heights offer a means of local control of pollutants discharged to the atmosphere from combustion and incineration plant and from industrial processes. They may be used to control the deposition of pollutants to the ground or their ambient concentrations over either long or short time scales, and for a variety of purposes including health effects and nuisance (due to odour for example). There are often additional controls on the scale of discharges from particular processes, both because of the requirements of BATNEEC to minimise discharge where practically possible and also to limit polluting discharges where the accumulation of a multiplicity of discharges may cause problems on larger scales, for example over the background level of pollutants in urban areas or where the accumulation of pollutants on continental or global scales is important. However, even when there are high levels of abatement, there is likely to be a residual discharge which must be effectively dispersed by means of an adequate chimney height.

Chimneys act as a means of control over local pollution levels by raising the polluting source to a sufficient height above the ground for the initial dispersion of the discharge plume, where pollutant concentrations are high, to occur away from the ground where most pollution problems occur. The chimney height is arranged so that the eventual contact of the plume with the ground results in pollutant concentrations at the ground within some prescribed limit value. This process is only effective within distances of about 50-100 chimney heights, much beyond which the effects of discharge height are no longer distinguishable. The highest pollutant concentrations usually occur within this range.

The calculation of effective chimney heights is thus a matter of great practical importance and there are a variety of methods of doing this, either by direct dispersion modelling or by using one of a number of guides for this purpose. For large plant, for example that defined as Part A processes (regulated for Integrated Pollution Control), it is common for individual dispersion modelling studies to be requested as a part of the authorisation process. Direct dispersion modelling may also be used for calculating chimney heights for smaller plant where there are complex problems due to the character of the dispersion or the nature of the discharge. However this is not usually practicable and there are several guides which allow chimney heights to be calculated more quickly and easily. These are discussed below. The majority of direct dispersion modelling uses computer models of varying sophistication. The USEPA models are the most commonly used (in the UK, along with the NRPB models), though they have distinct limitations in dealing with the more complex dispersion problems. Some complex dispersion problems also use small scale wind tunnel modelling to determine chimney heights.

For the great majority of smaller polluting discharges, chimney heights are determined using the published guides for this purpose. For many years chimney heights for conventional combustion plant (mainly heating and steam raising plant running on coal, fuel oil or gas) have been calculated using the 3rd Edition of the *Clean Air Act Memorandum "Chimney Heights"* which is still recommended for this purpose. More recently there has been a need to deal with newer types of combustion plant (combined cycle for example) and with the requirements for adequate discharge stack heights for the wide variety of smaller process plant classified as Part B processes under the *Environmental Protection Act*. This has been met with the HMIP Guidance Note D1, *Guidelines for Discharge Stack Heights for Polluting Emissions* (HMSO, 1993), which provides a systematic procedure for dealing with almost any type of polluting discharge. There is also specific advice on minimum chimney heights for discharge stacks in the Process Guidance Notes issued by the DETR Local Authority Unit dealing with the requirements for authorisation of various Part B processes. These also contain maximum pollutant emission limits for the processes. Guidance Note D1 is also used occasionally for setting chimney heights for Part A processes, but this requires specific approval in individual cases.

More information on the *Memorandum of Chimney Heights* and on Guidance Note D1 can be found in the background report (*Background Report to the HMIP Guidelines on Discharge Stack Heights for Polluting Emissions*, D.J. Hall, V. Kukadia, Building Research Establishment Report No. CR200/95); specific advice on calculating chimney heights for odorous discharges can be found in *Clean Air*, Voi. 24, No. 2, pp74-92, and in AEA Technology Report No. AEA/CS/REMA-038; on dealing with chimneys with low velocity discharges in *Clean Air*, Vol. 25, No. 3, pp128-339; and on chimney heights for emissions of volatile organic compounds in *Clean Air*, Vol. 25, No. 4.

(This appendix prepared by D.J. Hall at the Building Research Establishment, 1995)

APPENDIX 2.6

CLEAN AIR ACT 1993: SMOKE CONTROL

Section 18 of the *Clean Air Act 1993* allows a local authority to make Smoke Control Orders. When operative, it is an offence for an occupier of premises to allow smoke to be emitted from a chimney, unless the smoke is caused by an authorised fuel or the fireplace which the chimney serves is exempt from the order. The Department of the Environment is responsible for authorising fuels and exempted fireplaces.

Authorised fuels are listed below at Appendix 2.6a, and exempted fireplaces at Appendix 2.6b.

Appendix 2.6a: Smoke Control Areas (Authorised Fuels) Regulations 1991

Regulations covering authorised fuels were made under section 34(1) of the *Clean Air Act 1956* (*Clean Air Act 1993*, section 20) and apply to England, Wales and Scotland. The 1991 Regulations, which came into force on 1 July 1991 (amended 1992, 1993, 1996,1997 and 1998), consolidate all the Regulations covering authorised fuels made since 1956. All the earlier Regulations are revoked.

In addition to anthracite, semi-anthracite, electricity, gas and low volatile steam coals, the following are authorised under the Act:

1. **Phurnacite Plus**, manufactured by Coal Products Limited at Aberaman, Mid Glamorgan, which
   (a) comprise anthracite and coke breeze (as to approximately 75% of the total weight) and coking coal (as to the remaining weight):
   (b) were manufactured from those constituents by a process involving heat treatment, roll-pressing and further heat treatment at about 400°C;
   (c) are unmarked cushion-shaped briquettes and have an average weight of 40 grammes (Ancit 40) or 60 grammes (Ancit 60); and
   (d) have a sulphur content not exceeding 1.5% of the total weight.

1A **Aimcor Excel briquettes**, manufactured by Applied Industrial Materials UK Limited at Newfield, Co. Durham, which
   (a) comprise petroleum coke as to 60% to 75% of the total weight), low volatile coal and reactive coke (as to 20% to 25% of the total weight) and cold-setting resin binder (as to the remaining weight);
   (b) were manufactured from those constituents by a process involving roll pressing;
   (c) are unmarked pillow-shaped briquettes and have an average weight of 73 grammes; and
   (d) have a sulphur content not exceeding 2% of the total weight.

2. **Anthracine N20 briquettes**, manufactured by Agglonord, Agglomération du Nord, at Oignies France, which
   (a) comprise anthracite (as to approximately 95% of the total weight) and starch as binder (as to the remaining weight);
   (b) were manufactured from those constituents by a process involving roll-pressing and heat treatment at about 150°C;
   (c) are ovoids marked with one arrow and have an average weight of 20 grammes; and
   (d) have a sulphur content not exceeding 0.8% of the total weight.

3. **Anthranor briquettes & Energlo briquettes**, manufactured by Agglonord, Agglomération du Nord, at Oignies, France, which
   (a) comprise anthracite (as to approximately 95% of the total weight) and starch as binder (as to the remaining weight);

(b) were manufactured from those constituents by a process involving roll-pressing and heat treatment at about 150°C;
(c) are cushion-shaped briquettes with rounded corners and have an average weight of 30 grammes; and
(d) have a sulphur content not exceeding 0.8% of the total weight.

4. **Antrex briquettes**, manufactured by Agglonord, Agglomération du Nord, at Oignies, France, which
(a) comprise anthracite;
(b) were manufactured from the anthracite by a process involving roll-pressing and heat treatment at about 180°C;
(c) are pillow-shaped ovoids with three small grooves on one side and have an average weight of 40 grammes; and
(d) have a sulphur content not exceeding 1% of the total weight.

4A. **Black Diamond Gem briquettes**, manufactured by Coal Products Limited at Immingham Briquetting Works, Immingham, Humberside, which
(a) comprise anthracite duff (as to 20-30% of the total weight), petroleum coke (as to 40-45% of the total weight), bituminous coal (as to 12-22% of the total weight) and molasses and phosphoric acid binder (as to the remaining weight);
(b) were manufactured from those constituents by a process involving roll-pressing and heat treatment at about 300°C;
(c) are pillow-shaped briquettes marked with two parallel indented lines running latitudinally around the briquette and have an average weight of 160 grammes; and
(d) have a sulphur content not exceeding 1.5% of the total weight.

4B. **BFL Fireside**, marketed by British Fuels Limited and are the same as Supertherm briquettes as described in para 18 below.

4C. **Blue Flame briquettes**, manufactured by Eldon Colliery Limited at Newfield Works, Bishop Auckland, County Durham which
(a) comprise anthracite (as to approximately 30-50% of the total weight) and Long Beach petroleum coke (as to approximately 50-70% of the total weight) and a carbohydrate binder (as to the remaining weight);
(b) were manufactured from those constituents by a process involving roll pressing and heat treatment at at about 150°C;
(c) are unmarked pillow-shaped briquettes and have an average weight of 33 grammes; and
(d) have a sulphur content not exceeding 1.5% of the total weight.

5. **Centurion briquettes**, manufactured by Greystone Heating Marketing Limited at Hamilton, Lanarkshire, which
(a) comprise anthracite (as to approximately 90% of the total weight) and molasses and phosphoric acid as binder (as to the remaining weight);
(b) were manufactured from those constituents by a process involving roll-pressing and heat treatment at about 250°C;
(c) are unmarked ovoids and have an average weight of 35 grammes; and
(d) have a sulphur content not exceeding 1.5% of the total weight.

6. **Clean Flame briquettes**, manufactured by NSM Mining (South Wales) Limited at Llanelli, Dyfed which
(a) comprise a blend of anthracite and semi-anthracite coal (as to approximately 94.5% of the total weight) and hard grade bitumen binder (as to the remaining weight);
(b) were manufactured from those constituents by a process involving roll-pressing and heat treatment at about 250°C;
(c) are unmarked pillow-shaped briquettes and have an average weight of 100 grammes; and
(d) have a sulphur content not exceeding 1.5% of the total weight.

7. **Coalite** manufactured by Coalite Products Limited at Bolsover, near Chesterfield, Derbyshire and at Grimethorpe, Yorkshire using a low temperature carbonisation process.

8. **Coke** manufactured by
   (a) Coal Products Limited at Avenue Coking and Chemical Works, Wingerworth, near Chesterfield, Derbyshire and sold as "Sunbrite" or "Beacon Beans";
   (b) Monckton Coke & Chemical Company Limited at Royston, near Barnsley, South Yorkshire and sold as "Sunbrite" or "Monckton Boiler Beans";
   (c) Association Cooperative Zelandaise de Carbonisation at Sluiskil, The Netherlands and sold as "Dutch (Sluiskil) Coke Doubles";
   (d) Centrala Handlu Zagraniczengo Weglokoks, and sold as "Glowbrite";
   (e) SSM Coal Limited at Immingham Dock, Grimsby, South Humberside and sold as "Gloco";
   (f) British Steel Plc at Teesside Works, Redcar, Cleveland and sold as "Redcar Coke Nuts (Doubles)";
   (g) Coal Products Limited at Cwm Coking Works, Pontypridd, South Wales and sold as "Cwm Coke Doubles".

8A. **Ecobrite briquettes**, manufactured by Arigna Fuels Limited at Arigna, Carrick-on-Shannon. County Roscommon, which
   (a) comprise anthracite fines (as to approximately 96% of the total weight) and starch as binder (as to the remaining weight);
   (b) were manufactured from those constituents by a process involving roll-pressing and heat treatment at about 250°C;
   (c) are unmarked pillow-shaped briquettes in two sizes having an average weight of 37 grammes for the smaller size and 48 grammes for the larger size; and
   (d) have a sulphur content not exceeding 1.5% of the total weight.

9. **Extracite briquettes**, manufactured by Sophia-Jacoba Handelsgesellschaft GmbH at Hückelhoven, Germany, which
   (a) comprise anthracite duff (as to approximately 95.5% of the total weight) and ammonium lignosulphonate lye as binder (as to the remaining weight);
   (b) were manufactured from those constituents by a process involving roll-pressing and heat treatment at about 260°C;
   (c) are cushion-shaped briquettes with a silvery appearance and are marked with the letters "S" and "J" and have an average weight of 40 grammes; and
   (d) have a sulphur content of approximately 1.2% of the total weight.

10. **Fireglo briquettes**, manufactured by Les Combustibles de Normandie at Caen, France, and by La Société Rouennaise de Defumage at Rouen, France which
   (a) comprise washed Welsh duffs (as to approximately 92% of the total weight) and coal pitch binder (as to the remaining weight);
   (b) were manufactured from those constituents by a process involving roll-pressing and heat treatment at about 330°C;
   (c) are ovoids with three lines on one side and are smooth on the other side and have an average weight of 30 grammes; and
   (d) have a sulphur content not exceeding 0.8% of the total weight.

11. **Flamelite pellets**, manufactured by Alfred McAlpine Energy Limited at Rheola Works, Resolven, West Glamorgan, which
   (a) comprise pre-mixed anthracite duff and filter cake combined with a fixed proportion of starch-based binder;
   (b) were manufactured from those constituents by a process involving extrusion and heat treatment at about 100°C;
   (c) are unmarked pellets approximately 25mm in diameter and between 20mm and 35mm in

length; and
(d) have a sulphur content not exceeding 1% of the total weight.

12. **Homefire briquettes**, manufactured by Coal Products Limited at Coventry, Warwickshire, which
(a) comprise crushed bituminous coal;
(b) were manufactured from the coal by a process involving heat treatment at about 450°C and extrusion;
(c) are unmarked hexagonal briquettes and have an average weight of 200 grammes; and
(d) have a sulphur content not exceeding 1.5% of the total weight.

12A. **Kola briquettes**, manufactured by Allied Smokeless Fuels Limited at Foynes, County Limerick, which
(a) comprises anthracite fines and coal blends (as to approximately 70% of the total weight), petroleum coke (as to approximately 70% of the total weight), and molasses and phosphoric acid as binder (as to the remaining weight);
(b) were manufactured from those constituents by a process involving roll-pressing and heat treatment at between 250°C and 280°C;
(c) are pillow-shaped briquettes, with one indented line running latitudinally around the briquette, in two sizes having an average weight of 42 grammes for the smaller size and 85 grammes for the larger size; and
(d) have a sulphur content not exceeding 1.5% of the total weight.

12AA. **Homefire (R) briquettes**, manufactured by Coal Products Limited at Coventry, Warwickshire, which
(a) comprise anthracite fines (as to 40-60% of the total weight), char (as to 40-60% of the total weight), bituminous coal (as to 0-10% of the total weight) and an organic binder as to the remaining weight;
(b) were manufactured from those constituents by a process involving extrusion;
(c) are unmarked hexagonal briquettes having an average weight of 240 grammes; and
(d) have a sulphur content not exceeding 1.5% of the total weight.

12AB. **Island Lump and Island Nuts**, manufactured by Unocal Refinery, California, United States of America, which
(a) comprise petroleum coke;
(b) were manufactured from petroleum coke by a process involving heat treatment and steam injection;
(c) are unmarked random shapes and have an average weight of 80 grammes (Island Lump) or 30 grammes (Island Nuts); and
(d) have a sulphur content not exceeding 2% of the total weight.

12AAA. **Homefire Ovals (R)**, manufactured by Coal Products Limited at Chesterfield, Derbyshire, which
(a) comprise anthracite fines (as to approximately 50-75% of the total weight), petroleum coke (as to approximately 20-45% of the total weight), bituminous coal (as to approximately 5-17% of the total weight) and an organic binder (as to the remaining weight);
(b) were manufactured from those constituents by a process involving roll pressing;
(c) are pillow-shaped briquettes with two parallel indented lines running latitudinally around the briquette and have an average weight of 130 grammes; and
(d) have a sulphur content not exceeding 1.5% of the total weight.

12AAB. **Homefire (Improved) briquettes**, manufactured by Coal Products Limited at Coventry, Warwickshire, which
(a) comprise anthracite fines (as to approximately 40-70% of the total weight), petroleum coke (as to approximately 20-45% of the total weight), char (as to approximately 0-10% of the total weight), bituminous coal (as to approximately 5-30% of the total weight) and an organic binder (as to the remaining weight);

(b) were manufactured from those constituents by a process involving roll pressing;
(c) have a volatile content in the finished briquette of not less than 9% nor more than 15% of the total weight on a dry basis;
(d) are unmarked hexagonal briquettes and have an average weight of 140 grammes; and
(e) have a sulphur content not exceeding 1.5% of the total weight.

12B. **Long Beach Lump nuts** (otherwise known as LBL nuts), manufactured by Aimcor Carbon Corp. at Long Beach, California, USA, which
(a) comprise petroleum coke (as to approximately 85-100% of the total weight), limestone (as to approximately 0-10% of the total weight) and coal tar pitch (as to the remaining weight);
(b) were manufactured from those constituents by a process involving heat treatment and steam injection;
(c) are unmarked random shapes; and
(d) have a sulphur content not exceeding 2% of the total weight.

13. **Maxibrite briquettes**, manufactured by Maxibrite Limited at Llantrisant, Mid Glamorgan, which
(a) comprise anthracite fines (as to approximately 99% of the total weight) and bitumen as binder (as to the remaining weight);
(b) were manufactured from those constituents by a process involving roll-pressing and heat treatment at between 270°C and 300°C;
(c) are cushion-shaped briquettes marked with the letter "M" and have an average weight of 35 grammes; and
(d) have a sulphur content of approximately 1% of the total weight.

13A. **Maxiflame briquettes**, manufactured by Maxibrite Limited at Llantrisant, Mid Glamorgan, which
(a) comprise anthracite fines (as to approximately 99% of the total weight) and bitumen as binder (as to the remaining weight);
(b) were manufactured from those constituents by a process involving roll-pressing and heat treatment at between 270°C and 300°C;
(c) are cushion-shaped briquettes marked with the letters "MF" and have an average weight of 80 grammes; and
(d) have a sulphur content of approximately 1% of the total weight.

13B. Revoked by 1998 Regulations, SI 2154.

13BB. **Natura briquettes**, manufactured by NSM Mining (South Wales Limited at Taybrite Plant, Llanelli, Dyfed, which
(a) comprise anthracite fines (as to approximately 90% of the total weight) and molasses and phosphoric binder (as to the remaining weight);
(b) were manufactured from those constituents by a process involving roll pressing and heat treatment at about 250°C;
(c) are cushion-shaped briquettes with a red coating having a central line running latitudinally around the briquette and have an average weight of 48 grammes; and
(d) have a sulphur content not exceeding 1.5% of the total weight.

14. **New Taybrite briquettes**, manufactured by NSM Mining (South Wales) Limited at Llanelli, Dyfed, which
(a) comprise anthracite fines (as to approximately 94% of the total weight) and bitumen as binder (as to the remaining weight);
(b) were manufactured from those constituents by a process involving agglomeration with steam, roll-pressing and heat treatment at about 280°C;
(c) are cushion-shaped briquettes imprinted with a flame motif and have an average weight of 47 grammes; and

(d) have a sulphur content of approximately 1% of the total weight.

14A. **Newflame briquettes**, manufactured by Maxibrite Limited, at Llantrisant, Mid-Glamorgan, which

(a) comprise anthracite (as to approximately 75% of the total weight), petroleum coke (as to approximately 21% of the total weight) and starch with a catalyst binder (as to the remaining weight);
(b) were manufactured from those constituents by a process involving roll pressing and heat treatment at about 250°C;
(c) are unmarked pillow-shaped briquettes and have an average weight of 78 grammes; and
(d) have a sulphur content not exceeding 2% of the total weight.

15. **Phurnacite briquettes**, manufactured by Coal Products Limited at Immingham Briquetting Works, Immingham, Humberside, which

(a) comprise anthracite duff (as to approximately 65% to 85% of the total weight), petoroleum coke (up to approximately 20% of the total weight) and a molasses and phosphoric acid as binder (as to the remaining weight);
(b) were manufactured from those constituents by a process involving roll-pressing and heat treatment at about 300°C;
(c) are ovoid-shaped briquettes with two parallel indented lines running longitudinally around the briquette and have an average weight of 40 grammes; and
(d) have a sulphur content not exceeding 1.5% of the total weight.

16. **Pureheat ovoids**, manufactured by Applied Industrial Materials Corporation (AIMCOR) at Rotterdam, The Netherlands, which

(a) comprise petroleum coke (as to 60-75% of the total weight), bituminous coal (as to 10-20% of the total weight), limestone (as to 6-10 % of the total weight) and a coal tar pitch binder (as to the remaining weight);
(b) were manufactured from those constituents by a process involving roll-pressing, carbonisation for 30 minutes at 550°C to 600°C and hardening in sand at about 500°C for a further 30 minutes;
(c) are ovoids with two indentations on one side and one indentation on the other side running parallel to the longest side and have an average weight of 22 or 69 grammes; and
(d) have a sulphur content not exceeding 1.5% of the total weight.

16A. **Homefire ovals**, manufactured by Coal Products Limited at Immingham Briquetting Works, Immingham, Humberside, which

(a) comprise anthracite duff (as to approximately 57% of the total weight), petroleum coke (as to approximately 17% of the total weight), bituminous coal (as to approximately 13% of the total weight) and molasses and phosphoric acid as binder (as to the remaining weight);
(b) were manufactured from those constituents by a process involving roll-pressing and heat treatment at about 300°C;
(c) are pillow-shaped briquettes with two parallel indented lines running latitudinally around the briquette and have an average weight of 135 grammes; and
(d) have a sulphur content not exceeding 1.5% of the total weight.

16B. **Safelight Firelogs**, manufactured by Advanced Natural Fuels Limited, at Pocklington, East Yorkshire, which

(a) comprise woodchip (as to approximately 40% to 55% of the total weight) and Palm Wax binder (as to approximately 45% to 60% of the total weight);
(b) were manufactured from those constituents by a process involving pressing of the mixed ingredients at about 40° to 50°C;
(c) are rectangular hard finish Firelogs with two deep overlapping slots in the top surface, a single continuous slot in the base surface, and have an average weight of 1.8 kilogrammes; and
(d) have a sulphur content not exceeding 2% of the total weight.

17. **Sovereign briquettes**, manufactured by the Monckton Coke & Chemical Company Limited at Royston, near Barnsley, South Yorkshire, which
    (a) comprise anthracite (as to approximately 75% of the total weight), coal and reactive coke (as to approximately 21% of the total weight) and cold-setting resin binder (as to the remaining weight);
    (b) were manufactured from those constituents by a process involving extrusion;
    (c) are unmarked hexagonal briquettes and have an average weight of 130 grammes; and
    (d) have a sulphur content not exceeding 2% of the total weight.

17A. **Sunbrix briquettes**, manufacture by Yarraboldy Briquette Company Limited at Rockhampton, Queensland, Australia, which
    (a) comprise anthracite (as to approximately 90% of the total weight) and cold setting organic binder as to the remaining weight;
    (b) were manufactured from those constituents by a process involving roll pressing;
    (c) are unmarked ovoids which have an average weight of 50 grammes; and
    (d) have a sulphur content not exceeding 1% of the total weight.

17B. **Supacite briquettes**, manufactured by Maxibrite Limited at Llantrisant, Mid-Glamorgan, which
    (a) comprise anthracite (as to approximately 95% of the total weight) and starch and catalyst as binder (as to the remaining weight);
    (b) were manufactured from those constituents by a process involving roll pressing and heat treatment at about 240°C;
    (c) are unmarked ovoids and have an average weight of 45 grammes; and
    (d) have a sulphur content not exceeding 1.5% of the total weight.

18. **Supertherm briquettes**, manufactured by Thermac Fuels Limited at Shildon, County Durham, which
    (a) comprise a blend (in the proportion of 19:1) of anthracite and medium volatile coal (as to approximately 93% of the total weight) and cold-setting organic binder (as to the remaining weight);
    (b) were manufactured from those constituents by a process involving roll-pressing;
    (c) are unmarked ovoids and have an average weight of 160 grammes; and
    (d) have a sulphur content not exceeding 1.5% of the total weight.

18A. **Supertherm II briquettes**, manufactured by Thermac Fuels Limited at Shildon, County Durham, which
    (a) comprise anthracite (as to approximately 36-51% of the total weight), petroleum coke (as to approximately 40-55% of the total weight) and an organic binder (as to the remaining weight);
    (b) were manufactured from those constituents by a process involving roll pressing at the ambient temperature;
    (c) are unmarked ovoids and have an average weight of 140 grammes; and
    (d) have a sulphur content not exceeding 2% of the total weight.

18B. **Taybrite briquettes**, (otherwise known as Surefire briquettes), manufactured by Coal Products Limited at Immingham Briquetting Works, North East Lincolnshire, which
    (a) comprise anthracite (as to approximately 60% to 80% of the total weight), petroleum coke (as to approximately 10% to 30% of the total weight) and a molasses and phosphoric acid binder (as to the remaining weight);
    (b) were manufactured from those constituents by a process involving roll pressing and heat treatment at about 300°C;
    (c) are pillow-shaped briquettes with a single indented line running longitudinally along each face, offset from its counterpart by 10 millimetres, and have an average weight of 75 grammes; and
    (d) have a sulphur content not exceeding 2% of the total weight.

19. **Thermac briquettes**, manufactured by Thermac Fuels Limited at Shildon, County Durham, which
    (a) comprise anthracite (as to approximately 90% of the total weight) and cold-setting organic binder (as to the remaining weight);
    (b) were manufactured from those constituents by a process involving roll-pressing;
    (c) are unmarked pillow-shaped briquettes and have an average weight of 48 grammes; and
    (d) have a sulphur content not exceeding 1.5% of the total weight.

20. **Thermobrite briquettes & Thermaglow briquettes**, manufactured by Volkseigener Betrieb Gaskombinat "Fritz Selbmann" Schwarze Pumpe at Lauchhammer, Germany, which
    (a) comprise milled lignite;
    (b) were manufactured from the lignite by a process involving extrusion, drying and heat treatment at a temperature greater than 900°C;
    (c) are unmarked briquettes which are produced in three sizes: Thermobrite or Thermaglow Large, Thermobrite or Thermaglow Doubles and Thermobrite or Thermaglow Beans; and
    (d) have a sulphur content not exceeding 2% of the total weight.

Appendix 2.6b: Smoke Control (Exempted Fireplaces) Orders

(These Orders cover England and Wales. Similar Orders have been made for Scotland)

Class of Fireplace	*Conditions*
1970 Order (SI 1970 No. 615)	
1. Any fireplace specially designed or adapted for combustion of liquid fuel.	
2. Any fireplace (other than a fireplace fired by pulverised fuel) constructed on or after 31st December 1956 and installed before 1st May 1970 and equipped with mechanical stokers, or adapted between those dates for use with such stokers.	No fuel shall be used other than that for which the mechanical stoker was designed.
3. Any fireplace designed to burn coal (other than a fireplace fired by pulverised coal) with a heating capacity exceeding 150,000 Btu/hr constructed and installed on or after 31st December 1956 and equipped with mechanical stokers or adapted on or after that date for use with such stokers.	No fuel shall be used other than that for which the mechanical stoker was designed.
*4. The fireplace known as the Solid Fuel Ductair Unit, manufactured by Radiation Ltd.	
5. The fireplace known as the Fulgora slow combustion Stove, manufactured by Fulgora Stoves Ltd.	No fuel shall be used other than wood waste in clean condition.
*6. The fireplace known as the Housewarmer manufactured for the National Coal Board by Ideal Standard Limited and latterly by Stelrad Group Ltd.	No fuel shall be used other than selected washed coal marketed under the name Housewarm" by agreement with the National Coal Board.
*7. The fireplace known as Wood Chip Fired Air Heater, manufactured by Air Plants (Sales) Ltd.	No fuel shall be used other than clean wood waste of a size within the limits referred to in the manufacturer's instructions.
*8. The fireplace known as the Hounsell Sawdust Burning Stove, manufactured by John Hounsell (Engineers) Ltd.	No fuel shall be used other than wood waste in clean condition.
1970 No. 2 Order (SI 1970 No. 1667) The Fireplace known as the Triancomatic T 80 and manufactured by Trianco Ltd.	
**1971 Order (SI 1971 No. 1265)* The fireplace known as the Rayburn CB 34 and manufactured by Glynwed Foundries Ltd.	

Class of Fireplace	*Conditions*
1972 Order (SI 1972 No. 438) The fireplace known as the Parkray Coalmaster and manufactured by Radiation Parkray Ltd, now T. I. Parkray Ltd.	No fuel shall be used other than selected washed coal marketed under the name "Housewarm" by agreement with the National Coal Board.
1972 No. 2 Order (SI 1972 No. 955) The fireplace known as the Trianco TGB 17 and manufactured by Trianco Ltd.	
1973 Order (SI 1973 No. 2166) The fireplace known as the Rayburn Prince 101 and the fireplace known as the Rayburn Prince 301, both manufactured by Glynwed Foundries Ltd.	
**1975 No. 2 Order (SI 1975 No. 1001)* The fireplace known as the Riley Nihot Woodchip Fired Air Heater type NM011 manufactured by Clarke Chapman Ltd, latterly by NEI International Combustion Ltd, Riley Equipment.	No fuel shall be used other than clean wood waste of a size within the limits of the manufacturer's specifications and containing not more than 5% sander dust.
**1975 No. 3 Order (SI 1975 No. 1111)* The fireplace known as the Rayburn Prince 76, manufactured by Glynwed Domestic and Heating Appliances Ltd.	No fuel shall be used other than selected washed coal doubles and trebles.
1978 Order (SI 1978 No. 1609) The fireplace known as the Spanex Wood Fired Air Heater (types UL50, UL75 and UL100 only), manufactured by Spanex Sander GmbH KG of Volpriehausen, Solling, in the Federal Republic of Germany	1. The Fireplace shall be installed, maintained and operated so as to minimise the emission of smoke and in accordance with Issue No 1 of the manufacturer's instructions dated May 1978. 2. No fuel shall be used other than clean wood waste contaning not more than 5% sander dust and not more than 1% plastic contamination.
1982 Order (SI 1982 No. 1615) The fireplace known as the APE Saffire Boiler (in the sizes, expressed in BTUs per hour, as 1M to 8M, 10M and 12M) manufactured by Air Pollution Engineering Limited, now Air Pollution Equipment Ltd.	1. The fireplace shall be installed, maintained and operated so as to minimise the emission of smoke at all times and in accordance with the manufacturer's instructions dated 27 August 1982 and bearing the reference SAF 250-3000/HW & /S". 2. No fuel shall be used other than sawdust or shavings, or mixtures of sawdust, shavings and offcuts, being fuel containing (by weight) not more than 1 % of plastic material.

*No longer in production, but where such fireplaces continue in use they remain exempt.

Class of Fireplace	*Conditions*
1983 Order (SI 1983 No. 277) The fireplace known as the Rayburn Coalglo C-30 and manufactured, both as an inset model and as a freestanding model, by Glynwed Domestic & Heating Appliances Ltd, now Glynwed Appliances Ltd.	1. The fireplace shall be installed, maintained and operated so as to minimise the emission of smoke at all times and in accordance with the manufacturer's instructions which - a) in the case of the inset model, bear the date 1 September 1981 and the reference Code 510" or b) in the case of the freestanding model, bear the date 1 December 1982 and the reference Code 510 F". 2. No fuel shall be used other than selected washed coal doubles and trebles (also known as nuts and large nuts).
1983 No. 2 Order (SI 1983 No. 426) The fireplace known as the Talbott 500 Hot-air Heater (afterburn model) and manufactured by Talbott's Heating Ltd.	1. The fireplace shall be installed, maintained and operated so as to minimise the emission of smoke at all times and in accordance with the manufacturer's instructions dated 1 January 1983 and bearing the reference A1000. 2. No fuel shall be used other than wood off-cuts, woodwaste, pellets, chipboard, plastic covered chip-board (the plastic content of the covering being not more than 1% by weight), cardboard or paper. 3. The afterburn cycle shall last not less than 25 mins. and shall come into operation each time the loading door is opened.
1983 No. 3 Order (SI 1983 No. 1018) The fireplace known as the Trianco Coal King' Boiler and manufactured by Trianco Redfyre Ltd.	1. The fireplace shall be installed, maintained and operated so as to minimise the emission of smoke at all times, and in accordance with the manufacturer's instructions dated May 1983 and which - a) in the case of installation instructions bear the reference 47664' and b) in the case of the user, instructions bear the reference 47665'. 2. No fuel shall be used other than selected washed coal doubles or Union Coal Briketts, manufactured by Rheinbraun AG of Germany and comprising lignite compressed into briquettes of approximately 15 centimetres in length with square ends and with a sulphur content not exceeding 1 per cent.

Class of Fireplace	*Conditions*
1984 Order (SI 1984 No. 1649)	
The Parkray Coalmaster II manufactured by T.I. Parkray Limited, both as an inset model and as a free standing model.	a) installation instructions for for the inset model: reference List No. 1048/June 1983 8402"; b) installation instructions for the free-standing model: reference List No. 1058/February 1984"; and c) user's instructions for both models: reference List No. 1049/September 1983".
The Spacewarmer B200 manufactured by Clean Air Systems.	installation operation and maintenance instructions: reference B200/DEC 1983".
The Spacewarmer B500 manufactured by Clean Air Systems.	installation operation and maintenance instructions: reference B500/DEC 1983".
1985 Order (SI 1985 No 864)	
The SE60 Coalburner Stove manufactured by Jetmaster Fires Limited.	a) installation instructions: reference SE60/18/84"; b) operating and maintenance instructions: reference SE 60/28/84".
The Worcester Centair 40 Solid Fuel Warm Air Heater manufactured by Worcester Engineering Co. Limited	a) installation instructions: reference "BC40.1.2 July 1983; b) operating and maintenance instructions: reference "BC40.OM2 July 1983.
1986 Order (SI 1986 No. 638)	
The Triancomatic 60 boiler manufactured by Trianco Redfyre Limited.	1. The fireplace shall be installed, maintained and operated so as to minimise the emission of smoke at all times, and in accordance with the manufacturer's instructions dated 24 July 1985 and which - a) in the case of the installation instructions bear the reference No. 45576"; and b) in the case of the user instructions bear the reference No. 45574". 2. No fuel shall be used other than the washed coals recommended in the manufacturer's user instructions: reference No. 45574".
The Worcester Coalstream 17.5 kw underfeed stoker manufactured by Worcester Engineering Company Limited.	1. The fireplace shall be installed, maintained and operated so as to minimise the emission of smoke at all times, and in accordance with the manufacturer's instructions dated 1 August 1985 and which a) in the case of the installation instructions bear the reference No. ZKLIT 140"; and b) in the case of the user instructions bear the reference No. ZKLIT 139". 2. No fuel shall be used other than the washed coals recommended in the manufacturer's user instructions: reference No. ZK LIT 139".

Class of Fireplace	*Conditions*
The Corsair 300HW, 500HW and 750HW boilers manufactured by Erithglen Limited.	The fireplace shall be installed, maintained and operated so as to minimise the emission of smoke at all times, and in accordance with the manufacturer's instructions: reference 001 August 1985".
1988 Order (SI 1988 No. 2282) The Babcock Worsley Fluidised Bed Combuster manufactured by Babcock Robey Limited.	1. The fireplace shall be installed, maintained and operated so as to minimise the emission of smoke at all times, and in accordance with the manufacturer's instructions dated 30 April 1986 and which bear the reference No. C06/0016". 2. No fuel shall be used other than the waste derived fuel recommended in the manufacturer's instructions. 3. The fireplace shall be operated as a single unit with - a) the Tollemache Drier manufactured by Newell Dunford Limited; and b) The Venturi Scrubber manufactured by Air Pollution Control Limited.
The CBR Flexifuel Heater, models 300, 400 and 600 manufactured by CBR Fabrications Limited	1. The fireplaces shall be installed, maintained and operated so as to minimise the emission of smoke at all times, and in accordance with the manufacturer's instructions, which bear the reference FF/CBR Turbo Heat 88. 2. No fuel shall be used other than hard or soft wood off-cuts, chipboard or plastic coated chipboard. 3. The fireplace shall not be used to burn sawdust in bulk or plastic materials other than plastic coated chipboard.
The Eclipse Junior, Standard, Senior, Jumbo 30 and Jumbo 50 incinerators, manufactured by Northern Incinerators Limited.	1. The fireplaces shall be installed, maintained and operated so as to minimise the emission of smoke at all times, and in accordance with the manufacturer's instructions dated 21 June 1988 and which bear the reference NORCIN/ TECH/88". 2. No fuel shall be used, other than fuel consisting of paper, cardboard cartons, scrap wood, foliage, combustible floor sweepings and other waste from domestic, commercial and industrial activities containing no more than 20% of restaurant and cafeteria waste, and containing less than 5% by weight of coated papers, plastic or rubber waste.
The Haat LD, MD and HD Incinerators manufactured by Haat Incineration Limited.	1. The fireplaces shall be installed, maintained and operated so as to minimise the emission of smoke at all times, and in accordance with the manufacturer's instructions dated March 1988 and which bear the reference HAAT/I/CAA".

Class of Fireplace	*Conditions*
	2. No fuel shall be used, other than fuel consisting of paper, cardboard cartons, scrap wood, foliage, combustible floor sweepings and other waste from domestic, commercial and industrial activities containing no more than 20% of restaurant and cafeteria waste, and containing less than 5% by weight of coated papers, plastic or rubber waste.
The Holden Heat House 29.3kw and 45.4kw underfeed bituminous coal burning boilers manufactured by Holden Heat plc.	1. The fireplaces shall be installed, maintained and operated so as to minimise the emission of smoke at all times, and in accordance with the manufacturer's instructions which - a) in the case of the installation instructions bear the reference HH861B"; and b) in the case of the user instructions bear the reference HH861A". 2. No fuel shall be used other than the washed coals recommended in the manufacturer's user instructions.
The RanHeat Boiler Type RHA20, manufactured by RanHeat, Energy A/S.	1. The fireplace shall be installed, maintained and operated so as to minimise the emission of smoke at all times, and in accordance with the manufacturer's instructions dated 30 March 1988 and which bear the reference RHGBEA 30388". 2. No fuel shall be used other than hard and soft wood shavings.
The Talbott Pirojet P150 Heater manufactured by Talbott's Heating Limited.	1. The fireplace shall be installed, maintained and operated so as to minimise the emission of smoke at all times, and in accordance with the manufacturer's instructions dated February 1987 and which bear the reference No. P150-2-87". 2. No fuel shall be used other than hard or soft wood off-cuts, chipboard or plastic coated chipboard. 3. When the fireplace is used to burn chipboard and plastic coated chipboard, an afterburner which is supplied with the fireplace and which must be capable of continuously producing 20 megajoules of heat per hour, shall be used. 4. The fireplace shall not be used to burn sawdust in bulk or plastic materials other than plastic coated chipboard.
The Talbott Pirojet P300 Heater manufactured by Talbott's Heating Limited.	1. The fireplace shall be installed, maintained and operated so as to minimise the emission of smoke at all times, and in accordance with the manufacturer's instructions dated February 1987 and which bear the reference No. P300-2-87".

Class of Fireplace	*Conditions*
	2. No fuel shall be used other than hard or soft wood off-cuts, chipboard or plastic coated chipboard. 3. When the fireplace is used to burn chipboard and plastic coated chipboard an afterburner which is supplied with the fireplace and which must be capable of continuously producing 40 megajoules of heat per hour, shall be used. 4. The fireplace shall not be used to burn sawdust in bulk or plastic materials other than plastic coated chipboard.
The Talbott Pirojet P600 Heater manufactured by Talbott's Heating Limited.	1. The Fireplace shall be installed, maintained and operated so as to minimise the emission of smoke at all times, and in accordance with the manufacturer's instructions dated December 1986 and which bear the reference P600-12-86" 2. No fuel shall be used other than hard or soft wood off-cuts, or chipboard or plastic coated chipboard. 3. When the fireplace is used to burn chipboard, and plastic coated chipboard an afterburner which is supplied with the fireplace and which must be capable of continuously producing 75 megajoules of heat per hour, shall be used. 4. The fireplace shall not be used to burn sawdust in bulk or plastic materials other than plastic coated chipboard.
The Triancomatic 90 boiler manufactured by Trianco Redfyre Limited	1. The fireplace shall be installed, maintained and operated so as to minimise the emission of smoke at all times, and in accordance with the manufacturer's instructions dated July 1987 and which - a) in the case of the installation instructions bear the reference No. 46576"; and b) in the case of the user instructions bear the reference No. 46574". 2. No fuel shall be used other than the washed coals recommended in the manufacturer's user instructions.
The Triancomatic 140 boiler manufactured by Trianco Redfyre Limited.	1. The fireplace shall be installed, maintained and operated so as to minimise the emission of smoke at all times, and in accordance with the manufacturer's instructions dated November 1986 and which - a) in the case of the installation instructions bear the reference No. 48375"; and b) in the case of the user instructions bear the reference No. 48374".

Class of Fireplace	*Conditions*
	2. No fuel shall be used other than the washed coals recommended in the manufacturer's user instructions.
1989 Order (SI 1989 No. 1769)	
The Talbott T5-1M Automatic Heater manufactured by Talbott's Heating Ltd. *Class of Fireplace*	1. The fireplace shall be installed, maintained and operated so as to minimise the emission of smoke at all times, and in accordance with the manufacturer's instructions bearing the reference Jan. 89 T5-A-1-89. 2. No fuel other than softwood shavings, hardwood shavings or chipboard dust shall be used.
The Nordist Waste Fired System models 10, 11, 12, 13, 14, 15, 16, 17, 18, 19, 20, 21, 22 and 23 manufactured in part by Nordfab A/S and in part by Danstoker A/S.	1. The fireplace shall be installed, maintained and operated so as to minimise the emission of smoke at all times, and in accordance with the manufacturer's instructions bearing the reference P.S.501 9.12.88. 2. No fuel other than softwood shavings, hardwood shavings or sawdust shall be used.
The CBR Flexifuel Heater, models 150 and 200 manufactured by CBR Fabrications Ltd.	1. The fireplace shall be installed, maintained and operated so as to minimise the emission of smoke at all times, and in accordance with the manufacturer's instructions bearing the reference FF/CBR Flexifuel 150/200 1989. 2. No fuel other than hardwood or softwood offcuts, chipboard or plastic coated chipboard shall be used. 3. The fireplace shall not be used to burn sawdust in bulk or plastic materials other than plastic coated chipboard.
The Silent Glow Incinerator, models CCD 450, 600 and 750 manufactured by Silent Glow Incinerators Ltd.	1. The fireplace shall be maintained and operated so as to minimise the emission of smoke at all times, and in accordance with the manufacturer's instructions dated May 1989. 2. No fuel other than solid waste of the types specified in the manufacturer's instructions dated May 1989 shall be used.
The Hughes Edwards 45 Coalflow Boiler manufactured by Hughes Edwards Heating Ltd.	1. The fireplace shall be installed, maintained and operated so as to minimise the emission of smoke at all times, and in accordance with the manufacturer's instructions which: a) in the case of the installation instructions bear the reference II/02D/07-89, and b) in the case of the user instructions bear the reference UI/02D/07-89. 2. No fuel other than the washed coals recommended in the manufacturer's instructions bearing the reference II/02D/07-89 shall be used.

Class of Fireplace	*Conditions*
1990 Order (SI 1990 No. 345) The Haat Pioneer ABl Incinerators, models 12, 20, 28 and 36 manufactured by Haat Incineration Limited.	1. The fireplaces shall be installed, maintained and operated so as to minimise the emission of smoke at all times, and in accordance with the manufacturer's instructions bearing the reference HAAT/2/CAA/10/89". 2. No fuel shall be used other than the following fuels used in the mixtures by volume recommended in Appendix A of the manufacturer's instructions: paper, cardboard, corrugated paper, office or domestic waste, wood, polythene sheet or foam, polypropylene, nylon, polyethylene, rubber foam backed carpet, polystyrene, polyurethane and glass fibre reinforced plastics.
The Triancomatic 45 boiler manufactured by Trianco Redfyre Limited.	1. The fireplace shall be installed, maintained and operated so as to minimise the emission of smoke at all times, and in accordance with the manufacturer's instructions dated September 1989 and which - (a) in the case of the installation instructions bear the reference No. 44359"; and (b) in the case of the user instructions bear the referenceNo. 44358". 2. No fuel shall be used other than the washed coals recommended in the manufacturer's user instructions.
1990 Order (SI No. 2457) The Intrepid II woodstove manufactured by Vermont Castings, Inc.	1. The fireplace shall be installed, maintained and operated in accordance with the manufacturer's instructions bearing the reference AMENDED No. 20917C U.K. MAY 1990". 2. No fuel shall be used other than 16" firewood that has been split, stacked and air-dried.
The Spacewarmer B200 manufactured by Clearair Limited.	1. The fireplace shall be installed, maintained and operated in accordance with the manufacturer's instructions bearing the reference B200/DEC 83". 2. No fuel shall be used other than hardwood or softwood offcuts, a mixture of offcuts (hardwood or softwood) and sawdust with no more than 50% of the mixture being sawdust, chipboard offcuts or plastic coated chipboard offcuts. 3. The fireplace shall not be used to burn chipboard or plastic coated chipboard unless an afterburner, supplied by the manufacturer of the fireplace and capable of producing 50 megajoules of heat per hour, has been fitted to the fireplace.

Class of Fireplace	*Conditions*
The Spacewarmer B500 manufactured by Clearair Limited.	1. The fireplace shall be installed, maintained and operated in accordance with the manufacturer's instructions bearing the reference B500/DEC 83". 2. No fuel shall be used other than hardwood or softwood offcuts.
The Turbo' Heat, models 1000 and 1200 manufactured by CBR Engineers Limited.	1. The fireplace shall be installed, maintained and operated in accordance with the manufacturer's instructions bearing the reference CBR TURBO' HEAT 1000 TO 1200 1990". 2. No fuel shall be used other than hardwood or softwood offcuts, chipboard offcuts or plastic coated chipboard offcuts.
The Talbott's Energy Saving Wood Waste Burning Automatic Warm Air Heaters, models T1.5/A, T3/A, T5/A and TM/A manufactured by Talbotts Heating Limited.	1. The fireplaces shall be installed, maintained and operated in accordance with the manufacturer's instructions bearing the reference T/A JANUARY 1990". 2. No fuel shall be used other than hardwood or softwood shaving or sawdust.
1991 Order (SI No. 2892) The Hughes Edwards Model 65 hot water boiler manufactured by Hughes Edwards Heating Limited.	1. The fireplace shall be installed, maintained and operated in accordance with the manufacturer's instructions bearing the reference II/02D/11-90 and UI/02D/11-90". 2. No fuel shall be used other than bituminous Coalflow pearls distributed by the British Coal Corporation.
The Jansen Design stove, using the five channel system, manufactured by Kakkel ovnsmakeriet as.	1. The fireplace shall be installed, maintained and operated in accordance with the manufacturer's instructions bearing the reference CSC-JDS-OI dated 21/10/91". 2. No fuel shall be used other than wood.
The Resolute Acclaim woodstove manufactured by Vermont Castings, Inc.	1. The fireplace shall be installed, maintained and operated in accordance with the manufacturer's instructions bearing the reference AMENDED No. 200 - 0908 U.K. OCTOBER 1991". 2. No fuel shall be used other than 16" firewood that has been split, stacked and air-dried.
The Talbott's Warm Air Heaters Down Firing range models D250, D500 and D700 manufactured by Talbotts Heating Limited.	1. The fireplaces shall be installed, maintained and operated in accordance with the manufacturer's instructions bearing the reference MAY 1991 Ref No: D257". 2. No fuel shall be used other than hardwood or softwood offcuts, chipboard, plastic coated chipboard or cardboard.

Class of Fireplace	*Conditions*
1992 Order (SI No. 2811) The Cronspisen stove, using the five channel chimney system, manufactured by Cronspisen Produktion AB.	1. The fireplace is installed, maintained and operated in accordance with the manufacturer's instructions bearing the reference January 1992. Serial No: UM 351B". 2. No fuel is used other than firewood that has been split, stacked and air-dried.
The RanHeat Boiler Types RHA 160, 200 and 250, manufactured by RanHeat Energy GB Limited.	1. The fireplaces are installed, maintained and operated in accordance with the manufacturer's instructions dated 30th March 1988 bearing the reference RHGBEA 30388". 2. No fuel is used other than hard and soft wood shavings.
The Defiant Encore manufactured by VCW International Limited.	1. The fireplace is installed, maintained and operated in accordance with the manufacturer's instructions dated November 1991 bearing the reference 200-8632". 2. No fuel is used other than firewood that has been split, stacked and air-dried.
1993 Order (SI No. 2277) The Apollo incinerator types 10, 25 and 50 manufactured by Apollo Incineration Systems Limited.	1. The incinerators shall be installed, maintained and operated in accordance with the manufacturer's instructions dated 2nd November 1992 and bearing the reference Apollo 10-25-50". 2. No fuel shall be used other than wood, wood shavings, cardboard and polythene.
The Clearview models 650 and 750, and the Vision 500 model, manufactured by Clearview Stoves.	1. The fireplaces shall be installed, maintained and operated in accordance with the manufacturer's instructions dated 1st January 1993 and, in the case of the Clearview models 650 and 750, bearing the reference 1/42" and, in the case of the Vision 500 model, bearing the reference V1/42". 2. No fuel shall be used other than firewood which has been split, stacked and air dried.
The Farm 2000 boilers HT60, HT70, HT80 and BB154/2V manufactured by Farm 2000 Limited.	1. The boilers shall be installed, maintained and operated in accordance with the manufacturer's instructions which, in the case of models HT60, HT70 and HT80, are dated 1st July 1993 and bear the reference HT60/70/80", and, in the case of model BB154/2V, and dated 1st September 1993 and bear the reference 9/93". 2. No fuel shall be used other than cereal straw.

Class of Fireplace	*Conditions*
1996 Order (SI No. 1108) The Dovre woodstove models 500G and 700G manufactured by Dovre Castings Limited	1. The fireplaces shall be installed, maintained and operated in accordance with the manufacturer's instructions dated October 1993 and bearing the following reference :– (a) model 500G: "500G"; (b) model 700G:"700G". 2. No fuel shall be used other than wood.
The Farm 2000 boiler models BB154, BB154A and BB154/2 (when used with the Farm 2000 conversion kit BB154/2Vcx), maunufactured by Farm 2000 Limited.	1. The boilers shall be installed in accordance with the manufacturer's instructions dated May 1994 and bearing the reference "BB154/2VC", and maintained and operated in accordance with the manufacturer's instructions dated September 1993 and bearing the reference "BB154/2V". 2. No fuel shall be used other than cereal straw.
The Farm 2000 model HT6 (when used with the Farm 2000 conversion kit HT60cx), the HT6PLUS and HT600 (when each is used with the Farm conversion kit HT70cx), and the HT7 and HT8 (when each is used with the Farm 2000 conversion kit HT80cx), manufactured by Farm 2000 Limited.	1. The boilers shall be installed in accordance with the manufacturer's instructions dated May 1994 and bearing the reference "HT6780" and "HT 6781", and maintained and operated in accordance with the manufacturer's instructions dated 1 July 1993 and bearing the reference "HT60/70/80". 2. No fuel shall be used other than cereal straw.
The Jotul catalyst stove models 8TDIC and 12TDIC manufactured by Jotul Limited	1. The fireplaces shall be installed, maintained and operated in accordance with the manufacturer's instructions dated November 1995 and bearing the following references :– (a) model 8TDIC: "JT8/001" and "J/S/001"; (b) mode12TDIC: "JT12/001" and "JT/S/001". 2. No fuel shall be used other than wood.
The RanHeat appliances models MSU150, MSU300, MSU500, WA150, WA300 and WA500, manufactured by RanHeat Engineering Limited.	1. The appliances shall be installed, maintained and operated in accordance with the manufacturer's instructions dated July 1995 bearing the following references :– (a) models MSU150, MSU300 andMSU500: "MSU150/5001994"; (b)models WA150, WA300 and WA500: "WA150/5001994". 2. No fuel shall be used other chipboard, fibreboard, melamine coated chipboard, wood offcuts, softwood or hardwood shavings or dust.
The Talbott's Combustion Units, models C1, C2, C3 and C4, manufactured by Talbott's Heating Limited.	1. The fireplaces shall be installed, maintained and operated in accordance with the manufacturer's instructions dated August 1995 and bearing the reference "Issue: C1000/C/Range". 2. No fuel shall be used other than chipboard, or wood shavings, forestry chips or paper briquettes.

Class of Fireplace	*Conditions*
The Talbott's Heating models T75, T150, T300, D250B, D500B and D700B, manufactured by Talbott's Heating Limited.	1. The fireplaces shall be installed, maintained and operated in accordance with the manufacturer's instructions dated 1st January 1995 and bearing the following references :– (a) models T75, T150 and T300: "gen/sttech"; (b) models D250B, D500B and D700B: "Gen/Tech". 2. No fuel shall be used other than the following; (a) models T75, T150 and T300: wood offcuts, woodwaste pallets, chipboard, plastic coated chipboard, cardboard or paper; (b)models D250B, D500B and D700B: hardwood or softwood offcuts, chipboard, plastic coated chipboard or cardboard.
1997 Order (SI No. 3009) The Talbott's Energy Saving Wood Waste Burning Automatic Hot Water Heaters, models T1.5/AB, T3/AB, T5/AB, manufactured by Talbott's Heating Limited.	1. The fireplaces shall be installed, maintained and operated in accordance with the manufacturer's instructions dated October 1993 and bearing the reference "Issue: A1001". 2. No fuel shall be used other than hardwood or softwood shavings or sawdust.
The Talbott's Combustion Units, models CM1, CM2, CM3 and CM4, manufactured by Talbott's Heating Limited.	1. The fireplaces shall be installed, maintained and operated in accordance with the manufacturer's instructions dated August 1997 and bearing the reference "Issue: CM897". 2. No fuel shall be used other than wood-waste pallets, medium density fibreboard, melamine faced chipboard, cardboard, paper or untreated and airdried wood offcuts.

NB. There are no appendices for Chapter 3, Noise.

APPENDIX 4.1

WASTE MANAGEMENT PAPERS

This series of papers provides guidance on all aspects of waste management. Section 35(8) of the *Environmental Protection Act 1990* requires regulatory authorities to take account of guidance (such as WMPs) issued by the Secretary of State in the discharge of their licence functions. WMPs listed here were prepared by the Department of the Environment. They are published by The Stationery Office.

WMP 1	A review of options (second edition 1992)
WMP 2/3	[replaced by DOE Guidance, *Waste Management Planning - Principles and Practice* (1995)
WMP 4	The licensing of waste facilities (third edition 1994)
WMP 4A	Licensing of metal recycling sites (1995)
WMP 5	The relationship between waste disposal authorities and private industry (1976)
WMP 6	Polychlorinated biphenyl (PCB) wastes - a technical memorandum on reclamation, treatment and disposal (1994)
WMP 7	Mineral oil wastes - a technical memorandum on arisings, treatment and disposal (1976)
WMP 8	Heat treatment cyanide wastes - a technical memorandum on arisings, treatment and disposal (second edition 1985)
WMP 9	Halogenated hydrocarbon solvent wastes from cleaning processes - a technical memorandum on reclamation and disposal (1976)
WMP 10	local authority waste disposal statistics 1974/75 (1976)
WMP 11	Metal finishing wastes - a technical memorandum on arisings, treatment and disposal (1976)
WMP 12	Mercury bearing wastes - a technical memorandum on storage, handling, treatment, disposal and recovery (1979)
WMP 13	Tarry and distillation wastes and other chemical based wastes - a technical memorandum on arisings, treatment and disposal (1977)
WMP 14	Solvent wastes (excluding halogenated hydrocarbons) - a technical memorandum on reclamation and disposal (1977)
WMP 15	Halogenated organic wastes - a technical memorandum on arisings, treatment and disposal (1978)
WMP 16	Wood preserving wastes - a technical memorandum on arisings, treatment and disposal (1980)
WMP 17	Wastes from tanning, leather dressing and fellmongering - a technical memorandum on recovery, treatment and disposal (1978)
WMP 18	Asbestos waste - a technical memorandum on arisings and disposal (1979)
WMP 19	Wastes from the manufacture of pharmaceuticals, toiletries and cosmetics - a technical memorandum on arisings, treatment and disposal (1978)
WMP 20	Arsenic bearing wastes - a technical memorandum on recovery, treatment and disposal (1980)
WMP 21	Pesticide wastes - a technical memorandum on arisings and disposal (1980)
WMP 22	Local authority waste disposal statistics 1974/75 to 1977/78 (1978)
WMP 23	Special wastes - a technical memorandum providing guidance on their definition (1981; redraft due 9/97))
WMP 24	Cadmium bearing wastes - a technical memorandum on arisings, treatment and disposal (1984)
WMP 25	Clinical wastes - a technical memorandum on arisings, treatment and disposal (1983 - new draft expected 10/97)
WMP 26	Landfilling wastes - a technical memorandum on landfill sites (1986)

WMP 26A Landfill completion - a technical memorandum providing guidance on assessing the completion of licensed landfill sites (1994)
WMP 26B Landfill design, construction and operation (1995)
WMP 26D Landfill monitoring (draft published 1/96; publication due Spring 1998)
WMP 26E Landfill restoration and post closure management (draft 9/96; publication due 7/97)
WMP 26F Landfill co-disposal (publication due 7/97)
WMP 27 Landfill gas - a memorandum for local authorities on recycling (1991)
WMP 28 Recycling - a memorandum for local authorities on recycling (1991)

- Waste Policy Guidance: Preparing and revising local authority recycling strategies and recycling plans (DETR, 1998)

APPENDIX 5.1a

QUALITY REQUIREMENTS FOR BATHING WATER (76/160/EEC)

Parameters	*G (Guideline)*	*I (Mandatory)*	*Minimum sampling frequency*	*Method of analysis and inspection*
MICROBIOLOGICAL				
1Total coliforms /100 ml	500	10000	Fortnightly (1)	Fermentation in multiple tubes subculturing of the positive tubes on a confirmation medium. Count according to MPN (most probable number) or membrane filtration and culture on an appropriate medium such as Tergitol lactose agar, endo agar. 0.4% Teepol broth, subculturing and identification of the suspect colonies. In the case of 1 and 2, the incubation temperature is variable according to whether total or faecal coliforms are being investigated.
2Faecal coliforms /100 ml	100	2000	Fortnightly (1)	
3 Faecal streptococci /100ml	100	-	(2)	Litsky method. Count according to MPN (most probable number) or filtration on membrane. Culture on an appropriate membrane.
4 Salmonella / 1 litre	-	0	(2)	Concentration by membrane filtration. Inoculation on a standard membrane. Enrichment - subculturing on isolating - agar identification.
5 Entero viruses PFU/10 litres	-	0	(2)	Concentrating by filtration, flocculation or centrifuging and confirmation.

PHYSICO-CHEMICAL:

6 pH		-	6 to 9 (0)	(2)	Electrometry with calibration at pH 7 and 9.
7 Colour		-	No abnormal change in colour (0)	Fortnightly (1)	Visual inspection or photometry with standards on the Pt. Co scale.
		-	-	(2)	
8 Mineral oils	mg/litre	-	No film visible on the surface of the water and no odour	Fortnightly (1)	Visual and olfactory inspection or extraction using an adequate volume and weighing the dry residue.
		<0.3	-	(2)	
9 Surface-active substances reacting with methylene blue	mg/litre (lauryl-sulfate)	-	No lasting foam	Fortnightly (1)	Visual inspection or absorption spectrophotometry with methylene blue.
		<0.3		(2)	
10 Phenols (phenol indices)	mg/litre C_6H_5OH	-	No specific odour	Fortnightly (1)	Verification of the absence of specific odour due to phenol or absorption spectrophotometry 4-aminoantipyrine (4 AAP) method.
		≤0.005	≤0.05	(2)	
11 Transparency	m	2	1(0)	Fortnightly (1)	Secchi's disc.
12 Dissolved oxygen	% saturation O_2	80 to 190	-	(2)	Winkler's method or electrometric method (oxygen meter).
13 Tarry residues and floating materials such as wood, plastic articles, bottles, containers of glass, plastic, rubber or any other substance. Waste or splinters.		Absence		Fortnightly (1)	Visual inspection.

Parameters		*G (Guideline)*	*I (Mandatory)*	*Minimum sampling frequency*	*Method of analysis and inspection*
14 Ammonia	mg/litre NH_4			(3)	Absorption spectrophotometry. Nessler's method, or indophenol blue method.
15 Nitrogen Kjeldahl	mg/litre N			(3)	Kjeldahl method.
16 Pesticides (parathion, HCH, dieldrin)	mg/litre			(2)	Extraction with appropriate solvents and chromatographic determination.
17 Heavy metals such as	mg/litre			(5)	Atomic absorption possible preceded by extraction
– arsenic	As				
– cadmium	Cd				
– chrom VI	CrVI				
– lead	Pb				
– mercury	Hg				
18 Cyanides	mg/litre CN			(2)	Absorption spectrophotometry using a specific reagent
19 Nitrates and phosphates	mg/litre NI_1 PO_4			(2)	Absorption spectrophotometry using a specific reagent

G guide; I mandatory; (0) provision exists for exceeding the limits in the event of exceptional geographical or meteorological conditions; (1) When a sampling taken in previous years produced results which are appreciably better than those in this Annex and when no new factor likely to lower the quality of the water has appeared, the competent authorities may reduce the sampling frequency by a factor of 2; (2) Concentration to be checked by the competent authorites when an inspection in the bathing area shows that the substance may be present or that the quality of the water has deteriorated; (3) These parameters must be checked by the competent authorites when there is a tendency towards the eutrophication of the water.

APPENDIX 5.1b

THE BATHING WATERS (CLASSIFICATION) REGULATIONS 1991

Quality and Additional Sampling Requirements in Compliance with Directive 76/160/EEC

Parameter	*Parametric value*	*Minimum sampling frequency*	*Method of analysis and inspection*
MICROBIOLOGICAL			
1 Total coliforms	10,000/ 100ml	Fortnightly (1)	Fermentation in multiple tubes. Sub-culturing of the positive tubes on a confirmation medium.
			Either counting according to MPN (most probable number) or membrane filtration, culturing on an appropriate medium, subculturing and identification of the suspect colonies.
2 Faecal coliforms	2,000/	Fortnightly	The incubation temperature is variable according to
	100ml	(1)	whether total or faecal coliforms are being investigated.
3 Salmonella	Absent in 1 litre	(2)	Membrane filtration, culturing on an appropriate medium, sub-culturing and identification of the suspect colonies.
4 Entero viruses	No plaque forming units in 10 litres	(2)	Concentration (by filtration, flocculation or centrifuging) and confirmation.

	Parameter	Parametric value	Minimum sampling frequency	Method of analysis and inspection
	PHYSICO-CHEMICAL:			
5	pH	6 to 9	(2)	Electrometry with calibration at pH 7 and 9.
6	Colour	No abnormal change in colour	Fortnightly (1)	Visual inspection or photometry with standards on the platinum cobalt scale.
7	Mineral oils	No film visible on the surface of the water and no odour	Fortnightly (1)	Visual and olfactory inspection.
8	Surface-active substances reacting with methylene blue	No lasting foam	Fortnightly (1)	Visual inspection.
9	Phenols (phenol indices)	No specific odour	Fortnightly (1)	Olfactory inspection.
		≤0.05 mg/litre (C_6H_5OH)	(2)	Absorption spectrophotometry 4-aminoantipyrine (4 AAP) method.
10	Transparency	1 metre	Fortnightly (1)	Secchi's disc.

Notes

1. Samples may be taken at intervals of four weeks where samples taken in previous years show that the waters are of an appreciably higher standard than that required for the classification in question and the quality of the waters has not subsequently deteriorated and is unlikely to do so.

2. Samples must be taken in relation to this parameter when there are grounds for suspecting that there has been a deterioration in the quality of the waters or the substance is likely to be present in the waters.

APPENDIX 5.2a

QUALITY OF WATER FOR HUMAN CONSUMPTION (80/778/EEC): LIST OF PARAMETERS

Organoleptic Parameters

	Parameters	*Expression of the results* (')	*Guide level (GL)*	*Maximum admissible concentration (MAC)*	*Comments*
1	Colour	mg/l Pt/Co scale	1	20	
2	Turbidity	mg/l SiO_2 Jackson units	1 0.4	10 4	 Replaced in certain circumstances by a transparency test, with a Sechi disc reading in meters: GL: 6 m MAC: 2 m
3	Odour	Dilution number	0	2 at 12°C 3 at 25°C	To be related to the taste test.
4	Taste	Dilution number	0	2 at 12°C 3 at 25°C	To be related to the odour tests.

(') If, on the basis of Directive 71/354/EEC as last amended, a Member State uses in its national legislation, adopted in accordance with this Directive, units of measurement other than those indicated in this Annex, the values thus indicated must have the same degree of precision.

Parameters	Expression of the results [1]	Guide level (GL)	Maximum admissible concentration (MAC)	Comments
Physico-Chemical Parameters				
5 Temperature	°C	12	25	
6 Hydrogen ion	pH unit	6.5≤ Ph ≤ 8.5		The water should not be aggressive. The pH values do not apply to water in closed containers. Maximum admissible value: 9.5.
7 Conductivity	µS cm^{-1} at 20°C	400		Corresponding to the mineralization of the water. Corresponding relativity values in ohms/cm: 2,500.
8 Chlorides	Cl mg/l	25		Approximate concentration above which effects might occur: 200 mg/l.
9 Sulphates	SO_4 mg/l	25	250	
10 Silica	SiO_2 mg/l			
11 Calcium	Ca mg/l	100		
12 Magnesium	Mg mg/l	30	50	
13 Sodium	Na mg/l	20	175 (as from 1984 and with a percentile of 90)	The values of this parameter take account of the recommendations of a WHO working party (The Hague, May 1978) on the progressive reduction of the current total daily salt intake to 6g.

				150 (as from 1987 and with a percentile of 80) (these percentiles should be calculated over a reference period of three years)	As from 1 January 1984 the Commission will submit to the Council reports on trends in the total daily intake of salt per population. In these reports the Commission will examine to what extent the 120 mg/l MAC suggested by the WHO working party is necessary to achieve a satisfactory total salt intake level, and, if appropriate, will suggest a new salt MAC value to the Council and a deadline for compliance with that value. Before 1 January 1984 the Commission will submit to the Council a report on whether the reference period of three years for calculating these percentiles is scientifically well founded.
14	Potassium	K mg/l	10	12	
15	Aluminium	Al mg/l	0.05	0.2	
16	Total hardness				
17	Dry residues	mg/l after drying at 180°C		1,500	
18	Dissolved oxygen	% 0_2 saturation			Saturation value > 75% except for underground water.
19	Free carbon dioxide	CO_2 mg/l			The water should not be agressive.

Parameters	Expression of the results ([1])	Guide level (GL)	Maximum admissible concentration (MAC)	Comments
Substances Undesirable in Excessive Amounts				
20 Nitrates	NO_3 mg/l	25	50	
21 Nitrites	NO_2 mg/l		0.1	
22 Ammonium	NH_4 mg/l	0.05	0.5	
23 Kjeldahl Nitrogen (excluding N in NO_2 and NO_3	N mg/l		1	
24 (K Mn 0_4) Oxidizability	0_2 mg/l	2	5	Measured when heated in acid medium.
25 Total organic carbon (TOC)	C mg/l			The reason for any increase in the usual concentration must be investigated.
26 Hydrogen sulphide	S µg/l		undetectable organoleptically.	
27 Substances extract-able in chloroform	mg/l dry residue	0.1		
28 Dissolved or emul-sified hydrocarbons (after extraction by petroleum ether); Mineral oils.	µg/l		10	
29 Phenols (phenol index)	C_6H_5OH µg/l		0.5	Excluding natural phenols which do not react to chlorine.
30 Boron	B µg/l	1,000		
31 Surfactants (react-ting with methylene blue)	µg/l (lauryl sulphate)		200	
32 Other organochlorine compounds pounds not covered by parameter No 55.	µg/l	1		Haloform concentrations must be as low as possible.
33 Iron	Fe µg/l	50	200	

34	Manganese	Mn μg/l	20	50	
35	Copper	Cu μg/l	100 At outlets of pumping and/or treatment works and their substations. 3,000 After the water has been standing for 12 hours in the piping and at the point where the water is made available to the consumer.		Above 3,000 μg/l astringent taste discoloration + corrosion may occur.
36	Zinc	Zn μg/l	100 At outlets of pumping and/or treatment works and their substations. 5,000 After the water has been standing for 12 hours in the piping and at the point where the water is made available to the consumer.		Above 5,000 pg/l astringent taste opalescence and sand-like deposits may occur.
37	Phosphorus	P_2O_5 μg/l	400	5,000	
38	Fluoride	F μg/l			MAC varies according to average temperatue in geographical area concerned.
		8-12°C		1,500	
		25-30°C		700	
39	Cobalt	Co μg/l			
40	Suspended solids		None		
41	Residual Chlorine	Cl μg/l			
42	Barium	Ba μg/l	100		
43	Silver	Ag μg/l		10	If, exceptionally, silver is used non-systematically to process the water, a MAC value of 80 μg/l may be authorised.

APPENDIX 5.2b

WATER SUPPLY (WATER QUALITY) REGULATIONS 1989 AND PRIVATE WATER SUPPLIES REGULATIONS 1991

Table A

Item	*Parameters*	*Units of Measurement*	*Concentration or Value (maximum unless otherwise stated)*
1.	Colour	mg/l Pt/Co scale	20
2.	Turbidity (including suspended solids)	Formazin turbidity units	4
3.	Odour (including hydrogen sulphide)	Dilution number	3 at 25°C
4.	Taste	Dilution number	3 at 25°C
5.	Temperature	°C	25
6.	Hydrogen ion	pH value	9.5 5.5 (minimum)
7.	Sulphate	mg SO_4/l	250
8.	Magnesium	mg Mg/l	50
9.	Sodium	mg Na/l	150
10.	Potassium	mg K/l	12
11.	Dry residues	mg/l	1500 (after drying at 180°C)
12.	Nitrate	mg NO23/l	50
13.	Nitrite	mg NO22/l	0.1
14.	Ammonium (ammonia and ammonium ions)	mg NH24/l	0.5
15.	Kjeldahl nitrogen	mg N/l	1
Item	*Parameters*	*Units of Measurement*	*Concentration or Value (maximum unless otherwise stated)*

16.	Oxidizability (permangantate value)	mg O_2/l	5
17.	Total organic carbon	mg C/l	No significant increase over that normally observed
18.	Dissolved or emulsified hydrocarbons (after extraction with petroleum ether); mineral oils	µg/l	10
19.	Phenols	µg C_6H_5OH/l	0.5
20.	Surfactants (as lauryl sulphate)	µg/l	200
21.	Aluminium	µg Al/l	200
22.	Iron	µg Fe/l	200
23.	Manganese	µg Mn/l	50
24.	Copper	µg Cu/l	3000
25.	Zinc	µg Zn/l	5000
26.	Phosphorus	µg P/l	2200
27.	Fluoride	µg F/l	1500
28.	Silver	µg Ag/l	10(i)

Note: (i) If silver is used in a water treatment process, 80 may substituted for 10.

Table B

Item	*Parameters*	*Units of Measurement*	*Maximum Concentration*
1.	Arsenic	μg As/l	50
2.	Cadmium	μg Cd/l	5
3.	Cyanide	μg CN/l	50
4.	Chromium	μg Cr/l	50
5.	Mercury	μg Hg/l	1
6.	Nickel	μg Ni/l	50
7.	Lead nlpylg Pb/l	50	
8.	Antimony	μg Sb/l	10
9.	Selenium	μg Se/l	10
10.	Pesticides and related products:		
	(a) individual substances	μg/1	0.1
	(b) total substances (i)	μg/1	0.5
11.	Polycyclic aromatic hydrocarbons (ii)	μg/1	0.2

Notes:(i)The sum of the detected concentrations of individual substances.
(ii) 1642lylThe sum of the detected concentrations of fluoranthene, benzo 3.4 fluoranthene, benzo 11.12 fluoranthene, benzo 3.4 pyrene, benzo 1.12 perylene and indeno (1,2,3-cd) pyrene.nl

Table C

1.	Total coliforms	number/100 ml	0
2.	Faecal coliforms	number/100 ml	0
3.	Faecal streptococci	number/100 ml	0
4.	Sulphite-reducing clostridia	number/20ml	≤1(i)
5.	Colony counts	number/1 ml at 22°C or 37°C	No significant increase over that normally observed

Note: (i) Analysis by multiple tube method.

Table D(1)

Item	*Parameters*	*Units of Measurement*	*Maximum Concentration or Value*
1.	Conductivity	µlS/cm	1500 at 20°C
2.	Chloride	mg Cl/l	400
3.	Calcium	mg Ca/l	250
4.	Substances extractable in chloroform	mg/l dry residue	1
5.	Boron	µg B/l	2000
6.	Barium	µg Ba/l	1000
7.	Benzo 3,4 pyrene	µg/l	10
8.	Tetrachloromethane	µg/l	3
9.	Trichloroethene	µg/l	30
10.	Tetrachlorothene	µg/l	10

Note: (i) See regulation 3(3)(d).

Table E

Item	*Parameters*	*Units of Measurement*	*Minimum Concentration(i)*
1.	Total hardness	mg Ca/l	60
2.	Alkalinity	mg HCO_3/l	30

Note: (i) See regulation 3(4).

APPENDIX 5.3

THE SURFACE WATERS (DANGEROUS SUBSTANCES) (CLASSIFICATION) REGULATIONS 1989

Environmental quality standards relating to inputs of various EC "Black List" substances to inland, coastal and territorial waters.

	Inland	*Coastal and territorial*
	(&g/l, annual mean)	
Aldrin, dieldrin endrin & isodrin*	0.03 for total drins 0.005 for endrin	
Cadmium & compounds	5 (total)	2.5 (dissolved)
Carbon tetrachloride	12	12
Chloroform	12	12
DDT (all isomers)	0.025	0.025
pp-DDT	0.01	0.01
Hexachlorobenzene	0.03	0.03
Hexachlorobutadiene	0.1	0.1
Hexachlorocyclohexane (all isomers)	0.1	0.02
Mercury & compounds	1 (total)	0.3 (dissolved)
Pentachlorophenol & its compounds	2	2

* In July 1997 the Department of the Environment, Transport and the Regions expressed an intention to amend these standards as follows:

- aldrin 10 ng/l
- dieldrin 10 ng/l
- endrin 5 ng/l
- isodrin 5 ng/l

THE SURFACE WATERS (DANGEROUS SUBSTANCES) (CLASSIFICATION) REGULATIONS 1997 AND 1998

Schedules to the Regulations list concentrations of certain dangerous substances which should not be exceeded for meeting criteria for classification of either inland freshwaters or coastal and relevant territorial waters - see chapter 5, 5.15.2.

Schedules 1 and 2 to 1997 Regulations

Dangerous Substance	*Inland*	*Coastal and territorial*
	µg/l, annual mean	
Arsenic	50	25
Atrazine & Simazine (for the two substances in total)	2	2
Azinphos-methyl	0.01	0.01
Dichlorvos	0.001	0.04
Endosulphan	0.003	0.003
Fenitrothion	0.01	0.01
Malathion	0.01	0.02
Trifluralin	0.1	0.1
Tributyltin	0.02 µg/l	0.002 µg/l
Triphenyltin & its derivatives	0.02 µg/l	0.008 µg/l
Dichlorvos (used as a treatment For sea-lice infestation)		0.6 µg/l

Schedules 1 and 2 to 1998 Regulations

Dangerous Substance	*Inland*	*Coastal and territorial*
	µg/l, annual mean	
4-Chloro-3-methyl-phenol	40	40
2-Chlorophenol	50	50
2,4-Dichlorophenol	20	20
2,4-D (ester)	1	1
(Non-ester)	40	40
1,1,1-Trichloroethane	100	100
1,1,2-Trichloroethane	400	300
Bentazone	500	500
Benzene	30	30
Biphenyl	25	25
Chloronitrotoluenes	10	10
Demeton	0.5	0.5
Dimethoate	1	1
Linuron	2	2
Mecoprop	20	20
Naphthalene	10	5
Omethoate	0.01	-
Toluene	50	40
Triazaphos	0.005	0.005
Xylene	30	30

APPENDIX 5.4

THE SURFACE WATERS (RIVER ECOSYSTEM) (CLASSIFICATION) REGULATIONS 1994

These classifications apply to inland rivers and watercourses in England and Wales.

(1) Class	(2) Dissolved Oxygen % saturation 10 percentile	(3) BOD (ATU) mg/l 90 percentile	(4) Total Ammonia mg N/L 90 percentile	(5) Un-ionised Ammonia mg N/l 95 percentile	(6) pH lower limit as 5 percentile; upper limit as 95 percentile	(7) Hardness mg/l CaCO23	(8) Dissolved Copper pg/l 95 percentile	(9) Total Zinc pg/l 95 percentile
RE1	80	2.5	0.25	0.021	6.0-9.0	≤ 10 > 10 and ≤ 50 > 50 and ≤ 100 > 100	5 22 40 112	30 200 300 500
RE2	70	4.0	0.6	0.021	6.0-9.0	≤ 10 > 10 and ≤ 50 > 50 and ≤ 100 > 100	5 22 40 112	30 200 300 500
RE3	60	6.0	1.3	0.021	6.0-9.0	≤ 10 > 10 and ≤ 50 > 50 and ≤ 100 > 100	5 22 40 112	300 700 1000 2000
RE4	50	8.0	2.5	—	6.0-9.0	≤ 10 > 10 and ≤ 50 > 50 and ≤ 100 > 100	5 22 40 112	300 700 1000 2000
RE5	20	15.0	9.0	—	—	—	–	–

APPENDIX 5.5

THE SURFACE WATERS (ABSTRACTION FOR DRINKING WATER) (CLASSIFICATION) REGULATIONS 1996

Schedule 1: Criteria for Classification of Waters

(The limits set out below are maxima)

Parameters	*Units*	*Limits*		
		DW1	*DW2*	*DW3*
Coloration (after simple filtration)	mg/l Pt Scale	20	100	200
Temperature	°C	25	25	25
Nitrates	mg/l NO_3	50	50	50
Fluorides	mg/l F	1.5		
Dissolved iron	mg/l Fe	0.3		2
Copper	mg/l Cu	0.05		
Zinc	mg/l Zn	3	5	5
Arsenic	mg/l As	0.05	0.05	0.01
Cadmium	mg/l Cd	0.005	0.005	0.005
Total chromium	mg/l Cr	0.05	0.05	0.05
Lead	mg/l Pb	0.05	0.05	0.05
Selenium	mg/l Se	0.01	0.01	0.01
Mercury	mg/l Hg	0.001	0.001	0.001
Barium	mg/l Ba	0.1	1	1
Cyanide	mg/l CN	0.05	0.05	0.05
Sulphates	mg/l SO_4	250	250	250
Phenol (phenol index) paranitraniline 4-aminoantipyrine	mg/l C_6H_5OH	0.001	0.005	0.1
Dissolved or emulsified hydrocarbons	mg/l	0.05	0.2	1
Polycyclic aromatic hydrocarbons	mg/l	0.0002	0.0002	0.001
Total pesticides (parathion, hexachlorocyclohexane, dieldrin	mg/l	0.001	0.0025	0.005
Ammonium	mg/l NH_4		1.5	4

The classifications, DW1, DW2 and DW3, correspond to the 1975 Surface Water Directive's classifications of A1, A2 and A3; the limits specified are the maximum allowable for each classification; an annex to Directive 75/440 specifies the treatment required to bring the surface water up to drinking water standard in each classification:

- DW1: simple physical treatment and disinfection;
- DW2: normal physical treatment, chemical treatment and disinfection;
- DW3: intensive physical and chemical treatment and disinfection.

APPENDIX 6
THE EUROPEAN UNION AND THE ENVIRONMENT

The European Economic Community came into existence on 1 January 1958 following the signing of the 1957 *Treaty of Rome* by its six founder members - Belgium, France, West Germany, Italy, Luxembourg and The Netherlands. (These same six countries had, in 1951, formed the European Coal and Steel Community which created a common market in coal and steel.) The European Community was enlarged in 1973 when Denmark, Ireland and the United Kingdom joined; in 1981 Greece became a member, followed in 1986 by Spain and Portugal and by Austria, Finland and Sweden in 1995. The 1992 *Treaty on European Union* (the *Maastrict Treaty*) (see below) created the "European Union", the term by which the 15 member states are more usually called. In 1998 Cyprus, Hungary, Poland, Estonia, the Czech Republic and Slovenia began formal negotiations to join the EU.

The presidency of the European Union (EU) rotates every six months between Member States (as does chairmanship of the Council of Ministers). The 1957 *Treaty of Rome*, which has been amended a number of times, sets out the basic operating principles of the EU with the aim of ensuring a Common Market - that is the free movement of goods, people and services between Member States.

The European Union has become one of the most important international innovators on environmental issues and there are now over 560 legislative measures covering the whole spectrum of the environment; it should be noted however that a number of these are revisions or amendments of existing measures.

Although some of the EU's earliest environmental protection measures, on for example vehicle emissions, were adopted in 1970, it was not until 1973 that the *First Action Programme on the Environment* was adopted (see below). And it was not until 1986, when the *Single European Act 1986* was adopted, that the *Treaty of Rome* was also amended to make explicit mention of the environment.

Article 130R of the Treaty includes the following points:

a) Action by the Community relating to the environment shall have the following objectives:

- to preserve, protect and improve the quality of the environment;
- to contribute towards protecting human health;
- to ensure a prudent and rational utilisation of natural resources;

A further objective was added by the *Maastricht Treaty* and that was the need for EC environmental policies to contribute to international environmental measures to deal with regional and worldwide environmental problems.

b) Action by the Community relating to the environment shall be based on the principles that preventive action should be taken, that environmental damage should as a priority be rectified at source, and that the polluter should pay. Environmental protection requirements shall be a component of the Community's other policies.

c) In preparing its action relating to the environment, the Community shall take account of:

- available scientific and technical data;
- environmental conditions in the various regions of the Community;
- the potential benefits and costs of action or lack of action;
- the economic and social development of the Community as a whole and the balanced development of its regions.

This development, which had both legal and symbolic significance, was given further impetus through the *Treaty on European Union* (the *Maastricht Treaty*) signed in Maastricht in February 1992. Following ratification by all Member States, this came into force on 1 November 1993. The Treaty has as a principle objective "the promotion of sustainable and non-inflationary growth respecting the environment, including among the activities of the Community a policy in the sphere of the environment". The Treaty was further amended in 1997 to require the Union to promote "balanced and sustainable development of economic activities". It stresses that the policy should not only aim at a high level of protection for the environment but that environmental protection should be integrated into other areas of EU policy.

The *Maastricht Treaty* also gives further substance to the principle of "subsidiarity" and refers "to the process of creating an ever closer union among the peoples of Europe in which decisions are taken as closely as possible to the citizen". This principle has been included in the EU's Fifth Action Programme (see below).

Finally, the *Maastricht Treaty* created the European Union (i.e. all the countries within the Community) - this is made up of three sections: the European Community, Common Foreign & Security Policy and Home Affairs & Justice Policy. An amendment to the *Treaty of Rome* abolishes the European Economic Community (EEC) which becomes the European Community (EC). The Council of Ministers has become the Council of the European Community and the Commission of the European Communities the European Commission.

Legislative and Institutional Procedures

The *Single European Act 1986*, which came into force in July 1987, has as a principle objective the abolition of all barriers between Member States by 31 December 1992. To this end, new measures have been drafted and legislation amended with the aim of creating a single market in goods, services and employment - i.e. the right, subject to various safeguards, to trade and work in any Member State and the removal of technical, fiscal and other barriers. A fundamental objective to completion of the Single Market is that products and services legally sold or offered in one Member State should not be banned in another.

With regard to legislative proposals relating to the environment, those relating to product standards, competition or the "establishment and functioning of the internal market" (i.e. harmonising measures) are subject to majority voting under Article 100A. Other Directives relating to action on the environment are proposed under Article 130 and thus require unanimous voting under Article 130S. An amendment to this Article agreed in Maastricht enables some environmental measures to be adopted on a qualified majority. However, those incorporating, for example, fiscal, energy, planning and land use (excluding waste management) will still require unanimous approval. Article 130T permits Member States to adopt or keep stricter environmental protection legislation under certain conditions.

The European Commission - which can be seen as the "civil service" of the EU - is split into a number of Directorates-General (DG), each responsible for a particular area of the Commission's work. DG XI, the Directorate-General for Environment, Nuclear Safety and Civil Protection, is responsible for most environmental policy. The Commission is headed by a President and there are 20 Commissioners; although Commissioners are nominated by Member States' governments, they are expected to act independently of national interests. The Commission is responsible for developing and proposing new legislation and other initiatives. Proposals are published usually with the prefix "COM" - i.e. Communication [from the Commission to the Council and Parliament concerning ...], followed by the year and a reference number, e.g. COM(99) 00. Following adoption, they are published with a reference number preceded by the year of adoption (99/00).

EU measures are finalised as either

- **Regulations:** these are binding on all Member States in their entirety and take precedence over national legislation.
- **Directives:** these are binding on Member States as to the result to be achieved, while leaving a degree of flexibility on how the measure will be implemented in national legislation.
- **Decisions:** these are binding in their entirety and may be addressed to government, private enterprise or individual.
- **Recommendations and opinions:** these are not binding.

The Council of the European Community (i.e. Council of Ministers) is responsible for agreeing, amending or referring back to the Commission its draft proposals. The Council formally consists of the Foreign Ministers of the Member States, with the chairmanship changing every six months in line with the Presidency of the Community. Where, for example, environmental matters are to be discussed, then the Council will usually comprise the environmental ministers of the Member States. Initial discussions will have taken place between national governments' officials and also in the Committee of Permanent Representatives (COREPER), who will aim to reach agreement on proposals prior to discussion in the Council of Ministers. COREPER consists of each Member States' Ambassador to the EU.

The European Parliament is directly elected by electors in each Member State. Prior to ratification of the *Maastricht Treaty*, the EP had a rather limited role, being restricted to offering an opinion on Commission proposals; it was unable to amend or reject decisions reached by the Council, but could only ask them to reconsider. The only exception to this was the budget which it could reject.

The European Parliament now has the right to approve the appointment of the European Commission and of its President. On a majority vote it may also ask the Commission to produce a proposal for legislation in furtherance of the objectives of the Treaty. Under the co-decision procedure the Parliament may block a measure, even if approved by the Council of Ministers, if it is of the opinion that the proposal does not meet the purpose for which it is intended (Article 189B). If agreement cannot be reached on a proposal it is referred to a conciliation committee consisting of representatives of the EP and of the Council for further negotiation. The cooperation procedure (Article 189C) enables the Parliament on a second reading to propose amendments to proposals even though the Council of Ministers has already adopted a common position. The Commission then decides which of the European Parliament's amendments it can accept before the proposal returns to the Council of Ministers. The Council of Ministers can only reject or further amend the European Parliament's amendments which have been accepted by the European Commission by unanimous vote; most environmental measures are likely to be adopted under this procedure although the action programmes will be adopted under Article 189B.

Following adoption, the final text of Directives etc are published in the *Official Journal of the European Communities*. All legislation includes a date by which Member States must have incorporated it into national legislation. The amount of time allowed largely depends on the impact of the measure on national practice and the cost of implementation. In some instances, individual Member States will be allowed a derogation - i.e. extra time in which to comply.

In the UK EU measures are implemented either under the appropriate primary legislation, or where no suitable legislation exists, under the *European Communities Act 1972*.

The European Commission is also responsible for monitoring the performance of Member States in complying with Directives etc. Where it feels that a Member State is in breach of EU legislation it will first try to resolve the matter through informal discussion, correspondence, etc - there is a procedure for doing this. If however the Commission is still not satisfied, it can initiate legal action in the European Court of Justice. This is situated in Luxembourg with judges drawn from all Member States. Individuals in Member States may also complain to the European Court if they feel EU legislation is being breached. The European Court of Justice has the power to fine or levy a financial penalty on offenders.

European Environment Agency

Although agreement was reached on the establishment of the European Environment Agency (Regulation 1210/90) in 1990, it did not formally begin work until late 1993. The EEA's main task is to record, collate and analyse data on the environment, drawing up expert reports. These will enable both the European Commission and Member States to formulate appropriate environmental protection policies. A further aim of the EEA, which is based in Copenhagen, is to develop ways of harmonising measurement and forecasting methods. The Agency's remit initially includes air, water, soil, wildlife, land use, waste management and noise. Its remit may be extended in due course to include responsibility for monitoring implementation of EC legislation, establishing criteria for ecolabelling and for assessing environmental impacts, as well as the use and transfer of environmentally-friendly technologies.

The Agency's information network - EIONET: European Information and Observation Network - will help to coordinate the work and establish links between policy and research institutes throughout the EC. Information collected by the Agency will be publicly available and a report on the state of the environment will be published every three years.

EC Network of Environmental Enforcement Agencies

The permanent Network of Environmental Enforcement Agencies was founded in 1992 with representatives from all EC Member States. Its aims are to "provide a mechanism for the exchange of information and experience between environmental agencies in the EC in order to address issues of mutual concern and to enhance the quality of the environment". The Network operates mainly through four permanent working groups with specific areas of interest:

- technical aspects of permitting;
- procedural and legal aspects of permitting;
- compliance monitoring, inspection and enforcement;
- managing the enforcement process.

Action Programmes on the Environment

The United Nations Conference on the Human Environment, held in Stockholm in 1972, marked the beginning of global recognition of environmental problems which could only be solved by a sustained effort in all countries.

The European Community responded by drawing up its *First Action Programme on the Environment*; it covered the period 1973-76 and was adopted by the Council of Ministers in November 1973. This *First Action Programme* was a wide-ranging document containing a large number of measures designed to deal with already urgent pollution problems; it also took a longer term view of the future and sought the positive management of human activities in such a way as to prevent further problems arising. The First Action Programme also set out goals and objectives, defined principles, such as the Polluter Pays Principle, and recognised that prevention is better than cure. It adopted a comprehensive approach, tackling both air and water pollution, the management of wastes, noise pollution and the protection of wildlife and habitats. These ideas and principles were given further substance in three subsequent Action Programmes covering 1977-81, 1982-86 and 1987-92.

In 1993 the Commission's *Fifth Action Programme - Towards Sustainability* was approved by the Council of Ministers and the Parliament. In their Resolution adopting the Programme, the EC Environment Ministers ask the Commission to "ensure that all proposals relating to the environment properly reflect the principle of subsidiarity". They also note that further measures will be needed if the desire for sustainable development is to be achieved.

The Programme, which runs from 1993-2000, with a review in late 1995, stresses the need for all sectors of the community - governments, industry and citizens - to become involved in and to take responsibility for the protection of their environment. It says that environmental policies should be integrated into all areas of Community policy if the goal of sustainability is to be achieved. Sustainability in this context is defined as reflecting "a policy and strategy for continued economic and social development without detriment to the environment and the natural resources on the quality of which continued human activity and further development depend".

The Programme states that "the Community will take action, in accordance with the principle of subsidiarity, only if and insofar as the objectives of the proposed action cannot be sufficiently achieved by the Member States and can therefore, by reason of the scale or effects of the proposed action, be better achieved by the Community". It also recognises that in many areas, objectives will best be achieved through "shared responsibility" using a mix of "actors and instruments at the appropriate levels" - i.e. that action should be taken at Community, national or local level as appropriate.

Five areas requiring major effort because of the stresses each can place on the environment are targeted; these are industry, agriculture, energy, transport and tourism. The Commission suggests that these are all areas at which action for improvement can most efficiently and appropriately be taken at Community level. Within each of these target areas the Programme identifies a number of objectives aimed at achieving sustainable development while benefitting the sector concerned. The Programme also identifies a number of environmental issues which because of their transboundary or global nature should be dealt with at Community level. Again objectives and targets are set and a programme to be reviewed and developed is proposed. The environmental issues highlighted are climate change, acidification, air quality, urban environment (noise), waste management, protection of nature and biodiversity, management of water resources and coastal zones. The targets and actions proposed are summarised in the relevant chapters of the *Pollution Handbook*.

On the pages which follow, we list Community measures relating to air, noise, waste and water. Other measures of relevance are listed at Appendix 6.6.

Further Reading

A number of useful publications providing a more detailed discussion on the development of Community environmental policies and legislation, their implementation and the way in which the various Community institutions operate, are listed in the bibliography (General - European Issues) section of this Handbook.

APPENDIX 6.1:

ENVIRONMENTAL ACTION PROGRAMMES

Number	Title	adopted	brought into force	OJ No. and date Purpose
– Declaration of the Council of the European Communities and of the Representatives of the Governments of the Member States meeting in the Council on the Action Programme of the European Communities of the Environment. (1973-1976)	22.11.73	22.11.73	C 112 20.12.73	To lay down the objectives and principles of a Community environment policy. To describe measures to be taken to reduce pollution and nuisances and to improve the environment.
– Resolution of the Council of the European Communities and of the Representatives of the Governments of the Member States meeting within the Council on the continuation and implementation of a European Community policy and Action Programme on the Environment. (1977-1981)	17.05.77	17.05.77	C 139 13.06.77	To restate the policy objectives and principles. To describe measures to be undertaken to reduce pollution and nuisance, protect and manage land, the natural environment and resources and improve the environment.
– Resolution of the Council of the European Communities and of the Representatives of the Governments of the Member States meeting in the Council on the continuation and implementation of a European Community policy and and Action Programme on the Environment (1982-86)	07.02.83	07.02.83	C 46 17.02.83	To develop an overall strategy. To describe measures to be taken to prevent and reduce pollution and nuisance in the different environments, as well as the protection and rational management of land, the environment and natural resources.
– Resolution of the Council on the continuation and implementation of a European Community policy and action programme on the environment. (1987- 1992)	19.10.87	19.10.87	C328 07.12.87	To identify pollutants; to determine best focus for control measures; to set objectives to combat acid deposition and forest die-back; to reduce ambient pollutant concentrations; to develop appropriate management techniques.
Resolution of the Council on the fifth Community Policy and Action Programme on the Environment and Sustainable Development. (1993-2000)	18.03.92		C138 17.05.93	Define objectives for tackling a number of issues and for achieving sustainable development. Issues include climate change, acidification, air and water pollution, waste management.

APPENDIX 6.2: AIR POLLUTION

Industrial Pollution

Number		Title	Date adopted into force	brought and date	OJ No. Purpose
84/360/ EEC	"Framework" Directive on combating air pollution from industrial plants.	28.06.84	30.06.87	L 188 16.07.84	To implement measures and procedures designed to prevent and reduce air pollution from industrial plants within the Community.
88/609/ EEC	Directive limiting emissions of certain pollutants into the air from large com-bustion plants.	24.11.88	30.06.90	L 336 07.12.88	Sets emission standards SO_2, NOx and dust for existing and new plant; Reduction targets are to be met progressively by 1993, 1998, 2003 using 1980 levels as a base.
96/61/ EC	Council Directive concerning integrated pollution prevention and control	24.09.96	30.10.96	L257 10.10.96	To introduce a system of permitting for certain industrial installations.

Motor Vehicles and Fuels

Number		Title	Date adopted into force	brought and date	OJ No. Purpose
70/220/ EEC	Directive relating to measures to be taken against air pollution by gases from positive ignition engines of motor vehicles.	20.03.70	30.06.70	L 76 06.04.70	To set limit values for emissions of CO and HC from petrol-engined vehicles.
74/290/ EEC	Amendment Directive (1st)	28.05.74	01.10.74	L 159 15.06.74	To define specifications for acceptance tests, and reduce previous limits.
77/102/ EEC	Amendment Directive (2nd)	30.11.76	01.01.77	L 32 03.02.77	To fix permissible values for carbon monoxide, hydrocarbon fuels and nitrogen oxides and determine materials, conditions and methods for use in measuring levels of these substances.

Number	Title	Date adopted	Date brought into force	OJ No. and date	Purpose
78/665/ EEC	Amendment Directive (3rd)	14.07.78	01.01.79	L 233 14.08.78	To establish limits for exhaust emissions from road vehicles representing 35% for CO; 25% for HC; 15% for NOx.
83/351/ EEC	Amendment Directive (4th)	16.06.83	30.11.83	L 197 20.07.83	Reduce limits set in 78/665 of CO by 23%; HC and NOx by 20-30%; also limits pollutants from diesel engines.
88/76	Amendment Directive (5th): The Luxembourg Agreement".	03.12.87		L36 09.02.88	To set emission limits for CO, HC + NOx and NOx according to engine size.
89/458/ EEC	Amendment directive (7th) on gaseous emissions from private motor cars with a capacity of less than 1400cc	18.07.89		L226 03.08.89	To set mandatory limits on emissions of 19g/test CO and 5g/test HC + NOx for small sized cars. (Partially supersedes 88/76)
89/491/ EEC	Amendment Directive (9th)			L 238 15.08.89	Amends various directives with regard to fuel consumption.
91/441/ EEC	Amendment Directive (10th)	26.06.91	01.04.92	L 242 30.08.91	Extends emission standards set in 89/458 to all sizes of cars.
93/59 EEC	Amendment directive.	28.06.93	01.10.93	L186 28.07.93	To place emission limits on light commercial vehicles, off-road vehicles and heavy cars.
96/69	Amendment Directive	8.10.96		L282 01.11.96	Tightens emission limits for light commercial vehicles
72/306/ EEC	Directive on measures to be taken against emissions of pollutants from diesel engines for use in motor vehicles.	02.08.72	10.02.74	L 190 20.08.72	To lay down requirements relating to the type approval of diesel motor vehicles. To define standards for acceptance tests. To fix permissible values for fumes and determine materials, conditions and methods for measuring levels of the fumes.

88/436	Amendment Directive (6th) limiting gaseous pollutants from diesel vehicles up to 3.5 tonnes	16.06.88		L 214 06.08.88	To set standards for the emission of particulates of 1.1g/test for new engine types and 1.4g/test for new vehicles.
88/77	Directive on emission of gaseous pollutants from diesel lorries and buses.	03.12.87	01.10.90	L36 09.02.88	To control emissions of CO, HC and NOx in vehicles over 3.5 tonnes.
91/542	Amendment Directive of 88/77	01.10.91	01.01.92	L 295 25.10.91	Tightens limits set in 88/77 and introduces limits for particulates.
96/1	Amendment of Directive 88/77	22.01.96		L40 17.02.96	As above.
77/537/ EEC	Directive relating to measures to be taken against the emission of pollutants from diesel engines for use in wheeled agricul-tural forestry tractors.	28.06.77	30.12.78	L 220 29.08.77	To lay down requirements to the type approval of such vehicles. To fix permissible values for the fumes and determine materials, conditions and methods for measuring levels of the fumes.
97/68	Directive concerning emissions from non-road machinery	16.12.97		L59 27.02.98	To limit emissions of gaseous and particulate pollutants from internal combustion engines to be installed in non-road mobile macinery
75/716/ EEC	Directive relating to the approximation of the laws of Member States on the sulphur content of certain liquid fuels.	24.11.75	26.08.76	L 307 27.11.75	Repealed 1.10.94
87/219/ EEC	Amends Directive 75/716.	20.03.87	31.12.88	L 091 03.04.87	Repealed 1.10.94
93/12 EEC	Directive relating to the sulphur content of certain liquid fuels.	23.03.93	1.10.94	L74 27.03.93 01.10.96.	Reduces sulphur content of gasoils to 0.2% by weight by 01.10.94 and to 0.05% from
78/611/ EEC	Directive concerning the lead content of petrol.	29.06.78	05.01.80	L 197 22.07.78	Replaced by 85/210 – 31.12.85
85/210/ EEC	Directive on the approximation of Member State legislation on lead content of petrol, and the introduction of lead-free petrol.	21.03.85	01.01.86	L 096 03.04.85	Replaces Directive 78/611. Also fixes benzene content of leaded and unleaded petrol at 5% max. by volume.

Number	Title	Date adopted	Date brought into force	OJ No. and date	Purpose
87/416/ EEC	Amendment of Directive 85/210/EEC.	21.07.87	-	L 225 13.08.87	To permit Member States to ban the sale of regular grade leaded petrol after giving 6 months notice.
92/6 EEC	Directive on the installation and use of speed limitation devices for certain categories of motor vehicles.	10.02.92		L57 02.03.92	Speed limiters to be fitted to HGVs, buses and coaches.
92/55 EEC	Directive on vehicle emission testing.	10.06.92		L225 10.08.92	To harmonise in-service testing of vehicle emissions.
93/116/ EEC	Directive relating to the fuel consumption of motor vehicles.			L369 30.12.93	To set down procedure for determining CO2 emissions and require these to be recorded in document kept by vehicle owner.
94/63/ EC	EP and Council Directive on the control of VOCs resulting from the storage of petrol and its distribution from terminals to service stations.	20.12.94	31.12.95	C365 31.12.94	To reduce evaporative fuel losses.

Air Quality

Number	Title	Date adopted	Date brought into force	OJ No. and date	Purpose
96/62/EC	Directive on air quality assessment and management	24.09.96		L296 01.11.96	Framework Directive outlining system of monitoring and assessing air quality.
97/101/EC	Decision (superseding 82/459), establishing a reciprocal exchange of information and data from networks and individual stations measuring ambient air quality within Member States.	27.01.97		L 35 5.02.97	To set up a procedure for exchanging information between the Member States' measuring stations on a number of substances causing air pollution. To nominate a coordinating body. To arrange for the publication of a summary report.

80/779/ EEC	Directive on air quality limit values and guide values for sulphur dioxide and suspended particulates.	15.07.80	17.07.82	L 229 30.08.80	To lay down standards for sulphur dioxide and suspended particulates in the air, as well as the conditions for their application. To lay down the reference methods for sampling and analysis to be used.
–	Resolution relating to transboundary air pollution by sulphur dioxide and suspended particulates.	15.07.80	-	C 222 30.08.80	Calls on Member States to limit, and as far as possible reduce or prevent transboundary pollution in line with Directive
81/462/ EEC	Decision on the conclusion of the Convention on long-range transboundary air pollution. (The Geneva Convention).	11.06.81	-	L 171 27.06.81	To limit and as far as possible reduce and prevent transboundary air pollution.
86/277/ EEC	Council Decision concluding a Protocol to the 1979 Geneva Convention on Long-Distance Transboundary Air pollution concerning the funding of a long-term programme of cooperation for the constant monitoring and evaluation of the long-distance atmospheric transfer of pollutants in Europe (EMEP).	12.06.86	-	L181 04.07.86	See Title.
93/361	Council decision on the accession of the community to the Protocol to the LRTAP Convention on the control of emissions of nitrogen oxides or their transboundary fluxes.	17.05.93		L.149 21.06.93	
77/312/ EEC	Directive on biological screening of the population for lead.	29.03.77	31.03.78	L 105 28.04.77	To conduct two blood lead surveys, co-ordinated across the Community and separated by two years. The Directive prescribes surveys of three groups of people and defines reference' levels expressed in µg/100ml of blood to be applied to each group of people in assessing the results of the survey.

Number	Title	Date adopted	Date brought into force	OJ No. and date	Purpose
82/884/ EEC	Directive on a limit value for lead in the air.	03.12.82	10.12.84	L 378 31.12.82	To fix a limit value of 2 micrograms Pb/m^3 expressed as an annual mean concentration. To define characteristics to be complied with for choosing a sampling method and a reference method for analysing the concentration of lead.
85/203/ EEC	Directive on air quality standards for nitrogen dioxide.	07.03.85	01.01.87	L 087 27.03.85	To establish a limit value for NO_2 in air of 200 $\mu g/m^3$, expressed as a 98 percentile of the mean of one-hour measurements made throughout a year; also lower "guide values" for special protection zones.
87/217/ EEC	Directive on prevention and reduction of environmental pollution by asbestos.	28.03.87	31.12.88	L 085 28.03.87	To put controls on the pollution of air, water and land by asbestos from all significant point sources.
89/427/ EEC	Directive modifying 80/779 on limit values and guide values of air quality for sulphur dioxide and suspended particulates.	21.06.89			To harmonise measurement methods.
92/72 EEC	Directive on air pollution by ozone.	21.09.92		L297 13.10.92	To establish procedure for monitoring ground-level ozone, give information to the public and issue public alerts when levels are expected to be high.

Incinerators

Number	Title	Date adopted	Date brought into force	OJ No. and date	Purpose
89/369/ EEC	Directive on air pollution from new municiple waste incinerators.	08.06.89	01.01.90	L 163 14.06.89	To set emission limit values and operating requirements for new waste incinerators.
89/429/ EEC	Directive on air pollution from exisiting municipal waste incinerators.	08.06.89	01.01.90	L 203 15.07.89	To set emission limit values and operation requirements for existing waste incinerators.

Chlorofluorocarbons

–	Resolution on chlorofluorocarbons in the environment.	30.05.78	30.05.78	C 133 07.06.78	To limit the production of CFCs in the Community To encourage the search for substitute products. To promote elimination of CFCs.
87/412	Decision on the signing of a Protocol of the Vienna Convention for the protection of the ozone layer, relating to the control of chloroflourocarbons.	10.09.87	-		See title
88/540/ EEC	Decision implementing the Vienna Convention on protection of the ozone layer and the Montreal Protocol on substances which deplete the ozone layer.	14.10.88	-	L 297 31.10.88	See title
594/91/ EEC	Regulation on substances that deplete the ozone layer.	04.03.91	15.03.91	L 67 14.03.91	Repealed.
3952/92	Regulation amending 594/91	30.12.92		L405 31.12.92	Repealed.
3093/94 EC	Regulation on substances that deplete the ozone layer	15.12.94		L333 22.12.94	Tightens controls on CFCs etc and introduces restrictions on HCFCs and methyl bromide.

Energy Efficiency

93/76 EEC	Directive to limit carbon dioxide emissions by improving energy efficiency (SAVE).	13.09.93	31.12.94	L237 23.09.93	

APPENDIX 6.3: NOISE POLLUTION

Vehicles/Construction Plant/Aircraft

Number	Title	Date adopted	Date brought into force	OJ No. and date	Purpose
70/157/ EEC	Directive on the approximation of laws in the Member States relating to the permissible sound level and the exhaust system of motor vehicles.	06.02.70	10.08.71	L 42 23.02.70	To fix the permissible limits for the sound level, the equipment, conditions and methods for measuring this level.
73/350/ EEC	Directive adapting 70/157 to technical progress.	07.11.73	01.03.74	L 321 21.11.73	To prescribe measures for exhaust systems.
77/212/ EEC	Council amendment to 70/157	08.03.77	01.04.77	L 66 12.03.77	(Now superseded by Directive 84/424).
84/424/ EEC	Council amendment to 70/157	03.09.84	06.09.84	L 238 06.09.84	Amends noise limits set in 77/212; buses and lorries under 3.5 tonnes are categorised together, and those over categorised by horsepower.
92/97 EEC	Amendment to 70/157	10.11.92	01.07.92	L371 19.12.92	Reduces noise limits for cars, buses and HGVs by between 2-5 dB(A).
96/20 EC	Amends 92/97	27.03.96		L92 13.04.96	To make various chamges to noise level testing method.
78/1015/ EEC	Directive relating to the permissible sound level and exhaust system of motorcycles.	23.11.78	01.10.80	L 349 13.12.78	To fix the permissible limits for the sound level, the equipment, conditions and methods for measuring this level. To prescribe measures for exhaust systems.
87/56/ EEC	Amendment to Directive 78/1015	18.12.86	01.10.88	L 24 27.01.87	To modify the test procedure.
89/235/ EEC	Modification of Directive 78/1015 on sound levels of motorbikes.	13.03.89	01.10.90	L 98 11.04.89	To lay down common technical standards for exhaust systems; to provide a model EC type approval certificate.

74/151/ EEC	Directive relating to certain parts and characteristics of wheeled agricultural or or forestry tractors.	04.03.74	07.04.75	L 84 28.03.74	To fix the permissible limits for the sound level, the equipment, conditions and methods for measuring this level.
77/311/ EEC	Directive related to the driver-perceived noise level of wheeled agricultural or forestry tractors. (Extended by Directive 82/80.)	29.03.77	01.10.79	L 105 28.04.77	To fix the permissible limits for the sound level, the equipment, conditions and methods for measuring this level.
80/51/ EEC	Directive relating to the limitation of noise emissions from subsonic aircraft.	20.12.79	21.06.80	L 18 24.01.80	To make it compulsory for the Member States to apply annex 16 to the Chicago Convention on Subsonic Aircraft to establish mutual recognition of validity certificates. To determine exemptions.
83/206/ EEC	Amendment to 80/51		26.04.84	L117 04.05.83	To ensure that aircraft landing in the Community since 21.04.84 respect standards laid down by ICAO Chicago Convention.
89/629/ EEC	Directive limiting noise emissions from subsonic aircraft.	04.12.89		L 363 13.12.89	To prohibit registraton after 01.11.90 of aircraft unable to meet specific noise limits.
92/14 EEC	Directive limiting aircraft noise.	02.03.92		L 76 23.03.92	To ban all aircraft unable to meet Chapter 3 standards from operating into or out of EC after 01.04.95 and all Chapter 2 aircraft after 01.04.92.
79/113/ EEC	Directive on the approximation of the laws of the Member States relating to the determination of the noise emission of construction plant and equipment.	19.12.78	21.06.80	L 33 08.02.79	To define the sound level for construction plant and equipment. To define the criteria to use for expressing results, equipment and conditons for carrying out measurements and calculation method.
81/1051/ EEC	Amendment to 79/113	07.12.81	14.06.83	L 376 30.12.81	To determine the noise emitted to the operator's position by all categories of machines.
84/532/ EEC	Directive relating to common provisions for construction plant and equipment - "framework" Directive.	26.09.84	26.03.86	L 300 19.11.84	To establish a framework for avoiding barriers to trade for construction plant and equipment

Number	Title	Date adopted	Date brought into force	OJ No. and date	Purpose
84/533/ EEC	Directive on the limitation of the noise emitted by compressors.	17.09.84	26.09.89	L 300 19.11.84	To lay down maximum permissible values for sound levels and to prescribe methods of measurement of that sound.
84/534/ EEC	Directive on the approximation of the laws of the Member States relating to the permissible sound level for tower-cranes.	17.09.84	26.09.89	L 300 19.11.84	To lay down maximum permissible values for sound levels and to prescribe methods of measurement of that sound. (Amended 22 September 1986 - No. 86/491/EEC).
84/535/ EEC	Directive on the approximation of the laws of the Member States relating to the permissible sound power level of welding generators.	17.09.84	26.09.89	L300 19.11.84	To lay down maximum permissible values for sound levels and to prescribe methods of measurement of that sound.
84/536/ EEC	Directive on the approximation of the laws of the Member States relating to the permissible sound power level of power generators.	17.09.84	26.09.89	L 300 19.11.84	To lay down maximum permissible values for sound levels and to prescribe methods of measurement of that sound.
84/537/ EEC	Directive on the approximation of the laws of Member States relating to the permissible sound power level of powered hand-held concrete-breakers and picks.	17.09.84	26.09.89	L 300 19.11.84	To lay down maximum permissible values for sound levels and to prescribe methods of measurement of that sound.
86/662/ EEC	Directive on the limitation of noise emitted by earthmoving machinery (amended 1994).	22.12.86	26.09.89	L 384 31.12.86	To lay down noise emission levels for excavators, bulldozers, loaders and excavator loaders.
95/27	Directive on noise from earth moving machinery.	29.06.95	18.07.95	L168 18.07.95	Reduces emission levels set in 86/662

Lawn Mowers

84/538/ EEC	Directive on the approximation of the laws of the Member States relating to noise emitted by lawn mowers.	17.09.84	01.07.87	L 300 19.11.84	To lay down maximum permissible values for sound levels and to prescribe methods of measurement of that sound.
88/180/ EEC and 88/181/ EEC	Directives modifying Directive 84/538/ EEC on noise levels of lawnmowers.	22.03.88		L 81 26.03.88	To harmonise the legislation of the Member States on permitted noise levels for lawnmowers.

Household Appliances

86/594/ EEC	Directive on airborne noise emitted by household appliances.	01.12.86	04.12.89	L 344 06.12.86	To harmonise the methods of measuring the noise, arrangements for checking, general principles for publishing information on the noise emitted by these appliances.

Protection of Workers

86/188/ EEC	Directive on the protection of workers from the risks related to exposure to noise at work.	12.05.86	01.01.90	L 137 24.05.86	To protect workers from risks to hearing by setting limits on noise levels at which preventative action is required.

APPENDIX 6.4: WASTE

Waste

75/442/ EEC	Directive on waste.	15.07.75	18.07.77	L 194 25.07.75	To encourage the prevention and recycling of waste. To determine the arrangements to be made for the harmless disposal of waste. To provide administrative provisions for management and control. To provide a system of authorisations for firms responsible for collection, recycling or disposal.
91/156/ EEC	Directive amending 75/442/EEC on waste.	18.03.91	01.04.93	L78 26.03.91	Tightens up definition of waste and lists 16 specific categories. Obligations of 1975 Directive are expanded.

Number	Title	Date adopted	Date brought into force	OJ No. and date	Purpose
94/3	Commision decision establishing a list of wastes.	20.12.93		L5 07.01.94	
94/62 EC	EP and Council Directive on packaging waste	20.12.94	31.12.94	C365 31.12.94	To harmonise measures, reduce amount of such waste and its environmental impact; set up collection, recovery and re-use systems.
75/439/ EEC	Directive on the disposal of waste oils.	16.06.75	18.06.77	L 194 25.07.75	To determine the arrangements to be made for the collection and harmless disposal of waste oils. To require that priority is given to the regeneration of waste oils. To require a system of authorisations for plant either regenerating or burning waste oil. To prevent waste oils being mixed with toxic and dangerous wastes, in particular with PCBs.
87/101/ EEC	Amendment to above	13.01.87	01.01.90	L 42 12.02.87	
Hazardous Waste					
78/319/ EEC	Directive on toxic and dangerous wastes.	20.03.78	22.03.80	L 84 31.03.78	Repealed 27.6.95
91/689/ EEC	Directive on hazardous waste.	12.12.91	11.12.93	L 377 31.12.91	Updates 1978 Directive on hazardous waste management, defines various types of, and constituencies of hazardous wastes.
94/311/EC	Amendment of hazardous waste directive.				Sets implementation date of 91/689 at 31.3.95EC
84/631/ EEC	Directive on the supervision and control of transfrontier shipment of hazardous wastes within the European Community.	06.12.84	01.01.87	L 326 13.12.84	Repealed 6.5.94

90/170/ EEC	Decision on acceptance of OECD recommendation on control of trans-frontier shipment of hazardous waste.	02.04.90	-	L 92 07.04.90	See title.
91/157/ EEC	Directive on batteries and accumulators containing certain dangerous substances. Adapted by 93/72.	18.03.91	18.09.92	L 78 26.03.91	To reduce the amount of pollution from used batteries containing heavy metals; to encourage recycling and the production of batteries with lower levels of heavy metals.
259/93	Regulation on the supervision and control of shipments of waste into and out of the EC.	01.02.93	01.05.94	L30 06.02.93	Builds on and extends 1984 Directive and and implements Basel Convention on transboundary movements of hazardous waste.
93/98	Council decision on the conclusion of a convention of transboundary movements of hazardous waste and their disposal (the Basel Convention).	01.02.93		L39 16.02.93	
94/67/ EC	Directive on the incineration of hazardous waste.	16.12.94	31.12.94	C365 31.12.94	To reduce or prevent adverse environmental effects.
96/59 EC	Directive on the disposal of PCBs andPCTs	16.09.96	16.09.96	L 243 24.09.96	To identify PCBs and to control their disposal and elimination by 31.12.10
Recycling					
81/972/ EEC	Recommendation concerning the re-use of waste paper and the use of recycled paper.	03.12.81	-	L 355 10.12.81	To define and implement policies to promote the use of recycled paper and board.
85/339/ EEC	Directive on containers of liquids for human consumption.	27.06.85	03.07.87	L176 06.07.85	Repealed 30.6.96
Sewage Sludge					
86/278/ EEC	Directive on the protection of the environment, and in particular of the soil, when sewage sludge is used in agriculture.	12.06.86	17.06.89	L 181 04.07.86	To provide for a special regime concerning the spreading of sludge in agriculture and to fix sludge and soil analyses.

APPENDIX 6.5: WATER POLLUTION

Surface Water

Number	Title	Date adopted	Date brought into force	OJ No. and date	Purpose
75/440/ EEC	Directive concerning the quality required of surface water intended for the abstraction of drinking water in Member States.	16.05.75	18.06.77	L 194 25.07.75	To define the quality requirements for surface fresh water used for or intended for abstraction of drinking water. Provision of plans to clean up water. To define the requirements with which the quality measurements must comply.
79/869/ EEC	Directive concerning the methods of measurement and frequencies of sampling and analysis of surface water intended for the abstraction of drinking water in the Member States.	09.10.79	09.10.81	L 271 29.10.79	To lay down reference measuring methods for the parameters contained in Directive 75/440/EEC and sampling frequencies. To lay down the requirements with which these measurements must comply.
77/795/ EEC	Decision establishing a common procedure for the exchange of information on the quality of surface fresh water in the Community. Amended by 86/574.	12.12.77	12.12.77	L 334 24.12.77	To designate a coordinating body. To designate the stations taking part in the exchange of information. To define the parameters to be measured. To provide for the publication of a summary report.

Drinking Water

Number	Title	Date adopted	Date brought into force	OJ No. and date	Purpose
80/778/ EEC	Directive relating to the quality of water intended for human consumption.	15.07.80	19.07.82	L 229 30.08.80	To lay down standards for water intended for human consumption. To lay down sampling frequency, measuring methods and the requirements with which the measurements must comply. To lay down the conditions in which this quality is to be achieved.

Fresh Water

78/659/ EEC	Directive on the quality of fresh waters needing protection or improvement in order to support fish life.	18.07.78	20.07.80	L 222 14.08.78	To lay down the quality requirements for waters intended to support fish life. To lay down sampling frequency, measuring methods and the requirements with which the measurements must comply. To lay down the conditions in which this quality is to be achieved.

Shellfish Waters

79/923/ EEC	Directive on the quality required of shellfish waters.	30.10.79	30.10.81	L 281 10.11.79	To lay down the quality requirements for shellfish waters. To lay down the sampling frequencies, measuring methods and the requirements with which the measurements must comply. To lay down the conditions in which this quality is to be achieved

Bathing Water

70/160/ EEC	Directive concerning the quality of bathing water.	08.12.75	10.12.77	L 229 30.08.80	To define the quality requirements for bathing water. To define the sampling frequency, the measuring methods and the requirements with which these measurements must comply. To lay down the conditions in which this quality is to achieved.

Groundwater

80/68/ EEC	Directive on the protection of groundwater against pollution caused by certain dangerous substances.	17.12.79	19.12.81	L 20 26.01.80	To prevent the discharge of List I substances and restrict that of List II substances. To set up a system of authorisations and lay down the conditions for derogations. To prepare an inventory of discharge authorisations granted.

Dangerous Substances

Number	Title	Date adopted	Date brought into force	OJ No. and date	Purpose
76/464/ EEC	Framework directive on pollution caused by certain dangerous substances discharged into the aquatic environment of the Community.	04.05.76	04.05.78	L 31 05.02.76	To provide a system of authorisations for the discharge of dangerous substances into water. To provide limit values or quality objectives and monitoring procedures for List I substances. To provide quality objectives for List II substances. To adopt anti-pollution programmes for both types of substances and communicate them to the Commission. To draw up a list of discharges involving List I substances.
82/176/ EEC	Directive on limit values and quality objectives for mercury discharges by the chlor-alkali electrolysis industry.	22.03.82	01.07.83	L 81 27.03.82	To apply the Directive 76/464/EEC to the discharges from this industrial sector.
83/513/ EEC	Directive on limit values and quality objectives for cadmium discharges.	26.09.83	28.09.85	L 291 24.10.83	- as above -
84/156/ EEC	Directive on limit values and quality objectives for mercury discharges by sectors other than the chlor-alkali electrolysis industry.	18.03.84	12.03.86	L 74 17.03.84	- as above -
84/491/ EEC	Directive on limit values and quality objectives for discharges of hexachloro-cyclohexane (in particular lindane).	09.10.84	01.04.86	L 274 17.10.84	- as above -
86/280/ EEC	Directive setting out legal provisions applicable to various substances in List I of Annex to 76/464.	12.06.86	01.01.88	L 181 04.07.86	As above. To exend Directive 76/464/ EEC to cover discharges of DDT, carbon tetrachloride and pentachlorophenol.
88/347/ EEC	Directive on limit values and quality objectives for Hexachlorobenzene (HCB), Hexachlorabutadiene (HCBD), chloroform, isodrin, endrin, dieldrin and aldrin, discharges.	16.06.88	01.01.90	L 158 25.06.88	To extend Directive 76/464/EEC to cover discharges of the HCB, HCBD, chloroform and drins.

90/415/ EEC	Directive on limit values and quality objectives for certain List I substances.	31.07.90	01.01.92	L 219 14.08.90	To include 1,2 dichloroethane, trichloroethane, perchloroethane and trichlorobenzene.

Nitrates

91/676/ EEC	Directive on protection of fresh, coastal and marine waters from nitrate pollution.	12.12.91	19.12.93	L 375 31.12.91	To reduce and prevent nitrate pollution from agriculture, including nitrogen compounds on soils.

Waste Water

91/271/ EEC	Directive on urban waste water treatment.	21.05.91	30.06.93	L 135 30.05.91	To lay down minimum standards for the treatment of municipal waste water and the disposal of sludge.
98/51	Directive on urban waste water treatment.			L67 07.03.98	

Titanium Dioxide

78/176/ EEC	Directive on waste from the titanium dioxide industry.	20.02.78	22.02.79	L 54 25.02.78	To promote the prevention and recycling of such waste. To ensure its harmless disposal. To provide a system of authorisations for disposal operations. To lay down provisions governing immersion, discharge, storage and dumping. To enact provisions for monitoring long-established industries and to provide decontamination programmes with possible exceptions for new industries.
83/29/ EEC	Amendment	03.02.83		L 32 03.02.83	To provide a system of authorisation which will include a preliminary impact assessment. To determine the information to be notified to the Commission.

Number	Title	Date adopted	Date brought into force	OJ No. and date	Purpose
82/883/ EEC	Directive on procedures for the surveillance and monitoring of environments concerned by waste from the titanium dioxide industry.	03.12.82	10.12.84	L 378 31.12.78	To determine the parameters to be surveyed, the minimum sampling and analysis frequencies as well as the methods of measurement to be used in controlling the application of the Directive 78/176/EEC.
92/112/ EEC	Directive on procedures for the harmonisation of programmes for the reduction and eventual elimination of pollution caused by waste from the titanium dioxide industry.	15.12.92		L409 31.12.92	See title.
Barcelona Convention					
77/585/ EEC	Decision concluding the Convention for the Protection of the Mediterranean Sea against Pollution and the Protocol for the Prevention of the Pollution of the Mediterranean Sea by Dumping from Ships and Aircraft. (Barcelona Convention).	25.07.77	-	L 240 19.09.77	See title.
81/420/ EEC	Decision on the conclusion of the Protocol concerning cooperation in combating pollution of the Mediterranean Sea by oil and other harmful substances in cases of emergency.	19.05.81	-	L 162 19.06.81	See title.
83/101/ EEC	Decision concluding the Protocol for the protection of the Mediterranean Sea against pollution from land-based sources.	28.02.83	-	L 67 12.03.83	See title.

87/1125	Decision on mercury and cadmium discharges.	21.09.87	-		To allow the Commission to negotiate on behalf of the EEC, the adoption of measures relating to mercury and cadmium discharges as well as organosilicate components, within the framework of the convention for the protection of the Mediterranean Sea against pollution.

Paris Convention

75/437/ EEC	Decision concluding the Convention for the Prevention of Marine pollution from Land-based Sources. (Paris Convention).	03.03.75	-	L 194 25.07.75	Ratification by the Community of the Convention.
75/438/ EEC	Decision concerning Community participation in the Interim Commission established on the basis of Resolution No. III of the Convention for the Prevention of Marine Pollution from Land-based Sources.	03.03.75	-	L 194 25.07.75	To authorise the Commission to represent the Community in the Interim Commission responsible for administering the Paris Convention.
87/57/ EEC	Decision concluding the protocol amending the convention for the prevention of marine pollution from land-based sources.	22.12.86	-	L 24 27.07.87	To extend its scope to include airborne pollution.
98/249	Decision on the conclusion of the Convention for the protection of the marine environment of the north-east Atlantic - OSPAR			L104 03.04.98	

APPENDIX 6.6: OTHER EU MEASURES OF RELEVANCE TO POLLUTION CONTROL

Environmental Assessment/Access to Information

Number	Title	Date adopted	Date brought into force	OJ No. and date	Purpose
75/436/ Euratom ECSC/ EEC	Council Recommendation of cost allocation and action by public authorities on environmental matters.	03.03.75	03.03.75	L 194 25.07.75	To set out in detail the procedures for applying the Polluter Pays Principle, and to provide for some exceptions which may be made to this Principle.
79/3/ EEC	Council Recommendation to the Member States regarding methods of evaluating the cost of pollution control to industry.	09.12.78	09.12.78	L 5 09.01.79	To define the principles and methods to be followed by the Member States in assessing the costs of pollution control to industry.
85/337/ EEC	Directive concerning the assessment of the environmental effects of certain public and private projects.	27.06.85	03.07.88	L 175 05.07.85	To grant planning permission for projects which are likely to have significant effects on the environment only after an appropriate prior assessment of their environmental effects.
97/11 EC	Council directive amending 1985 directive			L 73 14.03.97	Amend 1985 Directive
85/338/ EEC	Decision on the adoption of a work programme for the first phase of the implementation of an information system on the state of the environment and the natural resources in the Community (1984-1987). (CORINE) (90/150 extends the programme pending establishment of European Environment Agency)	27.06.85	-	L 176 06.07.85	To fix a methodology framework and to apply it to: - biotopes of major importance for nature conservation. - protection of the Mediterranean environment. - acid deposition.
90/313/ EEC	Directive on freedom of access to information on the environment.	07.06.90	31.12.92	L 158 23.06.90	To oblige public authorities to provide access to environmental information, subject to certain restrictions.

1210/90	Regulation on the establishment of the European Environmental Agency and the European Environmental Information and Observation Network.	07.05.90	-	L 120 11.05.90	To set up a body to oversee the information network and ensure collection and objective data on environment.
880/92	Regulation on a Community eco-label award scheme.	23.03.92	23.03.92	L 99 11.04.92	To set up a Community scheme, define criteria and procedures, for awarding eco-labels; to promote the development of products with minimal environmental impact through their whole life-cycle.
1836/93	Regulation allowing voluntary participation by companies in the industry sector in a Community eco-management and audit scheme.			L168 10.07.93	To establish system of environmental management and auditing at industrial sites and provision of information to the public.
Chemicals					
82/501/ EEC	Directive on the major accident hazards of certain industrial activities (The Seveso Directive).	24.06.82	08.01.84	L 230 05.08.82	To establish a notification system of all dangerous substances, installations and major accident hazards. To ensure a better flow of information not only to the national and Community authorities but also to the workers and to the population concerned.
96/8/82	Directive on the control of major accident hazards (Seveso 2))	09.12.96		L 10 14.01.97	Tightens and extends provisions of earlier 1982 Directive which it will replace in 1998.
87/216/ EEC	Amendment to 82/501	19.03.87	-	L 85 28.03.87	To reduce the threshold triggering of notification system for certain products.
88/610/ EEC	Amendment to 82/501			L 336 07.12.88 public.	To increase scope of the Directive and clarify information to be made available to

Number	Title	adopted	Date brought into force	OJ No. and date	Purpose
Pesticides [see also water pollution: dangerous substances]					
76/895/ EEC	Directive on the fixing of maximum levels for pesticide residues in and on fruit and vegetables.			L 340 19.12.76	To protect consumers by setting limits on pesticide amounts on food.
86/362/ EEC	Directive on the fixing of maximum residues in and on cereals.			L 221 07.08.86	To protect consumers by setting limits on pesticide amounts on food.
86/363/ EEC	Directive on the fixing of maximum residues in and on products of animal origin.			L 221 07.08.86	To protect consumers by setting limits on pesticide amounts on food.
90/642/ EEC	Directive fixing maximum levels of pesticides in and on certain products of plant origin including fruit and vegetables.		31.12.92	L 350 14.12.90	Framework Directive providing for setting of mandatory maximum residue levels.
91/132/ EEC	Directive relating to undesirable sub-stances and products in animal nutrition.		01.08.91	L 66 13.03.91	Sets maximum permitted pesticide residues on or in animal feeds.
79/117/ EEC	Directive prohibiting the marketing and use of plant protection products containing certain substances.	21.12.78		L 33 08.02.79	Prohibits use of five mercury compounds and eight organochlorine compounds; also nitrogen 1,2 dibromoethane and 1,2 dichloroethane prohibited by subsequent amendments.
78/631/ EEC	Directive on classification, packaging and labelling of dangerous preparations.			L 206 29.07.78	To specify packaging and labelling labelling requirements for pesticides.
91/414/ EEC	Directive concerning placing of plant pro-tection products on the market.	15.07.91	26.07.93	L 230 19.08.91	To harmonise EC-wide registration of pesticides.
98/8/EC	Directive on placing of biocidal products on the marke	16.02.98		L123 24.04.98	To standardise way in which biocides are authorised throughout the EU; common principles, risk assesment criteria, etc.

Radioactivity

-	Resolution relating to the technological problems of nuclear safety.	22.07.75	22.07.75	C 185 14.08.75	To define guidelines for the progressive harmonisation of safety requirements and criteria.
80/836/ Euratom	Directive amending the Directives laying down the basic safety standards for the health protection of the general public and workers against the dangers of ionising radiation.	15.07.80	03.12.83 03.06.84	L 246 17.09.80	To establish a system of prior authorisation. To set doses for controllable exposures and principles governing operational protection of exposed workers.
87/600/ Euratom	Council Decision on Community arrangements for the early exchange of information in the event of a radiological emergency.	14.12.87	-	L 371 30.12.87	See title.
87/3954/ Euratom	Regulation laying down maximum permitted radioactivity levels for foodstuffs in the event of a nuclear accident.	22.12.87	-	L 371 30.12.87	See title.
89/618/ Euratom	Directive on informing the public in the event of a radiological emergency.	27.11.89	27.01.91	L 357 07.12.89	To require prior information on what to do in an emergency to general public likely to be affected and information about an accident to be communicated without delay to those affected; information on possible health risks to be given to all those giving emergency assistance.
90/143/ Euratom	Recommendation on the protection of the public against indoor exposure to radon.	21.02.90	-	L 80 27.03.90	See title.
90/641/ Euratom	Directive concerning protection of outside workers.			L 349 13.12.90 radiation.	Supplements 80/836 by setting standards for outside workers' exposure to ionising

Number	Title	Date adopted	Date brought into force	OJ No. and date	Purpose
96/29	Council Directive laying down basic safety standards relating to ionising radiation	14.05.96	13.05.00	L159 29.06.96	To protect workers and general public from dangers of ionising radiation
92/3/ Euratom	Directive on the supervision and control of shipments of radioactive waste.	13.02.92	01.01.94	L 35 12.02.92	To monitor and control transfrontier shipments of radioactive waste both between Member States and into and out of the Community.
1493/93	Regulation on Euratom shipments of radioactive substances between Member States.	08.06.93		L148 19.06.93	Similar to above.

Genetically Modified Organisms

Number	Title	Date adopted	Date brought into force	OJ No. and date	Purpose
90/219/ EEC	Directive on contained use of GMOs.	23.04.90	23.10.91	L 117 08.05.90	To establish notification, consent and emergency system to protect human health and the environment.
90/220/ EEC	Directive on deliberate release of GMOs into the environment.	23.04.90	23.10.91	L 117 08.05.90	To harmonise human health and environmental protection measures in Member States.

BIBLIOGRAPHY

GENERAL

European Issues

Caring for our Future: Action for Europe's Environment - European Commission, 1997.

EC Treaty and Environmental Law (second edition) - Krämer, L. Sweet & Maxwell, 1995.

EU Environment Guide (updated annually) - EC Committee of the American Chamber of Commerce, Avenue des Arts 50, Bte 5, B-1040 Brussels.

European Community Environment Legislation (Vol. 2 Air, Vol. 5 Noise, Vol. 6 Waste, Vol. 7 Water) - Commission of the European Communities, DG XI, 1993.

Manual of Environmental Policy: the EC and Britain - Haigh, N. Longman, 1992. (Updated twice a year)

Health

Environmental Health Criteria. International Programme on Chemical Safety. Series of reports on various pollutants evaluating effects on human health and the Environment. Nearly 150 reports have been published under joint sponsoring of UNEP, ILO and WHO. Further information available from the Office of Publications. WHO, Switzerland.

Legislation

Annual Catalogue of Standards. British Standards Institution. (Published in January.)

Encyclopedia of Environmental Health Law and Practice -

Cross, C (Ed). Sweet & Maxwell. (Updated)

Environmental Law - Burnett-Hall, R. Sweet & Maxwell, 1995.

Environmental Protection Act 1990, Part I. A Practical Guide - Central Control - Scottish Office, 1992.

The Environment Acts 1990-1995 - Tromans, S. Sweet & Maxwell, 1996. Texts and commentary.

The Green Triangle - an Environmental Legislation Guide for Businesses in Northern Ireland - ARENA Network (c/o Business in the Community, Airport Road West, Belfast BT2 9EA), 1997.

The Law of Nuclear Installations and Radioactive Substances - Tromans, S & Fitzgerald, J. Sweet & Maxwell, 1997.

Pollution Control: The Law in Scotland - Smith, C, Collar, N & Poustie, M. T & T Clark, Edinburgh, 1997.

Planning

Planning Pollution Prevention - Wood, C. Heinemann Newnes, 1989.

Planning Policy Guidance Notes - The Stationery Office. PPG 1: General Policy & Principles (1997); 6: Town Centres & Retail Development (1996); 7: The Countryside & the Rural Economy (1992, revised due April 1997); 9: Nature Conservation (1994); 10: Waste Disposal & Management (draft

1998); 12: Development Plans & Regional Guidance (1992, under review 1997); 13: Transport (1994); 14: Development on Unstable Land (1990); 18: Enforcing Planning Control (1991); 22: Renewable Energy & annexes (1993/94); 23: Planning and Pollution Control (1994); 24: Planning and Noise (1994).

National Planning Policy Guidance (Scotland) - General (1997); Provision of Roadside Facilities on Motorways & Other Trunk Roads (1996); 10: Planning & Waste Management (1996); Sport, Physical Recreation & Open Spaces (1996); Land for Housing (1996); 8: Retail Development (draft 1997); Skiing (1997); Planning for the Coast (draft 1997); Rural Development (draft 1997); Transport & Planning (draft 1997).

Planning Policy Guidance (Wales) - draft published 1995; will replace current 17 guidance notes.

Planning Policy Statements (Northern Ireland) - PPS 1: Planning System in NI (draft due 3/97); 2: Planning & Nature Conservation (due 3/97); 3: Development Control & Road Considerations (1996); 4: Industrial Development (draft due 3/97); 5: Retailing & Town Centres (1996). Other PPSs include Environmental Impact Assessment; Hazardous Substances.

Reference

Digest of Environmental Statistics (Annual) - Environment, Transport & The Regions Department of, The Stationery Office.

EC Eco-Management and Audit Scheme: A Participant's Guide - Department of Environment for UK Competent Body, 1995.

Eco-Management and Audit Scheme: A Practical Guide - Hillary, R. Technical Communications (Publishing) Ltd, 1993.

Environmental Health Reference Book - Jackson, MH and others. Butterworth, 1989.

Fundamentals of Environmental Chemistry - Manahan, SE. Lewis, 1993.

A Guide to Risk Assessment and Risk Management - HMSO, 1995.

Integrated Pollution Control - A Practical Guide. 1996. Environment, Department of. Available from DETR, 43 Marsham Street, London SW1P 3PY.

Our Common Future - World Commission on Environment and Development, Oxford University Press, 1987.

Pollution: Causes, Effects and Control - Harrison, R (Ed). Second Edition. Society of Chemistry Cambridge, 1990.

Silent Spring - Carson, R. Hamish Hamilton, 1962.

Royal Commission on Environmental Pollution Reports. First Report (1971); 2nd: *Three Issues in Industrial Pollution* (1972); 3rd: *Pollution in some British Estuaries and Coastal Waters* (1972); 4th: *Pollution Control: Progress and Problems* (1974); 6th: *Nuclear Power and the Environment* (1976); 7th: *Agriculture and Pollution* (1979); 8th: *Oil Pollution of the Sea* (1981); 9th: *Lead in the Environment* (1983); 10th: *Tackling Pollution - Experience and Prospects* (1984); 11th: *Managing Waste: The Duty of Care* (1985); 12th: *Best Practicable Environmental Option* (1988); 13th: *The Release of Genetically Engineered Organisms to the Environment* (1989); 14th: *GENHAZ - A System for the Critical Appraisal of Proposals to Release GMOs into the Environment* (1991); 15th: *Emissions from Heavy Duty Diesel Vehicles* (1991) 16th: *Freshwater Quality* (1992); 17th: *Incineration of Waste* (1993); 18th: *Transport and the Environment* (1994); 19th: *Sustainable Use of*

Soil (1996) - all published by HMSO. 20th: *Transport and the Environment - Developments since 1994* (1997); 21st: *Setting Environmental Standards* (1998) - The Stationery Office.

AIR

Acid Pollution

Air Pollution, Acid Rain and the Environment - Mellanby, K (Ed). Elsevier for Watt Committee on Energy, London, 1988.

The Effects of Acid Deposition on Buildings and Building Materials in the UK - Buildings Effects Review Group. HMSO, 1989.

Sulphur Dioxide, Acid Aerosols and Particulates - Advisory Group on the Medical Aspects of Air Pollution Episodes. HMSO, 1992.

Air Pollution

Air Pollutants and their Effects on the Terrestrial Ecosystem - Legge, A & Krupa, S (Eds). John Wiley and Sons, 1986.

Air Pollution and Plant Life - Treshow, M (Ed). John Wiley & Sons, 1984.

Air Pollution and Tree Health - Environment, Department of. HMSO, 1993.

Air Pollution in the UK: 1994 - Prepared by the National Environmental Technology Centre for DOE. AEA Technology, 1995.

Atmospheric Pollution, (Second Edition) Elsom D. Basil Blackwell, 1992.

Principles of Air Pollution Meteorology, Lyons, T & Scott, B. Belhaven Press, 1990.

The Politics of Clean Air - Ashby, A & Anderson, M. Clarendon Press, Oxford, 1981.

Air Quality

Air Quality Guidelines for Europe - WHO Regional Office for Europe. WHO Regional Publications, European Series; No. 23, 1987.

Expert Panel on Air Quality Standards - 1st report: *Benzene* (1994); 2nd: *Ozone* (1994); 3rd: *1,3 Butadiene* (1994); 4th: *Carbon Monoxide* (1994); 5th: *Sulphur Dioxide* (1995); 6th: *Particles* (1995); 7th: *Nitrogen Dioxide* (1996); Lead (1998) . The Stationery Office.

Department of the Environment, Transport & The Regions, Scottish Office & Welsh Office - Local Air Quality Management Guidance: *Framework for Review and Assessment of Air Quality* (LAQM.G1(97)); *Developing Local Air Quality Action Plans and Strategies: principal considerations*(LAQM.G2(97)); *Air Quality and Traffic Management* (LAQM.G3(97)); *Air Quality and Land-Use Planning* (LAQM.G4(97)). Technical Guidance: *Monitoring for Air Quality Reviews and Assessments* (LAQM.TG1(98)); *Preparation and Use of Atmospheric Emission Inventories* (LAQM.TG2(98)); *Selection and Use of Dispersion Models* (LAQM.TG3(98)); *Review and Assessment: Pollutant Specific Guidance* (LAQM.TG4(98)).

Quality of Urban Air Review Group - 1st report: *Urban Air Quality in the United Kingdom* (1993); 2nd: *Diesel Vehicle Emissions and Urban Air Quality* (1993); 3rd: *Airborne Particulate Matter in the United Kingdom* (1996). HMSO.

Smog Alert - Managing Urban Air Quality - Elsom D. Earthscan, 1996.

The United Kingdom National Air Quality Strategy - Department of the Environment & Scottish Office. The Stationery Office, 1997.

Global Warming

The Greenhouse Effect, Climatic Change and Eco-systems (SCOPE 29) - Bolin, B & others (Eds). John Wiley & Sons, 1986.

The Potential Effects of Climate Change in the United Kingdom - UK Climate Change Impacts Review Group, First Report, HMSO, 1991.

Health

Air Pollution and Health - Holman, C. Friends of the Earth, London 1989, revised 1991.

Department of Health, Advisory Group on the Medical Aspects of Air Pollution Episodes - 1st report: *Ozone* (1991); 2nd: *Sulphur Dioxide, Acid Aerosols and Particulates* (1992); 3rd: *Oxides of Nitrogen* (1993); 4th: *Health Effects of Exposures to Mixtures of Air Pollutants*. HMSO.

Department of Health, Committee on the Medical Effects of Air Pollutants - *Asthma and Outdoor Air Pollution* (1995); *Non-Biological Particles and Health* (1995), HMSO. *Handbook on Air Pollution and Health* (1997); *Quantification of the Effects of Air Pollution on Health in the United Kingdom* (1998), The Stationery Office.

Estimating Human Exposure to Air Pollutants - World Health Organisation. WHO Offset Publication No. 69. WHO, Geneva, 1982.

Lead, Mercury, Cadminum and Arsenic in the Environment (SCOPE 31) - Hutchinson, TC & Meema, KM (Eds). John Wiley & Sons, 1987.

Monitoring

Aerosol Sampling - Science and Practice - Vincent, JH. John Wiley & Sons, 1989.

Atmospheric Diffusion (3rd ed) - Pasquill, F and Smith, FB. Ellis Horwood Ltd, 1983.

Atmospheric Dispersion Modelling: Guidelines on the Justifiaction of Choice and Use of Models and the Communication and Reporting of Results - Policy Statement by Royal Meteorological Society, published in collaboration with Department of Environment, 1995. Available from RMO, 104 Oxford Road, Reading, Berkshire RG1 7LJ.

Characterisation of Air Quality BS 6069: Parts 1-4: 1990-1992. British Standards Institution.

Global Environmental Monitoring System - Assessment of Urban air Quality - Prepared by Monitoring and Assessment Research Centre for WHO and UNEP, 1988.

Methods for the Measurement of Air Pollution BS 1747: Parts 1-12; 1969-1993. British Standards Institution.

Odour

Latest Developments in Odour Measurement - Gibson, RN. IAPSC, Warren Spring Laboratory, 1992.

Odour at the Process Boundary - Pratt, M. Clean Air Vol 22, no. 3, 1992.

Odour Measurement and Control - An Update - Woodfield, M & Hall, D (Eds). AEA Technology, NETCEN, 1994.

The Control of Airborne Odours - Elvidge, AF & Blitz, J. IAPSC, Warren Spring Laboratory, 1992.

Ozone, Stratospheric

UK Stratospheric Ozone Review Group - Stratospheric Ozone (Fourth Report). HMSO, 1991.

Ozone, Tropospheric

Ozone - Advisory Group on the Medical Aspects of Air Pollution Episodes, 1991.

Radiation

Environmental Radon - Cothern, CR & Smith, JE (Eds). Plenum Press, New York, 1987.

Living with Radiation - National Radiological Protection Board, HMSO. 1989.

Natural Radiation Exposure in UK Dwellings - Wrixon, AD & others. HMSO for National Radiological Protection Board, 1988.

Radiation Exposure of the UK Population - Hughes, JS & others. HMSO for National Radiological Protection Board, annual.

Radiation: Doses, Effects, Risks - United Nations Environment Programme. UNEP, 1985.

Transport

Atmospheric Emissions from the Use of Transport in the United Kingdom - Fergusson, M, Holman, C, Barrett, M. Earth Resources Research. Worldwide Fund for Nature, 1989.

The Impact of Airport Operations on Air Quality - Raper, D, Longhurst, J. Clean Air, Vol. 20, no. 1, 1990.

Transport and the Environment - OECD, 1988.

Transport Statistics Great Britain - The Stationery Office, annual.

NOISE

Acoustics and the Built Environment - Elsevier, 1989.

Calculation of Road Traffic Noise - HMSO, 1988.

Fighting Noise in the 1990s - OECD, 1991.

Noise and Noise Law: A Practical Approach - Adams MS & McManus F. Wiley Chancery Law, 1994.

Noise Assessment, Information and Control, Noise Guides 3-8 - Health and Safety Executive. HMSO, 1990.

Noise at Work Regulations 1989. Noise Guides 1-2 - Legal duties to prevent damage to hearing - Health and Dafety Executive. HMSO 1989.

Noise Control in the Built Environment - Roberts, J & Fairhall, D (Eds). Gower Technical, 1988.

Noise Control: The Law and its Enforcement - Penn CN. Shaw & Sons, 1995.

Noise Pollution (SCOPE 24) - Saenz, AL & Stephens, RWB (Eds). John Wiley and Sons, 1986.

Planning and Noise (PPG 24). HMSO, 1994.

Rating Industrial Noise Affecting Mixed Residential and Industrial Areas, BS 4142. British Standards Institution, 1990.

PESTICIDES

Pesticide Related Law - Gilbert, D. & Macrory, R. The British Crop Protection Council, 1989.

The Pesticide Handbook - Hurst, P, Hay, A & Dudley, N. Journeyman, 1991.

Pesticide Users' Health and Safety Handbook - Watterson, A. Gower, 1988.

WASTE

Contaminated Land - Aspinwall & Co. for Institution of Environmental Health Officers. IEHO, 1989.

Cutting Your Losses: A further Guide to Waste Minimisation for Business - Trade and Industry, Department of. HMSO, 1992.

Reducing the Burden of Waste - Guidelines for Business - Confederation of British Industry, 1993.

The Environmental Impact of Refuse Incineration in the UK - Woodfield, M. Warren Spring Laboratory, 1987.

The Law of Waste Management - Pocklington, D. Shaw & Sons, 1997.

Waste Management Planning - Principles & Practice - Department of the Environment. HMSO, 1995.

WATER

Aquatic Pollution: An Introductory Text - Laws, WA, John Wiley & Sons, 1994.

Dangerous Substances in Water - A Practical Guide. Environmental Data Services Ltd, 1992.

The Law of the National Rivers Authority - Howarth, W. The National Rivers Authority/Centre for Law in Rural Areas, 1990.

Wisdoms Law of Watercourses, Fifth Edition - Howarth, W. Shaw and Sons, 1992.

JOURNALS

(Covering subjects relevant to material in the *Pollution Handbook)*

Air Quality Management (monthly). Information for Industry Ltd, 18-20 Ridgway, London SW19 4QN.

Atmospheric Environment (monthly). Pergamon Press, Headington Hill Hall, Oxford.

Clean Air (bi-monthly). Journal of the National Society for Clean Air.

ENDS Report (monthly). ENDS, Unit 24, Finsbury Business Centre, 40 Bowling Green Lane, London EC1R 0NE. News and analysis of current developments. Specialist reports on industry and the environment.

Environment Business (monthly). Information for Industry Ltd, 18-20 Ridgway, London SW19 4QN.

Environmental Health (monthly). Journal of the Institution of Environmental Health Officers, Chadwick House, Rushworth Street, London SE1 0QT.

Europe Environment (fortnightly). Europe Information Service, Av. Albert Elisabeth 46, 1200 Brussels.

Waste Manager. Environmental Services Association, 154 Buckingham Palace Road, London SW1W 9TR.

POLLUTION HANDBOOK INDEX